The Common Defense

STRATEGIC PROGRAMS

IN NATIONAL POLITICS

By Samuel P. Huntington

Columbia University Press

NEW YORK

FOR NANCY

INSTITUTE OF WAR AND PEACE STUDIES

In addition to *The Common Defense* the Institute of War and Peace Studies has sponsored the publication of *Defense and Diplomacy* by Alfred Vagts and *Man, the State, and War* by Kenneth N. Waltz. Members of the Institute have planned and edited three other volumes. These collections of essays are *Theoretical Aspects of International Relations*, edited by William T. R. Fox; *Inspection for Disarmament*, edited by Seymour Melman; and *Changing Patterns of Military Politics* (the 1961 volume of the *International Yearbook of Political Behavior Research*), edited by Samuel P. Huntington. There is now in press a volume on strategy, politics, and defense budgets which contains studies on the making of national security policy by Warner R. Schilling, Paul Y. Hammond, and Glenn H. Snyder.

ISBN 0-231-02518-1 *(cloth)*
ISBN 0-231-08566-4 *(paper)*

Copyright © 1961   Columbia University Press
Columbia Paperback Edition   1966

Printed in the United States of America
10 9 8 7 6 5 4 3

Foreword

The making of national security policy has been a major, though not an exclusive, concern of the members of Columbia University's Institute of War and Peace Studies for almost ten years. *The Common Defense* is one of the studies reflecting this concern. Also to be published in 1962 is a volume containing three other studies. All three deal with strategic choices and defense budgets and with the political process by which defense policy is made. The authors are Warner R. Schilling, Paul Y. Hammond, and Glenn H. Snyder.

Members of the Institute of War and Peace Studies exchange advice and criticism freely as they work on their closely related studies, but they are independent scholars. To the author of *The Common Defense*, therefore, belongs both the credit and the responsibility for its final form.

Samuel P. Huntington's first book on the military aspects of politics was *The Soldier and the State* (Cambridge, Mass., Harvard University Press, 1957). He has pioneered in the teaching of courses in the government and politics of American national defense at Harvard and Columbia Universities. He has edited and is the co-author of *Changing Patterns of Military Politics* (New York, Free Press, 1962), a collection of essays in comparative civil-military relations. In *The Common Defense* he has produced a systematic work of wide scope and consistent point of view. His book is not an analysis of contemporary alternatives in defense policy; much less is it a book-length exercise in pamphleteering in support of one or another of these alternatives. His focus, like that of his Institute colleagues in their studies of the making of national security policy, is on the policy process and ways for making that process yield better policies rather than on the policies themselves.

That large part of the research on *The Common Defense* done under the direct auspices of the Institute was made possible by a Carnegie Corporation grant in support of the Institute's general program of research on national security policy. It is a pleasure to acknowledge that support.

WILLIAM T. R. FOX
Director
Institute of War and Peace Studies

Preface

Between 1945 and 1960 American military policy changed rapidly. The purpose of this book is to analyze some of the patterns of politics and decision-making which shaped the speed and nature of those changes. In recent years, several social scientists have written penetrating analyses of military strategy, probing the rationality and desirability of alternative courses. This book is different. It is concerned not with what policy ought to be but with what it has been and why. It seeks to generalize about how military policy-making is made during a period of transition. It focuses specifically on one segment of military policy, strategic programs, that is, decisions on the overall size of the military effort, force levels, and weapons.

This book is not a history of military policy between 1945 and 1960. It treats no subject exhaustively, even in the area of strategic programs. Instead, it attempts to look at the politics of military policy from a number of different perspectives: the interaction between the desire for a stable military effort and the need to shift from a strategy of mobilization to a strategy of deterrence; the "legislative" character of the processes by which strategic programs are formulated in the executive branch; the competition among the components of the "Great Equation" and the ways in which Administrations attempt to balance that equation; the processes by which the strategic programs required for deterrence are innovated and those by which alternative programs are assimilated to a deterrent strategy; interservice rivalry and the competition among strategic programs. The generalizations which are advanced about these subjects are derived from a study of the events between 1945 and

1960. During these years, military policy was in a state of turmoil. It seems unlikely that stability will emerge in the immediate future. Certainly, the generalizations advanced here about military policy-making would have to be altered if it did. Even with continuing controversy, they may become less relevant. The immediate problems change, and each Administration develops its own ways of dealing with them. I would hazard the guess, however, that many of the patterns of behavior found to exist in the Truman and Eisenhower Administrations will continue to exist in future Administrations dealing with Cold War problems.

In the past, Americans often tended to think of military policy as something esoteric and remote. If this image was ever accurate, it certainly ceased to be so after World War II. For many years, political scientists have written books about American political ideas, institutions, and processes, and have paid little attention to the military activities and policies of the government. Conversely, analyses of strategy at times seem to assume that politics sets no limits on the military policies which the government can pursue, that strategic prescriptions can be made without reference to the constitutional habits and political idiosyncracies of the patient. This book is an effort to bridge the gap between the studies of American politics, on the one hand, and the substantive analyses of strategy, on the other. If this book has any distinctive message, it is that military policy can only be understood as the responses of the government to conflicting pressures from its foreign and domestic environments. Decisions on strategic programs, in particular, must be viewed in the broader context of American politics and government. This book is concerned with strategy, but the reader will find in it little information on missile capabilities and military concepts and much discussion of budget battles and political compromises.

The formulation of strategic programs differs in many important ways from the determination of foreign policy or from policy-making in the diverse domestic areas of governmental activity. In studying the development of military policy, however, one is struck more by its similarities to policy-making in these other areas than by its differences. Most of the distinctive characteristics of the American political process in general are also found in the processes by which military policy is made. Military policy cannot be separated from foreign policy, fiscal policy, and domestic policy. It is part of the warp and the woof of American politics. The roles of Congress and the President in the formulation of strategic programs can only be appreciated through a knowledge of the more general functioning of the separation of powers. The views of Republicans and Democrats on military policy are directly related to their stands on other issues. The processes of consensus-building and consensus-changing (innovation) in military policy do not differ significantly from those in other policy areas. The ups and downs of military spending reflect changes in the tax structure and the attitudes of the Administration in power toward welfare programs and unbalanced budgets. The competition among the services assumes a familiar aspect when it is viewed in terms of the patterns of competition which exist between the political parties and among other interest groups. Even the most penetrating criticisms of the strategy-making process echo the criticisms which have been made of other aspects of the government.

The political processes by which military policy is made thus do not vary greatly from the American norm. The issues at stake in military policy, however, may be much more significant than many of those at stake in domestic policy. The security and perhaps the survival of the nation depend upon the performance of the government in the military area. The key question is: Are the "normal" American ways of conducting politics capable of producing the military policies necessary for survival and security? Fifteen years furnish hardly enough evidence to answer this question. Yet, as the qualified optimism of my conclusion suggests, the question cannot now be answered in the negative, and we simply have not survived long enough to know whether it can be answered in the affirmative.

Elsewhere I have argued that military officers should approach policy issues from a professional military viewpoint. The corollary is that political officials should look at military policy from a broader viewpoint. Between 1945 and 1960 American military officers often forsook a professional military approach to military policy. Their role in key decisions, however, was not very important. The important decisions on strategic programs were made by the President or by other Administration officials acting in his name. These officials approached military policy with non-military or trans-military considerations high in their minds. If the officers abandoned their standards, the politicians held firmly to theirs. The decisions they made, which may seem incomprehensible when looked at "from a military viewpoint" or even from a national security viewpoint, become understandable, if not always justifiable, when placed in the broader context in which the Administration had to act. Military policy is *always* the product of politics. Good military policy is *only* the product of brave choice and ingenious compromise by experienced politicians.

I worked on this book on-and-off for three years. During this time I was helped by many individuals and organizations, none of whom, let me hasten to add, is responsible for its contents or defects. My early research in 1958 was aided by grants from the William F. Milton Fund and the Clark Fund of Harvard University and from the Social Science Research Council Committee on National Security Policy Research. The final manuscript was written in the fall of 1960 while I held the Ford Research Professorship in Governmental Affairs at Columbia University. In between, the great bulk of my research and writing was done under the auspices of the Institute of War and Peace Studies and supported by a grant from the Carnegie Corporation of New York. I am grateful to these groups for their financial assistance. I owe a special debt to Professor William T. R. Fox, not only for enabling me to be relieved of my teaching duties at Columbia, but also for encouraging my work on this manuscript in many other ways. In the Institute of War and Peace Studies Professor Fox has created a uniquely stimulating and informal setting for scholarly activity: the administrative support is efficient but unobtrusive; counsel and intellectual companionship are available but unintrusive.

The manuscript was read in its entirety by William T. R. Fox, Roger Hilsman, Louis Morton, and Harold Stein. Each of these scholars was extremely generous in the time and thought he devoted to it. Their advice saved me from many errors and ambiguities. Robert E. Osgood, Warner R. Schilling, and David B. Truman also read portions of the manuscript at various stages. Their expert comments on subjects where their knowledge far exceeded mine also enabled me to avoid many dead-ends and pitfalls. In the early phases of my research I was aided by Richard C. Johnson, Donald R. Reich, and Martin Shapiro, all of whom helped lighten the burden of reconnaissance in the uncharted areas of military policy. Vladimir V. Almendinger, Jr., was of expert assistance in the initial analyses of congressional voting on defense issues. In the last stages of research and writing, William E. Jackson, Jr., made an indispensable contribution in digging out and helping to organize the materials necessary to complete the research.

This book was written primarily from the public record. As the notes suggest, however, my analysis was enriched by a number of as yet unpublished studies of particular policy decisions which have been made by scholars who interviewed directly the principal participants. Among these studies, I am especially indebted to those of NSC 68 and the B-36 controversy by Paul Y. Hammond, the decision to rearm Germany by Laurence W. Martin, continental defense by Steven R. Rivkin, the FY 1950 military budget by Warner R. Schilling, the New Look by Glenn H. Snyder, and reserve forces policy by Charles D. Story. I am also grateful to the Viking Press for permission to quote extensively from *The Forrestal Diaries*, edited by Walter Millis, and to Harper & Brothers for permission to quote extensively from *The Uncertain Trumpet*, by General Maxwell D. Taylor.

Chapter III grew out of a paper I prepared for the Round Table on Civil-Military Relations of the International Political Science Association at Opatija, Yugoslavia, in September, 1959. An abbreviated version of it was published in the January, 1960, issue of *Foreign Affairs*. The contents of this article have been incorporated into the present manuscript with the kind permission of the copyright owner, the Council on Foreign Relations, Inc., New York. Chapter VI appears here in its third and fullest incarnation. It was prepared originally for the Ohio State University Conference on Civil-Military Relations, February, 1959, and a shorter version will appear in the volume of papers emerging from that conference, *Total War and Cold War* (Ohio State Press), edited by Harry L. Coles. Another briefer version was published in the March, 1961, issue of the *American Political Science Review*.

With infrequent complaints, uncommon patience, and unflagging encouragement, my wife suffered through the research and writing of this book. In manuscript and in proof, she read all of it twice and most of it three times. The extent of her contribution is perhaps indicated by her claim, which she can substantiate, that she is able to recite huge gobs of it from memory. Whatever stylistic virtues it may have are largely the result of her efforts. I only regret—although I know she doesn't—that time did not allow her a fourth reading.

SAMUEL P. HUNTINGTON

Sharon, Connecticut
September 1, 1961

Contents

Foreword, by William T. R. Fox ... iii
Preface ... v

I. THE DIMENSIONS OF MILITARY POLICY ... 1
    1. The Two Worlds of Military Policy ... 1
    2. Military Policy in the Cold War ... 14

II. THE SEARCH FOR A STABLE DETERRENT ... 25
    3. The Dual Quest ... 25
    4. The Interim Years: World War II to January, 1950 ... 33
    5. NSC 68 and Rearmament, 1950–1952 ... 47
    6. The New Look, 1953–1956 ... 64
    7. The New New Look, 1956–1960 ... 88
    8. Strategy and Change ... 113

III. STRATEGIC PROGRAMS AND THE POLITICAL PROCESS ... 123
    9. Structure, Strategy, and Process ... 123
    10. The Lobbying Functions of Congress ... 135
    11. Executive Legislation of Strategic Programs ... 146
    12. Criticisms of the Strategy-Making Process ... 166
    13. The Scope of Strategy-Making ... 174

IV. THE GREAT EQUATION ... 197
    14. The Politics of Fiscal Policy ... 197

15. External Influences: Tensions, Capabilities, and Deterrence 199
16. Domestic Influences: Spending, Taxes, and Balanced Budgets 207
17. The Administration and the Magnitude of the Military Effort 218
18. The Administration, the Public, and the Defense Effort 234
19. Parties and Elections 251
20. Drastic Changes in Military Magnitude 268
21. Appendix: The Magnitude of the Security Effort, 1945–1960 277

V. INNOVATION OF STRATEGIC PROGRAMS 284

22. Patterns of Innovation 284
23. Strategic Deterrence 298
24. European Defense 312
25. Continental Defense 326
26. Limited War 341
27. Assimilation of Alternative Programs 353

VI. THE COMPETITION OF STRATEGIC PROGRAMS 369

28. Service Interests and Interservice Competition 369
29. The Political Castellation of the Services 384
30. Conflict and Consensus in the Strategic Matrix 404

VII. THE POLITICS OF DETERRENCE 426

31. The Changes in Military Policy 426
32. Beyond Deterrence? 437

NOTES 449

INDEX 489

CHAPTER I

The Dimensions of Military Policy

1. THE TWO WORLDS OF MILITARY POLICY

The most distinctive, the most fascinating, and the most troublesome aspect of military policy is its Janus-like quality. Indeed, military policy not only faces in two directions, it exists in two worlds. One is international politics, the world of the balance of power, wars and alliances, the subtle and the brutal uses of force and diplomacy to influence the behavior of other states. The principal currency of this world is actual or potential military strength: battalions, weapons, and warships. The other world is domestic politics, the world of interest groups, political parties, social classes, with their conflicting interests and goals. The currency here is the resources of society: men, money, material. Any major decision in military policy influences and is influenced by both worlds. A decision made in terms of one currency is always payable in the other. The rate of exchange, however, is usually in doubt. Who knows the difference in international influence between a military budget of $35 billion and one of $40 billion? What will the commitment of six divisions to a nasty limited war cost in men, material, and domestic well-being? The uncertainty of the rate of exchange lies at the root of many of the dilemmas of military policy-making.

Military policy cuts clearly across the usual distinction between foreign policy and domestic policy. Domestic policy consists of those activities of a government which affect significantly the allocation of values among groups in society, while foreign policy consists of those activities of a government which affect significantly the allocation of values between it and other governments. The categories are not mutually exclusive. Foreign aid programs impose demands on the domestic economy; agricultural surpluses have implications for foreign affairs. Domestic politics serves as a constraint on the formulation of policies which are primarily responses to the external environment and have their principal impact on that environment. Conversely, international politics serves as a constraint on the formulation of policies which are primarily responses to the domestic environment and have their principal impact on that environment. With military policy, however, it is almost impossible to say which is the primary focus and which the constraint. It is neither primarily foreign nor primarily domestic. Instead it consists of those elements of both foreign and domestic policy which directly affect the armed forces. A commercial treaty and a collective security treaty are both foreign policy. A shift from excise taxes to income taxes and an across-the-board cut in governmental expenditures are both fiscal policy. The collective security treaty and the expenditures decision, however, are also military policy. The former directly affects the responsibilities of the armed forces, the latter their size and readiness.

THE COMPETITION OF PURPOSES

People sometimes argue that military policy involves the determination of the military programs and actions required to implement a given set of national goals. National policy or foreign policy or national security policy, they say, is decided first, and military policy then follows, subordinate to the more "ultimate" goals of higher policy. This image is a logical construct of what people think military policy ought to be. It is an image, however, which has little basis in fact. The crux of military policy, to be sure, is the relation of force to national purposes. But it is always national purposes in the plural, national purposes which are continually conflicting, often being compromised, and seldom being realized. Military policy is not the result of deductions from a clear statement of national objective. It is the product of the competition of purposes within individuals and groups and among individuals and groups. It is the result of politics not logic, more an arena than a unity. It is where a nation and its government come to grips with fundamental conflicts between those purposes which relate to the achievement of values in the world of international politics—conquest, influence, power, territory, trade, wealth, empire, and security—and those which relate to the achievement of values in the domestic world—economic prosperity, individual freedom and welfare, inexpensive government, low taxation, economic stability, social welfare. The competition between the external goals of the government as a collective entity in a world of other governments and the domestic goals of the government and other groups in society is the heart of military policy.

Broad goals, such as security, welfare, inexpensive government, are accepted as legitimate by most groups in society. But legitimacy does not necessarily imply compatibility. The realization of any one goal normally limits realization of the others. Because they are all legitimate they are all articulated, but also because they are legitimate the tendency of democratic politics is to obscure and to moderate the conflict among them. The latent conflict exists nonetheless, and it may well crystallize into actual conflict over specific issues, when, for instance, a government has to choose between balancing its budget and increasing its military security. In addition to general goals, particular groups participating in the policy process have their own specific, limited goals. The competition of purposes is not just among the broad goals of policy but also among the specific goals of these particular groups and between specific goals and broad goals. The fascination of military policy stems in large part from the intensity, complexity, and importance of the competing purposes which enter into its formation.

STRATEGY AND STRUCTURE

Military policy can be roughly divided into strategy and structure. Decisions made in the categories or currency of international politics may be described as *strategic* in character. Strategy concerns the units and uses of force. More precisely, strategic decisions may be subdivided into two broad divisions: 1) program decisions concerning the strength of the military forces, their composition and readiness, and the number, type, and rate of development of their weapons; and 2) use decisions concerning the deployment, commitment, and employment of military force, and manifested in military alliances, war plans, declarations of war, force movements, and the like. A strategic concept identifies a particular need and implicitly or explicitly prescribes decisions on the uses, strengths, and weapons of the armed services. *Structural* decisions, on the other hand, are made in the currency of domestic politics. They deal with the procurement, allocation, and organization of the men, money, and material which go into the strategic units and uses of force. Among the more important types of structural decisions are: 1) budget decisions concerning the size and distribution of funds made available to the armed forces; 2) personnel decisions concerning the number, procurement, retention, pay, and working conditions of members of the military services; 3) material decisions concerning the amount, procurement, and distribution of supplies to the armed forces; and 4) organizational decisions concerning the methods and forms by which the military services are organized and administered.[1]

The categories of decision—strategic and structural—are not independent of the purposes of decision. In general, when the goal of policy is related to the external environment, the decision is made in terms of the strategic categories. When the policy goal is domestic, it is made in terms of structural categories. Conversely, since any major issue in military policy inevitably has both strategic and structural implications, *how* the issue is defined for decision may well influence *what* the decision is. If another government becomes more and more powerful and unfriendly, the reaction may be to augment the military forces (the decision is made first in strategic terms) and then to increase the military budget, and perhaps as a result to multiply taxes and governmental borrowing or to reduce other programs. On the other hand, if the goal of policy is less governmental interference in the economy, the first step is a structural decision to reduce the military budget, and only later are decisions made to reduce force levels and perhaps foreign policy commitments. A category of decision, however, cannot simply be equated with any one particular purpose of decision. Military budgets go up as well as down, and, indeed, during a period of war mobilization budgets may be increased before strategy is formulated and before it is entirely clear how and for what the money will be spent.

In practice no sharp line exists between the strategic and structural elements in a military policy decision. This is particularly

1. THE TWO WORLDS

true of the overall magnitude of the military effort. This is determined by many strategic and structural decisions on force levels, budgets, personnel, and by other decisions which are not directly part of military policy at all. The determination of the resources available to the government and the allocation of those resources to military, domestic, and foreign purposes is, indeed, the crux of national policy. The determination of the magnitude of the military effort combines strategy and structure and also transcends them.

The various elements of military policy may conflict with each other or be compatible with each other. Obviously, a major action in any one area of strategy or structure implies demands upon the other areas. A decision to defend a certain territory with ground forces, for instance, is a strategic action on the use of force. It implies certain actions to insure that the forces and weapons necessary for the mission are in existence. These actions, in turn, may imply decisions on the budget (increasing ground force expenditures either by raising the total military budget or reallocating resources from other forces), on personnel (conscription or higher pay may be necessary to get the additional men required), on material (changes in procurement and base construction policies), and possibly on organization (enhancing the position of the ground forces in the overall defense organization). The failure to undertake any one of these structural actions may, at the extreme, negate the strategic decision or, at the least, create imbalances and contradictions in military policy. A decision to build a long-range missile within three years, for instance, is strategic. A decision to have it built by the Army in a government arsenal instead of a private company under contract with the Air Force is structural. But if it is technically or administratively impossible for the arsenal to construct the missile within the specified time limit while the private company could do so, the decision on structure will reverse the decision on strategy.

The more numerous the loci of decision-making, the more likely are there to be disharmonies among the various elements of military policy. In the American system of government, decisions on strategy are largely executive decisions, decisions on structure normally require both executive and legislative action. Within strategy and structure the decision-making process tends to be still further fragmented. One group of agencies is concerned with budgetary decisions; another with matters of organization; yet a third with personnel policy. Decisions on weapons may be made by one group and decisions on missions by another. To some extent each element of military policy is the product of a distinctive policy-making process. Many agencies, of course, play a role in shaping all or most of the components of military policy, but the broad scope of these agencies frequently hampers them in getting their views to prevail within any specific decision-making process. The likelihood of conflict is further increased by the different roles which individuals and groups play in making different types of decisions. A budgetary official with the power to grant or withhold funds may be on the periphery of the process of force level determination. Military men who decide upon the weapons they need may appear as claimants before civilians to get the money to procure the weapons. A politically appointed executive official, like the Secretary of Defense, who has much influence on the overall size of the military forces, may have little influence over their commitments and use. Each process of decision is unique, and even if the actors in the several processes are the same, their roles in those processes may vary considerably. The different processes necessarily produce policies embodying different and often conflicting goals.

The formulation of military policy is often discussed in terms of the contrasting roles and functions of civilian and military groups. Actually, the civil-military distinction is not very meaningful as far as policy is concerned. Rarely, if ever, does one find all the civilians ranged against all the military. Much more important is the distinction between the tendencies to think in terms of domestic goals and structural categories, on the one hand, and external goals and strategic categories, on the other. Both tendencies undoubtedly exist in some degree in almost all persons participating in the military policy-making process. Nonetheless, some individuals and groups tend to emphasize domestic goals and the structural categories, and other individuals and groups foreign goals and the strategic categories. The former may include budgetary officials throughout the government, some congressmen, many politically appointed civilian officials, and some high-ranking military officers. The latter group is more likely to include middle-ranking officials in the State Department and the military services, many congressmen, and some politically appointed executive officials. The clash between these two groups comes to a head in determining the magnitude of the military effort. The crucial differences over policy usually involve differences over concerns and values stemming from organizational and political position rather than from roles and occupations reflecting personal career lines and social background. Often the military are caught between a civilian State Department which expands their commitments and a civilian Budget Bureau which limits their resources. The relations of the military to these two agencies are two key foci of civil-military relations. Yet the conflicts involved are not fundamentally civil-military ones. They are between civilian-defined external policy goals and civilian-defined internal policy goals.

EQUILIBRIUM AND DISEQUILIBRIUM

The history of military policy, like that of other areas of public policy, can be divided into phases of controversy and change (or disequilibrium) and phases of harmony and stability (or equilibrium). Military policy is in equilibrium when: 1) no sharp conflicts exist among the dominant goals of domestic policy, military policy, and foreign policy; and 2) no major changes in policy are taking place. An existing policy equilibrium may be disturbed by a drastic change in either its external or domestic environment. When one environment is upset, disequilibrium ensues until that environment again becomes stabilized and the process of adjustment produces a new policy balance. A change in the external environment, for instance, such as a fundamental shift in the balance of power, the rise of new and threatening states, the decline of old and established empires, the acquisition or loss of territory, tends to produce changes in foreign policy which, in turn, disrupt the existing relation between foreign policy and military policy. Either military strategy and military structure adjust to accommodate these changes or continuing disharmony develops between foreign policy and military policy. The satisfactory adjustment of military policy to the external changes, in turn, may then force other changes in domestic policy or produce continuing disharmonies between domestic policies and military policy. Conversely, a major shift in the domestic condition of a country—the rise of new industries, the change from a predominantly rural to a predominantly urban society, a shift in government from absolute monarchy to democracy—may produce changes in domestic policies requiring adjustments in military policy and foreign policy. The adjustments may take years to work themselves out, and disequilibrium may continue for decades with foreign policy, domestic policy, and strategy and structure embodying competing values and purposes.

Policy reflects the power, interests, and attitudes of the public and private individuals and groups concerned with it and affected by it. A change in policy requires either a change in the attitudes of the groups which influence policy or a change in the groups themselves. A policy equilibrium, on the other hand, means that a stable and reasonably harmonious pattern of relationships exists among these groups. Needless to say, policies are never completely static, nor intergroup relationships completely harmonious. Equilibrium simply means relative stability and harmony as contrasted with the change and conflict characteristic of disequilibrium.

During a period of disequilibrium, more groups become concerned with the policy area. The area receives more time and energy of general policy-makers (Congress and the President) and assumes a larger role in public discussion and partisan debate than it does during periods of stability. The number of alternative future courses of action increases. The gap between what significant groups consider to be the felt needs requiring governmental action and the existing patterns of action widen noticeably. Maladjustments between various component elements of policy appear to increase. Disharmonies and fissions develop. Changes in policy are more frequent and more fundamental. During periods of equilibrium, on the other hand, the importance of the policy area appears to subside. The groups actively concerned with the policy decrease in number. Policy, in a sense, settles into a routine. The major choices have been made. The doors which were open have been closed, and the general course has been set. A balance exists among the goals and interests of the narrowed range of groups with continuing concerns in the area. Alterations in policy are few

1. THE TWO WORLDS

and of less significance. Balance, order, stability, consensus, and habit replace uncertainty, conflict, choice, change, and creativity.

In practice no sharp line divides equilibrium from disequilibrium. Over a period of time, however, it is possible to distinguish a rise and fall in the importance of any area of public policy and a corresponding expansion and contraction of the process through which it is made. Policy on the force levels of the Army, for instance, was in disequilibrium during the twenty years from 1790 to 1809: Congress changed the authorized unit strength of the Army eleven times during this period, and personnel strength fluctuated from a little more than 700 to a little less than 7,000. During the twenty years from 1878 to 1897 on the other hand, a stable equilibrium prevailed: the authorized unit strength of the Army remained constant at 25 regiments of infantry, 10 of cavalry, and 5 of artillery, and its personnel strength varied from a high of 28,265 to a low of 25,652. Stability and balance involved consensus and consistency. In 1801 the Jeffersonians reduced the Army by 30 percent. Democrats and Republicans, however, succeeded each other in office in the 1880s with no appreciable effect upon its force levels.

A classic case of prolonged disequilibrium between foreign policy and military policy occurred in France during the 1920s and 1930s. French foreign policy was concerned primarily with the problem of a resurgent Germany. Shortly after World War I the French negotiated alliances with the new states of eastern Europe, Poland and the Little Entente (Czechoslovakia, Yugoslavia, and Rumania) in particular, which implied that France would come to their aid if they were attacked by Germany. To fulfill this commitment, France would have to be able to launch or to threaten to launch an offensive against Germany if the latter menaced France's eastern allies. Hence, presumably France should have a professional, mobile army capable of quickly carrying out this mission. French military policy, however, did not correspond to these foreign policy needs. Instead it reflected the military experience of World War I and the ideologies and viewpoints of domestic political groups. The former bred the conviction within the French military establishment that the defensive was the superior form of warfare. The latter held that a democratic society was incompatible with a professional elite force and required universal short-term military service.

France built the Maginot Line and until 1935 maintained universal military service for one year. Instead of a ready professional force, French military strength consisted of large numbers of recently trained reserves. Military action of any sort required extensive mobilization, and offensive military action seemed "adventurous" when the elaborate strong points of the Maginot Line existed to protect France against invasion. For a decade or more French military policy and foreign policy were reasonably stable. But stability alone did not mean equilibrium. Foreign policy commitments, strategic programs, and manpower policies were fundamentally out of balance. The consequences of this lack of consensus were painfully obvious when the Germans remilitarized the Rhineland in 1936. The leaders of the French government asked the advice of the military chiefs on sending an expeditionary force into Germany. "Our military system," General Gamelin replied, "does not give us this possibility." The active units are but "the nucleus of the mobilized national army." Any rapid military operation in the Rhineland "even in a more or less symbolic form is fantastic." A significant military counterthrust would require the mobilization of a million reservists. To "chase three regiments of the Wehrmacht," in the words of the postwar Commission of Inquiry of the National Assembly, "it would have been necessary to put all the French army on a war footing." [2]

The lack of balance and harmony between French foreign policy and French military policy was not unnoticed during the interwar years. Many political leaders (including Paul Reynaud) and many military men (including Charles De Gaulle) pointed it out. But the conflicting goals and the system of decision-making made it impossible to bridge the gap. The requisite political strength did not exist to give France either the "army of her policy," as Reynaud wanted, or the "policy of her army," which some of the Rightists wanted. Changes in the attitudes or the power of either group were impossible, and the result was not equilibrium but conflict and stalemate.

The history of American military policy traditionally has been written in terms of the classic cycle of war and peace. During peace, the familiar story goes, America tends to neglect its military establishment: the armed services are starved for money and men and reduced to a small corps of regulars who struggle to keep alive military knowledge and the military spirit in an apathetic and indifferent country. As crises loom in the distance, the military warn the country of the need to rearm. The civilians, however, are slow to respond until war or national emergency is present or imminent. At this point the peacetime dike stopping the flood of military preparation gives way, the martial spirit seizes the populace, and the country rushes headlong into rearmament and the enthusiastic and successful prosecution of a war. Once the conflict is over, however, the country just as enthusiastically demobilizes, is outwitted at the peace conference, forgets the lessons of its prewar unpreparedness, and once again lets its military might decay.

There are substantial elements of truth in this picture. Military policy, however, is shaped by more than the cycle of war and peace. Only fundamental and permanent changes in a government's environment produce fundamental and permanent changes in its military policy. Wars may or may not involve such changes. If a war results in a marked extension of a state's territory and responsibilities, inevitably this is reflected in its military policy. It is the result of the war, however, rather than the war itself which produces the changes. On the other hand, a war which does not markedly alter the antebellum environment has little effect on military policy no matter how serious a conflict it may be. In such cases the war simply marks a temporary change in the environment of policy and produces only temporary changes in policy. After the war the prewar equilibrium is reestablished. The American Civil War was the biggest war of the century between 1815 and 1914 and yet it produced few significant changes in American military policy. But the Spanish-American War, a little war if not a splendid one, was associated with basic changes in military policy because it was part of a fundamental shift in the international position of the United States. The study of military policy and the study of war are two distinct although related pursuits.

This theory does not presuppose a mechanical or deterministic alternation of equilibrium and disequilibrium. It simply holds that at any given time military policy is a response to both its external and internal environments. If these environments are stable, a policy equilibrium *may* emerge; if not, disequilibrium prevails. The period of each may be long or short and bears no necessary fixed relationship to the other. Rapid changes in the environments might make disequilibrium rather than its opposite the rule in military policy. The theory assumes only that policy must be related to these environments, not that it moves through any necessary progression of phases. Before World War II American military policy evolved through three phases of equilibrium and two of disequilibrium.[3]

1. Neutrality and Eighteenth-Century Equilibrium. In the late eighteenth century, America was directly involved in European politics. To cope with this fact the Founding Fathers espoused a foreign policy of neutrality. The military system they inherited from the colonial period and which they attempted to refine and to develop reflected this policy. The Founding Fathers agreed that their principal military need was for a well-organized and trained militia which could protect the country against European invasion and yet not be a weight in European politics or a threat to domestic liberties. A standing army should be maintained only to the extent necessary to protect the frontiers against surprises. The Federalists wished the defense of American neutrality to include the protection of the neutral rights of American commerce. Hence they favored the maintenance of a navy adequate for this purpose.

2. Disequilibrium: Separation of Europe and America, 1803–1823. Between 1803 and 1823 the cession of Louisiana and Florida, the independence of Latin America, the end of the Franco-British wars, the maritime supremacy of the British fleet, and the Monroe Doctrine marked the separation of America from European politics. This fundamental change in the international environment led to equally drastic changes in military policy. By the mid-1820s a new military system had emerged.

3. Isolation and Continental Equilibrium. Isolated from Europe, the United States no longer needed a militia to protect itself against invasion, and the militia disintegrated as a military force. Military policy was shaped by the needs of continental and commercial expansion. The principal functions of the Regular Army became Indian fighting and the internal development of the country. War Department organization, the personnel system of the Army, its educational system, its lack of a general staff and reserve system, all reflected the primacy of these functions. The principal function of the Navy was the peacetime protection of American commerce abroad. Consequently it was dispersed about the world in a number of squadrons. Apart from these "police" duties, as Mahan contemptuously called them, the Navy had few military functions. As a result, it accumulated a variety of scientific and diplomatic activities. Once the basic missions and organization of the services emerged in the 1820s, they remained remarkably stable for sixty years.

4. Disequilibrium: Emergence on the World Scene, 1880–1916. In the last decades of the nineteenth century, fundamental changes in both the domestic and external environments again drastically altered American military policy. At home, the frontier disappeared and the country became industrialized. Abroad, the United States acquired interests in the Pacific, and the rise of Germany and Japan changed the European and Asian power balances. From the mid-1880s to World War I controversy and innovation characterized American military policy. The nineteenth-century military system disappeared and was replaced by a very different system.

5. Mobilization Strategy and the Interwar Equilibrium. The new military system reflected the old fact of American distance from Europe and Asia and the new danger of American involvement in European and Asian wars. Given this fact and this danger, the key to strategy was the concept of mobilization. In contrast to the dispersed naval vessels on "police" duty and the Indian-fighting Army of the continental period, the principal elements of the interwar equilibrium were: (a) a strong Navy and battlefleet, second to none, as a first line of defense capable of dominating the western Atlantic and eastern Pacific; (b) a small Regular Army devoted primarily to the preservation and increase of military knowledge and equipped with a general staff to plan for future wars; (c) a large manpower potential consisting in part of organized reserve forces and in part of untrained civilians who, it was assumed, could be mobilized and trained in an emergency; and (d) a strong civilian industrial economy capable of conversion to war production in an emergency. The principal ideas and features of this military system developed before World War I. From the end of the war to the beginning of the rearmament for World War II the military system remained remarkably stable. Equilibrium prevailed in military policy. The changes in the international environment which followed upon World War II made this system as obsolete as the continental system and introduced a new period of disequilibrium, change, and controversy in American military policy.

2. MILITARY POLICY IN THE COLD WAR
CHANGES IN EXTERNAL AND DOMESTIC ENVIRONMENTS

During World War II Americans expected that their postwar external environment would differ from their prewar environment. The old world of isolation and sporadic involvement in European wars to rectify or forestall changes in the European balance of power was to be replaced by a new world of internationalism and collective security. The United States and its major allies would participate in world affairs through a world organization. The full weight of this organization would be thrown against any aggressor. The American military system would consist of those forces committed to the world organization and relatively small additional forces to man the Atlantic and Pacific bases and provide the naval shield for continental security.

World War II did produce fundamental changes in the environments of American military policy. The realities of the postwar world, however, bore little resemblance to the wartime images of the postwar world. The domestic environment was characterized by relatively sustained prosperity and full employment. The external environment was dominated by at least five major features which few had anticipated while the war was in progress: the destruction of the European balance-of-power system and its replacement by the Soviet-American antagonism; the steady growth in power of the Soviet bloc; the Communist conquest of China and the emergence of Communist China as a major power; the decline

2. THE COLD WAR

of the old colonial systems and the emergence of new nations in Africa and southern Asia; and, finally, the development and proliferation of nuclear weapons.

CONTAINMENT AND ALTERNATIVE FOREIGN POLICIES

The disagreements with the Soviet Union over Germany, the United Nations, Poland, and Iran in 1945 and 1946 caused the wartime assumption of great power unity to be replaced by the postwar assumption of Soviet hostility. During 1946 and 1947 governmental leaders concluded that the United States must oppose further Soviet expansion and that the best means of dealing with the Soviets was through tough bargaining and negotiation from strength. This policy of "containment" was advocated within the government in 1946 and publicly stated in the Truman Doctrine and Mr. Kennan's "The Sources of Soviet Conduct" in 1947. It was, moreover, supported by the overwhelming majority of the American people. "The public," Gabriel Almond concluded from a study of attitudes on foreign affairs in the late 1940s, "apparently makes one primary requirement of American foreign policy: that it be resolute and firm in its opposition to Soviet expansion." [4] The American people were normally willing to support any action necessary to stop Soviet expansion. This was, as Almond pointed out, the central feature of the "foreign policy consensus" which emerged in the late 1940s.

Containment, however, was not without rivals. As reactions to the government's policy, alternative policies were brought forward by dissenters within the government or groups outside the government. Public debate of foreign policy usually came after policy had been made, rather than before, and was a result of governmental choice rather than a prologue to choice. The criticisms of the governmental policy also tended to confirm the choice and to make the adopted policy more conscious and explicit.

The first publicly debated alternative to containment was a policy of negotiation and concessions. This assumed that Soviet goals were limited and legitimate, and that Soviet expansion and intransigence were the products of fear, isolation, and insecurity. Responsibility for the antagonism between the two countries rested largely upon the negative and hostile attitude of the United States. The United States should reduce its military establishment and the influence of military men over its policy, stop brandishing the atomic bomb and backing British imperialism in the Middle East, and recognize the desirability and necessity of supporting "progressive" and socialist regimes in Europe and Asia. This policy received considerable support in the early years of the Cold War, between 1946 and 1949, particularly from liberal and left-wing groups but also from some conservatives. The conflict between it and the governmental policy was symbolized by the discharge of Henry Wallace as Secretary of Commerce in September, 1946, and, a few months later, the resignation of James F. Byrnes as Secretary of State in part because President Truman thought that he was too "soft" with the Soviets. The decisive defeat of Wallace as the Progressive Party candidate for President in 1948 signaled the rejection of the concessions and negotiation policy by the American people.

A second alternative to containment was the restriction of American concerns to the western hemisphere and the oceans surrounding it, a postwar version of the prewar policy of isolation. It argued that direct and continuing involvement in European affairs was detrimental to American interests. Militarily, American superiority in sea- and airpower meant that almost no changes in the balance of power on the Eurasian continent could directly threaten American security. Proponents of this policy usually made clear their hostility to the Soviet Union, but they also asserted that the United States should not attempt to restrict the growth of Soviet power until vital American interests were directly threatened. In various forms these policy attitudes undoubtedly had a widespread, if latent, popularity. They were articulately advanced as an alternative to containment only after some of the latter's unpleasant military implications became obvious in 1951 and 1952: the prolonged involvement in an old-style conventional war in Korea and the intensified involvement in Europe by the substantial increase in American forces stationed there. Support for a policy of withdrawal was openly and covertly expressed in Herbert Hoover's "Gibraltar" speech at the end of 1950, the "Great Debate" of 1951 over the dispatch of the additional troops to Europe, and the MacArthur controversy a few months later. Whatever chances of success this policy had, however, were ended at the Republican convention of 1952.

A third alternative to containment held that the United States should precipitate a showdown with the Communist powers. This policy, a product of dissatisfaction and irritation with the continuing demands of containment, was advanced when those demands were most onerous, during the years 1950–1952. This viewpoint rested, implicitly, upon the assumption that time was on the Soviet side and that the United States should use its superior strength before it was dissipated or neutralized. Showdown proposals took three forms. First, some advocated outright preventive war. Following Soviet explosion of an atomic bomb in August, 1949, it was argued that war between the two countries was inevitable sooner or later, and from the American point of view it would be desirable to precipitate a showdown while the United States still possessed a monopoly of operational nuclear weapons. Subsequently, after the outbreak of the Korean War, this line of argument was reinforced by the contention that the Soviets aimed to dissipate the strength of the United States in a series of limited wars with Soviet satellites. Hence, to avoid piecemeal destruction, the United States should act immediately against the source of the trouble. These preventive war policies never received substantial support within the government, and their rejection in the fall of 1950 was symbolized by the suspension of General Orvil A. Anderson, the resignation of Secretary of Defense Louis Johnson (who was reputed to be sympathetic to them), and the presidential censure of Navy Secretary Francis Matthews for expressing similar views.[5]

A much more significant version of the showdown policy developed during the winter and spring of 1951 as a result of the Chinese Communist intervention in Korea. This argued that the United States could not and should not continue to fight an indeterminate war in Korea but should bring the full weight of its sea- and airpower to bear upon the Communist Chinese to force them to withdraw from Korea and, in some versions, to surrender their control of the Chinese mainland. The supporters of this position differed sharply from those urging a showdown with the Soviet Union since they usually held that the United States could achieve a decisive victory over the Chinese Communists without provoking

Soviet intervention. The rejection of this alternative by the Truman Administration came to a dramatic climax in April, 1951, with the cashiering of General MacArthur, but it was reopened by the Republican victory in 1952. Indeed, President Eisenhower and his advisers partially adopted this viewpoint when they agreed that failing an early armistice in Korea they would authorize American attacks on Manchuria. In this case, the means which they were willing to adopt were those advocated by the supporters of a China showdown. The aim which they wished to achieve, however, was much more limited: agreement upon a divided Korea rather than the withdrawal of the Chinese from Korea, much less the destruction of Communist power in China itself. The successful conclusion of an armistice in July, 1953, however, made even a resort to the means unnecessary.

A final version of the showdown policy was much less specific than the others but like them was directed toward moderating the frustrations of the Cold War. This was the policy of "liberation," advocated in extreme form by several right-wing publicists in 1952 and 1953 and in a more tempered version by John Foster Dulles in the spring of 1952. Dulles argued that existing American policy was costing too much in taxes and loss of civil liberty and that it was "not designed to win victory conclusively." Its aim was not to solve the problem but to live with it "presumably forever." "Ours are treadmill policies," the future Secretary of State declared, "which, at best, might perhaps keep us in the same place until we drop exhausted." In their place Dulles urged a dynamic foreign policy which would deny the Iron Curtain, refuse to recognize Communist control of eastern Europe and China, and promote the creation of task forces to stimulate freedom in these areas. The satellites would be liberated not through military means but by "intelligent care." [6] During his campaign, General Eisenhower made the more cautious declaration that "We can never rest—and we must so inform all the world, including the Kremlin—that until the enslaved nations of the world have in the fulness of freedom the right to choose their own path, that then, and then only, can we say that there is a possible way of living peacefully and permanently with communism in the world." [7]

The liberation version of a showdown policy had considerable support among leading Republicans and, undoubtedly, considerable popularity among the voters. Once the Eisenhower Administration came into office, however, the policy received little more than token recognition. Chiang was "unleashed" in 1953 when he did not have sufficient force to do anything drastic, and then releashed in 1955 when it seemed that he might do something drastic. The East German uprising of 1953 and the Polish and Hungarian disturbances of 1956 provoked little positive response by the American government. Actually, of course, liberation was a long-term goal shared by the Eisenhower Administration and its predecessor; once in office, however, the former, like the latter, was unable to discover any effective means, apart from military force, of realizing it in the short run. The rejection of other alternative policies had been symbolized by the defeat or ouster of their supporters: Wallace, Taft, MacArthur, Anderson, and Johnson. The rejection of liberation was signaled by the triumph of Eisenhower, and the resulting absence of any fundamental change in American foreign policy. The foreign policy consensus was confirmed. For the rest of the 1950s no other significant groups advanced alternative foreign policies. In part this was because the Eisenhower Administration reduced the burdens of containment. In part, also, it was because the opportunity for choice, if it existed at all, was clearly passing, and it was recognized that the alternative policies were not so much ways of handling the problem of Soviet hostility as they were ways of avoiding it.

Publicly, the alternative policies were advanced at different times and debated in different arenas, depending upon the nature of the political situation. Nonetheless, their existence as formal alternatives to the current policy was recognized throughout most of the period. The two major overhauls of military strategy—NSC 68 and the New Look—included a formal canvass of these options. Drawn up in January and February of 1950, NSC 68 listed the four alternatives of American policy as: 1) continuation of the present course of action without strengthening American capabilities or reducing American commitments; 2) preventive war; 3) withdrawal to the western hemisphere, a Fortress America policy; and 4) the development of free-world capabilities and cohesion. The recommendation, of course, was in favor of the last, i.e., the continuation of existing policy and the build-up of American and allied strength.[8] Three years later, in May, 1953, the resurvey of American national security policy which General Eisenhower had promised before his election got under way with the appointment of three task forces to develop the cases for the existing policy of containment, a policy of drawing a sharp line and threatening devastating retaliation if the Soviets should cross the line, and a policy of liberation. Later, a fourth alternative, setting a time limit on negotiations and then threatening decisive action if agreements were not reached, was explored but rejected as too similar to "preventive war." Eventually, after the task forces had presented their cases, the NSC Planning Board, in NSC-162, recommended adherence to the existing policy with slight modifications favoring the second alternative.[9] The basic outlines of American foreign policy remained relatively unchanged from the first years of the Truman Administration until the end of the Eisenhower Administration.

THE ADJUSTMENT OF STRATEGY AND STRUCTURE

The reconstitution of foreign policy to meet the needs of the Cold War was reasonably rapid. The reconstitution of military policy was slower and more complex. It was relatively easy to visualize the Soviet Union as a major threat to the United States. It was more difficult to visualize what was demanded, particularly in the military field, to meet that threat. A foreign policy of containment implied that the aim of military strategy was to deter or to defeat Soviet aggressions. But what were the specific military requirements of such a policy? What did it mean in terms of the composition and uses of force, the size of the Air Force, Army, and Navy? What contingencies had to be prepared for or prevented from arising? Necessarily, the full implications of the Cold War for military policy were not seen immediately, nor would different groups of policy shapers recognize them at the same time. During the fifteen years after World War II American military policy was in a state of disequilibrium. The processes of adjustment were still underway in 1960.

The principal impetus to change, of course, came from the external environment. Foreign policy increased in importance relative to domestic policy. In military policy, a comparable revolution occurred in the relative importance of strategy and structure. Throughout the continental and the mobilization phases, military policy was defined largely in structural terms. Issues concerning the budget, personnel policy, and organization dominated the discussions of military affairs. Strategic categories were often ignored or left implicit, and strategic purposes were subordinated to the needs of the domestic environment. Civilian control was often defined in almost exclusively budgetary terms. Upton wrote *The Military Policy of the United States* as if the subject involved little beyond the methods of recruiting and organizing manpower for the armed forces. Similarly, the National Defense Acts of 1916 and 1920 essayed to define military policy, although they were conceived with little reference to the state of American foreign relations and the strategic categories of policy. The 1916 Act established a National Defense Council of five cabinet officers without including the Secretary of State. After World War II, on the other hand, external goals and strategy became increasingly preeminent. The great issues of military policy concerned force levels and weapons systems, alliances and interventions, limited war and massive retaliation, the innovation of new strategic programs, and, above all, the conflict of domestic and international goals in shaping the magnitude of the military effort. Structural issues concerning organization, personnel, procurement were still debated and fought over, but they were overshadowed by the strategic categories of policy more directly related to foreign policy needs.

Closely related to the shifts in the relative importance of strategy and structure were differences in the rate of change in the content of these categories. The new external environment required changes in all aspects of military policy. The different rates of change were the product of two factors: variations in the sensitivity of the individuals and groups concerned with the policy area to the changes in the external environment, and variations in the number and character of the individuals and groups involved in the policy area itself. The makers of foreign policy in the White House and the State Department naturally reacted first to the increased Soviet hostility in 1945 and 1946. Educating leading congressmen on the new problems and capitalizing on the inherent congressional suspicion of Communists, they were able to alter drastically American foreign policy in a very short time. The strategic aspects of military policy, on the other hand, took considerably longer to change. Involved here were great bureaucratic organizations, ongoing military programs, and, of critical importance, established patterns of thought. Diplomats value flexibility; military leaders value certainty and stability. Unlike the diplomats, the military are trained in doctrine, and doctrine inevitably changes slowly. In addition, alterations in strategy involved fundamental changes in the magnitude of the military effort which required the participation and acquiescence of a great many domestic agencies and interests. Adjustment in the various elements of structural policy required the acquiescence of even more specialized groups. Thus, changes in strategy tended to lag behind changes in foreign policy, and changes in structure behind those in strategy.

Structural issues will not be dealt with directly in the main part of this volume. This omission does not mean that structural issues were unimportant, even in the Cold War. Indeed, just as the nineteenth century seemed to assume that military policy should be made without reference to foreign policy, the mid-twentieth century seemed at times to assume that military policy should be made with reference only to foreign policy. Such a view was unrealistic in failing to appreciate the full scope and complexity of military policy and the conflicting values which necessarily enter into its formulation. Domestic values and structural categories were an inherent aspect of the policy-making process. In the long run, in fact, the mundane issues of budgetary procedures, administrative organization, pay and promotions may have just as decisive an influence on both the external and domestic aspects of policy as the more dramatic and glamorous issues of war plans, alliances, weapon systems, and force levels. The reason why at Balaklava was not the strategy, tactics, or weapons of the British Army but its system of officer recruitment.

While strategic issues increased in importance relative to structural issues, within strategy decisions on program assumed a new importance relative to decisions on the use of force. This was due not to the general character of the challenges stemming from the external environment but rather to the substantive character of the strategy that was adopted to meet those threats. The principal goal of a strategy of deterrence was to prevent other states from taking steps which would make conflict inevitable. The effectiveness of this policy depended upon proper communication of intentions and upon the size and nature of the forces of deterrence. Decisions on strategic programs, the size of the military effort, force levels, and weapons systems became the critical core of military policy. Previously, the admonition that military policy must reflect foreign policy normally meant that decisions on the use of military force must be compatible with the long-range foreign policy objectives of the state: that a nation should not go to war or commit its troops abroad except in support of those objectives. After World War II, the relation between foreign policy and military policy was equally close. But, given a policy of deterrence, the crux of the relation was whether the decisions on force levels and weapons were the proper ones to bring into existence and to maintain the military strength necessary to deter actions incompatible with American foreign policy objectives. The success of foreign policy now depended more upon *what* military forces were maintained rather than *how* those military forces were used. Indeed, if the proper decisions were made on forces and weapons, and if intentions were properly declared, it would seldom be necessary to use the forces and weapons.

The extent of the military strength required for deterrence meant that strategic program decisions had a greater impact upon society as a whole than they had ever had before in peacetime. They directly involved the allocation of approximately 10 percent of the national product. They had consequences for private well-being, business prosperity, fiscal policy, taxation, welfare programs, and many other activities. Not only determining the size of the overall military effort but also allocating the resources among competing military programs became a complex process involving the future of great political interests. Declaratory foreign policy usually concerned directly only the relations between the government and foreign powers. Strategic programs, however, directly affected both intergovernmental relations in the external world and intergroup relations within American society.

The remainder of this volume deals primarily with the adjustments in the magnitude of the military effort and the content of strategic programs during the first fifteen years after World War II. It is important to bear in mind, however, that these changes in strategic programs were but one part, albeit an extremely important part, of a general process of adjustment involving nonmilitary foreign and domestic policies, strategic declarations and actions, and the structural aspects of military policy.

CHAPTER II

The Search for a Stable Deterrent

3. THE DUAL QUEST

In the changed political conditions after World War II a strategy of deterrence demanded far more resources than the strategy of mobilization did during the interwar years. The military requirements of foreign policy conflicted sharply with the goals of the government and groups in American society to expand domestic governmental programs, to balance the budget, and to reduce taxes. These goals, in turn, directed the search for military programs toward the minimum deterrent adequate for security. The "ceilings" on the military effort were not the arbitrary caprice of short-sighted budget officials, but the product of important and legitimate social and political goals. The desire to minimize the military burden, moreover, was usually associated with the desire to stabilize it—to define once and for all the level of military effort necessary for security. Military policy between 1945 and 1960 was the outcome, first, of the conflict between the old strategy of mobilization and the new strategy of deterrence and, second, of the conflict between military and nonmilitary claims on resources. The interaction of these two sets of conflicting pressures produced a continuing search for a stable—and economical—deterrent.

CONTENT: MOBILIZATION AND DETERRENCE

The actual change in the content of strategy was slow and partial. In theory, however, the fundamental outlines of the new strategy, the Gestalt, as it were, of deterrence, differed distinctly from the strategy of the prewar years. Every strategy has its own semantics. The principal phrases and concepts of the prewar strategy were: total war, nation-in-arms, citizen-soldiers, industrial potential, M-day plans, mobilization requirements, hemispheric defense, preparedness, "the Navy as the first line of defense," no foreign entanglements. Those of the postwar strategy were: readiness, force-in-being, massive retaliation, limited war, graduated deterrence, continental defense, international balanced forces, collective security, military assistance, balance of terror.

Before World War II, American strategy implicitly assumed that the geographical remoteness of the United States from other powers, the superiority of the American fleet in western hemisphere waters, and the struggles which must ensue on the Eurasian continent before the balance of power there could be upset, all would give the United States sufficient time in a crisis to convert its manpower and industrial potential into operational military strength. Wars were caused by European developments beyond the control of the United States. After World War II American strategy came to be based on the assumption that the United States would have little or no warning of when or where military action might be required. War would begin with an attack on the United States or areas which the United States was committed to defend. The main purpose of postwar military policy was to reduce the probability of such attacks. Prewar strategy stressed mobilization potential; postwar strategy stressed ready forces-in-being. As one expert estimated, the value of force-in-being went up 10 percent per annum after 1945 and the value of reserve power declined proportionately.[1] The prewar concept of "preparedness" implied that peacetime military forces primarily affected the probability of victory or defeat in war, rather than the probability of peace or war. The term "preparedness" itself had passive connotations. In contrast, the postwar concept of "deterrence" had active connotations. Force was designed not to be adequate to anything that might happen, but to control and influence what would happen. In a mobilization strategy, military forces which were never used were a sign of poor planning; in a deterrent strategy, they were a sign of success. In a mobilization strategy, the usefulness of peacetime military forces was related to a hypothetical future contingency; in a deterrent strategy, the payoff of military forces was in the continuing present. In mobilization, the probability of future war shaped decisions on military strength; in deterrence, decisions on strength strongly influenced the probability of future war. In the old strategy, deterrence was impossible in peace; in the new strategy, mobilization was impossible in war.

Assuming the continuation of wartime harmony among the great powers and an effective system of collective security through the United Nations, Administration officials and other experts in 1945 generally expected that the future American military establishment would be an extension and development of the prewar system. Its key elements would be: 1) a contribution to the UN military forces; 2) bases in the Atlantic and Pacific to which American troops on the European and Asian continents would be withdrawn following the end of occupation; 3) a strong air force and navy in being; 4) continuation of the American monopoly of atomic weapons until an effective system of international controls was agreed upon; 5) a very small Regular Army; and 6) universal military training and a large, well-organized reserve of citizen-soldiers.[2]

The development of the Cold War made the expectations of 1945 almost as irrelevant as the realities of 1935. A new security system was necessary to replace evaporated distance, depreciated potential, and the disrupted framework of universal security. By 1955 it had become clear that the principal components of the postwar military system were: 1) a massive retaliatory force strong and ready enough to deter major Soviet aggression; 2) continental defense forces to protect the retaliatory force as a supplementary deterrent and to minimize damage if the deterrent should fail; 3) European defense forces, American and allied, to deter small-scale attacks on western Europe and to insure that any major attack would require a conscious choice of all-out war; and 4) American forces and allied forces (supported by American military assistance) strong enough to deter or, if this proved impossible, to suppress quickly small-scale aggressions or disorders inimical to American interests in the "gray areas" of the world. The usefulness of all these forces, moreover, varied directly with their readiness for action. The air crews of the Strategic Air Command, the carrier task forces in the Mediterranean and off Formosa, the interceptor squadrons and missile batteries of the Continental Air Defense Command, the tactical air wings and 7th Army divisions in Europe, the radar stations, planes, and ships of the Distant Early Warning Line, the STRAC units and Marine battalions earmarked for "brushfire" wars, all were required to achieve and to maintain a state of readiness without parallel in American history.

Previously American military alliances, effectually if not formally, were the products of war and were terminated in peace; they were instruments of mobilization. In the postwar period, however, military alliances were the products of peace, with the dual purpose of making clear the commitment of the United States to defend foreign territory and of increasing the combined military force which might be brought to the defense of a territory in which we had an interest. They were instruments of deterrence.

The process of change by which the deterrent forces were developed was confused, complex, and, at times, ponderous. Innovation, that is, changes in the attitudes, power, and functions of groups, was relatively easy in some areas, very difficult in others. Fifteen years after World War II the process of adjustment was still going on. Both established political ideas and military doctrine hampered change. Beliefs that the "military mind" was a threat to free institutions, that continued international friction must be resolved either in "real" peace or total war, that military forces caused war and arms races could only end in war, that war was justified only in defense of vital national interests and moral principles, that economic strength and manpower potential were the true sources of American military power, that the tough national decisions on foreign policy could somehow be avoided by reliance on the United Nations and collective security; these attitudes, held to varying degrees by military men and civilian statesmen, helped shape postwar American military policy. Reflecting earlier American experience and conditions, they complicated the process of adjustment to a new environment after 1945.

Changes in military systems frequently take place after major wars, but they are often shaped by wartime experience rather than postwar peacetime needs. After 1815 the War and Navy Departments carefully prepared plans to win the War of 1812. Similarly, after World War II most leaders assumed that the war of the future would be similar to the war just fought. The immediate postwar plans for unification of the military establishment, the coordination

3. THE DUAL QUEST

of foreign and military policy, the creation of mobilization planning agencies, universal military training, and the stress on strategic airpower reflected the needs and experiences of World War II. Programs and activities which demonstrated their value in World War II were continued into the postwar period. Defects and shortfalls in World War II were corrected in the postwar period. In many cases, these proposals, such as improved coordination between foreign and military policy, were highly relevant to the needs of the Cold War. In other cases, such as UMT, they were inappropriate to Cold War requirements.

SCOPE: SOVIET POWER AND STABILITY

The changes in content of American strategy contrast markedly with the desires of both the Truman and Eisenhower Administrations to achieve "stability" in military policy. Stability, however, did not mean technological stagnation or rigid adherence to old strategic concepts. Rather it meant stability in the overall level of military effort, a balance between military and nonmilitary claims upon resources, which could be continued indefinitely. It was equally the goal of military and civilians, executives and legislators, Republicans and Democrats. That everyone was for stability, however, implied of course that stability had many meanings. To some, stability meant stability of programs or forces; to others, stability in expenditures; and to still others, stability in the ratio of defense spending to the gross national product. Increases in expenditures were justified in terms of program stability, reductions in program in terms of expenditure stability.

The popularity of stability seemed to have four principal sources. First, people were aware that the Soviet threat was a continuing one and that many old policies were no longer acceptable. The tremendous expansion of the military establishment in war and its contraction in peace were characteristic of mobilization strategy. Rejection of this feast-and-famine pattern was thus, in a sense, "progressive." Implicitly also, however, people assumed that the opposite of feast-and-famine was stability and hence that it was an inherent characteristic of a deterrent strategy.[3] This proposition was more dubious. Conceivably, deterrence might require either a continually increasing effort or a continually decreasing effort. The opposite of a cycle is a secular trend which may be up, down, or steady.

Stability was also popular, particularly with civilian members of the Administration, because it was so easily associated with economy. A stable level of military effort usually meant a lower one than was otherwise contemplated: stability was more often an argument against imminent feast than against imminent famine. Inevitably, policy-makers feared that too high a military level would lose support and would be reduced. Hence, it was better to settle for a lower but more stable effort.

Third, the quest for stability often seemed to stem from a desire to define permanently the limits of the military problem, to establish once and for all what was adequate for security, and to be relieved of a succession of difficult choices between security claims and conflicting domestic demands. This view, in turn, was related to the expectation that military requirements could be precisely determined. They were fixed and definite—provided, of course, that they did not conflict seriously with other requirements. The military effort should be sufficient to provide the minimum necessary for security. Anything more was wasteful; anything less was dangerous. The defense effort must be established at a level determined by us and not subject to fluctuation with every change in the international climate or smile, threat, or feint of the Soviets. The quest for stability, in this respect, was related to the traditional American desire to find permanent solutions to continuing problems of political choice without reference to the baffling and complicating actions of foreign governments. Isolationism and the desire for final solutions frequently loomed in the background of the search for stability.

A fourth source of support for stability was the desire of the military themselves to have firm guidelines upon which to base their planning. "On and off," "stop and start," "up and down," policies are continuing targets of military criticism. Second only to the military desire for a clear definition of mission or goals is the military desire for a clear and stable definition of the resources available to achieve those goals. Both, the military believe, are essential to effective planning of forces and programs. "Lack of rea-

3. THE DUAL QUEST

sonable stability," General Taylor said, quoting Secretary Wilson, "is the most wasteful and expensive practice in our military establishment," as he argued the case for stability in the Army's missions, manpower, and money.[4]

For the politician, stability primarily meant isolating the level of military effort from the perplexing uncertainties of international politics; for the military man, it primarily meant isolating the military effort from the equally perplexing vagaries of domestic politics. The principal long-term threat to a stable military effort, however, undoubtedly came from the steady growth in power of the Communist bloc. Throughout the postwar period, the increase of Soviet economic and technological capabilities at rates apparently higher than those of the United States threatened to upset the balance of power essential for the security of the West. At the end of World War II American productive capacity was intact while that of the Soviet Union had been largely devastated. Soviet superiority in land power was counterbalanced by American superiority in air and sea power and the American monopoly of nuclear weapons. As late as December, 1947, Secretary of Defense Forrestal could list the "four outstanding military facts of the world" as:

(1) The predominance of Russian land power in Europe and Asia.
(2) The predominance of American sea power.
(3) Our exclusive possession of the atomic bomb.
(4) American productive capacity.[5]

The following decade saw the relative decline of each of the American sources of strength. Productive capacity tended to lose its military value in war, and American productive capacity had only limited military relevance in peace. The American monopoly of nuclear weapons disappeared. American predominance in seapower remained, but beneath it lurked the Soviet fleet of long-range submarines. During the same period, the Soviets developed an impressive number of nuclear weapons, the largest air force in the world, including a significant strategic capability, equality if not superiority in long-range missiles, and the second largest navy in the world. These military achievements rested upon the twin pillars of a rapidly growing economy and the sustained allocation of a substantial proportion of economic effort to military purposes.

In the three major wars of its history, time had always been on the side of the United States: the longer the war the greater the predominance of the United States and its allies over their opponents. In the Cold War, also, Americans initially assumed that "time is on our side" and that the Soviet Union would eventually collapse or mellow from internal stresses and strains. Yet the steady growth of Soviet power and the expansion of Communist influence in Asia were facts of the Cold War. American military policy confronted not a condition but a trend. It was a grim trend. It was a trend which could not be stopped. The problem was: Could it be duplicated or neutralized within the limits of a stable military effort?

THE PHASES OF MILITARY POLICY

The search for an adequate strategy of deterrence and a stable level of military effort continued throughout the fifteen years after World War II. The changing environment of military policy, however, made it necessary to sacrifice either one goal or the other. The effort to strike a balance went through four principal phases. In each phase policy in part reflected conscious efforts to spell out long-range goals and means (NSC-68, the New Look) and in part a series of specific adjustments to immediate needs. In each case the government attempted to define a course which would provide adequately for American security with a minimum sacrifice of other essential values. The strategy of each phase represented a different balance between mobilization and deterrence, between security needs and domestic demands, and among the major military programs. In no phase was military strategy "consistent"; change was slow and never complete; policy always involved conflicting purposes and conflicting programs. In each phase American policy-makers thought they had located a "plateau" where it would be possible to "level off" military efforts and maintain a "stable" policy. In each case the hopes for stability were dashed. Within a few years changes in the external or internal environments of policy compelled a new strategic adjustment. The relentless course of events over which the government had little or no control undermined ceilings and strategies, war plans and weapons systems.

4. THE INTERIM YEARS: WORLD WAR II TO JANUARY, 1950
COLD WAR AND DEMOBILIZATION, 1945–1946

During the eighteen months after V-E day, the World War foreign policy of great power unity gave way to the Cold War foreign policy of containment. During the same period, military policy changed fundamentally in scope but not in content: in classic fashion it simply shifted from the feast phase of a mobilization strategy to the famine phase. Foreign policy adjusted to the rise of a new opponent, military policy only to the defeat of old ones.

The change in foreign policy began before the end of World War II. On April 2, 1945, the Secretary of State advised the Secretaries of War and the Navy "of serious deterioration in our relations with Russia." A few days later Ambassador Harriman warned by cable from Moscow that we "must clearly realize that the Soviet program is the establishment of totalitarianism, ending personal liberty and democracy as we know and respect it." The Soviets, he said, were simultaneously pursuing three lines: collaboration with the United States and Great Britain in establishing a world security organization; creation of their own security system by extending their sway over their neighbors; and extension of their influence into other countries through local Communist parties and the opportunities offered by economic chaos and democratic freedoms. Arguing that the Soviets interpreted the "generous and considerate attitude" of the United States as a sign of weakness, he urged that the United States follow a tough policy, "that we should maintain positions that would be hard for the Soviet authorities if they maintained positions hard for us; and that we should hurt them if they hurt us." [6]

The cables from Harriman represented the first effort to assess the overall nature of the Soviet problem and to spell out an approach for dealing with it. Significantly, the initiative came from the Moscow embassy, that part of the government most exposed and most sensitive to the actions of the Soviets. In Washington, Forrestal, Leahy, and others accepted the Harriman analysis. The new President made it clear in the spring and summer of 1945 that he intended to bargain toughly with the Soviets on specific issues. He refrained, however, from formally endorsing the Harriman retaliation thesis and declined to utilize American forces in Europe to stop the extension of Soviet influence westward. Nevertheless, the controversies with the Soviets over Poland, the Balkans, UN procedures, Iran, the Dardanelles, and the Italian peace treaty underwrote the validity of Harriman's thesis, and in September, 1945, for the first time, the United States allowed a high-level conference (the Council of Foreign Ministers) to break down without agreement rather than make further concessions to Soviet demands.[7] Throughout the last six months of 1945, American policy-makers gradually came to agree on the need for a tougher line with the Soviets. The wartime image of postwar great power unity was slowly replaced by a new image of Soviet-American rivalry.

The expectations of conflict were formally confirmed on February 9, 1946. In a grim speech, which Justice Douglas labeled "The Declaration of World War III," Generalissimo Stalin argued that a peaceful international order was "impossible under the present capitalistic development of world economy" and announced a five-year plan for massive industrial expansion.[8] Almost simultaneously, in an eight-thousand-word cable from Moscow, George F. Kennan furnished the first overall postwar explanation of Soviet behavior and suggested a course for dealing with it. The Soviet leaders, he declared, had inherited "the traditional and instinctive Russian sense of insecurity," which reinforced their adherence to Marxist dogma and their view of the inevitability of conflict between the capitalist and communist worlds leading to the victory of the latter. Russia, he warned, would expand its influence through every possible means and attempt to fill every power vacuum. At times tactical considerations might lead the Soviets to appear more friendly and amenable, but such moves were only temporary maneuvers. In Kennan's words:

We have here a political force committed fanatically to the belief that with the U.S. there can be no permanent *modus vivendi*, that it is desirable and necessary that the internal harmony of our society be disrupted, our traditional way of life be destroyed, the international authority of our state be broken, if Soviet power is to be secure. This political force has complete power of disposition over the energies of one of the world's

4. THE INTERIM YEARS

greatest peoples and the resources of the world's richest national territory. ... The problem of how to cope with this force is undoubtedly the greatest task our diplomacy has ever faced and probably the greatest it will ever have to face.[9]

To meet this force Kennan urged "cohesion, firmness, and vigor" on the part of the West. His cable furnished the preliminary rationale for a policy of firmness which was reflected immediately in the sterner tones of Secretary Byrnes' February 28 speech to the Overseas Press Club, the decision to send the *Missouri* to Turkey, and the successful resistance to Soviet demands upon Iran.

Firmness, however, was presumably more than a matter of attitude. At the same time that American policy toward Russia was hardening, the armed forces which might, in the final analysis, have to underwrite that policy were melting away. Harriman, Kennan, Forrestal, and others could fairly easily reassess Soviet intentions. To reverse or even to redirect the disintegration of American military strength was quite a different matter. Initial plans for postwar demobilization had been drawn up in the midst of the war: the Joint Chiefs approved a system of individual rather than unit demobilization in September, 1943. Two years later the last and greatest postwar demobilization of the American armed forces got under way. Only war justified the maintenance of large military forces. The war was over. Hence there was no reason to keep men in the armed services against their will. Such was the logic of demobilization prevalent among the troops, Congress, and a large and articulate minority of the public. Congressmen were reluctant to undertake the responsibility for establishing demobilization policies themselves, but with a few exceptions they did not hesitate to flail the War and Navy Departments for their slowness in discharging their men.[10]

The pressure to "bring the boys home" produced one of the most rapid demobilizations in world history. On V-J day the Army had 8,020,000 men. By January 1, 1946, it had been cut almost in half to 4,228,936 men. By July, 1946, ten months after the end of the war, it was down to 1,889,690 men. On V-J day the Army Air Forces had 218 effective combat groups. By January 1, 1946, there were only 109 effective groups. The strength of the Navy on V-J day was 3,400,000 men. In March, 1946, it was less than half this size, 1,600,000 men. The decline in the military effectiveness of the armed forces, moreover, far exceeded the decline in their personnel strengths. The rapid loss of men affected almost all units. Frequently it was impossible to replace individuals with critical occupational specialities. It became difficult to maintain equipment. Turnover was huge. Replacements often were not properly trained. One month after the end of the war, the Joint Strategic Survey Committee reported that "... a year or more would be required to reconstitute our military position at a fraction of its recent power." The same month an Air Force general declared that the point was rapidly being approached when "the Army Air Forces can no longer be considered anything more than a symbolic instrument of National Defense." On November 15, the European and Pacific theater commanders estimated that their troops could operate at only about 50 percent of their wartime efficiency. "By the Fall and Winter of 1945-1946 the armies and the air forces that had been victorious in Europe and in the Pacific were no longer a closely integrated military machine, but rather had disintegrated to little more than large groups of individual replacements." [11]

As the leaders of the government were well aware, foreign policy and military policy were moving in opposite directions. Stimson, Marshall, and Forrestal, all warned against too rapid demobilization. Their words, however, did little to stem the tide, and the disintegration of American military forces inevitably affected American diplomacy. The public and congressional pressure to speed up demobilization in September and October, 1945, probably encouraged the Soviets in their stringent demands at the London Council of Foreign Ministers. In November Secretary Byrnes expressed concern to the Secretaries of War and the Navy that the reductions underway and contemplated would reduce American influence. On January 11, 1946, after the overseas riots and demonstrations of American servicemen, Under Secretary of State Acheson declared that demobilization "was a matter of great embarrassment and concern to his own Department in their conduct of our foreign affairs." Still later, at the Paris Peace Conference in September, 1946, the Secretary of State expressed concern and "almost alarm" at proposed further reductions in American forces in Europe. Subsequently, Byrnes argued that he consciously felt it nec-

4. THE INTERIM YEARS

essary to refrain from speaking out vigorously in the fall of 1945 because of American military weakness. Only when General Eisenhower assured him in February, 1946, that the reorganization of the Army was progressing satisfactorily did Byrnes feel that he could publicly espouse a stronger line.[12]

Demobilization obviously affected what American diplomats felt they could say and the results they were likely to achieve in international bargaining. What could be done to ease this constraint and close the gap between foreign and military policies? To stem the tide of demobilization would have required the President and the Administration bluntly and dramatically to warn the nation of the threat from the Soviet Union. It was just exactly this, however, which the Administration was reluctant to do during the winter of 1945–1946. Reversing the disintegration of American military strength would require a denunciation of Soviet Russia which would undermine completely our ultimate objective of arriving at an appropriate agreement with her. But, on the other hand, agreement was impossible without the strength to compel it. To speak out would reveal fully our military weakness; to remain silent would perpetuate it.

These issues were raised many times during the winter of 1945–1946. In the middle of October Forrestal argued that the President should fully reveal to the people "the details of our dealings with the Russians and with the attitude which the Russians have manifested throughout." Byrnes, however, opposed this on the grounds that it would justify to the Russians their hostile attitude toward us. In January Forrestal suggested that the President contact leading newspaper publishers and radio commentators and explain to them the seriousness of the situation, and Secretary Ickes urged that the State Department make a nationwide broadcast portraying the debilitating effects of demobilization on foreign policy. The following month, in his lengthy analysis of the nature of the Soviet threat from Moscow, Kennan similarly demanded that the truth be told to the American people:

We must see that our public is educated to the realities of the Russian situation. I cannot overemphasize the importance of this. . . . I am convinced that there would be far less hysterical anti-Sovietism in our country today if realities of this situation were better understood by our people.

There is nothing as dangerous or terrifying as the unknown. It may also be argued that to reveal more information on our difficulties with Russia would reflect unfavorably on Russo-American relations. I feel that if there is any real risk here involved, it is one which we should have the courage to face, and the sooner the better.[13]

No dramatic presentation of the type desired by Forrestal, Ickes, and Kennan was made. Demobilization moved into its final stages as the policy of firmness hardened into a more explicit policy of containment. The issue which was raised, however, returned at each subsequent major reconsideration of American strategy, in 1950, 1953, and 1957. Should the Administration present to the American people the grim facts about unpleasant developments in international politics? The negative answer of the Truman Administration in 1946 foreshadowed similar responses in later crises.

Critics later lamented the rapidity and scope of the demobilization of 1945–1946 and the unfortunate effects it had upon American foreign policy. They deplored the irresponsibility of the troops, the pressures from Congress and the public, the ineffectuality of the Administration. They argued that stronger and more courageous leadership would have prevented the disintegration of America's armed might. To be sure, the rapid demobilization did weaken the support for American diplomacy in the first eighteen months after the end of the war. It is a mistake, however, to think that any other course was possible. Demobilization was the last phase of World War II. As such, it was not the alternative to a wiser and more effective policy but rather a prerequisite to it. The citizen-armies mobilized to fight World War II were ill-adapted to the requirements of the Cold War. Military support of diplomacy is not just a matter of numbers; it is also a question of purpose and organization. The decks had to be cleared, the World War II force dissolved, before new armies could be brought into existence shaped and trained for the radically new needs of the Cold War. Delayed demobilization would simply have meant delayed adjustment. This sober truth was recognized by at least some military men.[14] The Navy and the Air Force, which completed their demobilization in 1946, were able to develop the forces required for the Cold War faster than the Army, which did not complete its demobilization until June, 1947. Demobilization, with its uproar and chaos, the 80,000 letters a week to congressmen, the speeches and editorials denouncing brass and militarism, the soldier committees and "I wanta go home," was the final violent swing of the pendulum of the old order, total peace to total war to total peace, an indispensable prelude to the somber greyness of the Cold War dawn.

POLICY CONFLICT, 1947–1949

Demobilization of the World War II military system was a necessary but not sufficient cause for the creation of a Cold War military system. The foreign policy upon which that system presumably would be based was succinctly and publicly expressed by George Kennan in the spring of 1947:

[T]he main element of any United States policy toward the Soviet Union must be that of a long-term, patient but firm and vigilant containment of Russian expansive tendencies. . . . Soviet pressure against the free institutions of the western world is something that can be contained by the adroit and vigilant application of counter-force at a series of constantly shifting geographical and political points, corresponding to the shifts and maneuvers of Soviet policy, but which cannot be charmed or talked out of existence.[15]

In late 1947 or early 1948 this policy was elaborated in one of the first papers, NSC 20, processed through the new national security policy machinery.[16] Early in 1947 the Truman Doctrine revealed some of the political and economic implications of containment. What, however, were the military requirements of containment? What sort of strategy was needed to support this policy?

The State Department furnished one answer in a June, 1948, paper on Soviet actions "affecting the nature of the U.S. defense arrangements." This analysis argued that "war is not a probability but is always a possibility." It did not emphasize the need to shape the military system to the requirements of a future war. Instead, the paper held that the main reason it was "necessary that the United States maintain armed strength" was to furnish "support for our political position." The other purposes of American forces were to act "as a deterrent," to serve "as encouragement to nations endeavoring to resist Soviet political aggression," and, lastly, to "wage war successfully in case war should develop." This hierarchy of purposes implied that the United States would have to maintain strong military forces to support policy for an indefinite period. A policy, the report said, "based on the maintenance of a permanent state of adequate military preparation is better than an effort pointed toward a given peak of danger." The paper, in short, outlined most of the military requirements of a strategy of deterrence to support a policy of containment. It was, perhaps, a landmark in the evolution of American strategic thought from the old strategy of mobilization for general war to a new strategy of deterrence. Significantly, it was produced by the State Department, not the Joint Chiefs of Staff.[17]

At that time a strategy for containment appeared to have two principal implications. First, it seemed to require stronger military forces than were then being maintained. American foreign policy was constantly brought up short by the inadequacy of American military forces. As General Marshall later recollected:

> I remember, when I was Secretary of State I was being pressed constantly, particularly when in Moscow [Fourth Meeting of Council of Foreign Ministers, March–April, 1947], by radio message after radio message to give the Russians hell. . . . When I got back, I was getting the same appeal in relation to the Far East and China. At that time, my facilities for giving them hell—and I am a soldier and know something about the ability to give hell—was 1⅓ divisions over the entire United States. That is quite a proposition when you deal with somebody with over 260 and you have 1⅓rd.[18]

Similarly, at a White House meeting in February, 1958, General Gruenther warned of the dangers of trouble in Greece, Italy, Korea, and Palestine. At that time those were the "geographical and political points," in Kennan's phrase, where the "adroit and vigilant application of counter-force" might be necessary. The forces available, however, were minimal. The total general reserve for emergencies consisted of some 70,000 Army and Marine troops. The employment overseas of anything more than a division, Gruenther emphasized, would require partial mobilization. As Marshall succinctly pointed out: [W]e are playing with fire while we have nothing with which to put it out." [19]

The problem for containment was not just the inadequacy of American military strength but also the nature of that strength. Two of Forrestal's three key components of American military power, exclusive possession of the atomic bomb and productive

4. THE INTERIM YEARS

capacity, were almost irrelevant to current "support for our political position," and the useful scope of the third, predominant seapower, was limited. The atomic bomb was of little help in preserving the integrity of Iran, suppressing guerillas in Greece, or deterring an attack in Korea. Ground troops were needed for containment, and in July, 1949, the author of containment warned the Joint Strategic Survey Committee that the United States was limiting its choice, in the event of Soviet aggression, either to replying with the atomic bomb or to doing nothing. He urged the desirability of having two or more mobile and mechanized divisions, trained and ready for instant use in "brush fire" wars. Other State Department officials thought that even larger forces were necessary and that American nuclear retaliatory power also needed strengthening.[20] Two factors, however, prevented the military requirements of containment from being realized.

First, domestic political considerations limited the size of the military effort. The logic of foreign policy might require larger military forces. Inevitably, however, the President and the Administration also thought in terms of the domestic environment. President Truman fought a continuing battle over taxes with the Republican majority in the 80th Congress. In January, 1947, he explicitly declared his opposition to a general tax reduction. Congress responded by passing H.R. 1, providing significant cuts in individual tax rates. The President vetoed the bill. Within a month Congress passed a revised version of the bill. The President vetoed that. Early in 1948 President Truman again declared that tax revenues should not be decreased but also recommended a tax credit of $40 for each individual taxpayer to be compensated for by enactment of a modified excess profits tax. This was election year politics to the Republicans. Congress approved a general reduction in individual income tax rates and an increase in individual exemptions which, it was estimated, would decrease revenues by about $5 billion. The President vetoed this bill, and Congress passed it over his veto. Despite the Democratic majority the following year, the President's recommendations for a $4 billion increase in taxes were ignored by Congress. No other significant change in tax rates was made until after the start of the Korean War.

The Administration thus faced a definite ceiling on its income.

Federal revenues in FY 1946 and FY 1947 were $39.8 and $41.5 billion, respectively. Following the passage of the 1948 act, they dropped to $37.7 billion in FY 1949 and, under the impact of the recession, to $36.5 billion in FY 1950. President Truman, moreover, as Forrestal said, was "a hard money man if ever I saw one," who was "determined not to spend more than we take in in taxes." [21] With this high priority for a balanced budget, expenditures had to be severely limited. Yet interest costs, which varied from $5 billion to $5.8 billion from FY 1947 through FY 1950, were unavoidable. Economic assistance to Greece and Turkey, interim aid to western Europe, the European Recovery Plan, and related activities were obviously of the highest priority. They took from $4.6 billion to $6.5 billion. The costs of domestic programs varied from a low of $11.6 billion in FY 1948 to a high of $16.1 billion in FY 1950. On the average, for the four years, the picture was:

Revenues		$38.9
Interest	$ 5.4	
Foreign aid	5.5	
Domestic programs	14.0	
Total		24.9
Available for security		$14.0

In actuality, from FY 1947 through FY 1950 security expenditures were: $14.4, $11.7, $12.9, and $13.0.* The subtraction of other expenditures from estimated revenues was exactly the means which the Administration used, with variations, to set the level of security expenditures. In May, 1946, the President decreed that in FY 1948 military activities could have one-third of the funds remaining after the fixed charges had been met. This was the initial appearance of the "remainder method" of calculating security expenditures which was to become a familiar feature of both Truman and Eisenhower peacetime budgets. (See Chapter IV, Section 17.) In all four fiscal

---

* *Expenditures* are actual disbursements of funds from the Treasury. *Appropriations* are the principal form of *new obligational authority* by which Congress authorizes expenditures. *Military expenditures* are those made by the Department of Defense and its predecessor agencies for military defense. *Major national security* includes spending for military defense, military assistance, atomic energy, stockpiling, and defense production. *International affairs and finance* includes funds for the conduct of foreign affairs, economic and technical assistance, and information activities. These are official budget terms. In this volume the phrase *total foreign policy expenditures* will also be used to refer to expenditures for major national security and international affairs and finance.

4. THE INTERIM YEARS

years from FY 1947 through FY 1950 the Truman Administration set and maintained reasonably firm ceilings on military appropriations and expenditures. In FY 1950, for instance, despite the initial high requests of the services and Forrestal's efforts to secure a $17 billion budget, the President established and held to a ceiling of $14.4 billion on new appropriations for the Defense Department. Actual military spending during that year came to only $11.9 billion. Early in FY 1950 the President set the ceiling for the FY 1951 budget at $13 billion. As he declared at the time:

> The budget policy on which my ceiling determinations for 1951 are based is that of (a) holding governmental expenditures as closely as possible to present levels and, in particular, (b) preventing the prospective large rise in the military area by adjustments in present plans. Even under this stringent policy the outlook is for sizable deficits, at least in the next two years, under present tax rates.[22]

This statement concisely revealed the implications for military spending of the desire of the Administration to balance the budget and the desire of Congress to reduce taxes.

These constraints upon the size of the military effort were one factor in preventing the development of the forces required for deterrence. They were not the only one. Even with an $11 billion budget, conceivably, as Kennan argued, it would have been possible to create the ground forces necessary to maintain some situations of strength if this need had been given sufficient priority. The second constraint on strategy was not civilian and budgetary but military and doctrinal. American military thinking was preoccupied not so much with the maintenance of forces-in-being with which to deter war but rather with the preparation of forces to win a major war if one should occur. The most probable and most serious danger was a Soviet attack on western Europe. Military planning was oriented toward this contingency. The overwhelming strength of the Red Army in Germany and eastern Europe made it unlikely that western Europe could be successfully defended on the ground without a major increase in the forces there. Consequently, American policy was directed to making clear the American commitment to defend Europe (North Atlantic Treaty, 1949), developing the nuclear weapons and airpower capabilities which would wreak havoc upon an aggressor, and making preparations to mobilize the industrial, manpower, and maritime strength of North America to rescue western Europe in the event of attack. Many military leaders, of course, were aware of other potential threats. The development of Soviet power would eventually require a continental defense system; the policy of containment, as Gruenther pointed out, required a readiness to use ground forces in many places about the globe. Nonetheless, given the budgetary limitations, the main emphasis of military policy was on preparation for general war with the Soviet Union.

This preoccupation was reinforced by the natural tendency to identify war with total war. "We can be certain [General Marshall declared in his final report as Chief of Staff in 1945] that the next war, if there is one, will be even more total than this one." Two and a half years later, General Eisenhower, in *his* final report as Chief of Staff, echoed these sentiments and urged more extensive preparation for the total mobilization which would be required in the future.[23] The other services shared similar expectations. The World War II experience, so recent and so compelling, furnished the basis for postwar requirements. "All advocates of every theory of American security," commented the House Armed Services Committee in 1950, "turn back to the experiences of World War II for historical examples—for illustration—to prove the soundness of their own arguments."[24] For the Army, in particular, the future total war would be World War II with additions. "Armed forces and the nature of war, if war comes during the next few years," declared the Army's leading planner in 1947, "will in general be similar initially to the closing phases of World War II."[25] Agreeing that the next war would be a total war, the Air Force and the Navy, however, were more reluctant to identify it with World War II. The Air Force, in particular, emphasized that the weapons of World War II were obsolete. Its image of total war assigned the initial and decisive role to airpower, with the surface services playing secondary and supporting parts. Navy opinion was hesitant about defining exactly what a new world war would be like. The Army view that it would be World War II over again implicitly held that it would be World War II in Europe over again. The Air Force view also left little room for the Navy. "I just feel that World War III," Admiral Radford argued, "is going to be different, and I

4. THE INTERIM YEARS

would hate to see our new organization patterned after the organization of World War II."[26] Nonetheless, the principal goals of all the services—UMT for the Army, 70 groups for the Air Force, the flush-deck supercarrier for the Navy—had been set before the end of World War II. Whatever relevance they had to the needs of the Cold War was fortuitous.

All the services recognized that American military forces would have to maintain an unprecedented degree of readiness in the future. For the Army, however, this meant not the abandonment of mobilization but its improvement. General Marshall admitted that the atomic bomb made it necessary to be ready to fight immediately and that the United States would not have time, allies, or oceans to protect it in World War III. Nonetheless, he also strongly argued that American security would be assured if it were possible to mobilize four million men within one year after an emergency developed.[27] In a similar vein, General Eisenhower interpreted "preparedness" to mean "a state of organized readiness to meet external aggression by a timely mobilization of public opinion, trained men, proved weapons and essential industries, together with the unmatched spiritual resources of America. . . . "[28] Such a concept was a far cry from the readiness which later became commonplace in the Cold War. The Air Force view was somewhat more advanced. "The first requirement of the peacetime Air Force," General Spaatz said, "is a combat force-in-being; ready for immediate employment; thoroughly trained; well equipped; wisely disposed on strategic bases; and capable of rapid concentration anywhere over suitable airways and connecting bases."[29]

In the immediate postwar years the concept of deterrence by forces-in-being had little place in military planning. The Joint Chiefs did accord a deterrent role to the atomic bomb, but deterrence was seen as a peculiar function of the bomb and strategic airpower, not of the armed forces as a whole. Army leaders maintained their prewar faith in industrial potential despite warnings that a revolution was taking place in military affairs. In 1946 in a remarkably prescient volume, five social scientists outlined the future effects of nuclear weapons and the requirements of a policy of "determent." Our military authorities, Bernard Brodie complained, "continue to think in terms of peacetime military establishments which are simply cadres and which are expected to undergo an enormous but slow expansion *after* the outbreak of hostilities." [30] Nevertheless, two years later the Army Chief of Staff endorsed Bernard Baruch's World War I views that war would require "a mobilization" of all the country's resources, "industrial, agricultural and financial," and the following year, after the Soviet atomic bomb, another Chief of Staff declared that "if there is any single factor today which would deter a nation seeking world domination, it would be the great industrial capacity of this country rather than its armed strength." [31]

Continued Army reliance on the industrial and manpower potential reflected in part the budgetary limits on the armed forces. As Eisenhower pointed out, the Army's M-Day requirement was 1,300,000 men. The Regular Army, he held, could never be this large. Ready reserve forces were necessary. Conditioned by the lean years of the 1930s, the military found it difficult to conceive of a situation in which American peacetime military force might decisively influence the behavior of foreign powers. In 1950 both Generals Bradley and Collins agreed that if war did come the budget was too little, and if war did not come the budget was too much. If we were sure, General Collins said, that there would be a war, we ought to be spending $50 billion a year on defense instead of $13 billion. The Joint Chiefs, he continued, did not advocate this, because if the war did not come, such a level of spending would unduly upset the economy.[32] The probability of a future war and the likely character of that war, in short, were the two factors which should determine the level and nature of military programs. Elsewhere Collins did state that it was necessary to begin thinking more about preventing war than preparing for war, but this axiom had not been integrated into the military planning process. In contrast, the State Department at the same time was taking the lead in developing a program estimated to cost up to $35 billion on the quite different assumption that such a program was necessary to deter war. The military, however, found it difficult to grasp the constructive, creative role which military force could play in peace to maintain peace.

Thus, from 1946 through 1949 the United States followed several different strategies, none of which it was willing to pay for. A

5. NSC 68 AND REARMAMENT 47

foreign policy of containment demanded not only airpower and nuclear weapons but ground forces to repulse local aggressions. The support for these forces came largely from the professional elements in the State Department and a few people, such as Gruenther, in the Pentagon. In general, however, the Army espoused an improved version of the prewar mobilization strategy. Necessarily, this limited the ability of the diplomats to develop high-level support for limited war forces. During 1947 and 1948, moreover, the most ardent and respected advocate of a mobilization strategy was the Secretary of State. General Marshall's great concern was with neither brushfire war divisions nor nuclear airpower but universal military training. On the other hand, the Air Force was certain that strategic airpower and nuclear weapons would not only deter a future general war but also would provide the easiest and most effective way of winning one. The implications of neither limited war, nor mobilization, nor nuclear airpower were fully spelled out. An inadequate balance existed but no overall strategic plan.[33] Budgetary policy gave domestic needs priority and left the country without the military forces to implement either the foreign policy of the diplomats or the strategy of the soldiers. The Army did not get UMT. The Air Force did not get the 70 wings it wanted. The State Department did not get its limited war divisions. The two great constraints on effective military planning, the doctrinal heritage from the past and the pressure of domestic needs, combined to produce a serious gap between military policy and foreign policy.

5. NSC 68 AND REARMAMENT, 1950–1952
NSC 68

Two portentous events in the external environment of American military policy occurred in the last six months of 1949. In August, three or four years ahead of most American estimates, the Soviets achieved their first nuclear explosion. A few months later the Chinese Communists completed their conquest of the Chinese mainland. In November, at the thirty-second anniversary of the revolution, the statements of Soviet leaders reached a new peak in truculence and hostility. These disturbing events highlighted the inadequacy of American military policy. They led to the first effort to define an overall strategy and supporting military programs for the Cold War.

The initiative for the reconsideration of American military policy came not from the military but from the State Department. In the fall of 1949 the services were deep in the B-36 controversy, fighting over how to fight another world war. In the summer of 1949, however, members of the State Department's Policy Planning Staff had been briefed by officers of the Joint Staff on the nature of the military program. They became convinced that budgetary limitations were seriously impeding the military implementation of foreign policy, and the Policy Planning Staff undertook a study of the relative capabilities of the Soviet and American economies to support large arms programs. During the fall members of the Staff attempted to trace out the implications of the new external developments for national policy. At the same time, the initial planning for the Mutual Defense Assistance Program (arms aid to NATO countries), money for which was appropriated by Congress in October, 1949, led the State Department to reassess the problems involved in the defense of Europe. The worsening of the international situation thus reinforced the feeling already developing in the State Department that a major reconsideration of national strategy was in order. This feeling was apparently shared by the Executive Secretary of the NSC, Sidney Souers, who, early in January, 1950, prompted the NSC to order a general strategic reassessment. The State Department immediately created a group to participate in this survey.[34]

The Soviet nuclear explosion also raised the question of whether the United States should develop a thermonuclear bomb. (See Chapter V, Section 23.) In September, 1949, members of the Policy Planning Staff argued that such a major undertaking demanded a general reconsideration of policy to relate the new program to other security activities. During the debate over the H-bomb in the fall of 1949, this viewpoint was reinforced by the hesitations of David Lilienthal, chairman of the Atomic Energy Commission, and others over the desirability of a crash program to build the bomb. They feared that this program would further unbalance the military program in the direction of weapons of mass destruction and neglect of conventional forces. As a result, when the President ap-

5. NSC 68 AND REARMAMENT

proved the hydrogen bomb program on January 30, 1950, he also approved a directive, drafted in the State Department, authorizing State and Defense, in the words of one commentator, "to make an over-all review and re-assessment of American foreign and defense policy in the light of the loss of China, the Soviet mastery of atomic energy and the prospect of the fusion bomb." [35]

State Department officials played a major role in shaping the document which eventually became NSC 68. The effect of the President's order of January 30 was to reassign responsibility for the survey from the NSC to a joint State-Defense *ad hoc* study group. During the next three months the strongest support for this group came from the State Department. The director of the State Policy Planning Staff, Paul Nitze, was chairman of the group. The Secretary of the Staff was secretary of the group. Three other members of the PPS participated actively and regularly in its work. Throughout, Nitze remained in close touch with Secretary of State Acheson, who strongly endorsed the project. Most significantly, the State Department members had the clearest understanding of the sweeping and radical character of the work which they were undertaking.

The participation of the Defense Department was hampered by the division of authority between the Secretary of Defense and the Joint Chiefs of Staff and even more by the prevailing attitudes in the Department toward the military budget. Secretary of Defense Johnson had been identified as the leader in the drive for economy in national defense. Any program for drastic rearmament would mean either a defeat for his views or a drastic change in them. Necessarily, he assumed a position aloof from the study. If his representatives had participated actively in the work of the group, they would have been forced either to obstruct that work or to turn their backs on Johnson. Significantly, the need for economy had also permeated the thinking of the Joint Chiefs of Staff. The previous fall, just as the State Department was beginning to move toward a greatly expanded foreign policy effort, General Bradley, Chairman of the Joint Chiefs of Staff, had assured Congress that:

Although your Department of Defense and their military planners are not responsible for the economic planning of our Government, we are at all times cognizant of the fact that a nation's economy is its ultimate strength in modern war. We realize, too, that our Nation's economy under existing conditions can afford only a limited amount for defense, and that we must look forward to diminishing appropriations for the armed forces.[36]

In January, 1950, Bradley declared that he supported the $13 billion ceiling, among other reasons, because a budget of $30 to $40 billion would disrupt the industrial capacity of the country. If the Joint Chiefs did not assume that the FY 1951 budget and similar subsequent ones were sufficient, he said, "the appropriation request which we would have to recommend would be out of all proportion to that which we believe this country could afford at this time" [37] Bradley later recanted these words, but at the time it seemed that the military, in effect, had accepted the economy position.

This acquiescence was reflected in their attitudes toward the strategic study. The State Department participants, as Paul Y. Hammond has put it, came "with a general though definite belief that the American response to the Soviet challenge was inadequate." On the other hand, "at least initially, and for the apparent purposes of the study group," General Landon, the military member designated by the JCS, "came committed to existing budgets, programs, and plans, although his commitment was an uneasy one." [38] His first paper assumed continuation of existing budget levels and advanced an optimistic assessment of Soviet and American capabilities. As a military man, he accepted what seemed to be the prevailing civilian philosophy. As he realized the direction of State Department thinking, he shifted his viewpoint. When the paper was completed in mid-March, Landon was an ardent supporter of it. At this point the study group circulated the paper throughout the higher reaches of the Pentagon and secured the endorsement of all three service secretaries and of all four Joint Chiefs. Outmaneuvered, Johnson had little recourse but to join Acheson in recommending the paper to the President. On April 12 the President implicitly gave it a preliminary approval by referring it to the NSC to estimate the programs and costs which would be involved in its implementation.

The document submitted to the President included a brief analysis of the purposes of the United States and the Soviet Union in world politics, the nature of the conflict between them, and an evaluation of their respective capabilities. The West, it argued, lacked conventional forces and was critically weak in Europe. The Soviet Union, on the other hand, possessed overwhelming superiority in ground troops and an expanding economy. By 1954, it was estimated, the Soviet Union would have the nuclear capability to launch a devastating attack upon the United States. The potential dangers confronting the United States and its allies were manifold: general war, piecemeal aggression, subversion, disunity in the western alliance, and loss of American will. The paper rejected the alternatives of doing nothing, engaging in preventive war, or withdrawing to the western hemisphere; it advocated, in the words of one of its principal authors, "an immediate and large-scale build-up in our military and general strength and that of our allies with the intention of righting the power balance and in the hope that through means other than all-out war we could induce a change in the nature of the Soviet system." [39] The report urged the expansion of American capabilities for both limited war and all-out war and the strengthening of the allies of the United States. All this would require a vast expansion of the security effort. The paper did not include any specific figures, but State Department officials estimated that defense expenditures of $35 billion a year would be required. In contrast, but in conformity with their tendency to think in terms of much lower spending levels, the leading military planners estimated its costs at about $17 to $18 billion a year—a modest increase over the existing $13 billion budget.[40]

Before NSC 68 all other NSC papers, with the possible exception of NSC 20, the containment paper, had dealt only with "particular areas and issues." [41] Even NSC 20, moreover, had not spelled out the economic and military implications of containment in concrete programs. NSC 68 was "the first comprehensive statement of a national strategy." [42] As such, it implicitly was directed toward the objectives of balance and stability in security policy: balance between economic and military programs and among the various military needs; stability in the need for a continuing policy. Here, for the first time, was an overall definition of goals and a general statement of methods oriented primarily to the needs of the Cold War. Unlike the programs and goals of the services dating back to World War II, this was a response to existing and future conditions.

NSC 68 was rational in terms of international goals, but was it feasible in terms of domestic politics? This issue confronted the

Administration in the spring of 1950. A clear gap existed between the "esoteric" strategy drafted by the State Department and the military and the "exoteric" strategy to which the Administration was publicly committed and which, it believed, represented the wishes of Congress and the people. NSC 68 had been drawn up in three months by those agencies of government most directly concerned with the external threat and the realization of external goals. The FY 1951 budget, however, had been in process for fifteen months. Its $13 billion ceiling had been set in July, 1949, long before NSC 68 and even before the Soviet nuclear explosion. The Administration was identified with austerity in the defense program. It was an election year. Presumably Congress was in no mood to approve larger defense expenditures or higher taxes. The Ways and Means Committee was changing an Administration tax revision bill into a tax reduction bill. In addition, the danger toward which NSC 68 was directed was still four years in the future: the drafters of the report did not expect major or minor Soviet aggressions until the Soviets obtained operational nuclear capabilities. Here was the crux of the issue: Without an immediate challenge or threat was it possible for a democracy to embark on a large and long-term program of rearmament designed primarily to meet a danger which would not become real for several years? In essence, the issue involved the feasibility of a policy of deterrence. NSC 68 was designed to deter future aggression by launching an immediate arms program. Could a democracy arm to deter or could it only arm to respond?

The resolution of the issue would involve either modifying NSC 68 to win the support of other groups whose primary interests and values differed from those of the State Department and the JCS or reducing the power and modifying the attitudes of those groups so that the State-JCS view could prevail. Conceivably, the Administration could do nothing, continue the existing arms program, and wait for future events to make NSC 68 more acceptable to Congress and the country. This could well mean too little too late and gravely endanger national security. The Administration could, on the other hand, dramatically attempt to arouse support for rearmament, which, under the prevailing assumptions about public opinion, might require a "scare" campaign, manufacturing

5. NSC 68 AND REARMAMENT

a minor crisis now to prevent a major crisis later. Despite the increased taxes which might be achieved, it would probably involve unbalanced budgets for the next few fiscal years. As a first step toward awakening public understanding of the new needs of national security and of bridging the gap between the esoteric and exoteric strategies, the joint study group had recommended the publication of its paper. The President, however, refused to approve this proposal. A third possible line of action, and the most probable one in May, 1950, was that the Administration would make small adjustments upward in the military budget to a level of $17 to $18 billion for the next fiscal year, beginning in July, 1951. Throughout the spring of 1950, however, the issue hung in the balance. In the words of the man at the center of the problem:

> Shortly after [the Soviet nuclear explosion] . . . I directed the top officials of our Government to make a new study of the foreign policies and the military potential of the Soviet Union. . . .
>
> These officials . . . came up with their preliminary answers in April, 1950. These answers presented us with some very difficult problems.
>
> It seemed clear, as a result of this study, that the United States and all other free nations were faced with a great and growing danger. It seemed clear that we could meet the danger only by mobilizing our strength—and the strength of our Allies—to check and deter aggression.
>
> This meant a great military effort in time of peace. It meant doubling or tripling the budget, increasing taxes heavily, and imposing various kinds of economic controls. It meant a great change in our normal peacetime way of doing things. These were the problems that were being laid on my desk . . . [in June] 1950.[43]

REARMAMENT

The issue was resolved on June 25. As President Truman went on to say, the Communist invasion of South Korea "made the danger clear to everyone." The policies which had been drawn up in response to two unpleasant external developments were made feasible by a third. The war raised the lid on taxes and on military expenditures. The tax revision bill was completely rewritten in the Senate to raise individual income and corporate tax rates and to increase revenues by an estimated $4.5 billion. In January, 1951, an excess profits tax was enacted. Pointing to the prospective war deficits, the President recommended more legislation to provide

$10.5 billion in additional revenue. These proposals went through a long, tortuous, and controversial legislative history. As eventually enacted they provided approximately $5.7 billion in new revenue.[44] This was the last general tax increase approved by Congress in the 1950s.

The increase in tax rates, the expansion of the economy, and the relative stability of domestic spending furnished the fiscal basis for rearmament. Federal tax revenues jumped from $36.5 billion in FY 1950 to $47.6 billion in FY 1951 and $61.4 billion in FY 1952. Expenditures for nonsecurity purposes declined slightly from $21.9 billion in FY 1950 to $18.6 billion in FY 1952. In contrast, expenditures for major national security programs rose rapidly to $22.3 billion in FY 1951, $44.0 billion in FY 1952, and reached a peak of $50.4 billion in FY 1953. The sharp rise in taxes permitted a surplus of $3.5 billion in FY 1951, but the subsequent flood of military expenditures produced deficits of $4.0 billion in FY 1952 and $9.5 billion in FY 1953. Between FY 1950 and FY 1953 federal revenues increased $28.3 billion, and security expenditures $37.4 billion. In calendar 1950 national defense consumed 5.2 percent of the gross national product; in 1953 it took 13.5 percent of a greatly expanded national product.

COMPETING PURPOSES

The rearmament effort that consumed these resources reflected three complementary but conflicting purposes: the immediate prosecution of the Korean War; the creation of a mobilization base which could be maintained over a long period of time and which would make possible rapid total mobilization in a general war; and the development of the active forces required to counterbalance the increase in Soviet strength and to deter further Soviet aggression.

The requirements of Korea necessarily received the greatest immediate emphasis. "In the summer of 1950," General Marshall later declared, "the build-up of the forces to halt the aggression in the Far East received the highest priority.... Combat-ready ground forces constituted the most urgent requirement."[45] Over 650,000 reservists and National Guardsmen were called to active duty during FY 1951. Selective service brought in 585,000 more men. Purchases of military equipment were speeded up to equip the new forces and to replace that consumed in Korea. During the first months of the war the Administration consciously chose not to push some long-range programs, such as UMT, which might divert energies and resources from the immediate task. Nonetheless, even in the summer of 1950 the Administration also stressed the fact that the rearmament effort involved far more than just a response to the challenge in Korea. "The purpose of these proposed estimates," President Truman told Congress on July 24, "is two-fold; first, to meet the immediate situation in Korea, and second, to provide for an early, but orderly, build-up of our military forces to a state of readiness designed to deter further acts of aggression." Six billion of the $10.5 billion requested in the first supplemental appropriation was for the general expansion of American military strength; only $4.5 billion was directly for the immediate needs in Korea.[46] In the later supplementals, the ratio of the former to the latter undoubtedly increased significantly, and the FY 1952 and FY 1953 military budgets were planned on the assumption that hostilities would be over before the fiscal year covered by that budget began.

From the viewpoint of the Administration, a limited war in Korea made rearmament possible, but rearmament was not primarily directed toward meeting the problem of limited war. On the one hand, the requirements of the conflict in Korea were viewed as a drain on the main effort, and, on the other, the requirements for possible future limited wars played only a minor role in the build-up which was concerned primarily with the deterrence of general war or the preparation for general war. Congress and the public, however, tended to believe that the expansion was required to serve the needs of Korea, and if it did not serve these ends, it ought to do so. The Administration, as Congressman Mahon pointed out, could get all the money it required for the war. The people would willingly support an additional $10 billion for that purpose. But they would be equally reluctant to spend more than $13 billion on the continuing military program.[47] Here, in a nutshell, was the difference between mobilizing support for a response to an immediate challenge and mobilizing support for a program to prevent future challenges.

Apart from the needs of Korea, the great issue of rearmament was: How much for mobilization and how much for deterrence? Many elements of rearmament contributed to both, but there were still differences in emphasis. NSC 68 had not directly confronted the issue; implicitly it had stressed the forces-in-being required for deterrence. Throughout the rearmament effort the build-up of the active forces had first priority. Nonetheless, the events of the winter of 1950–1951 and the influence of General Marshall made the development of a mobilization base a coequal goal with the creation of deterrent capabilities. The "two major objectives" of the military program, Marshall declared, were to create and maintain military forces for "an indefinite number of years" and to aim "at greatly increasing the readiness of American industry and manpower for full mobilization."[48] Simultaneously, the rearmament program held out the hope of deterrence and the need to prepare for general mobilization for another World War II-type war. These two goals necessarily had differing implications. A broad mobilization base and universal military training would speed mobilization for a general war but would probably contribute less to the deterrence of such a war than would substantial forces-in-being. On the other hand, the expansion of the means of strategic retaliation and the development of thermonuclear weapons presumably reduced the likelihood of major aggression, as well as contributing directly to current general war capabilities. If deterrence failed, the destructiveness of the weapons of deterrence seemed to indicate that industrial and manpower reserves would not be of decisive importance. Competitive and yet equally relevant, mobilization and deterrence marched shoulder-to-shoulder through the Korean War rearmament effort.

MOBILIZATION

The Chinese Communist intervention in Korea in November seemed to make general war with the Communist powers an imminent possibility. As American forces were hurled back the first week of December, a significant majority of the American people believed that, in effect, World War III had already begun. President Truman himself declared that the Communist powers were "now willing to push the world to the brink of general war." Throughout December, demands for total mobilization rose from Congress and the public.[49]

5. NSC 68 AND REARMAMENT

Responding to the deteriorating international situation and the domestic clamor for all-out mobilization, the Administration rushed the build-up of active military forces. Under the new plan, the "year of maximum danger" was moved forward from 1954, the time suggested in NSC 68, to 1952. More significantly, the Administration also stressed the desirability of achieving a state of partial mobilization as the indispensable and most feasible method of laying the groundwork for total mobilization should that become necessary. As Marshall explained the concept:

> This is a move to place us in a strong position from which we can go rapidly to the extent that may be developed as necessary. This is not full mobilization. This is . . . a raising up of the whole establishment to gain momentum from which we can open the throttle and go very quickly this way or that way. . . . In my own opinion, and that of my associates . . . the way to build up . . . to full mobilization, if that eventually is necessary, is first to get this [partial mobilization] program straightened out and put it on a very high level—you might say a high plateau—and to do it as quickly, as effectively, efficiently . . . as possible.[50]

In the summer of 1950 President Truman had identified the development of deterrent forces as a purpose second only to supporting the Korean War. In December, 1950, this second purpose was redefined as the preparation of the armed forces for action outside Korea if this should become necessary. The issue was total mobilization immediately versus partial mobilization justified on the grounds that it would greatly facilitate later total mobilization. With war apparently so imminent, the United States had lost its ability by changes in its military programs to influence the choice between war and peace. If the Communist powers had decided on war, the best the United States could do now would be to prepare for it. If they had not decided on war now, it was still desirable to create a state of continuing preparedness for possible mobilization in the future.

The impact of the immediate situation and the fear it engendered were reinforced by the strong adherence of General Marshall to the philosophy of mobilization. Marshall believed that in the absence of a general war the United States could not maintain for any length of time the mammoth forces required to fight a general war. It was necessary, he reasoned, to develop an economic and military base, reflecting a state of partial mobilization, from which it would be possible to build up rapidly the forces required for total war. In effect, he wished to bring into existence the quickly mobilizable reserve strength which America had lacked in 1916–1917 and 1940–1941. "Partial mobilization" meant for him more the maintenance of a mobilization base than the maintenance of active forces-in-being. The phrase, "In the event of war," which was continually on Marshall's lips during the winter of 1950–1951, implied that whether the "event" occurred or not was beyond our power.

In realizing "probably the most important" [51] purpose of rearmament, emphasis was placed upon the two traditional sources of American military strength: industrial capacity and manpower potential. A strategy of mobilization stressed the creation of a broad rather than a narrow base of military suppliers and the stockpiling of industrial facilities and raw materials rather than military end-items. Priority was given to the acquisition of industrial capacity rather than "the current accumulation of a large war reserve, much of which might be obsolete when most urgently needed." [52] The aim of procurement, Marshall reported, was "not merely to obtain as quickly as possible the matériel required for the current build-up but also to equip additional plants and assembly lines." These additional facilities would "enable the United States to expand military production rapidly in the event of a major war, thus greatly reducing the time factor for full mobilization . . ." [53] Simultaneously, the raw material stockpiling program was invigorated and expanded. From the passage of the Stockpiling Act in 1946 to the outbreak of the Korean War, Congress appropriated $1,065 million for the acquisition of raw materials. During the first year of the Korean War it appropriated $3,013 million for this purpose. Immediate demands for raw materials for the production of military goods limited the extent to which the stockpile itself might be expanded. Nonetheless, obligations of funds for this purpose in FY 1951 were approximately $2.1 billion, more than triple those of FY 1950. Concern with another war like World War II was also reflected in the creation of a civil defense organization and a permanent Office of Defense Mobilization.

The manpower equivalent of a broad mobilization base was

5. NSC 68 AND REARMAMENT

universal military training, which was a longstanding objective of General Marshall. In his view universal military training was the only alternative to the maintenance of large, burdensome, and potentially dangerous regular armed forces. With UMT, "In the event of a major war, the United States will be able to mobilize its combat strength within a considerably shorter time than heretofore. The reserve will no longer be perpetually understrength or inadequately trained."[54] In January, 1951, the Administration presented to Congress its recommendations for UMT. Five months later they were enacted in revised form. Universal military training was approved in principle. At least six months training was to be required of almost all young men, to be followed by seven-and-a-half years in the reserve. The act established a National Security Training Commission which was to draft a detailed set of proposals and to present them to Congress. The Commission's recommendations were considered by Congress in 1952 and rejected by the House of Representatives. UMT never came into operation.

DETERRENCE

From 1946 through 1950 a military balance existed between the Red Army and the American atomic bomb. The former held the countries of western Europe hostage against American pressure on the Soviet Union. The latter held the cities of Russia hostage against Soviet pressure on western Europe. In June, 1950, American armed forces included only 10 understrength Army divisions and 11 regimental combat teams, 671 ships in the Navy, 2 very understrength Marine divisions, 48 Air Force wings (including 18 in SAC), and a total personnel strength of about 1,461,000 men. If war broke out in Europe initial American capabilities would be limited to air-atomic strikes at the Soviet Union from the British Isles. The development of Soviet atomic weapons threatened to undermine this precarious balance. American nuclear capabilities would be counterbalanced by Soviet ones. The cities of the United States would be as vulnerable as those of Russia. In a nuclear stalemate, the overwhelming supremacy of Soviet ground forces might well be decisive. The balance of military power would swing dangerously in favor of the Soviet Union. NSC 68 anticipated this contingency by recommending the large-scale expansion of American nuclear and conventional forces before 1954, the date when, it was assumed, the Soviets would have enough nuclear weapons and delivery capability to launch a devastating attack on the United States. The requirements of deterrence thus combined with those of fighting the war in Korea and preparing for general war mobilization to make expansion of the active forces a top goal in the rearmament effort. This expansion was concentrated in two areas: the strengthening of the strategic retaliatory force so that even if it were hit by a surprise attack it would still be capable of effective retaliation against the Soviet Union; and the development of substantial ground forces in western Europe to counterbalance the Red Army. For both purposes allies were essential: the strategic retaliatory force depended upon overseas bases, and only the combined efforts of the free countries of the western world could bring into existence military forces comparable to those of the Soviet Union. Hence, the rearmament effort emphasized the strengthening of the mechanisms of collective security, particularly in the North Atlantic area.[55]

The first steps in the build-up of the active forces in the summer of 1950 were directed toward the 1954 target date. In their testimony on the Supplemental Appropriation Bill, Administration witnesses emphasized the extent to which the request for new funds was the outgrowth of careful and lengthy planning antedating the war and the extent to which it was simply the first increment on a long-range build-up which would presumably continue long after the war was over. The rearmament program, Secretary Johnson declared, would run for two or three years; the Korean War, it was hoped, would be over in six to eight months.[56] As the situation deteriorated in the fall, however, the JCS and NSC approved new force level goals for FY 1951, and on December 14, 1950, the NSC set the force levels to be achieved by the new time of maximum danger, July, 1952: 18 divisions and 12 regimental combat teams for the Army; 1,161 ships for the Navy; $2\frac{1}{3}$ Marine divisions; 95 Air Force wings; and total military personnel of roughly 3,600,000. The funds to achieve these goals were embodied in the FY 1952 budget presented to Congress in the late spring of 1951. On July 1, 1952, the armed forces did include 20 Army divisions and 18 regimental combat teams, 1,130 ships in the Navy, 3

5. NSC 68 AND REARMAMENT

Marine divisions and 3 Marine air wings, 95 Air Force wings, and a total military personnel of 3,636,000. Not all of these units were operational or at full strength. Nonetheless, the force-level build-up was a substantial and perhaps surprising success.

In the summer of 1951 the likelihood of general war in the immediate future appeared to decline. Consequently, weapons production was redirected toward the original target date of 1954. By this date Soviet air-atomic power would significantly affect the military balance, and the build-up of the Soviet satellite armies and the rebuilding of Soviet industry would be substantially complete. It would also be about the last year before the huge stocks of war material accumulated by the Soviets during World War II became obsolete. Most important of all, after 1954, it was estimated, NATO forces in Europe would begin to constitute a major obstacle to the Soviet conquest of western Europe. This was the date when Soviet military capabilities would be at their maximum compared to those of the West. It was both the most probable date for the Soviets to launch a war and also the beginning of a period of substantially increased danger.

In the light of these factors the Joint Chiefs reconsidered force-level requirements in the summer and fall of 1951. They endorsed the continuation of the 1952 force levels through 1954, with one significant exception. The Air Force, it was recommended, should expand from its existing level of 95 wings to 143 wings by mid-1954. The Administration approved this goal, but, in response to budgetary and political factors, set back the date for its achievement until July, 1955.

So long as the Soviet Union did not possess strong air-atomic capabilities, the United States strategic air force could remain relatively small. It was almost invulnerable to surprise attack, and its readiness to respond had to be geared only to the tempo of a Soviet ground attack on western Europe. Deterrence depended not upon the size of American air-atomic capability, but upon its monopolistic character. The breaking of the monopoly, however, made the question of relative size of decisive importance. The American force now had to be large enough so that it could not be eliminated in a surprise attack and ready enough so that it could strike back immediately at the enemy's strategic forces. The strengthening of the strategic deterrent between 1950 and 1953 included the development of thermonuclear weapons and the expansion of the nuclear stockpile, the drastic multiplication of the means of delivering these weapons against Soviet targets, and an intensive drive to increase the readiness of the retaliatory forces. (See Chapter V, Section 23.)

Before 1950 the United States had maintained occupation forces in Germany and Austria, naval forces in the Mediterranean, and strategic air forces in the British Isles. In addition, the NATO treaty had formally committed the United States to the defense of Europe, and the first mutual security funds had been approved by Congress in the fall of 1949. As yet, however, no European defense force existed strong enough to defeat a small-scale Communist attack or to delay a major attack long enough so that the bombers could reap their grim harvest before the Soviet Army reached the English Channel. The Korean War demonstrated that under certain circumstances the Communists would resort to force, and the development of Soviet nuclear capability forecast the neutralization of American strategic airpower. The construction of an effective European defense system in Europe thus became a major element in the rearmament effort. In the view of the American military the ground defense of Europe required a German contribution, and for the next three years the development of the terms and conditions for the participation of Germany in western defense efforts was a cardinal aim of American policy. More immediately, in the fall of 1949, it was decided to send four more American divisions to Europe, the 7th Army was created in Germany, and in early 1951 General Eisenhower established his command at SHAPE. (See Chapter V, Section 24.) The development of an overall NATO program was pushed. The Lisbon Conference in February, 1952, formally endorsed the goal of 90 divisions, half on active duty, by the end of 1952.

SLACKENING

The outbreak of the Korean War had made rearmament feasible. It had, in General Marshall's words, "clearly revealed to the American people the full menace of Soviet imperialism and made possible an upward adjustment of the armed forces to the realities

5. NSC 68 AND REARMAMENT

of the world situation." [57] In the summer of 1950 Congress approved anything the Administration asked because of the needs of combat in Korea. In the winter of 1950-1951 Congress approved anything necessary for what seemed to be an imminent general war with the Soviet Union. The absence of public debate over the long-term objectives and implications of the arms program speeded the process of rearmament in 1950 and 1951. The war made possible immediately the strategy and the armament without the major political effort which would have made them feasible permanently. As the war became increasingly unpopular in 1951 and 1952, so also did the rearmament program.

Within the Administration, domestic considerations began to play a more and more important role. The President's decision in the fall of 1951 to "stretch-out" the achievement of the 143-wing Air Force from 1954 to 1955 was dictated as much by political and fiscal considerations as by the problem of industrial feasibility. Throughout the first half of 1952, there were recurring reports of slippage and slow-down in weapons production. By July, 1952, the armed services, apart from the Air Force, had achieved their force level goals. Arms production, however, had climbed only two-thirds of the way to its goal.[58] The prolonged steel strike in the spring of 1952 was one reflection of the feeling of let-down and relaxation. More significant was the harsh treatment which Congress gave the Administration's request for $50.9 billion in the defense budget for FY 1953. Alarmed over the prospects of a substantial deficit, continued high taxes, waste and duplication in the Defense Department, and the relatively large carry-over ($38 billion) of unobligated funds, Congress cut $4.3 billion from the President's estimate, absolutely and proportionately the largest congressional cut in the military budget between 1946 and 1961.

The decline in the priority of security programs in the United States was part of a general relaxation throughout the western alliance. During the winter of 1951-1952 the European members of NATO began to stretch out their arms build-ups, reduce their military budgets, and cut the terms of service of their draftees. In the spring of 1952 the British, under the leadership of Prime Minister Churchill and the Chief of the Air Staff, Sir John Slessor, took the lead in what the former called a "reshaping of defense concepts."

They proposed less reliance on massive land armies and more reliance on the nuclear weapons which were becoming increasingly varied and increasingly available. The Administration in Washington was originally dubious, but in December, 1952, the North Atlantic Council approved a drastic reduction in the Lisbon force-level goals which had been formally agreed upon only the February before.

In 1952 the further expansion of the Air Force, the continued development and replacement of weapons and equipment, and the maintenance of 3,500,000 men in uniform, all indicated sustained, if not rising, defense costs for the immediate future. At the same time, the stalemate in Korea and the failure of other local wars or of general war to develop suggested an apparent improvement in the international situation. Implicitly, and to some extent explicitly, the goals of the rearmament effort were lowered or abandoned. This process was well under way in the last year of the Truman Administration. The low level of that Administration's strategic effort between 1946 and 1950 had created a gap between military policy and foreign policy. By 1952 the high level of its strategic effort had eliminated that gap but was creating another one between the military goals of the Administration and the domestic goals popular in both the Administration and Congress. It was obviously too late, however, for the Truman Administration to formulate a new relationship. The great problem of the Eisenhower Administration was to devise a new strategy adequate to foreign policy needs and feasible in terms of domestic realities.

6. THE NEW LOOK, 1953–1956
SOURCES AND CONCEPTS

The New Look of 1953 was more far-reaching than the NSC 68 program of 1950. The latter assumed that the economy could support, without extensive controls, a much larger defense program. But it did not attempt to balance the claims of national security as a goal against the claims of other goals. In contrast, the New Look was an effort to balance and to reconcile foreign and domestic, military and economic goals. The "New Look" in military policy was part of a "New Look" in domestic policy and fiscal policy.

6. THE NEW LOOK

Military policy is always affected by policies in these other areas, but for the first time a long-term military policy was consciously and directly related to other governmental ends. NSC 68 was national security policy; the New Look was national policy.

NSC 68 was primarily a response to the Soviet atomic bomb and the loss of China. It stemmed from the facts of increasing danger and existing military weakness. The New Look was the product of both domestic and external factors: the Administration's desires to reduce expenditures, balance the budget, and reduce taxes, on the one hand; the easing of tensions following the death of Stalin and the end of the Korean War, on the other. The prerequisite for the Eisenhower Administration's New Look was the Truman Administration's expansion of American military strength between 1950 and 1953. The basic military fact of the New Look was the overwhelming American superiority in nuclear weapons and the means of delivering them. In 1950, SAC could not have prevented the Soviets from occupying western Europe. By 1954, with its fleet of B-47s, its overseas bases, its large stockpile of improved fission bombs, and the increased readiness and competence of its crews, it could have effectively destroyed the Soviet Union with little likelihood of serious reprisal against the United States.[59] The years of the New Look were the high-water mark of relative American military strength in the Cold War.

Two concepts were important in shaping New Look military programs. First, the threat to national security was a dual one, economic and military, and a proper balance between a strong economy and strong military forces was necessary to meet this threat. NSC 68 aimed at a balanced military program, the New Look at a broader balance between a strong economy and strong military forces. Second, the dual threat was a continuing one. Once the proper balance between economic and military programs was achieved, it should be maintained indefinitely. Unlike the more specifically military aspects of the New Look, which did not take shape until the fall of 1953, the ideas of an economic-military balance and the long haul were advanced by General Eisenhower in his campaign and became active aims of the Administration in the first half of 1953. The rebalancing of the economic-military equation began with the revision of the FY 1954 budget; the "long-haul" concept was formally endorsed by the NSC in April, 1953. They were the two major themes of the President's general statement on defense policy of April 30, 1953. Together, they shaped decisions on specific military programs and activities.

The Dual Threat and the Economic-Military Balance. In reconciling the need to maintain substantial military forces with its domestic goals, the Administration assumed that the Communist threat was both military and economic, and that the economic threat was, if anything, more serious than the military. The Soviet leaders hoped, Eisenhower said, that their military threat would force upon the United States "an unbearable security burden leading to economic disaster.... Communist guns, in this sense, have been aiming at an economic target no less than a military target." As a result, the President believed that American security rested "not upon the military establishment alone but rather on two pillars—military strength in being and economic strength based upon a flourishing economy." [60] Security could become the criterion for the allocation of emphasis between military and economic programs. Since economic strength and military programs affected security, the military leaders should consider both in making their recommendations.

The economic collapse which the Administration feared could take two forms. Sustained excessive military programs could cause a spiraling inflation which would eventually lead to disaster. Or, the setting of a specific target date for the peak of the defense effort could cause a subsequent slump which, in turn, might lead to a disastrous depression. The New Look program was designed to avert both possibilities: the military program was to be reduced to avoid the danger of inflation and collapse; stabilization for the "long haul" would avoid the danger of peaking and depression. The President was particularly concerned about inflation. "Again and again," at the *Helena* conference in December, 1952, "he spoke of the urgent necessity of curbing inflation, referring to his European experiences and citing the destructive consequences he himself had witnessed." The United States, the President is reported to have argued, must have sufficent military strength, but "a prodigal outlay of borrowed money on military equipment could in the end, by generating inflation, disastrously weaken the economy and

6. THE NEW LOOK

thus defeat the purpose it was meant to serve." [61] A balanced budget and lower taxes were highly desirable goals in the economic philosophy of the Administration. They could also be justified on security grounds as two ways of strengthening and stabilizing the economy.

Stability and the Long Haul. The establishment of a new economic-military balance reconciling security needs, balanced budgets, and tax reduction was the first key element of the New Look. The second was the maintenance of this balance over the "long haul." The military program was to be sustained indefinitely without violent fluctuations in response to either temporary changes in world politics or economic discontent and pressures at home. No longer was the development of military strength to be directed toward any particular date or time as a "period of maximum danger." Eisenhower Administration leaders emphasized the extent to which their long-haul policy differed from the feast and famine and target date policies of the previous Administration. Actually, of course, a stable level of military preparation had been as much a goal of the Truman Administration as of its successor. The newness of the Eisenhower concept lay not in the stress on stability but rather in the context in which it was placed. For the new Administration, the duration of the effort became an argument for reducing its size.

Although at times Administration officials spoke of the need to have a "strong and expanding economy, readily convertible to the tasks of war," more often and more appropriately they defined the economic factor as the continuing partner of the military component of security. Economic strength was needed to sustain the indefinite and relatively constant military burden, not to be the foundation of a great wartime total mobilization. Under General Marshall permanent partial mobilization had been justified on the grounds that it was the indispensable prerequisite to rapid total mobilization in time of war or crisis. Under General Eisenhower the probability of total mobilization receded. A high level of military effort was justified not as a prerequisite to something else but rather as an intrinsically necessary continuing support for policy.

Another key difference between the Eisenhower long-haul and earlier policies lay in the concept of the external threat. The Truman Administration had identified 1954–1955 as a period of "maximum danger" because by that time the Soviets would have achieved a substantial air-atomic capability, and also because, at that point, Soviet military capabilities would reach their highest strength relative to those of the West. The Eisenhower Administration, in rejecting a "time of maximum danger," emphasized that the "Soviet Communists are planning for what they call 'an entire historical era,' and we should do the same." [62] No one in the Truman Administration would have disagreed with this diagnosis and prescription, as far as it went. The two Administrations differed, however, in their estimates of the future character of that danger. In the Truman view the threat was a continuing one, but it existed upon one level until approximately 1954–1955; thereafter it would continue upon a much more serious and threatening level. Underlying the Eisenhower Administration view, on the other hand, was the assumption that the threat would continue to exist at approximately the current level. Thus, no full-scale demobilization after the Korean War could be permitted, and no substantial increase in military effort was necessary. The target date in the Truman approach was not incompatible with a long haul but rather marked the beginning of the long haul. For the Eisenhower Administration a future target date was incompatible with a long-haul program which was to begin immediately.

In addition, in the Truman calculation, the year of "maximum danger" was a product of both Soviet and Western action. In 1954 or 1955 Soviet air-atomic capability would begin to counterbalance that of the West. Later, the rebuilding of Western conventional ground forces would begin to counterbalance those of the Soviet Union. The reduction in the military effort made by the Eisenhower Administration meant that the relative power of the Soviets would increase substantially after 1954. This removed one incentive to war, and the year of maximum danger tended to recede into the future. The reduction in the military effort invalidated the danger year assumption just as abandonment of the danger year justified the reduction in military effort.

For the Administration the future danger would not be significantly greater than the current one, and the current danger had lessened following the death of Stalin and the end of the Korean War.[63] The military programs, as Eisenhower said, must not shift up and down, "depending upon the state of world affairs." [64] The

6. THE NEW LOOK

Administration declined to postpone its reductions in the Army because of the Indochina crisis in 1954 or the Formosan crisis of 1955. The latter, Secretary Wilson declared, "is very important, but it doesn't change our military needs. Formosa is just a little ripple in our defense planning, and I am talking of planning for the long pull. But it is more than a ripple in international affairs." Similarly, after the 1955 Big Four Geneva conference, Wilson warned that the military effort should not be reduced because of "apparent changes in propaganda" or "wishful thinking at home." [65]

Presumably the security threat to the United States was a product of the hostile intentions of other powers and their capabilities. The Administration explicitly interpreted the hostile intentions of the Soviet Union as continuing and relatively constant. For its conclusions to be valid, however, the capabilities of the Soviet Union would also have to be relatively constant. Here was the principal lacuna in the Administration's analysis. NSC 68 had assumed that stability would be re-established in the future, after the Soviet Union had acquired an air-atomic capability and the West had acquired substantial conventional ground forces. The New Look assumed that the stability was inherent in the existing situation in which the Soviets lacked one and the West lacked the other. Administration leaders frequently deprecated Soviet capabilities, particularly in airpower, and some, like Secretary Wilson, placed the date of their acquisition of substantial air-atomic capabilities reasonably far in the future. Moreover, even when these future capabilities were admitted, they could still be discounted on the grounds that they would not significantly influence decisions on war and peace. Almost by its own logic, the Administration was driven to minimize the relevance of both temporary changes in international tensions and substantial changes in Soviet capabilities to the scope and nature of its military program. Potential conflict between domestic economic pressures and foreign military dangers was eliminated by assuming future dangers would require no larger program than was currently economically bearable.

THE FORMULATION OF POLICY

The New Look vs. the Old Strategy. The dialectic between the Administration's desires for economy and stability and the needs of strategy went through two phases, eventually producing in the fall of 1953 the distinctive military programs of the New Look. The initial phase, during the first nine months of 1953, involved the conflict between the new Administration's goals and the military strategy and programs inherited from the Truman Administration.[66] This conflict centered about the revision of the FY 1954 budget and the preliminary steps in the formulation of the FY 1955 budget. President Truman's FY 1954 budget estimated total revenues at $68.7 billion, expenditures at $78.6 billion ($46.3 billion military), leaving a deficit of $9.9 billion. It also requested new obligational authority of $72.9 billion ($41.5 billion military). The immediate goal of the Eisenhower Administration was to make as many inroads as possible on the Truman deficit. On February 3 the Director of the Bureau of the Budget reminded the heads of all executive departments and agencies that one of "the first and most important tasks of our new administration is . . . to proceed toward the accomplishment of a balanced budget." It was necessary "to reduce budgetary obligational authority; reduce the level of expenditures, critically examine existing programs, restrain commitments for new programs, and generally to drive for greater efficiency and reduced costs." No increases were desired in the rate of obligations; personnel vacancies were not to be filled except where clearly essential; new construction was to be limited. Each departmental head was to "initiate an immediate review within his department or agency calling for recommendations on the downward adjustment of program levels . . . " [67]

The results of the review were not encouraging to the Administration. Still hoping to balance the budget by FY 1955, the NSC on March 4 established a tentative expenditure limitation on the FY 1954 military budget of $41.2 billion, $5.1 billion less than the January Truman estimate, and directed the Defense Department to determine the impact of such a ceiling upon its programs. The Joint Chiefs reported back that such a limitation would seriously endanger national security. The NSC then asked the Chiefs what reductions would not endanger national security. A week later the Chiefs replied that any reduction would endanger national security. They reaffirmed the Truman Administration's planning assumption that the Soviets would achieve an effective air-atomic capability in 1954 or 1955 and argued that a decrease in the American air-

6. THE NEW LOOK

power build-up would increase the risks "beyond the dictates of national prudence."[68] An impasse existed between the new Administration, committed to economy and a stable program, and the old Joint Chiefs, committed to a substantial military build-up directed to the danger period of 1954-1955.

The Administration pursued its goal not by altering strategy but by evading it. The civilian leaders of the Defense Department made their own review and cuts in the FY 1954 budget with little help from or consultation with the old Truman Joint Chiefs. The cuts focused upon supporting activities, discrepancies among related programs, reduction in unobligated carry-over funds, and reform of administrative, personnel, and procurement practices. The Truman expenditures estimate was cut about $2.3 billion and his appropriations request about $5.2 billion. The bulk of the appropriations reduction came from the Air Force, whose new appropriations were cut from $16.8 billion to $11.7 billion. This was, in the words of the civilian leaders of the Defense Department, simply the "statistical result" of an across-the-board reconsideration of programs, and they expressed surprise that "most of the cuts seemed to show up in the Air Force program." [69] Although the Air Force would carry over into FY 1954 more than $28 billion in appropriations from previous fiscal years, such substantial cuts necessarily had some impact upon military programs. The Truman Air Force target of 143 wings by 1956 was officially abandoned and replaced by an "interim program" of 114 wings in FY 1954 and 120 wings in FY 1955.

The strong adherence of the Chiefs to the existing military program undoubtedly reinforced the Adiminstration's desire to replace them with a new group whose views would be more compatible. In addition, Republican leaders in Congress argued that a new overall strategy would be impossible unless new men were brought into office. The appointment of the new Chiefs, who would not take office until the summer, was announced early in May, after they had been cleared with Senator Taft. The first job of the Chiefs, even before they took office, was to begin the formulation of a new strategy.

In the absence of such a strategy, however, the conflict between the New Look goals of economy and stability and the existing military programs reappeared in the formulation of the FY 1955 budget. Secretary of the Treasury Humphrey still wanted to balance that budget, and at the end of May he recommended that federal expenditures be limited to $60 billion in FY 1955, which would have required almost a $10 billion reduction in the Defense Department budget. This, Secretary Wilson claimed, was almost impossible, and he was supported in his stand by the President. The issue, however, was reopened in July when the Director of the Budget Bureau wrote Wilson that the FY 1955 budget would have to show "substantial reductions" from the FY 1954 figures and that these reductions would "have to be at least equal to and may have to be greater than those already made in the fiscal year 1954 budget." Wilson objected to the directive, arguing that a "sound military budget" had to be based upon a "sound military plan." "Until the completion of the review of the military plan by the Joint Chiefs," he went on to say, "it would appear undesirable to make an estimate as to the amounts required. . ."[70] The absence of a new military strategy thus compelled the civilian defense leaders of the new Administration to oppose the efforts of other members of the Administration to reduce governmental expenditures.

It soon became evident, moreover, that the new Joint Chiefs would not complete their development of a strategic plan in time for the submission of the FY 1955 budget to the NSC and the Budget Bureau early in October. Instead, the new Chiefs produced an "interim look" to serve as the basis of the FY 1955 budget. Arguing that the threat to American security was no less than before, that no reduction had taken place in U. S. commitments, and that no new policies had been developed for the use of atomic weapons, the Chiefs endorsed the continuation through FY 1955 of the existing force levels of the Army, Navy, and Marine Corps, the buildup of the Air Force to 120 wings, and an expansion of continental defense. In the formulation of the FY 1955 budget the new Joint Chiefs simply repeated with some variations the behavior of the old Joint Chiefs in the formulation of the FY 1954 budget. These forces would require, the services estimated, expenditures of $41.5 billion and new appropriations of $34.5 billion, both representing slight increases over the current estimates for FY 1954. These figures

6. THE NEW LOOK 73

were presented to the NSC on October 13. Humphrey and Dodge were shocked. Humphrey had wanted defense expenditures of about $36 billion. Responding unfavorably to the Defense Department's proposals, the NSC decided that the budget should undergo further "refinement," and that the Joint Chiefs should speed up their overall strategic review so that it could be used in the final determination of the FY 1955 figures. Thus, for the third time, the economy desires of the Administration clashed with the existing military programs. In the spring the conflict had been evaded by making reductions which assertedly did involve changes in strategy. In the summer the conflict had been postponed pending the development of new plans. Now, the issue was again joined. In the absence of new decisions and a new strategy, the Joint Chiefs could only recommend the continuation of the old programs and the addition of obviously needed new ones. The resolution of the conflict in the FY 1955 budget would only be possible in the light of the new overall strategic appraisal.

The New Look's New Strategy. The reconsideration of overall strategy had been moving along concurrently with the development of the FY 1955 budget. It began in May when the President inaugurated "Operation Solarium," an effort to determine future national security policy in the broadest sense. The product of this study was a paper, NSC 162, in which the NSC Planning Board recommended a continuation of containment plus greater reliance on nuclear airpower in implementing that policy. The paper, which also warned of the continued growth of Soviet military power and recommended a substantial expansion of continental defense, was discussed by the NSC in the first part of October.[71] Meanwhile, in July, the new Joint Chiefs had begun their reassessment of American strategy. They were, the President directed, to consider not only military requirements but also the implications of those requirements upon fiscal policy and other areas of governmental activity. After a final August weekend session on the Secretary of the Navy's yacht, the *Sequoia,* the Chiefs came up with a paper which recommended the further development of United States air defenses and strategic retaliatory forces, the withdrawal of some American forces from overseas positions and creation of a mobile central strategic reserve, reliance upon allied forces for local defenses with the United States furnishing sea- and airpower, and strengthening of the reserve forces. This program, they estimated, would require approximately 2,900,000 men on active duty compared with the existing figure of 3,500,000.[72]

The trends of policy development represented by the FY 1955 budget, NSC 162, and the *Sequoia* study came to a head in the second half of October. The conflict between the desire for economy and the military requirements of security was resolved by adopting the strategy implicitly suggested by Admiral Radford in his presentation to the NSC on October 13: abandonment of the assumption that general war or large-scale limited war would be waged without recourse to nuclear weapons. This "basic decision" of the New Look was set forth in NSC 162/2, approved by the President on October 30. This document combined most of the ideas and proposals which had been stated in the *Sequoia* paper with a particular stress upon the role of nuclear weapons as the American contribution to the defense of the free world. It authorized the military to plan on using nuclear weapons in future conflicts where their use was desirable from a military viewpoint. No longer should the services attempt to prepare for purely conventional general war or large-scale limited war. The study emphasized both the importance of tactical nuclear weapons and the role of strategic airpower as a deterrent to aggression (thus laying the basis for Mr. Dulles' massive retaliation speech). The paper represented a major landmark in the movement of policy away from the idea that a future war would be like World War II. Its intent was, in the words of Glenn Snyder, "to foreclose any of the services—in particular the Army—from generating large requirements for manpower and conventional equipment based on an assumption that large-scale conventional war was possible." [73] Thus, technology mediated between conflicting political goals: strategic airpower and tactical nuclear weapons became the means by which lower military expenditures were reconciled with the foreign policy of NSC 162.

For six weeks after this decision the Joint Chiefs and their staff worked on the military plans for the long haul. These were finally embodied in a paper unanimously approved by the Chiefs and presented by Admiral Radford to Secretary Wilson on December 9. Along with the *Sequoia* paper and NSC 162/2, this paper was a key element in the New Look's long-haul strategy. It was directed to the military programs to be attained in June, 1957. These would be the targets for the three years of reduction in FY 1955, 1956, 1957 and also the programs which presumably were to be maintained indefinitely thereafter. In effect, its contents fell into three categories.[74]

First, the recommendations of the paper rested upon four crucial *assumptions:* 1) that no significant increase would take place in the existing level of international tension; 2) that no significant changes would occur in the existing ratio of Soviet to American power; 3) that American massive retaliatory capacity was the major deterrent to both general war and limited war; and 4) that nuclear weapons would be used in general war and in any limited war to the extent required by military exigencies. Following the President's directions, the Joint Chiefs also spelled out the economic assumptions upon which their analysis rested. Through the "remainder" method they calculated that military expenditures for FY 1957 should be between $33 and $34 billion. This was assumed to be the level which could be maintained for the long haul.[75]

In terms of *functional programs,* the Chiefs recognized the diplomatic problems involved in any massive redeployment of American forces from abroad but urged the withdrawal of all American troops from Korea and an eventual reduction of those committed to NATO. Primary responsibility for local defense, they said, should be left with the allies immediately concerned; the rearmament of Germany and Japan should be pushed; and effective use should be made of military aid to stimulate forces in allied countries which would best complement those of the United States. The American forces brought home should be assembled in a mobile, central strategic reserve (eventually to include six Army divisions). An effective continental defense system should be developed and provision made for an adequate mobilization base for general war.

In terms of *service force levels,* the Joint Chiefs agreed on a fairly substantial reduction in overall personnel strength from the December, 1953, level of 3,403,000 to a June, 1957, strength of 2,815,000. The Army was to drop from 1,481,000 to an even one million, the Navy from 765,000 to 650,000, the Marine Corps from 244,000 to 190,000, while the Air Force was to expand from 913,000 to 975,000. Reflecting its one-third cut in personnel the Army was to go from 20 to 14 divisions. The Navy was to drop from 1126 to 1030 combat ships, while the 3 divisions and 3 air wings of the Marine Corps were retained at reduced strength. The Air Force, on the other hand, was to expand from its existing strength of about 110 wings to 137 wings.

After a year of debate and uncertainty the Administration had achieved a new strategy and a long-range military program. In their final decisions on the FY 1955 budget in the remaining weeks of December, Administration leaders took their first steps to implement the new plans.

THE NEW STRATEGY IN PRACTICE

The same pressures for economy which had furnished the drive to formulate a new strategy also shaped its execution. In October, 1953, even before the new strategy had taken its final form, the services had been told that in FY 1955, "Additional economies and increased efficiency should be contemplated and costs projected accordingly on a somewhat lower basis." [76] After the new military strategy had been decided upon in November, the initial service requests for $35.9 billion in new obligational authority were cut back to $31.0 billion. Simultaneously, in the face of the economic downturn, the Administration began to reduce taxes. The personal income tax rates and excess profits tax enacted during the Korean War were allowed to expire at the end of 1953, cutting revenues by an estimated $5 billion. The following year the Excise Tax Reduction Act and the revisions of the internal revenue code eliminated $2.4 billion more. Thus, in January, 1955, the President could proudly declare that the $7.4 billion revenue cut "was the largest tax reduction in any single year in the country's history." "It was," he went on to say, "made possible only by large cuts in Government expenditures." [77] The President's cuts came entirely from national security. Non-security spending was $21.7 billion in FY 1953 and $21.8 billion in FY 1955. Security expenditures were $50.4 billion in FY 1953 and $40.6 billion in FY 1955. Military spending dropped $8.1 billion from its FY 1953 high of $43.6 billion.

Further efforts to curtail spending were made in the FY 1956 budget. The New Look manpower cuts originally scheduled for

6. THE NEW LOOK

achievement in FY 1957 were shifted to FY 1956. Initial service requests for $37.4 billion in new obligational authority were reduced to $32.9 billion. Military expenditures were estimated at $34 billion. Total revenues of $60 billion and expenditures of $62.4 billion would still leave a deficit in this, the third Eisenhower budget. Shortly after the fiscal year began, improved economic conditions and the resulting increase in revenues raised the possibility of balancing the budget by June, 1956, which, presumably, was attractive in an election year. Although upon his return from Geneva current estimates were still for a deficit of $1.5 to $1.7 billion, the President made a balanced budget in FY 1956 a primary objective. He pointed out to his cabinet that the expected deficit amounted to only 3 percent of the budget, and announced that "I am directing the Budget Director to deduct 3 percent of the expenditures planned for this year." [78] He indicated, however, that this was a goal rather than an absolute ceiling, and that he would entertain requests from departmental heads for exemption from it should it be demonstrated "that a cut of this size is an impossibility." At this point, the Defense Department was struggling to get down to the $34 billion level. The President's plan involved a reduction to $33 billion in expenditures, achieving the original New Look expenditure goal for FY 1957 in FY 1956. The military services vigorously opposed the further reduction, and both Dulles and Wilson warned of the serious effects it would have on the military establishment. The demands of the military, supported by the Secretary of State, triumphed over the drive for budget reduction. At this point, in effect, the New Look strategy and reduced expenditures parted ways. That strategy could not be invoked to justify expenditures of only $33 billion in FY 1956. Moreover, rising costs were already causing serious difficulties in getting expenditures down to even the $34 billion level. In actuality, they amounted to $35.8 billion. Total active duty manpower, however, did reach the original New Look goal of 2,815,000 in June, 1956, instead of June, 1957.

The failure of the efforts to reduce military expenditures did not prevent the achievement of a balanced budget. Although total spending increased by about $2 billion over FY 1955, revenues rose by over $7.75 billion and produced the Eisenhower Administration's first surplus, $1.6 billion. Increased revenues made feasible both a balanced budget and the maintenance of defense spending at approximately the FY 1955 level.

The strategic "mix," the allocation of emphasis and resources among military programs, of the New Look was significantly different from that which had prevailed during the Korean War. In part this was a result of the lower level of military effort and in part the result of technological developments and the multiplication of nuclear weapons. Even where the New Look program did not differ markedly from that of the earlier phase, as in the airpower build-up, the role and function of the program received a different emphasis in the declaratory policy of the Administration. The major changes of the New Look program were in: 1) continental defense; 2) conventional surface forces; 3) nuclear weapons; 4) reserve forces; 5) strategic airpower.

Continental Defense. The New Look has been often identified with offensive airpower. In program, however, strategic airpower received no greater emphasis than it had in the Truman Administration. The difference in the continental defense effort, on the other hand, was substantial. Here was the principal innovation of the New Look. (See Chapter V, Section 25.) In the formulation of the FY 1955 budget, the Chiefs "were given firmly to understand that they were expected to recommend an expansion in air defense ... " [79] The Secretary of Defense and the Joint Chiefs, Admiral Radford reported, were "agreed that continental defense programming is an increasingly important part of our national security planning." Strategic airpower and continental defense were, in Eisenhower's terms, the two key elements in a strategy of deterrence.[80] Quite possibly it was the increasing effectiveness of continental defense rather than the continued predominance of strategic airpower which the Administration saw as the principal counterbalance to the future strength of the Soviet strategic air force.

Conventional Ground Forces. The decision to expand the continental defense effort, combined with the desire to reduce overall military expenditures, required substantial cuts elsewhere in the military forces. The ground forces were the principal target. The Korean War was over. Administration leaders publicly rejected the idea that the United States would become tied down in a similar

6. THE NEW LOOK

conflict in the future. The overwhelming superiority of the Soviets in manpower meant that "there is no local defense which alone will contain" the Communists, and hence the free world "should not attempt to match the Soviet bloc man for man and gun for gun."[81] In addition, the principle of balanced collective forces required the United States to specialize in sea- and airpower: "the other free nations can most effectively provide in their own and adjacent countries the bulk of the defensive ground forces."[82] The needs which had been met by conventional ground forces could be adequately covered by other types of military force: tactical atomic weapons, ready reserve forces, nuclear airpower. While continental defense was the principal area of expansion in the New Look, conventional ground forces were the principal area of contraction.

The reduction in the ground forces was carried out expeditiously. During calendar 1954 the Army dropped from 1,480,-000 to 1,330,000 men and the Marines from 243,000 to 220,000 men. The FY 1956 budget proposed still speedier reductions. The Army goal for June, 1955, was set at 1,100,000 men (a decline of 73,000 from the goal established a year earlier), and its strength for June, 1956, was to be 1,027,000 men. Similarly, the Administration proposed to reduce the Marine Corps to 193,000 men by June, 1956, substantially achieving its original New Look goal (190,000 men in June, 1957) a year ahead of time. Congress objected to the reduction in the Marine Corps, and its strength stabilized through FY 1956 and FY 1957 at roughly 200,000 men. The Army manpower reductions, however, were carried out almost as scheduled. By the fall of 1956 the Army was down to the one million level, and its combat strength at 18 divisions and 10 regimental combat teams. The budgetary results of these reductions were impressive. Army expenditures in FY 1953, the last year of the Korean War, were $16,242 million. By FY 1956, they had been cut almost in half to $8,702 million.

Nuclear Weapons. The decision to place greater reliance upon nuclear weapons was a key aspect of the New Look. The military, as Secretary Humphrey put it, had been "trying to follow six strategies simultaneously—two for each service."[83] Considerable economies would result if the services planned to use nuclear weapons against any military targets where they would be effective, either in a general war or in a serious limited war. In the words of one White House adviser:

The President made it clear from the beginning that defense strategy plans were to recognize the existence of atomic weapons and the fact they would be used if needed. There was no hesitation in his mind. He became irritated with plans based on any assumption these weapons were not to be used. In effect, he told these people, "This isn't a debate any longer; we must face facts." He was very clear on the point that strategy and budgets be developed on that decision.[84]

Aircraft were still the principal means of delivering nuclear weapons; hence use of nuclear weapons implied a shift in emphasis from landpower to airpower. Also, ground forces with tactical atomic weapons, Wilson argued, could be much smaller than forces without them.[85] Such weapons, Mr. Dulles said, "can utterly destroy military targets without endangering unrelated civilian centers." If "the United States became engaged in a major military activity anywhere in the world . . . ," he continued, "those weapons would come into use because, as I say, they are becoming more and more conventional and replacing what used to be called conventional weapons." The President bluntly endorsed this view: "Where these things are used on strictly military targets and for strictly military purposes, I see no reason why they shouldn't be used just exactly as you would use a bullet or anything else." [86]

The decision to make nuclear weapons regular equipment in the ground forces and to use them where militarily needed was supplemented by the major shift in NATO strategy which also took place in 1954. By late 1952 it was obvious that it would be impossible to realize the ambitious Lisbon program to create a large conventional ground force in Europe capable of protecting Europe against a major Russian attack. Conceivably, however, tactical nuclear weapons could be substituted for more manpower in the NATO shield. In 1953 and 1954 the United States actively pushed the adoption of a nuclear strategy for NATO, and in July, 1954, a lengthy report prepared under the auspices of SHAPE recommended the integration of tactical nuclear weapons into the European defenses. In what was referred to as the "biggest U. S. diplomatic achievement since World War II," the North Atlantic Council in December, 1954, brought NATO strategy into line with American

6. THE NEW LOOK

strategy and authorized SHAPE to base its military planning on the assumption that nuclear weapons would be used in future conflict.

Reserve Forces. The cuts in the ground forces, Admiral Radford argued, would in part be compensated for by "an improved state of readiness of our Reserve forces." Similarly, Secretary Wilson held that "Strong Reserve Forces will make it possible to maintain the Active Forces at levels that will impose the least burden on the national economy and still provide for military strength as it may be needed." When General Ridgway protested that further reductions in the Army's strength left it unprepared to carry out its commitments, Secretary Wilson replied that "Reserves are the key to the solution of the Army's problem. . . . Even if millions of reserves or veterans are not properly trained, they could be regrouped or formed into effective reserves pretty quickly." [87]

Shortly after taking office the Administration directed the National Security Training Commission to study manpower and reserve problems. The Commission's report in December, 1953, urged the establishment of a large citizen reserve. Its essential ideas were embodied in the Administration's National Reserve Plan and then in the Reserve Forces Act of 1955. The goal of this legislation was 2,900,000 men in the Ready Reserve by 1960. To fill this massive reserve force, the Act obligated men who volunteered for or were drafted into the armed services to serve five years in the Active Forces and the Ready Reserves. In addition, the Act permitted 100,000 youths a year between the ages of seventeen and eighteen-and-a-half to enlist in a special six-month training program followed by seven-and-a-half years in the Ready Reserves. Under the stimulus of this act and other Administration encouragement, the number of reserve personnel in drill pay status increased from 578,000 in June, 1953, to 913,000 in June, 1956, and one million in June, 1957. During the same period direct expenditures upon the reserve components more than doubled, reaching $879.8 million in FY 1957.

The National Security Training Commission argued for reserves in terms of the needs of mobilization, attributing the slow and disorderly character of the mobilization in the country's last three wars to the absence of an effective reserve system. Its proposals and their rationale closely resembled Marshall's plans for UMT. The

Administration's support for a large and effective reserve program, on the other hand, stemmed less from the idea that it would be valuable in a future great mobilization than from the belief that it would be a reasonably inexpensive way to replace the active-duty manpower eliminated in the FY 1955 and FY 1956 budgets. The cost of one man on active duty, the Administration estimated, equaled the cost of ten reservists. The substitution of the latter for the former, of course, rested on the assumption that an equal or greater number of reserves could meet the same needs as the active-duty forces they were to replace. It presupposed an extremely high state of readiness for the reserves if they were to be capable of participating either in a limited war, in which nuclear weapons would probably be used, or in a general thermonuclear holocaust.

The predominance of the desire for economy over any doctrinal adherence to a mobilization strategy was also reflected in the Administration's policy toward the mobilization base. The Korean War rearmament effort had aimed at the development of a broad mobilization base, which, although more expensive than a narrow one, would greatly facilitate general mobilization in time of crisis. In this case the interests of economy did not coincide with those of a mobilization strategy. Under Wilson's prodding the Administration moved haltingly toward a narrower but less expensive mobilization base. In the words of General Ridgway:

Cutbacks and even cancellations of procurement contracts have had to be ordered and many currently active production lines are being placed in standby or will return to civilian production. This will narrow the operating production base and thereby reduce its capability after D-day.[88]

In effect, General Ridgway was arguing for a program more closely attuned to a mobilization strategy while the Administration, for economy reasons, was shifting to one more closely related to a strategy of deterrence. Secretary Wilson was less concerned with the "capability" of the production base "after D-day" than he was with current output and the feasibility of maintaining the production base for the "long haul." "If I had been doing it the last three years," he declared in 1953, ". . . I would have built more production and less mobilization base so I would have achieved a stronger military position quickly . . ."[89]

6. THE NEW LOOK

Strategic Airpower. Compared with the Truman Administration program, the New Look thus involved substantial reductions in military manpower and conventional ground forces and substantial increases in continental defense, reserve forces, and nuclear weapons. With strategic airpower, the picture is somewhat more complex. Compared with the Truman program, the New Look entailed slightly lower levels of total airpower and strategic airpower and yet greater emphases upon airpower in general and strategic airpower in particular.

The New Look Air Force goal was 137 wings by June, 1957. This included 126 combat wings, the same number that had been provided for in the Truman 143-wing program, with a reduction of 6 wings in troop carrier and air transport planes. Thus, the New Look's goal in overall combat air strength was similar to that of the Truman Administration but was pushed back eighteen months from December, 1955 to June, 1957. It also involved a redistribution of emphasis. In accordance with the stress on continental defense, the New Look program provided for 34 air defense wings instead of the 29 in the Truman program. Balancing this, the Strategic Air Command goal was reduced from 57 wings to 54 wings and the Tactical Air Command goal from 40 to 38 wings. "The 137-wing program," as Hanson Baldwin concisely put it at the time, "represents a slight decrease in numbers, a reallocation of wings, and a slow-down as compared to the prior 143-wing program of the Truman Administration." [90] The verbal stress on airpower, however, was much greater than it had been before. For FY 1955, the President declared, "heavy emphasis" was placed on airpower, and the budget pointed "toward the creation, maintenance, and full exploitation of modern air power." [91] This increased emphasis, however, was the product not of the expansion of airpower programs over the Truman goals but of a reduction in other programs: airpower was more important because it consumed a larger share of a smaller budget.

Strategic airpower assumed a new role in the functions which it was designed to perform. The actions and declarations of the Truman Administration had indicated that strategic retaliation with nuclear weapons would be a response only to a major attack upon western Europe or North America. The doctrine of massive retaliation raised the possibility that this capacity might be used to respond to less critical attacks in other parts of the world. Since massive retaliation was never ordered, it cannot be said that American policy was *to retaliate* massively against aggressions in the gray areas. On the other hand, with the speech of Mr. Dulles on January 12, 1954, it did become American policy *to declare* that we might respond by massive retaliation in such contingencies. This attempt to utilize nuclear airpower to deter lesser as well as major aggressions was another substitute for the conventional ground forces which might have been used for this purpose.

The New Look and Its Critics. The Joint Chiefs had originally agreed unanimously on the three-year New Look plan. It was, however, a tenuous agreement, dependent upon explicit and implicit assumptions. Explicitly they assumed that the international situation would get no worse and relative Soviet power not much greater during those three years. Implicitly, they assumed that the German and Japanese rearmament would move forward quickly, EDC would be ratified, Korea would remain calm and the build-up of South Korean forces continue, and that the Indochina situation would be resolved satisfactorily without American intervention.[92] Most significantly, implicitly they assumed that the reduction in conventional armed forces would be paralleled by increasing capabilities in tactical nuclear weapons. The Administration went ahead with its reductions, however, regardless of whether its assumptions were realized. Although he had agreed to the New Look goals, General Ridgway found himself dissenting from the first step toward their achievement: the reductions in the Army contained in the FY 1955 budget. He found some support in the Senate but not enough to get additional funds for the Army. The following year many of the assumptions upon which Ridgway had based his adherence to the original New Look program had still not been realized, yet the Administration speeded up its reductions. As a result, Ridgway was even more outspoken in his dissent.

This conflict over ground forces and conventional forces was the typical New Look pattern. The principal impact of the New Look program fell on those elements of the military forces, and, reinforced by the controversy over Secretary Dulles' "massive re-

6. THE NEW LOOK

taliation" speech, it was natural that this should become the principal focus of controversy. The 1953 battle over the initial "interim" reduction in the Air Force goals preceded the formulation of the new strategy and was the peculiar result of a peculiar, one-time cutback in airpower appropriations. From the presentation of the FY 1955 budget in January, 1954, until the displays of Soviet air strength in May, 1955, controversy over military programs focused on the reductions in manpower and ground strength. At the same time, a secondary stream of criticism pointed to the rate of the airpower build-up. This, however, was muted; although the Eisenhower program was less than the Truman program, it still provided for a substantial expansion over the existing levels and an even greater expansion in terms of its proportion of the total military effort. So long as the progress of the Soviet airpower build-up remained cloudy and uncertain, those who had doubts about the adequacy of the American build-up also had few concrete points upon which to hang their criticism.

SUCCESS AND FAILURE

In March, 1954, Walter Lippmann argued that the New Look involved "no radical change in our strategy policy." Three months later another well-informed observer declared: "The simple fact is that things *have* changed, and changed profoundly. Strategy has changed; the economics of strategy have changed; and the nature of war has changed." [93] Who was right? Was the New Look a significant change in American strategy?

The New Look did not mean a change in foreign policy. During the 1952 campaign Republican leaders had often talked of such changes, of liberation, the initiative, and bold, new, dynamic actions. Once the new Administration did come into office, however, these suggestions were quietly set aside. The foreign policy of the Eisenhower Administration was essentially that of its predecessor. The military strategy implementing that foreign policy, however, was different. The nomination of Taft would have meant a break in the foreign policy consensus and a major debate over the broad outlines of American foreign policy. As an internationalist Republican who had served the Truman Administration, Eisenhower could be expected to adhere to the existing foreign policy. As a general, he could be expected to devise more acceptable military means of implementing that policy. These were the expectations which, in a sense, the American people had voted for in the 1952 election.

The new strategy was part of a coherent set of economic, fiscal, and military policies. While differences, of course, existed among members of the Administration, unusual agreement also existed on the Administration's priorities: reduce expenditures, balance the budget, reduce taxes, in that order, while maintaining a military posture sufficient to preserve national security against the Soviet threat for an indefinite period of time. The New Look strategy which evolved in the fall of 1953 and was embodied in NSC 162/2 and the JCS paper of December 9 was designed to accomplish these goals. It was the appropriate military component of the Administration's overall policy. The New Look was one case where an Administration had its goals clearly in mind and pursued them with vigor and determination. The substance of its policy can be criticized; the absence of a policy cannot be.

The strategic changes of the New Look were the product of economic pressure and technological progress. In part these changes meant the addition of new programs and concepts: continental defense, tactical nuclear weapons, a declaratory policy of massive retaliation. To a much greater extent, however, what was new about the New Look was not the innovation of programs and concepts but their elimination. The Korean War rearmament had combined elements of mobilization and deterrence. In the New Look the balance shifted decisively toward deterrence. This was reflected in the reductions in conventional ground forces, the acceptance of the nuclear weapons as "conventional" where militarily needed, the narrowing of the mobilization base, the Dulles emphasis on clear-cut commitments and warnings of drastic action if these commitments were challenged. In 1951, strategy still admitted the possibility of fighting another general war similar to the closing phases of World War II. By 1955 this was no longer a probability. The dual pressures of technological progress and domestic demands squeezed the general war mobilization concepts out of strategy, except where, as in the case of the reserves, forces more appropriate for a mobilization strategy appeared to be a less expensive substitute for those more directly related to deterrence.

6. THE NEW LOOK

It has been suggested that the New Look was inevitable, that it would have come, in the words of Admiral Radford, "no matter what administration was in power." [94] A distinction must be made, however, between a new look and the New Look. The Korean War rearmament had begun to lose its direction and momentum. If the Truman Administration had remained in office, undoubtedly the military programs in practice would have become even further removed from the strategic concepts which originally inspired them. Any *new* Administration, Democratic or Republican, would have made significant changes in military policy, particularly when confronted in its first year in office with the death of Stalin, the end of the Korean War, and the Soviet explosion of a thermonuclear weapon. It was not inevitable, however, that these changes take the course which they did take. As Glenn Snyder has accurately pointed out, the "Soviet hydrogen explosion *might* have been interpreted by another set of Chiefs as indicating an imminent decline in the effectiveness of the U. S. nuclear deterrent, and as requiring stronger ground defense forces as a substitute . . . " [95] A new look was inevitable. The New Look was the special reflection of the values and goals of Dwight Eisenhower, George Humphrey, John Foster Dulles, Arthur W. Radford, their associates in the Administration, and the dominant groups in the Republican Party.

In the fall of 1955 the New Look's goals were apparently certain of achievement. A new balance between military requirements and domestic economic demands was in sight. Governmental expenditures had been reduced by almost $10 billion, and taxes by an estimated $7.5 billion. A balanced budget was in prospect, and, in fact, it did materialize nine months later. A stable military program was about to be realized. Military expenditures for FY 1956 were $35.8 billion, less than one percent higher than those of FY 1955. National security expenditures for both FY 1955 and FY 1956 were stable at $40.6 billion. By June, 1956, total military personnel strength leveled off at the hoped-for goal of about 2,800,000, which was maintained with little change throughout FY 1957.

Stability was the great theme of the FY 1957 military budget. In October, 1955, Secretary Wilson declared that no major changes would take place in the level of military spending or the size of the military forces in FY 1957. The budget document presented to Congress in January estimated military expenditures at $35.5 billion, more than the current estimates for FY 1956 but roughly the same as the actual total expenditures for FY 1955. The projected manpower strengths for the end of FY 1957 were not very different from those for the end of FY 1956: 200 men more for the Army, 599 less for the Navy, 4,735 more for the Marine Corps, and, the only substantial change, 20,000 more for the Air Force. The FY 1957 budget, the *Army-Navy-Air Force Journal* declared, indicated a "period of stability in military strength" and provided for "unprecedented stability in Army, Navy and Marine Corps manpower plans." [96] Moreover, the budget of FY 1957 provoked little dissent in the Pentagon. In FY 1955 and FY 1956 the executive branch had been divided over the reductions in the ground forces; in later budgets major battles were to occur over the adequacy of airpower and missile programs. Although Air Force leaders were already beginning to have their doubts about this adequacy, the FY 1957 budget nonetheless represented a brief moment of peace in the Pentagon between the battles over one strategy and those over another. In the fall of 1955 security, harmony, economy, stability, all seemed within reach. The New Look's moment of success, however, was a fleeting one. Already well under way was the increase in Soviet capabilities which was to undermine its assumptions and goals.

7. THE NEW NEW LOOK, 1956–1960
THE STIMULI

The Balance of Terror. In 1954 the United States possessed the ability to destroy the war-making capacity of the Soviet Union with little likelihood of serious reprisal. A few years later this was no longer the case. The emergence of the "balance of terror" was the decisive military fact of the mid-1950s. It undermined the New Look's two key assumptions: that the 1953 ratio of Soviet to American power would not begin to change drastically before the late 1950s and that American nuclear retaliatory forces could deter both large and small aggressions.

The balance of terror was a product of two factors: the development by the Soviet Union of substantial delivery capabilities in jet bombers and ballistic missiles, and the development by both sides of a significant stockpile of thermonuclear weapons. That the Soviet Union would achieve such capabilities had, of course, been foreseen and had been the principal reason for the New Look emphasis on continental defense. The Administration had not anticipated, however, that the Soviet Union would counterbalance American strategic superiority until the end of the decade.[97] Yet in 1955, the Soviets demonstrated that they were far advanced in the production of long-range bombers and that they were qualitatively abreast of the United States in aircraft design and development. About the same time, newly installed radar devices picked up evidence that the Soviets were testing large numbers of 800-mile range ballistic missiles. The Administration-appointed Killian committee warned that unless the United States made additional efforts the Soviets would achieve a decisive lead in strategic missiles by 1960.[98] Two years later, in August, 1957, the Soviets announced the successful firing of an intercontinental missile, and the sputniks a few months later dramatized their capabilities. In 1959 and 1960 the United States continued to be superior in long-range bombers, but the Soviets were probably ahead in deploying operational long-range missiles. Massive retaliation had become a two-way street.

The balance of terror was reinforced by the growing number of thermonuclear weapons on both sides of the Iron Curtain and the increasing appreciation of their awesome destructiveness. The United States carried out its first thermonuclear explosion in November, 1952, the Soviets theirs in August, 1953. By 1955 and 1956 the accumulation by both sides of substantial stockpiles of thermonuclear weapons marked a drastic change in the military situation. "There is," as Winston Churchill declared in March, 1955, "an immense gulf between the atomic and the hydrogen bomb. The atomic bomb, with all its terror, did not carry us outside the scope of human control or manageable events in thought or action, in peace or war." A general war in which hydrogen weapons were used would be disastrous for all participants. The power of the weapons reduced the delivery capabilities needed to use them effectively and made the problem of defense extremely difficult. In 1950 and 1951 the Administration had prepared for what seemed like an imminent conflict with the Soviet Union. In 1953 and 1954 a different Administration not only had placed reliance upon the ability of nuclear air power to deter major and minor aggressions but also had indicated that it would not hesitate to use nuclear weapons where they would be militarily effective. Two years later, however, willingness to use nuclear weapons required also a willingness to face the possibility of thermonuclear devastation. The great powers, as Churchill put it, were reaching a stage "where safety will be the sturdy child of terror, and survival the twin brother of annihilation."

Easing of International Tensions. The horror of military weapons perhaps contributed to the lessening of international tensions which had begun in 1953. In 1955, the Geneva conference, the Austrian peace treaty, the UN agreement on the admission of new states, the establishment of diplomatic relations between the Soviet Union and the German Federal Republic, all seemed to indicate a thaw in the Cold War. Bulganin declared that 1955 would "go down in history as the year of a definite turning point in the tense international situation which has existed in recent times." Secretary Dulles agreed that ". . . there has been some considerable diminution of international tensions; I think it is generally agreed that there is less risk of general war than has been the case heretofore." At the Twentieth Party Congress in February, 1956, Khrushchev declared that "there is no fatal inevitability of wars." [99] Major crises occurred over Hungary, Suez, Lebanon, the offshore islands, Berlin, the U-2, but the behavior of the major powers underlined the extent to which both were reluctant to let any crisis get out of hand. These developments coincided with evidence that the Soviet Union, while restricting the use of force to achieve its goals, was putting greater emphasis upon diplomatic, psychological, and economic means. In 1955, Soviet bloc countries began to supply arms to Egypt, and the Soviet Union itself offered to assist the economic development of the Arab states. As the danger of war receded, the intensity of the economic and diplomatic conflict increased.

Domestic and Economic Factors. Three factors successively dominated the domestic-economic environment of the military budget. First, federal expenditures on nonsecurity programs had been remarkably stable for five years: they were $16.1 billion in FY 1950, $15.4 billion in FY 1955. By 1956 an expansion in domestic program spending could no longer be delayed. "For years," the President said in his FY 1957 budget message, "many activities which are desirable for fostering sound economic growth have been postponed because of the overriding needs of war and defense." Now, however, "new and expanded programs" could be undertaken in school construction, highways, housing, domestic airways, the merchant marine, and "the expansion of research and training in science, health, and agriculture." This marked the beginning of a 50 percent rise in domestic federal expenditures over the next five years, a rise in which the Administration acquiesced reluctantly but which numerous critics argued was still insufficient to meet the need for public services. Second, prices, which had remained relatively stable between 1953 and 1955, started to move up in 1956 and despite the 1957–1958 recession generally continued to increase throughout the period. This continuing inflation made the Administration all the more anxious to balance the budget during the nonrecession years. Finally, at the end of the decade the "weakening" of the dollar internationally added still another constraint on federal spending in general and overseas expenditures in particular. The cumulative effect of these three factors was a strong incentive to keep military expenditures at the minimum consistent with a reasonable degree of national security.

ADMINISTRATION STRATEGY

The emergence of a balance of terror had two implications for American military policy. Conceivably both the strategic force and the defense system of one country could be far superior to those of another and yet not superior enough to prevent the retaliatory devastation of the stronger country by the strategic forces of the weaker. Larger forces might be desirable for other purposes—prestige, political influence, deterrence of other actions—but, if governments acted rationally, they were not essential to deter direct attack on vital interests. Second, strategic nuclear forces were less relevant to the deterrence of local aggressions. As long as each major power had the ability to devastate the other, it would be in the interest of neither to use its strategic forces in response to small-scale attack. A key element of the New Look was undermined. The threat to use the strategic forces lost credibility as a deterrent to local aggression. Other tactical and conventional forces were required to supplement the decreased efficacy of the strategic forces for this purpose.

The balance of terror thus implied that for purposes of deterrence there was a maximum strength beyond which strategic retaliatory forces need not go and a minimum strength below which limited war forces should not be allowed to go. The Administration partially accepted these implications. The relaxation of Soviet-American tensions and the domestic-economic constraints, however, precluded any substantial increase in overall military expenditures. The Administration attempted to develop a new strategy for mutual deterrence by adjusting programs, assumptions, and goals within the existing level of military effort. The dominant features of this "New New Look" were: 1) continuing efforts to stabilize military expenditures; 2) downgrading of mobilization potential and reserve forces; 3) acceptance of a future retaliatory capability sufficient, but only sufficient, to deter a direct attack on American territory or equally vital interests; and 4) a slowly growing recognition of the need to maintain capabilities for limited war. The great debates over strategy in the second Eisenhower Administration concerned the wisdom of the Administration's sufficient-deterrent policy, the adequacy of its provisions to implement that policy, and the adequacy of its provisions for limited war.

THE STRUGGLE FOR STABILITY

A distinguishing feature of the New New Look was the Administration's effort to maintain stable levels of military programs *and* expenditures *despite* the significant changes taking place in the foreign and domestic environments of military policy. The struggle between the Administration and the forces pushing programs and expenditures upward evolved through three phases.

Program and Expenditure Stability, 1956–1957. The New New Look properly began in December, 1955, when Secretary Wilson directed the Joint Chiefs of Staff to make a "complete and careful" study of the nation's defense problems during fiscal years 1958, 1959, and 1960. Wilson did not, however, expect the Joint Chiefs to revolutionize strategy, and his confidence in existing programs was confirmed by the Joint Chiefs in March after a six-day meeting in

7. THE NEW NEW LOOK

Puerto Rico. The Chiefs concluded that no increase in military personnel was necessary and that no substantial shift in emphasis among military programs was desirable. Both military chiefs and Administration leaders recognized, however, that no hope existed of stabilizing military expenditures at the early New Look goal of $34 billion. Military expenditures for FY 1956 were $36.7 billion, their low point in the Eisenhower Administration. The new goal was to keep them below $38 billion. The Chiefs, however, estimated that $38 billion would be "the minimum sum needed to carry on necessary programs" and that possibly $40 billion would be required. Secretary Wilson more accurately predicted that even $40 billion would be insufficient.[100]

The difficulties involved in reconciling program stability with expenditure stability became clear in the summer of 1956. Despite the Joint Chiefs' acceptance of the $40 billion limit, the initial requests of the services for FY 1958 were $48.6 billion for the continuation of existing programs. Admiral Radford argued that stability in expenditures required a drastic reduction in military programs, including a cut in personnel from 2,800,000 men to 2,000,000 men. Secretary Wilson attempted to steer a middle course, rejecting both the "Radford plan" and $48 billion in military expenditures as "extreme." No "responsible person," he declared, had ever advocated the reduction and withdrawal of forces contained in the "Radford plan." The three-year plan approved by the Secretary proposed a more moderate cut in manpower strength of about 300,000 to be carried out during FY 1959 and FY 1960 as a result of the development and adoption of new weapons. Yet Secretary Wilson also limited the increase in military expenditures, rejecting the initial service FY 1958 estimates out of hand as "unrealistic" and "completely out of trend with the requirements of the nation."[101] The Administration's FY 1958 budget thus attempted to combine program and expenditure stability. Projected military personnel strength for June, 1958, was only slightly above the existing strength in December, 1956; a few shifts were made in service force level goals. New obligational authority of $38.5 billion was requested from Congress, while expenditures were estimated at $38 billion. As in the previous year, the keynote of the budget was "the importance of our stable force concept." "We are set," Chairman Vinson declared, "upon a stable goal for the indefinite future." [102]

Program vs. Expenditure Stability, 1957. FY 1958, however, rushed the season. During the winter and spring of 1957 a marked upsurge took place in military spending. The rate of military expenditures, which had been $37 billion a year in the first half of FY 1957, rose to $40.2 billion by the end of the fiscal year. As a result, total expenditures for FY 1957, estimated at $36 billion in January, were $38.4 billion. This sharp increase was a concrete indication of the difficulty of combining program stability and expenditure stability. It was primarily due not to an expansion of programs but to inflation and to changes in procurement practices. In July, 1956, the wholesale price index was 114.0. A year later it was 118.2. The costs of the goods and services required by the Defense Department reportedly rose more rapidly than those in the economy in general; Secretary Wilson estimated that between January and August, 1957, the overall price tag on Defense Department programs had jumped by 5 percent. An unanticipated acceleration also took place in military procurement. Fewer slippages than normal occurred due to strikes and material shortages. The Administration's tight money policy stimulated contractors to speed up their collections. Research and development projects moved forward more quickly than anticipated. Reversing the usual procedure, more defense contracts were placed in the first half of FY 1957 than in the second half, and until stopped in May, the Air Force followed a policy of partial financing: initiating procurement programs for which full obligational authority had not yet been obtained from Congress.[103] Defense Department officials predicted that unless drastic action were taken to reverse the upward trend in spending, military expenditures for FY 1958 would amount to about $42 billion, $4 billion more than had been approved by the President. In addition, the national debt in the summer of 1957 was about $273 billion. The increased defense spending which seemed likely would require the Administration to ask Congress to raise the statutory debt limit of $275 billion. The Administration clearly confronted the issue: either military programs must go down or military spending (and the national debt) must go up.

7. THE NEW NEW LOOK

The Administration's choice was unequivocally in favor of stability of expenditures rather than stability of programs. The spending rise, in the words of the Defense Comptroller, was "incompatible with the basic defense policy of a stable, steady effort over the long pull." The increases in costs, Secretary Wilson said, made an expenditure level of $38 billion an "impossible one without an adjustment in the program. So we are in the process now of adjusting our programs downward." The cuts were "an effort to stabilize (military) costs at the $38,000,000,000 level." [104] A 200,000-man reduction in military personnel to 2,600,000 was ordered. The Army lost 2 divisions, 38 anti-aircraft battalions, and 2 atomic support commands. The Navy lost 20 warships and 59 other vessels. The Air Force, which had momentarily achieved its long-sought goal of 137 wings in June, 1957, was cut back below the original FY 1958 goal of 128 wings to 117 wings. Installations and depots were closed, overtime work on defense contracts curtailed, civilian personnel cut by over 68,000 places, progress payments on military contracts limited. Development of many weapons was canceled, including the Navaho and Triton missiles, the F-103 all-weather interceptor, a Navy jet bomber, and a long-range early warning patrol plane. Production of the C-132 transport plane was stopped, and production of other Air Force and Navy fighters and bombers was cut back or stretched out. "We were working late into the night and week-ends," one official later declared, "trying to cut expenditures to meet fixed spending ceilings—in a rush, too, cutting an Army division here, laying up a dozen ships there." [105] The efforts, however, were successful: military expenditures dropped from their peak rate of $40.2 billion in June, 1957, to $39.2 billion in the first quarter of FY 1958. Simultaneous with the reduction in current expenditures, the Administration, "apparently on written orders from the President," imposed $38 billion ceilings on both new appropriations and expenditures for FY 1959 to guide the services in their decisions on force levels and to prevent a recurrence of the previous year's experience when the initial service requests were $10 billion more than the Administration was willing to allow.[106] The all-out effort was on to hold the $38 billion expenditure line.

Restabilization, 1958-1960. Whether this effort would have succeeded in the absence of the Soviet sputniks and the domestic recession remains a fascinating but unanswerable question of military policy. Despite these developments and the pressure from Congress, the Gaither Committee, and other informed opinion, the Administration only reluctantly agreed to increases in programs and expenditures. Immediately after the first Soviet sputnik the Administration ordered a speed-up in the long-range ballistic missile programs, to be accomplished, however, within the framework of the $38 billion budget. By the end of October the Administration admitted that defense expenditures would probably exceed $38.4 billion in FY 1958. At the same time, "The informed word from the Defense and Treasury Departments . . . was that the Administration's economy effort had not been abandoned, and that the defense breakthrough would be a reluctant one and no larger than absolutely necessary." [107]

Reflecting this approach, the FY 1959 budget did not represent any marked change in the level of national defense effort. The President estimated that military spending in the current 1958 fiscal year would be $38.9 billion, and he recommended FY 1959 expenditures of $39.8 billion. This rise would, as Charles Wilson said, "hardly cover the increased cost of inflation." [108] Higher expenditures for missile and other priority programs were balanced by reductions in military personnel, cutbacks in conventional active forces and in the reserves, closing of installations, and reduced procurement of older weapons.

Actually, under the impetus of the increases in missile and related programs and the delay in the reductions in the conventional forces caused by the Lebanon and Quemoy crises in the summer of 1958, FY 1959 expenditures amounted to $41.2 billion. This set the level of the new plateau. The FY 1960 budget reflected the Treasury's concern over the growing "softness" of the dollar internationally and the President's belief that the Republican defeats in the 1958 congressional elections had been due to the party's failure to convey to the voters the importance of sound fiscal policy. He made strenuous efforts to prevent any major rise in defense spending and presented to Congress a budget with a narrow estimated surplus of $100 million and with military expenditures of $40.9. A year later the President affirmed his intention to maintain this level of spending for both FY 1960 and for FY 1961. Actual mili-

7. THE NEW NEW LOOK

tary expenditures were $41.2 billion for both FY 1959 and FY 1960 and $43.2 for FY 1961. In its last three years the Eisenhower Administration briefly succeeded in stabilizing military spending at $7 billion more than the original New Look goal and $3 billion more than the pre-sputnik New New Look goal. At least half of the FY 1958–1961 increase over the $38 billion goal, however, was due to rising prices. In constant dollars, total national security expenditures were less in calendar 1960 than they had been in any year since 1951. Total foreign policy spending (major national security programs and international affairs and finance) was more than 60 percent of the federal budget. Yet from FY 1958 to FY 1961 it increased only $3.4 billion—slightly more than half the $6.2 billion increase in other federal expenditures, largely for agriculture, labor and welfare, commerce and housing, and interest on the national debt. Given rising Soviet strength abroad and rising prices at home, the Eisenhower Administration did remarkably well in its struggle for stability.

MOBILIZATION BASE AND RESERVE FORCES

The New New Look marked another stage in the shift from mobilization potential to force-in-being. The New Look tendency to minimize the significance of a broad industrial mobilization base continued. Under prodding from the Air Force, the services adjusted their procurement policies to the expectation that a general war would be decided in a few months. The "traditional concept of a prolonged industrial build-up after attack," in the words of one early Air Force directive, "must be replaced with a 'readiness' program." [109] Service schedules of "full-mobilization requirements" for major weapons and equipment were slashed 50 to 65 percent. Companies not engaged in military production in peacetime were warned that there was little likelihood of their receiving military contracts in wartime. Multiple sources of supply were eliminated and stand-by equipment and factories reduced in number.[110] Abandoning plans for the mobilization of the nation's resources more than six months after the start of hostilities was, as Hanson Baldwin put it, a "marked concession to the school that holds that any future war must be fought with what the services have at the outbreak." [111] The intensity with which these policies were followed in the economy wave of 1957 once again indicated how, under the appropriate circumstances, economy stimulated the evolution of policy from mobilization to deterrence.

During the New Look large reserve forces had been viewed as an economical substitute for active forces. During the New New Look it became apparent that large reserve forces were not the most economical way of meeting the force requirements of mutual deterrence. Hardly more than a year after the Administration had successfully piloted the Reserve Forces Act of 1955 through Congress, it shifted its advocacy from a massive reserve to a smaller, better trained, readier one. Under the 1955 act, the draftees coming out of the active army in the summer of 1957 would be required to serve three years in the reserves. This promised mounting costs for a program which, in the view of the Administration, no longer met a major military requirement. In December, 1956, the Defense Department announced that it was planning to reduce the costs of the reserve program, to cut the size of the reserve forces, and to place emphasis on quality rather than quantity. This was an effort, the Assistant Secretary of Defense declared, to develop a reserve which would "tie in with actual military needs." The Joint Chiefs of Staff reportedly felt that "new strategic plans and concepts make obsolete many previous plans for development and utilization of Reserve Forces." Significant changes were necessary "in order to prevent runaway costs and to bring Reserve and Guard units into line with current military planning and requirements." [112] In October, 1956, as the first steps in this direction, the Army suspended the formation of most new reserve units and in January, 1957, announced that it would require new National Guard recruits to undergo six months of active duty training.

In the summer of 1957, under the impetus of the economy drive, the Administration and the Joint Chiefs pushed forward the "new look" at the reserves in formulating the FY 1959 budget. "Many military leaders," it was reported, "now think that a cutback in Reserve manpower should be considered in view of the rising costs and the budget ceiling." The deleterious effects of the larger reserve program for a strategy of deterrence were pointed out by Army Secretary Brucker when he warned that the influx of volunteers into the Army's six-month training program would "place an in-

7. THE NEW NEW LOOK

creased training burden upon our strategic Army forces at a sacrifice of over-all combat readiness." Secretary of Defense Wilson was said to have demanded a "searching review" of the reserve forces in the hope of reducing them to "something manageable." [113]

The results of this review were revealed in January, 1958. The Administration proposed to reduce the Army National Guard from 400,000 men to 360,000 men and the Army Reserve from 300,000 men to 270,000 men. In addition, in March, 1958, the Army announced a plan to eliminate 6 Guard and 4 Reserve divisions, to reduce and consolidate smaller units, and to change the remaining 27 divisions into "pentomic" units with fewer men and more nuclear weapons. In this and succeeding years, however, the opposition of the National Guard and the Reserve Forces defeated the Administration's efforts to cut their manpower and forced the Army to modify its reorganization of their force structure. While the interests of economy led the Administration to de-emphasize reserve forces, the political strength of the reserves, and particularly their support within Congress, prevented the Administration from carrying out its policies.

THE SUFFICIENT DETERRENT

The New Look had been based upon the overwhelming American superiority in nuclear airpower. The development of Soviet planes, ballistic missiles, and nuclear weapons threatened drastically to reduce that superiority and to eliminate its significance. What should be the response of American policy? Three alternatives were posed in 1956. One, the Radford Plan, proposed to continue the existing level of military expenditures but to maintain a clear superiority in nuclear and strategic forces by major cutbacks in conventional strength. The plan assumed that any war would be short and would involve the use of nuclear weapons. Military manpower would be reduced by 800,000 men with the bulk of the cut, 450,000 men, coming from the Army. The reduction in the Army and the gradual shift in reliance in the Strategic Air Command from the medium-range B-47 to the long-range B-52 would permit the withdrawal of American troops from overseas and the retention of only token forces in Europe.[114] The stress on nuclear weapons and strategic airpower, the withdrawal of forces from overseas, the reduction in conventional forces and in tactical airpower, and, most significantly, the assumption of the absolute necessity of keeping a tight lid on military expenditures—all represented the logical extension of the policies of the New Look, which Admiral Radford had helped to formulate three years earlier.

A second alternative was debated in Congress. "Soviet Russia," the House Appropriations Committee declared, "will probably equal the United States in offensive airpower capability within a very few years unless the United States is to expand the overall size of its Air Force and substantially step up the production of aircraft." The issue, the Committee said, is "what to do about it. Should we attempt to stay ahead of the Soviets in the overall size of our Air Force and in the numbers of aircraft to be produced or should we attempt to maintain what is determined to be a sufficient Air Force equipped with the best modern aircraft to act as a deterrent to any possible aggression?" The Committee supported the second alternative.[115] Senate Democrats, however, responded to the warnings of Air Force leaders by proposing a $900-million increase in Air Force appropriations "to maintain our supremacy in airpower . . . " Airpower superiority, they argued, was required to insure the effective deterrence of a Soviet attack and to maintain the prestige of the country and the confidence of its allies.[116] Like Admiral Radford, they accepted superiority as a primary goal. Unlike him, they proposed to achieve that goal not at the expense of conventional forces but by raising the general level of military expenditures.

The Administration chose a third course. It agreed with Radford that military expenditures should be stabilized and with the Senate Democrats that no new drastic reduction should take place in conventional forces. It disagreed with both by refusing to make the maintenance of American strategic superiority a continuing requirement of policy. In 1953, 1954, and 1955 the Administration had insisted that the United States have the best Air Force in the world and "maintain its lead in airpower and the technology that produces that power." [117] In 1956, in effect, it abandoned that position. In actual fact, for the rest of the decade, American strategic airpower was superior to that of the Soviets, but this was more a product of Soviet action than American intentions. In responding

7. THE NEW NEW LOOK

to its critics in 1956 the Administration defined the goals which were to guide its decisions during the following four years. Here was the critical turning point in the adjustment of American policy to the balance of terror.

The rationale of the Administration's policy was the doctrine of "sufficiency" elaborated by Secretary Quarles in August, 1956. At the moment, Quarles said, "United States airpower is clearly out ahead of its nearest competitor." The Air Force, however, "will have a problem next year." Why? Because "there comes a time in the course of increasing our airpower when we must make a determination of sufficiency." The requirements of sufficiency cannot be expressed in any fixed figure, such as 137 wings; they "must be determined period by period on the basis of the force required to accomplish the mission assigned." The "build-up of atomic power" on both sides of the Iron Curtain, he went on to say, "makes total war an unthinkable catastrophe for both sides." Hence, he declared:

Neither side can hope by a mere margin of superiority in airplanes or other means of delivery of atomic weapons to escape the catastrophe of such a war. Beyond a certain point, this prospect is not the result of *relative* strength of the two opposed forces. It is the *absolute* power in the hands of each, and in the substantial invulnerability of this power to interdiction.

Because of the great destructiveness of "even a single weapon," each side "could possess what might be called a 'mission capability'" relative to the other, "even if there is a wide disparity between the offensive or defensive strengths of the opposing forces." Quarles went on to say that the United States possessed this "mission capability" and must continue to maintain it, evaluating carefully at each stage what was required to insure it in the future. If a potential enemy, for instance, he said, should score "some unforeseen technological breakthrough" and increase the effectiveness of its air defenses two- or threefold, it would be necessary to re-evaluate immediately the requirements for sufficient mission capability. It was, however, "not likely" that technological changes would "occur in such a revolutionary fashion." The guiding standard must be not the abstract comparison of American forces with Soviet forces but rather the capability of the American forces to launch a devastating retaliation against the Soviet Union. "It is neither necessary nor desirable in my judgment," Quarles said firmly, "to maintain strength above that level." [118]

The balance of terror and the desire for economy necessarily yielded a strategy of sufficiency. Indeed, the basic weakness of the Radford plan was that in a situation of mutual deterrence "massive retaliation" was no longer the path of economy. Even the Radford plan's drastic cuts in conventional and tactical capabilities probably would not have yielded enough savings to cover the costs of maintaining the air-atomic supremacy required to deter both large-scale and local aggressions. The New Look assumed superiority in strategic capabilities and inferiority in conventional forces. The New New Look assumed superiority in neither but adequacy in both. Moreover, the New Look strategy assumed that overwhelming American superiority in strategic forces could be maintained at reasonable cost. With the Soviet air-atomic challenge, the maintenance of that overwhelming superiority would become increasingly expensive: every increase in Soviet strategic capabilities would require a much greater increase in American strategic capabilities if they were to deter more than a direct attack upon the United States or western Europe. The costs of the strategic superiority required for this purpose would soon exceed the costs of maintaining tactical-conventional forces adequate to deal with the more likely limited war situations. The Radford plan, with its complete derogation of conventional-tactical forces, pointed in the direction of ever-increasing expenses. In 1953 nuclear weapons and economy provided the rationale for limiting American conventional forces. In 1956 thermonuclear weapons and economy provided grounds for limiting American strategic retaliatory forces. Once again, technological developments walked hand in hand with economy, but, perversely, this time they provided the justification for limiting the forces which were going to use them.

During the next four years the Administration consistently adhered to the course it had embarked upon in 1956. Its critics challenged it on two grounds. First, there was the question of the desirability of the policy itself. In 1956 this issue had been debated in terms of a sufficient air force vs. a superior air force. In 1958 and 1959, the debate was resumed in different terms. Should the

7. THE NEW NEW LOOK 103

United States pursue a counterforce or "infinite" deterrent strategy or should it pursue a countercity, finite, or minimum deterrent strategy?* As long as the Soviet nuclear striking power was small and consisted principally of airpower, any strike by the American strategic force presumably would be directed primarily at its Soviet counterpart. This would be the obvious strategy if SAC struck first in response to a Soviet ground attack in Europe. It would also be a rational strategy even if the Soviet strategic air force attacked first, as long as the surviving forces of SAC could eliminate the Soviet strategic capabilities. As the Soviets multiplied their means of delivery, however, and in particular as they developed a substantial missile capability, the requirements for an American counterforce capability multiplied rapidly. Eventually, when the Soviet Union came to rely primarily upon hardened and mobile missiles, its attacking force would become virtually invulnerable. In the late 1950s this was still many years in the future, and the United States continued to possess a significant counterforce capability. The issue in 1958 and 1959, however, was: What effort should be made to prolong the maintenance of this capability during the interim period before it became technically unfeasible?

The principal support for a continued counterforce capability came from the Air Force. Like Admiral Radford earlier, the Air Force wanted to maintain the New Look position in which the American strategic force was strong enough to deter aggressions other than a direct attack on the United States. A counterforce capability, it was argued, lessened the requirement for specialized limited war forces and avoided the frightening and restraining implications of mutual deterrence in which both states possessed substantially invulnerable retaliatory forces. For the Army and the Navy, on the other hand, a minimum deterrent policy created the need for limited war forces and also promised to make such forces more feasible budgetarily. The Administration also inclined toward a finite strategy—the natural extension of its earlier emphasis

---

* In a counterforce strategy, the principal target of the nuclear air-missile forces is the opponent's nuclear air-missile forces. In a countercity strategy, the principal target is the opponent's population centers and industries. In actuality, neither strategy would be pursued in pure form; the differences would always be a question of degree.

on sufficiency. The United States, Secretary McElroy declared, had no intention of attempting to match the Soviet Union missile for missile; it was apparently willing to accept a temporary three to one Soviet superiority in long-range missiles in the early 1960s. The key criterion was not the "missile gap," but the "deterrent gap." The development of two mutually invulnerable and invincible retaliatory forces would represent a stable balance in which neither power would have an incentive to resort to general war. Most important from the Administration viewpoint, a "finite" capability, like a "sufficient" air force, placed a definite limit upon the resources required for the strategic deterrent.[119]

The debate over a finite vs. counterforce strategy was supplemented by a second debate over a closely related issue. Assuming a finite strategy to be necessary, if not desirable, did the Administration's programs adequately provide for such a strategy? The issue here was not whether the United States should have a counterforce capability, but rather whether it was doing enough to prevent the Soviets from developing such a capability. With its existing programs, the critics argued, the United States faced a "gap" in the early 1960s in which the balance between Soviet offensive and defensive forces, on the one hand, and the American strategic offensive forces, on the other, would be such that the Soviets might conclude that a surprise attack would reduce their losses to acceptable limits. The key issue, highlighted by the Gaither Committee report in the fall of 1957, was the vulnerability of the American retaliatory forces. In response to its critics, the Administration conceded a Soviet lead in long-range missiles or at least the capacity to build long-range missiles. It maintained, however, that the numerous and varied forms of retaliation which the United States possessed precluded their destruction by the Soviet Union. The Administration made some program adjustments to increase the future effectiveness of the strategic deterrent forces, but in neither 1958 nor 1959 did it take all the actions demanded by its "missile gap" critics. At the same time the Chief of Staff of the Army and the Chief of Naval Operations were arguing that the strategic forces had absorbed too many resources and that the United States possessed an "overkill" capacity.[120] The Administration comfortably

7. THE NEW NEW LOOK   105

maintained its position between those military experts who held that its retaliatory force was too weak and those who held it was too strong.

LIMITED WAR

The doctrine of sufficiency was one adjustment to mutual deterrence. The other area in which adjustments were made was limited war. The extent of the adjustments, however, was more ambiguous. Sufficiency coincided with the Administration's desires for economy and stability in military expenditures. But the needs of limited war seemed to require increases in force levels and expenditures. In 1955, the Administration recognized "for the first time . . . the possibility of a condition of mutual deterrence and the importance in such a period for the United States to have versatile, ready forces to cope with limited aggression." [121] In later years, however, it backed away from the budgetary implications of this policy. The Administration allowed the services individually to take steps, within prescribed budget limits, to improve their limited war capabilities. Administration leaders, however, refused to take the initiative in spurring the development of these forces. Instead, they held that if the government was prepared to deter or to fight a major war, it was also prepared to deter or to fight a smaller one. In strategic retaliation, the Administration adjusted its goals downward to fit existing programs. In limited war, the Administration accepted new goals but did not significantly expand existing programs upward to meet them. (See Chapter V, Section 26.)

The manner in which the Administration attempted to relate existing programs to the needs of limited war is well illustrated by its changing interpretation of the role of nuclear weapons. The creation of a varied arsenal of tactical nuclear weapons had been a key New Look objective. Throughout the New Look period, however, this goal usually had been linked closely with stress on air-atomic forces in general. In 1953 and 1954 Administration spokesmen did not clearly differentiate between different types of nuclear weapons and the different purposes to which they might be put. A distinguishing characteristic of the New New Look period was the direct mating of tactical nuclear weapons with the idea of limited war. The appearance of the weapons in sufficient numbers for battlefield use in 1954 and 1955 helped to legitimatize limited war in the thinking of the Administration. Beginning in 1955, Administration spokesmen continually referred to the possibilities of meeting limited aggression with limited use of nuclear weapons. In the late spring and summer of 1957 the State Department apparently took the lead in urging that more extensive consideration be given to the potentialities of tactical atomic weapons for limited conflict. In September, 1957, Secretary Dulles declared that "in the future it may . . . be feasible to place less reliance upon deterrence of vast retaliatory power" because the "nations which are around the Sino-Soviet perimeter can possess an effective defense (in limited nuclear warfare) against full-scale conventional attack and thus confront any aggressor with the choice between failing or himself initiating nuclear war . . ." [122] The wheel had come full circle from the early days of the New Look. In 1953 emphasis on tactical nuclear weapons had been part of the reaction against the concept of limited war. By 1957 it had become the means by which the United States proposed to implement that concept in any conflict of consequence.

CHALLENGE AND RESTRAINT: THE GAITHER COMMITTEE

The Administration's response to the sputnik crisis and the Gaither Committee report of 1957 demonstrated the extent of its commitment to stabilizing the level of military expenditures, maintaining a "sufficient" but no more than sufficient deterrent, and accepting the possibility of limited war but not the need to make substantial new preparations for it. Between a counterforce strategy and a minimum deterrent lay the possibility of providing forces capable of deterring not only a direct attack on the United States but also other major provocations beyond those which could be met by a "limited war" response. Such forces, labeled a "Type II" deterrent by Herman Kahn, would be largely defensive in nature. Stronger active defenses and substantial civil defense preparations would increase the credibility of massive retaliation as a response to attacks on important but less than vital interests. The potentially significant role of civil defense led the Federal Civil Defense Administration in the spring of 1957 to submit to the NSC a proposal for blast and fall-out shelters for the protection of the civilian population which would cost about $40 billion over several years. The President replied that obviously before a program of that magnitude could seriously considered, it would have to be related to the entire defense effort. He appointed a committee of eleven individuals from outside the government to evaluate shelter needs. The committee soon decided that it could not properly make recommendations concerning civil defense without also judging other defense requirements. The committee's report, finished in October, was an overall assessment of the state of national defense and its needs for the immediate future.

The Administration and the committee had access to the same intelligence reports. Yet their policy recommendations differed greatly. The committee concluded that if the United States did not change its policies, it was in danger of becoming a second-class power.[123] Even if the United States made the most strenuous efforts, it would be impossible to overcome the Soviet lead in ballistic missiles until 1960–1961. Soviet strategic power was developing to the point where it could substantially cripple the Strategic Air Command. Soviet air defense was rapidly increasing in effectiveness. These capabilities, in conjunction with the new stress on "preemptive" war in Soviet military writing, suggested that the Soviets might conclude that a surprise attack could reduce their losses from SAC to an acceptable level. "I felt," one member of the committee was reported to have declared, "as though I was spending ten hours a day staring straight into hell." [124]

To remedy this situation, the committee assigned first and overriding priority to reducing the vulnerability of SAC and insuring second-strike capabilities sufficient to pose unacceptable losses to the Russians. The committee warned against placing too much weight upon the initial destructive power of SAC and too little on the destructive power which actually could be delivered after a Soviet attack. In this respect, the committee did not directly challenge the Administration's policy. Instead, it drew from intelligence reports more pessimistic conclusions than the Administration did about future Soviet capabilities and urged that stricter criteria be used to judge the adequacy of the programs necessary for an invulnerable second-strike capability. The committee urgently recommended the protection of existing SAC forces through dispersal of planes, an airborne alert for some planes, and a "ready" alert for others. It also urged the speedy development and production of IRBMs and ICBMs with particular attention to those which could be placed in hardened or mobile sites. Complementing these recommendations, the committee called for intensive efforts to develop an effective warning system and active defense against missiles.

Tracing out the implications of mutual deterrence for local aggressions, the committee also urged the need to develop conventional, limited war capabilities. Here the committee directly challenged the view accepted by many in the Administration that existing general war capabilities were also sufficient to handle likely limited war aggressions. The committee also challenged the Administration's position on passive defenses. It did not endorse the mammoth $40 billion blast and fallout shelter program proposed by the FCDA, but as a first priority measure it urged the investment of several hundred million dollars over a period of years in intensive research and preliminary planning on civil defense needs. As a second priority project, after the research phase, it recommended a $22 billion fall-out shelter program.[125] Finally, the Committee also proposed a reorganization of the Pentagon, particularly the strengthening of the unified and specified commands, increased spending for basic scientific research, and more extensive foreign aid, particularly economic aid for underdeveloped areas.

The committee's recommendations required "substantially increased expenditures." [126] Aside from the shelter program, whose implementation would need an additional $5 billion a year for several years, the committee estimated that its proposals would require by FY 1961 an increase of at least $8 billion over the existing level of $38 billion. It stressed that any immediate prospects of a tax cut should be ruled out and that the debt ceiling would have to be raised. Tax increases should be studied but the committee did not think they would be mandatory.

The recommendations of the Gaither Committee might have been quietly dropped and forgotten or in part quietly adopted if it had not been for the demonstrations of Soviet prowess which accompanied their presentation to the Administration. In August the Soviets announced the successful test of an intercontinental ballistic missile. In October and November they launched the first

7. THE NEW NEW LOOK

man-made earth satellites. Almost immediately, the favorable public environment for the Administration's defense policies disappeared: a sense of crisis and urgency swept the nation. The new atmosphere was an opportunity for the Administration to change its programs if it desired to do so. It also was a challenge to the Administration to prevent changes in those programs which it did not wish changed. The Gaither Committee report had brought most of the proposals for change together into a single package. The sputniks now brought them into the realm of political feasibility.

The public reaction of the Administration to the Soviet sputniks was, in part, to mimimize their military significance. Simultaneously, however, it was confronted with the Gaither Committee report, which claimed that all was not well with military security. It was, in a sense, retreating to a dubious battlefield. The Gaither report was discussed in the National Security Council on November 7. The President's address in Oklahoma City the following week set the tone for the Administration's reaction to the Gaither recommendations and the sputnik crisis. The time had come, the President said, "for another critical re-examination of our entire defense position." He indicated, however, that this re-examination would not lead to any fundamental or willing change in the Administration's existing New New Look policies of stable expenditures, a sufficient deterrent, and no expansion of conventional forces. The Administration recognized the need to strengthen the strategic deterrent and improve other aspects of the defense program. The President hoped, however, that the "substantial costs" which these actions entailed would be met in part by reductions elsewhere in the budget. In effect, the Administration accepted the proposals of its critics in so far as they did not conflict seriously with existing policies or did not require substantial net additional expenditures.

Responding to one line of action proposed in both the Gaither and Rockefeller reports, the President announced in January his intention to reorganize the Defense establishment. After an extensive study the Administration presented its recommendations to Congress in April. With some changes these were enacted by Congress in the Defense Department Reorganization Act of 1958. The Administration also acted on those proposals which, although they involved increased expenditures, were directly related to the maintenance of a sufficient deterrent force. Steps were taken to protect and improve the effectiveness of the airpower deterrent during the period in which the Soviets were developing an increasing missile capability. In February, 1958, Congress, acting upon the Administration's recommendations, appropriated funds to accelerate the dispersal of SAC bombers to additional bases, to place a greater proportion of the SAC force on an "alert" status, and to improve the effectiveness of the early warning system for aircraft. Both the Army's Jupiter and the Air Force's Thor IRBMs were ordered into production, and at the NATO conference in December negotiations were begun to secure launching sites for them in Europe. Overtime restrictions on the ballistic missile programs were removed. Development of the Atlas and Titan liquid-fuel intercontinental missiles and of the solid-fuel Minuteman ICBM and Polaris submarine-based IRBM was accelerated. Congress, however, felt that the Administration's action did not go far enough, and in the summer of 1958 it appropriated more funds than the Administration requested for the ICBM and Polaris programs. The Administration also accelerated efforts to develop an anti-missile early warning system and active defenses against missiles. More stress was placed on the development of anti-submarine warfare capabilities. Funds for basic research were also increased. Recommendations designed primarily to strengthen scientific education were enacted by Congress in the National Defense Education Act of 1958.

The Administration took little or no action on those Gaither Committee proposals which required substantial new expenditures not directly related to strategic deterrence or which involved substantial deviations from current policy. The demands for increased conventional war capability and a more substantial airlift for the Army were rejected. The FY 1959 budget proposed to eliminate one more Army division, to drop a number of tactical air wings, and to reduce the manpower of all four services. No bold new foreign aid programs were launched. The Gaither recommendations for a substantial passive defense research program and for a large-scale fall-out shelter program were quietly sidetracked. The Gaither Committee and the Rockefeller Brothers panel had urged an increase in defense spending to $46–48 billion in FY 1961. The Administration's FY 1961 estimate was $41.0 billion. The difference was an accurate measure of its commitment to stability and its unwillingness to expand beyond the minimum essentials of a second-strike deterrent and existing limited war preparations.

The Administration's response to the Gaither Committee report and the sputnik crisis may be profitably compared with the Truman Administration's response to NSC 68 and the Korean War in 1949 and 1950.[127] In 1957, as in 1949, a firm ceiling existed on military spending and an economy move was underway with which the leadership in the Defense Department was identified. In each case the development by the Soviet Union of new military capabilities—atomic bombs and long-range missiles—aroused concern about the adequacy of American defense policies. In each case the consideration of one or more specific policy proposals to meet this new situation—construction of the hydrogen bomb, the FCDA proposals for shelters—led the Administration to appoint an *ad hoc* group to make a broad survey of defense policy. In each case, the group came up with proposals for a major change in existing policies and significant increases in the level of military spending: a 25 percent increase by the Gaither Committee, a 300 percent increase in NSC 68. In each case, also, the consideration of the report in the government coincided with a dramatic challenge from the Communist states: Korea and the sputniks. In each case this challenge produced widespread public demands for a vigorous governmental response. Yet, in one case a major change took place in military policies and in the other only minor adjustments.

The difference in response would appear to be related to two other differences in the situation. In 1949 and 1950 the new policies which were proposed had powerful support within the Administration; in 1957 and 1958 they did not. Many members of the Gaither Committee, of course, had close connections with the Administration, but the committee still could not develop significant sources of institutional support within the executive branch. Administration officials were reported to feel that, as the committee had expanded its concerns outside its initial focus on civil defense, it had allowed its fears to run away with its judgment; it had "tended to become stampeded, and was carried away to too alarmist conclusions." In 1950 the Joint Chiefs eventually endorsed the NSC

68 recommendations. In 1957 the Chiefs reportedly agreed with Charles Wilson that the committee had largely "just aired old problems." [128] In 1950 the Administration's acceptance of the need to raise military expenditures to implement the NSC 68 recommendations facilitated support for them by executive agencies. In 1957, as Morton Halperin has pointed out, the Administration's reluctance to increase spending made each agency view the Gaither recommendations to increase other programs as direct threats to its own programs. The FCDA was dissatisfied with the stress on strategic deterrence. The military services had little enthusiasm for civil defense and were unwilling to admit that they were as unprepared as the Gaither report seemed to suggest. In both 1950 and 1957 the Secretary of Defense opposed the new program. In 1950, however, the replacement of Johnson by Marshall symbolized a change in policy, while in 1957 the replacement of Wilson by McElroy was purely coincidental. Undoubtedly it did permit the Administration to make a more flexible response than would otherwise have been the case—but a flexible response within the framework of the same policies. Finally and most significantly, in 1950 Secretary Acheson strongly supported the NSC 68 recommendations. In 1957, however, Secretary Dulles dealt the *coup de grâce* to the more extensive Gaither recommendations: increased conventional forces, he held, were not necessary for the defense of the gray areas, and the shelter recommendations would disturb our allies.[129] Here was the crucial difference. While the Truman Administration had hesitated to make public the rearmament proposals until Korea forced its hand, the Eisenhower Administration consistently rejected the demands of congressional leaders that it make public portions of the Gaither report.

The second difference between 1950 and 1957 was in the nature of the catalysts: in the one case an act of aggression, in the other a demonstration of superior scientific and possibly military capabilities. The latter was an indirect challenge rather than a direct one. As a scientific achievement, sputnik could only be greeted with praise, an epoch-making accomplishment of the human race. The aggression against South Korea, on the other hand, was a gauntlet flung in the face of the United Nations and the Western collective security system. Inevitably, the Administration could reason, the impact of

Sputnik upon the willingness of the American public to bear an increased military burden would be less than that of Korea. At the NSC meeting on November 7 Robert Lovett and John J. McCloy assured the President that the financial community would support the additional expenditures required to implement the committee's recommendations. The President, however, indicated that he still had "a nagging fear that the American people would balk at paying the bill, even though he said he personally would like to do the things called for in the report." The President reportedly feared that the "gloomy findings in the report would panic the American people into going off into all directions at once." [130] In the absence of a war the Eisenhower Administration adopted and put into effect about the same proportion of the Gaither Committee recommendations as the Truman Administration probably would have done with the NSC 68 program in 1950—in the absence of a war. Sputnik simply did not furnish as much of an opportunity and a compulsion to change existing policies as did Korea.

8. *STRATEGY AND CHANGE*
STRIKING THE STRATEGIC BALANCE

Military strategy was shaped by the domestic and international goals of the Administration in power. Even those broad efforts to develop an overall national security policy, such as NSC 68 and the Gaither Report, succeeded only when they were related to foreign and domestic goals. NSC 68 became a reality when a war changed those goals. The Gaither program was adopted only in so far as it did not seriously disturb existing goals. Major alterations in military policy were associated with basic changes in both its political and economic environments.

The Administration in power originated and decided upon major changes in the strategic balance. Public opinion, nongovernmental experts, the press, and Congress played peripheral roles in determining overall strategy. The effective adoption of NSC 68 in the fall of 1950, indeed, was accompanied by very little public debate or understanding of its meaning and significance. Popular discontent with the Korean War helped bring the Republicans to power in 1953 but did not point toward any particular strategy. The New

Look strategy of 1953–1954 and the New New Look strategy of 1956–1957 were the products of the Administration. In both cases, the Administration's policies were extensively debated and criticized, but the debate came after the policy had been shaped and the Administration was committed. (See Chapter III, Section 13.) In each case, the critics of the Administration attempted to broaden the arena of policy-making, but in neither were they successful. The experience of the Gaither Committee, moreover, suggests that even *ad hoc* groups created by and reasonably close to the Administration cannot produce major changes in the established policies of the Administration.

Within an Administration, changes in policy must be proposed, approved, and then implemented. It is not surprising that military leaders played a key role in implementing policy and that they seldom actually made important decisions on policy. Perhaps more striking is the relatively unimportant role which they played in proposing changes in policy. In no case did military leaders initiate major new policies and in no case did they effectively prevent changes in old ones. Undoubtedly, they generally favored changes which increased the level of military effort and disapproved those which did not. But, more than anything else, one is struck by the tendency of the military to embrace the broad policy *status quo*. In 1949 and 1950 the Joint Chiefs accepted the limits of the Johnson budgets: General Bradley defended them before Congress (despite his disapproval of them, which he later recorded); General Landon was much more ready to accept existing policy than the State Department members of the NSC 68 drafting group; after the document was drafted, the military estimated it would require only a $5 billion increase in defense spending compared to the $25 or $30 billion increase which the State Department leaders had in mind. Again in 1953, first the "old" Truman Chiefs, in the revision of the FY 1954 budget, and then the "new" Eisenhower Chiefs, in the initial formulation of the FY 1955 budget, recommended the continuation of existing programs and expenditures. Admiral Radford probably played a more important role in shaping strategy than any other military man in military office between 1946 and 1960. Nonetheless, even in the New Look the initiative for a new strategy and its principal ideas came as much from the President, Humphrey, and Dulles as from Radford. Similarly, in 1956 the Joint Chiefs followed the Administration in endorsing the continuation of the existing level of military effort and the prospect of $38 to $40 billion military budgets. Puerto Rico produced nothing new. A year later it was the civilian Gaither Committee, not the Joint Chiefs, which challenged existing policy and succeeded in producing minor changes in it. The initiative in military policy rested with the civilian executives, the decision on military policy with the President.

Three factors seem to be responsible for military passivity. First, at least until the Reorganization Act of 1958, the military had no effective way of developing a unified military strategy. On any issue of importance the services were divided. Each service Chief was a service spokesman, and the JCS Chairman was an Administration spokesman. Second, the devotion of the military leaders to the principles of civilian control made them hesitate to challenge the political and economic assumptions of military policy defined by Administration leaders. Finally, and most important, military strategy, impinging as it did upon so many aspects of domestic and foreign policy, could only be changed by groups possessing a broad sense of overall policy priorities. Even if the Chiefs had been united, the initiative in strategy would have been beyond them. It is not enough to assume that the resources will be available to implement broad national security policies. The issue is seldom one of resources; it is always one of goals. The goals of policy, foreign and domestic, are the preserve of the civilian Administration leader. The military could not challenge these goals because they were in no position to propose alternatives. Inevitably and appropriately their viewpoint was parochial. Individual military men, like Denfeld or Ridgway, might dissent from specific aspects of Administration strategy directly concerning their services. But they could not and did not effectively challenge the strategic balance as a whole or propose an alternative to it. At best the military were the draftsmen of strategy. The civilian leaders of the Administration were always the architects.

ECONOMY AND STRATEGY

The balancing of international and domestic goals by the Truman and Eisenhower Administrations produced a continuing search for the minimum military effort required to prevent Communist aggression. This goal reflected the influences of international politics and the desire to minimize the impact of these influences upon American society. The interaction and balancing of the conflicting pressures was a difficult political task, and, in many respects, the most important one confronting the Administration in power.

The overall reconsideration of military policy was usually associated with the emergence of an apparently major new need plus environmental changes which made a policy change feasible. In 1949 and 1950 the development of Soviet nuclear weapons led, first, to the decision to go ahead with the development of thermonuclear weapons, and then to a complete reshaping of strategy which was subsequently made feasible by the Korean War. In 1953 the need to develop a continental defense program and to adjust military policy to the end of the Korean War led to a re-evaluation of strategy, and a new Administration, pledged to the development of a new strategy, made it feasible. In 1956 the emergence of the balance of terror was a fundamental change in the external environment. The absence of any major change in the factors affecting feasibility, however, limited the adjustments which were made. In 1957 the demand for an increased civil defense program also led to a review of strategy which, unlike those of 1950 and 1953, was abortive in the absence of favorable environmental circumstances.

Usually the expansion of the American economy has permitted new groups to rise to affluence and to secure a claim on resources without directly dispossessing established groups. Similarly, in American government new programs have normally been added without abolishing old ones. In both cases expansion has eased innovation. The peculiarly mixed conservative and revolutionary character of the American economy and government reflect this ability to perpetuate the old and to add the new. Within the Cold War military establishment, however, the rate of expansion lagged behind the pressure for innovation. Competition between old and new was intensified. Usually a new program could only be added by subtracting one which already existed. The need to resolve these intense conflicts between old and new, "to establish priorities," produced unprecedented peacetime demands upon the government.

8. STRATEGY AND CHANGE

The expansion and the contraction of the military effort affected the adjustment of strategy both positively and negatively. The rise in military expenditures between 1950 and 1952 eased the innovation of programs for strategic deterrence and European defense. The absence of a full-scale demobilization after the Korean War helped the innovation of continental defense. The efforts to stabilize spending in the mid-1950s slowed the development of limited war programs. Expansion of the military sector, however, did not necessarily mean the addition of new programs and forces more relevant to the new strategy than to the old. A large part of the great Korean War expansion was devoted to reinforcing the country's mobilization capacity. J. K. Galbraith has suggested that the continued expansion of the American economy will not necessarily rectify what he considers to be the imbalance between the public sector and the private sector of the economy. Similarly, the simple expansion of the military budget does not necessarily produce a better balance between strategies and programs. At the very best, expansion adds needed new programs without eliminating unneeded old ones. At worst, it adds unneeded new activities which later complicate the addition of needed new ones.

The pressures for economy frequently buttress policies such as the maintenance of substantial reserve forces which are more directly relevant to mobilization than to deterrence. Also, they may slow the development of new weapons and limit the number of weapons under development at any one time. On the other hand, they may stimulate policy-makers to search out new weapons and forces as cheaper substitutes for existing ones. Most important, low priority programs, however defined by the Administration and the services, are eliminated *only* when intense pressures curtail the scope of the military effort. Before the Korean War, economy pressures compelled the United States, in contrast to the Soviet Union, to disband its World War II army and to rely heavily upon nuclear weapons as a deterrent and as a weapon. In 1953 they led to a reduction in conventional forces, a narrowing of the mobilization base, and the increased probability that nuclear weapons would be used in general war or limited war where they would be militarily valuable. In the late 1950s, the desire to limit military expenditures led to the slow abandonment of the effort to maintain an overwhelmingly superior first-strike capability. The economy waves of 1948–1949, 1953–1954, and 1957 caused the elimination of older programs and concepts. While pressure for economy does not itself produce the innovations, technological or otherwise, necessary for an evolving strategy, it does increase the importance of innovations which are made and hasten the change in overall strategy. Obviously, a roller-coaster defense effort is undesirable. Prolonged stability, however, also has its costs. Over the long run, alternating periods of expansion and contraction may well produce a "better defense" than a fixed high-level military effort.

Among the three major powers the rate of technological innovation and the rate of overall policy change and program elimination appeared to be almost inversely related. The pressures to reduce the military effort tended to restrict the one and to speed the other. These pressures presumably were strongest in Great Britain, moderate in the United States, and least in the Soviet Union. Its more limited resources caused Great Britain to lag behind the other two powers in the development and production of nuclear weapons and missiles. Similarly, pressures of economy at times delayed technological innovations in the United States and were one reason why the Soviet Union achieved a lead in strategic missiles and some other weapons. On the other hand, the policy changes of the three powers, especially the overall allocation of resources between new and older forms of military force, followed almost exactly the reverse pattern. Changes in American military policy often came two or three years after changes in British military policy. The New Look originated with Churchill and the British Chiefs of Staff in 1951 and 1952; it became American policy in 1953 and 1954. The British began to reduce and redesign their reserve forces in 1955; the Americans followed suit in 1958. The British announced in 1957 their intention of eliminating conscription by 1962; in 1960 American policy was edging in this direction. While the wealthier country was able to develop new weapons earlier than the poorer one, nonetheless, the poorer one, largely because of its more limited resources, often was first in adjusting its military policies to the new technological developments.

Similarly, the pressures which tended to cause the American rate of technological innovation to fall behind that of the Soviets

8. STRATEGY AND CHANGE

also tended to produce more rapid changes in American policy than in Soviet policy. In comparison with American strategy, Soviet strategy adjusted slowly to the new conditions of the nuclear age, evolving through the same phases as American strategy but at slightly later times. American strategy was dominated by the experience of World War II from 1945 until 1950. Soviet strategy was dominated by World War II experience until after the death of Stalin in 1953. The strategic position of the Soviet Union in the late 1940s, as Garthoff has pointed out, was completely different from what it had been before 1945. The principal enemy was no longer a Eurasian landpower but a western hemisphere sea-air power. Yet the principles of "Stalinist military science" remained fixed; this was a period of "stagnation" in military thought.[131] Technologically, the Soviets pushed ahead rapidly in developing nuclear weapons while, doctrinally, they continued to adhere to the ground forces strategy of World War II.

Between 1953 and 1955 Soviet strategy escaped from its World War II fixation[132] and changed to a new pattern resembling a cross between the American strategy of the Korean War rearmament and the New Look. The shift in emphasis from the "permanently operating factors" of Stalinist military science to the limited (in the sense of distinguishable from economic and political considerations) and yet universal (in the sense that its laws apply equally to capitalist and socialist societies) character of military science implied increased stress upon the role of military force-in-being.[133] For the first time Soviet military writers began to highlight the importance of "surprise" in warfare.[134] As Soviet nuclear capabilities and delivery capabilities developed, Soviet military officers articulated the doctrine of "pre-emptive war." In many respects the Soviet equivalent of massive retaliation, the theory of pre-emptive war held that if an enemy was clearly about to launch a nuclear attack on the Soviet Union, the Soviets must be able to strike first and blunt the prospective enemy attack.[135] Such a theory presupposed, of course, that both sides possessed counterforce capabilities. Simultaneous with this new emphasis upon nuclear weapons, surprise, and force-in-being, the Soviets announced two major reductions in military manpower: 640,000 men in August, 1955, and 1,200,000 men in May, 1956. Economic factors apparently played a major role in bringing about these cuts.[136] The Soviets also ceased to push the build-up of their surface fleet, turning their attention to submarines, and abandoned the attempt to create a strategic bombing force equal to that of the United States, substituting a major drive to develop ballistic missiles. Thus, as a result of decreased international tensions, increased domestic economic pressures, and increased availability of nuclear weapons, the Soviets moved in 1955 and 1956 toward a "selection" of military forces comparable to that which the United States had made in 1953.

At the same time, however, the Soviets did not abandon the doctrine of "balanced forces" nor the idea that a future war was likely to be a prolonged struggle. Despite their manpower reductions, they maintained overwhelming superiority in conventional ground forces. In this respect, they combined elements of the American New Look strategy with the continued achievement of the unrealized goal of the American Korean rearmament strategy: the maintenance of forces capable of fighting and winning a non-nuclear major war.[137]

In 1956 and 1957, as the Soviets moved toward a counterforce strategy, the United States began to move away from such a strategy in response to the conditions of the balance of terror. In 1960, however, Khrushchev's report to the Supreme Soviet indicated that Soviet strategy was turning the same corner which American strategy had passed a few years earlier. Khrushchev now officially accepted the doctrine of "mutual deterrence." Surprise was no longer a decisive factor. "A state subjected to surprise attack—provided, of course, it is a big state—," Khrushchev declared, "will always be able to give the aggressor a worthy rebuff."[138] In effect, the Soviet shifted toward the acceptance of a second-strike deterrent strategy. Only a "madman," Khrushchev emphasized again and again, would start a war under present conditions. "The present means of warfare," he said, "do not give such advantages [of a first-strike strategy] to any side." In the new era, a surprise attack would be the equivalent of self-destruction.

In 1958, Garthoff observed, "the Soviet strategic concept does not require the employment of an intercontinental striking force to gain a victory, while in the American concept and under current policy such use is assumed to be necessary."[139] In 1960, however,

8. STRATEGY AND CHANGE 121

Soviet strategy was apparently moving toward the American position and reducing its capability to fight a large-scale conventional war, which had been the most significant element distinguishing its strategy from that of the United States. "Our Armed Forces," Khrushchev said, "have been regeared to a considerable degree to rocket and nuclear weapons." In announcing Soviet intention to cut 1,200,000 more men from the armed forces, Khrushchev emphasized the extent to which firepower could replace manpower. Development of new armaments, he said, "allows us to reduce our armed forces without any detriment to the defense potential of the country." Since 1955 military manpower had been reduced by one-third, but "firepower has increased many times over during the period, owing to the development and introduction of new military techniques." In effect, Khrushchev held forth the Soviet equivalent of "a bigger bang for a buck." "While reducing the numerical strength of our Armed Forces," he continued, "we shall not be diminishing their firepower. This, on the contrary, will increase manifoldly in terms of quality." Khrushchev suggested that even an alteration of the hallowed Soviet doctrine of balanced forces might be in the wind. A "country's defense capacity," he declared, "depends *decisively* on the firepower and the means of delivery it possesses." Here he came close to espousing the older American concepts of the decisive character of strategic nuclear capabilities, which a few years before Soviet military men had denounced as "false" and "adventuristic." He held out the prospect of a ruthless elimination of older weapons and forces, including airplanes and surface ships. A year after Khrushchev's talk, the shift from the traditional Russian emphasis on ground forces was further marked by Marshal Sokolovsky's declaration that "strategic rocket forces" had become "the *principal arms* of the armed forces of the U.S.S.R."[140]

Khrushchev denied that the reductions in Soviet military manpower were caused by its difficulties in fulfilling the seven-year plan. The reduction in the Armed Forces, however, would save 16 to 17 billion rubles annually, which, he said, "will be a very tangible savings for our people and country. This will give us much added strength for fulfilling and overfulfilling our economic plans." The money "will be used more effectively" than for military purposes. Echoing the rationale of the American New Look six years before, Khrushchev argued that the large armies of the West were the "allies" of the Soviet Union. They would help the Soviets "achieve our main objective of surpassing the most advanced capitalist countries in every respect—in science, in the manufacture of machinery and means of production, in the production of consumer goods, and in meeting the people's needs." Technological developments and domestic economic pressures thus moved Soviet strategy in the same direction as American strategy. The search for a *stable deterrent* seemed likely to produce a situation of at least temporary *stable strategic deterrence* in which both sides possessed reasonably invulnerable retaliatory forces.

CHAPTER III

Strategic Programs and the Political Process

9. STRUCTURE, STRATEGY, AND PROCESS

The complexity and diversity of military policy are reflected in the processes through which it is made. Three categories of governmental groups are concerned with military policy. The Administration includes the elected and politically appointed leaders of the executive branch: President, Vice President, agency heads, secretaries, under-secretaries. Bureaucratic groups include the Foreign Service, the military services, the civil servants in all bureaus and agencies. Together the Administration and the bureaucracy make up the executive. The third category exists in Congress and includes primarily the members of the Foreign Affairs, Foreign Relations, Science and Astronautics, Aeronautical and Space Sciences, and Armed Services committees, the Military Appropriations subcommittees, and the Joint Committee on Atomic Energy. Within the executive branch the groups are arranged in two overlapping structures. In the hierarchical structure, all officials and agencies are in theory arranged in superior-subordinate relationships in the classic pyramid culminating in the President. Superimposed upon the executive hierarchy is a second, conciliar structure. It includes many interdepartmental and interagency boards and committees, the most important of which are the National Security Council and the Joint Chiefs of Staff. The hierarchical structure of the executive provides a vehicle for vertical communication between superiors and subordinates; the conciliar structure supplements this and also provides a formal means for lateral communication among agencies or officials at similar levels in different hierarchies.

These officials and bodies play different roles in the determination of different military policy issues. Deterrent commitments may take the form of force deployments ordered by the President, treaties negotiated by the executive and ratified by the Senate (NATO, SEATO), joint declarations of Congress passed on the recommendation of the executive (Formosa resolution, Eisenhower Middle East doctrine), or statements by the President or Secretary of State (Dulles' September, 1958, warnings on the offshore islands). Action commitments or interventions are made by the President in consultation with the Secretary of State, the military chiefs, and other executive officials. In the decisions on the Berlin crisis and Korea in the Truman Administration, congressional leaders apparently were informed after the executive branch had determined policy. In the Indochina and Lebanon crises in the Eisenhower Administration, congressional leaders were informed before final action by the President, and in the Indochina crisis in the spring of 1954 the doubts of the congressional leaders (together with those of the British) apparently persuaded the Administration to reverse its inclination to intervene. In each case, however, the final decision on peace or war always rested with the President, and presidential decisions were not formally ratified by Congress. The military and diplomatic conditions of the mid-twentieth century made obsolete the congressional declaration of war. In a small-scale intervention or limited war a congressional declaration was unnecessary and undesirable; in a general war it would, in all probability, be impossible.

Structural issues of military policy are usually handled through what might be termed the domestic legislative process. Proposals usually originate in the executive branch or in advisory groups close to the executive branch. They are advanced through the executive hierarchy, modified, and eventually approved by the appropriate secretaries, the Budget Bureau, and the President. They are then recommended to Congress as Administration measures and referred to the Armed Services committees or other congressional bodies, which hold hearings and act upon them: substantially approving the Administration's recommendations, amending them significantly, or at times rejecting them. The action of the committees is usually approved by their respective houses; the

9. STRUCTURE, STRATEGY, AND PROCESS 125

differences are ironed out in conference; and the measure becomes law. In this process the President, the leaders of the Administration, and, usually, the heads of the President's party in Congress act as legislative leaders, focusing the attention of Congress on the proposals which they support and compelling Congress to act upon them in one way or another. The decisions on their proposals, however, are made in the committees and houses of Congress, and the political processes of arousing support or opposition are directed toward these multiple decision-making foci in Congress.

Between 1945 and 1960 the major issues of structural policy were resolved through this process. These included the organization of the military establishment and the individual services,* military pay scales and the conditions of service and retirement,† conscription and military training,‡ the disciplinary law of the services (Uniform Code of Military Justice, 1950), and basic policy on procurement (Armed Services Procurement Act, 1947). Although they involved strategic issues as well as structural ones, major policies concerning the reserves (Armed Forces Reserve Act, 1952; Reserve Forces Act, 1955) were also determined in a similar manner. For much of the period between 1947 and 1960, the House Armed Services Committee maintained subcommittees which specialized in pay and promotion matters, material and procurement, reserve policy, and real estate and construction. The members of these groups developed a recognized expertise in their subjects. There "is no man on this committee, or in Congress," the Republican chairman of the Armed Services Committee declared in 1953, "who knows more about it [personnel] than Mr. Kilday"—the ranking Democrat on the personnel subcommittee.[1] Similarly, Representative Overton Brooks, chairman of the reserves subcommitttee, was the acknowledged congressional expert on reserves. On these struc-

---

* For example, National Security Act, 1947; Security Act Amendments, 1949; Reorganization Plan No. 6, 1953; Defense Department Reorganization Act, 1958; Navy Organization Act, 1948; Army Organization Act, 1950; Air Force Organization Act, 1951.

† For example, Officer Personnel Act, 1947; Army and Air Force Vitalization and Retirement Equalization Act, 1948; Career Compensation Act, 1949; Uniformed Services Pay Increase Act, 1952; Reserve Officer Personnel Act, 1954; Career Incentive Act, 1955; Military Pay Act, 1958.

‡ For example, Extension of World War II Selective Service, 1946; Selective Service Act, 1948, and extensions, 1950, 1954, 1959; Universal Military Training and Service Act, 1951; universal military training bills, 1947, 1948, 1952.

tural issues the congressmen and senators acted with competence and authority. They did not hesitate to revise or to reject Administration measures. UMT legislation was repeatedly turned down, organizational proposals to centralize authority in the Pentagon weakened, pay legislation reworked. On these matters, the executive proposed and Congress disposed.

The process of policy formation on strategic programs differs significantly from both the familiar processes of congressional legislation of domestic policy and executive decision in foreign affairs. It tends to be executive in locale but legislative in character. In the formulation of strategic programs the need for legislation is recognized by an executive agency or by some skill group (nuclear physicists) or consulting group close to the executive branch. The agency or group develops proposals to deal with the new problem. It arouses support for them among other executive agencies, congressional bodies, and, possibly, some nongovernmental groups and foreign governments allied with the United States. Opposition develops from some of these agencies and groups. Alternative solutions to the problem are proposed; in some cases, the existence of the problem or the need to do anything about it may be denied. A process of negotiation, bargaining, and conflict ensues among the various executive agencies and groups. Many of these efforts to arrive at a compromise take place in the budgetary process, the Joint Chiefs of Staff, and the National Security Council. Eventually, an agreement is reached among the interested agencies, it is approved by the President, and it is then implemented by the executive branch. Sometimes the presidential decision is announced to the public, or the implementation of the decision reveals the fact of decision, or an executive official dissatisfied with the decision finds means of expressing his dissatisfaction. Discussion and debate flare up in Congress and the press. The Administration attempts to suppress evidence of dissension in the executive ranks. Its leaders either refuse to confirm the fact that a decision has been made, refuse to comment on it, defend it when challenged, or, perhaps, if the criticism has been particularly widespread and effective, modify the policy in practice while staunchly defending it in debate. Eventually the discussion subsides and the executive agencies

9. STRUCTURE, STRATEGY, AND PROCESS

continue to implement the policy, modified or unmodified, while controversy and interest turn to other issues.

In one sense, in American government there are no final decisions. Almost every decision by one body or in one forum can be appealed to another body or another forum. It is possible, however, to speak of "effective decisions," of decisions which in the normal process of politics settle the issue, at least temporarily; because although the possibility of appeal exists, it is seldom exercised. In this sense, effective decision on structure rests in Congress, and effective decision on strategic programs rests in the executive.

A significant gap thus exists between the theory and practice of the Constitution. Few constitutional principles are more firmly established than that which gives Congress the final say on the size and composition of the nation's armed forces. The "whole power of raising armies," Hamilton declared, "was lodged in the *Legislature,* not in the *Executive* ..." The authority of the President as Commander in Chief "would amount to nothing more than the supreme command and direction of the military and naval forces, as first General and admiral of the Confederacy; while that of the British king extends to the *declaring* of war and to the *raising* and *regulating* of fleets and armies,—all which, by the Constitution under consideration, would appertain to the legislature." [2] Later commentators emphasized again and again the authority of Congress over all aspects of military policy.[3] The President could command only the forces which Congress placed at his disposal. After World War II, however, the division of authority between Congress and President no longer coincided with the division between policy and command. The great powers of Anglo-American legislatures over the size and composition of the armed forces, so bitterly fought for in the seventeenth and eighteenth centuries and so carefully inscribed in the Bill of Rights, the Mutiny Acts, the Declaration of Independence, and the Constitution of 1787, had faded away. The loss of power by Congress, however, did not necessarily mean an equivalent increase in the power of the President. Congress lost its power not to the President but to the executive branch. Just as power to legislate strategic programs was at one time, at least in theory, shared by President and Congress, so it is now, very much in practice, shared by the President and a variety of agencies within the executive branch.

In the post-World War II period, the executive determined the overall level of military effort and the strategy by which it was shaped. The executive decided whether the Air Force should have 95 or 137 wings, the Army 14 or 24 divisions, the Navy 200 or 400 warships. The fundamental decisions to maintain a massive nuclear retaliatory force, to construct a continental defense system, and to develop or not to develop forces for conventional limited wars were all made in the executive branch. The decisions on whether to build hydrogen bombs, "super-carriers," long-range jet bombers, intermediate-range and intercontinental ballistic missiles, nuclear-powered submarines and planes were also executive decisions. This is not to say that congressional groups played no role in these decisions. In a variety of ways they could influence them, and in some cases compel the Administration to pay a high price to get what it wanted. But they could not make the decisions. The effective, final "yes" or "no" rested with the executive branch.

In addition to individual legislative acts on specific problems, three regular pieces of executive legislation dealt with strategic programs in general. The annual NSC paper, "Basic National Security Policy," a brief document of about twenty-five pages, contained "a broad outline of the aims of U. S. national strategy and a more detailed discussion of the military, political, economic, and domestic elements to support the overall national strategy."[4] Much of this document did not change from year to year. Nonetheless it did reflect shifting emphases in policy. The first of the series, NSC 68, in 1950 provided the framework for the Korean War rearmament. In 1951 the paper stressed continental defense and civil defense, and in 1952 new efforts in the Middle East and southern Asia, although in neither year were the programs fully implemented. In 1953 the Eisenhower Administration adopted the New Look, NSC 162, reducing military spending and increasing the emphasis upon nuclear weapons. In 1954 nuclear weapons were again stressed. The 1955 paper shifted away from nuclear weapons and massive retaliation, recognizing the emergence of mutual deterrence and the need to have forces for limited wars. In 1957 and in 1958 the stress was on the stabilization of defense expenditures.[5]

9. STRUCTURE, STRATEGY, AND PROCESS

The JCS counterpart to the NSC annual policy paper was the Joint Strategic Objectives Plan, which annually defined the military programs required three years in the future. It "estimates the military requirements for cold, limited, or general war, and includes a determination of the military forces together with their dispositions and employment necessary to implement the military strategy derived from the 'Basic National Security Policy.'" [6] In the Eisenhower Administration, the Basic National Security Policy paper was usually formulated in May. It then became the basis for the third regular piece of executive legislation: the annual formulation of force requirements by the military chiefs, which, when approved by the Administration, became the grounds for the appropriation and expenditure requests by the military services in the executive budgetary process ending in December.[7] Through these three mechanisms the Administration and the executive agencies annually shaped the strategic programs of the government.

In many, if not most, areas of domestic policy, statutory authorizations prescribe fairly explicitly and in detail the amounts of money which are authorized to be appropriated for various projects. As a corollary, the appropriation of funds for any project which has not received prior statutory authorization is subject to a point of order in Congress. Before 1961, however, except for military aid, military public works, and a few weapons, little legislation existed to guide the Appropriations committees in acting upon the military budget. General authorizations, of course, furnished the legal basis for Army, Navy, and Air Force appropriations, but in most cases no statutory authorization existed for the specific programs which the military might be pursuing at any particular moment. The same statutes could furnish the legal base for a budget of $15 billion or $50 billion. As a result, military programs were in effect authorized through the machinery of the JCS and the NSC. In 1953 the Eisenhower Administration initiated the practice of including cost estimates in a financial appendix to NSC papers. This was the executive equivalent of the congressional practice of requiring legislative authorization before money can be appropriated for support of a program.[8] Only in military policy were programs involving the expenditure of billions of dollars determined in the executive rather than through the traditional process.

The decision to have a national highway program requiring the eventual expenditure of $20 billion, for instance, was legislated in the normal way through Congress. The decision to have a continental defense program involving a comparable level of expenditures was made through executive processes: the Joint Chiefs of Staff, advisory committees, the National Security Council, and the President. The only significant exceptions to the pattern of executive decision were reserve force levels and military public works. Here Congress played a more aggressive and assured role than it did on weapons and the size of the active forces. Even so, the final power to say "no" rested with the executive.

Congressional incapacity to determine force levels and strategic programs is frequently attributed to the lack of proper information and technical competence on the part of congressmen. This may indeed be a factor, but it is only a contributory one. In the first place, it is striking, as one acute observer has noted, "how well informed some members of Congress are" on foreign and military policy.[9] Congressmen who have specialized in military affairs for a decade or more are at least as knowledgeable and competent as most Administration officials. In addition to all the informal sources and mechanisms by which strategic information is fed to Congress from competing services and departments, well-established formal procedures also exist to provide the principal congressional groups with basic information on existing and proposed strategic programs. Nor is the problem of classified information a significant one. Congressmen do receive classified information in briefings and appropriations hearings, and the amount of additional security information required to enable them to reach conclusions on major strategic programs would not be substantial. Much information on the considerations for and against an executive decision on a strategic program comes out after the decision is made. Presumably the release, officially or informally, of the same information to Congress before the decision was made would not involve any greater security risk except as it might require greater revelation of the Administration's assumptions and intentions. In addition, the more important a policy issue is, the less important becomes detailed technical information and the more relevant become broad judgments on goals and values, i.e., political judgments, where

9. STRUCTURE, STRATEGY, AND PROCESS

presumably the congressman's competence is greatest. Yet congressmen themselves, as Lewis Dexter has pointed out, often tend to view broad questions of general military policy as "technical" and therefore beyond their competence, although they do not hesitate to probe thoroughly and to render judgments concerning highly specialized and detailed questions of military administration.[10]

Congress is unable to play a decisive role in strategic programs not for technical reasons but for political ones. In the late 1930s, when the country was split over isolationism vs. interventionism, Congress actively considered and, at times, rejected strategic programs (naval base construction on Guam). The Administration was then moving toward a foreign policy which did not command general support until after the outbreak of the war in Europe. In the late 1940s, on the other hand, a general consensus among people, Congress, and Administration quickly emerged on the need to maintain whatever military programs were required to prevent the expansion of Communism. With a few exceptions members of Congress did not espouse conflicting foreign policies with conflicting implications for strategic programs. General agreement on the goals of policy meant that controversy centered on the relative usefulness of alternative programs to achieve those goals. The groups primarily interested in these issues were the agencies of the executive branch.

The initiation and elimination of programs and the apportionment of resources among them, nonetheless, remain political decisions involving competing interests and groups. The military programs have to be weighed against each other, against conflicting interpretations of the security threats and military requirements, against the needs of domestic and nonmilitary foreign policy programs, and against tax revenues and the requirements of fiscal policy. No congressional committee is competent to do this, not because it lacks the technical knowledge, but because it lacks the legal authority and political capability to bring together all these conflicting interests, balance one off against another, and arrive at a compromise or decision. This can only be done by bodies before which or in which all the conflicting interests can be brought together. The issues of whether the federal government should build schools or regulate the internal affairs of labor unions are contested by coalitions of private interest groups. The issue of whether the federal government should build greater limited war capabilities is contested by the Army, Navy, Air Force, Marines, Defense Department, State Department, Budget Bureau, Treasury, and a few other officials. The diversity of interests is just as great as on many domestic policy issues, but the interested groups are almost entirely executive agencies. Moreover, they do not function, as often is the case in domestic policy, as representatives of other interests outside the government. They are more principals than agents, and they trade on their own account. They are not adequately represented in any single congressional body. The Armed Services, Appropriations, Ways and Means, Finance, Foreign Relations, Foreign Affairs, and Atomic Energy committees all participate in the process. No congressional body gets more than a partial view of the interests involved in the determination of any single major strategic program. Every congressional action in military affairs is to some extent *ex parte*. Consequently, congressional bodies may become advocates of particular programs, but they lack sufficient political competence to determine an overall program. The key interests can only be brought together in the executive branch. If "the group interests work out a fair and satisfying adjustment through the legislature," Bentley wrote in 1908, "then the executive sinks in prominence . . . when the adjustment is not perfected in the legislature, then the executive arises in strength to do the work . . . the growth of executive discretion is therefore a phase of the group process . . ."[11]

After World War II congressional groups rarely prevented the Administration from going ahead with a strategic program which it deemed necessary. Although not perhaps obsolete, like the Crown's veto over legislation, the veto power of Congress over military programs certainly was dormant. At times in the past Congress formally legislated and limited military programs through unit and personnel authorization, appropriations, and the authorization of weapons development. As instruments of control and elimination, these have fallen into disuse. Throughout the nineteenth century Congress established by legislation the number and type of regiments and other units permitted the Army. This practice came to an end in 1920. Before World War II Congress legislated the maximum personnel strengths of the services, although the appropriated strengths seldom approximated the authorized strengths. In 1945, General Marshall and other representatives of the executive branch appeared before Congress as supplicants, pleading for congressional approval of the force levels which they believed necessary. Once the Cold War began, however, Congress ceased to exercise a negative over executive force level recommendations. In the 1946 debates hardly a member of Congress challenged the validity of the executive goal of a 1,070,000-man Army; what they debated was whether such a force could be maintained through volunteers or whether continuation of selective service was required. In the Selective Service Act of that year Congress accepted Administration recommendations and set ceilings, effective July 1, 1947, of 1,070,-000 men for the Army, 558,000 for the Navy, and 108,000 for the Marine Corps. In 1948, after the establishment of the independent Air Force and in response to the spring crisis of that year, Congress authorized a strength of 837,00 enlisted men for the Army, 666,882 enlisted men for the Navy and Marine Corps, and 502,000 officers and men for the Air Force. After the start of the Korean War Congress first suspended these ceilings and then established a general ceiling of 5 million military personnel on all the armed services. At the peak of the Korean War mobilization, however, the strength of the services amounted to only 3,600,000, so this high overall ceiling had little practical effect on policy. The suspension of the individual service ceilings was renewed in 1954, 1957, and 1959. "These ceilings," as Senator Russell explained, "apply in normal times, when we are not engaged in either hot wars or cold wars, to the Armed Forces of the United States." [12] In effect, Congress ceased to set the maximum personnel strengths for the services.

Similarly, throughout the dozen years after World War II, except when confronted by similar competing programs, Congress never vetoed directly a major strategic program, a force level recommendation, or a major weapons system proposed by the Administration in power. In 1908 Congress did not hesitate to slash in half Theodore Roosevelt's requests for battleships. After World War II the chairman of the House Appropriations Committee fought a lonely and unsuccessful battle against the Navy's requests for Forrestal-class carriers. During the Cold War Congress was simply not going to assume the responsibility for weapons selection. The most that congressional groups could do was to use their veto authority to compel the executive to make a choice.[13] In addition, while the practice of congressional authorization of (as well as appropriation for) the warships of the Navy had been well established in earlier years, this practice did not initially carry over to airplanes and missiles. In 1959 the Armed Services committees asserted their right to authorize airplane and missile procurement.[14] Their first exercise of this power in 1961, however, suggested that it would seldom be used to veto executive requests. Nor did Congress ever eliminate programs or weapons, with one partial exception (the Navy's second nuclear carrier), through the failure to appropriate the funds recommended by the executive. While the Appropriations subcommittees did not hesitate to decide structural issues through the budget, they usually avoided strategic ones. Almost regularly, of course, Congress reduced the *total* military appropriations request, but it almost never did so in a manner which seriously affected a major strategic program. The relative inviolability of the military estimates throughout this period was striking when compared with the appropriations requests for nonmilitary security programs, such as foreign aid and civil defense, and for many domestic programs. Between 1950 and 1958, for instance, Congress reduced military appropriations requests by roughly 3 percent; during the same years foreign aid requests were reduced by about 18 percent. A strong tradition in Congress, stemming in part from the experience of the Committee on the Conduct of the War during the Civil War, holds that Congress should not interfere in wartime strategy. During the Cold War congressmen have also felt ill-equipped to be responsible for the military security of the country. They have generally recognized and accepted the decisive role of the executive in formulating strategic programs. The areas of congressional responsibility, the chairman of the Senate Military Appropriations subcommittee argued, are essentially structural: "the four M's . . . money, men, material, and management." Never, he proudly declared, has "Congress cut Defense Department requests so as to impair the carrying out of the overall strategic concepts of the establishment." The Armed Services committees may have subcommittees on personnel and real estate, the Appropriations subcommittee panels on the Army, Navy, and Air Force; but the congressional bodies do not have special groups concerned with strategic deterrence, continental defense, or limited war. "God help the American people," Senator Russell once said, "if Congress starts legislating military strategy." [15]

10. THE LOBBYING FUNCTIONS OF CONGRESS

The unwillingness of Congress to exercise a veto over strategic programs does not mean that Congress has no role in the formulation of those programs. On the contrary, with strategy Congress has, like Bagehot's queen, "the right to be consulted, the right to encourage, the right to warn." The most prominent congressional role is that of prodder or goad of the Administration on behalf of specific programs or activities. With the executive the decision-maker, Congress becomes the lobbyist. The absence, apart from the State of the Union Message and the budget, of a general statement of the Administration's overall military program leaves congressional groups free to push particular projects or activities without directly confronting the effects of their actions on the military program as a whole. The presence of dissenting agencies within the executive gives congressional groups a fulcrum for leverage. Just as in other areas the Administration uses pressure and persuasion to move its legislation through Congress, so in military policy congressional groups often engage in sustained campaigns of pressure and persuasion to produce action on the part of the Administration. Congress as a whole, of course, does not lobby with the executive, but particular groups within Congress do: committees, blocs, or even an entire house. As lobbyists, the congressional groups are in a peripheral bargaining position with the Administration. Although unable to impose their will on the Administration, they can, through public criticism and encouragement of executive dissidents, force it to pay a substantial price for the military policy it wants. In lobbying with the executive, congressional groups use three major techniques: representation, investigation, and authorization and appropriation.

REPRESENTATION

Before the executive decides an issue, congressional groups may attempt to influence the decision by representations, including letters and visits to the President or Secretary of Defense, speeches in Congress, encouragement of similar-minded groups within and without the executive, release of information and statements to journalists, and addresses to groups outside Congress in an effort to arouse broader support for the program. Outstanding among the congressional groups using these tactics is the Joint Committee on Atomic Energy. Unlike the Armed Services committees and the Military Appropriations subcommittee, the Joint Committee has a special concern in military affairs. As a result, it emerged as virtually a built-in lobby on behalf of nuclear weapons, nuclear means of propulsion, and related weapons systems. Most congressional lobbying with the executive necessarily comes after the Administration has made a decision. The Joint Committee, however, was well-enough informed about developments in the nuclear field to bring pressure upon the executive before decisions were made. Hence, it could rely primarily upon informal representational means of influencing the executive instead of the formal and traditional techniques of appropriation, authorization, and investigation.

In the fall of 1949, Senator McMahon, chairman of the Joint Committee, was a leading advocate of building the hydrogen bomb. He prodded the Defense Department to take an active interest in the weapon, appointed a special subcommittee to investigate scientific opinion at Los Alamos, and wrote a number of letters to President Truman. Later, he and other members of his committee urged the executive to back Dr. Teller in his efforts to secure a second laboratory to speed up weapons research. In 1951 and 1952 the Committee took the lead in pushing the expansion of the production facilities for nuclear weapons. In 1955, Senators Anderson and Jackson urged upon the President the importance of accelerating the intermediate-range ballistic missile program. The Joint Committee, Senator Jackson declared, "played a major role in accelerating it—in the form of urgent representations and recommendations to the executive branch of the Government." [16] Senator Jackson also consistently advocated the expansion and acceleration of the Polaris submarine program. In 1957 the Joint Committee took the lead in authorizing an expansion of plutonium-producing facilities despite the opposition of the Administration. Also in

10. LOBBYING FUNCTIONS OF CONGRESS

1957, Congressman Durham and Senators Anderson and Jackson opposed Budget Bureau reductions in the nuclear rocket program. With the help of sputnik, the "intense pressure" of the Joint Committee eventually produced a speed-up in this program in the spring of 1958.[17]

Illustrative of the Joint Committee's role in weapons development was its activity on a nuclear powered aircraft. In 1949 the Joint Committee urged the AEC to set up a special group to explore the project's feasibility. The Research and Development subcommittee, under Representative Price, continued support for the program throughout its ups and downs in the executive branch. In 1953 when Secretary Wilson wanted to terminate the project, Representatives Price and Hinshaw from the Joint Committee intervened to keep the program in existence although on a reduced basis. As Secretary Wilson declared, "it was being pushed, under pressure from the special committee of the Senate and House—the Atomic Energy Committee." In 1957 the Joint Committee was influential in getting the program reorganized and in focusing responsibility for it in a single office. In October, after a trip to the Soviet Union, Price wrote the President urging that every effort be made to get a nuclear-powered plane into the air at the earliest possible date because of the impact which such an achievement would have on world opinion. After two-and-a-half months of discussion, deliberation, and controversy in the executive branch (involving some interservice rivalry), the President in March, 1958, finally ruled against the "fly early" proposal and decided that highest priority should go to "an operational military aircraft" rather than "the first nuclear flight." [18]

The lobbying activities of the Joint Committee in the military area were paralleled by similar efforts concerning peacetime uses of atomic energy. Consequently, they reflected the Committee's concept of its proper role regarding atomic energy rather than a concept of the proper role of a congressional committee in military affairs. Nonetheless, the activities of the Committee were an example of the influential role which congressional committees could assume with respect to strategic programs. Like any lobbyist, of course, the Committee was not 100 percent successful in its efforts. It did not, for instance, secure the action it wished on either the

Polaris speed-up or the aircraft nuclear propulsion program. Its success depended upon the unanimity and involvement of its members and the existence of some support for its view among important officials in the Administration.

INVESTIGATION

A long-standing constitutional dictum holds that congressional power to investigate rests upon congressional power to legislate. Actually, however, Congress often investigates, in the grand manner, matters which are impossible for it to legislate (witness the activities of Senators McCarthy and Kefauver). Similarly but more responsibly, congressional bodies, especially the two Armed Services committees, regularly investigate strategy and strategic programs. Although they usually possess the power of decision on structural issues, the Armed Services committees have a minor role in the appropriations process, and before 1961 they had little opportunity to use their authorization powers to lobby with the executive. Hence, investigation was the most effective means by which they could influence the content of strategic programs. The subjects which the Armed Services committees investigated often contrasted markedly with those upon which they legislated. In the spring of 1958, for instance, the Senate Preparedness subcommittee extensively investigated strategy, weapons, and forces, but the actual military legislation in committee for decision concerned structural matters: reserve bills, the Cordiner pay-increase proposals, and the President's recommendations for reorganizing the Pentagon.

In January and February of each year the two Armed Services committees are formally briefed by the top military and civilian leadership of the Defense Department on the state of existing programs and on the new program proposals embodied in the budgetary estimates concurrently under consideration by the Appropriations committees. These hearings are not directed to any specific legislative product. However, they give the Administration an opportunity to defend its policies, and they offer the members of the two Armed Services committees a regular opportunity to inform themselves about strategic programs and to put pressure on the Administration to alter them. In addition, on occasion the two committees launch major investigations into strategy: the 1949 hearings on

"Unification and Strategy," the 1951 MacArthur investigation, the 1956 Symington airpower hearings, and the Johnson missile investigation of 1957–1958. None of these directly produced legislation, but they did compel the Administration to make a public defense of its policies, enable Congress to bring pressure to bear on the executive, and help educate the attentive public on strategic issues.

Even before an investigation is launched, the possibility that one may be undertaken undoubtedly affects the Administration in shaping its policies. The Administration may attempt to head off the investigation or to soften the criticism by altering its programs. The chairman of the Senate Armed Services Committee, for example, formally authorized the Symington airpower investigation on February 24, 1956. Hearings began on April 16. On March 1, however, the Secretary of the Air Force directed that a study be made of B-52 production capabilities. On April 12, the Secretary approved an increase in production from seventeen to twenty a month. On April 13 the President forwarded a supplemental appropriation request of $248.5 million to finance the accelerated production. Reportedly, Republican members of the Symington subcommittee "had persuaded the White House to propose the increase in an effort to take the steam out of the Symington engine before it could get started." [19] Similarly, alterations in the missile and space programs followed the launching of Senator Johnson's investigation in the fall of 1957.[20] Investigations offer executive dissenters from Administration policies an unusual opportunity to express their viewpoints publicly. In many instances, of course, investigations by the Armed Services committees develop a record which leads the Appropriations committees to increase appropriations over Administration requests. If this does not occur, members of the Armed Services committees may attempt to amend the Defense appropriation bill when it comes up on the floor.

APPROPRIATION AND AUTHORIZATION

The ancient congressional powers of authorization and appropriation were originally designed for the negative purpose of stopping the executive from maintaining military forces without the consent of the legislature and the people. After World War II, congressional groups attempted to use these powers for the positive ends of placing floors under rather than ceilings over military programs and forces. Congress tried to convert a veto power into a lobbying device. The issue in the seventeenth century was whether the legislature could prevent the executive from maintaining forces which the legislature did not want. The issue in the mid-twentieth century is whether the legislature can urge or compel the executive to maintain forces which the executive does not want.

The success of congressional groups in lobbying with the Administration over force levels and spending depends upon the unity which exists in Congress and the form which the congressional action takes. If the key centers of congressional power, the two Armed Services committees and the two Military Appropriations subcommittees, agree on a policy opposed to that of the Administration, the Administration usually comes to terms. More often, however, only one or two committees actively oppose Administration policy, and only rarely does congressional action assume a mandatory form. The principal means open to Congress are, in order of decreasing permissiveness: 1) resolutions expressing congressional opinion but lacking the force of law; 2) authorization of weapons or forces above those requested by the Administration; 3) increases in military appropriations above Administration requests: 4) provisos in appropriation acts declaring that particular military forces "shall" be maintained at certain stated strengths; 5) formal legislative prescriptions of the minimum strengths for the services; and 6) prohibitions in appropriations acts against the use of funds to reduce programs or forces.

Only once, in the Marine Corps Act of 1952, did Congress legislatively prescribe minimum unit strengths for a service. The mandatory nature of this action and the almost unanimous support for it in both House and Senate led the Administration to maintain the Corps at the prescribed levels of 3 divisions and 3 air wings, even though it reduced Marine personnel strength from 249,000 to 175,000 men between 1953 and 1959. In three instances Congress wrote provisos into appropriations acts that the Army National Guard and the Army Reserve should be maintained at personnel strengths higher than the Administration wished. Again, these actions encountered virtually no opposition in Congress, and the Administration adjusted its policies to accord with the congressional

10. LOBBYING FUNCTIONS OF CONGRESS

action. In one case, the Administration made use of an increase in the appropriation for the Army reserves even though the House had refused to approve the proviso which the Senate had written into the bill. In all other instances where Congress simply added funds without a minimum strength proviso, the Administration refused to accept the congressional action. In most of these cases Congress was divided against itself. In 1949, for instance, the House of Representatives insisted upon appropriating funds for a 70-group Air Force over Senate objections, and the President impounded the money. In 1956 the Senate, by a close partisan vote, gave the Air Force additional funds while a similar amendment had been "shouted" down in the House as "[l]arge numbers of Democrats and Republicans joined in smothering by voice vote" the proposed increase. The Administration indicated that it would apply the funds against its requests for the next fiscal year.[21] In 1955, the Administration proposed to cut the Marine Corps back from 215,000 men to 193,000 men The House and Senate Appropriations committees and the House itself approved the reduction. The Senate added funds to maintain the Corps at its existing strength by the narrow margin of 40 to 39. The Administration did not use all the money, although it did stabilize Marine strength at 201,000 men. "I was not conscious that you had any special hearings on this matter," Secretary Wilson pointedly told a congressional committee, "or that the Marines themselves were insisting they should have more people."[22] Similarly, in 1958, Congress added funds to maintain the Army and Marine Corps at 900,000 men and 200,000 men, respectively, but refused to write in the provisos which in the same bill were attached to increased appropriations for the National Guard and the reserves. The Administration refused to use the additional funds and cut back the Army to less than 870,000 men and the Marine Corps to 175,000 men. The next year Congress again appropriated money for 200,000 Marines and the Administration again kept the force at 175,000 men.

In the spring of 1959 the Senate attempted to compel the Administration to maintain a 900,000-man Army by writing into a supplemental appropriation act the requirement: "That no part of the funds herein appropriated shall be used for the purpose of reducing the strength of the active Army below 900,000, nor be expended directly or indirectly for the purpose of transporting any person or persons pursuant to any plan or program for reducing the strength of the Army below 900,000." Unlike the National Guard, Reserve, and Marine Corps provisos, this was a limitation on the use of funds and thus not subject to a point of order as legislation in an appropriation bill. It represented perhaps the most sophisticated effort to use the negative appropriations power of Congress for the positive purpose of placing a floor under a service. House members objected to it, however, and the Senate proviso was dropped in conference.[23] Disagreements within the executive branch enable congressional groups to push force-level proposals opposed to those of the Administration. Disagreements within Congress usually enable the Administration to reject the congressionally sponsored alternatives.

In one sense the freedom of Congress to vote monies for stronger forces than requested by the Administration rests upon the failure of Congress to authorize force levels through the traditional legislative process. If force level maxima were approved by the Armed Services committees, it would, of course, be out of order for the Appropriations committees to appropriate funds for larger forces than those authorized. Force levels, however, are determined in the executive, and, as a result of the separation of powers, the congressional Appropriations committees remain free to accept or to exceed that authorization. This freedom was limited by the procedure initiated in 1961 of making annual congressional authorizations for airplanes, missiles, and warships. Such a practice enhances the lobbying role of the Armed Services committees and restricts that of the Appropriations committees; the latter can not appropriate more money than the former authorizes.

Because increases were in the final analysis permissive and decreases mandatory, Congress naturally tended toward the former rather than the latter. It warned the executive but left the final responsibility with the Administration. Congress, to the extent that it was able to induce the Administration to accept its floors, complicated the process of bargaining and adjustment among other programs and interests. The Administration was forced either to increase its total military budget or to reduce other activities. In either event its freedom of action was circumscribed. Congress, however, still had no reason to feel responsible for reducing other programs. All it had done was to urge an increase in one program and to leave the Administration free to deal with the rest as it pleased. The gain to the favored program was clear and concrete; the loss, if any, to the others was diffused and obscure. Extended to a wide variety of programs and forces, of course, congressional floors and favoritism might eventually seriously restrict the freedom of the Administration to allocate funds in what it thought to be the most rational and efficient manner, and the problems of change and innovation would thereby be seriously complicated.

ADMINISTRATION AND CONGRESSIONAL ATTITUDES

Both the Truman and Eisenhower Administrations objected to congressional efforts to limit or to eliminate executive freedom to determine force levels and military spending. In 1945, for instance, the House Naval Affairs Committee reported and the House passed a concurrent resolution declaring that the Navy "should consist of not less than" certain specified numbers of vessels. Although this was the mildest form of congressional action, President Truman objected to it as a "usurping of executive functions,"[24] and the resolution did not come up in the Senate. In 1951 the Administration also objected strongly to the initial version of the Marine Corps Bill, which proposed both a minimum personnel strength of 400,000 for the Corps and a minimum unit strength of 4 *full strength* divisions and 4 air wings. In 1959 the President termed the National Guard and Reserve provisos written into the defense appropriations act in 1958 "an unprecedented departure from past policy," "wasteful of resources that can be more appropriately applied elsewhere," "entirely inconsistent with a policy of promptly adjusting our military forces and concepts to rapidly changing world conditions and revolutionary advances in science and technology."[25] Similarly, the White House was reportedly "deeply concerned" over the prohibitive proviso which the Senate added to the Supplemental Appropriations Bill in 1959.[26]

At times the Administration reached agreements with congressional groups on service force levels. Later Administration efforts to change the agreed-upon strength, however, normally produced violent congressional reactions. In 1955, for instance, reportedly the Administration persuaded Representative Vinson not to attack its reduction in the Army by promising that in the future the Army would be maintained at not less than 900,000 men. Three years later the Administration's proposal to cut the Army to 870,000 was approved by the House Appropriations Committee but was overturned on the floor in a move led by the members of Mr. Vinson's committee.[27] In 1957 Representative Overton Brooks helped negotiate an agreement among the Army, the National Guard, and the Armed Services Committee under which, in return for other concessions, the Army agreed to maintain the Guard at 400,000 men. The following year the Administration proposed reducing the Guard to 360,000. Representative Brooks took the lead in securing House approval of a resolution declaring that it was Congress's intention that the Guard be maintained at 400,000.[28] Once having reached an agreement with congressional groups on force levels, the Administration has to pay significant political costs if it unilaterally attempts to break the agreement and to reassert executive prerogative.

The attitudes and expectations of congressmen on their efforts to affect executive decisions were mixed. Often they solemnly cited their constitutional responsibility to provide for the armed forces and warned the Administration against intruding upon congressional prerogatives. Congressional authority over force levels, however, was easy to assert but difficult to exercise. Even Congressman Vinson, the most influential and articulate defender of congressional powers, recognized the existing limitations on Congress. As a remedy, he advocated congressionally established floors for all the services and legislation requiring the Administration to consult with the Appropriations committees before reducing any appropriation by more than 5 percent. Congressmen generally seemed to feel that there should be some means by which Congress could, if it so desired, make its floors effective against the Administration. Congressmen also recognized, however, that in the normal course of events the power of decision on strategic programs had to rest with the Administration. They regularly criticized the Administration for "ignoring" or "violating" the intent of Congress, but at the same time they accepted the legitimacy if not the advisability of the Administration's actions. Congressional willingness to accept executive actions tended to increase during the postwar decade.

10. LOBBYING FUNCTIONS OF CONGRESS

In 1949 and 1950, both the House Appropriations Committee and the House Armed Services Committee denounced vigorously President Truman's impounding of Air Force funds. In 1956, the Appropriations Committee comment upon the Administration's failure to use Marine Corps funds was comparatively restrained.[29] In the late 1950s most congressional leaders agreed that the Administration effectively controlled service force levels and the size of the military establishment.[30]

THE ROLE OF LOBBYING

Congressional lobbying plays a vital although not decisive role in the process of strategy-making. The activities of the congressional groups bring issues to the top where they cannot be ignored by the President and other chief policy-makers of the executive. In the debate over the hydrogen bomb and intermediate-range missile programs, the letters from the Joint Committee to the President helped to focus the problem and to make it clear that these were major issues which had to be decided. Similarly, Representative Price's representations on the aircraft nuclear propulsion program forced the President to make a definite choice between a "fly early" policy with the advantageous effects it would have on world opinion and a "military utility" policy with its greater benefits for long run military effectiveness. The existence of conflicting values and needs was clearly recognized: "in present circumstances," as the President said, "they meet head on." Similarly, congressional appropriation of more money than the Administration requests usually reflects a significant policy divergence between the Administration and Congress.[31] It is a means through which congressional groups express their opinion on what policy should be; and it puts the responsibility squarely on the executive either to accept their views or to reject them. In 1949, when Congress appropriated money for a 70-group Air Force, the Administration was clearly compelled to choose between principal reliance on airpower and continued adherence to its goal of "balanced forces." In 1956 the Senate's increase in Air Force appropriations posed the issue of "sufficient" airpower vs. "superior" airpower. Less clearly, the congressional increases in Army and Marine Corps funds raised the issue of the adequacy of preparations for limited conventional war. Within the recesses of the JCS-NSC machinery, strategic alternatives may be compromised and obscured. Congressional challenges to policy, even when they come after the Administration position has been determined, at least force the Administration to confront the issue again and to articulate a defense of its course.

11. EXECUTIVE LEGISLATION OF STRATEGIC PROGRAMS

Strategic programs are determined in the executive rather than in Congress. The process of decision within the executive, however, bears many striking resemblances to the process of decision in Congress. It retains a peculiarly legislative flavor. Legislative and executive *processes* of policy-making do not necessarily correspond to the legislative and executive *branches* of government. A policy-making process is legislative in character to the extent that: 1) the units participating in the process are relatively equal in power (and consequently must bargain with each other); 2) important disagreements exist concerning the goals of policy; and 3) there are many possible alternatives. A process is executive in character to the extent that: 1) the participating units differ in power (i.e., are hierarchically arranged); 2) fundamental goals and values are not at issue; and 3) the range of possible choice is limited.

Strategic programs, like other major policies, are not the product of expert planners, who rationally determine the actions necessary to achieve desired goals. They are the result of controversy, negotiation, and bargaining among officials and groups with different interests and perspectives. The conflicts between budgeteers and security spokesmen, between the defenders of military and nonmilitary programs, among the four services, and among the partisans of massive retaliation, continental defense, and limited war, are as real and as sharp as most conflicts of group interests in Congress. The location of the groups within the executive branch makes their differences no less difficult to resolve. The variety and importance of the interests, the intensity of the conflicting claims, the significance of the values at stake, all compel recourse to the complex processes of legislation. The inability of Congress to legislate strategic programs does not eliminate the necessity to legislate them but simply focuses it in the executive branch. To be sure, many "rules of the game" for innovating proposals, mobilizing support, distracting and dissuading opponents, and timing decisions in the executive "legislative" process differ from those in the congressional "legislative" process. Each of the leaders of Congress depends, in the last analysis, on the support of a unique constituency. All the leaders of the Administration depend in part on the support of a single constituency: the President. Much greater publicity usually attends the processes of congressional legislation than those of executive legislation. The two processes are thus not identical; nonetheless, they remain very similar. In its broad outlines the development of a major strategic program, such as continental air defense, lacks none of the phases involved in the passage of a major piece of domestic legislation through Congress. The locus of decision is executive; the process of decision is primarily legislative.

STRATEGY AND BARGAINING

The development of a consensus for a strategic program involves elaborate processes of bargaining, as complex and subtle as those required for either domestic policy or foreign policy.[32] In domestic policy the primary participants are often private groups, with governmental agencies playing secondary or refereeing roles. In contrast, the relative absence of nongovernmental groups concerned with strategy enhances the extent and the importance of the bargaining roles of govermental officials and agencies. Strategic bargaining is seldom, if ever, a simple two-way process. The significance and far-reaching effects of any major strategic decision mean three or more groups normally participate in the determination of any issue. All issues are shaded and all (or nearly all) groups divided. The demands of the military compete with those of the supporters of nonmilitary security programs, domestic programs, and reduced governmental expenditures. The four services struggle concurrently with each other and against the budgetary pressures from the Comptroller and the Bureau of the Budget. The process is both subtle and complex, formal and informal. Bargaining proceeds along vertical, horizontal, and diagonal axes. The lines of communication, alliance, and conflict are vines woven about the hierarchical and conciliar trellis of the executive branch; in some cases they reinforce the formal structures, in some cases they weaken or break those structures.

In almost no executive hierarchy is the flow of influence all in one direction: actual feedback and anticipated reactions limit the influence of administrative superiors over administrative inferiors.[33] Underlying the hierarchy is a set of bargaining relationships explicit or implicit. The dispersion of power in American society and the separation of powers in government reinforce this characteristic. Agencies and officials in subordinate positions often are substantially independent of their administrative superiors. At best the superior may be able to persuade; at worst he may be openly defied. In large part his success depends upon the extent to which he can use superior status, prestige, and influence in other areas to help the subordinate and so persuade him to comply with his wishes. Even within the military services skill at persuasion and manipulation competes with hierarchical position as the source of power and authority.[34]

Vertical bargaining in the upper reaches of the American executive reflects what might be called the principle of the inverse strength of the chain of command. On the organization chart, the lines of authority fan out from the top executive down level by level to the lowest subordinate. Actually, however, the lines at the bottom of the chart usually should be darker than those at the top, which might well be dotted or light gray. As one moves up a hierarchy the links in the chain of command weaken and even tend to dissolve. Hierarchical control becomes less important; bargaining relationships more important. The reasons include the greater difficulty in replacing top level personnel, the wider span of lateral associations possessed by top executives, and their broader and more diversified fields of responsibility (which make it more difficult for the superior to enforce his will on any single issue). The President may be the most powerful man in the country, but relatively speaking he has less control over his cabinet than a lowly VA section chief has over his clerks or a corporal over his squad. Consequently, at the higher levels of government, relationships, even among hierarchical superiors and subordinates, tend towards egalitarianism and usually involve substantial bargaining.

The process of vertical bargaining over strategic programs is

11. EXECUTIVE LEGISLATION

strikingly reflected in the efforts of the Administration to secure the concurrence of the Joint Chiefs of Staff, individually and collectively, in its budgetary and force-level recommendations to Congress. Typically, the military seek refuge in the formula that as hierarchical inferiors they have "accepted" the decisions of higher authorities, while the higher authorities, on the other hand, stress the autonomy of their subordinates and argue that "acceptance" actually means independent "approval." The dual relationship inevitably produces ambivalent attitudes toward the legitimacy of policy differences between superior and subordinate. On the one hand, "parochial" views by administrative subordinates may be recognized as natural, if not legitimate. "I'd be worried," Secretary Wilson once declared, "if Ridgway didn't believe in the good old Army." On the other hand, an administrative decision derives its legitimacy (as well as its effectiveness) in part from its acceptance and support by the subordinate officials and agencies affected by it. Great efforts are made to secure their concurrence. "The pressure brought upon me to make my military judgment conform to the views of higher authority," General Ridgway has declared, "was sometimes subtly, sometimes crudely applied." [35] The intensity of the pressure applied was tribute to the value of the approval sought.

The interweaving of hierarchical and bargaining roles also creates many opportunities for confusion and ambiguity, both designed and unanticipated. At the Key West conference in March, 1948, for instance, Secretary Forrestal told the Joint Chiefs that the President had approved construction of a flush-deck carrier by the Navy.[36] The Chiefs "said that they would go along with it because it was in the President's program." Two months later Admiral Denfeld, Chief of Naval Operations, announced that the Joint Chiefs had approved the carrier. The Air Force Chief of Staff denied this. To clear up the ambiguity, Denfeld again presented the carrier proposal to the Joint Chiefs who approved it by a 3 to 1 vote. In April, 1949, Secretary of Defense Johnson asked the Chiefs for their opinion on the carrier, and this time they disapproved it by a 2 to 1 vote, General Bradley now being recorded against it. Later asked to explain his change, Bradley argued that his apparent approval of the carrier in May, 1948, "was based upon my understanding that it had been approved by those in authority and I accepted it as a fait accompli. Therefore, I was merely noting, in effect, a decision that had already been made by higher authority. I did not offer opposition to it until I found, in April, 1949, that the matter was then open for formal decision."[37] As Paul Hammond has pointed out, Bradley's argument that he never approved the carrier in 1948 when it had been referred to the JCS a second time to clear up the uncertainty over the previous JCS action would, if carried out logically, mean that the Joint Chiefs could never give their opinion on an Administration policy until the Adminstration revoked the policy.

Similarly, in defending the New Look the Adminstration argued that General Ridgway failed to dissent positively from the Administration's FY 1955 program when it was submitted to the Chiefs at the end of the budgetary process.[38] Ridgway, on the other hand, held that he did not file a dissent because he had previously indicated his objections to the Administration's proposals, he now assumed that the decision had been made by the Administration, and he accepted it in silence as an obedient subordinate. To the Administration the absence of formal dissent meant approval, to Ridgway it meant acceptance. Ridgway, as Glenn Snyder points out, learned his lesson. In similar circumstances the following year, he did file a formal dissent. In a comparable instance, when the Army vigorously protested an across-the-board cut of 10 percent in its funds, Defense Department officials acknowledged the dangers involved but asked the Army to prepare a list of the reductions which it would make if it did have to take a cut. Then, after the Army had returned with its paper, it was told: "That is very good. I am glad to see you think that way. The program that you have recommended is approved." "Thus the burden of cutting," General Gavin comments, "is shifted to the Chief of Staff."[39] His development, as a subordinate, of a program based upon certain assumptions which he had received from a superior was interpreted as independent approval of those assumptions as a bargaining equal.

Where agreements between the Administration and the Chiefs on major budgetary matters are not based upon ambiguity or misunderstanding, they frequently are tenuous and limited. In the development of the budget for FY 1960, for instance, the Administration was able to secure the agreement of the Chiefs to the following statement:

The Joint Chiefs of Staff consider that the FY 1960 proposed expenditure figure of $40,945,000,000 is adequate to provide for the essential programs necessary for the defense of the nation for the period under consideration. They find no serious gaps in the key elements of the budget in its present form, but all have reservations with respect to the funding of some segments of their respective Service programs.[40]

Under the loop-hole in the final clause, each Chief presented to Congress an extensive list of the additional needs of his service. The Chiefs found the budget adequate for "essential programs," but who furnished the criterion of essentiality? Were the needs which the Chiefs listed under the loop-hole clause unessential in their view? They carefully hedged their finding to "no *serious* gaps in the *key* elements of the budget *in its present form* . . ." What was meant by the phrase "period under consideration"? The expenditures in FY 1960 would shape the defense of the nation for several years to come. Did the Chiefs believe that the defense provided by the budget was "adequate" only for FY 1960 or did they also believe that it would provide "adequate" defense for FY 1961 and FY 1962?

A hierarchical superior can control his subordinate by determining the goals which the subordinate is to pursue, controlling the resources available to the subordinate, or doing both. Vertical bargaining in the military establishment tends to divide these functions between superior and subordinate. The superior finds the limitation of resources easier than the definition of goals: previously Congress and now the Administration have relied heavily on the budget as an instrument of "civilian control." In addition, as the demands of the service chiefs amply demonstrate,[41] the subordinate, if forced to choose, normally prefers fewer resources and greater freedom to allocate them as he sees fit than more resources less subject to his control. The result is a balance in which the subordinate acquiesces in the authority of the superior to limit resources while the superior leaves to the subordinate a relatively free hand in how he uses them.* Obviously, the superior's allocations are influenced by the subordinate's choice of goals, and the subordinate's goals are influenced by his conception of the superior's priorities. Yet if the superior wishes to push one particular

---

* This is the administrative counterpart of the distinctive American operational practice of giving a field commander a general mission and specified forces and leaving it to him to determine how to use the latter to achieve the former.

purpose, he usually can do this only by increasing the resources available to the subordinate and earmarking the increase specifically for that purpose. Otherwise, his principal means of control is that formally used by the Eisenhower Administration: the request by a subordinate agency for more resources to pursue a new or newly important goal had to be accompanied by an indication of what activities related to other goals were to be eliminated to furnish those resources. The Administration's control thus tends to be negative rather than positive.

On any policy issue of significance, agreement is necessary not only between superior and subordinate but also among subordinates on the same level in the administrative hierarchy. This agreement may be produced either by direct negotiation among the subordinates (informally or through an interdepartmental committee) or by mediation and negotiation by a superior to the subordinates. In the latter case, the superior consults and negotiates simultaneously with his subordinates, performing the typical "broker" role of the politician and, often, the initiating role of the political leader. To act in this manner, the superior's self-image must stress the political dimensions of his job. If he is the President or Secretary of Defense, however, the responsibilities of his position require him to delegate many of these "coordinating" or "consensus-building" functions to individual assistants. The assistants, in turn, as one observant Washington correspondent has noted, must make "judicious use" of their access to the superior while they "burrow and bully their way to . . . . the problems that may lay hidden; negotiate the gaps between agencies; and attain co-ordination by putting major decisions before their boss." [42] The advantage to the superior of this method of producing agreement among subordinates is that it offers him some protection against the subordinates' arriving at an agreement which is more satisfactory to them than it is to him. Horizontal bargaining, informally or through interdepartmental committees, however, also offers advantages to both superiors and subordinates. Subordinates are freed from the ambiguities of maintaining both hierarchical and bargaining relationships with their superiors. Superiors, if they can define the framework or the assumptions upon which the horizontal bargaining of the subordinates is based, are likely to achieve a more economical

11. EXECUTIVE LEGISLATION

and effective realization of their interests than if they relied upon vertical bargaining. Conflict among subordinates is substituted for conflict between superior and subordinates, and this is something which both superior and subordinate have reason to prefer. The roles of vertical and horizontal bargaining in producing agreement among subordinates may well vary from time to time. Horizontal bargaining was undoubtedly more important in the Eisenhower Administration than in the Kennedy Administration. Nonetheless, the variety of interests in the executive branch means that neither can be dispensed with completely.

The compromising and balancing of interests required in the horizontal process tends to focus about two key committees: the Joint Chiefs of Staff and the National Security Council. They are probably the two most important committees in the executive branch of the national government. On the surface, it seems strange that two committees should play such important roles in military affairs and national security policy, the one place where one might expect clear-cut lines of authority, hierarchy, and executive decision-making. No executive committees of comparable importance exist in domestic areas of policy-making, such as agriculture, labor, commerce, or natural resources.* The significance of the JCS and NSC, however, derives from the fact that they perform essentially legislative rather than executive roles. To be sure, they are formally designated as advisory committees to the executive decision-makers, the President and the Secretary of Defense, but in actual practice these officials can devote only a small portion of their time to the determination of strategy. Necessarily, this process devolves upon the machinery of the JCS and NSC, in which the principal interested groups are represented. One does not make war or even conduct diplomacy by committee, but one can rarely legislate without one. In an emergency, the normal NSC and JCS procedures, like the normal congressional procedures, are often bypassed. The emergency generates a sense of unity and willingness to accept presidential decision. When the emergency subsides, the consensus and

---

* Significantly, the most important other group of noncongressional committees in the government consists of the independent regulatory commissions. These bodies were given committee form and established outside the executive hierarchy partly because it was recognized that many of their functions, e.g., rate-making, were inherently legislative in nature.

unity disintegrate, and policies again are hammered out through negotiation among conflicting interests.

The JCS and NSC have what Congress lacks: the political capability to legislate strategy. Just as agricultural policy is the product of conflict, bargaining, and compromise among the interested groups in Congress, military strategy is the product of conflict, bargaining, and compromise among the interested groups in the JCS and the NSC. Just as Congress often wrote tariff legislation by giving each industry the protection that it wanted, so at times the NSC and JCS make decisions on weapons by giving each service what it wants. The individual members of the JCS and NSC suffer the classic role conflict which afflicts the members of representative and legislative bodies. It is expected that they will defend the interests of their services or departments; at the same time, their decisions are presumed to be in the national interest.

The utility of the conciliar structure in producing a consensus within the executive branch is evidenced in its different roles in making strategic decisions within the executive and in formulating Administration recommendations to Congress. In the latter case, where Congress has the effective final word on whether the policy becomes law, the formulation of the executive proposals usually is handled primarily through the hierarchical structure. Obviously the conciliar bodies are consulted and frequently their advice and approval may be critical. In general, however, their role is less significant in the preparation of executive recommendations to Congress than it is in the disposition of matters which lie exclusively or primarily within the competence of the executive branch. The NSC advises the President more in his role as a *decider* of policy within the executive branch than in his role as a *proposer* of policy to Congress. Executive recommendations on personnel legislation, organization, reserve forces legislation, universal military training, military pay, and the like, although they are often endorsed by the Joint Chiefs of Staff, usually are not put together through the JCS or NSC machinery.[43] However, major strategic programs—not subject to congressional ratification except indirectly through the budget—are handled through the JCS and NSC. If the final decision on the matter is within the executive branch, the concurrence of all the interested agencies is essential. If the executive is merely making proposals to Congress and if the final decision lies in the Armed Services committees or other bodies of Congress, the Bureau of the Budget may play a key role in shaping Administration recommendations. Much of the political process for the integration of ideas and the mobilization of consent, however, takes place before, through, and within the congressional bodies. If any executive agencies have doubts or reservations about the legislation, they can express them directly, if informally, to Congress. The congressional body, not the executive branch, has the onerous political responsibility of working out the language which will secure the largest measure of acceptance. Also, proposals which come before Congress often directly affect nonexecutive groups, and the executive branch is probably incapable of fully integrating the entire range of interests which has to be accommodated.

UNANIMITY AND THE STRATEGIC LEGISLATURES

A majority vote normally produces action in a legislative assembly. If the schisms in the legislature are so deep or minorities so well entrenched that majority action becomes impossible, the legislature loses power and respect and may suffer a complete breakdown. The strategic legislatures of the executive branch operate under even more difficult requirements. If a significant majority of the committee is strongly convinced of its position, it can probably overpower weak or indifferent dissenters. Usually, however, the effectiveness of the committee depends upon the ability of its participants to produce not just majority opinion but unanimous opinion. In theory the strategic legislatures possess few, if any, legal powers of decision. If, however, the members of the committee agree among themselves, rarely will the executive superior override their recommendations. Between October 6, 1955, and March 31, 1959, for instance, the Secretary of Defense rejected only four of 2,954 unanimous papers produced by the Joint Chiefs of Staff.[44] The record of the President on the National Security Council recommendations is probably not quite so conclusive, but it must be rare that he goes against the unanimous advice of his principal assistants. On the other hand, the failure of the strategic legislatures to produce agreement necessarily transfers responsibility for decision to the executive decision-maker and to the vertical system of bargaining. The authority and effectiveness of the legislatures depends upon their unanimity.

Unanimity is difficult to achieve. Any participant can, by persistent objection, block action upon a measure. In miniature, the JCS and, to a lesser extent, the NSC embody in practice Calhoun's theory of the concurrent majority. Even during World War II, as Secretary Stimson pointed out, the Joint Chiefs "remained incapable of enforcing a decision against the will of any one of its members." The JCS, he went on to say, "was an exact counterpart in military terms of the Security Council later established by the United Nations; any officer, in a minority of one, could employ a rigorous insistence on unanimity as a means of defending the interests of his own service." [45] Nonetheless, while the difficulties in producing agreement are great, both the executive decision-maker and the subordinate participants in the strategic legislature have strong incentives to welcome and to encourage unanimity.

The interests of the subordinate members of the legislature in unanimity are fairly obvious. Each participant must balance the gains and losses of compromising with his peers against the potential gains and losses of appealing to the executive superior. This choice must reflect not only the effects of appeal upon the immediate issue at hand but also the interest of the participant in the continued functioning of the legislature. The situation is a mixed game, with the committee members balancing the promotion of their individual interests against their collective interest opposed to change in the locus of decision-making.[46] The change in locus may be quite undesirable if the superior official has options open to him which are denied to the committee. On a question of allocating $100 million among three services, two services may agree upon a 40-40-20 allocation while the third might insist upon a 30-30-40 division. As long as the framework of decision remains constant, the three services have relatively little to lose in allowing the issue to go to the superior official. Presumably he will approve some compromise, say 35-35-30. The superior official, however, is not necessarily bound by the same limitations as the members of the committee. Conceivably, he could agree with each service's statement of its maximum needs and make available $20 million more to permit a 40-40-40 distribution. More likely, however, he will use one service as a check upon the other, and accepting the minimum estimates for each service, decrease the total available to $80 million and allocate it on a 30-30-20 basis. The common interest of the services thus puts a high priority on agreement. "[T]here is always tremendous self-imposed pressure," the Air Force Chief of Staff has declared, "to do the best job possible because . . . a compromise solution of a military problem arrived at by the Joint Chiefs of Staff is usually better than a compromise decision made by civilian authority." [47]

The greater the tendency of favorable executive decisions to be distributed randomly among the committee members, presumably the more equally distributed among the members will be the desire for unanimity. If the executive decision-maker, however, demonstrates a strong partiality towards one participant in the committee deliberations, the tendency of that participant to resist compromise with his colleagues will be increased, as will, conversely, their desire to avoid appeal to the executive superior. Between 1955 and 1959, for instance, in acting upon twenty-three split JCS papers, the Secretary of Defense supported the Air Force in seventeen cases and the Army in only three.[48] Presumably the willingness of the Air Force to insist upon its viewpoint within the Joint Chiefs even to the point of a split opinion was considerably greater than that of the Army. Given a reasonable balance, even if not complete equality, of executive decisions on appeal, however, the common interest of the committee members in resolving the issue at their level presumably will be greater than the expectations of gain to be achieved by dissent and appeal.

It is frequently argued that while subordinates favor unanimity, the superior must encourage "split opinions" among his advisers so he may pick and choose and thereby maximize his own power. Otherwise, it is said, he may become a figurehead, the prisoner of his aides. In actuality, however, the superior also has a strong interest in unanimity, provided he defines the framework or limits within which the subordinate committee members must arrive at a decision. In 1953 President Eisenhower reportedly told the top military and civilian leaders of the Pentagon that he wanted only unanimous reports from the Joint Chiefs.[49] This has often been interpreted as an abdication of presidential responsibility and a weakening of presidential power. In many respects, however, it was more an assertion of power than an abdication of it. In effect, the President demanded that the military chiefs reach agreement among themselves on the basis of the policy assumptions and budget limitations which he and the civilian members of his Administration determined. Certainly General Ridgway, the principal dissenter on the Joint Chiefs in 1953 and 1954, did not feel that the Administration's desire for unanimity was a sign of Administration weakness. Eisenhower's action was similar to Secretary Forrestal's demand in 1948 that the Joint Chiefs agree on an allocation of a $14 billion budget although they insisted that at least $3 billion more was necessary. In eventually compelling the Chiefs to agree on a division of the $14 billion budget, Forrestal imposed his will on them. Similarly, President Roosevelt's desire in World War II for unanimity among his military advisers did not reflect a failure to use presidential power but rather an acute awareness of the methods by which it could best be employed and the issues toward which it should be directed: "fear of his displeasure frequently forced compromise agreement in the Joint Chiefs of Staff." [50]

A superior can encourage his subordinates to come to agreement by threatening to decide the issue himself. In 1951, for instance, the Air Force demanded a new build-up goal of 163 wings. The Army and the Navy opposed it. The issue became stalemated in the Joint Chiefs. Immediately after assuming office in September, Secretary of Defense Lovett indicated his intention to resolve the issue himself if the services did not agree. On October 2 it was announced that the Chiefs had finally agreed upon an airpower goal of about 140 wings. Lovett, it was reported, had "notified the chiefs with some firmness that it was their responsibility to come forward with positive recommendations for consideration by the civilian heads . . ." [51] Lovett's practice of sitting in with the Chiefs when they disagreed on major issues was duplicated upon a more formal basis by Secretary Gates in the last year of the Eisenhower Administration. This procedure undoubtedly stimulated the Chiefs to agree among themselves, and, where agreement was impossible, it insured that the issues would be quickly resolved by the Secretary. In the first six months of 1960 Secretary Gates participated in 21 meetings of the Chiefs and made decisions on six issues unresolved

11. EXECUTIVE LEGISLATION

by the Chiefs within a week after they were submitted to him. The result was, in the words of the Army Chief of Staff, a "great advance . . . in dealing with controversial problems and issues more quickly, resolving them, providing a decision, and getting on with the business." [52]

A committee may dispose of issues by spontaneous agreement, artificial agreement, or disagreement. Spontaneous agreement occurs when all the committee members initially come to the same conclusion on one issue. At the other extreme are the tough issues where the participants are unable to agree and which are left unresolved or submitted to the executive superior for resolution. If a committee produced nothing but spontaneous agreement, it would be unnecessary. If it produced nothing but disagreement, it would be a failure. The function of the committee is to create ultimate agreement from initial disagreement, and a principal measure of its effectiveness is how well it does this job. In the Eisenhower Administration spontaneous agreement apparently occurred on about one-third of the issues which came before the National Security Council, but unfortunately no evidence is available on the disposition of the other two-thirds.[53] It is possible, however, to get some picture of the record of the Joint Chiefs in producing agreement.

JCS members and others familiar with its operations have repeatedly stated that the Chiefs reach unanimous agreement on at least 90 percent of the issues which come before them. The unanimity of opinion on unanimity is overwhelming and conclusive. Yet surely here is a paradox. During these same years in which JCS actions were 90 to 100 percent unanimous, interservice rivalry was a commonly recognized fact of life in the military establishment. How is it possible to reconcile the continuing and sometimes acrimonious service rivalry with the apparent harmony in the Joint Chiefs? Could the Chiefs avoid disagreeing in private on the issues which they were not infrequently debating in public?

The explanation of this apparent paradox lies in part in the nature and importance of the issues upon which the Chiefs reached agreement and disagreement. The Chiefs found it relatively easy to agree on war plans for the immediate future. Assuming that each service had its current capabilities, the Chiefs could determine how these forces should be used in the various contingencies which might arise. This is "military planning" in its purest form. The greatest range of disagreements occurred over issues involving the futures of the services: roles and missions, budgets, and the allocation of weapon systems.[54] Here, of course, the Chiefs function not as experts planning the employment of given forces in a hypotheti-

TABLE 1. REPORTED JCS ACTIONS AND SPLIT PAPERS

Period	Total JCS Actions	Split Papers
1947–49 [a]	not available	5–6
1949 (fall)–1951 (spring) [b]	not available	0
1951–52 [c]	1,650	5
1953–55 [d]	2,000	20
1955 (Oct. 6)–1959 (Mar. 31) [e]	2,977	23
1956 (Dec. 15)–1958 (Jan. 22) [f]	884	3

[a] Lt. Col. J. D. Hittle, "Sea Power and a National General Staff," 75 *U.S. Naval Institute Proceedings* (Oct. 1949), 1100–2.
[b] *U.S. News & World Report*, May 18, 1951, p. 14.
[c] Gen. Omar Bradley, *New York Times*, Jan. 10, 1953, p. 4.
[d] Vice Admiral H. E. Orem, "Shall We Junk the Joint Chiefs of Staff?" 84 *U.S. Naval Institute Proceedings* (Feb. 1958), 59.
[e] Gen. Maxwell D. Taylor, *The Uncertain Trumpet* (New York, 1960), p. 91.
[f] Hanson W. Baldwin, *The Great Arms Race* (New York, 1958), p. 85.

cal situation but as political representatives protecting the interests of their services. Moreover, the rationality and relevance of JCS war planning could be tested only in the rare instances where the nation was compelled to utilize military force. In the day-to-day operation of the military establishment inevitably the bread-and-butter decisions affecting relations among the services seemed much more important. It would not, perhaps, be accurate to say that the more important the issue the less the likelihood of agreement among the Chiefs, but there is little doubt that the disagreements "involve some transcendent issues." [55] Expounding the accepted viewpoint, even after his ouster as Chief of Naval Operations, Admiral Denfeld once declared that "On nine-tenths of the matters that come before them, the Joint Chiefs reach agreement themselves." The effect of his declaration was somewhat mitigated by the sentence immediately following: "Normally the *only* disputes are on strategic concepts, the size and composition of forces, and budget matters."! [56]

In the decade after World War II the Joint Chiefs disagreed on an impressive list of major issues. In 1948 and 1949 they split over the desirability of the Navy's projected flush-deck carrier. In

11. EXECUTIVE LEGISLATION   161

formulating the FY 1951 budget they disagreed over whether the Air Force should have 70 groups and over whether the Navy should have 8 combat carriers (the Navy figure), 4 (Army), or none at all (Air Force). In wrestling with the FY 1953 budget in the autumn of 1951 the Chiefs initially disagreed over the proper build-up goal for the Air Force. In 1953 the Chiefs split over the 137-wing program for the Air Force. In 1953 and 1954 General Ridgway dissented from the Joint Chiefs' recommendations concerning force levels for FY 1955 and 1956. In 1956 the Chiefs were unable to arrive at an agreement on aviation and missiles. Between 1955 and 1959 General Taylor reports that the Chiefs disagreed over such questions as:

Should the Army be permitted to have an intermediate-range ballistic missile?
What is the best possible composition of the atomic stockpile in types and yields of weapons?
What authority should be given the Commander-in-Chief of the North American Defense Command?
How should the Pacific Command be organized and staffed?
Should a top priority be given to development of small tactical atomic weapons?
How should the Nike-Hercules and Bomarc surface-to-air missiles be employed?
Is there sufficient troop lift available for limited wars?
Should the "Basic National Security Policy" be modified to place greater emphasis on the possibility of limited war? [57]

All the issues upon which the Joint Chiefs were unable to agree were obviously important and the bulk of those upon which they agreed were unimportant. Nonetheless, the small absolute number of split papers indicates that the Chiefs must have been able to agree on many significant issues. Was such agreement spontaneous or artificial? On many of the lesser issues undoubtedly it was often spontaneous. "Most of the papers considered by the Chiefs," General Taylor reports, "are quickly disposed of. Others, however, may be carried forward for weeks on the agenda. These are generally the involved papers bearing upon the long-range plans of the services." [58] On important matters artificial agreement was probably the prevailing pattern.* The rarity of split papers on important issues is

* Field-Marshal Montgomery reports that during his membership on the Chiefs of Staff Committee, 1946–1948, the only instance of "real unanimous

tribute to the effectiveness of the mechanisms used by Chiefs for compromising differences and producing agreements.

PRODUCING AGREEMENT IN STRATEGIC LEGISLATION

The Joint Chiefs of Staff, except when the Secretary of Defense participates, is exclusively military. The National Security Council, except for its military adviser, is exclusively civilian. At stake in the deliberations of both, however, are personal and organizational interests, values, and perspectives. Both resort to the same methods for resolving or disposing of controversial issues. These are the traditional means of the congressional legislative process. They may be grouped into four categories.

1. Avoiding controversial issues, delaying decision on them, referring them to other bodies for resolution. If an issue appears highly controversial, members of the strategic committees, like members of Congress, attempt to avoid considering it. Since "one dissenting Chief can prevent action on an issue for long periods," General Taylor has written, "it is difficult to force consideration of matters unpalatable to one or more of the services." [59] If the strategic legislature is unable to avoid formal responsibility for the issue, it may still avoid facing it directly by postponing consideration of it or by devolving responsibility for it to other agencies. Decision delayed is disagreement avoided. Unless serious differences exist, little reason exists to delay decision on an issue, and yet delay has been an oft-commented-upon aspect of JCS operations. Some issues simply invite delay. "Even under the stress of war," General Marshall remarked, "agreement has been reached in the Joint Chiefs of Staff at times only by numerous compromises and after long delays . . ." [60]

The proliferation of committees is a useful political device to facilitate and, in some cases, legitimate the avoidance of decision. Issues can be referred from committee to committee, up and down the hierarchy, and since the same service and departmental interests are usually represented on all the committees, agreement in one is

---

agreement," i.e., spontaneous agreement, was on his proposal that the Chiefs ask the Prime Minister for a new Minister of Defence. "In all other cases agreement was reached only by compromise." Even in the case he cites, the spontaneous agreement was only temporary. *The Memoirs of Field-Marshal Montgomery* (Cleveland, 1958), p. 438.

11. EXECUTIVE LEGISLATION   163

just as unlikely as agreement in another. The hope always exists, however, that further study may illuminate new avenues of agreement. The tendency is to "sweep controversial issues under the rug, where they lie dormant for indefinite periods." [61]

Controversial decisions may also be avoided by devolving them from the Joint Chiefs back upon the services. Thus, while the Chiefs authorize force levels, they do not specify particular types of forces and weapons. The number of attack carriers comes before the JCS; whether they are nuclear powered or conventional powered, large or small, is left for the Navy and the Budget officials to decide. The advantages of a live-and-let-live philosophy on weapons development were underlined by the B-36 controversy of 1949. In formulating the force levels for FY 1960 the Joint Chiefs did not specifically consider "whether the Army should be maintained at 870,000 or 900,000, whether funds should be sought for a Navy carrier, and what should be done with reference to the B-52 bomber program." [62] Agencies are naturally reluctant to bring programs of great importance to themselves before the NSC or JCS for consideration.[63]

Decision on major issues also may be avoided by devoting more time to minor ones. The relations among the services tend to inflate relatively unimportant administrative questions into major interservice political issues. Even so, the resolution of those issues undoubtedly is considerably easier than the resolution of the major ones on strategy, missions, and budgets. One-third of JCS decisions in 1951 and 1952 dealt with administrative matters other than strategy. The JCS "dips into matters it should avoid," Vannevar Bush complained, "it fails to bring well-considered resolution to our most important military problems, and it fritters away its energy on minutiae." Departmental representatives in the NSC machinery, a Senate study said, aim "to bypass the committees while keeping them occupied with less important matters." [64] The Chiefs and the NSC, however, were treading a well-worn legislative path. In almost identical terms, political scientists have for years accused Congress of refusing to grapple with major issues of public policy and of wasting time and energy on minor matters of administrative detail.

2. *Compromise and logrolling, that is, trading off subordinate interests for major interests.* If an issue cannot be avoided, recourse

is frequently had to the classic political processes of compromise and logrolling. In the executive as in the legislature, different interests can agree upon the disposition of the immediate issue before them without agreeing upon the long-range goals of policy.[65] Where the framework of decision is authoritatively set from the outside, the logic of compromise demands service equality. As the $14 and $13 billion ceilings firmly succeeded each other in the late 1940s, the tendency to divide the funds equally among the three services became more and more pronounced. If, however, the limits permitted by superior executive authority are broad or undefined, logrolling enables each service to obtain what it considers most important. In "Operation Paperclip," Army, Navy, and Air Force proposals are added together and called a joint plan. In 1947, for instance, the President's Air Policy Commission criticized the duplication between the Air Force and naval aviation and asked the Chiefs to prepare an integrated plan. In the paper which the Chiefs submitted, however, "agreement was reached between them by avoiding that issue [of overlap], for the paper merely approved the statement of requirements each service presented—14,500 aircraft for Naval aviation and a 70-group Air Force." [66] During the Korean War General Vandenberg reportedly secured support for additional Air Force wings by agreeing to the Navy's program for Forrestal class carriers. A "tacit agreement" developed among the Joint Chiefs that no one chief would oppose the purchasing program of another.[67] Interservice conflicts over the control of weapons systems inevitably tended toward duplication: Thor and Jupiter, Nike and Bomarc. Duplication is simply the price of harmony. It is hardly surprising that JCS should be referred to as "a trading post." As one congressman remarked to his colleagues:

If you are concerned, you politicians, with getting unanimity of action, I refer you to the Joint Chiefs of Staff. There is a classic example of unanimity of action on anything: You scratch my back and I will scratch yours. "Give me atomic carriers," says the Navy, "and you can have your B-52s in the Air Force." I do not know why General Taylor is going along, because I have never been able to find anything that the Army is getting out of the deal.[68]

3. Expressing policies in vague generalities representing the "lowest common denominator" of agreement in which all can acquiesce. If jurisdiction over an issue cannot be avoided and if trading or logrolling is impossible, policy may still be defined in vague words and phrases lacking operational meaning. Referring to the annual NSC statement of national security policy, General Taylor has declared:

> The end product . . . has thus far been a document so broad in nature and so general in language as to provide limited guidance in practical application. In the course of its development, the sharp issues in national defense which confront our leaders have been blurred in conference and in negotiation. The final text thus permits many different interpretations. The protagonists of Massive Retaliation or of Flexible Response, the partisans of the importance of air power or of limited war, as well as the defenders of other shades of military opinion, are able to find language supporting their divergent points of view. The "Basic National Security Policy" document means all things to all people and settles nothing.[69]

Similarly, when the Secretary of Defense compels the Joint Chiefs to consider a disagreeable issue, their answer often "may be 'waffled,' i.e., made ambiguous or incompletely responsive to the fundamental question." [70] In effect, this frequently means that the decision is referred back to the services or subordinate committees, for it is they who must make the policy in the process of executing it. Decisions become more of a way of producing agreement among equals than of producing action by subordinates.

What may seem to be insignificant struggles over semantics and phraseology thus assume importance as methods of securing general endorsement of a policy by the interested parties. The Joint Chiefs, as Hanson Baldwin declared in 1951, "often argue over phraseology, instead of substance, and try to reach agreement by compromises in semantics." [71] In formulating a statement of China policy, for instance, the NSC's predecessor, the State-War-Navy Coordinating Committee, carefully interlarded words and phrases from the State Department, on the one hand, and the military, on the other hand, to produce a balance which became national policy, a process no different in its essentials from that by which a congressional committee produces a statute.[72]

4. Basing policies upon assumptions which may or may not be realistic. An alternative to agreement on the vague generality is agreement upon specific policies or programs which are based upon unrealistic assumptions. Usually these are assumptions that the domestic situation will permit larger forces than would actually be the case or that the international situation will permit weaker forces than appear to be warranted. In 1948 the Joint Chiefs easily agreed on a budget on the assumption that the Administration would make $23 billion available to the military. In the late 1950s the mid-range plans of the Chiefs (the Joint Strategic Objectives Plans) reflected assumptions that $48 to $58 billion would be available. On this basis the Chiefs could agree. In actuality, the Administration was attempting to hold military spending at about $40 billion and rejected the Chiefs' "Blue Sky planning." The mid-range plans were also criticized on the grounds that they set goals for the pre-D-day procurement of mobilization reserves which were totally unrealistic in terms of the national fiscal limitations on the military budget.[73]

Agreement on strategic programs may also be based upon tenuous assumptions about the state of the world. Thus, General Ridgway agreed to the three-year New Look program with the understanding that it was based on the assumptions: "1) that there would be no new outbreak of war in Korea, 2) that the political situation in Korea would become stabilized, 3) that the build-up of the German, Korean and Japanese armed forces would proceed on schedule, 4) that the war in Indo-China would be ended and the political situation there stabilized, 5) that the European Defense Community plan would be ratified, and 6) that there would be no further deterioration in international political conditions." In the final New Look paper, however, some of these assumptions were transmuted into "implementing actions," that is, the paper recommended that the German and Japanese rearmaments be hastened rather than assuming that they would be hastened.[74] The approval which Ridgway gave the paper was apparently contingent upon the realization of the assumed conditions, not merely upon their encouragement. Until the assumptions clearly were not realized, however, presumably the New Look commanded the unanimous support of the Chiefs.

12. CRITICISMS OF THE STRATEGY-MAKING PROCESS

Curiously enough, the location of the point of decision on strategic programs in the executive rather than in Congress has occasioned only sporadic criticism from American commentators. In-

12. CRITICISMS

stead, dissatisfaction has focused upon the importation into the executive branch of the processes and characteristics of policy-making common to the legislative branch. The most common criticisms are: 1) National security policy has lacked unity, coherence, and a sense of direction; decisions have been made upon an *ad hoc* basis, uninformed and unguided by a common purpose; 2) National security policies have been stated largely in terms of compromises and generalities; clear-cut alternatives have not been brought to the highest level for decision; 3) Delay and slowness have characterized the policy-making process; 4) The principal organs of policy-making, particularly the NSC, have not been effective vehicles for the development of new ideas and approaches; they tend to routinize the old rather than stimulate the new; 5) The procedures of policy-making tend to magnify the obstacles and difficulties of any proposed course of action; 6) The above deficiencies are primarily the product of government by committee, particularly when the members of the committee necessarily represent the interests of particular departments and services.

To remedy these deficiencies, the critics urge reducing the role of committees and enhancing the role of individual executive decision-makers, developing more effective, farsighted, and more powerful executive leadership, imbuing the executive branch with a greater sense of purpose and direction, and, in general, rationalizing the structure of the executive to achieve a greater correspondence between organization and purpose.[75]

Almost all these allegations of fact are accurate. The strategy-making process *is* slow, prone to compromise, given to generalities, strewn with reefs and shoals, and unlikely to produce clear-cut, coherent, and rational policies. Judgments of the effectiveness of a policy-making process, however, must be based upon at least two criteria. In strategy, as elsewhere, meaningful policy requires both content and consensus. Strategic policies, like statutes or treaties, are both prescriptions for future action and ratifications of existing power relationships. A strategy which is so vague or contradictory that it sets forth no prescriptions for action is no strategy. So also, a strategy whose prescriptions are so unacceptable that they are ignored is no strategy. Consensus is a cost to each participant in the policy-making process, but it is a prerequisite to any policy.

Critics raise two issues. First, is the "better" policy, however defined, more likely to be the product of a single responsible official or agency or the product of negotiation and compromise among a number of officials and agencies? The answer depends largely upon whether one thinks that the policy views of the single responsible official or agency will coincide with one's own policy views. The Framers of the Constitution, believing that it was wiser not to take chances, devised a remarkably complex system of dividing power and responsibility. Bagehot, on the other hand, argued that the American Constitution was based "upon the principle of having many sovereign authorities, and hoping that their multitude may atone for their inferiority." [76] The question of who was right need not be answered here. The second issue raised by the critics is the more relevant one: To what extent is policy made through a single responsible official or agency feasible in the American system of government? Madison not Bagehot wrote the Constitution. In the course of a century and a half, constitutional pluralism has been supplemented by socio-economic pluralism and bureaucratic pluralism. One can accept the premise of the critics that greater purpose, unity, and direction are needed for a good policy, but one must also accept the fact of American politics that agreement among a number of groups and agencies is needed for any policy. One perceptive critic, for instance, has argued that ". . . the conclusions of both the Joint Chiefs of Staff and the National Security Council reflect the attainable consensus among sovereign departments rather than a sense of direction." [77] Some measure of departmental concensus, however, is essential to any policy. If it is a good policy, it will also have direction and purpose. But the direction can only be a product of the consensus, not an alternative to it. Professor Morgenthau has struck directly to the heart of the problem and argued that:

> The policy decisions of the Executive Branch of the Government, like the decisions of the business executive or any decision an individual must make in his private affairs, are fundamentally different from the legislative decision. The latter is supposed to represent divergent interests brought to a common denominator or one interest which has won out over the others. The executive decision is supposed to be, first of all, the correct decision, the decision which is more likely than any other to bring forth the desired result.
>
> The committee system is appropriate for the legislative process, and

it is not by accident that it originated and was institutionalized there. The executive decision requires the mind and will of one man who, after hearing the evidence and taking counsel, takes it upon himself to decide what is the right action under the circumstances.[78]

"Divergent interests," however, exist within the executive as much as within Congress. Lower taxes, domestic welfare programs, balanced budgets, massive retaliation, limited war, foreign assistance —these are only a few of the foreign and domestic goals and needs represented by executive agencies. That the conflict among them takes place within the executive branch of government does not make that conflict any less real or the values at stake any less important.

Committees have proliferated within the executive branch precisely because the "committee system is appropriate for the legislative process." At times, of course, the President does act against the advice of his associates. Major decisions on strategic programs, however, can seldom be the result of the "mind and will of one man." Like major decisions on domestic programs in Congress, they require the participation and consent of many men representing many interests. If the negotiation and bargaining do not take place in committees, they take place outside them. On the principal issues which come up within the executive branch, there is no single "correct decision." There may, indeed, be no decision at all if the interests involved cannot discover some basis of agreement; the form which that agreement may take is as unpredictable as the final version of a bill in the legislative process in Congress. In the executive as in Congress, the major problem is not to discover rationally what is required to bring forth "the desired result" but rather to reconcile conflicting views of what results are desirable. The problem of consensus always exists, and there are costs involved in winning support for any policy proposal or decision. Many practices which critics properly deplore because they weaken the content of policy contribute directly to the development of a consensus for policy.

The political and legislative character of the strategy-making process also casts a different light on the argument that the NSC and JCS have failed to initiate new policy proposals. As one observer of the domestic legislative process has commented, "Very little legislation ever originates within a legislature." [79] Hence, it is to be expected that original contributions and policy proposals would come from the service staffs rather than the Joint Staff, which functioned as a negotiating agency. In view of the significance of this function for the NSC, the JCS, and their subordinate bodies, the absence of originality among them hardly seems so crucial. Similarly, as the critics argue, the committee system facilitates the raising of objections to any particular proposal. If a function of the committee, however, is to elicit consent, to devise the policy upon which all can agree, the airing of all major objections to that policy becomes an essential part of the process.

Just as much of the early criticism of Congress stemmed from failure to appreciate the political roles of that body, so much of the criticism of the NSC and JCS stems from the application to these bodies of nonpolitical standards. In the past, it has been assumed that through investigation and debate all members of a legislative body should arrive at similar conclusions as to where the public interest lay. More recently, conflict within a legislature has been viewed as normal rather than reprehensible, and policy thought of as the result, not of a collective process of rational inquiry, but of a mutual process of political give and take. Analyses of Congress seldom criticize it now because of the conflicts and disagreements among its members. To a considerable extent, however, the JCS and the NSC are judged by the earlier theory: in them disagreement is still considered inherently evil. As one naval officer wryly commented: "How curious it is that the Congress *debates,* the Supreme Court *deliberates,* but for some reason or other the Joint Chiefs of Staff just *bicker!*" [80]

Significantly, next to the supposed lack of agreement among the Joint Chiefs, those aspects of their operation which receive the greatest criticism are precisely their mechanisms for reaching agreement: delay, devolution, referral, platitudinous policies, compromise, logrolling. Assuming agreement among the Chiefs to be natural and rational, the critics have almost as little use for artificially produced agreement as they have for the inherent tendencies toward disagreement. At the same time the Chiefs are criticized because they can not resolve major issues, they are also criticized because they do resolve them through the classic means of politics.

12. CRITICISMS

Much criticism of strategic decision-making fails to appreciate the tenuous and limited character of hierarchical authority in American government. Reacting against the prevalence and visibility of horizontal bargaining, the critics almost unanimously advocate the abolition of committees and the strengthening of executive controls. In temporary periods of emergency and crisis presidential coordination may partially replace the normal bargaining processes.[81] But no presidential laying on of hands can accomplish this on a permanent basis. Decisions on strategic programs are simply too important to be fitted into a symmetrical and immaculate model of executive decision-making. Clarifications of the chain of command and legal assertions of formal authority may reduce bargaining, but they can never eliminate it. Each of the three reorganizations of the military establishment after 1947 purported to give the Secretary of Defense full legal authority to control his department and yet each succeeding Secretary found his control circumscribed. The existence of counterparts to the NSC and JCS in almost every other modern state suggests that the causes which have brought them into existence may be pervasive and inherent in the problems with which they deal.

The problem of legislating strategy is the dual one of producing both content and consensus. The problem can be solved neither by denying its complexity nor by looking for relief in institutional or administrative reforms which are not based upon underlying political realities. The abolition of committees or a reduction in their importance, for instance, may not necessarily strengthen executive leadership. What strength the administrative hierarchy does retain is at least partially derived from the fact that it does not have to bear the entire burden of bargaining, that much of the responsibility for developing a consensus within the executive establishment has been transferred to horizontal mechanisms such as the NSC and the JCS. The emergence of these committees in the executive branch was, in part, an effort to avoid the problems and difficulties of bargaining along the vertical axis. Abolition of the committees would transfer many questions now resolved by negotiation among bureaucratic equals back to the administrative hierarchy to be resolved by negotiations between an administrative superior and a multiplicity of subordinates. The result could overload the hierarchy, increase the ambiguities and misunderstandings resulting from the confusion of hierarchical and bargaining roles, and dissolve still further the authority of the superior over his subordinates.

"Nobody stands sponsor for the policy of the government," one critic has written. "A dozen men originate it; a dozen compromises twist it and alter it; a dozen offices whose names are scarcely known outside of Washington put it into execution." These words sum up the case against the strategy-making process. They were written, however, by Woodrow Wilson in 1885.[82] The new criticism of strategy-making falls into a classic pattern of criticism of American governmental processes. The ideas, fears, goals, and even phrases of the strategic reformers echo those not only of Wilson, but those of the progressives in the first part of the twentieth century, the devotees of economy and efficiency of the 1920s, and, most particularly, the complaints of the liberal reformers of the 1930s and 1940s on domestic policy and economic planning. In each case, the critics concluded that certain critical policy needs demanded prompt, coherent action, and that the governmental machinery was incapable of giving these needs the priority which they deserved. The targets of the liberal reformers and the strategic critics were the same: the dispersion of power, the absence of sharply defined alternatives, the dangers of stalemate. The liberal critics saw policy as the product of compromise among pressure groups with narrow interests; the strategic critics see it as the product of compromise among agencies and departments with narrow purposes. The liberal criticism complained that political parties cohered only long enough to produce an electoral majority at the polls; the strategic criticism argues that the policy-making committees cohere only long enough to produce a unanimous report. The old criticism argued that the absence of disciplined and responsible parties prevented the voters from making a clear choice between sharply different policy proposals; the new criticism argues that the proliferation of committees prevents executive officials from making a clear choice between sharply different policy proposals.

The liberal criticism wanted to organize the majority so that it could work its will despite interest groups, local bosses, and the constitutional separation of powers; the strategic criticism wants to organize the executive so that presidential leadership can override semi-autonomous departments, parochial interests, and bureaucratic inertia. The principal reforms advocated by the old critics were responsible parties, modification of the separation of powers, and presidential leadership. The principal reforms advocated by the new critics are elimination of committees, vitalization of the chain of command, and presidential leadership. What the old criticism found inadequate in Congress, the new criticism finds inadequate in the executive.

The prophecies of economic calamity by the old critics proved erroneous and their demands for reform superfluous. The American people moved out of the depression without resorting to constitutional reform, disciplined parties, or cabinet government, and even in the face of a gradual decline in the effectiveness of presidential leadership from its high point of 1933–1935. This was due more to fortuitous circumstance, which moderated and redirected the challenge, than to the demonstrated ability of the governmental system to meet the challenge. The economic challenge disappeared in World War II and was replaced by the strategic challenge. The likelihood of fortuitous circumstance's moderating or eliminating the latter appears reasonably remote.

Criticism of strategy-making is thus the latest phase in a prolonged confrontation or dialogue between American intellectuals and reformers and American political institutions. It is directed at the appearance in the strategy-making process of characteristics pervasive in American government. On the one hand, the critics express the need to recognize new policy imperatives, to establish priorities, and to reflect felt needs in an adequate manner and with a sense of timeliness. On the other hand, the persistent and pervasive dispersion of power and authority in American government insures the representation of all claims but the priority of none. The criticisms of the strategic reformers go to the very roots of the governmental system. In many ways they are much more profound than the critics themselves seem to realize. The condition which they protest is not a passing one, the product of particular men or events. The defects which they highlight are not easily remedied by exhortations to unity, assertions of executive authority, or changes in personnel or Administration. They are endemic to the political system.

13. THE SCOPE OF STRATEGY-MAKING
THE PUBLICS OF STRATEGY

Strategy-making is carried on largely within the executive, and the consensus arrived at, if any, is primarily an executive one. The consensus is often tenuous and tentative. Repeal or modification of an Administration decision usually faces fewer procedural and institutional obstacles than repeal or modification of an act of Congress. Groups which are not fully satisfied with the policies developed within the executive branch are tempted to express their dissatisfaction and appeal their cases to groups outside the executive branch. Although the effective power of decision on strategy rests with the Administration, the possibility always exists that external forces could impose such high political costs for adherence to a decision that the Administration would prefer to reverse it. The world outside the executive branch is a continuing potential threat to executive strategic decisions. Hence, the activity of the Administration is more often devoted to defending a policy which has been decided upon than advocating a policy which has yet to be adopted.

In the traditional legislative process, an issue is debated first within the executive and then publicly within and about Congress. All the debate contributes directly or indirectly to shaping the final product: to pushing the legislation through without change, amending it in one direction or another, or defeating it entirely. In strategy-making, predecision debate among the various executive agencies and related groups (and, in some cases, foreign governments) also contributes directly to shaping the measure. Once the decision is made by the President and the NSC, this debate subsides. Once the decision becomes known, however, to nonexecutive agencies and groups, the postdecision public debate begins. The likelihood of such debate may affect executive policy-makers before they decide, but their anticipation of public reactions often is, at best, an informed hunch and, at worst, a rationalization that

13. THE SCOPE OF STRATEGY-MAKING 175

the public will not accept policies which they do not accept themselves. Public debate of a strategic decision may also affect its implementation and may influence subsequent decisions. Coming after the initial decision, the debate conceivably may undermine the decision but it cannot constructively shape it.

The public debate usually is triggered either by the official announcement of the policy decision (hydrogen bomb, massive retaliation) or by the public dissent from the decision by an executive official or group (airpower sufficiency, missile gap). Often public announcement and public dissent occur almost simultaneously. Some dissent within the executive branch is a *sine qua non* to public debate of the decision outside the executive branch, and on major policy issues this *sine qua non* is almost never absent. Executive dissenters not only aid the opponents with information and arguments, but also assure them that they are not completely "on the outside," and making criticisms which are irrelevant or quite detached from reality. Outside criticism of Administration policies can be effective only if it is supplemented by inside opposition. Inside opposition to Administration policies can be effective only if it is supplemented by outside criticism.

The tentative quality of the executive consensus is enhanced by the uncertain interest and influence of nonofficial groups.[83] In other policy areas, strong private groups link the policy-makers within government to the publics outside government. They mobilize and structure opinion and interests. For most of the period between 1945 and 1960, however, strategy-making lacked a large stable system of private interests through which public opinion could be formulated, directed, and structured. Toward the end of this period a limited system of private interests in strategy was beginning to emerge. The alumni of executive branch positions concerned with military affairs were growing in number. Private scholars and experts were responsible for a rapidly expanding literature on strategic issues. Many university centers, other private research groups, and specialized journals focusing upon the problems of war and peace had come into existence. Interservice competition had stimulated the development of a variety of organizations and interests about each of the services. Scientists and other technical specialists outside the government participated more regularly in the consideration of strategic problems. Industrial and regional interests became more conscious of their stakes in defense programs. The emergence of this private system of interests was a natural result of the disequilibrium in military policy. Nonetheless, in 1960, the system of private interests was still uncertain and fragmentary. The outside individuals and groups concerned with strategy were all closely associated with the executive branch, and strategy-making was still dominated by executive officials. Individual outside experts experienced considerable frustration in attempting to play a positive role in the bureaucratic process. The other concerns of service-oriented groups often tended to obscure the debate of strategic problems. The books and articles on strategy were often seized upon as weapons in the intra-executive struggle, playing more of an instrumental than a creative role. The economic interests of the industrial concerns—potentially the most powerful of the outside groups—usually did not extend to major strategic issues. The companies tended to accept the decisions on basic strategy and then, within that framework, compete for contracts for their products and services. It is doubtful, for instance, that the aircraft industry—more involved with military policy than any other industrial complex—influenced the decision on massive retaliation or even that it played an important role in determining the size of the Air Force.[84] In the future, the influence of some outside interests in the formulation of strategy probably will increase. Between 1945 and 1960, however, their role was distinctly peripheral.

Throughout most of the Truman and Eisenhower Administrations, strategic programs received only occasional attention from the general attentive public: the leading quality media of communication, interest groups such as the major business and labor organizations which have concerns with most areas of public policy, congressmen not on the military committees, and the like. Groups and media with broad interests in public policy often feel much more confident in expressing themselves on foreign policy issues than on strategic programs. The AFL-CIO and the American Farm Bureau Federation, for instance, not only take stands on most issues of domestic policy, but also on the key issues of foreign policy such as ratification of the UN Charter or the North Atlantic Treaty.

13. THE SCOPE OF STRATEGY-MAKING

What interest does the AFL-CIO or the AFBF have, however, in massive retaliation, continental defense, the adequacy of limited war forces, the relative merits of a minimum deterrent versus a counterforce strategy? The implications of strategic programs for specific domestic interest groups are often obscure, and tradition holds that military questions are technical and outside the competence of all but a few.

Public debate can most easily come to grips with issues which are simple and discrete: to pass or not to pass a bill, to ratify or not to ratify a treaty, or to intervene or not to intervene in Korea, Indochina, Formosa. The issues relating to strategic programs, however, are complex and continuing, seldom simple and dramatic. As Roger Hilsman suggests, efforts are regularly made to dramatize issues in simple quantitative terms: Should the Air Force have 48 or 70 wings, more or less planes than the Soviet Union?[85] Inevitably, however, most program issues decided within the executive branch are less dramatic. The question is allocating an extra hundred million dollars to one multi-billion dollar program or to another, and the decision is complicated by the fact that it must be related to earlier and later decisions involving similar issues. The same problem will come up the following year and the year after that. Issues are seldom resolved; they are simply rendered tolerable. As a result, they arouse little interest outside a small number of groups composing the attentive public.

Strategic programs thus differ significantly from the structural areas of military policy, which have reasonably stable systems of concrete interests whose views must be taken into consideration in the policy-making process. UMT legislation activates veterans, educational, religious, farm, and labor organizations; reserve legislation, the various reserve and National Guard organizations; personnel legislation, the military welfare groups and retired officers' groups. The public of strategy, however, goes through an accordian process of expansion and contraction. The expression, "The public won't stand for it," is frequently heard in discussions of military policy as executive officials attempt both to predict nonexecutive reaction and to invoke their predictions to support the policy of their choice. (See Chapter IV, Section 18.) In contrast, one rarely hears the phrase, "The public won't stand for it" in connection with agricultural policy, resources policy, or labor policy. In these areas, the structure of interests concerned with policy is relatively stable, the limits within which those groups primarily concerned can make policy are reasonably well-defined, and the demands which the semi-autonomous policy-making areas impose on the political system as a whole are reasonably constant, expected, and accepted. The instability of the strategy public is characteristic of an area where policy is in a state of disequilibrium and change. Instability in the public of military policy goes hand-in-hand with instability in its substance.

PARTISANSHIP AND STRATEGIC PROGRAMS

The normal process of legislation in American government goes through phases of debate, consensus, and decision. This same process goes on, more or less, in executive development of strategy. So far as public debate is concerned, however, the process is more one of decision, debate, controversy. The occurrence of the debate after the decision leaves little room for the constructive discussion of the issues, the narrowing of the points of contention, the gradual development of a consensus. Instead, since the decision has been made, discussion tends to polarize opinion. Opponents of the Administration can only criticize; they have little expectation of being able to improve. Supporters of the Administration, on the other hand, may have doubts about the policy but they too are prevented from improving it and become committed to its defense in the form in which it was made. The Administration has little direct interest in the debate. Discussion can only restrict its freedom of action in carrying out the policy. In domestic policy, the course of the debate sets the character of the policy. In strategy, the character of the policy sets the course of the debate.

Party voting in Congress prevails on some issues of domestic legislation. On other issues, however, the coalitions cut across party lines: sectional blocs, congressional committees, economic groupings, personal cliques, ideological affiliations often are significant in the legislative process.[86] In particular, successful legislation usually requires a wide degree of consensus within the committee which is responsible for it. An effective committee, in the long run, is not divided along party lines. The Armed Services

13. THE SCOPE OF STRATEGY-MAKING 179

committees and the Military Appropriations subcommittees take great pride in their nonpartisan approach to the structural issues of military policy. On these issues, Democrats and Republicans respond similarly to the demands of farm groups, reserve organizations, industrial lobbies, and veterans organizations.

On major issues of foreign policy a different pattern of bipartisanship has existed. Instead of the natural bipartisanship of policy legislation within Congress (because other affiliations are more significant to congressmen than partisan ones), formal, artificial procedures have been developed for consultation between congressional leaders of both parties and Administration leaders. The prevalence and usefulness of these procedures has apparently varied considerably, but if an Administration wishes to utilize them, particularly in moments of crisis, they are normally available. Bipartisanship in foreign policy thus tends to come from above, the conscious product of collaboration between executive and legislative leaders.[87] Bipartisanship on domestic policy, however, tends to come from below, the natural outgrowth of sectional and economic divisions which cut across party lines.

Strategic program determination falls somewhere between the artificial bipartisanship of foreign policy and the natural bipartisanship of domestic policy. The process of strategic program decision-making inherently encourages partisanship. Developed primarily within the executive, strategic programs are a rare instance in American government: the responsibility for policy belongs clearly to one party; the other party is clearly excluded from responsibility. Political leaders argue that national defense is above partisanship, but the record of debate and voting on strategic programs suggests that strong pressures exist in the opposite direction. When confronted with an Administration decision on weapons or force levels, the natural tendency of the opposition party members is to react negatively. The absence of other groupings with easily identifiable interests in major strategic issues enhances the importance of party groupings. Lacking clear-cut constituency or other interests, a congressman is more likely to react to an Administration decision on strategy in terms of his general attitude toward the Administration rather than in terms of the specific merits or demerits of the Administration's policy. Moreover, the inhibitions which restrict congressional criticism of the more strictly foreign policy actions of the Administration do not have the same effect on strategic programs. After the President's March, 1959, speech on the Berlin crisis, for instance, congressional Democrats unanimously endorsed his strong declaration of American intentions to stay in Berlin. The other portion of his speech, however, dealing with the defense budget, was vigorously criticized by many leading Democrats as an inadequate response to the crisis. Thus, public debate over strategic programs is largely the result of opposition party attacks upon Administration policy. In the debates over massive retaliation, sufficient airpower, the missile gap, limited war, the lines were fairly sharply drawn between the Administration and its party supporters in Congress and the opposition party leaders. In strategic program decisions, the United States almost has a form of semi-parliamentary government.*

If the distinction between strategic and structural issues suggested above is valid, a marked difference should exist between the degree of partisanship in congressional votes on strategic matters and votes on structural issues. Table 2 shows this to be the case.

Amendments increasing funds in the military appropriations bill give Congress almost its only opportunity to record itself formally on major issues involving strategic programs.[88] Sharp cleavages between the parties occurred on over 90 percent (11 out of 12) of the votes in this category, and on slightly over 40 percent (7 out of 16) of the votes on other appropriations issues. In contrast, in no category of structural issue were there sharp cleavages on more than 40 percent of the votes. Sharp cleavages occurred on 64.3 percent of the total votes on appropriations but on only 20.4 percent of all the votes on structural issues. The appropriations votes made up 34.1 percent of the total number of votes in the analysis, but they furnished 62.1 percent of the votes on which there were

---

* "Several members of the Congress occupying important foreign policy positions feel that the United States is moving toward the 'British system,' as they interpret it, in foreign policy. Congress is playing more the roles of critic, reviewer and supporter of executive-initiated policies. Increasingly, these men do not regard the anticipated trend with alarm. Indeed, they express the thought with mild enthusiasm." Holbert N. Carroll, "Congressional Politics and Foreign Policy in the 1960's," Paper presented at the Annual Meeting, American Political Science Association, New York, N.Y., Sept. 8–10, 1960, p. 12 (footnotes omitted).

TABLE 2. PARTISANSHIP ON CONTROVERSIAL MILITARY POLICY ISSUES, 1946–1960

Partisan Cleavage	TYPE OF ISSUE						
	Amendments to Increase Appropriations	Other Appropriations Votes	Selective Service	UMT-Reserve	Pay	Organization	Total Issues
Sharp cleavage	11	7	..	6	1	4	29
Moderate cleavage	..	4	2	4	..	3	13
Little cleavage	1	5	18	5	8	3	40
Total issues	12	16	20	15	9	10	82

Note: Controversial issues are those in which more than 10 percent of one party was in a minority. Sharp cleavage means an index of likeness of less than 50; moderate cleavage, index of likeness, 50–65; little cleavage, index of likeness, 65–100. The index of likeness is calculated by subtracting the percentage of "yes" votes cast by one party from the percentage of "yes" votes cast by the other party, and subtracting the result from 100. See Julius Turner, *Party and Constituency: Pressures on Congress* (Baltimore, 1951), pp. 36–38, 69–71.

sharp cleavages. Thus, partisanship is less on structural issues, where the decisive roles rest with Congress and its committees, than on strategic issues, which come before Congress in the form of budgetary recommendations to implement policy decisions already made in the executive branch. The relatively high degree of partisanship in voting on strategic programs undoubtedly in part reflects differences in the constituencies of the two parties.* It is also, however, in part the result of the process of strategic decision-making which makes these decisions the responsibility of a single party. In effect, only those nonbureaucratic forces, ideas, and groups which can express themselves through the party in control of the executive branch are in a position to influence significantly the determination of strategic programs.

THE ADMINISTRATION'S DEFENSIVE ROLE

Both the Truman and Eisenhower Administrations, as different as they were otherwise, have been criticized for not exercising "leadership" in national security policy. In each case, it is alleged, the President failed to take the initiative in bringing strategic is-

---

* For analysis of the differences between the parties on strategic issues, see Chapter IV. The analysis here is designed only to show the tendency toward partisanship in strategy as compared with other military policy issues, not to analyse the substance of the party positions.

sues to the people, in arousing support for foreign and military policy proposals, and in educating the public to its responsibilities in the nuclear age. Clearly, this criticism assumes that the President should play the same leadership role in strategic matters that he does in domestic legislation. In the latter, the President must be the source of energy for his program; it is usually in his interest to dramatize the issue, broaden public concern with it, and take the lead in presenting the case for it to as many groups and in as many forums as possible. The concept of presidential leadership is that of Theodore Roosevelt, Wilson, FDR, rallying support for a legislative program being urged upon a recalcitrant Congress. In the strategy-making process, however, the President's role is very different, and the domestic model is inapplicable. In strategy, the President and his Administration have no reason to desire public debate and many reasons to fear it. The decision has been made; the policy is being implemented. The expansion of the public concerned with the policy can only lead to pressure to change it in one way or another and to the exploitation of the issue by the opposition party. While executive dissenters from Administration policy—the Crommelins, Ridgways, Gardners, Taylors—attempt to expand the public concerned with strategy, the Administration's role is defensive: to protect the balance of interests, the policy equilibrium which has been arrived at within the executive, against the impact of profane forces and interests outside the executive.

The interest of an outside group in any particular aspect of strategy, its efforts to shift the emphasis from one program to another or to correct an inadequacy or deficiency in one portion of the military effort, inevitably appears to the Administration as a threat to the entire strategic balance, involving the reopening of all the issues which have been laboriously settled. Mr. Cutler put the case very bluntly:

There is another seamlessness in our complex world: the fabric of our national defense. Perhaps the most potent argument against public disclosure of secret projects or of short-falls (which inevitably always exist) in any one aspect of our national defense is that such disclosure builds up a Potomac propaganda war to rectify that defect or over-finance that project. But if you devote larger resources to one area of national defense, you are apt to imbalance the rest.[89]

13. THE SCOPE OF STRATEGY-MAKING

Other members of both Administrations have shared Mr. Cutler's fears. When President Truman impounded the extra funds which Congress voted for the Air Force in 1949, for instance, he declared that this money "must be viewed in the light of total national policies and it must be evaluated in terms of our present commitments, . . . the effect of large military expenditures on our economy, . . . security needs in the light of our foreign policy and the economic and fiscal problems facing us domestically." [90] Similarly, in the formulation of NSC 68, George Kennan was concerned over the consequences of revealing its general policies to the public. He predicted, not entirely inaccurately, that the balance which the members of the Administration saw as desirable would be upset, that military programs would get priority over economic programs, and that military programs related to the massive deterrent would get priority over those designed to deal with less drastic contingencies. "If you tell Congress nothing," Forrestal quoted Reston as saying, "they go fishing; . . . if you tell them all, they go wild." [91]

The fear which executive leaders have of the impact of external influences on national security policy decisions is, in their own terms, a legitimate one. In the abstract, it can even be argued that while it is rational to debate the merits of one possible strategic balance over another, any balance put together with some consideration for all the elements entering into the picture is to be preferred to a mauled and disrupted strategy, the product of the pulling and tugging of a variety of groups with limited concerns and *ex parte* interests. The problem is that once the executive has produced a strategic program no other groups can approach it as a whole. They can change parts of it, but they cannot change it systematically in terms of an alternative strategy which they prefer. The realization of its incapacity to legislate a strategic program as a whole is one reason why Congress usually treats the military budget as gently as it does.[92] In cold outrage, Stewart Alsop quotes one NSC member as declaring, "Policy decisions of the National Security Council are not a fit subject for public discussion." [93] Yet, in a sense, the official is right. Once the decision is made, the time for debate is past. If it is to make a positive contribution to the shaping of policy, discussion must come before the decision, not after it.

Taken singly, persuasive and compelling cases can be made for more limited war forces, civil defense, military aid, antisubmarine forces, long-range missiles—not to mention domestic programs, a balanced budget, and tax reduction. To produce favorable action toward any one of these goals, its proponents must build up support, arouse interest, inspire publicity, reach influential congressmen and journalists, and utilize all the other techniques of political persuasion. The interest of the supporters of each program is to widen the public concerned with that program. The job of the Administration, on the other hand, is to impose discipline, restraint, and balance. The strategic balances themselves—between security programs and domestic programs, military ones and nonmilitary ones, among Army, Navy, and Air Force, massive deterrence, continental defense, limited war—are hardly merchandisable commodities. The Administration may well have struck the best balance possible, but inevitably every one on the outside will have a different perspective. The Administration can win the point, but it can seldom really win the debate. It can only attempt to discourage debate.

The new techniques of presidential leadership are directed primarily to developing and preserving consensus within the executive branch. While congressional groups are the targets of the old forms of presidential leadership in domestic policy, executive groups are the targets of the new forms of presidential leadership in strategy. These "defensive" weapons of presidential leadership are as important to the Administration in the determination of strategic programs as the familiar "offensive" techniques are in the promotion of domestic legislation in Congress.

1. Restrictive information policies. Both Administrations tended to restrict the flow of information to the public. As the Moss Subcommittee investigations amply demonstrated, the technical requirements of military security hardly justified many actions which were taken. Supplementing the technical needs of security, the demands of consensus building within the executive branch lead the Administration to attempt to curtail the flow of information out of the executive branch. The limitation of the flow of information to that which makes a "constructive contribution" to the mission of the Defense Department is a normal reaction of an Administration trying to prevent releases "destructive" of the policy consensus it is attempting to develop.

2. Suppression of leaks. The establishment of broad policies limiting the flow of information out of the executive branch inevitably leads to circumvention and evasion. The pressures upon the dissenting executive officials to make their dissent known outside the executive branch are just as strong as the pressures on the Administration to maintain a united front. Hence the phenomenon of the "leak" has become a common, although unofficial, governmental practice. Presidents may express their disapproval in the strongest terms, but staff officers and commanders will still find means of getting to sympathetic newsmen and congressmen. The services, Truman observed, "wanted to boast openly of their top-secret achievements. I directed that the strictest measures be taken to stop these leaks to the press by anyone in the government." "This leakage," Eisenhower declared "is something that's got to stop." [94] Yet, just as it was natural for the Administration to classify as "confidential" General Ridgway's retirement letter expounding his views, so also was it natural for the *New York Times* to acquire and publish the letter.

3. Minimizing of Soviet achievements. The leaders of both Administrations tended to minimize the significance of Soviet achievements in weapons and foreign policy. This was in part due to a fear of public hysteria which might upset the policy plans of the Administration. In the case of the Soviet atomic bomb, the Administration took the lead in breaking the news to the public to soften the impact of the news. In 1955, on the other hand, the Administration, apparently from the same motive, was slow in releasing any official statement on the new Soviet aircraft. Similarly, in 1957 the Administration knew of the Soviet ICBM tests before the Russian announcement in August and had been warned of the imminence of a Soviet satellite launching. In each case, however, the Administration refused to reveal its information to the American public, and when the announcements were finally made by the Russians, Administration leaders (with a few exceptions) minimized their significance. Throughout both Administrations, the American people were assured either that new Soviet developments were unimportant or that they had already been taken into account by existing American policies. Significantly, not once did either Administration attempt to seize upon a Soviet technological advance as a means of intensifying or expanding the American military effort. When some changes in program were made, as in 1955 and 1957, they were more a reaction to the congressional and public reaction to the Soviet achievement than a direct response on the part of the Administration itself.

4. Minimizing American deficiencies. Once the Administration has adopted a program its natural tendency is to obscure any deficiencies in it both to protect its own reputation and, as Mr. Cutler suggests, to prevent the unbalancing of the program by efforts to remove the deficiencies. In addition, of course, a strong case can always be made for obscuring any deficiencies in American military strength because of the effects their revelation would have on enemies, allies, and neutrals. The public exposure of a deficiency may at times be necessary to remedy it; its exposure, however, may also enable the enemy to capitalize upon it. Inevitably, if forced to make a choice, an Administration tends to choose silence rather than self-criticism. In general, the Administration attempts to maintain an air of calm assurance, an imperturbable facade.

5. Reluctance to make formal pronouncements on strategic programs. Both Presidents Truman and Eisenhower only addressed the country on national security programs when they were compelled to answer criticism or when they desired to push through Congress measures on which that body retained the power of final approval. The hesitancy about publicizing the implications of NSC 68 in the spring of 1950, the abandonment of Operation Candor in 1953, the effort to suppress General Ridgway's statement of his views in 1955, the refusal to reveal the contents of the Gaither Report in 1957, all indicate a desire to shy away from a general public debate of military force levels and weapons.

The contrast between the Administration's roles in strategic programs and in structural measures is clearly seen in President Eisenhower's two addresses to the nation after sputnik, in October and November of 1957, and his speech on behalf of his defense reorganization plan in the spring of 1958. The former were defensive in character: the President had no alternative but to defend the past record of his Administration. On the other hand, his speech on reorganization was advocatory, a plea to Congress and the public to support his proposed reforms. The general tone of the post-sputnik speeches was reassuring; that of the reorganization plea was demanding. Both were reasonably successful in achieving their purposes. The sputnik talks calmed the public and encouraged the feeling that no substantial increases in the defense program were necessary. The reorganization speech was followed by a marked change in public attitudes toward Pentagon reform, and directly helped the presidential recommendations in Congress.[95]

Public debate and questioning of strategic programs may also be reduced by distracting public attention from these issues. By proposing major changes in structural policy the Administration may shift the debate to issues for which Congress rather than the Administration is primarily responsible. In 1947 and 1948, when Congress was urging the Administration to increase the strength of the Air Force, the Administration proposal of UMT forced Congress to assume responsibility for limiting the trained manpower reserve. In 1955 the Eisenhower Administration's reserve forces legislation shifted attention away from the second stage of the New Look. In 1958 the Administration's proposals for reorganization and military pay increases distracted attention from the state of the strategic programs. In this instance, the insufficiency of some programs could hardly be denied. By identifying interservice competition and lack of effective centralized authority in the Defense Department as contributing causes to the deficiency, however, the Administration successfully compelled Congress to assume partial responsibility by enacting the Administration's reorganization proposals.

6. Restriction of testimony before congressional committees. The problem of the freedom of executive officials (and particularly military officers) to express their views before congressional committees when those views conflict with the policy of the Administration is an extremely difficult one.[96] The problem comes up in two different forms. With normal legislation, such as a reorganization bill or a military pay bill, where the effective power of decision rests with Congress, the process of consensus development within the executive branch usually does not proceed as far as in the instances where the policy decision is made within the executive. Consequently, dissenting executive officials are freer to express their views before the congressional committees. The Administration will, of course, attempt to discourage such activity—witness Secretary McElroy's rebuke of Admiral Burke in the 1958 reorganization debate—but the logic behind Congress' hearing all views on a proposal upon which it must make the final decision is fairly overwhelming. The Administration usually is more anxious to cover up expression of executive dissents from Administration strategic programs where the final power of decision rests with the Administration. In these cases the expression of military dissent before Congress cannot be justified on the grounds that it is essential to help Congress make a decision. Indeed, if the dissents come after the formulation of Administration policy, they can be justified only in terms of the pressures and incentives which they might generate to get the Administration to alter its policy. If they come before the Administration has determined its course of action, they are even more vigorously resisted by the Administration as attempts to limit its freedom of action and prejudice its decision. Both the Truman and Eisenhower Administrations tried to define as broadly as possible the obligation of military officers to support Administration programs before Congress.[97]

LEGISLATIVE LEADERSHIP IN STRATEGY

In the traditional legislative process, interest groups and executive agencies originate proposals, the President integrates them into a legislative program, Congress debates, amends, and decides. In the executive legislative process, executive officials and related groups originate proposals, and the President and Secretary of Defense, working through the mechanisms of the NSC and JCS, debate, amend, and decide upon them. Who, however, plays the role of legislative leader? Who winnows out the various ideas and proposals in the light of an overall set of priorities or grand strategy and then integrates these proposals into legislative programs which can then be discussed, amended, and ratified? Paradoxically, it is in executive leadership of legislation that the executive legislative process is weakest. In a hierarchy, ideas and proposals presumably bubble up from below; individual executives decide on programs and proposals, rejecting some, approving others and pushing them along to the next higher level. The highest executive makes decisions; he does not formulate proposals to present to some other body.

The concept of a superior executive official drafting a program and submitting it to a committee of subordinates for approval is not generally accepted; on the contrary, it is the function of the committee of subordinates to formulate the program and submit it to the executive for approval. Hence, the issue: Who leads the subordinate committee? Throughout the decade after World War II this problem was never absent from the operations of the NSC and the JCS. If the President or the Secretary is the final decider or ratifier of strategic programs, one of two things happens: initiative comes from a variety of uncoordinated sources and the committee is never confronted by an integrated legislative program; or some other body or official drafts such a program and presents it to the committee, which then discusses, amends, and decides upon it and presents recommendations to the President and Secretary. The problem in the executive legislatures is to develop something comparable to the dialectic of proposal and decision which exists between the President and Congress in domestic legislation. The body which has the final decision on policy issues should not also have complete and exclusive control over its own agenda. Otherwise the temptation to avoid the tough issues become almost irresistible. In presenting his legislative program to Congress, the President often compels Congress to face up to issues which it would be happy to avoid. In the executive legislative process, the problem has been to develop sources of initiative and leadership which can compel the NSC and the JCS, the President and the Secretary of Defense, to face up to issues which they might just as well wish to avoid, and to present the strategic legislatures with general strategic programs initially drawn up from a broader viewpoint than that which they are collectively capable of producing.

Congressional groups are able to seize upon specific issues and proposals which might be lost in the executive machinery and bring them up to the top where the principal executive decision makers must come to grips with them. Congressional groups cannot, however, perform the function of legislative leadership. Necessarily, they deal with only parts of the whole picture. Similarly, ad hoc committees and study groups, such as the Finletter Commission, the Lincoln Summer Study Group, the Killian Committee, or even the Gaither Committee, can help to prompt an executive decision on a particular policy proposal, but usually they cannot develop an overall strategic program. Largely recruited from outside the government and limited in existence to a year or so at the most, these groups serve as temporary stimuli but not as continuing leaders. Even when the group develops a broad concern with a wide variety of defense policy problems (as the Gaither Committee did), its inevitable termination means that it is in a poor position to force an Administration to make a clear decision on its proposals (much less make a favorable decision) as long as the Administration wishes to temporize and avoid them. Congressional committees and citizens' committees thus may be able to focus attention upon a particular policy issue, but they lack either the scope or the longevity to play a continuing role as effective legislative leaders.

Other difficulties hamper the ability of executive groups to play leadership roles. The stress upon the concept of "civilian control" inhibits both military and civilians. The military tend to accept as fixed the existing political and economic assumptions of policy. Apart from the Chairman of the Joint Chiefs of Staff, the military leaders themselves have "parochial" concerns. Consequently, they usually lack the scope to come forth with a broad, balanced defense program, and, frequently, they feel that this is not their responsibility. The initiative for a general reappraisal of defense programs and strategy seldom has come from the military. (See Chapter II, Section 8.) The stress on "control" in civilian control also discourages civilian initiative, and encourages reliance upon the allocation of resources rather than the definition of goals as the means of insuring civilian supremacy. The prevailing concept of "civilian control" thus fits in perfectly with the idea that the executive decision-maker is a judge rather than a leader, that it is his function to say yes or no to programs proposed by others rather than to originate programs himself. Civilian control is rarely thought of in terms of policy leadership in the formulation of military programs.

Critics of both the NSC and the JCS have regularly stressed the desirability of greater initiative and leadership from above by the President and the Secretary of Defense. They have often urged the

13. THE SCOPE OF STRATEGY-MAKING

enlargement of the NSC staff so that it could play a policy-formulating role rather than simply a coordinating and processing role. They have also advocated a civilian-military policy staff for the Secretary of Defense. The inherent difficulties of placing responsibility for both the formulation of policy proposals and the final decision on policy proposals on the same agency have prevented much development along this line. The problem is: Who can propose an overall policy without committing the Administration? The President is in a poor position to do this. In actuality, the leadership of the strategic legislatures has fallen to members of the legislatures: the Department of State in the NSC and the Chairman of the Joint Chiefs. The problem has perhaps been less acute in the NSC than in the JCS. After 1950 the President kept in close contact with the operations of the NSC; not until 1959 was a regularized procedure developed for the participation of the Secretary in the deliberations of the JCS. In addition, the presumption of absolute equality which existed with respect to the services in the JCS did not prevail in the NSC. Instead, the State Department was recognized as the first among equals. The primacy of the Department of State among cabinet departments has long been recognized by tradition and statute. In both the Truman and Eisenhower Administrations roughly three-quarters of the papers considered by the NSC originated in the State Department. Until the Vice-President was added to the NSC in 1949, the Secretary of State chaired the NSC deliberations in the absence of the President. In addition, until 1960 the Under Secretary of State chaired the Operations Coordinating Board. For a decade, during the most critical years of the Truman and Eisenhower Administrations, the Department of State was headed by two individuals who combined sustained tenure in office with the highest confidence of and closest relations with the President. Mr. Acheson and Mr. Dulles also brought to the deliberations of the NSC superior minds, great force of character, and unusual skill in articulation and debate. All these factors combined to give the Secretary of State a position of leadership in the operations of the National Security Council. On the other hand, the Secretary of State can never be more than first among equals under the President. Conceivably, as Herman Kahn has urged, if backed by an expanded staff, the Special Assistant to the President for National Security Affairs could become the "party leader" in in the National Security Council.[98]

The high premium placed upon the formal equality of the service representatives precluded a similar development in the Joint Chiefs. However, the normal absence of the Secretary of Defense from JCS deliberations permitted the emergence of a separate chairmanship. Although the position of chairman was not formally established until 1949, since their creation in 1941 the Joint Chiefs have almost always had a chairman in practice, and from 1949 down through 1958 the powers of the Chairman grew steadily. In 1953 and again in 1958 his authority over the Joint Staff was increased, and, particularly during the incumbency of Admiral Radford (1953-1957) the Chairman played an active and creative role in formulating strategic ideas and plans. Under Radford, as General Taylor put it, the Chairman came "to be a sort of party whip . . . "[99] The principal limitation on his development of this role rested in the character of the Joint Staff. While the Chairman himself was divorced from and independent of service interests, the staff upon which he had to rely was not. Despite the efforts which were made to stimulate a "joint" outlook on the part of the Joint Staff members, their future careers still lay with the services, and the principle of equal representation of the services strengthened the assumption that the members had some representative responsibilities. The replacement in 1958 of the committees in the Joint Staff with a more strict system of executive hierarchical control in the long run would help the Chairman of the Chiefs to play a more independent role as a legislative leader.

Just as the desirability of greater leadership from the presidential level in the formulation of NSC policy has been urged, so also it has been frequently argued that the Secretary of Defense should play a more active role in the initial development of policy proposals in his department. Secretaries Forrestal and Lovett and other informed observers urged the creation of a policy staff, usually to be composed of both civilian and military personnel, to enable the Secretary to play this role. Such a staff would, at the least, give him an independent source of advice, and, at the most, enable him to be a leader in making strategic decisions.

In due course, either the leadership functions of the Secretary of State and the Chairman of the Joint Chiefs will become more fully recognized and clarified, or the Special Assistant and Secretary of Defense will develop the staff facilities necessary to perform these functions. This development would not only facilitate consensus but would also probably improve the content of strategic decisions. The form in which issues are presented for decision affects the nature of the decision. The problem in the executive legislative process is not the presence of bargaining but rather the point at which bargaining starts. Bargaining cannot be eliminated, but the development of more effective leadership organs in the NSC and JCS would limit it and focus it. The starting point would become not three separate proposals advanced by three separate departments but one set of proposals advanced by the legislative leaders. The requirements of consensus might still cause those proposals to be torn apart tooth and limb, but, at the very least, the clear visibility of the mutilation would have certain restraining effects. It has had them in Congress.

A striking feature of the past dozen years has been the extent to which expressions of alarm at the decline of presidential leadership have occurred simultaneously with expressions of alarm at the growth of executive power. This apparent paradox simply reflects the fact that the very ability of the executive to make the crucial decisions on strategic programs has undermined the ability of the President to lead. The more the President becomes, at least in theory, the judge, the less he can be the advocate. This shift inevitably has had its effect upon the personal role and influence of the President. The President's ability to lead in the process of congressional legislation is a very real one. No one else can focus attention on a legislative program, arouse support, dramatize the issues, as effectively as he. He can, if he so desires, almost monopolize this role. His power to decide strategic issues within the executive branch, however, is more difficult to exercise and to monopolize. To be sure, the President appoints the members of the NSC and the JCS, and they are theoretically only his advisers. No policy exists until he has approved it. Yet in part this is a myth to preserve the appearance of presidential decision-making.

The President does not override unanimous or near-unanimous recommendations of his advisers much more often than he vetoes acts of Congress. The theory that the President makes the decisions, in short, serves as a cloak to shield the elaborate processes of executive legislation and bargaining through which the policies are actually hammered out. As a decision-maker, the President may, in many respects, have less influence on strategic programs than as a legislative leader he has on domestic policy in Congress. The leadership function is personal to him. Decision-making he shares with a variety of groups in the executive branch. The development of stronger sources of legislative leadership in strategy within the executive branch, however, would enhance the power of the President "as a court of last appeal" on strategic programs.[100]

In discussing the processing of papers through the NSC machinery Robert Cutler raises the issue: "[A]re we to let in the public while this preparatory work goes on? Are the propagandists of one view or another to be given the opportunity to argue the pros and cons in the press?" His answer is a resounding "No!" It is based upon the concept that in the process of strategy-making, "nothing has happened" until the President "has approved a policy recommendation made to him by the National Security Council . . . " All the arguments and advice before this "are personal to the Chief Executive . . . "

> It is my concept [Mr. Cutler declares] that all papers, all considerations, all studies, all intelligence leading to the formulation of national security policy recommendations to the President, are the property of the Chief Executive. They are his working papers; they have no other standing to be recognized. Only he can dispose of them.

This argument is buttressed by the claim that a decision by the President on national security is of the same order as the decision of a corporation executive on plant location:

> While the staff of a business executive is working up a problem to present to him, the working papers and the preliminary views which fluctuate and change in successive conferences are kept under lock and key. If this confidential procedure is sensible for decision-making in business, surely it is doubly so in matters of national security which affect the lives of our people and the survival of the Republic.[101]

To question Mr. Cutler's views it is not necessary to invoke democratic theory as to the possible *right* of the people in a democracy to be informed of the considerations which go into national

13. THE SCOPE OF STRATEGY-MAKING 195

security policy. The problem is rather the conflict between the rationale and reality. The concept that "nothing has happened" until the President has approved an NSC recommendation is a legal fiction. The fact is that by that point almost everything in the policy-making process has happened. Mr. Cutler's argument amounts to saying that nothing has happened in the domestic legislative process until the President has signed a bill into law or that nothing has happened in the judicial process until the Supreme Court has rendered a decision on appeal. The theory is one of pure presidential decision; the actuality is executive agencies hard at work legislating strategic programs. The representatives of these agencies no more function simply as personal, confidential advisers to the President than the witnesses in a congressional hearing function as personal, confidential advisers to the committee. They act as representatives of the interested groups, and, it might be argued, it is precisely the claims which they make and the compromises which they arrive at which should be opened as far as possible to public view.

The struggle between the Administration, attempting to capitalize upon its advantages of hierarchy, and the subordinate executive agencies, attempting to appeal to a broader forum is a continuing one, as much a part of the system of strategy-making as the struggle between President and Congress is a part of the governmental system in general. The Administration can never be sure of its policy so long as potential sources of opposition exist outside the executive branch, and the executive agencies can never expect to exercise a greater influence on the policy outcome so long as the public statement of their views comes after rather than before the Administration decision. Policy on a controversial issue can be free of tentativeness and certain of support only when it emerges from a process in which all the potentially interested groups have an opportunity to make a contribution. Public interest in strategic program decisions, knowledge of the considerations entering into those decisions, and discussion and contribution to the making of the decisions depend upon the revelation of conflicting views within the executive branch before the Administration makes its decision. Nongovernmental groups, and even nonexecutive groups, can seldom originate policy proposals and alternatives, but they can consider those espoused by responsible executive groups, make clear the implications of the proposals for themselves and other groups in society, and indicate the extent to which they are willing to support one against another.

The opening up of policy proposals for more extensive debate before an Administration position is reached might have several results. It would enable congressional and public groups to play a more effective and recognized role in the discussion of policy alternatives. It would broaden the consensus supporting the policy which is finally adopted. It would remove the need and the opportunity for dissident executive groups to appeal their cases to the public after the decision. It would minimize post-decision debate and lessen doubt about the finality of the presidential action. It would mitigate many of the defects of the policy-making process which disturb the critics. One effect of congressional lobbying has been to bring issues to the top and compel a personal and explicit presidential decision on them. Broader public debate of strategic issues would, in all probability, have the same effect. The attention and the interest which would be aroused on particular strategic issues would compel them to be resolved by presidential decision. Greater publicity and more participation by nonexecutive groups in strategy-making might also restrain the tendencies toward "horse trading" which exist within the executive. It might both enhance the roles of public and congressional groups and, at the same time, strengthen the hand of the President. In addition, the sense of purpose which the critics have found lacking in the policy-making process, if it is to be developed at all, can only be developed from society at large. Common purpose can only emerge out of broadly based policy discussion and widespread participation in the policy-making process. It cannot be decreed from on high. Broadening the scope of the policy consensus may well go hand-in-hand with improving the quality of the policy content.

CHAPTER IV

The Great Equation

14. THE POLITICS OF FISCAL POLICY

The pre-inaugural planning of the Eisenhower Administration on the cruiser *Helena,* according to one of the participants, focused primarily on "balancing what we came to call the Great Equation—how to equate needed military strength with maximum economic strength."[1] The choice of topic was hardly accidental. The most persistent, difficult, and significant issues faced by the government after World War II were balancing the needs of national security against other social needs. (See Section 21.) Before 1946 the magnitude of the security effort was not a major issue in American politics. In peacetime, military forces consumed only a fraction of the national product. In wartime, military needs were overriding. During the fifteen years after World War II, however, defense absorbed an average of 10 percent of the national effort. It imposed definite limits on the resources available for other purposes and directly affected the allocation of resources among the major interests of society. Conversely, the demands of other social needs limited the strategic options of the government. The size of the defense effort became a key issue in the new pattern of fiscal politics, focused upon the allocation of resources between the public and private sectors of the economy and among the various purposes of government. Each Administration had to balance a Great Equation in which the major components were: 1) Domestic programs for agriculture, housing, highways, veterans, education, and the like, loosely identifiable as serving the *welfare* purposes of government; 2) Foreign policy programs, including military defense, foreign aid, atomic energy, and space exploration, loosely related to the goal of *secu-*

rity; 3) Tax limitation and reduction, justified in terms of *private consumption and investment;* and 4) Balanced budgets, justified during prosperity by a number of goals, including the prevention of inflation and the reduction of the national debt, related to the value of *fiscal integrity.*

These were the four components of the Great Equation with which the Administration was most immediately concerned. Lurking behind them, however, was a fifth. In the long run, conflict among the four goals could only be moderated by the steady expansion of the economy as a whole. Except for the Korean War period. however, governmental programs were not usually directed exclusively to the goal of economic expansion. In some cases, the expansion of national security programs, domestic programs, or private expenditures could be achieved through the expansion of total economic activity. Beyond a certain limit, however, the expansion of any one sector required the contraction of the others. The goals of security, welfare, tax reduction, and balanced budgets might all be legitimate but that did not necessarily make them compatible. Even when they were compatible, the belief that the expansion of one would require the contraction of others had much the same effect as if it did require that contraction. If consumers believed that an increase in national defense expenses meant higher taxes and businessmen believed that high taxes restricted private investment, these beliefs had significant political results regardless of whether they were grounded in sound economics.

Before World War II agriculture, business, and labor were, in a sense, the basic interests in American politics. Post-World War II politics rested upon the general prevalence of full employment, the decisive role of the government in the economy, the international responsibilities of the government, and the continuing presence of inflationary tendencies. The old conflict among producer interests was supplemented by the new struggle among the proponents of welfare, security, tax reduction, and fiscal integrity. Each year the many decisions on the Great Equation were shaped by the competing political forces and interests which made up the Administration and its environment.

Despite the interdependence of the components of the Great

Equation, persistent tendencies existed either to treat each segment in the equation separately, something to be considered "on its merits" without reference to other goals, or to assume that one goal was of overriding importance and must have absolute priority over the others. Many politicians talked and acted, for instance, as if domestic needs could be met independent of security needs. Often it was alleged that an absolute limit existed on what "the economy could afford" for defense. On the other hand, statesmen and experts concerned with security problems often failed to look at the domestic side of the equation. They at times assumed that the requirements of security were absolute and that the only legitimate limit on their fulfillment was the physical capacity of the economy. They balanced the "requirements" of security against economic capability rather than against requirements derived from legitimate but competing purposes of government and society. In reality, however, no single factor—the "absolute" requirements of the military or the "absolute" limits of the economy or of public opinion—did or could determine the level of the defense effort.

15. EXTERNAL INFLUENCES: TENSIONS, CAPABILITIES, AND DETERRENCE

Threats from the external environment influence the size of the military effort in so far as they are perceived, evaluated, and responded to by the leaders of the executive branch. Obviously the external situation was responsible for the general level of the military effort. Postwar occupation duties and other responsibilities compelled the United States to maintain a military establishment much larger than it maintained during the 1930s. After 1949 the antagonism of the Soviet Union caused it to triple even that establishment. Beyond this, however, to what extent did external factors influence the specific size of the military effort? Of primary relevance were the conflicts of interest (tensions) which existed between the United States and other countries and the relative power (capabilities) of those other governments to injure American interests. In the mid-1950s the influence of tensions on the size of the military effort seemed to decrease without, however, a marked increase in the influence of capabilities. This situation was partly responsible for the major role which domestic politics played in shaping the size of the defense effort.

Traditionally, the size of the American military effort varied almost directly with the probability of war. Both the Truman and the Eisenhower Administrations were convinced that this pattern of "feast and famine" would have to be broken. The need for stability in the military effort was universally recognized by military and civilians, Republicans and Democrats. (See Chapter II, Section 3.) Stability implied that the magnitude of the military effort should be reasonably independent of changes in the tensions of international relations. Nonetheless, many traditional American ideas persisted which linked the maintenance of military forces to the likelihood of war. The intentions of other states seem more important than their capabilities. If there are no issues which seem likely to give rise to war, why maintain a military force large enough to fight a war? When the Soviet sputniks stimulated an increase in the American military effort, two distinguished congressmen argued persuasively that the Soviet Union did not want war and hence the United States should not rush into a precipitate expansion of its defense programs.[2] In part, this attitude was a holdover from the earlier periods in American history when the capabilities of other states were often less directly relevant to the size of the American defense establishment. If the intentions of another state became hostile, allies and distance gave the United States an opportunity to increase its military capabilities before the potential enemy could capitalize upon its initial superiority. The size of the military budget, in short, should reflect the likelihood of war, not the power of possible enemies. This attitude persisted into the post-World War II period. Military and political leaders often attempted to deflect criticism of their budget decisions by arguing that if war came they were spending too little while if it did not come they were spending too much.[3]

A strategy of deterrence implied that military magnitude would be directly related to the military force-in-being of a potential enemy. Nonetheless, many people continued to associate the maintenance of large military forces or an increase in military forces with the likelihood of war. This association partly reflected the fear that any significant increase in American military capability might precipitate an attack by the Soviet Union, i.e., that military strength might be a provocation rather than a deterrent.[4] Closely related to this was the more widely accepted belief that an arms race could only end in war. Increases in armaments increase the likelihood of war; hence, only an increase in the likelihood of war justifies an increase in armaments.

Before the mid-1950s, major changes in the magnitude of the American military effort coincided with shifts from war to peace and vice versa. During the post-World War II demobilization, defense spending dropped $80.6 billion. The Korean War stimulated an increase of $38.5 billion. The close of that war brought a reduction of $12.1 billion. Similarly, the 25 percent increase of $2.8 billion in defense spending in 1948 and 1949 was largely a product of the "war scare" in the spring of 1948 at the time of the Czech coup and Berlin crisis; the subsequent decline of $2.1 billion in 1949–1950, although primarily the result of domestic considerations, was aided by the failure of war to materialize. The feasibility of a major increase in defense spending in the absence of war or crisis would have been tested in 1950 if the Korean aggression had not taken place. With the war, the State Department's goal of a $35 billion increase in defense spending was realized. Without the war, the increase probably would have been about the size of that of 1948–1949, $3 or $4 billion.

After the post-Korean decline in military magnitude, variations in both international tensions and in Soviet capabilities had only moderate influences on the level of military effort. The Administration consciously attempted to prevent passing crises from affecting the size of military programs. The Indochinese, Formosan, Suez, and Hungarian crises of 1954, 1955, and 1956 came and went without producing major alteration in the size of the military effort. The Lebanese and Formosan crises of 1958, however, did delay reductions in the Army and Marine Corps, and the post–U-2 crisis in the summer of 1960 led to some increases in military programs. No one of these crises, of course, involved American forces in actual shooting war; this fact and the feeling that in a state of mutual deterrence no country would let a crisis emerge into war contributed to the reluctance to adjust the military effort to changes in the international temperature. In addition, no increase in military force as the result of a crisis was likely to be relevant to the settlement of that crisis except to offer concrete evidence of a determination not to yield. Even in its crudest forms, it takes a year or more to bring military strength into being. Consequently, while some people argued in the spring of 1959 that the Berlin crisis required an expansion, if not mobilization, of American military strength, others could with equal logic reply that no expansion of effort would significantly affect the resolution of the immediate issues in Berlin.

The post-Korean military effort also seemed to be only partially responsive to changes in Soviet capabilities. The major increase of $5.8 billion in military spending in 1956 and 1957 and the later brief decline of $1.2 billion were almost entirely produced by domestic causes. The $2.1 billion increase in defense spending in 1958 and 1959, on the other hand, was more directly the result of Soviet achievements in missiles and space. Nonetheless, the Gaither and Rockefeller groups considered this only a minimal response and urged a much greater military effort to meet the threat of the missile gap. Soviet advances brought an end to the 1957 economy wave and the $38 billion ceiling on military expenditures, but they did not produce a major increase in the magnitude of the effort. Indeed, measured in constant dollars, less was spent on defense in 1958 than in 1957.

The failure of major changes in Soviet capabilities to produce major changes in the overall magnitude of American defenses reflected both the remoteness of foreign capabilities and the immediate presence and pressure of competing domestic needs. Changes in the power of other states are not really felt until they are used or threatened to be used. Then the threat to society becomes obvious, a sense of common danger and common purpose develops, other interests are subordinated, and increased efforts are devoted to counterbalancing the external danger. Increases in the capabilities of other states divorced from open increases in hostilities do not necessarily have the same effect. They do not reduce demands for domestic programs, increase the willingness to accept higher taxes, or produce that subordination to a common purpose which occurs in time of war or crisis. In addition, it is difficult to estimate changes in capability. As Colonel G. A. Lincoln has pointed out, until it is exercised, power is what people think it is. Until power is exercised, the strength of another nation can be judged in many ways. The intensity of a conflict with another nation, on the other hand, cannot be ignored.

Even with the relatively simple question of judging military capabilities, two major problems arise. First, how important are military capabilities in relation to overall national strength? After World War II it was frequently argued that efforts to increase military strength at the sacrifice of other values would weaken rather than strengthen the country. Economic strength, political strength, and spiritual strength, it was contended, were more important than military strength. Throughout the postwar years many agreed with the New Look concept that American power rested "not upon the military establishment alone but rather on two pillars—military strength in being and economic strength based upon a flourishing economy." [5] The reiteration of the idea that Soviet strategy was to drive the United States into inflation and bankruptcy and, in the words of one congressman, "take over in the ensuing chaos and confusion" "without firing a shot," was regularly adorned with purported quotations from Lenin—not found in any of his published works.[6] In effect this belief held that military strength could destroy the only goal which justified it. Consequently, at some point in the expansion of military strength the conflict between security needs and other needs ceased to be real. The satisfaction of the other needs also strengthened security. At times, however, it was also possible to argue that military strength was much more important than other elements in the competition. The Administration tended to denigrate the importance of the sputniks as largely a propaganda stunt, of some psychological and political value but of less importance scientifically and still less militarily. It implied that the military balance of power was of primary significance, and, as Secretary McElroy declared, neither sputnik directly affected that balance. Thus, the significance of any particular Soviet capability can always be minimized by emphasizing the totality of the Soviet threat.

Second, additional difficulties arose simply in estimating military capabilities themselves. Habit as well as interest complicated the problem of assessing Soviet strengths and weaknesses. The traditional view of the Soviet Union as industrially, technologically, and scientifically backward competed with new images of the Soviet Union as the leader of the race into space. Some observers argued that the lack of freedom in a totalitarian society inevitably discouraged and retarded scientific and technological development. Others held that the dissatisfaction of Soviet citizens with the quantity of consumer goods and the opposition to the regime in general were major flaws in the Soviet structure. In a manner faintly reminiscent of *1984*, Allen Dulles said that "Russia's growing strength could be a weakness." [7] One recurring American tendency was to overestimate the time it would take the Soviets to develop particular types of weapons. When they once developed those weapons, it was commonly argued that they were only prototypes and that it would be years before they could be in mass production. Yet other informed analysts warned of the accelerating rate of Soviet achievement and prophesied the day when the Soviet Union was likely to have a decisive military superiority over the United States. Usually, only a dramatic Soviet achievement—such as its first nuclear and thermonuclear explosions—would "trigger" substantial innovations in American strategic programs. (See Chapter V.)

The problem was not only varying estimates of Soviet capabilities but also the absence of any clear set of criteria by which to assess these estimates. The level of military magnitude necessary for deterrence under one set of assumptions and conclusions could be two or three times the size of that required under another set. How could valid argument be distinguished from interested pleading? The difficulty in judging capabilities increased the tendency to subordinate capabilities to tensions and strengthened the role of domestic forces in determining the level of military magnitude. As Warner Schilling has pointed out, no formula exists to relate the probabilities of occurrence of particular events to the quantities of preparation required to deal with those events.[8] Even more troubling was the absence of any clear formula by which to relate Soviet capabilities to the American capabilities required for deterrence. Governmental leaders could almost always find a reasonable interpretation of enemy capabilities which supported their policy preferences. More than that, the differences in interpretation and assessment made a wide variety of other considerations necessary to guide policy-makers to decisions on specific issues.

The difficulties in estimating the strength and relevance of Soviet capabilities inevitably raised doubts about the justification of American military requirements. The consequences of a cutback in defense spending may be concrete for specific military programs but they are seldom concrete in long-run policy implications. Military spending is the largest element in the federal budget; it can always be argued that room exists to eliminate waste and duplication without significantly affecting military strength. The Administration, for instance, may estimate that a half-billion cut in its total spending will mean the difference between a balanced and an unbalanced budget. A reduction of this size would eliminate completely or severely cut any other program of the government. After the Korean War, however, it would have amounted to less than 1.5 percent of the military budget. An Administration naturally feels that such a reduction can be made without seriously affecting the substance of important military programs. Even if the cut does affect the substance of programs and requires, for instance, the elimination of an Army division, it is still difficult to identify precisely what effects that elimination will have on policy. A deterrent can only be shown to be insufficient when it fails to deter. The longer a given level of military force is apparently adequate for deterrence, the greater is the temptation to assume that a slightly lower level might be equally adequate.

Apart from the deterrence of direct aggression, it is also difficult to estimate the effects which any given level of armaments has upon the diplomatic position of the country. In 1957 and 1958, for instance, the Administration declined to implement many recommendations of the Gaither Committee. It did not significantly increase foreign military aid, add to its conventional and limited war capabilities, or construct fall-out shelters for the civilian population. Two years later, how did its failure to do these things affect the American bargaining position in the negotiations over Berlin or its position in the crisis over the U-2? Would the implementation of the Gaither recommendations have deterred Khrushchev from reopening the Berlin question and restrained him from torpedoing the Paris conference? The questions are important but impossible to answer. Despite the common phrase, risks cannot be calculated, they can only be felt. The inability to determine the precise impact of force levels on foreign policy encourages an Administration to believe that the effects of not increasing those levels or of making a small reduction in them will not be very great.

Military magnitude thus tended to be very sensitive to major changes in international tensions but less sensitive to changes in foreign capabilities or minor shifts in international temperature. Without war or crisis, the technological advances and secular growth in the military strength of the Soviet Union and other states appeared insufficient impetus to alter the established equilibrium in American society and to produce corresponding changes in the military strength of the United States. In the absence of changes in the international climate, the domestic political-economic system adjusts to the existing level of military magnitude and perpetuates it. Hence, serious problems appear in the relation between military magnitude and deterrence. If a potential enemy greatly increased its military capabilities, a strategy of deterrence might require a comparable increase in the magnitude of the American effort in order to maintain the existing balance and to reduce the likelihood of war. Changes in the magnitude of the American effort, however, apparently depend upon changes in the likelihood of war. If there is "no alternative to peace" there may also be no alternative to the existing general level of armaments. The success of American policy in avoiding any further limited engagements, such as the Korean War, may also reduce the possibility of any significant increases in the defense effort. If this situation were to continue for long, conceivably the future effort required to increase American military magnitude to deter war might in itself increase the likelihood of war. Barring this, a minor war scare could be the alternative to war itself. As Herman Kahn has suggested, awareness by the Soviet leaders of this relationship between international tensions and American defense activities is probably a primary deterrent to major Soviet provocations and minor aggressions.[9] Soviet interests would be best served by relative international harmony and continued development of Soviet military capabilities.

Thus, in a sense, the long-run success of deterrence may depend upon its short-run failure. The prevention of minor aggressions may lessen the ability of the democratic states to prevent a major aggression. In all states, the development of military forces to meet probable future threats presents serious political difficulties. Even in the Soviet Union, dangers have to be located in the immediate future to have significant immediate impact upon military capabilities.[10] Certainly in the United States predictions of future unfavorable changes in relative military capabilities are unlikely by themselves to produce immediate major increases in military magnitude. By 1960 the old feast-and-famine pattern had only partially disappeared, and a new sensitivity to the balance of power had only partially emerged. American military capabilities were shaped more by current political demands and needs than by expert predictions of the future balance of military forces.

16. DOMESTIC INFLUENCES: SPENDING, TAXES, AND BALANCED BUDGETS

Inability to define precisely the needs of national security enhanced the role of domestic influences and pressures in the Great Equation. The size and shape of the military effort were molded by the political struggles among the supporters of security programs, domestic programs, lower taxes, and balanced budgets. This conflict continued throughout the post-World War II years. After 1955, however, the emergence of the balance of terror reduced the importance of specific changes in Soviet and American capabilities. After 1953, the absence of war involving American forces also moderated the impact of changes in the international temperature. On the other hand, the pressure of the components of the "Great Equation" became more intense after 1955, and domestic considerations became more important in shaping the size of the military effort. In the competition among them, domestic programs and tax stability seemed to have definite advantages over balanced budgets and military programs.

DOMESTIC PROGRAMS

From the late 1940s until 1955–56 federal domestic spending was remarkably stable. In FY 1949, budget expenditures for domestic programs—excluding national security, international affairs and finance, and interest—were $15.1 billion. In FY 1955, they were $15.3 billion, a substantial reduction if inflation is taken into account. Total nonforeign policy budget expenditures increased by only about one billion dollars during those six years. Cash expenditures increased more substantially, but this increase was just a foretaste of things to come. Between 1956 and 1960 budgetary expenditures for domestic programs rose from $15.3 billion to $19.8 billion. Total cash expenditures for nonforeign policy purposes increased by over $18 billion to a level more than double that of ten years earlier. Comparable increases took place in state and local spending, which rose from $31.3 billion in 1954 to $50.9 billion in 1960.

The increases in domestic spending reflected powerful and diverse political forces and demands. Many programs in agriculture, natural resources, labor, and welfare dated back to the 1930s or middle 1940s. By the mid-1950s they had become accepted responsibilities of the government. In most cases, they were supported by potent domestic interests. One group which favored curtailing these programs reluctantly admitted in 1959:

We are not sanguine about the possibilities of holding non-security expenditures to the total budgeted by the President. The lobbies for veterans, agriculture, housing and many other Federal programs affecting particular groups, industries, and regions, have amply demonstrated their ability to protect, and even to enlarge, the gains they have made at the expense of the mass of taxpayers. Recent experience shows how difficult it is for the Congress to reduce spending in the face of the unrelenting pressures of self-interest groups. And there is no indication that the Congress will be able to resist these pressures any better this year than it has in the past.[11]

Laws often authorized and required expenditures when certain criteria were met or certain conditions prevailed. Congressional legislation removed from the annual control of Congress and the executive agencies the rate and level of spending for veterans benefits, grants-in-aid to states for public assistance, federal highway grants, agricultural price supports, and of course, interest on the public debt. Between FY 1950 and FY 1955 these "relatively uncontrollable major programs" absorbed between $12 to $15 billion dollars a year and made up from 55.7 percent to 68.2 percent of the non-national security expenditures of the federal budget.

In addition to the older, established programs, newer ones came

TABLE 3. BUDGET EXPENDITURES IN TERMS OF CONTROLLABILITY
        FOR FISCAL YEARS 1950–1955 ($ billion)

	1950	1951	1952	1953	1954	1955
National security	13.0	22.3	43.8	50.3	46.5	40.6
Relatively uncontrollable major programs	15.6	12.1	12.3	14.9	14.3	16.3
All other	11.0	9.6	9.3	9.2	7.0	7.6
Total	39.6	44.0	65.4	74.3	67.8	64.6

Source: *The Budget of the United States Government for the Fiscal Year Ending June 30, 1955*, p. M37; *ibid., Fiscal Year 1956*, p. M24; *ibid., Fiscal Year 1957*, p. M13.

into existence reflecting the emerging needs of the 1950s and 1960s. Even the Eisenhower Administration recognized that the postponed demands for domestic spending programs could no longer be resisted, and inaugurated or accepted new programs for highways, education, civil aviation and communications facilities, medical research, peaceful use of atomic energy, small business loans, and expansion and modernization of the postal service.[12] Other services and programs in housing, urban redevelopment, and public assistance demanded more and more funds. Many individuals and groups vigorously criticized the Administration for not allocating enough to these needs. The "low" projection of the report of the Rockefeller Brothers Fund on American economic and social needs forecast an increase in nondefense spending at all levels of government of over $40 billion by 1967. The growth of the governmental programs was solidly rooted in an affluent society's deficits in public services.[13]

The Eisenhower Administration came into office committed to a reduction in federal spending. After only a few months, however, Budget Director Joseph M. Dodge "lamented the difficulty of putting through budget cuts which collided with the local interests of members of Congress, particularly when these cuts affected social welfare, veterans' benefits, and public works." The President later argued that:

If balancing the budget was everything, why should only the military programs on which the security of the country depended be sacrificed? Why shouldn't the sacrifice be spread through veterans' benefits, the farm program and grants-in-aid to the states—obligations, he said, which had been assumed at a time when the country was not under compulsion to spend heavy sums for security?[14]

Despite the President's desires, the reductions in total spending which his Administration achieved in its first two years came entirely from national security. After the Soviet sputniks demonstrated the need for increased security expenditures, the President again announced his intention to reduce domestic spending. Defense, he said in his Oklahoma City speech, required "tax money, lots of it." The principal source of these funds would have to be drastic reductions in domestic spending: "savings of the kind we need can come about only through cutting out or deferring entire categories of activities." Despite presidential pressure, budgetary officials found it almost impossible to make large reductions in the major nondefense programs. The President's January budget, the biggest in peacetime history, proposed an increase of $800 million in foreign policy expenditures for FY 1959 over estimated expenditures for FY 1958 and an increase of over $300 million in domestic spending. Even so, the reports that a number of proposed programs in labor, welfare, and resources had been eliminated from the budget stimulated protests from both Republicans and Democrats in Congress.[15] The prospects for any really significant reductions in nondefense spending had thus disappeared even before the full impact of the recession dealt them the *coup de grâce*.

If the general economic conditions of the 1950s continued, no Administration was likely to reduce domestic expenditures significantly. Under an Administration more favorably inclined toward welfare objectives and a broad role for the government in the economy the rate of increase probably would be much faster. "If George M. Humphrey could not cut down government spending," David Demarest Lloyd inquired, "who can?" [16]

TAXATION

While some political pressures drove domestic expenditures relentlessly upward, others tended to freeze the federal tax structure. General increases and decreases in tax rates were usually linked with shifts from war to peace. Reductions in rates were approved in 1945, 1948, and 1954. Increases were voted in 1950 and 1951. For fifteen years after World War II no general increase in tax rates occurred in peacetime. Decreases in rates were more frequently considered and presumably were easier to achieve than increases—a tax reduction bill was on its way through Congress when the Korean War broke out—but even decreases pose difficult political problems. Major changes in the structure, upward or downward, mean the adjustment of a complex political-economic balance involving a large number of groups. General agreement could exist on the desirability of an increase or decrease in rates, yet change could still be stymied by the difficulties of allocating the benefits from the reductions and the burdens of the increases. The status quo tends to be perpetuated because each group fears that it may be worse off after a general revision of taxes than it had been before.

The changes which did take place in the tax structure usually dealt with particular rates and provisions. Increases in social security taxes and the highway excise tax added to federal revenues although they were not recorded in the administrative budget. More significant was what one tax expert described as the "accelerating trend" toward special tax provisions and preferential tax treatment for particular groups.[17] Special tax benefits for one group stimulated claims for similar treatment by other groups, and the result was an increasing complexity in revenue legislation and a growing gap between the nominal statutory rates and the effective rates paid by many influential groups. In a sense this was piecemeal tax reduction, in which those groups with the greatest political influence secured tax benefits first and then other groups, with less political power but in comparable economic circumstances, attempted to secure similar benefits in the name of equity. The "erosion" of the revenue structure made the tax rates less progressive in actuality than they appeared on the surface. Just as the political system seemed to encourage expenditure programs desired by special groups, so also it seemed to encourage tax benefit provisions desired by special (and in a few cases the same) groups.

The more difficult it is to make fundamental changes in the tax structure, the more tax revenues reflect the general level of economic activity. Receipts go up in prosperity, down in recessions. Despite the erosion of the tax base, moreover, the income tax is still fundamentally progressive in nature. Thus, increases in national income, whether real or inflationary, increase tax revenues at an even quicker rate. Between calendar 1955 and calendar 1958, for instance, the gross national product increased by 9.9 percent. Between FY 1955 and FY 1958, federal tax receipts increased by 14.4 percent in the administrative budget.[18] In part the increase in revenues represented the governmental share of the real growth of the economy. In part it was simply the result of inflation, which had roughly the same effect on taxes as an across-the-board increase in tax rates. To some extent, of course, the increases were self-defeating; as more taxpayers moved into upper brackets the demands for special benefits also increased. So long as the economy continued to expand, however, the political stalemate over tax legislation did not necessarily mean no increases in tax revenues. The growth of revenues was a graphic and concrete, albeit only a partial, example of how in American society political problems can be dissolved in economic abundance. It was an open question, however, whether even continuing prosperity would increase federal revenues at a rate sufficient to offset increased expenditures for domestic and foreign policy programs. The federal budget was unbalanced in eight of the first fourteen years of the Cold War, although at least three of the eight were recession years. Despite an expanding economy, the political stalemate over tax rates usually meant either lower expenditures or unbalanced budgets.

BALANCED BUDGETS

Throughout much of the period between 1945 and 1960 strong inflationary pressures existed in the economy. Between 1945 and 1948 prices increased drastically as a result of the removal of controls and the release of the pent-up demand accumulated during World War II. Once this pressure had exhausted itself, prices stabilized and even declined slightly between 1948 and 1950. A second inflationary movement got under way shortly after the start of the Korean War, largely the result of scare buying and the expectation of shortages. Prices reached their peak in 1951 and then leveled off. They remained fairly stable from 1952 through 1955. In the spring of 1956, however, they started upward. After a rise of about six points, the wholesale price index stabilized at about 119 during the 1958 recession. Consumer prices, on the other hand, rose steadily past their previous peak of 115.4 to a new high of 126.8 in September, 1960. Unlike the other two inflationary movements this price increase was not related to wartime shortages—actual or anticipated. Economists differed over its immediate causes, but all agreed that it reflected forces which could be expected in the normal peacetime economy of the Cold War.

Both Administrations employed many means to curb the recurring inflationary pressures. Key figures in both, however, believed that an unbalanced federal budget was a major stimulus to inflation; consequently, both made major efforts to balance the budget. Undoubtedly other motives also contributed to the desire to balance the budget, but the fear of inflation was a primary one. The increasing numbers of white collar workers, the aged, the beneficiaries of pension and retirement plans, fixed-salaried individuals, all had a clear interest in the maintenance of the purchasing power of the dollar. No politician could explicitly endorse inflation. The leaders of both Administrations were convinced that inflation was a bad and potentially disastrous phenomenon for the country. Mr. Truman, as Forrestal said, was "a hard-money man if ever I saw one . . ." A balanced budget was always a major goal of the Truman Administration; this goal led it to oppose the tax reductions in 1947 and 1948 and to urge tax increases in 1950 and 1951. One of Mr. Truman's proudest boasts was that, except for its last fiscal year, his Administration took more money into the Treasury than it paid out.[19] President Eisenhower's even greater concern apparently dated back to his observation of the effects of the runaway inflations in wartime and postwar Europe. At the *Helena* conference Eisenhower stressed the overriding need to achieve a stable dollar.[20]

During the Eisenhower Administration's first term, prices remained reasonably stable. The upswing which began in 1956, however, stimulated the Administration to make extensive use of monetary and fiscal policy to limit the inflationary movement. When prices continued to rise during and after the 1957–1958 recession, the Administration gave increasing prominence to the campaign against inflation. This campaign centered upon the need to balance the budget. The June, 1959, report of the Cabinet Committee on Price Stability for Economic Growth, chaired by Vice President Nixon, declared that "Not only is it imperative that the budget be balanced in the fiscal year starting next month, but it is important that the national debt be reduced." The committee warned of "strong pressures for irresponsible spending" and declared that to yield to these pressures "would create serious inflationary forces." Simultaneously the President, in speeches and at his news conferences, was actively arousing public support to hold down expenditures and to balance the budget.[21] The President's appeals on the inflation issue struck a responsive chord with the public and helped temper congressional desires to increase spending.

The pressures to increase domestic spending and to stabilize the tax structure came largely from nongovernmental groups. Many business and other groups also supported a balanced budget, but the initiative in the efforts to achieve this goal rested largely with the Administration. The Administration's ability to achieve its goal, however, was uncertain. Before World War II, price movements had generally been cyclical in nature. Upward trends were counterbalanced by subsequent deflationary movements. After World War II, however, powerful forces created a secular movement upward. The movement was occasionally halted (1948–1950, 1952–1955) but it was never clearly reversed. The government was always on the defensive in its struggle against inflation. The budget surpluses which the Administration achieved in prosperity never equalled the deficits occasioned by recessions. The Administration simply lacked the power to control the inflationary forces in the economy. The extent to which its spokesmen urged the leaders of business and labor voluntarily to act responsibly to ease inflationary pressures was in some measure an indication of the weakness of its position.

MILITARY PROGRAMS

The forces supporting domestic spending, those obstructing major change in the tax structure and simultaneously eroding the existing structure, and the strong pressure to balance the budget, all were part of the framework within which the magnitude of the military effort was considered. In addition, of course, other influences and considerations existed more directly related to security needs and the military effort. In large part, these influences consisted of the Administration's direct perceptions of and reactions to the international environment. In part, however, they also involved the structure of the political interests supporting the military effort. In a crisis or war, support for defense spending comes from the community at large: everyone is for whatever is necessary for survival, security, or victory. Such widespread support is a temporary phenomenon. Normally, most groups in society have other primary concerns than national security. In the absence of acute international crisis or war, Administration decisions on the size of the defense effort balance the relative strength of competing demands for resources, on the one hand, and the strength of the permanent structure of interests and forces supporting military claims, on the other.

The traditional feast-and-famine cycle in military spending reflected the old pattern of widespread but transitory support for military needs. Presumably a stable military effort had to rest upon a stable structure of political interests which would lead to a reasonable balance of power or equilibrium between military claims and competing claims on resources. The development of a stable structure of support for the military effort, however, was affected by three key factors.

1. In the American system of government, stable and secure claims on resources usually rest upon well-organized political interests with effective access to key decision-making points in the government.[22] The principal organized groups supporting military claims were the armed services. As executive agencies and also as military agencies, however, the freedom of the services to promote their claims was limited. They were much more susceptible to control by the Administration than were the supporters of the more significant domestic programs. The distinguishing aspect of the military programs, as compared with most major domestic programs, was the relative weakness of their organized support outside the executive branch. Military programs had a widespread latent general popularity, but loosely structured favorable public attitudes could not be turned into effective political support against the wishes of the Administration in power. For organized support, the crucial governmental group, apart from the military, was the State Department. The State Department, however, suffered from the same disability as the military; it was subject to Administration control as an agency of the executive branch, and it lacked a well-organized domestic clientele. Its head, however, was usually a much more important member of the Administration than the Secretary of Defense or the Chairman of the Joint Chiefs of Staff. In both

the Truman and Eisenhower Administrations the support of the Secretary of State was the decisive element in expanding or maintaining the military effort. Alone, the military were no match for the Treasury and the Bureau of the Budget. In 1948 Secretary of State Marshall was busy with mutual assistance and did not back Forrestal's unsuccessful efforts to increase the defense budget.[23] In 1950 the leadership of the State Department would have made possible some increase in military spending even without the Korean War, despite the unfavorable attitudes of the civilian leadership of the Defense Department. In the summer of 1955 a strong economy movement was underway to achieve a balanced budget in FY 1956. The Secretary of State successfully helped the Defense Department to resist these pressures. At best, however, the State Department was an uncertain ally of the military. It had other, sometimes conflicting, primary interests. Secretary Acheson was almost alone among the Cold War Secretaries of State in giving extensive attention to military programs. Secretary Dulles, in contrast, usually "seemed not to be well informed on military-scientific developments having an important bearing on foreign policy and tended to regard budgetary questions as being outside his proper concern." [24] In 1957 and 1958 Dulles opposed the Gaither Committee recommendations and refused to back expansion of limited war capabilities.

Apart from congressmen and the State Department the only other potentially important source of organized support for military programs was the private groups which benefited from the programs. A sustained high level of military spending created powerful political interests—a "military-industrial complex," in Eisenhower's words—in its continuation. Undoubtedly, a drastic decrease in arms spending would stimulate intense and far-reaching opposition. (See Section 20.) There was, however, less of a "munitions lobby" than there were "munitions lobbies." The Department of Defense had some 40,000 prime contractors.[25] Many industrial, commercial, and geographical groups did what they could to protect and to expand their own shares of the defense program. In particular instances group pressure secured the continuation of a program which might otherwise have been suspended or the award of a contract which might otherwise have received a low priority. From the viewpoint of the executive attempting to formulate a coherent and rational military program, these pressures tended to produce a misallocation of resources. It is unlikely, however, that their activity significantly increased the overall defense effort. Each group was primarily concerned only with those programs or contracts which affected it. No one group or even coalition of groups existed to mobilize support for the defense program as a whole. The victories of one firm or one locality usually represented defeats for another firm or a different locality. The activities of the defense contractors were much more relevant to interservice competition than they were to competition between civil and military purposes. (See Sections 28 and 29.)

2. Not only did the claimants for the defense programs lack support outside the executive branch, but as military agencies they were presumed to be subject to "civilian control." If this term had any operational meaning, it was that the Administration had more authority over the armed services than it had over the normal domestic agency. In part this control reflected the inability of congressional or private groups outside the Administration to affect the size of the military effort. In part, also, it reflected the willingness of the military leaders to acquiesce in the legitimacy of the limits and conditions which the Administration might lay down. By and large the military were acutely aware of the specialized nature of their competence and the fact that the overall size of the defense effort had to reflect a wide range of nonmilitary considerations. To a degree the military were themselves the prisoners of a feast-and-famine psychology, accepting as proper the restrictions imposed on them.*

3. The reluctance of the military to challenge the external limits placed upon the defense effort stimulated their criticism of each other's requests and programs. The disunity of the military, in turn, tended to strengthen the Administration and to increase its ability to limit the defense effort. Whenever the Administration wished to reduce the program or funds of one service, it could almost always count upon the acquiescence or support of the other services. Expert military opinion usually could be as effectively in-

* On military acquiescence in established policy, see Chapter II, Section 8, Chapter V, Section 22, and Chapter VI, Section 28.

voked to justify cuts as to justify expansion. No Administration was ever confronted with a united military establishment backing a single coherent military plan. If an Administration had ever been so confronted, it would have been extremely difficult and perhaps impossible for the Administration not to have acquiesced in the military demands. Divided against themselves, however, the military limited themselves. Interservice rivalry was a key element in the control of the Administration over the size of the defense effort.

17. THE ADMINISTRATION AND THE MAGNITUDE OF THE MILITARY EFFORT
THE ADMINISTRATION'S PROBLEM

Writers on military affairs often implicitly assume that a major problem for an Administration is how to secure the support of Congress and the public for the level of military effort which it thinks necessary. Actually, however, the Administration's problem, as the two Administrations saw it, was a different one. Both Administrations were more concerned with finding means of keeping the level of military spending down than with finding means of pushing it up. The persistent controversy was between military and congressional groups supporting the multiplication of programs and increases in military spending, and the Administration struggling to control the military effort. Two factors were primarily responsible for this situation.

First, the concerns of the President transcend national security. He has to take into account other needs and is responsible for other goals. "It is inherent in the obligation of an administration," the Secretary of Defense declared in 1959, "to consider not only what its obligations are in national security, but what its obligations are in the administration of the resources of the country for the various projects that have to be taken care of by the whole thing.... [T]here is no other branch of the Government that has the responsibility for putting all of these needs of the United States together and taking the responsibility for submitting a single program." [26] Harry S. Truman agreed that through the budget, "one of the most serious responsibilities of the President," the Administration seeks to achieve "the proper relation between the long-range integrity of our debt management, the basic and pressing economic and social needs of the people of the United States, and the needs of our allies." [27]

From the presidential viewpoint national defense is a special interest, even though an extremely important one. Hence both Presidents tended to view the military claimants more as antagonists than as allies. All of the services, Truman recalls, "made excessive demands" and "frequently brought pressure to force me to alter the budget which had been carefully worked out to achieve balance with the other needs of the government and our economy as a whole." As a result, he "compelled the three branches to be specific and exact about the requirements they considered essential. Every single item in the military budget had to be justified to me and to the Secretary of the Treasury." [28] Similarly, President Eisenhower denounced the "parochial" generals who were dissatisfied with their funds and demanded equally strict justifications of military appropriations requests.[29]

As a conflict between "generalist" and "specialist" the struggle between the Administration and the military might be assumed to be less intense than that between the Administration and claimants for goals less general than national security. In actuality, however, the conflict was in many respects more intense in the military area than in other areas because of the differences in Administration power over the components of the Great Equation. The Administration can influence the number and scope of domestic programs. But, as the record of the Eisenhower Administration amply demonstrates, the interested groups and their supporters in Congress can establish and expand domestic programs despite the opposition of the Administration. Also, the Administration cannot exercise exclusive control over the tax system. Tax legislation requires the acquiescence not only of the Ways and Means and Finance Committees but also of other groups with varied and conflicting interests. In contrast, the Administration is relatively free to unbalance the budget if it desires to do so. Both the Truman and Eisenhower Administrations, however, were reluctant to accept this alternative. As a result, their tendency was to restrict the national security effort. This was within their effective control. Neither Congress nor the public was willing to prevent the Administration from maintaining the forces which it thought necessary, and neither was able to compel the Administration to maintain more than it thought necessary. For the Administration, a cut in national security spending is easier to achieve than a cut in most domestic programs, and the Treasury can more easily impose a ceiling on the military budget than it can secure increased taxes from Congress. The groups directly interested in domestic programs and tax decisions play a greater role in making those decisions than the military services play in determining the level of the military effort. The arena of decision-making for domestic programs, in short, is broader than it is for military programs, and the freedom of action of the Administration is correspondingly less. The greater power of the Administration over the military budget is the crucial factor limiting that budget. An aggressive, confident, hard-driving Administration can win a struggle with the military while it may face defeat on other fronts. Throughout the period from 1946 to 1960 the ceiling on the military effort was set not by Congress, not by public opinion, and, most certainly, not by the economy, but by the deliberate choice of the Administration.[30]

Both Administrations made continuing efforts to keep military spending within prescribed limits and also launched major economy drives in 1949, 1953, and 1957. In comparison, only once during peacetime, in 1948, when war seemed imminent, did the Administration attempt to stimulate a rearmament movement; as soon as the likelihood of war decreased, it immediately reversed that movement. In four instances, when the Administration was urged by groups within its ranks or closely associated with it to arouse public support for additional military effort, the Administration consciously and consistently refused to do so. In 1945 and 1946, Forrestal, Harriman, Kennan, and other members of the Truman Administration wanted the President to explain to the nation our deteriorating relations with Russia and thereby curb the drastic reductions in American military might. The President refused to do so. In the spring of 1950 the authors of NSC 68 wanted the President to make public the essence of their findings to pave the way for doubling or tripling the military budget. Again the President refused to act. In 1953 the Eisenhower Administration was urged to launch an "Operation Candor," informing the public of the horror of nuclear weapons to arouse support both for defensive measures and an arms agreement. The President watered down these recommendations until they finally emerged as the "atoms-for-peace" proposal. In 1957, the members of the Gaither Committee urged that the substance of their report be released to arouse public support for their program. Again the President refused to act. The 1948 spring rearmament drive stands alone as a conscious attempt by the Administration to increase significantly the level of military effort in peacetime.

The indeterminacy of the external factors affecting the magnitude of the military effort and the influence of domestic needs were reflected in the "remainder" method by which the Administration calculated its goal in military spending.[31] In both the Truman Administration before the Korean War and in the Eisenhower Administration after the war, the tendency was: 1) to estimate the revenues of the government or total expenditures possible within the existing debt limit; 2) to deduct from this figure the estimated costs of domestic programs and foreign aid; and 3) to allocate the remainder to the military. In 1946, for instance, the President informed the Secretaries of War and the Navy that the armed services could have one-third of the total budget for FY 1948 after fixed charges had been met. "It was here," Walter Millis points out, "that President Truman for the first time laid down the arithmetical approach that he was to adopt toward the military budget in the ensuing two years." [32] In 1949 and 1950, as tax revenues decreased, the Administration's goal in military spending moved down with them. In the debate over NSC 68 in early 1950, the Director of the Budget Bureau, Frank Pace, continued to insist upon adherence to this formula.[33] During the first two years of the Korean War the remainder method was not used. Immediately after the war, however, it reappeared in the development of the military spending estimates for the New Look by a JCS subcommittee working with advice from the CEA, the Budget Bureau, the Treasury, and the Defense Department Comptroller. "From figures that we obtained on prospective national income over the long pull," Admiral Radford said, "we eliminated the more or less fixed expenses, and within the remaining estimated amount, we did feel ... that we came up with a military program which was adequate for the security of the

United States."³⁴ Three years later, Charles Murphy reported that "there is only one hard-and-fast restriction that the President has imposed upon the Pentagon in its development of forces: that the cost of the forces be financed on a pay-as-you-go basis—that is, within a balanced budget."³⁵ Amid the welter of contingencies and risks, probabilities and predictions concerning the international situation, the remainder method enabled the Administration to produce a definite dollar figure for the military budget. Yet it also reflected the political fact that it was easier for the Administration to limit military spending than it was to reduce domestic spending or increase revenues. The method was, in short, both precise and practical.

Decisions to add or to expand military programs and decisions to reduce them were usually made through different processes. Reductions usually took place in the budgetary process. They were formulated first in terms of the limited funds available and then translated into changes in programs and goals. Decisions to add or increase individual military programs, on the other hand, were usually made through the Joint Chiefs and NSC. They were formulated in strategic categories; they dealt with the ends of policy and the substantive programs necessary to achieve those ends. In effect, program increases required previous authorization from the NSC, JCS, or other authoritative official or agency to justify a claim on the resources apportioned through the budgetary process. Even so, prior authorization did not guarantee a program funds. The continuing concern of the Administration to restrict military spending thus made the budgetary process a focal point in the determination of military policy. It also made the Bureau of the Budget the Administration's key instrument in achieving its policy objectives. As a result, much criticism which could have been directed at the Administration was directed instead at the Bureau.³⁶

The military budgetary process is divisible into three phases: the pre-Congress executive phase, the congressional phase, and the post-Congress executive phase. For the overall magnitude of the military effort and the scope of major programs, the first and the third are far more important than the second. The economizing process is essentially executive in nature. The military effort is limited by the Bureau of the Budget and the Treasury, not the

Appropriations committees. The budget is still a principal means of civilian control of the military, but it is a weapon wielded by executive agencies, not congressional ones.

PRE-CONGRESS CONTROLS

In the pre-Congress phase of the budgetary process the Administration can control estimated levels of appropriation and expenditure by means of ceilings, reductions, and indoctrination.[37] Except during the Korean War, initial ceilings on the military budget were a common phenomenon in both the Truman and the Eisenhower Administrations. The Truman Administration established ceilings of $11.5 billion in FY 1948, $11 billion in FY 1949, $15 billion in FY 1950, and $13.5 billion in FY 1951. These ceilings were issued at the beginning of intensive work on the budget in May, June, or July of each year. In each case the ceilings were effective: the presidential appropriations request or expenditure estimate sent to Congress in January was always lower than the ceiling announced six to eight months earlier.[38]

After the Korean War the Eisenhower Administration returned to ceilings on both a three-year and an annual basis. In the formulation of the New Look military program for FY 1955–1957, the Joint Chiefs set $32.9 billion as the level of expenditures to be maintained over the long haul.[39] Three years later, in the New New Look studies of 1956, Administration leaders and the Joint Chiefs agreed on a ceiling of $40 billion for FY 1958–1960. These goals were supplemented by additional ceilings laid down at the beginning of the annual budgetary process. In the summer and fall of 1953, for instance, the Bureau of the Budget suggested a ceiling of $40 billion on military expenditures and $30 billion on new appropriations for FY 1955. A year later it directed that expenditures and appropriations for FY 1956 should be less than those for FY 1955. In October, 1955, the Administration set an expenditure goal of $34.5 billion for FY 1957. In the summer of 1957 Secretary Wilson imposed a ceiling of $38 billion on military appropriations and expenditures for FY 1959. In the summer of 1958 a ceiling of $41.75 billion was established on expenditures for FY 1960. Except when rising costs or Soviet sputniks intervened, the Administration's January budget requests and estimates usually fell below the ceilings established at the beginning of the executive budgetary process.[40]

The great advantage of an early ceiling to the Administration was that it helped to head off large military requests which the Administration would then be forced to reduce. Ceilings, however, also made the Administration peculiarly vulnerable to the charge that it was putting fiscal considerations before national security. Before the military implications of the Cold War were fully appreciated, this was not very significant, and in the late 1940s the Truman Administration did not hesitate to call a ceiling a "ceiling." Subsequently, Administrations became more cautious in their terminology. The NSC established a "point of departure" of $45 billion for new military appropriations for FY 1953. In 1953 the President and the NSC established a "projected level" of military expenditures for FY 1955, and in 1958 the Administration spoke of an "initial budget planning target" for FY 1960.[41] While the phrases changed, the reality remained the same. When the ceilings were not supplemented by other means of control, the Administration had to compel the military services to divide among themselves the total which was allocated to defense. As the experience of the FY 1950 budget suggests, this was no easy task. Nonetheless, even in this case, neither the Chiefs nor Secretary Forrestal were able to dissuade the President from his course. In general, early Administration ceilings which had firm presidential and Budget Bureau support effectively limited both military appropriations requests and actual military spending.

Often the ceiling was supplemented by other forms of control. Also, in some years the Administration established no ceiling at all; in these cases it usually had no alternative but to make substantial reductions in the budgetary requests of the services. How substantial these reductions were over the years is almost impossible to say because of the difficulty of identifying what the initial service requests were. Naturally, these requests were "fundamentally for planning and negotiating purposes." [42] They were made to be cut, and the real meaning of the overall cuts which were made by the Administration would be visible only to those who were privy to the intentions and tactics of both sides in the vertical bargaining process. The reductions by the Administration, however, were always substantial, varying from a low of about 10 percent to a high of about 40 percent. The difference between the service requests and the Administration requests was always much greater than that between the Administration requests and the congressional appropriation.

Although the budget estimates may have been in the process of formulation for six to nine months, the crucial reductions usually came at the very end of the executive budgetary process, in November and December, just before the budget was submitted to Congress. "In this process," as one Hoover Commission task force pointed out, "90 percent or more of the previously prepared detailed estimates become practically useless. Tens of thousands of man-hours of time reflected in the preparation of the detailed estimates is pushed aside as the top program and budget officials make hasty and relatively arbitrary cuts in order to bring the totals of the detailed estimates in line with the much lower budgetary targets." [43] Key issues were often left to the very last moment. In the development of the FY 1950 budget, for instance, it was not until December 20 that Forrestal made his last effort to get presidential approval for $700 million more than the $14.4 billion ceiling which the President had established earlier. In 1951 the presidential decision to stretch out the Air Force build-up and to reduce the military budget request by $3 billion was made in December. On December 5, 1953, the military services requested appropriations of $35.9 billion for FY 1955. Within ten days the Department of Defense whittled these requests down to $31.2 billion and submitted them to the Bureau of the Budget on December 15. On December 11 the National Security Council reduced the Army's FY 1955 year-end strength from 1,281,000 men, earlier approved by Secretary Wilson, to 1,164,000 men (later increased to 1,172,000 men).[44] The number of divisions in the Army remained in doubt right up to the last minute; Secretary Wilson stated on January 8 that the Army divisional strength "wasn't settled yet." [45] The next year the pattern was repeated. The Defense Department originally planned total manpower of 2,945,000 at the end of FY 1956. Just before the Department submitted its final estimates to the Budget Bureau, however, the President suggested that the Secretary of Defense "take another look at the situation." The result was a cut in the planned goal to 2,815,000 men, announced to the press by the Secretary of Defense on December 20. After vigorous protests from the Army, the President, on January 5, 1955, eased this cut, establishing yet another goal of 2,850,000 men.[46] Similarly, in the development of the FY 1958 budget, Secretary Wilson reduced the original service requests of over $48 billion to $40 billion. He presented this figure to the President on December 7, 1956. Over the objections of the Secretary of Defense, the President reduced the figure to $38.5 billion. This, of course, necessitated further last-minute cuts in programs, and the Secretary of Defense returned from his Christmas vacation on December 27 still uncertain how many wings would be in the Air Force.[47] * The final stages in the formulation of the FY 1961 budget saw the elimination of the Air Force F-108 fighter, the reduction in the B-70 bomber program, cuts of 5,000 men each in the Air Force and the Navy, and the elimination of a second nuclear-powered aircraft carrier. Even so, a National Security Council meeting of November 25, it was reported, left "some major policy issues . . . still unresolved."[48] The process of agency request and Administration reduction inevitably meant that often the most important decisions were made at the end of the executive consideration of the budget. Almost always the process culminated in last minute personal decisions by the President, in which he completed the reductions begun by the Defense Department Comptroller and the Bureau of the Budget.

The extent to which an Administration relies upon early ceilings or last-minute reductions directly affects the role of civilian and military officials in the budgetary process. If primary reliance is placed upon an early ceiling, the heavy work of reducing military budget requests and allocating the total funds for defense among the services tends to fall upon the military themselves. In the FY 1950 budget a hard ceiling was established early in the process and firmly maintained by the President and the Budget Bureau. As a result, the National Military Establishment had to make repeated

---

* On December 7, 1956, President Eisenhower commented that: "You know, I've been working on this budget one way or another since 1928, and I'll be darned if I've ever seen it fail—in the last ten days every one goes into a flap." *New York Herald Tribune*, Dec. 8, 1956, p. 7.

efforts to produce an agreed-upon allocation within the presidential limit of $15 billion. Early in the summer of 1948 Forrestal directed the Joint Chiefs to establish a Budget Advisory Committee. In August, this committee, known as the McNarney Board and including officers representing all three services, began to review and reduce the service requests. These initially totaled $30 billion. By the end of September the McNarney Board had brought them down to $23.6 billion. The presidential ceiling, however, was still $15 billion, and on October 6 Forrestal demanded from the Joint Chiefs "a definitive recommendation from you, as an entity, as to the division of funds in the 1949–50 budget—specifically as to the allocations to the respective Services, under a ceiling of $14.4 billion." [49] The following day the Chiefs reported they were unable to agree upon a division of this figure. During the next month, however, they did work up an agreed-upon allocation of a budget of $17.5 billion. The President, however, stuck by his $15 billion ceiling. Finally, in the face of this pressure, the Chiefs and Forrestal produced on December 1 an apportionment of funds based on a budget of $15,022,000,000.*

The procedure in the development of the FY 1952 budget was very different. No ceiling was laid down in advance, and initial uncoordinated service requests amounted to $104 billion. The job of reducing this amount to what the Administration believed desirable and feasible fell largely to the civilians. A Budget Advisory Committee was created, consisting of the Under-Secretaries of the Navy and the Air Force and the Assistant Secretary of the Army. This committee made a detailed and intensive review of the military budget from the middle of February to the middle of April (because of the Korean War the normal budget schedule was delayed about four months). Personnel from the Defense Department Comptroller's office and the Budget Bureau worked with the committee. By the elimination of duplication, over-financing, and items considered desirable but unnecessary, the Budget Committee brought the appropriations request down to $60 billion. The work

* The formulation of the FY 1951 budget, which also was developed under a firm ceiling, followed a similar pattern, with the Joint Chiefs collectively, Generals Eisenhower and Bradley as presiding officers of the Chiefs, and a military Budget Advisory Committee under Admiral Carney all playing significant roles.

of the committee also revealed a number of important policy questions which were resolved in a two-day conference of the service secretaries, the Chiefs of Staff, and representatives of the Budget Bureau and the Secretary of Defense. In the ceiling process, the final work on the budget devolved on the military men and agencies. In the reduction process, it was done by the civilian secretaries and budget agencies.

Early ceilings and late reductions were "objective" means of control by the Administration over the military effort.[50] Either the Administration defined its position first and held it against military pleas or the military advanced their claims first and the Administration reduced them. Either procedure involved conflict and bargaining. The Administration in particular, but also the military, had distinct interests in minimizing this overt conflict. Consequently, the Administration often made considerable efforts to change the preferences and demands of the military leaders by broadening the range of factors which the military considered and making it coincide more with that of the Administration. In effect, these were efforts to persuade and to educate, attempts to ease the conflicts inherent in objective control by the Administration over the military by substituting for it a form of subjective control.

In the formulation of the FY 1951 budget Administration leaders persuaded General Bradley and other members of the Joint Chiefs that the economy could not afford more than a $13 billion budget. Taking these economic and military factors into consideration, the military supported the Administration's budget figures before Congress. In 1953 the new Administration's philosophy that a strong economy was a fundamental basis of national security implied that the military should consider the effects of their programs and spending on the economy. In the formulation of the New Look and in the preparation of the FY 1955 budget the Chiefs accepted and implicitly approved the fiscal limitations developed by the Administration and, in form at least, even participated in the making of these calculations.[51] In 1958, the Chiefs attempted to convince the President of their need for more funds, but after dinner together, apparently he convinced them. "When the meeting was over, it was the President's understanding that he had won the chiefs' support for the budget and that they would endorse it, however regretfully, as the best possible when Congress holds its annual budget hearings." The same year the Chiefs were also briefed by the Secretary of the Treasury "about the danger to our economy of increased defense spending . . ." After the briefing, the Chiefs "had another look [at the budget] and decided there were some things that were not absolutely vital that could be squeezed out." [52] The ability of the Administration to persuade the military to accept responsibility for limiting the budget reflected the fact that it is always easier to plead for the consideration of a wider range of factors and a broader viewpoint than it is to limit the range of considerations and to maintain a "parochial" viewpoint. The importance of the whole is an argument which can be used to reduce each of the parts. Efforts to cut the military budget are almost invariably prefaced by expressions of concern for either "the overall picture" or for "the long run."

POST-CONGRESS CONTROLS

The Administration's pre-Congress controls are directed toward executive appropriations requests and expenditure estimates for a fiscal year more than six months in the future. After the fiscal year starts, the Administration still can control directly the level of spending. It can order new decreases in expenditures and programs not provided for in the budget document, or it can permit increases in expenditures within the limits of the available obligational authority. In FY 1953 through FY 1955 the actual level of spending was much less than had been predicted in the Administration's budget. From FY 1956 through FY 1959 actual spending was more than the Administration had predicted. The increases, however, were not the result of voluntary, conscious decision on the part of the Administration. The low estimates of expenditures reflected what it wanted to do, and the tendencies toward a higher actual rate of expenditures were often stimuli for it to reduce substantially particular programs and funds. Administration refusal to spend monies Congress appropriated in excess of Administration requests reflects differences in policy between the Administration and Congress. Administration reductions from its own estimates reflect changes in its policies or efforts to adjust old policies to new circumstances.

The imposition of post-Congress controls on expenditures began in the first full fiscal year after World War II, when the President in August, 1946, set ceilings of $8 billion and $5.6 billion on War Department and Navy Department expenditures for the current 1947 fiscal year. This caused the Navy to reduce its anticipated expenditures by about $650 million.[53] In the summer and fall of 1949, an even more intensive reduction campaign was instituted to bring FY 1950 expenditures down to the level of $13 billion projected for FY 1951. In August, 1949, Secretary Johnson appointed a National Defense Management Committee to recommend economy measures, and in September the Committee proposed cuts of $800 million in the service programs, amounting to 9 percent of the Navy spending estimates, 8 percent of the Army, and 3 percent of the Air Force.[54] Despite service opposition, particularly from the Navy, these cuts were put into effect with only minor modifications. In the first year of the Korean War, of course, the Administration greatly increased spending over the original estimates, receiving from Congress supplementary appropriations for this purpose. In the first year after the war, however, the new Administration reduced the Army by one division in the midst of the fiscal year. For the next year, FY 1955, the budget presented in January, 1954, estimated expenditures at $37.6 billion. In September, 1954, however, after Congress had voted the FY 1955 appropriations, the Administration announced a reduction of more than $2 billion in its FY 1955 spending estimates, to come primarily from procurement programs.[55] A few months later, in January, 1955, the Administration announced a new reduction of 70,000 men in the Army, to be completed before the end of the fiscal year. These post-Congress cuts brought FY 1955 expenditures down to $35.5 billion. Also in January, 1955, in an unusual move, the Administration announced in advance its intention of reducing the FY 1956 expenditure estimates of $35.75 billion by $1.75 billion during the course of that fiscal year. This figure was carried in the budget document as an "unallocated reduction in estimates." In the summer and fall of 1955 serious consideration was given to attempting a still further reduction in FY 1956 expenditures to $33 billion. Actually, however, total FY 1956 expenditures were almost exactly what had been predicted without the unallocated reduction. More successful reductions in spending and programs were made shortly after the beginning of FY 1958, when the Administration launched a major economy drive, eliminating several missile programs and cutting back the Army by three divisions rather than the one-division cut which had been forecast in the budget.

Post-Congress expenditure cuts were thus an important means by which the Administration limited or reduced the magnitude of the military effort. In making such cuts, however, the Administration always had to watch the potentially critical reactions of a jealous Congress. If military spending was to be reduced, the congressmen wished to get a share of the credit for it. Congressmen reacted very negatively to situations in which Administration and military officials first appeared before the Appropriations committees to insist that the full funds they asked for were essential to national security and then, after Congress appropriated the funds, retired to the Pentagon to make substantial reductions in the expenditures. In the fall of 1949, for instance, the FY 1950 cuts in the military program were proposed while Congress was still in session and considering the FY 1950 budget containing the funds which the Administration desired to cut. Secretary of Defense Johnson, Representative Vinson declared, "to make his record of saving $800,000,000, says Congress is giving more money than he needs and he lets Congress go along and do it and then he says, 'I will cut it out and it will reflect credit on my great ability to save the taxpayers' money.'" "You," he told Mr. Johnson, "should have come up to the Appropriations Committee and told the committee that, after a reevaluation of the appropriations, you found that you probably could make savings, and you should have given the committee an opportunity to have made a good record as well as enabling our distinguished Secretary of Defense to make a good record."[56] Similarly, in 1957, the Administration vigorously attacked the cuts which the House made in FY 1958 appropriations and successfully persuaded the Senate to restore many of them. Then the Administration itself began to cut back FY 1958 spending to avoid breaching the debt limit; the Budget Director asked all agencies to keep their spending for that year at or below the level for FY 1957. This request became public on July 10. "The apparent purpose of the letter," Richard E. Mooney reported, "was to induce further economizing in the Government without going through the slow details of revising appropriations requests to Congress."[57] Its intentions to reduce expenditures exposed to public view, the Administration was forced to abandon its earlier position on the defense budget and to acquiesce in a cut of $142 million from the Senate-approved figure. Stimulated and incensed by this shift, the conference committee approved a figure $774 million less than that of the Senate and only $197 million more than that of the House.[58]

The troubles of the Administration with Congress in 1949 and 1957 largely stemmed from the fact that it began to reduce expenditures for the new fiscal year before Congress had completed appropriating money for that year. In 1955 Vinson apparently sympathized with the reduction in the Army but again objected to the Administration's making the change without getting congressional approval.[59] The Armed Services Committee could investigate the Administration's Army reductions because they were announced with the presentation of the FY 1956 budget to Congress in January, 1955. For the Administration the best time to make expenditure cuts was early in the fiscal year, after Congress adjourned in the summer and before it reassembled in January.

ECONOMY DRIVES

The Administration continually attempted to limit and to control the level of military spending. At times, however, these efforts were intensified into full-fledged economy drives. In these instances all the various means of control, pre-Congress and post-Congress, were used to the full: programs were slashed; restrictions imposed on spending and obligations; personnel cut; bases closed. The overriding concern in the Defense Department became the reduction of military spending or reversal of an upward movement in military spending.

Between the post-World War II demobilization and the end of the Eisenhower Administration major economy drives took place in 1948–1949, 1953–1954, and 1957. The second drive differed somewhat from the other two; it was associated with a change of Administration, the end of a war, and a conscious reshaping of strategy. The influence of the last two factors, however, can be overestimated: the economy drive was well underway five months before the war ended and nine months before the New Look strategy emerged. The other two economy drives involved clearcut efforts by the Administration to reverse an upward trend in military spending. The upward movement in 1948 was stimulated by the rearmament measures initiated in the spring of that year. The upward movement in 1957 was largely the product of economic and administrative causes. In both cases the rise in military spending threatened other policy goals of the Administration. The 1948 upswing came just as Congress reduced taxes and complicated the Administration's effort to achieve a balanced budget. The 1957 upswing came just as the Administration was already perilously close to the legal debt limit and threatened to compel it to ask Congress to raise that limit. The efforts of the Administrations to reverse these movements have many similarities, some of which are shared with the economy drive of 1953–1954. In each economy wave the emphasis upon the strategic deterrent-massive retaliation forces tended to increase, with the major reductions in manpower, conventional forces, and surface forces. In 1948–49 and 1953–54, reductions in active forces were coupled with increased emphasis upon the importance of reserve forces. All three drives tended to increase interservice competition. The first two drives were also associated with efforts to reorganize the military establishment aimed, among other goals, at securing greater economy and efficiency. Each drive also compelled difficult choices among competing weapons systems. Major weapons programs in the process of research and development were reduced or eliminated: the Navy's flush-deck carrier in 1949, the nuclear-powered airplane in 1954, the Navaho missile in 1957. On the other hand, other weapons were pushed ahead as a result of the choice: the B-36 in 1949, tactical nuclear weapons in 1953–54, the Snark in 1957. Each economy drive also produced demands to reduce overseas deployments of forces. The 1948–49 drive led to the withdrawal of American troops from Korea. The 1953–54 drive produced a reduction in forces in Korea and elsewhere in the Far East, rumors of possible cuts in our NATO forces, and official endorsement of the idea of creating a mobile general reserve in the United States and relying upon allied forces for local defenses. The 1957 drive again stimulated talk of possible reductions in the European forces.

The theory that the natural tendency of the Administration is to increase the defense effort implies that the stronger the Administration is the greater would be the tendency toward a high level of military spending. Actually, however, not the weakness but the strength of the Administration limits the scope of the defense effort. A strong Administration securely in power can maintain the desired balance between military expenditures and other needs without recourse to an economy drive. A feeble Administration may be unable to push through a drive. All three economy drives between 1947 and 1960 came immediately after the Administration had scored an electoral victory and was anxious to assert its control over the military establishment. A new Administration, of course, may have to launch one, as in 1953–1954, to achieve the balance which it thinks desirable. Older Administrations may have to resort to them if they become lax, indifferent, or distracted from the job of keeping tight control of military spending. "While we were all sweating to win the election," as a close associate of the President explained the 1957 rise in expenditures, "and while the President was also concentrating on the Suez business, shoring up the world alliance and all that, we plumb forgot about our own bureaucrats." When the President turned his attention again to the defense establishment, he was appalled to discover that Secretary Wilson "had lost control of the Pentagon's fiscal machinery." [60] Fresh from a decisive electoral victory, the Administration was able through vigorous efforts to reestablish its control, to halt and to reverse the upward trend. Like the cashiering of MacArthur or the dispatch of troops to Little Rock,[61] however, its action was an extreme assertion of Administration power in response to a threat which conceivably could have been headed off by a milder but more timely exercise of that power.

18. THE ADMINISTRATION, THE PUBLIC, AND THE DEFENSE EFFORT

"The rule to which there are few exceptions," Walter Lippmann wrote in 1955, "... is that at the critical junctures, when the stakes are high, the prevailing mass opinion will impose what amounts to a veto upon changing the course on which the government is at the time proceeding. Prepare for war in time of peace? No. It is bad to raise taxes, to unbalance the budget, to take men away from their schools or their jobs, to provoke the enemy." The people, he went on to say, "have compelled the governments, which usually knew what would have been wiser, or was necessary, or was more expedient, to be too late with too little, or too long with too much . . ." [62] Mr. Lippmann's indictment of the ills of modern democracy is long and complex. This section is concerned with only two of his propositions. The first, concerning the strength of public opinion, holds that in a democracy the policies of the government, including military policy, are shaped by public opinion. The second holds that public opinion not only determines the level of military magnitude but that it also tends to restrict, reduce, and limit that magnitude. The public is insensitive to the requirements of national security and insistent that the security budget be limited to avoid the curtailment of more popular domestic programs and to achieve a reduction in taxes.

An analysis of governmental action and popular opinion between 1945 and 1960 suggests that Mr. Lippmann's indictment attributes to the mass public a power which it did not possess and an attitude which it did not hold. "Mass opinion" is difficult to identify, much less to measure. Public opinion polls have their limitations, but they are the best source available; their evidence is so overwhelming that even a wide margin of error would not invalidate the conclusions drawn from them. In contrast to Lippmann's hypothesis, the polls suggest that public opinion has been hostile to only one major element of the national security effort, foreign aid. With military programs and the defense budget, on the other hand, public opinion tended to follow the lead of the Administration where the Administration took a definite position; where the Administration did not take a strong stand, public opinion was, at the least, passive and permissive, and at the most, very favorably disposed toward stronger defenses. Opinion on this issue may be analysed in terms of: 1) the relation of public opinion to governmental action; 2) the popularity of defense programs vs. other programs; and 3) the popularity of defense spending vs. a balanced budget or lower taxes.

PUBLIC OPINION AND GOVERNMENTAL ACTION

Governmental policy and mass opinion on the level of military effort have frequently differed, but in every case the Administration has been in favor of less military effort and public opinion in favor of more. This pattern was consistent throughout the Cold War. In

May, 1946, in the midst of demobilization after World War II, a Roper survey asked: "In order to have the United States accomplish what you think it should accomplish during the next 20 years or so, do you think we have enough military strength now, or should we have more?" Thirty-eight percent of the sample thought we had enough; 52 percent thought we should have more.[63] The following year, when reductions in the defense budget were debated in Congress, Gallup inquired: "Do you think Congress should reduce the amount of money which the Army and Navy have asked for?" The response was: yes, 35 percent; no, 60 percent.[64] The results of a series of Gallup polls in 1948, 1949, and 1950 show, with one minor exception (the Army in February, 1949), more than 2-to-1 majorities in favor of increasing the size of all three services. The February, 1948, poll immediately preceded the spring crisis and the President's request for UMT, selective service, and a supplemental defense appropriation. A year later the economy wave was in full swing, and the majorities in favor of a larger military establishment sagged somewhat but still remained overwhelming. Immediately after the outbreak of the Korean War opinion was virtually unanimous on the need for military strength. Clearly, mass opinion supported the expansion of the Air Force, which the Administration vetoed, as well as the demands of the other services for larger forces. Equally clearly, mass opinion did not furnish a primary impetus to the cutbacks in the military program which began in the summer of 1948 and were carried through to the beginning of the Korean War.

Question A. Do you think the United States should increase the size of its Army? Navy? Air Force?

		Increase Army	Increase Navy	Increase Air Force
February, 1948	Yes	61%	63%	74%
	No	29	26	17
	No opinion	10	11	9
February, 1949	Yes	56	57	70
	No	29	27	17
	No opinion	15	16	13
July, 1950	Yes	85	85	89
	No	9	9	6
	No opinion	6	6	5

Source: Gallup Surveys 412K, 436K, 458.

This conclusion is reinforced by other polls early in 1950. In January, when asked what governmental programs should be reduced or cut out, only 3 percent of a national sample mentioned military expenditures.[65] In February, Gallup asked: "Do you think the amount of money we are now spending on the Army, Navy, and Air Force is too much, too little, or about right?" Forty-three percent of the public were satisfied with the status quo, 25 percent thought too little was being spent on the military, and only 15 percent thought too much was being spent.[66] In March, 1950, Gallup asked the public whether spending should be increased, decreased, or remain the same for a number of governmental programs. The results for national defense were: increased, 64 percent; decreased, 7 percent; remain the same, 24 percent; no opinion, 5 percent.[67]

These polls suggest that the potential public support for NSC 68 may have been much greater than either its supporters or opponents appreciated. Certainly, they indicate little positive public support for the vigorous efforts to keep the defense budget at $13 billion during the fall and winter of 1949–1950. The responsibility for American military weakness at the outbreak of the Korean War may be assigned to many sources, but it can hardly be laid at the door of public opinion.

During the Korean War mass opinion tended to support a high level of mobilization. In July, 1950, when the American position in Korea was still tenuous, Gallup asked whether "U. S. industry (factories) should or should not begin now to produce planes, tanks, guns, and other war equipment on a full war-time basis and cut out making autos, refrigerators, television sets and other items which people may want and need?" Sixty-six percent of the sample voted for tanks and planes; 26 percent for autos and refrigerators.[68] In November, before the intervention of the Chinese Communists became known, the Gallup survey told its sample that the government planned to increase the armed forces from their pre-Korean level of 1,500,000 men to 3,000,000 men, and asked what they thought of the latter figure. Seven percent thought it was too high; 50 percent thought it was about right; 33 percent thought it was too low. A month later, 70 percent of the public approved doubling United States defense expenditures in the coming year; 17 percent disapproved of this proposal.[69] Thus, the support for substantial mobilization during the first year of the Korean War was almost overwhelming. Significantly, however, after the MacArthur hearings, the stalemate, and the debate over Korean strategy in the 1952 election, the willingness of the public to spend more money on defense declined noticeably. In a November, 1952, poll Gallup asked: "Do you think the government should spend more money or less money for defense purposes?" The results were: more, 30 percent; less, 25 percent; same, 27 percent; no opinion, 16 percent, miscellaneous, 2 percent.[70] Although the results indicate a wide division of opinion on defense spending, even at this point more people favored more money for defense than for either of the other possibilities.

The public opinion polls also suggest that there was little public demand for the reduction in the military effort which came after Korea. In July, 1951, just as the armistice talks were getting under way, Gallup asked the public: "If the Korean war is brought to an end soon, do you think the United States should continue our defense program as planned, or do you think the defense program should be reduced?" Eighty-four percent thought the program should be continued as planned; 11 percent thought it should be reduced.[71] Almost two years later, in April, 1953, when the armistice was on the verge of reality, the response was similar. Gallup asked: "At present there are about $3\frac{1}{2}$ million men in our Armed Forces, both in the U. S. and overseas. If a truce is reached in Korea, do you think we should cut down the size of our Armed Forces, or not?" Seventy-one percent thought that the United States should not reduce its strength; 19 percent thought that it should. Simultaneously, however, the new Administration proposed a reduction of $5 billion in the military appropriations for FY 1954. In August, 1953, the Budget Director, Joseph Dodge, urged the Secretaries of the Army, Navy, and Air Force to reduce expenditures "to meet public demand."[72] The same month, Gallup asked the public whether too much or too little of federal taxes was being spent for defense. The results indicated general satisfaction with the existing level of defense spending: too much, 19 percent; too little, 22 percent; about right, 44 percent; no opinion or no answer, 15 percent.[73]

In less than twelve months, however, the Administration cut the armed forces by a quarter of a million men; military expenditures went down from the Korean War peak of $43.6 billion in FY 1953 to the post-Korean low of $35.5 billion in FY 1955. Despite Mr. Dodge, these reductions can hardly be attributed to an overwhelming demand on the part of public opinion.

The tendency either to favor the status quo in military magnitude or to support larger military forces was underlined in subsequent polls. In September, 1955, when additional proposals to cut defense spending were under consideration, Gallup asked whether "we should keep on spending as much as we do now for our defense program, or should we cut down on the amount we spend for defense?" Seventy-two percent of the sample favored continuation of the current spending level; 19 percent were in favor of a cut.[74] In December, 1956, according to Secretary of Defense Wilson, the President drastically reduced the Defense Department requests because he "sensed this budget-cutting thing in the wind." "Obviously," Mr. Wilson said, "the people in the country are in no mood to spend more dollars." Congressional reductions in the budget, he argued, reflected "the opinion of the people that we have got to cut down our military expense."[75] Yet the 1957 polls indicate no widespread belief that military spending should be reduced. In February, 1957, just as the budget cutting wave was gathering force, Gallup asked whether the "biggest part of government spending" going for defense "should be increased, decreased, or kept about the same." A substantial majority, 60 percent, favored the latter course; 22 percent thought that defense spending should be increased; 9 percent thought it should be cut.[76] In May, 1957, 47 percent of the people in a Gallup survey favored cutting the President's budget and 32 percent opposed cutting it. Only 42 percent of those in favor of cutting the budget (20 percent of the total sample), however, favored a *major* cut in the budget. Of those in favor of a major cut, only 7 percent (less than 2 percent of the total sample) thought that it should come in the defense area.[77] Despite Mr. Wilson, the 1957 military cuts hardly seem to be the result of mass public demand.

In summary, if the polls give an accurate picture of mass, unstructured public opinion, that opinion never favored a major reduction in the country's military strength during the Cold War.

The reductions in military magnitude in 1949–1950, 1953–1954, and 1957 were not the result of any swelling popular pressure against defense expenditures. Before the Korean War the general public overwhelmingly favored increases in all the armed services and particularly in the Air Force. In the initial phases of the war, public opinion tended to favor steps approaching all-out mobilization. At the end of the war there was no demand for a substantial reduction in the size of the military effort. After 1954 opinion usually favored the existing level of forces; again there were no substantial demands for any decrease in military strength. On specific issues of military policy, moreover, the public tended to favor measures which symbolized or could be interpreted as meaning greater military preparedness. In a series of nine surveys on UMT from December, 1945, to January, 1956, for instance, only once did the majority in favor of UMT drop below 65 percent and only once did the minority opposed to it rise above 25 percent.[78] (The exception was in March, 1952, when the results were: favor, 60 percent; oppose, 33 percent.)

The tendency of public opinion to favor large military forces was in part balanced by another tendency to acquiesce in the decisions of the Administration. While a substantial majority might oppose a cut in the armed forces before it was made, a substantial majority also might approve the cut after it was carried out. In April, 1953, for instance, 70 percent of the sample favored maintaining the existing strength of the armed forces if a truce were concluded in Korea. But in July, 1953, after the Administration and Congress had reduced the funds in the FY 1954 budget, Gallup asked: "Do you agree, in the main, with those people who say the defense budget has been cut so much that the nation's safety is threatened—or with those people who say only waste and extravagance have been cut out of the budget?" Fifty-three percent thought that waste alone had been cut; 17 percent thought that safety had been threatened.[79] Interviewing in the Middle Atlantic states immediately after the first Soviet sputnik, Samuel Lubell also found a tendency of voters to put their faith in the President and to accept his estimate of the situation and his proposals for action as the right ones. "In no community" did he find "any tendency on the part of the public to look for leadership to anyone else—to their

18. THE ADMINISTRATION, THE PUBLIC, AND DEFENSE

newspapers or radio commentators, to Congressmen, or to men of science." [80] In April, 1960, after two years of attacks on the Administration by congressmen and non-official opinion leaders over the "missile gap," the mass public was generally satisfied with the Administration's position. Forty-five percent thought that the Administration was spending "about the right amount" on defense, 21 percent thought it was spending too little, 18 percent thought it was spending too much.[81] The reliance of the public upon executive leadership in this area partly reflects the public's own estimate of its lack of competence and a feeling of detachment from military problems. The average citizen could hardly have more than the foggiest idea of the implications of alternative military strategies either for foreign policy or for himself. While favorably disposed toward greater military strength, the public also did not feel strongly on the issue, did not usually express its views positively to congressmen and other decision-makers, and tended to wait upon the leadership of the Administration.[82]

Mass opinion thus did not dictate limits on the strength of the armed forces. Each Administration was able to follow military policies which when inaugurated had little support from the people. In 1948 and 1949, 70 percent of the public and the House of Representatives were unable to compel the Administration to maintain a larger Air Force. This was a strategic issue whose decision rested with the Administration. At the same time, 70 percent of the public and the Administration were unable to persuade Congress to approve universal military training. This was a structural issue whose decision rested with Congress. In both cases, the appropriate agencies of the government, not public opinion, had the final word.

These conclusions also suggest that those who criticize the Administration for spending too little on defense may face an insoluble dilemma. In the absence of any debate over the size of the military effort, public opinion favors a larger effort. If the critics vigorously and articulately attack the Administration for reducing military strength, the Administration eventually is forced to make a public defense of its policies. The public listens to the Administration, not the critics, and the reassurances of the Administration induce mass acquiescence in its policies. Thus, in terms of mass opinion, criticism of the Administration tends to convert an anti-

Administration majority into a pro-Administration majority. By initiating a debate over defense the critics insure that they will lose the debate.

DEFENSE PROGRAMS AND OTHER PROGRAMS

The popularity of a large military establishment becomes clear when public attitudes toward military programs are compared with public attitudes toward other governmental programs. The results presented in Question B are typical public ratings for the late 1940s and early 1950s. A 1957 poll inquiring of those favoring a major cut in governmental expenditures where they thought such a cut should be made produced these results: foreign aid, 52 percent; overall, 10 percent; domestic affairs, 9 percent; war defense, 7 percent; personnel, 4 percent; farm program, 2 percent.[83] In the spring of 1959, Gallup again queried the public on the spending for various programs, but came up with slightly different results (Question C).

Question B. Do you think U. S. Government spending should be increased, decreased, or remain about the same on the following?

	Increased	Decreased	Same	No opinion
National defense	64%	7%	24%	5%
Public works—dams, airports, roads, etc.	52	14	27	7
Federal housing	46	24	21	9
Social welfare, health, and social security	42	16	37	5
Veterans benefits	30	18	47	5
Farm subsidies	16	52	22	10
Marshall Plan aid to foreign countries	12	46	33	9
General expense of government	7	66	20	7

Source: Gallup Survey 454K, March 24, 1950.

Question C. Do you think there is anything for which the government should be spending MORE/LESS *money than it is at present?*

Should be spending MORE for		Should be spending LESS for	
Schools, education	11%	Foreign aid	17%
Defense	9	Government expenses, salaries	13
Unemployment benefits	3	Defense	9
All other items	15	Farm subsidies	4
Nothing	62	All other items	9
		Nothing	48

Source: AIPO Release, May 1, 1959.

These and similar polls suggest three general conclusions: 1) Military spending is usually more popular than any other form of government spending; 2) Although foreign aid programs may be just as essential for security, they are usually the least popular governmental activity; 3) The popularity of defense spending may have declined in the late 1950s. At least in 1959 about the same number of people wanted to decrease defense spending as wanted to increase it. This could mark the beginning of a permanent change in public opinion, or it could be simply the result of the Administration's response to its critics.*

DEFENSE, BALANCED BUDGETS, AND LOWER TAXES

The crucial test of the willingness of the public to support a large defense establishment comes when it is asked to choose between that goal and the payment of less taxes or the achievement of a balanced budget. The public can never realize the implications of its choice of one goal over another in the way the Administration can. Nonetheless, the extent to which the public is favorably disposed toward one goal rather than another gives the Administration some indication of the extent of its freedom to choose.

The view which holds that public opinion is the principal restraint upon the size of the military effort assumes that if given a free choice, the public will choose lower taxes rather than more defense. The evidence offered by the polls, however, suggests that the truth is not so simple. The figures presented in Question D indicate that during periods of tension or war majorities favored an increase in the military forces even if it meant an increase in taxes. Even in a noncrisis time, such as February, 1949, very large minorities of the total sample indicated that they would be willing to pay higher taxes to support a larger Army and Navy, and a ma-

* American attitudes toward governmental spending programs, at least before 1959, may be contrasted with British attitudes, which gave a defense cut priority:
"If the government wants to cut down its spending, which of these would you put first?"

Defense	32%	Health service	4%
Food subsidies	21	Roads	3
Atomic power development	17	Housing	2
Schools	4	Don't know	17

British Gallup Survey, *New York Herald Tribune,* Oct. 17, 1955, p. 2.

jority of the sample was willing to contribute more taxes for a larger Air Force.

Question D. Would you be willing to pay more money in taxes to support a larger Army? Navy? Air Force?

		Army	Navy	Air Force
February, 1948	Yes	55%	55%	63%
	No	36	35	28
	No opinion	9	10	9
February, 1949 *	Yes	44	45	54
	No	9	9	12
	No opinion	3	3	4
July, 1950	Yes	71	71	73
	No	23	23	21
	No opinion	6	6	6

* Question in this survey asked only to those who answered yes to Question A.
Source: Gallup Surveys 412K, 436K, 458.

On the other hand, even during the Korean War, the tendency to favor higher taxes for the other fellow was noticeable. When asked in the fall of 1950 how money should be raised to support the war effort, the public responded:

Borrowing	8%	Higher taxes on higher	
Taxes (unspecified)	14	income groups	7%
Corporation, business taxes	25	Lottery	2
Sales and excise taxes	13	Reduce governmental	
Higher income taxes for all	14	expenditures	5

Significantly, also, the public was split almost evenly over whether Congress should raise personal income taxes again to cover the increased costs of defense. Forty-four percent approved such action; 48 percent disapproved.[84] In January, 1958, after the Soviet sputniks, however, 63 percent of a Gallup sample were willing to approve an increase in their own income taxes "to build up our military strength here and abroad." [85] In 1960 when Gallup asked its sample to suppose that a presidential candidate had said "that America is falling behind Russia in such fields as science and missile development, and that to catch up the American people will have to pay more taxes," 50 percent of the sample said this statement would help him in their eyes, 28 percent said it would hurt him.[86]

Evidence on public attitudes toward the choice between defense spending and a balanced budget is not so readily available. Question E, however, presents the results of one *Fortune* poll in 1946 in

18. THE ADMINISTRATION, THE PUBLIC, AND DEFENSE

which an overwhelming majority preferred strong military forces to a balanced budget, and a substantial majority preferred a balanced budget to lower taxes. In general, it is clear that tax reduction rates low in the hierarchy of public preferences and that military power rates high. Willingness to support higher taxes for more defense, however, varies with the type of military strength and with the nature and incidence of the tax.

Question E. If we can't do both at the same time, which do you think we should do first:

See that our military forces are kept at about their present strength, or balance the national budget?

Keep up forces	71%
Balance budget	17
Express no opinion	12

Continue to send food to needy countries, or balance the national budget?

Send food	56%
Balance budget	31
Express no opinion	13

Reduce taxes, or balance the national budget?

Reduce taxes	33%
Balance budget	53
Express no opinion	14

Continue making loans to foreign nations, or balance the national budget?

Continue loans	14%
Balance budget	70
Express no opinion	16

Source: *Fortune* Survey 57, December, 1946.

THE REASONS FOR PUBLIC SUPPORT

Too much should not be read into the survey data which has been presented. Substantial public support for a large defense effort does not necessarily rest upon widespread public understanding of the relation between force and foreign policy or widespread acceptance of the requirements of a strategy of deterrence. In fact, while the polls conclusively demonstrate the popularity of a large military establishment, the very continuity and breadth of that popularity imply that it did not reflect a highly structured or discriminating set of attitudes. Analysis of the polling data in sectional, income, partisan, and educational groupings indicates that no group consistently opposed higher defense spending. Occasionally, some groups turned in slight majorities in favor of reducing defense expenditures, but these were always exceptions to a normal pattern of support. Variations also existed in the degree to which different groups supported a strong military establishment. The relevant point here, however, is the marginal character of these variations and the relatively even distribution of pro-defense opinion across sectional and social-economic lines.

Public support of defense was not only widespread but also fairly constant. Public attitudes toward the defense effort in 1937, 1938, and 1939 before the outbreak of the European war did not differ significantly from public attitudes after the outbreak of the Cold War. The same questions in the 1930s produced the same answers they did in the 1940s. In October, 1935, 75 percent of the public wanted to increase the size of the Army and Navy. In October, 1938, 66 percent of the sample thought the Army should be increased in size, and 71 percent thought the Navy should be increased. Fifty-three percent were willing to pay more taxes to support a larger Army, 56 percent a larger Navy. In January, 1939, when respondents were asked whether the spending for particular programs should be increased or decreased, the relative popularity of national defense and the other programs differed very little from the answers to the same question eleven years later.[87]

In itself this evidence proves nothing about the influences shaping public opinion. Conceivably, in 1938 and 1939 the majority had become convinced that the international situation and the course of American foreign policy required stronger military forces. Equally conceivably, a similar line of reasoning produced a similar conclusion in the 1940s and 1950s. This is possible, but not very probable. The more likely explanation is that public support for strong military forces is not limited to any specific opinion on foreign policy. In 1937 the country was strongly isolationist. In 1938 and 1939 the swing toward intervention was just getting under way. In the 1940s and the 1950s the nation was involved in world politics in a way in which it never had been before. Yet through all these changing circumstances public attitudes toward military force remained relatively constant. Similarly, during the Cold War it seems likely that support for stronger military forces was much broader than the "foreign policy consensus" which Gabriel Almond has described. Between 1946 and 1948, as he points out, perhaps a quarter of the population was susceptible to the appeals of reactionary and nationalistic foreign policies, and some, although not all, of the organizations espousing such policies also supported a strong defense effort.[88] Isolationists, nationalists, collective-security minded internationalists, preventive war enthusiasts, liberationists, and backers of containment and deterrence, all might have their own reasons to support stronger military forces. None of the underlying currents of hyperpatriotism, xenophobia, isolationism, and fundamentalism, which Edward Shils found to exist in American culture, would be incompatible with a major defense effort.[89] In a sense, strong military forces were a means which could be related to a variety of ends, the lowest common denominator among many conflicting foreign policies.

The great gulf between the popularity of the military program and the unpopularity of the foreign aid program implies that military forces had a certain inherent appeal and attractiveness apart from their connection with any foreign policy. Increased American military strength may by itself be a source of satisfaction, pride, and excitement. Many citizens may, like the citizens of prewar Germany and Japan, achieve psychological benefits from identification with the military might and achievements of their country. Foreign aid programs, although they may in fact be equally or more important to the nation's security than the military programs, produce no similar satisfying feeling. Instead, they arouse the suspicion that perhaps the United States is being taken in by wily foreigners and that other countries are simply freeloading off the United States, consuming resources which would much better be spent at home for real "American" purposes.

The variety of considerations which may lead people to support military forces is also suggested by the extent to which this support varies inversely with education and information. In the fall of 1939, for instance, 50 percent of American social scientists supported an increase in the armed forces, while 75 percent of the population as a whole favored such an increase.[90] Similarly, in June, 1946, it was found that while all information groups favored maintaining armed forces larger than the government was maintaining or planned to maintain, those with high information on public affairs favored smaller armed forces than those with low information. While the variation among the groups did not correlate perfectly with differences in information, at the extremes the gap was very noticeable. The median size of the Army supported by the No. 1, or high information group, was 2,140,000 men; the median size of the army supported by the No. 7, or low information group, was 3,470,000 men.[91] This difference was one aspect of a broader difference in outlook and attitudes among information groups. Those with less information were generally more pessimistic, nationalistic, and militaristic; the better informed were more optimistic, idealistic, and internationally minded.[92] Other analyses have confirmed the existence of these Hobbesian and Lockean attitude sets. However, a decade of Cold War probably created among the better informed more favorable attitudes toward the military forces needed for foreign policy. It seems at least doubtful that social scientists in the late 1950s were as far behind the rest of public opinion in supporting military forces as they were in the late 1930s. Nonetheless, differential support along information and education lines probably still remained. In three Gallup polls in 1950, 1952, and 1957 concerning increasing or decreasing the size of the armed forces, only one educational group (in terms of primary, high school, or college education) ever showed a larger percentage in favor of decreasing the military forces than in favor of increasing them. This was the college group in 1952.[93] This variation in opinion supporting military forces is almost exactly the reverse of that supporting foreign aid. A 1958 Gallup survey, for instance, revealed that 46 percent of those who were uninformed, 56 percent of those who were partially informed, and 63 percent of those who were well informed were in favor of foreign aid.[94]

IMAGES OF PUBLIC OPINION

If public opinion significantly influenced military policy, it did not do so directly but rather through the images which governmental leaders had of public opinion and the extent to which they were able to persuade other leaders that their images were accurate. Governmental leaders projected onto the public their own values and concerns. Their images of public opinion derived from their policy preferences and their responsibilities in the policy-making process.

18. THE ADMINISTRATION, THE PUBLIC, AND DEFENSE 249

The congressional image of public opinion on military magnitude was mixed, but congressional leaders tended to emphasize the popular support for the defense effort. This inclination was the natural counterpart of the tendency of congressional groups to favor substantial increases in specific military programs.[95] Within Congress, of course, those congressmen who opposed defense spending saw public opinion backing their position, while those who supported increases naturally stressed the extent to which the public favored a stronger defense. "If there is one thing the American people demand," Representative Arends declared in 1957, "it is that we make certain we have the proper national defense. Anyone who votes against a national defense need is certain to have to make an accounting with the people he represents." He then described the difficulties he had with his Illinois constituents when he voted against the refortification of Guam in the 1930s. Other congressmen, Democrats and Republicans, joined in this estimate.[96] In the 1956 airpower debate, when Secretary Wilson suggested that the supporters of larger defense expenditures were unwilling to back higher taxes, Senator Chavez indignantly replied that "there has not been any complaint from the American taxpayers or the American people. No Senator has received a single communication objecting to sufficient funds for national security." [97]

The dominant congressional image of public opinion on defense was not shared by either Administration. Given the generally favorable attitude of the public toward a large military establishment revealed by the polls, how was it possible for Administration leaders to maintain a contrary image of public opinion? The answer, of course, is that the images which governmental leaders have of public opinion have very little to do with the actual substance of public opinion. The difference between the congressional and Administration images of public opinion on defense need not and probably did not reflect significant differences in their ability to estimate that opinion. Instead it reflected the fact that the Administration had the responsibility for determining the size of the military effort while congressional groups were free to espouse the claims of executive groups that felt they had been unjustly cut in the executive branch. An Administration cannot avoid allocating scarce resources among conflicting goals, and no goal receives the resources which its principal supporters would like it to receive. Inevitably, the Administration must legitimate its action by invoking general values which command broad support. Demands for reduction in military expenditures are resisted in the name of a high goal—national security. It is, however, almost impossible to be against security, which is assumed to be a basic and absolute value. Reductions in security expenditures, therefore, cannot be justified in terms of a higher value.

An Administration may sincerely and with good reason believe that it is more important to balance the budget than to maintain security expenditures, but if it is wise it will seldom justify its actions on this ground. Instead, it is forced to invoke a legitimate restraint upon its action. The policy-maker frequently develops restrictions upon his own behavior to reduce the alternatives open to him, to simplify his choice, and to justify the choice he eventually makes. The search for decision is often a search for constraints.[98] In determining the magnitude of the military effort, three constraints are often invoked: absolute requirements of what is needed for security, absolute limits on "what the economy can afford," and absolute limits on "what the people will support." All three are artificial constructs invoked by participants in the policy-making process. No absolute requirements exist which, if met, will make the country secure and which, if unmet, will leave it insecure. Short of total mobilization, no definable limit exists on what the country can afford without risking economic disaster and bankruptcy. So also, the idea of an absolute limit on defense spending in public opinion has little basis in reality. Nonetheless, it is continually invoked to facilitate and to legitimatize Administration decisions. The invocation is an effort to externalize and to objectify the values which the Administration holds, to make desire into necessity.

Images of what the public desires thus mirror what public officials want. The extent to which an Administration's image of public opinion is shared by other groups is some measure of how successful it is in developing a consensus for its policies. A statement by a leading Administration official that "the public will not support" a particular policy is usually a self-confirming hypothesis. The public and the communications elites look to the Administration for leadership on defense matters; they interpret such a statement to mean that the public should not or need not support a larger defense effort. In most cases, this is what the official does mean. An official who thought that a larger defense effort was necessary would seldom publicly declare that the public would not support what he wanted even if he privately estimated that this was indeed the case. Public acceptance of an Administration's policy preferences and an Administration's images of public opinion go hand-in-hand. The true success of an Administration is revealed by the extent to which informed and articulate critics of its policies accept its image of public opinion. Many individuals attacked the Eisenhower Administration for not providing enough for national defense; at the same time they denounced its subservience to public opinion and its acceptance of that opinion as something fixed and given rather than something to be informed and created.[99] In a sense, the critics of the Administration allowed themselves to be deceived by the rhetoric of the Administration. At least with the level of the defense effort, whenever the Administration invoked public opinion, it was very probably opposing public opinion. The critics, however, berated the Administration for succumbing to opinion rather than for defying it. From their viewpoint, they assumed that the public was wrong and the Administration was weak, whereas, if anything, from their viewpoint, the public was weak and the Administration was wrong.

The level of defense spending was determined not by external limits upon the Administration but by conflicting demands within the Administration. The Administration's image of public opinion derived not so much from the substance of public opinion as from its responsibility in the policy-making process and from its identifying with public opinion its own choices among conflicting demands. The public opinion which Lippmann and the other critics feared, which the generals revered, and which the budget-cutters invoked was real because the image of it in their minds was real.

19. PARTIES AND ELECTIONS
THE PARTY RECORDS

The Administration has the decisive voice in determining the magnitude of the military effort. The opposition party in Congress, however, has the initiative in defining the issues.* The Administration strikes a balance among the competing claims on resources, makes the decisions on force levels and the budget, and formally reveals them to Congress in January of each year. The opposition leadership in Congress must either acquiesce in Administration decisions, attack the level of military magnitude for being too high, attack it for being too low, or do all three. The responsibilities of Congress, as was pointed out in Chapter III, usually lead congressional groups to advocate increases in particular programs. Congressmen act, however, not only in institutional roles but also in partisan roles, which, conceivably, could lead them in either direction. The Administration, in short, determines its position, but the opposition party determines the front upon which the Administration defends that position.

Party attitudes on public policy may reflect their constituencies and their responsibilities. To the extent that a party attitude reflects its constituency, the attitude remains fairly stable as the party moves in and out of office. To the extent the attitude is shaped by responsibility, it changes with changes in party control of the Presidency and Congress. In the 1920s and 1930s, party attitudes on defense varied with party control of Congress and the Administration: during the 1920s the Republicans were more favorable to a large Army and Navy than were the Democrats; during the 1930s the Democrats were more favorable to strong defenses than were the Republicans. In his analysis, Julius Turner classifies armament as an issue on which the cleavage between the parties was "moderate" and "inconsistent," that is, it varied with control of the executive branch. In this respect, voting on military measures resembled voting on foreign policy measures generally.[100]

After World War II, voting on foreign aid seemed to adhere to the interwar pattern and to change with changes in control of the Administration. During the Truman Administration, Democrats supported foreign aid and Republicans tended to oppose it. During the Eisenhower Administration, Democratic support for foreign aid, particularly among Southerners, decreased, while Republican

* The phrase "opposition party" is used throughout to describe the non-Administration party in Congress irrespective of whether it is the majority or minority party in Congress.

support increased significantly.[101] Voting on military issues, however, deviated markedly both from prewar voting on military and foreign affairs issues and from the postwar voting on foreign aid. The difference between the parties on military issues remained about what it had been before, but party attitudes did not change with changes in Administration. Throughout the fifteen years, the Democrats favored a higher level of military effort than did the Republicans. Consistent Administration support for foreign aid, in short, was linked with changes in party attitudes in Congress. Consistent party attitudes on military issues in Congress were linked with changes in Administration attitudes.

The interwar and Cold War patterns of congressional voting on military issues are presented in Tables 4 and 5. The data are not absolutely comparable, but the differences in voting are sufficiently striking to be independent of this minor difference in the issues included in the analysis.* In the interwar period, with a single exception (Senate Republicans and Navy), each group of congressmen voted significantly more "pro-defense" when its party was in power than it did when its party was out of power. Table 5, on the other hand, reveals a remarkable consistency in party voting in the Truman and Eisenhower Administrations. The only major change between Administrations involved the Senate Republicans, whose pro-defense score *went down* 14.1 percent from the Truman Administration to the Eisenhower Administration. Democratic pro-defense voting dropped slightly from the Truman to the Eisenhower Administration but not enough to be significant. Largely as a result of the attack on the military budget in 1957, the Democratic pro-defense score in the second Eisenhower Administration was less than it had been in the first Eisenhower Administration. Even in the second Eisenhower Administration, however, the Democrats were much more pro-defense than the Republicans. The generally consistent pattern of voting on military issues contrasts with the marked change in party voting which Jewell found on foreign aid measures (Table 6).

* Grassmuck employed all roll-call votes on armaments issues. My analysis is limited to those on "controversial issues," i.e., issues on which at least 10 percent of one party was in the minority. Included in the tabulation are votes on appropriations, force levels, selective service, universal military training, and military pay.

TABLE 4. PARTY ATTITUDES ON ARMY AND NAVY LEGISLATION, 1921–1941, EXPRESSED IN FAVORABLE ROLL-CALL VOTES CAST BY CONGRESSMEN OF MAJOR PARTIES (in percent)

	ARMY		NAVY	
	Democrats	Republicans	Democrats	Republicans
House				
1921–1932	53.3	74.6	66.2	73.0
1933–1941	76.4	44.3	89.8	63.8
Senate				
1921–1932	51.1	67.6	61.2	67.8
1933–1941	70.2	54.2	83.0	70.4

Source: George L. Grassmuck, *Sectional Biases in Congress on Foreign Policy* (Baltimore, 1951), p. 33.

TABLE 5. PARTY ATTITUDES ON CONTROVERSIAL ISSUES AFFECTING MILITARY MAGNITUDE, 1946–1960, EXPRESSED IN PRO-DEFENSE VOTES CAST BY CONGRESSMEN OF MAJOR PARTIES

		PRO-DEFENSE VOTES (in percent)	
	Number of Issues	Democrats	Republicans
House			
1946–1952	24	80.7	54.8
1953–1960	7	71.2	50.4
Senate			
1946–1952	34	79.8	47.1
1953–1960	14	76.9	33.0

TABLE 6. PARTY ATTITUDES IN THE SENATE ON FOREIGN AID AUTHORIZATIONS AND APPROPRIATIONS, EXPRESSED IN FAVORABLE VOTES

	VOTES FOR HIGHER LEVELS OF FOREIGN AID (in percent)		
Period	Northern Democrats	Southern Democrats	Republicans
1949–1950	90	64	36
1957–1958	63	39	73

Source: Malcolm E. Jewell, "Evaluating the Decline of Southern Internationalism through Senatorial Roll Call Votes," 21 *Journal of Politics* (Nov. 1959), 629.

The continuing differences between the parties are also revealed by the changing dialectic between Administration and opposition over military appropriations. Before the Korean War, the principal budgetary issue, the size of the Air Force, found House Republicans and Democrats solidly arrayed against the Administration and Senate Republicans and Democrats. The efforts by the congressional Republicans in 1951 and 1952 to reduce military appropriations suggest that the earlier pre-Korean War Truman budgets may have been low enough so that the opposition party, which did not have the desire to increase military spending, was also denied the room to decrease it. In nine attempts to amend the military budget in Congress during the Truman Administration, a majority of Republicans once supported the Administration by voting for a lower figure, once supported the Administration by voting for a higher figure, and seven times opposed the Administration by voting for a lower figure. The Democrats in Congress, in contrast, supported the Administration on every vote, voting once for the lower figure and eight times for a higher one. Although somewhat obscured before the Korean War, the dominant pattern was one in which the Administration and the congressional Democrats supported a higher level of military effort and the congressional Republicans supported a lower level.

Party differences became more marked during the Eisenhower Administration. In every year of the Eisenhower Administration except 1957, congressional Democrats attempted to increase the military budget. In 1957 they attempted to reduce it. In eight years a majority of Democrats twice supported the Administration in voting for a higher figure and once opposed the Administration in voting for a lower one. All three instances occurred in 1957. The other nine roll-call votes in Congress always found the Democrats voting for a higher figure and the Administration defending a lower one. In all twelve cases a majority of congressional Republicans supported the Administration, voting for a higher figure three times and a lower figure nine times. Thus, on ten votes a majority of Democrats opposed the Administration and a majority of Republicans; in nine of those instances the Democrats supported the higher level of military effort and the Administration and the congressional Republicans the lower level.

While the nature of the party division shifted from inconsistent to consistent after World War II, the extent of that division remained significant but not extreme. On 37 of the 79 controversial issues from 1946 through 1960, majorities of both parties voted pro-defense; on three issues, bipartisan majorities voted anti-defense. On 37 of the remaining 39 issues a majority of Democrats voted pro-defense and a majority of Republicans anti-defense. On only two issues were the positions of the parties reversed. Thus, a majority of Democrats voted pro-defense on 74 of the 79 issues, while a majority of Republicans voted pro-defense on only 39 of the 79 issues. On all the controversial issues from 1946 through 1960, Democratic Senators voted 78.8 percent pro-defense and Republican Senators, 43.0 percent; Democratic Representatives voted 78.4 percent pro-defense and Republican Representatives, 53.8 percent. From 1946 through 1960, 132 of 178 Democratic Representatives voted pro-defense on 70 percent or more of the issues, while only 45 of 170 Republican Representatives did so. If the 348 congressmen are divided into quartiles on their defense voting, the high pro-defense group is composed of 77 Democrats and 10 Republicans, while the low pro-defense group is composed of 14 Democrats and 73 Republicans. As Table 7 suggests, Democratic opinion is heavily pro-defense while Republican opinion is almost evenly distributed across the entire scale of attitudes.

TABLE 7. DISTRIBUTION OF REPRESENTATIVES BY PRO-DEFENSE VOTES AND PARTY, 1946–1960

Percentage Pro-Defense Votes	NUMBER OF REPRESENTATIVES		
	Democrats	Republicans	Total
0 – 9.9	0	7	7
10.0– 19.9	2	3	5
20.0– 29.9	1	17	18
30.0– 39.9	2	23	25
40.0– 49.9	7	15	22
50.0– 59.9	11	27	38
60.0– 69.9	23	33	56
70.0– 79.9	33	24	57
80.0– 89.9	45	20	65
90.0–100.0	54	1	55
Totals	178	170	348

Note: These 348 representatives include those who voted on at least 16 of the 31 controversial issues dealing with the magnitude of the military effort from 1946 through 1960.

Hence, in 41 of the 79 controversial issues little apparent difference existed between the parties: the index of likeness was 70 or more. In the 38 issues where the difference was significant, however, the contrasting party stands are clearly revealed. In 25 of the 26 votes where a sharp cleavage existed between the parties (index of likeness less than 50), the Democrats supported the pro-defense position. In 11 of the 12 instances where a moderate cleavage existed (index of likeness 50–69.9), the Democrats were the pro-defense party.[102] As was pointed out in Chapter III, partisanship tended to be much greater on budget votes where strategic issues were at stake than on votes concerning structural issues where Congress had the decisive say.

In his analysis for the 1920s and the 1930s, Turner found distinct sectional patterns in both Democratic and Republican congressional voting on defense issues. In both parties congressmen from the coastal areas were more favorably inclined toward a strong Army and Navy than congressmen from the Lake States and the Plains States. In the Democratic Party, Southern and Border congressmen were neither significantly pro- or anti-defense in the 1920s; they were strongly pro-defense in the 1930s, their views changing more directly with the change of Administration than those of congressmen from other sections.[103] Except for the absence of any marked change in Southern and Border voting with changes in Administration, the Cold War patterns of sectional difference within the parties resembled the interwar pattern. Within the Democratic Party, congressmen from New England and Middle Atlantic, Southern, Border, and Pacific States generally voted more pro-defense than those from the Lake and Plains States, with Mountain State Democrats in an intermediary position. Within the Republican Party the sectional breakdown was much more marked. Republican representatives from New England and Middle Atlantic, Southern, and Pacific States all averaged more than 60 percent pro-defense votes; those from the other sections all averaged less than 50 percent. The contrast between the coastal and interior areas in Republican Senate voting was equally distinctive.

TABLE 8. PRO-DEFENSE VOTING BY PARTY AND SECTION, 1946–1960 (in percent)

Section	DEMOCRATS		REPUBLICANS	
	House	Senate	House	Senate
New England and Middle Atlantic	78.9	84.5	71.4	49.8
South	79.7	77.7	61.3	...
Border	82.2	86.3	45.4	38.0
Lake	73.7	66.7	40.6	31.9
Great Plains	64.5	66.7	40.1	39.4
Mountain	76.0	77.6	44.9	34.6
Pacific	76.9	83.1	66.1	66.5

If Republican representatives are grouped into quartiles, in terms of their pro-defense voting record, the sectional breakdown is striking: 38 of the 43 Republican representatives in the high pro-defense group come from the Northeast and the Pacific Coast; 38 of the 42 low pro-defense Republican representatives come from the Lake and Plains States. In the Democratic Party, on the other hand, the distribution of sectional groups among the pro-defense categories was much more even.

TABLE 9. DISTRIBUTION OF REPRESENTATIVES BY PRO-DEFENSE VOTES AND SECTION

DEMOCRATIC

Quartile	Range	New England, Middle Atlantic, and Pacific Coast	South and Border	Lake, Plains, and Mountain	Total
High	91.3–100	12	28	5	45
Med.–High	82.8– 91.3	8	28	8	44
Med.–Low	69.6– 82.8	12	27	6	45
Low	15.0– 69.6	7	25	12	44
Total		39	108	31	178

REPUBLICAN

Quartile	Range	New England, Middle Atlantic, and Pacific Coast	South and Border	Lake, Plains, and Mountain	Total
High	70.4–100	38	0	5	43
Med.–High	57.1– 70.0	26	3	13	42
Med.–Low	37.5– 56.0	13	3	27	43
Low	0.0– 37.0	2	2	38	42
Total		39	8	83	170

Note: The 348 representatives in these tables include those who voted on at least 16 of the 31 controversial issues dealing with the magnitude of the military effort from 1946 through 1960.

The greater degree of sectionalism within the Republican Party is reflected in the differences between sectional extremes in the two parties (Table 10). Republican ambivalence toward defense thus rested on a sectional basis. The interior Republicans tended to be moderately anti-defense, coastal Republicans moderately pro-defense. In each case, however, the sectional patterns existed within the overall difference between the parties on defense. In every section, the Democrats were significantly more pro-defense than the Republicans, with the differences, of course, much greater in the interior sections than in the coastal ones. Also, in the Senate every sectional group of Democrats had a higher pro-defense score than any sectional group of Republicans. This was also true in the House except that the highest scoring Republican section, the Northeast with 71.4 percent, had a higher score than the lowest scoring Democratic section, the Plains States with 64.5 percent.

TABLE 10. DIFFERENCES BETWEEN SECTIONS MOST AND LEAST PRO-DEFENSE

	DEMOCRATS			REPUBLICANS		
	Section Most Pro-Defense	Section Least Pro-Defense	Difference (in percent)	Section Most Pro-Defense	Section Least Pro-Defense	Difference (in percent)
House	Border	Plains	18.7	New England and Middle Atlantic	Plains	31.3
Senate	Pacific	Lake and Plains	19.6	Pacific	Lake	34.6

ELECTIONS AND DEFENSE

The consistent and fairly significant differences between the parties on the magnitude of the defense effort suggest that it should have a role in national elections. Actually, however, it was a significant issue in only one of the four presidential contests during the Truman and Eisenhower Administrations. In 1948 both candidates avoided foreign policy issues. In 1952 Eisenhower vigorously criticized the Administration's conduct of the Korean War. Popular discontent, however, focused upon the inconclusiveness of the war rather than upon its domestic economic burden. The two military policy issues raised in the 1956 campaign were ending the draft and nuclear weapons tests. Only in 1960 did the size of the defense effort play a positive role in presidential politics. Comparison of the 1956 and 1960 experiences suggests that whether the magnitude of the defense effort becomes an important campaign issue depends not only on the differences between the parties on that issue but also on their stands on other issues.

The failure of the magnitude of the security effort to become an issue in the 1956 campaign is particularly striking. For three years Democrats had vigorously attacked the New Look and the reductions in conventional forces. On few issues during Eisenhower's first term were the two parties more sharply divided in Congress. In every one of seven key roll-call votes between 1953 and 1956, 78 percent or more of the Democrats voting favored increasing military appropriations; 88 percent or more of the Republicans voted against increasing them. Not once in the seven votes was the index of likeness between the parties more than 27 percent. At 1956 congressional hearings, both Army General Ridgway and Strategic Air Command chief General Curtis LeMay deplored the deficiencies of the Administration's military effort. In the late spring the airpower issue came to a head with the acrimonious exchange between Secretary Wilson and Democratic senators and the addition by the Senate Democrats of $800 million to the Air Force budget. In July the revelation of the "Radford Plan" stirred up further criticism against the proposed cut-backs in ground forces. The Democratic critics of the Administration, moreover, included senators from northern industrial states, the south, and western states. Apparently here was an issue where the lines were clearly drawn between the parties and where both parties were unusually united within themselves. "For the first time in the history of the Eisenhower Administration," the Alsops wrote, "the Democrats plan to make a major issue of the Administration's defense policy." The Administration, they predicted, would claim credit for reduced taxes and a balanced budget, while the Democrats were "eager to impress the voters with the fact that both have been achieved wholly at the expense of heavy cutbacks in the defense and security area." [104]

Yet the magnitude of the defense effort did not become a major issue in the presidential campaign, and the ending of the draft and of atomic bomb tests did. Why was this? The usual explanation stresses the Democratic candidate's reluctance to challenge the President's military judgment. The congressional Democrats, however, had continually challenged the President on the issue of military preparedness. They had not been intimidated by the five stars. Why should Stevenson have been? During the campaign Stevenson did question the Administration on the draft and nuclear tests, although presumably the President's military judgment was just as formidable and relevant here as it was on divisions and B-52s. On the latter issues the Democrats could marshall on their side the testimony of an impressive number of military men. Yet they challenged the President on two issues of military policy where they could get little support from other significant military opinion.

The reasons for this apparently strange behavior lie not in the nature of defense as a political issue but in the identification of the parties with other issues. The Korean War had been the dominant issue in 1952. Eisenhower had restored peace. When questioned about which party was more likely to prevent a future war, the voters invariably chose the Republicans by a substantial margin.[105] The Democrats active in the presidential campaign were determined to weaken or to remove the "war party" stereotype in the minds of the public.

A dichotomy thus existed between the logic of foreign policy and the logic of domestic politics. Democratic and Republican military policy assumed that peace could be maintained only by deterring Soviet aggression and that deterrence required strong American military forces. The adequacy of those forces was questioned by Generals Ridgway, Taylor, Twining, LeMay, and Partridge. These challenges were encouraged by the opposition party in Congress. The issues of deterrence were understood in Washington, but were they understood on Main Street? For over a century war and arms had been linked together in official and popular thinking. In foreign policy, strong armaments were a prerequisite to peace; in domestic politics, strong armaments were identified with war. To counteract their identification with war, which was unpopular, the Democrats had to play down their identification with armaments, which were popular. The real issues of military magnitude debated in Washington were not debated in the campaign. Instead, the Democratic candidate challenged the Administration on nuclear tests and the draft. Through these issues he dramatized his opposition to horrendous weapons, onerous military burdens, and therefore, presumably, his opposition to war.

The Administration, the military chiefs, and the congressional leaders were deeply divided over the proper magnitude of the military effort. A presidential candidate, however, like any politician running for office, wishes to avoid divisive issues and to search for causes which are generally popular. By espousing these first, he may be able to embarrass his opposition and compel it to take the unpopular side. The possibility existed that the Administration itself might endorse the termination of the draft and the suspension of H-bomb tests. Stevenson later asserted that there was "reason to believe that the National Security Council itself *between September 5 and September 19* had voted 'unanimously' in favor of a similar superbomb proposal; but this decision had then been set aside for obviously political reasons..." [106] The accuracy of Stevenson's information is less significant than the fact that the Democrats thought that it was true. The revelation of the Radford Plan in July, 1956, also stimulated speculation that the Administration was moving toward the abolition of the draft.* If the Administration did have either of these proposals under consideration, Stevenson, by raising them first in the campaign, induced the Administration to reverse its course and to denounce them as unrealistic and dangerous. Thus, the campaign may have forced the Administration to reject policies which it had been thinking of approving; and by bringing the issues into the campaign, the Democrats may have reduced the likelihood that the policies they supported would be carried out if their opponents won. The effect of the campaign may have been to disrupt an emerging consensus and to create differences between the two parties; at the same time it produced a tendency to ignore the issues of the adequacy of our defense forces, upon which the two parties had been divided for four years.

This experience, if true, points out the extent to which the "real" issues of military policy arise out of the recurring debates and disagreements among the principal interested parties within the executive branch when those issues are appealed to Congress and the public by dissenters within the executive branch. In 1952 the Republicans capitalized on the dissatisfaction of the military commanders and the public with the conduct of the Korean War. In this instance, it seemed "good politics" to espouse the views of

---

* "One explanation for the curious interpolation," T.R.B. remarked of Stevenson's draft proposal, "was that he had got a tip that Ike would himself make such a dramatic proposal in the final week of the campaign—like his celebrated 1952 'I will go to Korea' maneuver. The Democrats were not taking chances. Furthermore (the argument seemed to run) how better to answer the GOP charge that the Democrats are the 'war party' than to raise the subject of the draft, or remind those who are lulled by the White House boast of 'peace' that the draft still continues." [135] *The New Republic* (Sept. 17, 1956), 2.

the military dissenters from the Administration's conduct of the war. In 1956 it was not "good politics" for the Democrats to espouse the views of the military dissenters from the Administration's decisions on weapons and forces. Instead, the logic of politics compelled the opposition candidate to espouse two issues which would weaken the image of the Democratic Party as the "war party" and on which there was probably no real disagreement between the parties or even, possibly, within the Administration itself. The major issues of military policy which are debated within the executive branch, in short, are not necessarily the major issues of military policy which are debated in an electoral campaign.

The political situation of 1960 was different enough from that of 1956 to change significantly the role of the defense issue in the campaign. In 1958, 1959, and 1960, Democratic congressmen had attacked the Administration on the missile gap and the allegedly inadequate preparations for limited war. In the winter of 1960, in particular, a prolonged, highly technical, and rather confusing debate developed between Administration spokesmen and congressional leaders over conflicting reports of Soviet capabilities. The voting records of the two parties over defense, however, were not as far apart in the second Eisenhower Administration as they had been in the first. Thus, in terms of the issue itself, there seemed to be little reason for defense to play a larger role in 1960 than it had in 1956. Other factors, however, dictated a different course. Seven years had elapsed since the Korean War, and the identification of the Democratic Party as the "war party" had weakened substantially. Four more years of defense debate over deterrence presumably had further enlightened the public on the relations between arms and war. In addition, both Kennedy and Johnson had been among the leading congressional critics of Administration policy.

These circumstances made likely a prominent role for the defense issue in the campaign. The Administration was willing and able to respond positively to this line of criticism. Nixon was reported to be favorably inclined toward stronger defenses, and he was obviously not as strongly committed as the President to existing Administration policy. To head off conflict, Nixon came to an agreement with Governor Rockefeller on the party platform. As amended, the defense plank pledged the Republicans to accelerated missile programs, "intensified development of an active civil defense," and "strengthening of the military might of the free-world nations..." In August the Administration released about $476 million previously appropriated by Congress for more Polaris submarines, increased dispersal of SAC, increased capability for an airborne alert, deployment of more aircraft carriers to the Pacific and the Mediterranean, modernization of Army weapons, greater airlift capability, accelerated development of the B-70 bomber, and intensified work on reconnaissance satellites. These actions did not, of course, eliminate defense as a campaign issue. Both candidates made several speeches touching upon military policy and related matters. Senator Kennedy demanded "new defense goals" and attacked the Republicans for not doing enough. Vice President Nixon argued that the United States was militarily the strongest nation in the world but that it would have to make additional efforts to maintain that position. The overall effect of the campaign carried forward and encouraged the narrowing of the gap between the two parties. Unlike 1956, the Democrats felt free to press the issue, and the Republicans were able to adjust their platform and actions to take the edge off the Democratic attacks. Avoidance of the issue of military magnitude in 1956 thus intensified disagreement over other issues. Debate over military magnitude in 1960 narrowed the differences between the parties.

THE PATTERN OF PARTY POLITICS

Since general agreement existed on the need for strong strategic retaliatory forces, support for a larger military effort was usually associated with "strategic pluralism" and, particularly, concern for limited war demands.[107] It seems unlikely, however, that party views on magnitude derived from strong commitments on strategy. There appears to be no inherent reason why Democrats should be more inclined to strategic pluralism and a limited war strategy than Republicans. Similarly, there would seem to be no inherent reason why Republicans led by an Army general should be more inclined toward "strategic monism" and a nuclear strategy than the Democrats. More probably, the views of political leaders on strategy reflected their views on military magnitude rather than vice versa, and their views on military magnitude, in turn, reflected their overall political and economic outlook. Since consistent differences between the parties on this issue did not exist in the 1920s and 1930s, the development of this difference probably was related to changes in the political issues between the 1930s and the 1950s and to changes in the constituencies of the parties.

During most of the nineteenth century the parties were primarily coalitions of agrarian interests, and the issues which divided them were primarily sectional issues. The key groups in national politics were the hay and dairy farmers of the Northeast, the tobacco planters of the upper South, the cotton planters of the lower South, the corn farmers of the Middle West, the wheat growers of the frontier. Writing in the first year of the New Deal, Arthur Holcombe saw a fundamental change taking place in American politics with the rise of a "new party politics" reflecting the processes of urbanization and industrialization. "The old party politics is visibly passing away. The character of the new party politics will be determined chiefly by the interests and attitudes of the urban population. It will be less rustic than the old and more urbane. There will be less sectional politics and more class politics." The differences among the city dwellers were not related to climate, soil, and rainfall. They derived instead "from the differences between the various classes of urban society." Rural interests and rural politics would "never again have the same importance as formerly. The new urbane class politics will increasingly dominate the national political scene." [108]

Holcombe correctly forecast the politics of the succeeding quarter century. Both parties tended to become national organizations. Even the Solid South heard rumblings of Republicanism, and the number of distinctly one-party states declined noticeably. The distribution of voters between the two parties was largely in terms of income, wealth, and education. In the era of sectional politics the Republican Party had been the party of the hay and dairy farmers, the Democratic Party the party of cotton, and both had competed for the support of the corn and wheat farmers. In the new class politics, the Republican Party was the party of the upper income groups, the better educated, and the property owners. The Democratic Party was the party of the lower income groups, wage labor, the propertyless, and, generally, the more recently arrived immigrant groups. Both competed for the vote of the urban white-collar middle class. The principal domestic issues of the New Deal and Fair Deal periods were conflicts between urban conservatism (usually allied with rural interests) and urban liberalism.

In the 1950s sectional interests still existed and the class differences between the parties were still fundamental. The issues over which the parties clashed, however, had changed in content. The great issues of the 1950s concerned the allocation of resources to the goals of welfare, security, consumption, stability, and expansion. In the politics of fiscal policy the policy attitudes and party allegiances of groups reflected their relation to the taxation and spending programs of the federal government. Given the nature of American parties, the differences between them over these goals could never be absolute. They could, however, have different tendencies or inclinations. Setting aside economic expansion, which all favored and which primarily involved judgments of what other values contributed to it or should be sacrificed to achieve it, priority lists could be constructed for the two parties on the basis of the stands of Administration and congressional leaders:

Democratic Priorities	*Republican Priorities*
1. Domestic welfare programs	1. Fiscal integrity
2. National security programs	2. Lower taxes (consumption)
3. Lower taxes (consumption)	3. National security programs
4. Fiscal integrity	4. Domestic welfare programs

Obviously, in neither case were these absolute priorities. Republicans did not propose to eliminate all welfare programs to reduce taxes. Nor were the Democrats completely insensitive to the dangers of inflation. In addition, of course, vast differences existed within the parties: Rockefeller's priorities were very different from Goldwater's, and Hubert Humphrey's from Senator Byrd's. The priority lists were, however, a rough approximation of the dominant tendencies within the two parties in the allocation of marginal resources among policy goals. Significantly, the priority hierarchy of one party was just the reverse of that of the other.

The differences between the parties on defense policy can thus be understood only in the context of these broader party viewpoints. The principal Republican goals of fiscal integrity, balancing the budget, and lower taxes required lower expenditures. These led directly to efforts to reduce the military budget to the lowest level consistent with the minimum requirements of national security. The principal Democratic concern with domestic welfare programs did not conflict as directly with national security spending unless it was also linked with a high priority for a balanced budget or tax reduction. When confronted with the political necessity of cutting domestic programs or foreign programs, Democrats tended, as the experience of 1949 and 1957 demonstrated, to reduce the foreign programs. When not confronted with this necessity, they tended to maintain taxes or to unbalance the budget rather than drastically to reduce programs. The natural tendency of the Republicans, on the other hand, was to cut domestic programs, although the political obstacles to accomplishing this might well compel them, as in 1953 and 1957, to reduce national security programs in their efforts to balance the budget and lower taxes.

Party differences in goals were the natural outgrowth of the alignment of interests between the parties. As the party of the poor and underprivileged, the Democrats traditionally favored cheap money and governmental intervention in the economy. As the party of business and the upper classes, the Republicans usually believed in less government and lower taxes. Although the evidence is scattered, Democratic voters apparently tended to be more partial than Republicans to higher levels of defense spending.* In the sputnik crisis, low-income groups and the unemployed—traditional sources of Democratic support—favored expansion of the military effort, while middle-income groups—wary of inflation and more Republican-oriented—opposed substantial increases in the military budget.[109] Party attitudes on the magnitude of the defense effort were thus an inherent part of the overall political structure and outlook of the parties.

* In 1946 the Cornell survey found that the only significant difference between Republicans and Democrats on questions concerning atomic energy and foreign policy was over the desirable size of the peacetime army. The median size preferred by Republicans was 2,276,000 men, that by the Democrats, 2,786,000 men. Cornell University, *Public Reaction to the Atomic Bomb and World Affairs: A Nationwide Survey of Attitudes and Information* (Ithaca, March 1947; mimeo.), p. 8, Table 84. Gallup Surveys 453 (Feb. 1950) and 579 (Feb. 1957) did not show any significant difference between Republicans and Democrats on a larger defense effort. Gallup Survey 508 (Nov. 1952), however, revealed a slight Republican preference to decrease the defense effort and a fairly strong Democratic preference to increase it. In April, 1960, Gallup found that 15 percent of the Republicans polled and 24 percent of the Democrats favored an increase in defense spending. *New York Herald Tribune*, Apr. 10, 1960, p. 23.

20. DRASTIC CHANGES IN MILITARY MAGNITUDE

A prolonged limited war or a sudden turn for the worse in the Cold War might lead an Administration to try to increase drastically the magnitude of the military effort. Conversely, a marked lessening of tensions and substantial agreement on disarmament proposals could lead an Administration to try to decrease drastically the size of the defense effort. This section analyzes not the probability of a drastic move in one direction or the other, but rather the probable political consequences if such a move were attempted. For the purposes of this discussion, a "drastic change" in military magnitude will be defined arbitrarily as a 50 percent increase or decrease in defense spending within three years.

In the 1950s economists generally agreed that there were few economic reasons why the United States could not change drastically the size of its military effort without deleterious economic consequences. A profound confidence existed in the flexibility, resiliency, and adaptability of the American economy. On the one hand, they argued that a substantial increase in national security expenditures was possible without damage to the economic system. On the other, they held that a substantial reduction in security spending might require some adjustments, but that these would be temporary and other sources of demand would quickly replace the military. In discussing the capacity of the economy to absorb substantial increases in defense spending, it was usually argued that the level of military effort should be determined by security considerations alone: "Changes in such outlays," as one economist put it, "should not be manipulated for reasons other than their strategic rationale itself." [110] Failure to provide adequately for security was unjustified on economic grounds. The questions asked were: "If it should be determined that international considerations of military and political strategy make advisable a substantial increase in our present defense program, could we afford it?"; "How much can the economy stand?"; "How much defense can the economy stand?" [111] The common answer to these questions almost invariably was that "The defense we need is the defense we can afford." [112] The economy could "afford" a particular level of defense spending, the economists argued, if that level did not materially interfere with the growth of the economy by lessening private and public investment and did not stimulate sustained inflation incapable of control by monetary or fiscal measures within the existing tax structure. The economy could not afford a level of defense spending, it was suggested, which would require drastic changes in the tax structure or comprehensive controls on prices, wages, and raw materials. In some cases, economists suggested that the economy could not stand a level of defense spending which would restrict personal consumption or lead to a decline in net per capita disposable income.

Economists generally agreed that the economy could afford much more defense spending than existed in the late 1950s. In 1953, national security expenditures were roughly $53 billion, and the Administration planned to reduce them to $42 billion by 1956. The National Planning Association, however, estimated that an increase of expenditures to between $62 and $75 billion in 1956 "would lie within the nation's financial and economic capacity without necessitating wartime controls." Early in 1957 another NPA study estimated that the existing level of $42 billion in national security expenditures could be raised to $54 billion by 1960 if no tax reductions were made; to $64 billion if taxes were returned to their Korean War level, some domestic programs were delayed, and tight credit controls were maintained; and to $75 billion if comprehensive direct controls were introduced. The Committee for Economic Development held that the "risk that defense spending" of up to 15 percent of the GNP "or if necessary even more, will ruin the American way of life is slight indeed," and a Harvard professor argued that "As a matter of economics there is no question that we could afford a hundred [billion] for defense." [113] Actual federal purchases for national security in 1957 were $44.3 billion, just 10 percent of the gross national product.

A similar optimism pervaded estimates of how large a reduction in national security spending the economy could stand. All "our witnesses thus far have exemplified a great deal of optimism," Senator Humphrey declared in a hearing on this subject, "as to the ability of the American economy not only to absorb a so-called $20 billion cut in defense expenditures, but actually be much better off . . . " The economists recognized that "adjustments" would be needed to compensate for the decline in military spending, but no one of them thought that military expenditures were required for American prosperity.[114] On the same page in which they argued that the economy could afford a 50 percent increase in the defense program, the CED Research and Policy Committee also held that "we should not fear that contraction of defense markets would cause a depression." [115]

The prevailing optimism on the economic feasibility of major increases or decreases in defense spending pointed up the extent to which the problems of drastic change were political rather than economic. Arguments that significant increases or decreases in defense spending were economically feasible rested on the assumption that there would be widespread public support for such changes. Additional "defense expenditures are feasible without necessarily creating inflation," one NPA study declared, "*if* the increase in Government spending is accompanied by other appropriate Government measures and by a cooperative attitude on the part of business, labor, and the people in general." [116] The political problems of increasing the defense budget were much more widely recognized than the political problems involved in decreasing it. Great differences of opinion existed, nonetheless, as to how the United States could compensate for a drastic decrease in defense spending. Some stressed the importance of expanded governmental expenditures for domestic programs and, particularly, for public works and other forms of investment expenditures which would have a multiplier effect throughout the economy. Schools, highways, slum clearance, local transportation, reclamation, soil conservation, hospitals, even "publicly supported repertory theaters, opera companies, and symphony orchestras" [117] were suggested. Others urged some reduction in taxes and some increase in other federal expenditures. Still others emphasized the reduction of taxes and an increase in private consumption. "There is, in fact," as one CED study put it, "no end of desirable uses to which the resources freed by a reduced armament burden could be applied." [118]

From an economic viewpoint this multiplicity of alternatives eases the problem of adjustment; from a political viewpoint, however, it complicates the problem. Too many opinions on how to use a substantial reduction in defense spending could reduce the likelihood of such a reduction. The "liberal" may want more public works, the "conservative" lower taxes; both may accept national security expenditures as a lesser evil, as one means of resolving what would otherwise be an intense and bitter political conflict. A drastic reduction in military spending, in short, could have just as disruptive a political effect as a drastic increase. A substantial reduction in national security expenditures might not greatly affect American prosperity. It might, however, have very far-reaching results for the degree of consensus existing in the American political system.

The inner, or normal, limits on military spending are set by the demands for domestic programs, lower taxes, and a balanced budget. In an international crisis, these limits may be transcended. Taxes may be increased, deficits accepted, domestic program expansion curtailed. If the military increase is a drastic one, some form of economic controls probably becomes necessary. At this point, however, the outer limits of expansion may be reached. The experience of the Korean War demonstrates that this outer limit is a political reality.

Immediately after the start of the Korean War widespread support existed for a comprehensive system of economic controls. In the Defense Production Act of September, 1950, Congress gave the Administration more than it asked for, including power to impose priorities and allocations, to requisition facilities required for defense purposes, to expand productive capacity, to stabilize prices and wages, to set up machinery for the settlement of labor disputes, and to control consumer and real estate credit. The Act, however, restricted the Administration from using compulsory price controls until it had first tried voluntary measures. An Economic Stabilization Agency was established in the fall of 1950, and business groups were urged to curtail price increases. The wholesale price index, however, jumped from 100.2 (1947–1949 equals 100) in June, 1950, to 115.0 in January, 1951. In December, 1950, selective controls were imposed on automobiles and a few other products. In January, 1951, a general ceiling price regulation froze prices at their highest point during the period from December 19 to January 25. The problem was squarely presented: Could a pluralistic democracy effectively impose economic controls during a period short of total war?

The record of the following two years was not an encouraging one.[119] Each major economic group resisted the controls affecting its interests, and each was able to find or to create within the government at least one source of support for its viewpoint. Farm and business groups had access to Congress, labor groups access to the President. The difficulties of imposing controls on agricultural prices even in a total war crisis had been evident in 1941 and 1942 when the farm bloc in the House and Senate riddled the Administration's proposed price control legislation with special provisions and exemptions for a wide range of farm commodities.[120] Similar difficulties arose with Korean War price controls. The original act provided that no ceilings could be set below the parity prices of farm products or the May-June, 1950, level of farm prices, whichever was higher. Since farm prices were generally below parity, this provision permitted a 26 percent increase in wholesale farm prices during the first eight months of the war. Parity prices, moreover, were calculated monthly; this made administration of price controls based on them almost impossible. In the spring of 1951, the Administration proposed legislation to establish parity prices on a yearly basis. Congress refused to pass the bill. The Administration also attempted to bring meat prices under control by establishing a quota system allocating meat to processors and by rolling back beef prices, which had risen to 152 percent of parity. The roll-back order was issued on April 28. On May 2, the Senate Agricultural Committee demanded its immediate revocation. The House Banking and Currency Committee wrote into the extension of the Defense Production Act the Fugate amendment which prohibited two of the three Administration roll-backs. In addition, the meat industry launched an intensive lobbying campaign against quota controls, and both houses of Congress passed the Butler-Hope amendment providing that "No restriction, quota, or other limitation shall be placed upon the quantity of livestock which may be slaughtered or handled by any processor." [121] In August, 1951, a major battle developed when the Administration tried to get Congress to repeal this ban. "Mr. DiSalle [OPS Administrator]," the

20. DRASTIC CHANGES IN MILITARY MAGNITUDE

National Independent Meat Packers Association declared, "has said that price control on meat will not work without quota power. This makes it terribly important to do everything we reasonably can to defeat quotas, if we want to put an end to price control." [122] The meat packers won. The House Rules Committee shelved the bill, and in the absence of House action the Senate refused to pass it. The next year further amendments were written into the act to benefit the farmer, on the one hand, and the food industries, on the other.

A somewhat similar pattern prevailed in manufactured articles. In 1951 the congressional committees adopted the Capehart amendment, which not only prohibited roll-backs in manufacturers' prices but also permitted individual increases in prices, to take account of cost increases up to July, 1951. The amendment was written in by the conference committee on the DPA extension act without testimony from the price control agencies. This provision, "affecting the pricing of millions of manufactured items, placed upon the agency an administrative task completely beyond the experience of price control in this country." [123] The Administration valiantly attempted to secure repeal of the individual price adjustments clause. Repeal legislation cleared the House and Senate Banking and Currency Committees but was blocked by the House Rules Committee. Also, in 1951 Congress added the Herlong Amendment to the act, prohibiting any further regulations which did not insure distributors their pre-Korea percentage markups. The amendment, as one authority put it, allowed distributors "to pyramid every increase at the producer level." [124] The Administration objected strongly to this provision, but again its efforts to secure repeal failed. The following year, indeed, strenuous efforts were made to guarantee the margins of individual distributors, since the Herlong amendment had been applicable only to "groups of sellers." The Administration was able to defeat an amendment granting individual markups to all distributors, but Lyndon Johnson was successful in adding to the bill a provision granting individual mark-ups to Texas automobile dealers (the so-called "Lone Star Statute"). In a short while, of course, equity required the price control authority to extend "Johnson relief" to automobile dealers in other states.[125] In the American system of government, pluralism fosters special privilege and democracy universalizes it.

Farm and business groups were able to undermine price controls through the process of congressional amendment. Labor was similarly able to weaken wage controls through its access to the Presidency. In two years three different wage boards came and went. Each included representatives of labor, management, and the public. The first, established in September, 1950, proposed that wages be stabilized at a rate 10 percent above that existing in January, 1950. The labor members protested this formula and walked out. The United Labor Policy Committee, a joint CIO-AFL group dealing with mobilization problems, withdrew the labor members from all economic mobilization agencies as a protest against the dominance of industry representatives. In April, 1951, the labor walk-out achieved its goal. The President abandoned the old wage board and created a new one, which was given power over both wage and non-wage issues in union-management disputes. It granted wage increases higher than those proposed by the first board. The second board lasted a year and came to a dramatic end in the steel wage crisis in the spring of 1952. In this case the public and labor members of the board recommended a settlement agreeable to labor. The Director of Defense Mobilization, Charles Wilson, was willing to approve the increase in wages only if the industry were granted a substantial price increase. The President refused to grant the increase industry wanted. Wilson resigned. The steel workers went on strike. The government seized the steel mills. The Supreme Court ruled the seizure illegal. A lengthy steel strike resulted which seriously affected the production of ammunition and other supplies for the armed forces. Eventually a settlement was reached in July, 1952. The same month a third wage board was created with its powers limited purely to wages. It had a brief existence, coming to grief in the fall of 1952 over the issue of raising coal miners' wages. The industry and public members refused to approve an increase. Labor protested. The President overruled the board. The chairman and the industry members walked out. Thus, in each case the President intervened in the settlement of wage disputes on the side of labor, twice to overrule the rcommendations of a majority of the wage board and once to back the majority of the board against his own mobilization director.

The political system proved incapable of maintaining an effective system of price and wage controls. As so often happens in American experience, however, economic expansion removed the need for political discipline. In 1950 the federal government undertook a major program of industrial expansion, including accelerated depreciation of industrial plants, guarantee of private loans for industrial expansion, direct federal loans for this purpose, and commitments to purchase the products of such plants. The overall expansion goals were achieved. In 1949, the gross national product (in 1958 prices) was $324 billion, and in 1950 it was $352 billion. In 1953 it had risen to $411 billion. The index of industrial production stood at 97 in 1949. By 1952 it was 124; in 1953 it was 134. When the new Administration came into office in January, 1953, political pressures had eviscerated the system of controls. The expansion of the economy, however, had also made controls unnecessary. The first major action of the new Administration was to remove them. The government could not maintain controls in a time of shortage, but it could, through subsidies and other means, stimulate the economic expansion which made controls unnecessary.

During the Cold War the country had no drastic decrease in military spending comparable to the Korean War increase. The demobilization of 1945–1947, of course, reduced military spending 85 percent in two years. The reduction, however, was from near-total mobilization; stockpiled civilian demand created economic conditions not likely to be present in any cut in "normal" Cold War military spending. Apart from this, the largest decrease in military spending took place after the Korean War, when national security outlays dropped more than 20 percent, from $50.5 billion in the second quarter of 1953 to $38.4 billion in the fourth quarter of 1954. This reduction was a principal cause of the 1953–1954 recession.[126] The recession was stopped by the $7.5 billion reduction in taxes in 1954 and by relaxation of the Administration's monetary policy.

Reductions in military spending in 1957 were, on the whole, fairly minor, and they were probably a less important factor in stimulating the 1957–1958 recession than they had been in stimulating the 1953–1954 recession. Among the other developments leading to the 1957 downturn were the decline in exports, the decline in plant and equipment spending following the boom conditions of 1955–1956, and reduced purchases of automobiles. Nonetheless, the 1957 defense economy drive also helped reduce business confidence. In the words of Charles Silberman and S. S. Parker:

> The cutbacks in the second half of 1957 did not cause the recession. But they did contribute to its severity. From mid-1957 to the first quarter of this year [1958], the Defense Department reduced its annual spending rate by $2 billion—more than two-thirds of the cut was in procurement—and this touched off an additional $2-billion decline in the rate of inventory purchase by aircraft and other contractors. And the psychological effects were even more severe. When the cut-backs were made, it was widely assumed that tax reduction would follow. Instead the Soviet Union's startling successes in rocketry shelved the plans for tax reduction while not immediately increasing military orders. The result was a sharp decline in business expectations.[127]

The economy drive directly affected many communities primarily dependent on defense industries. The cancellations in airplane and missile procurement contributed to extensive unemployment in the aircraft industry. In the early fall of 1957 it was expected that employment in the aircraft industry would decline by over 100,000 by the first of the year. Los Angeles, Long Island, Seattle, Buffalo, New Jersey, all were severely hit by defense cutbacks.[128]

The decline in defense spending contributed to the 1957–1958 recession. More important politically, perhaps, was the role which later increases in defense spending played in bringing the country out of the recession. Many proposals were made for dealing with the slump. Those who wanted tax cuts were divided among some who wished to raise the $600 personal exemption, others who wished to reduce tax rates, and still others who supported alternative tax plans. Those who wished to increase domestic spending were divided among the advocates of different programs. Amid the conflicting theories and programs, however, the Soviet sputniks offered one possible course of action upon which almost all could agree: a reversal of the downtrend in defense spending. At first the Administration apparently considered a tax cut as the primary means of dealing with the recession; after the sputniks, however, it shifted emphasis to an increase in military expenditures.[129] Although the Administration did not adopt their more expensive recommendations, the Gaither and Rockefeller Committee reports gave the impression that vast increases in defense outlays were likely. Critics of the Administration, such as George L. Meany, President of the AFL-CIO, might demand an increase in the personal exemption which the Administration was unwilling to approve, but they could also endorse "increases in defense spending" which the Administration was willing to employ.[130] Defense orders, which had amounted to $7 billion in the last six months of 1957, jumped to $13 billion in the first six months of 1958. Among the conscious actions of the government to halt the recession, the "most important was probably the sharp reversal of the defense order situation. The Russian sputniks of October, 1957, were far more important than the slump in achieving this most desirable result." [131]

The 1958 increase in defense spending, of course, was not overwhelming, and military expenditures were only one of a number of steps taken to improve economic conditions. Nonetheless, the experience of that recession suggests that any drastic decrease in expenditures may well be self-limiting. The economic conditions created by a drastic decline may well give rise to political pressures and demands which can be met by an increase in military spending. With or without sputniks, such increases can always be justified as essential to national security. Most important, such increases avoid the controversies which are inevitably stimulated by most other anti-recession actions. They do not get caught in the cross-fire between liberals and conservatives, domestic spenders and tax reducers, the defenders of consumer buying power and those of business expenditures. A severe recession is likely to be caused in part by reductions in defense spending. It is even more likely to be remedied in part by an increase in defense spending.

21. APPENDIX: THE MAGNITUDE OF THE SECURITY EFFORT, 1945–1960

Comparison of the military effort of one government with that of another is extremely difficult. Using a monetary measure, however, it is possible within any one society to compare the military effort with the resources devoted to other activities and to compare military efforts at different points in time. When approached in these terms, on a quarterly basis, the evolution of the size of the American security effort after World War II can be broken into eleven periods.

1. Demobilization: April, 1945–June, 1947. National defense expenditures reached their World War II peak annual rate of $90.9 billion in the first quarter of 1945. A few months later a steady decline set in which did not come to a halt until the second quarter of 1947, when defense expenditures hit an annual rate of $10.3 billion, their lowest point after World War II. This marked the end of the demobilization period. The official termination of Army demobilization was June 30, 1947, and all selective service men were released from the Army by that date.

2. Stability: July, 1947–June, 1948. For a year, FY 1948, defense expenditures remained relatively stable, varying from a low of $10.7 billion to a high of $11.5 in the second and third quarters of 1947. The Administration wished to balance its overall budget. European recovery loomed as a major claim upon resources. Firm peacetime ceilings were placed upon defense spending. This was the pause between the immediate aftermath of World War II and the first military stimuli of the Cold War.

3. Spring Crisis Rearmament: July, 1948–September, 1949. In the spring of 1948, the Czech coup and the first Soviet moves against Berlin stimulated fear of imminent war and prompted the Administration to secure from Congress selective service legislation and supplemental defense appropriations. These were reflected in the steady increase in defense spending from the summer of 1948 to a peak of $14.1 billion in the summer of 1949.

4. Economy Drive: October, 1949–June, 1950. Hardly had defense spending started up in the summer of 1948 when governmental policy shifted, and a major economy wave began in the fall of that year. It reflected the easing of the Berlin crisis, the tax reduction of 1948, the role of the Fair Deal programs in the 1948 election, and the large expenditures required for European Economic Cooperation. It was intensified after Louis Johnson became Secretary of Defense in March, 1949. It did not produce a turnabout in the trend of defense spending, however, until the end of 1949. By that time, State Department officials and others were already concluding that a considerable increase in the military effort was required.

5. *Korean War Rearmament: July, 1950–June, 1953.* The Korean War led to a sustained three-year increase in national security expenditures from $12.0 billion in the second quarter of 1950 to $50.5 billion in the second quarter of 1953. Spending started upward immediately after the beginning of the war, but the major increases occurred in 1951, after the passage of the supplemental appropriation acts in the summer and fall of 1950. Taxes were also increased, and federal domestic spending was kept relatively constant.

6. *Post-Korean Decline: July, 1953–December, 1954.* The end of the Korean War and the advent of the New Look saw a steady decline in defense spending over an eighteen-month period, reaching a post-Korean low of $38.4 billion at the end of 1954. This decline coincided with increased emphasis on nuclear weapons, cutbacks in conventional forces, and major tax reductions in 1954.

7. *Stability: January, 1955–June, 1956.* The decline was followed by a long period of relative stability in defense spending. For eighteen months the quarterly rates only varied between a low of $38.8 billion and a high of $39.2 billion. For three successive quarters, spending was $39.1 billion. In part, this stability reflected improvements in the international situation and strenuous efforts to bring the overall federal budget into balance. In part, it also reflected a balance between New Look cutbacks in personnel and conventional forces, on the one hand, and rising prices and increased expenditures for missiles and other weapons, on the other.

8. *Administrative Increase: July, 1956–June, 1957.* The stability was disrupted by the steady rise of defense spending throughout FY 1957. Within a year expenditures went up almost 15 percent, to $44.9 billion in the summer of 1957. This increase was not primarily the result of a planned expansion of programs. Missile expenditures were increased during the year, but the more significant factors responsible for the overall increase were rapidly rising prices, accelerated payments to contractors, and more rapid deliveries than had been anticipated.

9. *Economy Drive: July, 1957–December, 1957.* The unplanned increase was followed by a planned decrease. The rapid rise in de-

fense spending in the spring of 1957 threatened to force the Administration to ask Congress to increase the ceiling on the federal debt. To avoid this, a vigorous, if shortlived, economy drive was started in the summer of 1957. Drastic cuts were made in force levels and personnel; severe restrictions were imposed on spending. The increase in expenditure halted in the summer of 1957. As the effects of the policy changes were felt, the rate of spending eased off moderately by $1.0 billion to $43.9 billion at the end of 1957.

10. *Sputnik Expansion: January, 1958–June, 1959.* Hardly had the economy wave got under way in the fall of 1957 when the Soviet sputniks and the beginnings of the recession produced another turnabout in policy. New programs and expenditures were undertaken in missile and allied fields. Expenditure restrictions were lifted. The reversal in policy produced a shift in spending in the

TABLE 11. NATIONAL DEFENSE SPENDING, 1945–1960:
SEASONALLY ADJUSTED QUARTERLY TOTALS
AT ANNUAL RATES ($ billion)

Calendar Year	QUARTER			
	First	Second	Third	Fourth
1945	90.9	(1) 89.8	73.9	49.2
1946	24.5	19.4	16.3	15.0
1947	13.0	10.3	(2) 10.7	11.5
1948	11.2	11.3	(3) **11.8**	12.1
1949	13.5	13.7	14.1	(4) **13.0**
1950	12.6	12.0	(5) **14.1**	18.3
1951	24.3	31.2	38.1	41.8
1952	43.0	46.2	47.0	49.3
1953	49.8	50.5	(6) **49.3**	47.6
1954	44.8	41.5	40.0	38.4
1955	(7) **39.2**	38.8	39.2	39.1
1956	39.1	39.1	(8) **41.0**	42.1
1957	43.7	44.9	(9) **44.9**	43.9
1958	(10) **44.0**	44.3	44.5	45.3
1959	45.8	46.2	(11) **46.1**	45.5
1960	44.9	44.7	45.1	45.7

Note: Boldface figures and numbers in parentheses mark beginning of various periods or trends discussed in text.

Sources: U. S. Department of Commerce, Office of Business Economics: *National Income: 1954 Edition,* p. 224; *U. S. Income and Output* (1958), pp. 120–21; *Survey of Current Business* (Feb. 1960), p. 11, (Nov. 1960), p. 10, (Feb. 1961), p. 12.

These figures are federal government purchases of goods and services for national defense. This category corresponds closely to the classification "major national security" in the annual budget. The latter includes expenditures for the military programs of the Department of Defense, atomic energy, military assistance, stockpiling, and defense production.

TABLE 12. NATIONAL DEFENSE SPENDING, 1947–1960: ANNUAL TOTALS
AND SEASONALLY ADJUSTED QUARTERLY TOTALS
AT ANNUAL RATES (1954 $ billion)

Calendar Year	Annual Total	QUARTER			
		First	Second	Third	Fourth
1947	14.1	16.0	12.7	13.5	14.0
1948	13.7	13.5	13.5	13.9	14.0
1949	15.5	15.4	15.8	16.2	14.3
1950	16.0	13.9	13.9	15.8	19.9
1951	34.3	24.5	32.1	38.6	42.0
1952	46.8	43.5	47.2	47.2	48.9
1953	50.0	50.2	51.4	50.2	48.2
1954	41.2	45.0	42.0	39.7	38.0
1955	37.6	38.5	37.6	37.1	37.0
1956	37.0	36.3	36.5	37.6	37.9
1957	38.4	38.6	39.2	38.2	37.4
1958	38.0	37.4	37.7	37.6	38.3
1959	37.7	38.2	38.6	37.9	36.7
1960	35.8	36.3	36.2	35.2	35.5

Sources: These figures were obtained by dividing federal government purchases of goods and services for national defense in current dollars (Tables 11 and 13) by the implicit annual and quarterly price deflators for all federal purchases of goods and services. U. S. Department of Commerce, Office of Business Economics; *U. S. Income and Output* (1958), pp. 222–23; *Survey of Current Business* (Feb. 1959), p. 24, (Feb. 1961), p. 12. Quarterly price deflators for federal purchases are not available before 1947. Since federal purchases for national defense are usually about 80 percent of total federal purchases, no very great distortion is involved in not having price deflators specifically for national defense purchases.

spring of 1958. Over a fifteen-month period, expenditures rose from $44.0 billion in the first quarter of 1958 to $46.2 billion in the second quarter of 1959.

11. Uneasy Stability: July, 1959–December, 1960. The efforts of the Administration to stabilize spending brought the rise to a halt in the third quarter of 1959. Expenditures dropped off to a low of $44.7 billion in the second quarter of 1960 as the Administration fought off its missile gap and limited war critics. In the summer of 1960, spending began to inch up again as the Administration accelerated programs after the break-up of the Paris summit talks.

The Administration acts to increase or decrease defense spending in response to the policy requirements and political pressures which it faces. Consequently, changes in policies are best reflected in changes in defense spending in current dollars. To compare, apart from other considerations, the size of the military effort at one time with its size at another time, however, figures in constant dollars are necessary. Such figures on a quarterly basis are not calculated by the Department of Commerce. They have, however, been closely approximated by the data in Table 12. The ups and downs in military magnitude caused by changing policy priorities as revealed in Table 11 can also be seen, in moderated form, when the changing value of the dollar is eliminated. Probably the outstanding feature revealed in Table 12 is the extent to which the Eisenhower Administration, despite its shifts in policy and direction, did succeed in achieving a reasonably stable absolute level of defense spending. For five years, from the third quarter of 1954 to the third quarter of 1959, the quarterly rate of defense spending was never more than $39.7 billion and never less than $36.3 billion.

The proportions of governmental and national effort devoted to defense purposes differed markedly in the pre-Korean, Korean, and post-Korean periods. The relevant figures are presented in Tables 13 and 14.

At the peak of World War II almost 42 percent of the GNP went to war purposes. After demobilization and before the Korean War about 5 percent of the GNP was devoted to national security.

TABLE 13. GROSS NATIONAL PRODUCT AND NATIONAL DEFENSE SPENDING, 1944–1960

Calendar Year	Gross National Product ($ billion)	National Defense Spending ($ billion)	Percent
1944	211.4	88.6	41.9
1945	213.6	75.9	35.5
1946	210.7	18.8	8.9
1947	234.3	11.4	4.9
1948	259.4	11.6	4.5
1949	258.1	13.6	5.3
1950	284.6	14.3	5.0
1951	329.0	33.9	10.3
1952	347.0	46.4	13.4
1953	365.4	49.3	13.5
1954	363.1	41.2	11.3
1955	397.5	39.1	9.8
1956	419.2	40.3	9.6
1957	442.8	44.4	10.0
1958	444.2	44.8	10.1
1959	482.1	46.0	9.5
1960	503.2	45.1	9.0

Sources: U. S. Department of Commerce, Office of Business Economics; *U. S. Income and Output* (1958), pp. 118–19; *Survey of Current Business* (Feb. 1960), p. 11, (Feb. 1961), p. 12. For nature of "national defense spending," see Table 11 above.

TABLE 14. TOTAL BUDGET EXPENDITURES AND MAJOR NATIONAL SECURITY EXPENDITURES, FY 1946–FY 1961

Fiscal Year	Total Expenditures ($ million)	Major National Security Expenditures ($ million)	Percent
1946	60,448	43,507	72.0
1947	39,033	14,392	36.9
1948	33,068	11,675	35.3
1949	39,507	12,902	32.7
1950	39,606	13,009	32.8
1951	44,058	22,306	50.6
1952	65,408	43,976	67.2
1953	74,274	50,363	67.8
1954	67,772	46,904	69.2
1955	64,570	40,626	62.9
1956	66,540	40,641	61.1
1957	69,433	43,270	62.3
1958	71,936	44,142	61.4
1959	80,697	46,426	57.5
1960	77,233	45,627	59.1
1961 prelim.	81,500	47,389	57.8

Source: *Budget of the United States Government for the Fiscal Year Ending June 30, 1955*, pp. 1165, 1167; *ibid., 1957*, pp. 1164–65; joint statement, Secretary of the Treasury and Director of the Bureau of the Budget, July 20, 1961.

During the Korean War, the percentage rose to a peak of 13.5 percent in 1953. From 1955 through 1959 it remained remarkably stable at about 10 percent. Similarly, before the Korean War roughly one-third of federal expenditures was devoted to security purposes. Rearmament increased this to a peak of 69.2 percent in FY 1954. In the following years the ratio of national security spending to total federal budget expenditures hovered about 60 percent.

CHAPTER V

Innovation of Strategic Programs

22. PATTERNS OF INNOVATION
DETERRENCE AND INNOVATION

In 1940 the principal elements of American military might were the strongest navy and the largest industrial potential in the world, a small regular army and air force, and large untrained and semitrained manpower reserves. In 1945 most military and civilian leaders thought that once again these would be the core of American military strength and that to them would be added a strong air force and nuclear weapons. In 1946 the United States did not have a strategic retaliatory force designed to deter major Soviet aggression, European defense forces to deter or to defeat attacks on western Europe, continental defense forces to protect North America against direct attack, or limited war forces designed to deter or to defeat Communist aggressions elsewhere in the world. Fifteen years later it did have such programs. The innovation of these "functional" strategic programs was revolutionary in its scope and rapidity. Concurrently, two other programs—civil defense and arms control—were proposed which rested on substantially different strategic conceptions. As the national commitment to deterrence hardened and as the requirements of deterrence changed, these alternative programs were slowly and partially assimilated into the deterrent strategy. This was innovation, but innovation different from that involved in the creation of the major functional programs.

Between 1945 and 1949 the great issues of military policy involved conflicting service program goals. In the 1950s the significant military policy issues stemmed from the innovation of the functional programs of deterrence: the 1949–1950 debate over construction of the hydrogen bomb; the 1950–1951 "Great Debate" over troops to Europe; the 1952–1953 struggle over the continental defense of North America; and the continuing controversy after 1954 over limited war forces. Controversy focused upon these issues even more than upon the broader questions of the strategic balance and the relation between security and nonsecurity needs. The innovation of these programs reflected the changing requirements of deterrence which, in turn, stemmed primarily from the development and expansion of Soviet strategic capabilities. Soviet acquisition of nuclear weapons, added to Soviet superiority in ground forces, required a strong, ready American strategic retaliatory force. The growth of Soviet air-atomic strength and the apparent willingness of the Soviets to risk war stimulated the creation of defense forces in western Europe. As the Soviets further developed their striking power, continental defenses became necessary to minimize first-strike damage to American strategic forces. Finally, Soviet acquisition of thermonuclear weapons and long-range missiles created the impetus for limited war forces to handle the small-scale disturbances which might take place within the framework of mutual strategic deterrence. In retrospect the desirablility of each of these innovations seems clear. When first suggested, however, each was the target of vigorous opposition. In each case the question was *whether* or not the proposed program was desirable or necessary. Eventually each program won either general acceptance or, in the case of limited war forces, partial acceptance. Then lesser but continuing battles went on over *how much* effort should be devoted to the new program.

In earlier periods of military policy disequilibrium, changes occurred in the goals of the military services and in service programs. The activities of each service implemented one or more policy purposes which might change but which were quite different from the purposes implemented by the activities of the other services. Functional programs related to particular policy goals either coincided with service programs or were components of service programs. In the first part of the nineteenth century, for instance, the Army developed its activities designed to protect the frontier against the Indians. In the first part of the twentieth century, the U. S. Marine Corps acquired a distinctive purpose in amphibious warfare and developed an amphibious warfare program involving a fourfold expansion in personnel, the development of new tactics and weapons, and the creation of the Fleet Marine Force. Immediately after World War II, the principal military program goals were service goals: universal military training, 70 Air Force groups, larger aircraft carriers. The functional programs required by a continuing peacetime strategy, however, cut across service boundaries. They developed within the service framework, but eventually transcended any one service. In little over a decade the World War II-oriented service programs had been transformd into Cold War-oriented functional programs.

The innovation of a major functional program reflects a new purpose in military policy. Strategic program innovation usually includes changes in weapons, forces, organization, personnel, and deployments, but innovations in any one of these elements need not be associated with innovations in strategic programs. Innovations in weapons, in particular, occur much more frequently than innovations in major programs. The construction of thermonuclear weapons and the expansion of the Air Force between 1950 and 1953 were part of the emergence of a new program of strategic deterrence. The innovation of long-range ballistic missiles after 1954, on the other hand, was simply a new means of implementing that program. It was a change in armaments but not a change in purpose. Similarly, while major innovations in organization are usually associated with program innovations, organizational changes may also be substitutes for program changes. Changes in weapons and organizations are easier to identify than innovations in major programs, and numerous studies have been made of individual weapons innovations and individual organization innovations.[1]

THE PROCESS OF INNOVATION

Significant differences existed in the innovation of the four major functional programs. Technological issues, for instance, played a major role in strategic deterrence and continental defense; diplomatic issues were more important in European defense and limited war. The innovation of strategic deterrence and European defense was accomplished earlier and more easily than the innovation of continental defense and limited war programs. Despite their distinctive characteristics, however, all four shared many common elements. Generalizing from these four cases, it is possible to construct a "model" which describes no actual innovation but which does embody the key elements of the innovation process.

Program innovation is complex, slow, and controversial. It requires the addition of new military activities to service programs, the adjustment of old service programs, and, often, changes in service concept and doctrine. It also requires time. The "effecting of large scale changes," as Ginzberg and Reilley have said, "is never an event but always a process." [2] The emergence of a functional program usually consumed four or five years. The controversy over the maintenance of the strategic deterrent force lasted from about 1948 through 1951, that over European defense from 1948 through 1952, that over continental defense from 1951 through 1954, that over limited war capabilities from 1954 to the beginning of the Kennedy Administration. Innovation involves major political struggles among many groups: military and scientific, industrial and political, governmental and private. These groups have different perceptions of strategic needs and different preferences about the ways in which those needs should be met. The conflicts ebb and flow about a variety of specific issues and proposals. In "the discovery and elaboration of new programs," March and Simon have observed, "the decision-making process will proceed in stages, and at no time will it be concerned with the 'whole' problem in all its complexity, but always with parts of the problem." [3] Innovation is more the result of accretion than of any single decision.

Innovation begins when groups sensitive to the new need take uncoordinated steps toward meeting it. In due course, the activities of these groups produce a "critical program," which assumes decisive importance in the minds of both the supporters and the opponents of the overall innovation: the hydrogen bomb, troops to Europe, a distant early warning system, larger Army forces. The critical issue becomes the focus of debate, requiring decision at the highest level of government. An affirmative decision on it is a necessary although not sufficient condition for the emergence of the program as a whole.

The desirability of innovation does not become equally visible to all groups simultaneously. A group can take the lead in breaking the previously existing consensus, or in "creating an issue," only if it is both sensitive to the need and also free to propose and to push programs to meet the need. The sensitivity of military groups to new program needs depends largely upon service doctrine and service interests. The Air Force was active in pushing strategic deterrence and the Army in innovating European defense since each program was closely related to existing service doctrine. All the services were hesitant in pushing continental defense and limited war, however, which were alien to traditional service doctrines. In addition, military groups occupy a fixed position in a highly formal structure of authority, and they accept budget ceilings and other elements of policy as predetermined, limiting their own area of possible innovation. "In general, the proposer of an innovation will regard elements of structure and existing programs that are more than one or two steps removed from him in the formal structure as 'given' and unchangeable." The activities of military groups, moreover, are highly programmed, and in general, "vigorous innovative activity will take place only in organizational units that are not assigned substantial responsibilities for programmed activity."[4] The initiative in program innovation, as in weapons or organization innovation, often rests with civilians or military who are "unconventional" or "outsiders."[5] The smaller the stake which a group has in existing programs, the more likely it is to push new programs.

The intra-executive debate and controversy produces reasonably well-defined alignments of groups supporting and opposing the innovation. Military services, civilian executive groups, and "outside" or fringe groups may be on both sides of each issue, and the groups which enthusiastically support one innovation often oppose others. Scientists who had been against the development of the hydrogen bomb ardently pushed European defense (Conant) or continental defense (Oppenheimer). Those closely identified with established functional programs view unfavorably the innovation of new ones. The Air Force, for instance, played a major role in developing strategic deterrence. The innovations of the other strategic programs were, in a sense, the result of the prospective or actual expansion of Soviet retaliatory capability and the relative decline of its American counterpart. Airpower supporters, particularly those closely identified with strategic airpower, tended to oppose the program innovations designed to adjust American strategy to the developing needs of deterrence. Throughout the 1950s, in technological innovation, the Air Force was the most advanced of the services; in program innovation, it was the most conservative.

Budgetary officials and other governmental leaders concerned primarily with economy oppose program innovations. Whether or not the addition of a new program would actually be more expensive than the expansion of the old program, which might be the only substitute, the addition of new programs seems more expensive.[6] The opposition of the economy supporters was not significant in the development of strategic deterrence or the expansion of American forces in Europe during the Korean War. It delayed considerably, however, approval of the continental defense program, and it was a major factor in the continuing reluctance of the Eisenhower Administration explicitly to endorse additional limited war programs.

The proposal of the critical program is met by counterproposals from other groups and by the outright opposition of still others. The issue is studied and debated at length.[7] One or more of three factors work to prolong the process. First, both supporters and opponents of the innovation assume that their disagreement can be resolved through analytic rather than through political means. It is to be expected, as March and Simon have argued, that disputes "will be defined as problems in analysis, that the initial reaction to conflict will be problem solving and persuasion, that such reactions will persist even when they appear to be inappropriate, that there will be a greater explicit emphasis on common goals where they do not exist than where they do, and that bargaining (when it occurs) will frequently be concealed within an analytic framework."[8] The man who was Secretary of Defense longer than anyone else during the Truman and Eisenhower Administrations reportedly displayed in his office the sign: "Reasonable, intelligent men with a common objective, in the presence of the facts, do not have too much trouble coming into agreement."[9] From this belief it is but a small step to the assumption that disagreement must be due to the absence of the facts. Issues are subjected to relentless study and investigation in an effort to resolve conflicts over goals by research into data and to solve by experts problems which require politicians.

Secondly, decisions promoting innovation differ from decisions allocating resources among existing programs because they are distinctly asymmetrical in character.[10] Failure to decide whether the Army or the Navy should receive an additional $50 million may or may not have different consequences for the programs of the two services. Failure to decide on innovation, however, is a decision not to innovate, and most decisions not to innovate are made in this manner. To resolve the issue is to innovate; to postpone the issue always is not to innovate. Rarely if ever is there a conscious decision against innovation. Evasion and delay are key methods of preventing innovation, and referral of the proposed program to committees and study groups becomes a means by which its opponents attempt to defeat it. Moreover, a negative decision, or rather the absence of a decision, can be continually challenged and usually remains reversible. A decision to innovate, however, is much more difficult to change.

Finally, the supporters of innovation may have their own reasons to favor delay. The asymmetrical character of the decision-making process imposes peculiar burdens on them. "Individuals and organizations give preferred treatment to alternatives that represent continuation of present programs over those that represent change."[11] Consequently the supporters of innovation can succeed only by arousing support from strategically located officials and groups. This requires time and effort. Research and study groups are often valuable instruments of "education."

The decisive factor in the innovation of a functional program is the extent to which it is supported by executive groups and congressional or other groups closely associated with the executive branch. If the executive groups substantially favor innovation, not much else is required to make it a reality. If they substantially oppose it, nothing else can make it a reality. If serious disagreements exist within the executive branch, the proponents and the opponents of innovation engage in "outflanking movements," attempting to mobilize additional supporters. In bureaucratic struggles as in military ones, Cannae is a model of success. The side which seems to be losing at the moment takes the initiative in seeking to expand the arena of decision. Sometimes the encircling movements include only groups within the executive branch. When the struggle is intense, however, one or both sides may appeal to outside publics. The more prolonged the discussion within the executive branch, the more extensive are the lobbying efforts of congressional and other groups to influence the decision. In general, the greater the agreement in the executive branch, the less time is required for the Administration to reach a decision, the less need and opportunity there are for dissatisfied groups to appeal to the outside public, the less public debate there is about the issue before the decision is made, and the greater the likelihood there is that the opponents of innovation will stimulate extensive public debate after the decision. This was the pattern with the hydrogen bomb and the European reinforcements. On the other hand, the greater the opposition to innovation within the executive, the more prolonged is the discussion within the executive, the more extensive are the efforts of the proponents of innovation to arouse support outside the executive, and, hence, the more extensive is the public debate of the issue stimulated by the proponents of innovation before the Administration makes its decision. This was the pattern with continental defense and limited war. Thus, where the decision to innovate occurs quickly, the opponents appeal for public debate; where it is delayed, the supporters do. The extent of the debate varies inversely with the support for the program. The question of what is the proper decision gives rise to a corollary debate on what is the proper locus of decision.

The decisions on critical programs are almost invariably made by the President, working through the National Security Council machinery. In some instances, the decision grows naturally out of the process of debate and consideration. Innovation is always easier during a transition from war to peace or peace to war or immediately after a change of Administrations. In other instances, a stalemate may develop among the interested groups; the pressures for innovation are insufficient to overcome inertia and resistance. In these cases, a dramatic development or "trigger event" may play a decisive role in bringing about a decision. In decisions on the allocation of resources among existing programs it is always possible to compromise and split the difference between the two competing programs. Innovation, however, involves the balancing of two incommensurables: time and resources. The decision-maker weighs the potential consumption of time in not innovating against the potential consumption of resources in innovating. Temporal accountability is usually less exacting than financial accountability; as long as time appears to be in reasonable supply, the balance is tilted against innovation. The function of a trigger event is to clarify and dramatize the shortage of time. Its message is: "There is no time." In some cases, such as the hydrogen bomb, a trigger event may stimulate the initiation of a critical program. In others, such as continental defense, it may bring to an end a prolonged period of discussion and controversy with an authoritative decision by the President and the NSC.

Favorable Administration decision on the critical issue, although not necessarily designed to do so, commits the government irrevocably to the new policy and purpose. Inevitably, however, the overall purpose can only be realized by many additional decisions which offer the opponents of the program further opportunity for obstruction and "foot-dragging." Often the exact meaning and implications of the Administration action are questioned. Changes in the policy environment are held to justify modification of the decision or postponement of its implementation. Further reconsideration is urged. These efforts within the executive branch may be linked with public questioning of the decision outside the executive branch, as the supporters of innovation make additional, continuing efforts to secure the cooperation of other groups. Final acceptance of the program is usually marked by two developments: the emergence of autonomous organizational units devoted exclusively or primarily to it and the broadening of the participation in the program to other groups originally unsympathetic or opposed to it.

A strategic program requires men, weapons, equipment, installations. The program only becomes a continuing reality, however, when these raw materials are brought together in an organizational unit devoted primarily or exclusively to the program. Organizational identity is essential for the program to be a continuing force. It may be achieved either by revivifying an existing organizational unit or by creating an entirely new unit to embody the new purposes. SAC, SHAPE, CONAD, and STRAC are, in their different ways and strengths, organizational embodiments of functional programs. The emergence of an autonomous organization strengthens the program in competition with other programs and usually leads to a marked increase in the resources allocated to the program.[12] Organizational independence becomes a guarantee of program permanence. Abandonment of the program requires a new battle to disestablish the organization or to change its purpose.

Isolation or withdrawal thus sharpens the identity of the program and the organization, removing doubts of its proponents and opponents as to the program's existence. At the same time, however, the political stability of the program also requires broadening the support for the program and acceptance of the organization among other groups. The more groups affiliated with the program, the more secure is its existence. Developing organizational autonomy and broadening affiliations are, in a sense, opposing tendencies, yet they both contribute to the same end. Usually the achievement of organizational autonomy comes earlier than the broadening of affiliations, but the two processes always overlap to some degree. The crucial aspect of innovation is the change in the attitudes of the groups affected by the program. Innovation is successful to the extent that these groups become affiliated with the program, participate in it, support it, or at least acquiesce in its existence. Innovation begins with the disruption of an existing consensus by those proposing a new program. It ends with the appearance of a new consensus accepting the existence of the program. It is the process by which the unfamiliar becomes the accepted.

THE DIALOGUE OF INNOVATION

Different substantive policies are debated in each innovation. Certain types of issues and patterns of argument, nonetheless, tend to recur. Four key issues are: 1) the relevance of the proposed program to a strategy of deterrence; 2) its feasibility and appropriateness in the light of its purported objectives; 3) its effects on other programs and the extent to which it sustains or upsets the strategic balance; 4) and the immediate need for the innovation of the program, its timing.

Deterrence. The proponents argue that the new program is necessary to supplement the old deterrent programs which no longer meet the prospective or actual growth of Soviet capabilities. For example, the two crucial questions concerning the hydrogen bomb were, as Harry Truman said, "Can the Russians make this thing? And if so, how can we help making it?" [13] Or, a year later Acheson argued that the NATO countries must build up their ground forces in Europe to "continue to deter aggression after our atomic advantage has been diminished." [14] Continental defense was justified because it would protect SAC and increase SAC's deterrent value, and because it would complicate the problems of a potential aggressor and be "a disincentive—a defensive deterrent—to the Soviet Union." [15] Similarly, a balance of terror with neutralized strategic retaliatory forces, it was held, required stronger limited war forces to deter local aggressions.

The opponents of innovation argue that such programs will not deter, that they may provoke or invite aggression, and that they will decrease the deterrent effectiveness of existing programs. American development of a hydrogen bomb, it was held, would provoke Soviet development and eventually precipitate thermonuclear war. The use of the weapon was the inevitable result of its existence. If, on the other hand, the United States refused to develop thermonuclear weapons, the Russians probably would refrain from doing so also; if they did develop them and the United States did not, the balance of military power would not be greatly affected.[16] In the summer of 1950, the opponents of the NATO build-up argued that "it would provoke a preventive attack by the Russians long before Western defenses had been adequately strengthened." [17] Ground forces would not significantly help to deter war. "[T]he big deterrent to war for the next 2 or 3 years is still going to be American air power," General LeMay argued, "and not any divisions that we could muster and put in Europe or any divisions that the Allies could produce themselves." [18] The Air Force opposition to continental defense held that it added little deterrent strength and that the "long-range retaliatory power of the Strategic Air Command is as important for our defense as are interceptor planes and aircraft warning systems." [19] Development of a continental defense system, the opponents held, would indicate that the United States did not expect to deter war and that it was returning to isolationism, abandoning its European allies to their own fate. Similarly, opponents argued that the preparation of special forces to deal with limited aggressions would decrease the credibility of the massive deterrent and invite local aggressions. The innovation of all three programs other than strategic deterrence was opposed on the grounds that it would undermine the effectiveness of SAC as a deterrent, thus attributing the decreased effectiveness of SAC to an increase in other American capabilities rather than to an increase in Soviet capabilities.

Feasibility. Innovation, March and Simon have argued, is most likely under conditions of "optimal stress," that is, "when the carrot is just a *little* way ahead of the donkey—when aspirations exceed achievement by a small amount." If the gap is too small, too little dissatisfaction exists to produce innovation; if it is too large, frustration results and "neurotic reactions interfere with effective innovation." [20] Hence, the proponents attempt to advance a program which is sufficiently large and radical (technologically or diplomatically) to achieve their goal and yet sufficiently small and familiar to be feasible. Usually they focus their argument on fairly concrete and easily dramatized proposals. The opponents, on the other hand, can argue that the program itself may not be feasible or that it will be so large and expensive as to be prohibitive. Many scientists had their doubts, for instance, about the practicality of the hydrogen bomb, although opposition to the bomb was based more on the fear that it would be feasible than upon the fear that it would not be. The difficulty of defending Europe successfully on the ground led the Joint Chiefs to insist upon German rearmament and furnished the public opponents of the program ample opportunity to deplore the American "expendables" who would be the victims of a "massacre" if the Soviets attacked.[21] Similarly, the Secretary of the Air Force argued in 1950 that "a thorough air defense is not now feasible, nor does it seem attainable in the immediate future." Three years later the defenders of the Lincoln Summer Study Group replied at length that their recommendations were technically feasible and that the costs of a continental defense system would not be excessive.[22] In the debate over limited war, it was held that the United States simply could not afford to match the Communists "man for man" and to be prepared for every possible contingency. The only feasible course was to concentrate upon what Admiral Radford called our long suits: airpower and naval power. The supporters of limited war forces, on the other hand, argued that only a small additional effort was required to maintain an efficient three- or four-division force, which would be much less expensive than the prolonged maintenance of a first-strike capability.

Balance. Closely related to the feasibility issue are the effects of the proposed innovation on the balance among strategic programs. The supporters of innovation hold that failure to innovate will restrict the flexibility of American diplomacy, close off potentially desirable policy options, and condemn the United States to an all-or-nothing response. The new program, they argue, will not replace existing programs or detract from them. Instead, it is a necessary supplement to them. The supporters of innovation tend to suggest, although seldom to assert, that their program is the "absolute" answer to a new "absolute" danger. This leads the opponents to argue that the new program will upset the "balance" in strategy and that it will be overemphasized, excluding or subordinating existing programs. In addition, the opponents argue that innovation will divert men, money, and materials from established and successful programs to a dubious undertaking.

Members of the AEC General Advisory Committee felt that the hydrogen bomb would "give us a false impression of security and illusion of security that we had gained a decisive or absolute weapon ... an overvaluation of the security that could be secured from large bombs alone as distinguished from a balanced military establishment." [23] A year later the opponents of the European reinforcements argued that the proposed deployment would further aggravate what they considered the existing unbalance in favor of a surface force strategy. "Two-thirds ground and sea and one-third in the air," Lt. Gen. Harold George, USAAF (Ret.), said, "is out of balance." [24] The supporters of the move, however, argued that all three forms of military power were equally essential. A large continental defense program, it was held, would upset the existing strategic balance. The proponents of continental defense, one Air Force official said, believed "it was necessary not only to strengthen the Air Defense of the continental United States, but also to give up something, and the thing that was recommended that we give up was the Strategic Air Command, or more properly I should say the strategic part of our total air power, which includes more than the

Strategic Air Command."[25] The Air Force argued that any available resources should be used not to construct a new distant early warning line but "to improve the air defense system then in existence."[26] The supporters of the hydrogen bomb in 1950, Conant argued, had been pushing "sort of a Maginot Line psychology"; the supporters of continental defense, the Chief Scientist of the Air Force held, "recommended a Maginot Line type of concept."[27] Similarly, it was argued that if the United States was prepared to fight a large war successfully, it must also be prepared to fight a small one, and hence any special program for limited war would unbalance the military establishment and misuse resources.

Timing. The proponents of innovation usually attempt to act in terms of what might be described, parallel to the concept of "optimum stress," as the concept of optimum timing. The danger to be met by the proposed program is usually located about three years in the future—distant enough so that a program can still be inaugurated but close enough so that the inauguration cannot be delayed. The danger is also described in fairly concrete terms. The proponents of the hydrogen bomb argued that, regardless of whether the United States made one or not, the Soviets would have one in three or four years. Hence, a "crash" program was essential. The backers of European defense in 1950 declared that in the "danger year," 1954, the Soviets would be in their best position to assault western Europe. "The need for the strength to deter aggression is immediate," Acheson said, ". . . the greatest risk of all is that we might once again hear the bitter refrain: 'Too little and too late.' And this time there may be no opportunity to remedy the mistake."[28] The supporters of continental defense pointed to the immediate need to bring a defense and warning system into existence before the Soviets developed substantial strategic capabilities. The proponents of limited war forces, however, were handicapped by their inability to locate the danger at some specific point in the future and to develop a sense of urgency for their program.

The opponents of innovation usually hold that a more thorough study of the issue is required and that while they do not necessarily oppose the new program in principle, they do oppose the waste, expense, and deleterious effects on other programs which are involved in innovating a program on a crash basis. The opponents of the hydrogen bomb argued that the whole question needed further study in a larger framework. In recommending postponement of the decision on the hydrogen bomb, Lilienthal also urged that atomic weapons be improved, that they be increased in variety and mobility, that the Air Force be strengthened, and that renewed efforts be made to reach agreement with the Russians to control all means of mass destruction.[29] Hoover and Taft argued that the American reinforcements to Europe should be delayed until the Europeans themselves had created a defense force strong enough to stand off the Russians. When continental defense came up before the NSC, the Air Force opposed construction of the distant early warning line on a crash basis.

23. STRATEGIC DETERRENCE

In March, 1949, Winson Churchill declared that "It is certain that Europe would have been communized and London under bombardment some time ago but for the deterrent of the atomic bomb in the hands of the United States." [30] Churchill expressed a prevailing view. Few dissented from the proposition that the American atomic bomb monopoly was the principal deterrent to Russian aggression. Split by interservice rivalry, the Joint Chiefs of Staff unanimously agreed to rely upon "atomic bombing as a deterrent to war . . ." [31] The idea of atomic deterrence was accepted because it seemed so obvious: What else was stopping the Red Army from marching to the Channel? The means of deterrence were a legacy from World War II. Until 1949 the legacy was sufficient; no substantial new effort was required to supplement it or even to maintain it. Deterrence was easy and uncontroversial, an accident of history not a creature of policy.

The proposal to build the hydrogen bomb was the first major innovation to raise directly the issue of strategic deterrence as a matter of choice. At stake in the debate over the bomb was the nature of the Cold War and the viability of deterrence as a policy. Would a more powerful weapon be a more powerful deterrent to war or only a more awful weapon of war? Could the United States forestall an arms race with the Soviet Union? Did an arms race

23. STRATEGIC DETERRENCE

necessarily mean war? These were the issues. The justification of the bomb rested on its contribution to deterrence rather than victory. The consequences of its use were stressed not by its supporters but by its opponents. The innovation of the hydrogen bomb was the critical program in the emergence of a policy of strategic deterrence. It shaped the evolution of American strategy during the following decade. Inevitably it led to long-range ballistic missiles, earth satellites, and space probes. It laid the basis for the nuclear stalemate of the 1950s and the resultant need for limited war forces.

The critical nature of the hydrogen bomb innovation is underlined by the contrast between the esoteric debate within the executive branch over its construction and the simultaneous public debate before Congress in the B-36 investigation.[32] The B-36 debate marked the end of the old era, the hydrogen bomb debate the beginning of a new one. With a few exceptions, most of the participants in the B-36 hearings agreed that the atomic bomb had been the great deterrent of Soviet aggression. They debated, however, not the requirements of future deterrence but the requirements of future wars. The Navy disputed the effectiveness of the Air Force's long-range bombers in a future war and the military efficiency, political wisdom, and general morality of employing strategic nuclear bombing in a war. The focus of the strategic debate was the allegation by "[a]lmost the entire high command" of the Navy "that the present military strategy of the United States has been erroneously founded on the premises that (1) should war begin, the United States will immediately resort to atomic warfare, and (2) the United States will employ such warfare against large urban areas." As the investigating committee stated, neither side in the debate "can be proved right or wrong except through the supreme test of actual war and the nature of the peace that follows." [33] If a general war had broken out in the following year or two, the B-36 debate would have seemed extremely important. One side or the other would have been vindicated. Instead, the issues turned out to be irrelevant. The specific and fairly minor issue, for instance, of whether the B-36 would be a success in combat was never resolved; the B-36 became a success because it never went into combat. The issue in the B-36 hearings was how the United States should prepare to fight another war. The issue in the hydrogen bomb debate was whether the United States should through armaments attempt to prevent another war.

During World War II top priority was given to the development of a fission bomb; only theoretical work was done on thermonuclear weapons. At the end of the war, scientists differed on the practicality and desirability of making a major effort in this field. Such a program, however, was impractical in the immediate postwar atmosphere; at least one, and possibly two, committees of scientists recommended that no major development effort be made but that research be continued. In 1947 the AEC General Advisory Committtee and in 1948 the Research and Development Board of the Military Establishment and the Joint Chiefs of Staff urged continuation of the research. Throughout this period a small group of scientists at Los Alamos did do basic research on the problems of thermonuclear reactions. There the matter rested until the announcement of the Soviet atomic explosion in September, 1949.

The initiative for making a high priority effort to develop the hydrogen bomb came primarily from civilian scientists.[34] They were quickly joined by the members and staff of the Joint Committee on Atomic Energy and then by the military. Although generally favoring the bomb, the military were not the first to push it. Immediately after the announcement of the Soviet atomic explosion on September 23, two scientists, Ernest O. Lawrence and Luis Alvarez, at the University of California in Berkeley, began to stimulate the interest of other scientists and consulted with Edward Teller at Los Alamos. At about the same time, AEC Commissioner Strauss urged the project on the other commissioners. Writing on October 21, 1949, Oppenheimer observed that ". . . two experienced promoters have been at work, i.e., Ernest Lawrence and Edward Teller. The project has long been dear to Teller's heart; and Ernest has convinced himself that we must learn from Operation Joe [the Soviet atomic explosion] that the Russians will soon do the super, and that we had better beat them to it. . . . Ernest spoke to Knowland and McMahon, and to some at least of the joint chiefs." [35] The scientists, an Air Force officer later said, "urged that the military express its interest in the development of this weapon." As a result, General Vandenberg, Air Force Chief of Staff, speaking for the JCS, "strongly urged the development of this thermonuclear weapon" at a meeting between the Chiefs and the Joint Committee on Atomic Energy on October 14. Three days later the Chiefs wrote the AEC requesting information about thermonuclear weapons and expressing concern that funds had not been already secured for the project. The "joint chiefs," Oppenheimer stated on October 21, "appear informally to have decided to give the development of the super overriding priority, though no formal request has come through." On October 29 when General Bradley met with the General Advisory Committee, however, he seemed uncertain about possible military uses for the bomb. Clearly, in the events immediately following the Soviet nuclear explosion, the initiative lay with the civilians, who stimulated the interest of the military and found an especially sympathetic response in the Air Force. Before that time, as Oppenheimer emphasized, "there had been no great expression of interest on the part of the military in more powerful weapons. The atomic bomb had of course been stepped up some, but we had not been pressed to push that development as fast as possible. There had been no suggestion that very large weapons would be very useful. The pressure was all the other way; get as many as you can." At no time before the AEC report to the President on November 9 did the military specify the relative priority which should be assigned to expanded A-bomb production and H-bomb development.[36]

The four months of active consideration of the hydrogen bomb between September, 1949, and January, 1950, were devoted less to efforts to find an "analytic" solution to the differences between its supporters and opponents than to the efforts of both to arouse support for their viewpoints and the efforts of the opponents to delay decision on the issue. The outflanking maneuvers of both sides followed classic patterns. In the first phase of the controversy, active opposition to the bomb seemed to be confined to the Chairman of the AEC, David E. Lilienthal, and to some members of the Commission's staff. The promoters of the project tried to outflank the Commission by arousing the support of the members and staff of the Joint Committee and of the military. To the opposition, these methods of broadening the arena of discussion "were not proper." [37] At the request of Commissioner Strauss, the most ardent advocate of the bomb on the AEC, the General Advisory Committee of the AEC was called into session to advise the Commission on the desirability of a crash program for the hydrogen bomb and to recommend other measures in the light of the Soviet achievement. At its meeting on October 29, the General Advisory Committee unanimously opposed an immediate hydrogen bomb effort. The Committee became the center of a growing opposition to the bomb, as other scientists expressed themselves against it. Confronted with the Committee's advice, the Atomic Energy Commissioners themselves were unable to reach agreement. On November 9 they urged the President to explore further the foreign policy implications of the bomb and appended to their report their separate opinions on its desirability. Chairman Lilienthal and Commissioner Pike were against the proposal; Commissioners Strauss and Dean were for it; Commissioner Smyth occupied a middle position. Uncertain, President Truman on November 10 referred the problem to a special committee of the NSC consisting of Secretary of State Dean Acheson, Secretary of Defense Louis Johnson, and Chairman Lilienthal.

At this point the initial successes of the proponents of the bomb had been counterbalanced by the rallying of the opposition. The issue was now in doubt, and the process of consideration moved into its third phase as the proponents regrouped their forces and intensified their efforts. Strauss aroused Johnson's interest in the proposal. A military committee was appointed to advise Admiral Souers of the NSC Staff. The Weapons System Evaluation Group endorsed the bomb. Within the AEC, the director of the Division of Military Application also supported it. Senator McMahon spoke personally to the President several times and wrote five letters to him arguing the need for the bomb. In the State Department, the chairman of the Policy Planning Staff, George Kennan, recommended against immediate development, but the Secretary of State favored it: "it became clear that the State Department felt that no international advantage would be gained by postponing the H-bomb program (although the AEC did not receive a formal statement of this)." [38] For slightly different reasons, Defense and State thus joined in support of an immediate start on the bomb, the military fearing a war in which Russia had the bomb and the United States did not and the diplomats fearing the negotiating leverage and blackmail opportunities which exclusive possession of the bomb would give the Soviet Union. Although the services were denouncing each other publicly in the B-36 hearings, Chairman Lilienthal was unable to detach the Army from the united military front.[39] The opposition coalition did not pick up significant new strength; as the lines of division became clearly drawn, the substantial weight of opinion and activity was in favor of development.

Aware that they had been outflanked in the executive branch, the opponents of the bomb considered expanding the arena of debate further by appealing to groups outside the executive. Although Oppenheimer did not approve of Lawrence's going to the Joint Committee without first consulting the AEC, he also did not approve of the limitation of the debate to the executive branch. Writing four years after the events, Lilienthal argued that those who opposed the hydrogen bomb and who wished to deal more broadly with the deficiencies in American defenses "had a most difficult task of persuasion, and an almost impossible one when the facts were kept secret from the people of the country—as most of them still are." He went on to argue:

For had even a part of the essential facts and implications become known to the public, vast new Congressional appropriations and heavy new taxes would have been required at once. The "economy drive" which had brought the military establishment to a low ebb of strength would have come to an abrupt end. Young men would once more have been drafted. But the H-bomb, as a program in itself, did not require facing the music on such unpleasant realities as these.[40]

Proponents and opponents of the bomb leaked material to the press and made other moves toward broadening the arena of decision. For the proponents, however, such action became increasingly unnecessary. For the opponents it would have been disastrous. Facing defeat within the executive branch, the opponents seemed to assume almost automatically that expansion of the arena of debate would redress the balance in their favor. Of course, public discussion of the hydrogen bomb probably would have tilted the scales even more against them. Certainly, simple revelation of the "facts" to the public would in itself have had little political effect. Congress and the public would have been guided in their appraisal of these facts by the views of the Chiefs of Staff and the civilian State and Defense Department leaders.

Closely linked with the opponents' desire to expand the arena of controversy were their efforts to delay decision upon the bomb. Indeed, delay was almost a prerequisite to further discussion. Thus, at the meeting of the Committee of Three on January 31, 1950, Acheson and Johnson recommended approval of the program. Lilienthal, however, urged that a broader study was necessary: "a re-examination of our objectives in peace and war and of the effect of these objectives on our strategic plans in the light of the probable fission bomb (atom bomb) capabilities and the possible thermonuclear capabilities of the Soviet Union." [41] The effort to delay, however, was unsuccessful. The President approved both a general resurvey of American security policy, which eventually produced NSC 68, and also an immediate start of work on the hydrogen bomb without waiting for the results of the overall study.

The initiating trigger of the intra-executive debate was, of course, the Soviet atomic explosion in the last days of August. American intelligence experts had estimated 1952 as the earliest date of a Soviet atomic explosion. Others had put it still farther in the future.[42] The trigger effect of the bomb was enhanced by its unexpectedness. The future had suddenly materialized. The BAS clock jumped from eight to three minutes of midnight. President Truman's reported expression on hearing the news, "That means we have no time left," defined perfectly the meaning of a trigger event: the possibilities of procrastination were over. The Soviet explosion, as Teller later put it, meant "that the arms race was no longer a possibility but a frightening reality." [43] Everyone agreed action was necessary. But what action? The Berkeley scientists filled the need. The Joint Committee on Atomic Energy, as Oppenheimer observed, which had "tried to find something tangible to chew on ever since September 23rd, has at least found its answer." [44] In a sense, the proponents simply moved in response to the demand. The trigger event fired the charge, they supplied the projectile.[45]

The subject of the President's decision precluded extensive public discussion of the wisdom of the decision. Only nuclear scientists not currently in government employ and members of the Joint Committee on Atomic Energy were ready for informed discussion. In Congress, Representative Cole opposed the decision, Representatives Holifield and Jackson supported it. Senator McMahon argued that it was necessary but warned that an unrestrained armaments race could only end in disaster and urged international control of atomic energy as a step toward the reallocation of funds from weapons to economic aid and the peaceful uses of atomic energy.[46] A few scientists directly challenged the desirability of building the bomb, Dr. Hans Bethe on grounds of morality and Dr. Robert Bacher on its military value. More frequently, the scientific critics warned of the horrible consequences of the use of the bomb by any nation. The implications of this admonition were that it made little sense to manufacture a weapon which would not be used. Twelve leading physicists declared that the H-bomb "is no longer a weapon of war but a means of extermination of whole populations. Its use would be a betrayal of all standards of morality and of Christian civilization itself.... To create such an ever-present peril for all the nations in the world is against the vital interests of both Russia and the United States." Still more frequently, the critics expressed concern with the process by which the decision was made. "There is grave danger for us," Oppenheimer declared, "in that these decisions have been taken on the basis of facts held secret." Other scientists urged that more information be presented to the public. The AEC responded in the middle of March by first instructing, and then requesting, AEC and contractor employees to "refrain from publicly stating facts or giving comment" on the thermonuclear program.[47] Three months after the decision the limited public debate was virtually over.

The President's decision of January 31 was the turning point in the development of the hydrogen bomb and a decisive step in the emergence of a program of strategic deterrence. It was, however, only one part of a long process. To be meaningful it had to be implemented. To be implemented, its own meaning had to be understood and accepted. Initially, considerable doubt existed about what the President's action did signify. The President, as Warner Schilling's penetrating analysis shows, had made the decision without resolving many of the crucial issues at stake in it. It was a minimal decision, with the President seeking "that course of action which would close off the least number of future alternatives, and which would avoid the most choice." The decision rejected delay in order to negotiate with the Russians or to complete a general survey of

American strategy; but, on the other hand, the presidential directive following the decision "had not endorsed an intensive H-bomb program" and did not authorize the construction of production facilities for the bomb.[48] Without production facilities, of what use would be the bomb? The Secretary of Defense and the Joint Chiefs returned to the fray on February 24 with a recommendation for the "immediate implementation of all-out development of hydrogen bombs and means for their production and delivery." [49] The President again referred the issue to his three-man NSC committee. Sumner Pike had replaced Lilienthal as AEC Chairman, and he agreed with the military that it would make little sense to develop a successful bomb only to wait several years before producing it in quantity. While the State Department officials did not wish to make an early commitment to quantity production, they could not oppose this logic, and on March 10 the President approved the military recommendations. Thus, as Warner Schilling has put it, "the minimal decision [of January 31] permitted the Department of Defense to achieve its objectives in two bites and to take its possible opponents one at a time, and while the January decision might not have prejudiced the chances of an unfettered look at the H-bomb program, the March decision certainly did." [50]

The criticisms voiced publicly by leading scientists and the well-known initial GAC opposition may have had adverse effects upon the recruitment of scientists to work on the development of the weapon at Los Alamos. The principal scientific figure in the development of the bomb has claimed that during this period the General Advisory Committee was "serving as a brake rather than encouragement." Oppenheimer and others have denied that any conscious effort was made to obstruct the recruitment of scientists or in any other way to delay the development of the bomb.[51] Shortly after the President's decision, however, apparently both Oppenheimer and Conant considered resigning from the GAC because of their opposition to the bomb, but were urged not to do so by Dean Acheson. In the summer of 1950, when Gordon Dean became chairman of the AEC, Oppenheimer debated resigning as Chairman of the Advisory Committee because on "a very major point of policy" he "had become identified with a view which was not now national policy. I thought that there could be stronger arguments for having as chairman of that committee someone who had from the beginning been enthusiastic and affirmative." [52] Chairman Dean, other commissioners, and members of the GAC urged him to remain as chairman, which he did. When his membership on the General Advisory Committee expired in 1952, however, President Truman did not reappoint him. The issues left unsettled by the presidential decisions in the winter of 1950 came up again and again in the following two years. Even in the fall of 1952, influential figures, including apparently some members of the State Department's advisory committee on disarmament, urged the United States not to test its H-bomb until it had negotiated with the Russians for a ban on such tests or at least to postpone the test until the new Administration had come into office.[53]

Furthermore, during the winter of 1951–1952 Teller insisted that thermonuclear work was not proceeding satisfactorily at Los Alamos and argued vigorously that a new laboratory was needed to speed the development of the bomb. This idea was strongly backed by the Air Force and the Joint Committee on Atomic Energy. The establishment of a new full-scale laboratory was opposed almost unanimously by both the Commission and the General Advisory Committee. In the late spring of 1952, however, the Commission, the GAC, and the other groups concerned agreed upon a second, more limited, weapons laboratory under Teller's direction at Livermore, California. All the principal work on the hydrogen bomb, nevertheless, was done at Los Alamos.[54]

In 1951 and 1952 the Air Force sponsored two studies: Project Lincoln on air defense and Project Vista on tactical nuclear weapons. Both projects led to major innovations in strategic programs. Both were also, however, viewed with suspicion and even outright opposition by those elements in the Air Force associated with the Strategic Air Command and primarily concerned with the development of the forces required for strategic deterrence. Conversely, many scientists who had initially opposed the hydrogen bomb played an active role in pushing these later projects. The line-ups in the battles over thermonuclear weapons, air defense, and tactical nuclear weapons were remarkably similar. Clearly, with the supporters of the hydrogen bomb there can be little doubt that this was a case of once-successful innovators opposing subsequent innovations which might lay competing claims on resources. It is likely also that the support which the scientists gave to air defense and tactical weapons was related to their opposition to the hydrogen bomb. This group of scientists seemed to progress through three phases: active opposition to the hydrogen bomb before the President's decision; uncertainty and lack of enthusiasm for the bomb after the President's decision in 1950 and 1951; enthusiastic and positive support for air defense and tactical weapons innovations in late 1951 and 1952. In this way, continued dissatisfaction with one innovation eventually hastened other innovations.

The development of one weapon, of course, did not create a program of strategic deterrence. This required many other actions on many other programs. No one of them, however, aroused controversy comparable to that over the hydrogen bomb. The Atomic Energy Commission carried out a major expansion of its facilities for the production of fission weapons and preparation for the production of fusion weapons. During the Korean War the Air Force began to expand, with eventual agreement on a 143-wing goal in the fall of 1951. The B-36 bombers were improved, and production of B-47 medium jets was accelerated. Under the leadership of Secretary Finletter overseas bases were established in Europe, North Africa, Greenland, and the Far East. The acceptance of strategic retaliation as a major deterrent program was also aided by the Korean War, which opened up for the Navy the hope that it too could acquire the means for long-range nuclear bombing. Beginning in 1951 Congress authorized a series of large aircraft carriers comparable to the carrier whose cancellation in 1949 had provoked the B-36 controversy. In 1956, the Navy also began to develop the Polaris missile for submarine use. In addition, in the mid-1950s it seemed for a time that the Army might share in the strategic retaliatory mission or at least in the development of weapons for that mission.

The creation of the bombs, the planes, and the bases for strategic deterrence became meaningful as they were integrated into an organization clearly devoted to strategic deterrence. Only in 1949 did such an organization begin to emerge. Along with the Air Defense and Tactical Air Commands, the Strategic Air Command had been created in March, 1946. General George Kenney commanded it until October, 1948. During this period, SAC had the top priority within the Air Force, and, unlike Air Defense and Tactical Air, it maintained a continuous existence as a major combat command. It was, however, a very different organization then from what it was later. In the summer of 1946 it had only one group capable of delivering the atomic bomb, and only slowly did it expand this capacity. It was, of course, equipped exclusively with World War II aircraft. During this period, in the words of one semi-official account, "SAC lacked planes, bases, equipment, and trained men." [55] During these years, two SAC admirers agreed, "SAC gradually degenerated into a second-, and then third-rate military force. . . . SAC's pilots, who flew only ordinary routine cross-country flights, grew lax and lazy, 'just boring holes in the air,' as one airman put it." [56] The need for a highly ready strategic deterrent force was not clearly perceived. SAC existed as a skeleton, but its mission, in a sense, did not.

The "rejuvenation" of SAC and its emergence as the primary organizational embodiment of strategic deterrence took place between 1949 and 1954. It was one of the most significant developments in the American military establishment after World War II. It marked a fundamental change in the composition of American military forces, comparable to the development of the battlefleet by the Navy at the turn of the century. Moreover, because it was carried out within an existing organizational structure, it was accomplished with no legislation and little or no public debate and discussion. The rejuvenation of SAC required, of course, demands upon scarce resources and conflicts with other groups. Its most significant aspect, however, was an internal matter: not the acquisition of resources, but the creation and acceptance of the purpose and concept which would shape the use of the resources. Unlike the military services, SAC was a single-purpose organization. That purpose was the most important one in American military policy. It could be clearly grasped and understood both by the members of SAC and by the general public. It could furnish clear-cut criteria for judging the priorities of programs and standards of performance.

Outstanding in the recreation of SAC as the organization for strategic deterrence was Lt. Gen. Curtis E. LeMay, who succeeded

General Kenney as its commander in October, 1948. LeMay represented a type of "bureaucratic innovator" which has been reasonably common in American civilian bureaucracy but not so common in the military bureaucracy. The bureaucratic innovator identifies himself with a specific and easily understood public purpose and either creates an organization to embody this purpose or revamps an old organization to identify it with this purpose. The former course usually demands congressional legislation and requires the innovator to work with and through members of Congress. In the other instances, however, the innovator, with little or no additional legislative authority or direction, recreates an organization by giving it new purpose. Often the innovator takes over the organization a few years after its establishment, at a time when its existence is accepted but its purposes, self-image, and functions have yet to be authoritatively defined. Civilian examples of the species include: John Wesley Powell, who in 1881 became the second head of the Geological Survey founded two years earlier and who served until 1894; Gifford Pinchot, who in 1898 became the second head of the Forest Service founded in 1886 and who served until 1911; and J. Edgar Hoover, who in 1924 became the sixth head of the Bureau of Investigation founded in 1908 and who was still serving in 1960. A comparable military figure would be Sylvannus Thayer, who in 1817 became the fourth head of the United States Military Academy founded in 1802 and who remained until 1833.

The parallel between LeMay and J. Edgar Hoover is particularly close. Both took over organizations with potentially very important purposes but which had become "lax and lazy." Both were charged by their superiors (Attorney General Stone, General Vandenberg) with reform of the organizations and were given the full backing of the superior in their efforts against any opposition (congressional patronage seekers, competing military groups). Both had considerable prior experience in the work of the organization (Hoover with the Bureau since 1917, LeMay with the 20th Air Force in World War II). Both infused their organizations with a new sense of mission, stressing the need for professionalism and imposing new standards of competence and discipline upon their personnel. Both presided over major expansions of the organization while refusing to take on functions not closely related to its fundamental purpose. Both cultivated reputations for themselves as tough, no-nonsense, hard-driving administrators, and for their agencies as efficient, technically expert, hard-working organizations, employing the most up-to-date devices of technology in the singleminded pursuit of their mission. They encouraged the dissemination of the image of their organizations as the protector of the nation against the horrible evils of crime and subversion, on the one hand, or devastation, on the other, through press, radio, books, and articles. Their personalities and personification of their programs made both into public figures usually better known and often much more influential than their immediate superiors in the administrative hierarchy. Both commanded the support, respect, and at times the deference of congressmen. Both succeeded in identifying their organizations with the symbols of American strength and national spirit so that criticism of them seemed to verge on the unpatriotic. Both aroused the suspicions of liberal groups.

LeMay was able to work his transformation of SAC because he commanded it for over eight years. This was "the longest tenure of major command in the history of the Air Force," [57] and it was a significant departure from the normal military practice of rotating officers through three- to four-year tours of duty. Rotation was introduced by Elihu Root to break the political power of the Army's long-entrenched Washington bureau chiefs. By preventing any single individual from becoming identified with a particular office or organizational unit and from building up continuing sources of support for that office or unit, it strengthens civilian control and stimulates identification with the service as a whole. As a corollary, it also reduces the effectiveness of the officer in any single job. Rotation conflicts with innovation. When not only the commander but all senior personnel change every few years, no one individual has the incentive or time to make major changes. Routine and formalized procedures are employed because they can be known by all and because they minimize the disruptive impact of continuously changing personnel. As in the Fourth Republic, discontinuity in personnel reflects institutional rigidities, on the one hand, and creates additional obstacles to change, on the other. LeMay's eight-year tenure at SAC gave him a unique opportunity both to make fundamental changes in his organization and to develop substantial public support for its program.* He neglected neither opportunity.

LeMay's achievement was a military organization in which all else was ruthlessly subordinated to combat readiness and effectiveness justified in terms of the mission which the organization served. This identification required the differentiation of the organization from other groups, symbolized perhaps by LeMay's transfer of SAC headquarters from Bolling Field near Washington to Offut Air Force Base in Nebraska a month after assuming command. It was further emphasized by creating the expectations that special demands would be made on SAC personnel, that special standards of readiness were required of SAC units, that special measures of security were required for SAC bases, that special standards of performance were required of SAC crews, and that special benefits and rewards were available when those standards were exceeded. Indefinitely, SAC was to remain keyed up for instantaneous combat. Upon its readiness depended the security of the nation. "What keeps SAC on edge with drive and *esprit*," John McDonald wrote, "is this principle of combat capability and war readiness, plus the knowledge of where it fits into the whole defense of the U. S., plus a commander who is a warrior and an exacting organizer." [58] Under LeMay SAC became an elite force, with distinctive purpose and pride. As such, among major U. S. commands, its only counterpart was the United States Marine Corps.

24. EUROPEAN DEFENSE

The development of American policy for the defense of western Europe involved three critical innovations, the last of which produced a major deterrent program involving American forces. The first innovation, the North Atlantic Treaty, grew out of the deteriorating relations with the Soviet Union which culminated in the breakup of the Council of Foreign Ministers meeting in December, 1947. This stimulated the British to take the lead in initiating the

---

* Similarly, Admiral Rickover's continued specialization—at variance with normal Navy practice—was responsible for the early innovation of nuclear propulsion.

Brussels Treaty with France and the Benelux countries. After the Czech coup in February and "with encouragement from the United States," as Dean Acheson put it, the treaty was signed in March 1948.[59] Concurrently, American leaders explored with the European powers the possibility of a broader regional arrangement in which the United States could participate. The Administration, however, wished to move cautiously and not to precipitate another major foreign policy issue before the 1948 election. At the same time it seemed desirable to prepare the way for such a move. Working in close collaboration, Under Secretary of State Robert Lovett and Senator Vandenberg drafted the text of a Senate resolution which, among other things, endorsed the "Association of the United States by constitutional process, with such regional and other collective arrangements as are based on continuous and effective self-help and mutual aid, and as affect its national security."[60] The Senate approved the resolution in June, 1948. Shortly thereafter the State Department initiated conversations with the western European powers on regional security and military assistance. These discussions produced a decision in October to give first priority to the negotiation of a North Atlantic security pact.[61] Throughout the fall and winter the terms of the pact were formulated, with the State Department simultaneously negotiating with representatives of the eleven nations involved and with the members of the Senate Foreign Relations Committee. The text of the treaty was agreed upon in March. It was signed in April and after extensive hearings and debate ratified by the Senate in July, 1949. The key figures in this successful innovation were Lovett, Vandenberg, and Acheson.

For the United States the North Atlantic Treaty was, in effect, a deterrent commitment based on the belief that if American intentions to prevent the upset of the European balance of power were made clear in advance, the likelihood of a challenge to that balance would be greatly reduced. It reflected the lessons of 1917 and 1941: "[W]hen Mr. Hitler was contemplating World War Two," as Senator Vandenburg put it, "I believe he would never have launched it if he had had any serious reasons to believe that it might bring him into armed collision with the United States. I think he was sure it would not do so because of our then existing neutrality laws. If an appropriate North Atlantic Pact is written,

I think it will exactly reverse this psychology so far as Mr. Stalin is concerned if, as and when he contemplates World War Three." [62] The treaty formalized the intention of the United States to protect western Europe. Its effect upon a potential aggressor depended, however, not only on the strength of the intention but on the force behind it. To some of the treaty's supporters, such as Vandenberg, the deterrent power behind the treaty was the American military potential: "It is not the military forces-in-being which measure the impact of this 'knock-out' admonition, important though they are," he said in his speech to the Senate. "It is the potential which counts, and any armed aggressor knows that he forthwith faces this potential from the moment he attacks." [63] Other supporters of the treaty in the executive branch stressed the extent to which the treaty brought western Europe under the deterrent umbrella of the American atomic monopoly. The Europeans welcomed the commitment and the umbrella, but they were also concerned about their own military weakness. The American deterrent, moreover, might fail to deter, and, in any event, it was likely to be decreasingly effective. The Europeans did not wish to be subjected again to the cycle of destruction, occupation, and liberation. An American survey of European defenses in the spring of 1949 convinced the leaders of the executive branch that major efforts would be needed to bolster them.[64] Before signing the treaty eight European countries filed requests for military aid, and immediately after ratification of the treaty in July the Administration presented to Congress its recommendations for a military assistance program. The support within Congress for military aid, however, was by no means as extensive as it was for the treaty. After three months deliberation and the Soviet atomic explosion, the Mutual Defense Assistance Act was passed in October, 1949.

Three key assumptions seemed to underline the development of NATO and the military assistance program in the winter and spring of 1949–1950. First, the Soviet threat to western Europe was not viewed as immediate. NSC 68, then in the process of formulation, pointed to 1954 as the year in which the Soviets would probably have sufficient nuclear air capability to launch a serious attack against the United States. NATO planning worked on a similar timetable. Until the Soviet Union had such capability, the likelihood of aggression appeared relatively remote. The goal of NATO planning, it was reported, was 36 divisions by 1955. Second, the military assistance itself was viewed as a short-run program, lasting, perhaps, four or five years, the assistance to come largely from American stocks of surplus weapons.[65] After the initial phase, the European powers would be expected to sustain their own defense efforts. Partly for this reason, the Mutual Defense Assistance Act gave the goal of economic recovery clear priority over that of rearmament. Finally, the unified defense plan agreed to by the NATO powers in the winter of 1949–1950 embodied the principle of "collective balanced forces," under which each nation undertook to concentrate its efforts upon those forces most needed for the overall buildup. The principal American contributions were to be strategic airpower and naval forces; Great Britain and France were to share responsibility for tactical airpower; and the continental countries were to be primarily responsible for ground forces. Thus, in the spring of 1950, the principal military threat to western Europe still seemed several years in the future; the United States was committed to a temporary effort to get the rearmament of the European countries underway; and a unified defense plan had been agreed to under which the principal American contributions were to be air and naval forces.

The third great innovation in American policy for the defense of Europe was the indefinite deployment of American forces in Europe under an international command headed by an American general. Neither the deterrent commitment of the treaty itself nor the military assistance program was unique in American policy. The Rio treaty was agreed to a year before the North Atlantic Treaty; later, the United States entered into similiar commitments in the Southeast Asia Treaty, bilateral agreements with Korea, Japan, and Nationalist China, and by its support of the Baghdad Pact. Military assistance to western Europe was preceded by the Greek-Turkish aid programs, and military assistance was also made available to many other countries in Asia and Latin America. The permanent stationing of American forces abroad under an international command, however, was unique to NATO. It was the final critical step in the development of American policy for the defense of Europe. The changes made in the 1950s in NATO strategy, force level goals, and weapons were all made within a context presupposing American forces.

The decision to increase American forces in Europe was intimately connected with the decisions to establish a supreme command in Europe and to press for the rearmament of Germany. All three ideas had, of course, been considered before June, 1950. Several Europeans had advocated the permanent commitment of an American garrison to Europe. Other Europeans and Americans had urged the need for a supreme commander of the allied forces.[66] Still other Europeans and Americans had spoken of the necessity of facing the problem of German rearmament. In the fall of 1949, the U. S. Army General Staff took the initiative in drafting a plan for the creation of German divisions. Despite urgings from the State Department to move slowly, the Joint Chiefs of Staff endorsed the Army plan on April 30, 1950.[67] All three proposals were thus under consideration before the outbreak of the Korean War. Nonetheless, at the outbreak of the war American policy was opposed to all three. An "overall commander," Secretary Johnson declared early in June, "we deem neither advisable nor necessary." [68] Similarly, the United States had no intention of rearming Germany: "Our policies are fixed in that matter," Acheson declared. ". . . Germany is to be demilitarized. . . . That is our policy and we have not raised it or revalued it." [69] Administration spokesmen were not quite so definite in rejecting the possibility of an increase in American forces in Europe. Nonetheless, no decision had been made to do so. Asked if a stronger NATO meant more U. S. troops, Secretary Johnson declared, "No, sir, not necessarily. I am talking about the potential forces of the western European democracies. They have more manpower than they have equipment. . . . It is the furnishing of equipment largely by us to those existing military organizations in Europe that I was talking about . . . " [70] In short, in June, 1950, all three moves were considered as conceivable developments in the distant future, but all three were contrary to current policy.

The invasion of South Korea abruptly changed the Administration's time perspectives and program priorities. The willingness of the Communists to use force to achieve their goals was, as General Bradley said, "a fundamental change and it has forced a change in our estimate of the military needs of the United States." [71] More than a score of Soviet divisions were in East Germany; the East Germans themselves had a substantial "police force." The parallel between North and South Korea and East and West Germany aroused general concern about the defense of western Europe. The assumption that Communist aggression was unlikely until the Soviets had built up a nuclear arsenal had been disproved: "all previous time schemes had been invalidated by the aggression in Korea." [72] Soviet aggression against western Europe was possible at any time. The new goal proposed by the United States was 36 NATO divisions by 1952, or 1953 at the latest.

The assault on Korea thus triggered the active consideration of the third major innovation in American policy for the defense of Europe. As in the case of the hydrogen bomb, however, the initial trigger itself might not have been enough to produce a decision to innovate. After the first shock of the Korean attack, the sense of urgency began to dissipate in the mid-summer of 1950. "As matters began to look brighter in Korea, however," Walter Millis has written, "new pressures were arising against the whole NATO concept. . . . The NATO idea, abruptly reinvigorated at the end of June, was again languishing by the end of August." [73] Secretary of Defense Johnson became convinced that the western Europeans were unwilling to cooperate fully; isolationist senators began to demand extensive European efforts and German rearmament before the United States invested greater resources in the defense of Europe; the Joint Chiefs of Staff delayed action on State Department proposals. European defenses were threatened by an Alphonse-Gaston stalemate. "In Congress," Harry Truman has written, "there were demands for proof that the Europeans would carry an appropriate share of the burden of common defense. In Europe, just as understandably, there was reluctance to extend risks and expenses until America's participation was clearly evident." [74] Throughout August the Administration was under this double fire.

Fortunately, the Administration was also under pressure to resolve the stalemate and to formulate its own position as quickly as possible. The North Atlantic Council was scheduled to meet in the middle of September. That meeting would be a decisive point in the development of western European defenses. If, in the words of L. W. Martin, "it failed to mark a decisive step forward, the flimsy defensive structure might crumble." [75] A policy had to be ready before then. The deadline stimulated Acheson to ask the President to demand agreement between State and Defense on an appropriate course. At a conference with Acheson, Johnson, and the Joint Chiefs on August 26, the President set a deadline of September 1, later extended to September 5, on the recommendations he wanted. On September 4 the *ad hoc* State-Defense group made its report. The President approved it on September 8 and on September 9 announced that substantial American reinforcements would be sent to Europe. On September 12, Acheson presented the complete American proposals, including German rearmament, to the British and French foreign ministers.[76] Clearly, this was a case where a previously agreed-upon schedule imposed deadlines upon the making of policy. In a sense, the foreign ministers' meeting in September had the same effect upon the formulation of American policy for European defense that the annual budget message deadline has upon the formulation of the budget. Without the foreign ministers' meeting the formulation of American policy would have been considerably more leisurely, and the August apprehension over who would take the first step might well have hardened into firm mutual reluctance to act.

While the deadline furnished by the North Atlantic Council meetings was a stimulus to decision, it was not, of course, sufficient cause for decision. Even with the stimulus, the Administration might have been unable to formulate a policy, and the meeting could have been a quiet debacle. The deadline pressure worked, however, because substantial agreement existed within the executive branch on the measures which should be taken. The European allies, the State Department, and the Pentagon all endorsed replacement of "collective balanced forces" by an integrated force under a supreme commander who would be an American. They were also generally agreed upon the need for substantially greater American military assistance to Europe, although some differences existed about the exact amounts required. The only major difference was the relative priority and emphasis which should be given to American (and British) reinforcements in Europe and the rearmament of Germany. The continental allies wanted a reinforced and permanent American garrison in Europe. In the absence of such a commitment they feared that the United States would be preoccupied with the Far East, that an adequate European defense could not be brought into existence, and that their own efforts to rearm might provoke Soviet attack while at the same time leaving them quite incapable of defeating such an attack. Sympathizing with their concern and acutely aware of the difficulty which the absence of firm American guarantees was creating for European rearmament, the State Department took the initiative in pushing American reinforcements within the excutive branch. Thus, while the State Department pressed for a major change in American military programs, the American military pushed for German rearmament. The Joint Chiefs of Staff had endorsed this in principle in April, and in June General Bradley had argued in favor of it "from a military viewpoint," although recognizing that broader political considerations made it unfeasible at that time. After the Korean attack the Joint Chiefs were consistently unwilling to agree to American reinforcements unless sufficient European forces, including German troops, were also available to make an effective defense probable.

The contrast between the JCS and State Department approaches can be seen in the differing plans which they proposed for western European defense. In July the Joint Chiefs recommended to the NSC that a "ready force" under a permanent commander replace the "balanced collective forces" and that German divisions be established with some restrictions on their equipment and staffs.[77] The State Department, however, prevented the approval of German rearmament at that point. A month later, the State Department submitted to the military its proposals: an integrated force under a single commander, military assistance to the European powers dependent upon their cooperation, and the deployment of 4 to 6 more American divisions to Europe. The Joint Chiefs and the Army accepted these proposals and "conceded that some of the additional divisions be American, as and when such units were formed." [78] They insisted, however, that German troops were necessary to insure that the supreme commander had sufficient forces to perform his mission. High Commissioner McCloy in Germany also warned the State Department of the potential dangers from the East German police force, and their own evaluation of the situation was leading the State Department leaders to accept the inevitability of German rearmament. Anxious to arrive at a policy, the State Department leaders agreed to the JCS amendments. The Chiefs promised quick action on their part.

Even after State "had definitely informed the JCS of its readiness to endorse German rearmament," however, the military still hesitated to approve American reinforcements because of their "serious misgivings" about "the prospect of a long and hazardous commitment to a collective defense effort which would not even be under the sole control of the United States." The Chiefs, in Martin's account, insisted "that the American proposals to NATO be made strictly conditional upon iron-clad commitments by the Europeans to their own contributions, and in particular, upon unequivocal acceptance of an immediate start on German rearmament in a form technically acceptable to American strategists." [79] Faced with this demand, the State Department agreed to a hard-and-fast bargain linking American reinforcements to an American supreme commander and an immediate start on the formation of German military units. On the surface, the military had reshaped American foreign policy. The Joint Chiefs, however, should have realized that the State Department was promising something which was beyond its power to deliver. Given American leadership in NATO, the Chiefs could hardly assume that if our allies or the Germans refused to approve German rearmament immediately that the American reinforcements would be held up until they did. The Joint Chiefs continually emphasized that all three proposals were part of a "single package." [80] Yet they had traded an American decision for an American position. The decision was implemented while the position was debated. A year after the bargain the American divisions the State Department wanted were in Europe. Six years later the German divisions which the Joint Chiefs wanted were still being organized. If anyone came out on top in the deal, it was the civilians, not the military.

In a little over two months the United States had decided, as Acheson said, "to take steps which were absolutely unprecedented in our history, to place substantial forces in Europe, to put these forces into an integrated force for the defense of Europe, to agree to a command structure, to agree to a supreme commander, to join in a program for integrating European production, to take far reaching steps in the financial field . . . "[81] The speed with which these decisions were taken contrasts with the prolonged consideration given the other major measures in defense of western Europe. Two reasons for the speed were the sense of urgency after the attack on Korea and the high degree of agreement which existed within the executive branch. "By August, 1950," as Martin has said, "the difference between the Pentagon and the State Department had dwindled to one of method and timing."[82] Given the general agreement on the need to press forward in the creation of a western European defense system, State and the Chiefs could freely bargain and arrive at a policy which satisfied both. This agreement was sufficient for those portions of the bargain which were within the power of the executive branch to determine. The ability of the executive to determine strategic programs was thus a key factor in the speed with which the decision was made to increase American forces in Europe. The North Atlantic Treaty had required agreement among eleven other governments, plus the State Department, the military, the Senate Foreign Relations Committee, and the Senate. The process of resolving differences among these groups took over a year. Similarly, with MDAP, the State Department had to mediate between the requests from the European powers and its estimate of the attitudes and intentions of four committees and two houses of Congress. The Administration took more than four months to formulate its initial proposals to Congress, and Congress took another four months to pass the legislation. In these instances, the initiative for policy came from the State Department or from Europe. In the case of German rearmament, consensus was even more difficult to achieve. The American Chiefs of Staff, supported by many congressmen, were pressing for action, but the State Department had to secure the agreement of Germany and the European allies. Given the situation, the State Department was remarkably successful in achieving in September the general, although reluctant, approval of all the other NATO powers except France to the principle of a German contribution to western defenses. Later the State Department found itself a mediator, attempting to reconcile French demands for restrictions with German demands for equality.

The decision to increase American forces in Europe encountered no such problems. The European allies were heartily in favor of it. The top leaders of the State Department were for it, and the Joint Chiefs had no basic objection to it. Within the executive, Louis Johnson was perhaps least sympathetic, but he was on the sidelines; after the Korean invasion he was overshadowed by Bradley and the Joint Chiefs. Later it was revealed that elements in the Air Force had doubts about the wisdom of the move, but during the two months of decision-making in the summer of 1950 these had neither the time nor the opportunity to make their opinions known. Executive branch consensus was reasonably quickly produced, and, so far as the American reinforcements were concerned, executive branch consensus was all that was needed. Six months later, of course, groups in Congress challenged the exclusion of Congress from the decision-making process. This challenge stimulated public debate of the executive's policies, but the outcome of the challenge simply underwrote the power of the executive to make the decisions. The broad agreement within the executive branch also meant that there was no need for extensive campaigns within the executive to arouse support for the innovation and little opportunity for the opponents of innovation to delay it. In addition, the agreement between State and Defense minimized the pressure to find analytic solutions to the problem. Sharing so much in common, the two agencies could afford to bargain more or less openly with each other.

The views of the Air Force leaders and airpower supporters indicate both the extent and the limits to which the identification of airpower with strategic retaliation would produce opposition to the innovation of other deterrent programs. Five Air Force officers, on active duty and retired, testified before the Senate hearings in the Great Debate. General Vandenberg, the Chief of Staff, and his predecessor, General Spaatz, wholeheartedly endorsed the troop movement. The commanders of the Strategic Air Command and the Air Defense Command expressed reservations about the policy, particularly its effect on the allocation of funds to their forces. A retired Air Force officer, Lt. Gen. Harold George, expressed more vigorous objections to the policy, although he recognized that "we have already committed ourselves." [83] Civilian supporters of airpower were much more active than the military airmen in denouncing the policy, and other opponents to the move advanced an air-naval strategy as the alternative to fighting a land war in Europe.

In 1950 a brief but intensive public debate followed presidential announcement of the hydrogen bomb decision. No such debate immediately followed President Truman's disclosure on September 9 that substantial reinforcements would be sent to Europe. The announcement itself was vague enough to make criticism difficult. Congressional groups and potential critics were perhaps ill-prepared to explore the implications of the decision, and their attention was focused upon other issues.[84] Most importantly, the general consensus within the executive meant that no significant executive group felt the need to appeal to a larger forum; those groups outside the executive which were generally critical of its policies had no sure allies within the executive to lend weight to their position and to encourage them in their stand. Criticism of the decision and efforts to broaden the arena of discussion thus did not immediately develop. Even the Administration's most stringent critic, Senator Taft, was careful not to go on record as opposing the move.[85]

In the absence of differences over Europe within the Administration and so long as it seemed to be winning the Korean War, the opposition had neither the incentive nor the strength to launch a full-scale attack on the Administration's plans for Europe. Once the debacle developed in Korea and the Administration limited the use of force against Communist China, however, the way was opened for a more thorough probing of its defense policies in other areas. The disaster in Korea lent cogent support to the argument that the United States should avoid ground wars with the Communist powers on the Eurasian continent. Early in December Taft indicated that while he favored an increase in ground forces he did not think that they should be sent to Europe until the Europeans had made greater efforts in their own defense. The full-scale public debate came with Hoover's "Gibraltar" speech on December 20, the day after Truman announced that Eisenhower would be appointed European supreme commander and that the United States would speed the dispatch of the reinforcements to his command.[86] Hoover's speech attacked the Administration's overall military policy in general and its policies for Europe in particular. No American troops should be sent to Europe, he argued, until the Europeans were ready to defend themselves. Immediately after the assembly of the 82d Congress in January, Senator Wherry introduced his resolution to investigate whether or not the Senate should declare "that no ground forces of the United States should be assigned to duty in the European area for the purposes of the North Atlantic Treaty pending adoption of a policy with respect thereto by the Congress." The Great Debate thus got under way four months after the issues at stake had been resolved in the executive branch.

The form in which the Administration's opponents launched their attack indicated the essential weakness of their position. Lacking significant support from within the executive branch, they could not hope to show that the State Department had overriden the Chiefs of Staff, that the leadership of any one service had vigorously opposed the action, or that the views of the commander in the field had been disregarded. Of course, if they had probed hard enough they might have revealed the doubts of the Chiefs the previous summer and the ironclad commitments which they had demanded before agreeing to the move. The right-wing Republican critics, however, were almost as suspicious of the Chiefs as they were of the Administration's political leaders, and they never capitalized upon this potential rift. Instead, the absence of serious division within the Administration and their inability to make use of those differences which did exist in the executive forced the critics to define the issue as one of Congress vs. the President. To expand the arena of decision-making, they were driven back upon formal constitutional arguments on legislative and executive authority. As a result, compared to the B-36 hearings fifteen months earlier, the MacArthur hearings three months later, or even the subsequent Symington and Johnson investigations of the Eisenhower Administration, the Great Debate hearings were rather unexciting. LeMay came closer than other executive officials to criticizing Administration policy, but even he indicated that he thought the ground defenses of Europe should be bolstered and that if he were a senator he would vote against the Wherry resolution. Faced with executive unanimity and the staunch defense of the Administration's position by three of the nation's four most popular soldiers (Marshall, Eisenhower, Bradley), the opposition senators failed to define any clear alternatives to the Administration's action, much less to influence or to reverse the character of that action. No responsible executive official espoused an alternative to the Administration's plan. In the absence of this precondition for public discussion of strategic issues, the Great Debate fizzled.

The four divisions moved to Europe between May and December, 1951. The creation of the organizations to execute and to represent the new policy began much earlier.[87] On the lower level, the Seventh Army was formally activated in November, 1950. This became the American ground combat force in Europe. Within two years it quadrupled in size. As with SAC, more significant than the quantitative increase was its change in mission. Before 1951 American forces in Germany were largely concerned with occupation duties. The primary goal of Lt. Gen. Manton S. Eddy, the Seventh Army's commander, like that of LeMay, was to make his organization into a combat-ready force. As with SAC, this meant a new emphasis upon training, equipment, installations, maneuvers, and deployments, all directed to the goal of instantaneous fighting readiness. The new resources of the command reflected its new purpose, and only the new purpose could shape and make effective the new resources. The increase in American land forces in Europe, of course, was also accompanied by substantial increases in the tactical air forces. The British created the Army of the Rhine, and the European allies increased their military forces available for the integrated defense. In the following years an elaborate infrastructure was created, including bases, depots, and transportation and communication facilities. The supply lines of the American forces in southern Germany, for instance, which had run parallel to the East German border to Bremerhaven, were redirected back from the front to French ports.

The key role in the development of the European defense forces was, of course, played by the integrated command which was established early in 1951. The diplomatic Eisenhower was the European defense equivalent of the hard-driving LeMay of strategic retaliation. Although Eisenhower stayed with his command little more than a year, he was indispensable in bringing it to being. Once created, SHAPE, of course, became a continuing institution representing the common interests of the NATO powers in the defense of Europe. Except during Ridgway's brief tenure, its later commanders, Gruenther and Norstad, had been with it since the beginning. They furnished the continuity in leadership essential to the development of an organization with a life and interest and will of its own. On the one hand, the development of SHAPE was made possible by the general consensus within the American government and among the NATO powers on the needs of European defense. On the other hand, as the institutional embodiment of European defense, SHAPE and its Supreme Commander also stood ready to oppose any efforts to change that purpose or to reduce the resources devoted to it.

25. CONTINENTAL DEFENSE

NSC 68 fixed 1954 as the target date for the defense build-up because by that year the Soviet Union probably would have sufficient nuclear capability to attack the United States. Among other provisions NSC 68 directed that high priority be given to the development of a continental defense system. Earlier, in August, 1949, the Soviet atomic explosion had triggered the development of the hydrogen bomb and of strategic retaliatory forces. Later, in June, 1950, the Korean War triggered the indefinite assignment of American forces to an international command for the defense of Europe. The war also led to a flood of military appropriations. On the surface it would seem that this combination of events should have produced a major effort at continental defense in 1950, and indeed several piecemeal steps were taken. Construction was begun of a "Permanent System" of seventy-five radar stations in the United States and Alaska which had been authorized by Congress in 1949. In July, 1950, the Army Antiaircraft Command was created. In January, 1951, the Air Force Air Defense Command came into existence as a permanent major combat command. Also in 1951 the Air Force began to acquire all-weather fighter interceptors, and agreement was reached with Canada for the construction of the "Pinetree" radar line along the northern boundary of the western United States and across southern Canada. Yet these steps were both discrete and incomplete. They did not represent a major coordinated effort to develop a continental defense system. Despite policy directives and apparent needs, the critical turning point in continental defense did not come until 1953. Four factors were responsible for the delay.

First, until the summer of 1952 the technological difficulties in the way of an effective continental defense system seemed almost insuperable. In World War II a 10 percent "kill-rate" of attacking aircraft constituted effective defense. With atomic weapons, however, the kill-rate would have to be at least 50 percent and probably more. In 1950, the possibilities of achieving this goal seemed remote, and little study had been devoted to the ways in which the obstacles might be overcome. Policy alternatives were unexplored. Potential programs were undefined and had not been subjected to discussion and controversy. In a sense, as far as continental defense was concerned, there was nothing for the Soviet atomic bomb or the North Korean aggression to trigger. They simply came too early in the policy process to precipitate action.

Second, the Korean War made other needs seem more immediate. The war itself had first claim on resources. Beyond this, the most immediate danger seemed to be an attack on Europe. American concern over this possibility and the fears of the continental NATO countries led to a strong effort to bolster western defenses in Germany. During the next few years expanded and strengthened American retaliatory forces would help to deter an attack on Europe; after that they would be essential to counterbalance Soviet air-atomic power. Compared to the threats of possible aggression overseas the danger of direct attack on North America still seemed remote in 1950.

Third, continental defense marked a much sharper break with the earlier tradition and doctrine of the services than did strategic deterrence and European defense. Strategic retaliation required new weapons and the expansion of the air-atomic forces, but it did not require the creation of radically new types of forces not previously in existence. The weapons and doctrine of strategic bombing could easily be adjusted to the new need. Similarly, the defense of western Europe was a natural outgrowth of American experience in the two world wars and the feeling that these wars might have been avoided by an earlier commitment of American strength. The permanent stationing of American forces in Europe was, to be sure, a major innovation, but the continued presence of American occupation forces in Europe after the war made it appear less radical than it actually was. (If American forces had been withdrawn in 1947 or 1948, would they have ever returned short of a Soviet attack?) Continental defense was a much greater innovation. Not since the War of 1812 had the continental United States been the probable target of foreign attack. The doctrines of all three services were based on the assumption that the best defense is the offense. Each of the services also had other primary concerns which led it to assign a secondary priority to continental defense.

Finally, the problems which continental defense posed for the American military were most acute for the Air Force, which had principal responsibility for continental defense. In 1950 and 1951 the Air Force was primarily concerned with the build-up of SAC, with the conduct of air operations in Korea, and with the creation of tactical air forces for the defense of Europe. The Air Force was particularly imbued with the spirit of the offensive and with a strong doctrinal belief in the efficacy of strategic air warfare: "The bomber always gets through." Yet air defense was one of its three major combat responsibilities. The attitude of the Air Force was ambivalent. Continental defense was innovated in part with its support and in part over its opposition.

The critical decision in the innovation of continental defense was made by the Eisenhower Administration in the fall of 1953, when it approved a series of recommendations which had grown out of a scientific study group in the summer of 1952. "Our real problem and decision," two leading experts wrote in the fall of 1953, "are not concerned with any one separate concept, such as early warning, but the whole system of air defense and what will make it effective as a system. . . . Only the concept of an effective over-all air defense system is meaningful when we consider capital and operating costs . . ." [88] In effect, the critical decision on continental defense, made in October, 1953, was to create this type of system and to recognize continental defense as a major defense need, to treat it on an integrated basis, and to give it extensive budgetary support. The decision paved the way for the development of a distant early warning system, new communications systems, improved means of interception, and, eventually, the estab-

25. CONTINENTAL DEFENSE

lishment of a single continental defense command for North America.

The initiative for this decision arose under Air Force auspices but not entirely with Air Force blessing. In response to the directives in NSC 68 and the desire on the part of Air Force Chief of Staff Hoyt Vandenberg and Air Force Chief Scientist Louis Ridenour to mobilize more effectively American scientists on Air Force projects, early in 1951 the Air Force contracted with the Massachusetts Institute of Technology for a study (Project Charles) of the best means of tackling the air defense problem. Two MIT physicists, A. G. Hill and George E. Valley, Jr., who had been interested in air defense, played leading roles in the study. Project Charles recommended that a permanent laboratory be established for continuing work on the technical problems of air defense. In September, 1951, the Lincoln Laboratory formally came into existence as the result of a contract between the Air Force and MIT. The laboratory, in the words of Secretary of the Air Force Finletter, was to be the "Manhattan Project of air defense." [89] Throughout the winter and spring of 1951–1952 the Lincoln scientists worked on the problems of detection and interception.

In the summer of 1952 a group of Lincoln and non-Lincoln scientists was brought together to survey the achievements up to that point and to lay out future courses of action. The report of the Summer Study Group: 1) estimated that in two or three years the Soviet Union would have sufficient planes and atomic weapons to cripple the United States in a surprise attack; 2) declared that existing and planned American defenses were inadequate and improperly integrated and that under optimal conditions would achieve only a 20 percent kill-rate; and 3) argued that new and probable technological break-throughs made it feasible to develop an air defense system which could hope to achieve a kill-rate of 60 to 70 percent. Specifically, the report recommended the construction of a distant early warning radar line across northern Canada to give three to six hours warning of approaching enemy bombers, an integrated and fully automatic communications system for air defense forces, and improved fighter planes and homing missiles for interception. Finally, the report urged that the distant early warning system be given top priority. The estimated costs of these improvements varied greatly, but all of the Study Group's recommendations together probably required several billion dollars.[90]

The high degree of consensus within the executive branch on European defense policy resulted in a short period of discussion and decision-making. Those differences which did exist were quickly resolved by direct negotiation between the State Department and the Joint Chiefs. The formulation of continental defense policy was very different: the development of the policy spanned two Administrations, and major differences existed among executive branch agencies. The Summer Study Group report received such extensive consideration that it almost became a classic case of a proposal which was studied to death. All three reasons for a prolonged innovation process played major roles. The opponents of continental defense attempted to delay decision by referring proposals to additional study groups. The supporters of continental defense hoped to arouse support. The President and other leaders of the Administration wished to find some means of resolving the dispute with the least sacrifice of the conflicting values. "As might be expected," the Alsop Brothers wrote in revealing the Summer Study Group recommendations, "one of the governmental responses to the dilemma has been that of a man who hopefully consults other doctors, seeking a pleasanter verdict, when his own physician orders him to a painful and dangerous operation." [91]

The Lincoln Summer Study Group recommendations were part of an Air Force project. Neither the Air Force nor the Department of Defense, however, initially approved the Group's recommendations, and the Air Force refused to recommend the report to the NSC. At the very beginning of the policy process, consequently, the proponents of continental defense had to outflank the opposition. In September, 1952, they made the report available to the National Security Resources Board. Jack Gorrie, chairman of the NSRB, brought it before the National Security Council with the recommendation that construction begin immediately on the distant early warning line, which, the NSRB estimated, would require a billion dollars during the first three or four years. The Air Force reportedly charged that it had been "by-passed" by the scientists.[92] Through the fall of 1952, the Truman Administration considered the needs of air defense. In its last months in office it was not in a position to innovate a major program. It did, however, prepare a general survey, NSC 141, of the defense problems confronting the incoming Administration which analyzed at length the implications of Soviet accumulation of nuclear weapons and which recommended much more intensive efforts in air defense, civil defense, and in military assistance to the Middle East and Far East.[93] Secretary of Defense Lovett also appointed a civilian committee under the chairmanship of Mervin J. Kelly, president of the Bell Telephone Laboratories, to study the air defense problem and to make recommendations on the possibilities of an improved warning system, the relation of such a system to other aspects of continental defense, and the "over-all policies and programs to achieve a more effective defense of North America against atomic or other airborne attack." [94] The purpose and membership of the committee were cleared with the prospective leaders of the Eisenhower Administration. In effect, the Truman Administration left to the Eisenhower Administration a warning that substantial additional efforts in continental defense would be necessary and a study-in-progress designed to review and to evaluate the concrete recommendations of the Lincoln Summer Study Group.

The Eisenhower Administration thus confronted a major policy dilemma the moment it assumed office. On the one hand, it had NSC 141 and the Summer Study Group proposals for a greatly enlarged continental defense program. On the other hand, it brought into office expectations and promises that it would substantially reduce expenditures, balance the budget, and reduce taxes. During February and March the National Security Council debated this dilemma. Vice President Nixon, Secretary Dulles, Under Secretary of State Bedell Smith, and Mutual Security Administrator Harold Stassen, all favored a more extensive effort, while Secretary of the Treasury Humphrey and Budget Director Dodge vigorously opposed it. In normal circumstances, the support of the Secretary of State would have tipped the balance in favor of action. Apparently, however, Secretary of Defense Wilson also supported the proponents of economy. Given this stalemate within the Administration, a group of consultants, the "Seven Wise Men," was appointed to study the problem from a business viewpoint. They, too, supported a go-slow policy. Caught between the conflicting demands of defense and economy, the President reportedly told senators and congressmen that "his dilemma was giving him sleepless nights." [95]

The dilemma was not relieved by the report of the Kelly Committee in May. The report was a masterpiece of compromise, so much so, in fact, that Charles J. V. Murphy could label it an "impressive rebuttal" of the Lincoln Summer Study Group recommendations while the Alsop Brothers could argue that the "Lincoln warnings have been fully confirmed." [96] As did the Lincoln report, the Kelly Committee noted Soviet capability to launch a surprise attack against the United States which would "cause large loss of life and major property damage and possibly temporarily lessen the capability of the U.S. to support a major war effort." The Committee recommended the creation of a "continental air defense system much better than that which is assured under present programs." But in opposition to the general tenor of the Lincoln report, the Committee stressed the need to deter attack and "the importance of continued development of a powerful U.S. atomic offensive capability, reasonably invulnerable to initial attack, as a vital, major part of the over-all defense system." The Committee also "expressed concern about the recent public advocacy of a program which would purportedly give nearly perfect protection against air attack." Such protection, the Committee said, "is unattainable and in any case completely impractical, economically and technically . . ." Finally, the Committee played down the need for haste in continental defense and rejected the idea of a "crash" program.[97]

The Kelly Committee report came just as the Administration was launching its overall survey of national security, Operation Solarium. (Chapter II, Section 6.) Since the report urged stronger air defenses but minimized the need for haste, it seemed unnecessary to take any immediate action on it until the Administration's "new look" had been completed. In addition, before embarking on the Kelly Committee recommendations, members of the Eisenhower Administration, including Secretary Wilson, were anxious to have the problem studied again by some of their "own people." [98] Another study group was appointed under the chairmanship of an old associate of the President, Maj. Gen. Harold Bull. The Bull Committee, whose members were drawn from within the government, presented its report to the NSC in July. Its recommendations covered more ground than those of the Kelly Committee and urged much more extensive measures which, it was estimated, would cost $18 to $27 billion over a five-year period. The need for action was further emphasized by the report of yet another committee, under Lt. Gen. Idwal Edwards, which had been appointed to estimate Soviet air-atomic capabilities.[99] The NSC was impressed but again remained stalemated during the summer. Up to this point the principal efforts to resolve the differences between the economizers and the proponents of air defense had been through increasingly detailed studies of the nature of the threat and of technological capabilities and potentialities. This path had proved unsuccessful in providing analytic solutions to the policy differences. Frustrated in this direction, the Administration started to search for a solution by broadening the framework within which the problem was considered.

Conceivably, a decision to go ahead with continental defense would have been made in any case as part of the Administration's new defense policy. More likely, the decision would have been blurred and still further delayed. The Soviet explosion of a hydrogen bomb in August, however, triggered action on continental defense. The Soviet bomb, in the words of Steven Rivkin, "broke the back of resistance to air defense within the Administration." [100] The paper drawn up by the Joint Chiefs after their *Sequoia* cruise on August 6 identified continental defense and massive retaliation as the two principal military problems facing the country. On August 26 Admiral Radford, in his first press conference as Chairman of the Joint Chiefs, declared that the Soviet hydrogen bomb meant that the United States must review and strengthen its air defenses. Meanwhile, the NSC Planning Board was working on the report of Operation Solarium, NSC 162. In evaluating this report, the Council employed yet another group of six consultants, including General Bull, who had headed the earlier survey favorable to continental defense, and James Black, president of Pacific Gas & Electric Company, one of the "Seven Wise Men" who had urged the priority of economy.[101] On September 25 the NSC considered the continental defense problem in a large meeting attended by the consultants as well as by the service secretaries and the Chiefs of Staff. Two weeks later, on October 6, the NSC approved NSC 162.

This paper identified the Soviet threat as "total," declared that the Soviets had the ability to launch a nuclear attack against the United States, argued that national defense had to have clear priority over other goals, and recommended that a much greater effort be made to improve continental defenses. NSC 162 included almost all the proposals recommended a year earlier by the Lincoln Summer Study Group, although the priorities among them were slightly shifted. It contemplated spending $20 billion over a five-year period for continental defense.[102] Operation Solarium, which had begun in May as an overall survey of national security requirements, ended in October with its principal focus on continental defense.

Throughout the air defense controversy the most active group supporting an expanded program was the scientists who had been associated with Project Lincoln. The principal opponents were the defenders of governmental economy and strategic airpower. Budgetary considerations had played only a minor role in the executive debates over the hydrogen bomb and European reinforcements. In the consideration of continental defense they were a major factor. Almost all the top leaders of the Eisenhower Administration were dedicated to the reduction of the governmental budget. During the nine months in which the continental defense program was debated within the Administration, the principal opposition came from Budget Director Dodge and Secretary Humphrey. Dodge remained in opposition right through the final approval of NSC 162 in October.[103] Throughout the debate, moreover, the head of the governmental department principally concerned, Secretary Wilson, had, for budgetary reasons, voiced little enthusiasm for the innovation.

The Summer Study recommendations also received little active support from the military. General Bradley, JCS Chairman until August, 1953, wanted to "move faster in matters of manufacture, installation and over-all organization," but he vigorously opposed giving first priority to the distant early warning line. He argued, instead, that continental defenses should be built from the "inside out," with initial efforts concentrated on close-in defenses and radar.[104] Many Air Force officials had serious reservations on strategic grounds. They feared that undue emphasis on continental defense would adversely affect the Strategic Air Command. In the spring and summer of 1952 the Chief Scientist of the Air Force, acting apparently with the knowledge of its Secretary, attempted to delay and to limit the work of the Lincoln Summer Study Group. In the fall of 1952, the Air Force, according to two of its supporters, was "disturbed" by the Summer Study Group report. Continuously, the Air Force opposed the construction of the distant early warning line on a crash basis.[105] "For reasons known only to the Armed Forces . . . " Lloyd Berkner wrote two years later, "many efforts were made to ignore or to suppress the findings of the Lincoln Summer Study and little effort was made to demonstrate how the ideas might work out. . . . the Armed Forces refused to recognize the serious state of the air-defense problem or to admit that it could be improved by radical measures." [106] The presidential decision on continental defense eventually led to the development of an extensive program and organization under the direction of the Air Force, but it did not drastically change the dominant doctrine of the Air Force.

The double role of the three principal outside groups appointed to study continental defense—the Kelly Committee, the "Seven Wise Men," and the NSC consultants—was well illustrated by the conflicting interpretations of the significance of the "Seven Wise Men." On the one hand, it was held that they were appointed at the urging of the President to develop support for continental defense among business, educational, and labor leaders; on the other hand, it was argued that they were a "packed jury" appointed at the urging of Budget Director Dodge to hold up action on continental defense.[107] The twenty-one positions in the three groups were filled by nine business executives, five educators, two labor leaders, one lawyer, one publisher, one military officer, one foundation executive, and one business consultant. The outside committees helped to delay decision and at the same time helped to broaden support and understanding for the needs of continental defense. The one thing they did not do was to contribute new ideas and proposals. The initiative for and against the innovation rested with the scientists and the governmental agencies principally concerned. The most significant contribution was made by the Kelly Committee, whose compromise report anticipated in many respects the eventual action of the Administration.

The periods of intense executive decision-making on the hydrogen bomb and European defense lasted approximately four months and two months, respectively. Public debate came after the decisions in the form of questions and criticisms by the opponents of innovation. The air defense controversy followed a different pattern. Executive consideration was so prolonged that the moves for public debate were made by the proponents of innovation before the presidential decision rather than by the opponents of innovation after the decision. Realizing the strength of the opposition within the executive branch, the supporters of air defense argued that the problems involved in continental defense should be presented to the people. They were leading supporters of "Operation Candor."

In 1952 and 1953 many individuals and groups urged the Administration to present to the people the facts concerning the destructiveness of nuclear weapons, the approximate relative magnitudes of the American and Russian stockpiles, and the probable nature and results of a nuclear war. Such a presentation, the advocates of candor argued, would inform people generally about the dangers of the world in which they lived and also would stimulate support for continental defense measures and for intensified negotiations with the Russians to end the arms race. One influential source of the demand for candor was a committee on disarmament policy appointed in 1952 to advise the Secretary of State. The chairman of the committee was J. Robert Oppenheimer, who had been a leading participant in the Lincoln Summer Study Group. The committee submitted its report in January, 1953, just as the Truman Administration went out of office, and in the spring of 1953 Oppenheimer presented it again to the Eisenhower NSC. Two of the committee's five recommendations were for candor and continental defense. In 1950 *after* the hydrogen bomb decision, Oppenheimer had warned that "There is grave danger for us in that decisions have been taken on the basis of facts held secret." In 1953 *before* the continental defense decision, he again warned that "We do not operate well when the important facts, the essential conditions, which limit and determine our choices are unknown.

We do not operate well when they are known, in secrecy and in fear, only to a few men."[108] The first need, he argued, is for "candor—candor on the part of the officials of the United States Government to the officials, the representatives, the people of their country."

Throughout the spring and summer of 1953 most of those who supported candor also supported continental defense. Their demands for the former helped to direct public attention to the latter. The Alsops extensively publicized the Summer Study Group recommendations, while other expert journalists, such as C. J. V. Murphy in *Fortune* and Hanson Baldwin in the *New York Times*, emphasized the desirability of moving slowly. In May, Lloyd V. Berkner urged the physicists to take the lead in pushing a new approach to continental defense. In June, Oppenheimer argued that a "reasonable" defense against attack was possible.[109] Thus, even though the President did not make a dramatic presentation of the facts of the atomic age to the people, considerable public discussion of continental defense took place before the President and the NSC reached their decision. In the absence of decision, however, the proponents remained unsatisfied. "Long carried on behind closed doors, the debate on the issues posed by our present vulnerability to atomic attack should now come into the open," two supporters of continental defense wrote in the fall of 1953, "for our government must have—and knows it must have—the help of informed public opinion in dealing with the problem."[110] In the end, the country had a debate over candor but a decision on continental defense. The decision, in turn, removed a principal stimulus to the drive for candor. The emphasis of that project shifted toward a "positive" proposal, and eventually resulted in the President's "Atoms for Peace" speech to the United Nations in December, 1953.[111]

The Joint Committee on Atomic Energy had played a significant role in the pre-decision debate over the hydrogen bomb. Despite the greater publicity, Congress played a less important role in the pre-decision debate over continental defense. Congress was preoccupied with other matters in the first months of a new Administration, and no congressional group had the background in continental defense which the Joint Committee had in nuclear weapons.

Also, whether or not to build a hydrogen bomb was a fairly concrete and simple issue compared to the complexities of continental defense. Congressional action, like executive decision, was triggered by the Soviet hydrogen bomb. Two days before the NSC meeting at which NSC 162 was approved, Representative W. Sterling Cole, chairman of the Joint Committee on Atomic Energy, urged additional expenditures of up to $10 billion a year for continental defense and civil defense and declared that "the time has arrived when more revelations should be made" to the public about the force, if not the number, of hydrogen weapons. Other congressmen expressed similar views. Six days later Senator Kefauver demanded a "complete review" of the continental defense situation in hearings before the Senate Armed Services Committee, and Senator Saltonstall, chairman of the Preparedness Subcommittee, announced the appointment of Robert C. Sprague to conduct a study of continental defense on behalf of the committee. The hearings requested by Kefauver were never held, however, and Sprague did not submit his report to the subcommittee and to the President until March, 1954. Apparently, he made several recommendations for improvements in continental defense but generally found that the existing programs were an adequate "minimum" and that, in Senator Saltonstall's words, they "combine to constitute a sound overall continental defense program." [112]

The culmination of the executive policy-making process on the hydrogen bomb and European reinforcements was marked by presidential announcements of the innovation decision. No such announcement was made after the approval of the continental defense program embodied in NSC 162. At about the time of the NSC action several Administration leaders and Chairman Cole issued conflicting estimates of Soviet atomic capabilities. On October 8, two days after the NSC discussion of NSC 162, the President declared that "the Soviets had the capability of atomic attack on us, and such capability would increase with the passage of time." He also, however, declared that he did not intend to disclose the "details" of American atomic strength. "The President's statement," Reston reported, "was something of a victory for those members of his Cabinet who have argued against dramatic disclosures in the field of atomic energy." The President said that studies of continental defense "were not complete" and "were going forward." Ten days later Secretary Wilson warned that continental defense needed better means of detection and interception and declared that the Administration had adopted the principle of Project Lincoln together with several other recommendations. The next month the American and Canadian Chiefs of Staff approved plans for an early warning system, and President Eisenhower declared in Ottawa that: "We must be ready and prepared. The threat is present. The measures of defense have been thoroughly studied by official bodies of both countries. The permanent joint board on defense has worked assiduously and effectively on mutual problems. Now is the time for action on all agreed measures." [113] Apart from these statements, no official declaration was made of the decision to go ahead with the continental defense program. In this respect, the Administration definitely did not choose candor.

Administrations are fully committed only when they are publicly and explicitly committed. Even in the case of the hydrogen bomb the vagueness of the language in the presidential directives permitted conflicting interpretations of their meaning. The reticence of the Administration about continental defense undoubtedly encouraged even greater uncertainty and offered the opponents of innovation additional opportunities for obstruction. Indeed, probably one reason for the reticence, as Stewart Alsop suggested, was that many members of the Administration accepted the necessity of continental defense but still hoped that it would be possible to avoid substantial additional expenditures.[114] On October 6, the day of the NSC meeting on NSC 162, Secretary Wilson minimized the likelihood of vast new expenditures for continental defense and suggested that only $500 million would be added to the FY 1955 defense budget for this purpose. A week later the Vice Chief of Staff of the Air Force warned that the "safest and surest defense" was a strong retaliatory force and that to neglect this force "because of preoccupation with last-resort defenses would be suicidal." [115]

Despite the continued budgetary and strategic reservations about continental defense the NSC action did mark a turning point. After the President's visit in November the Canadian government indicated that new steps of "great magnitude" would be undertaken and that measures "recommended by the Chiefs of Staff on the basis of recent studies have been agreed to . . ."[116] The New Look paper submitted by the JCS in December stressed the importance of continental defense and laid down a three-year program for its development. The revised FY 1955 budget provided about $1 billion more for continental defense than was provided in FY 1954.[117] In early 1954 the final American decision was made on the construction of the DEW line, and in April, 1954, the Canadian and American governments announced their agreement in principle to proceed with its development, on which preliminary work was "already well advanced."[118]

Construction on the line was begun in 1955, and it became operational in the summer of 1957. In 1956 the Air Force began to extend the warning system from Alaska through the Aleutians, and the Navy undertook to establish sea extensions to Midway and across the North Atlantic with the establishment of the Pacific and Atlantic Barrier Commands. In 1958 the complex SAGE system communications system, linking the warning units and interception units, became operational. Meanwhile in 1954 the Army began to install Nike antiaircraft missiles at key points and by the end of that year over fifty Air Force squadrons had been equipped with all-weather interceptor aircraft.

The expansion of the continental defense activities required forces and resources from all three services and thus tended to involve the services and to commit them to continental defense as a program. At the same time, however, interservice rivalry delayed the establishment of an autonomous command devoted exclusively to continental defense. The Joint Chiefs had debated the desirability of a joint American defense command since 1947 without ever reaching agreement on its organization. The services did agree that in an emergency the Air Defense Command could exercise control over Army and Navy forces, but the peacetime relation among the air defense components of the three services was based upon voluntary cooperation rather than unity of command. The 1953 decision to go ahead with a major continental defense effort, however, eventually broke the interservice stalemate, and in September, 1954, the Continental Defense Command was established under General Benjamin W. Chidlaw, commander of the Air Defense Command. General Chidlaw's command extended to the Army Antiaircraft Command and to the naval forces assigned to continental defense. The assignment of Army and Navy officers to the Continental Defense Command headquarters helped to strengthen the identification of these two services with the Command, but, even so, friction and dissatisfaction still existed, with the Army in particular complaining of its allegedly "subordinate" position. In September, 1956, partly as a result of Army protests, CONAD headquarters was separated from that of the Air Defense Command. Neither General Chidlaw nor his successor in 1955, General Partridge, was able to dramatize their function and to exert the personal prestige and influence which General LeMay had done with SAC and General Eisenhower with SHAPE. Nonetheless, the continental defense command slowly grew in size and authority, and in 1957 an international command, the North American Air Defense Command, was established to exercise integrated control over both Canadian and American forces. The emergence of an autonomous organization and the recognized need for contributions from all three services eventually produced a firm foundation for continental defense.

26. LIMITED WAR

The innovation of limited war programs was more difficult and less advanced in 1960 than that of other functional programs. Four factors were responsible for this lag. First, in the three earlier programs, the threat was fairly specific and easy to visualize, and the needed response seemed obvious and definite. The requirement for a limited war capability, however, was not the direct result of a need to match some clearly identifiable increase in Soviet capabilities. In fact, throughout most of the period Soviet doctrine minimized the possibility of limited war between the major powers. The need for limited war forces flowed instead from Soviet development of strategic forces designed for general war. Logically, the argument that a nuclear balance of terror increased the likelihood of limited war seemed irrefutable. It did not, however, produce a concrete threat in terms of an increase in Soviet capabilities which could serve as a stimulus and a standard for the development of comparable American capabilities. The danger of limited war was vague and seemingly remote. Because of its unspecific nature, the possible responses to deal with the danger were varied. By the late 1950s almost everyone recognized the possibility of limited wars, but many, including top officials in the Administration, argued that no special programs were needed to deter or to prepare for limited war, that if the country was properly prepared for a major war, it was naturally prepared for a small war. Those particularly sensitive to the dangers of limited war were divided over the means required to meet those dangers. Some stressed reliance on tactical nuclear weapons; others argued that conventional forces were needed. Some argued that a "mobile general reserve" was required, ready to move quickly to snuff out brush-fire conflicts any place in the world. Others held that extensive overseas deployments in the likely trouble spots were essential to deter such wars. To some, limited war was the principal mission of the Army; to others, the Marine Corps seemed the obvious nucleus of a limited war force. Further divisions existed between those who emphasized American responsibility to develop limited war forces and those who argued that priority should be given to strengthening allied forces through military aid programs.

Second, like continental defense, limited war marked a major change in earlier military strategy and programs. The concept of limited war was alien to traditional American ideas on war and peace. Initially, it was also alien to the prevailing doctrines of all the services. The need to maintain regular forces in a high degree of readiness for such conflicts was in itself a drastic change from the mobilization strategy of the interwar period.

Third, the Korean War permitted the major expansions of strategic deterrent and European defense forces and stimulated serious exploration of continental defense programs. Paradoxically, however, the war did not directly encourage the development of continuing limited war programs. The creation of forces to fight a war in progress did not imply a decision to maintain indefinitely in peacetime similar forces to deter similar wars in the future. In 1953 and 1954 massive retaliation to deter future limited wars was still a viable policy. The policy requirement for limited war forces stemmed not from American experience in Korea but Soviet achievements after Korea. Instead, the experience with one limited war in Korea led many members of the Eisenhower Administration to decide that this was one experience they did not wish to see repeated. In General Taylor's words, ". . . the ultimate effect of the Korean experience, oddly enough, was not to weaken faith in atomic air power but rather to strengthen it." [119] Only after the impact of the Korean War had abated and mutual deterrence had become an accepted feature of the international scene did special limited war programs begin to be feasible.

Fourth, the greater the delay in innovating a strategic program, the greater the difficulty in making the innovation. Inevitably, the limits on the overall military effort tended to increase the opposition to each successive program. Only so much room existed under the ceiling, whose level was usually determined by exogenous factors. Innovation of new functional programs was much easier during the Korean War than during the subsequent years of peace. Each potential additional claim on resources was usually opposed by the programs with established claims on resources. Budgetary considerations were of little importance in strategic deterrence and European defense; they played a greater role in the year-long debate over continental defense; and they were crucially important in the continuing debate in the 1950s over limited war.

In neither the Truman nor the Eisenhower Administrations did the supporters of limited war muster enough strength to gain high-level Administration approval of a unified program for limited war forces. In the Truman Administration, civilian leaders in the State Department and elsewhere viewed sympathetically the need for limited war forces. Many anticipated the development of Soviet air-atomic capabilities; others were concerned with the possible demands upon American military strength arising from the aftermath of World War II (e.g., China) or other local situations not directly involving Communist aggression (e.g., Palestine). George Kennan and members of the Policy Planning Staff of the State Department urged upon the Pentagon the desirability of providing forces to deal with small wars and local aggressions. Similarly, Oppenheimer in 1948 and Lilienthal two years later warned the military to consider the need for a flexible response and to avoid over-emphasis upon weapons of total destruction.[120] Before the Korean War, however, budgetary limitations and the concern of the military with the danger of general war precluded more entensive preparations for local conflicts.

During the first Eisenhower Administration the Army emerged as the principal supporter of limited war programs. This involved a major change in Army strategic thinking. Traditional Army doctrine and preparations had been directed to total war and the great mobilization of massive ground forces through universal military training and reserve forces programs. As a result, the Army was ill-prepared for the Korean War. It viewed the war as a "unique" experience which should not distract Army attention from its primary concern with the preparation for general war in Europe. In October, 1950, General Bradley declared that "We will refuse absolutely to allow local wars to divert us unduly from our central task. They must not be allowed to consume so much of our manpower as to destroy our strength and imperil our victory in a world war." [121] Similarly, early in 1951 the Army Chief of Staff elaborated at length the Army view that Korea was abnormal and of secondary concern:

> ... we must not permit recent experience to obscure what we may need in the future. For example, we must guard against the tendency to look upon the Korea fighting as a "Preview of Future War."
>
> The war in Korea has been a reversion to old-style fighting—more comparable to that of our own Indian frontier days than to modern war. Although some of the equipment and some of the tactics the enemy has used are undoubtedly similar to what we might expect to face in a war of the future, I do not believe the Korea fighting is typical of future war. ...
>
> To prevent an invasion of western Europe, the area most coveted by the Communists, we would have to fight an altogether different war than we have been fighting in Korea.[122]

The western European orientation of the Army and its involvement in the controversy over the strengthening of American defenses in Europe reinforced its tendency to think of Korea as an aberration and to assume that future wars would be very different.

During the Korean War some civilians and junior military officers began to develop ideas on the significance of limited war. Nonetheless, the thinking of many leading figures in the Army remained focused upon the problem of total war. Thus, in the fall

26. LIMITED WAR

of 1953, after the Korean War was over and just as the New Look was being formulated, the Army's new Chief of Staff, General Ridgway, still rejected Korea as a prototype for the future: "The day when wars had limited effects is past. . . . War, if it comes again, will be total in character. It will affect the whole social, economic and political fabric of the nations involved. . . . Today, war would not be waged solely between military forces, but between entire societies. . . . If we must fight, we must win. There can be no other goal. There must be no other outcome."[123] Significantly, perhaps, this speech was reproduced in the Army's official magazine in the spring of 1954. Down through 1953 and even into 1954 important elements in the Army still thought in terms of a future total war and depreciated the relevance of the Korean War to Army planning and strategy. On the one hand, the Korean War caused the Administration to view with extreme distaste the possibility of future limited conflicts, and, on the other, it did not immediately develop great enthusiasm for a limited war mission among many leaders of the Army.

The Army was pushed toward a limited war program not so much by what happened on the battlefield but by what happened in Washington. Army espousal of limited war was primarily a reaction to the New Look and the threat which it posed to the Army's missions. Continued preoccupation with total war in an age of thermonuclear weapons and long-range jet bombers clearly meant the acceptance of a subordinate role for the Army in peacetime. Service interest compelled the Army to make a bid for long-range missile and space programs, on the one hand, and yet to break radically with its doctrinal heritage of total war, on the other. The New Look and the emergence of the nuclear stalemate caused the Army to espouse the concept of limited war and to take the lead in developing programs which, in turn, eventually modified the massive retaliation strategy of the New Look.[124]

The rapidity with which the Army adopted the doctrine of limited war was remarkable. In the spring of 1954, for the first time, Army leaders stressed in budget hearings the danger of limited war breaking out in a number of places and the "unique" ability of the Army to deal with this type of war.[125] In August, 1954, Reston reported that ". . . the foot soldiers at the Pentagon are beginning to make some headway with the idea that what is really needed to supplement the 'capacity for massive retaliation' is a military 'old look' that can deal with the threat of limited wars." [126] In September a new version of the Army basic field manual on operations, FM 100-5, reflected the changing doctrine. Although the role of the Army in general war still received much attention, the manual pointed to the local aggressions in Greece, Korea, and Indochina and the probability that "political considerations" would prevent the use of maximum airpower against other aggressors and their supporters. "The continuing possibility of such limited wars," the manual declared, "requires the maintenance in being of Army forces capable of immediate commitment and fully organized, trained, and equipped for combat, and at the same time possessing a capability of strategic mobility." [127] Early in 1955, General Ridgway, in a marked change from the views which he had expressed only fifteen months earlier, also argued the case for the Army in terms of both general and limited war: ". . . armies are an essential element in our ability to conduct global war successfully, regardless of whether or not atomic and hydrogen bombers are used. The importance of the Army's role in geographically limited wars is equally clear." [128] Several months later, on his retirement, Ridgway pointed to the emerging nuclear stalemate, argued that the United States must be "prepared to meet and defeat limited aggression in small perimeter wars, whether or not nuclear weapons are used," and declared that the present "preoccupation with preparations for general war has limited the military means available for cold war to those which are essentially by-products or leftovers from the means available for general war." [129] Immediately after succeeding Ridgway, General Taylor declared that "If we are to assure that the disastrous big war never occurs, we must have the means to deter or to win the small wars." Taylor systematically elaborated the requirements of national military policy in which the deterrence of and preparation for limited wars received equal emphasis with the deterrence of general war, and the limited war function was defined as one which the Army was peculiarly qualified to perform. The development of the theory of limited *nuclear* war particularly fitted the Army's purposes, combining a distinctive mission, on the one hand, with a persuasive claim for nuclear weapons, on the other. Under Taylor's leadership the Army, in his words, became "the principal spokesman for increasing the United States capability in limited war." [130] Five years after one Army Chief of Staff had warned that Korea was not the prototype of future wars, another Chief of Staff was describing the Army's needs for limited war forces "[b]ased on our Korean experience . . ." [131]

The importance of the Washington political situation in the change in service attitudes toward limited war is pointed up by the contrast between the Army and the Navy. Although it had previously espoused a general war strategic concept, the top leaders of the Army identified themselves with limited war needs several years earlier than did the top leaders of the Navy. Massive retaliation and the prospective nuclear stalemate moved the Army toward a doctrine of limited war in 1955. Navy leaders, on the other hand, did not embrace the limited war doctrine with the same enthusiasm until 1957 and 1958, even though the Navy had always viewed itself as the principal military instrument of diplomacy, traditional naval doctrine was much more sympathetic to limited war concepts than traditional Army doctrine, and junior naval officers had actively articulated limited war ideas in the early 1950s. The hesitancy of the Navy in identifying itself with limited war was partly due to the influence of Admiral Radford, but it also reflected the fact that the New Look did not threaten the Navy as it did the Army. With its aircraft carriers and later its missile-firing submarines the Navy was able to look forward to an increasingly important role in the deterrence of general war. Only after the retirement of Admiral Radford in 1957 and the shift in State Department thinking away from massive retaliation did naval leaders become outspoken advocates of greater limited war preparations.[132]

During the first Eisenhower Administration the Army was almost alone in the executive branch in urging increased preparations for limited war. Increasingly, however, it began to receive more and more support from informed civilian opinion outside the executive branch. Early in 1952 at least one civilian expert advised the government on the need for a permanent limited war strategy and program. (In contrast, the first National War College theses on limited war were written in 1955.) After 1952, former members of the Truman Administration, such as George Kennan, began to criticize the new Administration for neglecting this need, and Secretary Dulles' massive retaliation speech in January, 1954, stimulated still more criticism along this line. In the fall of 1954 William W. Kaufmann and Bernard Brodie published systematic critiques of massive retaliation, arguing the probability of limited wars and the need for continuing forces to deal with this contingency.[133] "It was from unofficial critics of national defense," General Taylor has written, "that the public first was to receive intimations of the limitations of dependence on a nuclear strategy. . . . [These writings] from unofficial sources represented the first public questioning of the validity of the New Look policy of Massive Retaliation and I welcomed them warmly. Their acuity was all the more remarkable from the fact that the authors did not have access to complete information with regard to atomic weapons effects." [134] Limited war programs received additional support from the publication of Kaufmann's *Military Policy and National Security* in 1956 and Kissinger's *Nuclear Weapons and Foreign Policy* and Osgood's *Limited War* in 1957. The external critics, however, did not have a decisive influence on Administration policy. In 1952 and 1953 the physical scientists backing continental defense eventually secured Administration endorsement of their principal proposals. Reflecting perhaps the differences in status, access, and influence of the two professions, the social scientists supporting limited war programs did not meet with comparable success.

In the executive branch the opposition to any substantial limited war program remained predominant. On the one hand, the Air Force continued to advocate the absolute priority of strategic deterrence and the desirability of maintaining a counterforce capability requiring sustained large investments in missiles and planes. On the other hand, proponents of economy within the Administration, centered in the Budget Bureau and the Treasury, joined the surface services in opposing the Air Force's demands for a stronger strategic deterrent and joined the Air Force in successfully opposing Army-Navy demands for stronger limited war forces.

Throughout the 1950s opportunities presented themselves for a critical program decision on limited war comparable to the critical decisions which had been made on the other functional programs. In the face of the opposition to limited war programs and the weight which this carried with the President, however, the Army, Navy, and Marine Corps were unable to develop the support to bring about a radical change in Administration policy. The year-long debate within the executive branch over the Summer Study Group recommendations had permitted some public discussion of continental defense before the decision in the fall of 1953. The continuing refusal of the Administration to initiate a major limited war program resulted in even more extensive public discussion of limited war needs as Generals Ridgway, Gavin, Taylor, and other dissenters appealed their case to the public. Continued public demands for greater limited war strength thus coincided with the continuing reconsideration of the issue within the executive branch.

Prospective American intervention in the Indochina crisis in the spring of 1954 raised the possibility that, in the words of Secretary Wilson, "a soul-searching review" of American military policy might be necessary. The President was reported to have under consideration a second "new look" or "general revision of military plans," including cancellation of the proposed reductions in Army strength from 19 to 17 divisions.[135] Senate Democrats, led by Senator John F. Kennedy, attempted to increase Army funds for this purpose. The Administration and Senate Republicans, however, maintained their position, and with the resolution of the crisis by the Geneva partition agreement, the need for additional limited war forces apparently subsided.

A second opportunity for a possible increase in limited war capabilities appeared the following spring. It was related not to an immediate international crisis but rather to the developing Soviet air-atomic capabilities. The Basic National Security Policy paper developed in January, 1955, gave recognition "for the first time to the possibility of a condition of mutual deterrence and the importance in such a period for the United States to have versatile, ready forces to cope with limited aggression." [136] Although recognizing the threat of local aggressions, this paper did not authorize any specific new programs to deal with it. Army leaders talked of the desirability of establishing a "Free World Strategic Reserve" of ten Army and Marine Corps divisions deployed in four corps in Southeast

Asia, the Middle East, the Japan-Korea area, and the United States.[137] Pursuing its decision to hasten reductions in the military forces, however, the Administration rejected this proposal. In 1956, under the leadership of General Taylor, the Army made further efforts to increase its limited war capabilities. The Joint Chiefs apparently endorsed the view that limited war was the most likely contingency, but at the Puerto Rico meeting in March General Taylor was unable to persuade them to give limited war forces equal priority with the strategic deterrent forces. "It was too early," he later said, "to obtain a consideration of fundamental changes at a time when the other services were quite content with the *status quo*. But the issue was only postponed, not settled." [138]

In the spring of 1958 the Army, spurred on by Secretary Dulles' interest in the development of tactical nuclear weapons for limited wars, made a major effort to change Administration policy. Simultaneously Congress demonstrated new support for limited war needs and voted more funds for Army and Marine Corps divisions and for Army airlift. The Army itself completed in May, 1958, an extensive study detailing its requirements for manpower and conventional forces. At the urging of the Army, the Joint Chiefs launched a study of the adequacy of the military airlift, which, however, apparently concluded that the existing airlift was sufficient.[139] Most important, however, was a joint State Department-Defense Department study stimulated by the Army's urgings, the State Department's uneasiness, and the Gaither Committee's recommendations. This study attempted to estimate the American forces which would probably be required to deal with local aggressions in the different areas of the world. It was, in the words of Hanson Baldwin, "voluminous and thorough." [140] It did not, however, produce a major change in policy. In the debate over the Basic National Security Policy paper for 1958 the Navy and the Marine Corps joined the Army in urging "changes that would take into account the implications of nuclear parity, establish finite limits on the size of the atomic retaliatory force, and in general make for a flexible strategy for coping with limited aggression." What was required, General Taylor argued at the NSC meeting, was "an overall concentration of attention on limited war comparable to that which we had bestowed in the past upon general war." Generals

26. LIMITED WAR

Twining and White, in turn, argued against any change in the previous year's language. The members of the NSC sided with the status quo. As a result, the "meeting broke up without a decision being announced but in reality our cause was lost for the time being.... The eventual decision was to retain the language of the old guidance for the purpose of formulating the 1960 budget, but to keep the controversial parts under continuous review." [141] No Administration is likely to start major military programs in its last twelve to eighteen months in office, and the failure to provide more substantially for limited war needs in 1958 meant that few changes were likely until 1961.

During its four years of active effort to alter Administration policy and to introduce substantial limited war capabilities the Army had built up considerable support for its proposals in Congress and among the informed public. Unable to secure the active support of the State Department at the critical moments, however, it was also unable to produce a change in Administration policy. Although State Department officials often expressed concern over the effects of American military posture on the confidence of our allies, they did not take the lead in pressing for substantial changes in military programs. In 1956 and 1957 the attitude of the State Department, General Taylor regretfully observed, was "one of curious detachment. It was as if they felt that the conflicts in the Pentagon were what the Japanese call 'a fire on the other side of the river.'" Although Secretary Dulles and other State officials expressed interest in the development of tactical nuclear weapons for limited wars in the latter part of 1957, at the key NSC meeting on the Basic National Security Policy paper in 1958 "Secretary Dulles and his advisers did not provide the strong support for a new strategy" for which General Taylor had hoped.[142] In the absence of positive and continuing leadership from the State Department, efforts to increase limited war capabilities inevitably were doomed to failure. Thus, in the Truman Administration the State Department had pushed limited war needs while the Army was unsympathetic, and in the Eisenhower Administration the Army pushed limited war needs while the State Department was unsympathetic.

The difficulty in changing limited war programs was increased by the absence of a trigger event which might have precipitated a favorable decision. To be effective a trigger event has to dramatize a probable danger three or four years in the future; this makes the immediate innovation of programs to deal with that danger both necessary and feasible. By its very nature as a consequence of Soviet air-atomic build-up, the need for limited war forces was denied this type of impetus. The possibilities of limited war were so varied and its probabilities so uncertain that the supporters of greater limited war forces could not identify a definite future danger. The supporters of limited war capabilities could never argue, for instance, that "the Viet Minh build-up means an attack on South Viet Nam three years from now; therefore we must have two more Army divisions." The foreign developments which affected the level of Army forces, conventional forces, and limited war forces were not so much changes in the capabilities of potential enemies as diplomatic crises. The crises, however, could only have negative rather than positive effects. The Suez and Hungarian crises in the fall of 1956, sputnik in the fall of 1957, and the Lebanon and Quemoy crises in the summer of 1958, all caused either the cancellation or postponement of additional cuts in the Army. No crisis, however, could justify an increase in forces since any increase would not be available until long after the crisis had been resolved.

Throughout the Eisenhower Administration, programs especially designed for limited war never received the strong push from the top which other functional programs had received. Nonetheless, after 1955 almost all leaders of the executive branch did agree that limited war was a probable danger and that some forces were required to meet this danger even if they were only those also designed for general war. In this sense, the needs of limited war were on a sounder basis in the late 1950s than the needs of continental defense had been before 1953. Within the restrictions laid down by the Administration the military services and other agencies took many specific actions to increase American readiness and ability to deter or to win limited wars. The Administration refused to approve suggestions for a "Free World Strategic Reserve," but the Army was able to bring into existence its own Strategic Army Corps in 1958. Similarly, the Tactical Air Command created "composite air strike forces" to deter or to respond to local aggressions. The

Navy also prepared its carrier task forces for limited war missions, and the Marine Corps, of course, continued to be a prime component of American limited war capability. These developments, however, were largely initiated from below by the military leaders of the services, and they had to be implemented within the budgetary restrictions imposed by the Administration. Thus, in 1959, reductions in Army manpower caused it to cut back the Strategic Army Corps from four to three divisions. In addition, the unwillingness of the Administration to push the development of limited war forces meant that it did not bring into existence a headquarters or unified command especially concerned with limited war problems. Consequently, the requirements for limited war forces could not be formulated on a integrated basis; instead they were developed primarily within the individual services. The forces which might be used in a limited war were "a composite of Army, Navy, Marine, and Air Force units entirely unrelated to each other in planning and training." No approved joint plans existed "for the assembling, training, and rapid outloading of these heterogeneous forces, which represent our principal resources, to reinforce our overseas garrisons or to cope with the brush fires of limited war." [143] The individual services made their own specific preparations to deter limited war, but in the absence of enthusiastic Administration support, these capabilities lacked both a commander to coordinate them and a spokesman to represent their integrated needs within the government. Innovations were made to meet the threat of limited war, but they were made piecemeal, without the unity, direction, and strength which can only come from the highest levels of government. These had to await the Kennedy Administration.

27. ASSIMILATION OF ALTERNATIVE PROGRAMS
CIVIL DEFENSE AND ARMS LIMITATION AS ALTERNATIVE PROGRAMS

For most of the years from 1945 to 1960 civil defense and arms limitation were the country cousins of American strategy. They never quite "belonged," yet they could not be disowned. They existed on the periphery of policy, admittedly important but also strangely different. The military programs of the Defense Department, the weapons activities of the AEC, the foreign aid operations of the State Department, all seemed to share something in common which was denied to these two areas of policy. Almost all the other programs were related directly or indirectly to the needs of deterrence. The "outsider" quality of civil defense and arms limitations stemmed precisely from the fact that initially neither seemed directly related to or required by a strategy of deterrence. They were both alternative programs beyond the scope of the foreign policy-strategic consensus. Strategic deterrence and limited war were competitive, but competitive within the framework of common strategic assumptions. Civil defense and arms limitation initially rested on other assumptions. However different they were in substance from each other, these two programs were strikingly similar in their relations to the main course of American strategy, the remedies they proposed, the political positions which they occupied, and their eventual partial assimilation into a strategy of deterrence. Their similarities derived from their common character as alternatives to deterrence.

Both civil defense and arms limitation were originally based on the belief that security could not be permanently assured by the accumulation of armaments. Eventually the nuclear arms race would erupt into war. The United States must have an alternative to "peace through strength." American policy must either, as the supporters of disarmament argued, end the arms race before war occurred, or, as the supporters of civil defense maintained, it must be able to mitigate the horrors of war when it did occur. Behind both programs was the assumption that deterrence could not last. Civil defense was insurance against its failure, arms limitation the means of avoiding failure. In the immediate post-World War II years, disarmament proposals reflected the implicit assumption that it would be possible to return to the situation of great-power harmony which had existed during the war and had been envisioned in the drafting of the UN charter. As late as 1957 the Humphrey subcommittee argued that the need for disarmament derived from the "limitations" of "nuclear deterrence as a means of maintaining our national security..." Based upon the weaknesses rather than the strengths of the dominant American policy, disarmament tended

27. ASSIMILATION OF ALTERNATIVE PROGRAMS 355

to be "given a rather low priority in foreign policy matters" and "to be divorced from other and related aspects of foreign policy." [144]

While disarmament policy had its origins when it seemed that continued deterrence could be avoided, civil defense policy came into existence when it seemed that deterrence had failed. The Federal Civil Defense Act was a product of the dark days of December, 1950, when general war with the Soviet Union seemed highly probable. It was at this point that the emphasis in military programs shifted from the long-range build-up programs to the mobilization programs which would be more useful in a general war in the near future. The civil defense program was a product of this shift. Indeed, not waiting for congressional action, the President on December 1, 1950, created the Federal Civil Defense Administration by executive order. Like the other general war programs, the initial plans and activities in civil defense were largely based on the World War II experience. Only a small planning office, however, had remained in existence after World War II. Consequently, the creation of a new civil defense agency and program in 1951 represented the innovation of a defense program directed primarily to preparation for general war. In this respect, civil defense differed significantly from the military defense of North America. The latter was an essential element of deterrence. Early warning was necessary to speed the departure of the retaliatory force; anti-aircraft and anti-missile defenses were necessary to reduce the damage to that force. By increasing the size of the aggressive force necessary for a successful attack and multiplying the contingencies with which the aggressor would have to deal, military defense contributed significantly to deterrence. Initially, civil defense did no such thing. It was designed not as a contribution to deterrence but rather as a hedge against its failure.

ASPIRATION AND ACHIEVEMENT

Some gap between goal and program is essential to the continued existence of an administrative organization. The force-level goals of the armed services were seldom achieved under the circumstances for which they had been prepared. In general, however, the interaction between goal and program was a dynamic one involving the continuing realization of some goals and development of new ones. In arms limitation and civil defense, however, agencies and groups postulated far-reaching goals but made very little progress toward them. In contrast to the gradual innovation of the deterrent programs, the gap between goal and reality in the alternative programs remained almost constant. Unreality and futility suffused these two areas of activity. Virtually no one ever opposed civil defense or disarmament in general. All other military measures, it was repeatedly argued, were only temporary substitutes until an effective system of arms control could be agreed upon. Similarly, few editorial writers would openly attack the desirability of some civil defense. Yet despite this general agreement in principle, or perhaps because of it, civil defense and arms control plans went unrealized in practice.

From the viewpoint of deterrence, civil defense was directed to a contingency of low probability and maximum disaster, disarmament to a contingency of low probability and maximum desirability. Inevitably the supporters of both programs minimized the considerations of probability, and instead stressed the horrors "if nuclear war should come" and the benefits "if the arms race could be ended." If it were accepted that continued reliance on deterrence must result in war, the argument for either arms limitation *or* civil defense was irrefutable. Consequently, supporters of each stressed the horrors of thermonuclear war and argued that these must either be avoided or mitigated. On the one hand, it might seem somewhat incongruous for the Civil Defense Administrator to suggest that it was "entirely possible" that American cities would be uninhabitable after an atomic attack as support for an additional appropriation of $16 million. On the other hand, the argument that an atomic attack might kill fifty million Americans was not enough to generate approval within the Administration or Congress for $20 or $30 billion dollars for shelters. The magnitude of the threat justified almost any expenditure on civil defense. The probability of the threat, however, clouded the issue. Indeed, if resources allocated to civil defense were subtracted from deterrent programs, a larger civil defense effort would increase the probability of the danger with which it was meant to deal. Supporters of the alternative programs regularly pointed out that the FCDA spent less than one one-thousandth of the military budget and that the State Department wanted less than one one-thousandth of one percent of the military budget for disarmament studies.[145] These ratios dramatically reflected the distance between the two programs and the main thrust of American policy.

Continuing gaps existed between the plans and proposals advanced for civil defense and arms limitation and the programs which materialized. The FCDA was unique among federal agencies in the extent to which Congress cut its appropriations requests. In late 1950 federal officials estimated that civil defense would require $1.67 billion in federal funds during the next three years. Actual appropriations were less than 10 percent of this amount. From FY 1951 through FY 1957 the Department of Defense requested $300.3 billion from Congress and received $289.2 billion. During the same period, the FCDA requested $1,931 million and received $398 million, a gross cut of 79 percent. (Even foreign aid funds were seldom cut more than 20 percent.) In 1952 Project East River outlined a massive attack on the civil defense problem, urging the need for a national program to decentralize urban and industrial areas, improve warning time, and construct a strong, permanent civil organization. Three years later a panel established to review this report noted some improvements but concluded that "the nation's preparations and progress in non-military defense are still far from what they should be . . . the gap between the threat and the non-military defenses has widened." [146] When the Administration rejected the FCDA proposal for blast and fall-out shelters costing approximately $32 billion, congressional supporters warned that a "vast and dangerous gap" existed "between civil defense as it is and civil defense as it should be." [147] In 1951 the Civil Defense Administrator declared that not one city in the United States "has even approached the point where it could withstand an atomic attack now." Eight years later, a survey reported that "Home-front defenses are not ready for a massive nuclear attack. At present there are no guarantees when they may be." [148] Congress consistently reduced the agency's funds on the grounds that its plans were "unrealistic." The lack of funds, in turn, compounded the "unrealism" of the agency's activities. What was realistic in terms of the magnitude of the threat was unrealistic in terms of an overall policy of deterrence designed to prevent the threat from materializing.

A similar gap between aspiration and achievement pervaded American arms limitation policy. Civil defense plans were unrealized because they conflicted with American deterrent needs. Arms limitation plans were unrealized because they conflicted with either American deterrent needs or Russian military interests. The negotiations over disarmament consisted largely of the presentation of opposing grand plans for disarmament. These included, for the West, the Baruch proposals of June, 1946, the American "Proposals for Progressive and Continuous Disclosure and Verification of Armed Forces and Armaments" and "Essential Principles of a Disarmament Program" of April, 1952, the Anglo-French Plan of June, 1954, the "Open Skies" proposal of July, 1955, the revised Anglo-French Plan of March, 1956, the American partial disarmament proposals of April, 1956, and the Western "Proposals for Partial Measures of Disarmament" of August, 1957. These were matched by the Soviet plan for outlawing atomic weapons of June, 1947, the proposed General Assembly resolution for "strengthening the peace" of October, 1950, the new Soviet proposals of May 10, 1955, the Bulganin recommendations of November, 1956, and the Soviet London proposals of April, 1957. Like the grand plans for civil defense, the grand plans for disarmament, whether Soviet or American, went unrealized. All were discussed, none agreed upon. The first ten years of negotiations were "a decade of deadlock." The negotiators were no more successful in reaching agreement among themselves than the advocates of civil defense were in securing appropriations from Congress. Inevitably, as it became obvious no agreement would profit both sides, each side sought to profit from disagreement. Unlike the civil defense proposals, unrealistic disarmament plans did have a certain usefulness in the propaganda battles of the Cold War. The more unrealistic the plans were, the easier it was to secure agreement upon them within the government proposing them. On the one hand, the ardent supporters of disarmament favored a "comprehensive" approach; on the other, those officials primarily concerned with the maintenance of deterrent strength could rest assured that the more comprehensive the proposal the

27. ASSIMILATION OF ALTERNATIVE PROGRAMS

less likely it was to be accepted by the opposing side. Each disarmament program usually had a "joker" in it which made it unacceptable to the other government. A disarmament plan had to be unacceptable to the opponent but appealing to everyone else.[149] The utility of the arms limitation proposals thus came to rest upon their unreality.

THE POLITICAL POSITION OF THE PROGRAMS

As alternative programs civil defense and arms limitation had difficulty in securing continuing organized support within the government. Although few officials ever openly opposed civil defense or arms limitation in principle, equally few ever strongly supported either in particular. The ambivalent position of the programs as policy was matched by their organizational dilemma. The assignment of the program to an independent office or agency responsible for that program alone stimulated opposition from other agencies concerned with deterrence. Assignment of the program to an agency with deterrent responsibilities inevitably resulted in the subordination of the alternative program. The choices seemed to be ineffectiveness by remoteness or ineffectiveness by subordination. Civil defense was the responsibility of the FCDA from 1951 to 1958. Disarmament was the responsibility of Harold Stassen as Special Assistant to the President from 1955 to 1958. Neither became a major influence in the executive branch of the government, and eventually their activities were transferred to other agencies.

The position of the FCDA was distinctly marginal. It shared control over civil defense not only with state and local agencies but, within the federal government, first with the National Security Resources Board and then the Office of Defense Mobilization. The head of FCDA was a member of neither the NSC nor, initially, the Cabinet. The agency was in recurring difficulties with Congress over funds, personnel, and policies. Given their concern with deterrence, the military services simply refused "to accredit civil defense as a partner along with the Army, Navy, and Air Force on the national security team." [150] Taking seriously its own warnings on dispersal, FCDA further damaged its standing by moving from Washington to Battle Creek, Michigan. This move was not only "responsible for some temporary paralysis in effectiveness," but it also permanently "crippled" the ability of the agency to maintain contact with other federal agencies. Reviewing FCDA history in 1955, one expert panel concluded that the agency "does not yet have the stature, prestige, acceptance, or effectiveness with Congress, with other governmental agencies on the local, state, and Federal level, or with the people of the country that it so badly needs and should have." [151]

During most of the first Eisenhower Administration the FCDA put primary emphasis upon the development of plans for the evacuation of key target areas in the likelihood of atomic attack. It adhered to this policy because it was not well informed by the Defense Department and the AEC on fall-out dangers and the prospective evaporation of warning-time with the development of ballistic missiles. For this adherence it was vigorously criticized by the House Military Operations Subcommittee, one of the few congressional groups interested in civil defense problems. When the FCDA changed its position in 1956 it did so with a vengeance, recommending to the Administration a $32 billion construction program for fall-out and blast shelters. This recommendation received the enthusiastic support of Representative Holifield's subcommittee, but it was adamantly opposed by the Administration, which appointed the Gaither Committee to study the problem. The Gaither Committee suggested a $22 billion fall-out shelter program as a second-priority measure. This, however, was opposed by the Budget Bureau and the Treasury for economy reasons, the military because it would encourage a "Maginot line mentality" (and might possibly result in lower military appropriations), and by the State Department because of the psychological impact it would have on our allies and encouragement it might give to neutralist tendencies.[152] In 1958 the Administration eventually asked for $13 *million* for research and prototype construction, and Congress cut this figure to $4.5 million. Thus, despite support from the National Academy of Sciences, the Gaither Committee, and the Holifield Subcommittee, the FCDA was frustrated in its principal program recommendations. Shortly after rejecting the shelter program, the Administration merged the FCDA and the ODM. The new agency remained in the Executive Office of the President, and Gordon Gray, former head of ODM, became head of the combined OCDM. Thus subordinated, civil defense officials were unlikely to come up with further expensive recommendations to embarrass the Administration.

27. ASSIMILATION OF ALTERNATIVE PROGRAMS

The life of the Office of the Special Assistant for Disarmament was briefer and even stormier than that of the FCDA. Appointed to this post in March, 1955, Harold Stassen found himself in a running battle with officials of State, Defense, and AEC. Like the civil defense officials, he was an outsider backing a policy which ran counter to the presuppositions of deterrence. Just as the FCDA in 1957 came forward with its independent shelter proposals, so in 1957 Mr. Stassen stepped forward to play a significant role in the London disarmament negotiations with the Soviet Union. Reportedly twice exceeding his specific instructions in order to encourage agreement, Stassen ran into opposition from the foreign affairs agencies of the government and from our allies. "[I]n the main," Secretary Dulles commented, "the military people do not have great confidence in the efficacy of any attainable control or inspection system." [153] Admiral Radford argued that the United States could not "trust the Russians on this or anything." The "professionals beneath the political level at the State and Defense Departments," it was said, were highly dubious about Soviet intentions.[154] Scientists and AEC officials, led by Chairman Strauss, influenced the President to insist on the stopping of nuclear weapons production as a necessary condition for the suspension of nuclear tests. Military leaders were "worried about the psychological effect that prolonged disarmament talks might have on the military budget." [155] Chancellor Adenauer expressed concern over any agreement for aerial inspection of Germany. French leaders were dubious about any agreement limiting the nuclear club to three. British and French officials were also concerned about Stassen's by-passing them and dealing directly with the Russians before a common western position had been agreed upon. Secretary Dulles, of course, was highly sensitive to these European fears. Initially, the President supported Stassen, but eventually he was persuaded to stiffen the American position. In the end the Russians shifted their line before the full consequences of the opposition to Stassen within the Administration and the NATO alliance became apparent. That opposition, however, made his success in negotiation about as unlikely as Administration approval of the FCDA shelter request.

The final break came the following winter when Stassen apparently forced the issue between himself and Dulles over the possibility of bilateral arms negotiations between the United States and the Soviet Union. The issue, as Stassen's chief assistant defined it, was between those who favored "relaxation of tension" and those who favored "increased pressure" on the Soviet Union.[156] Although he seemed to favor a more liberal approach to arms negotiations, the President sided with Dulles. When Stassen resigned to run for Governor of Pennsylvania, the White House Disarmament Staff was transferred to the State Department and placed under the direction of the Secretary's special assistant on atomic energy. The abolition of the White House post, the President was reported to have said, reflected the fact that "the emphasis would soon be on other aspects of American foreign policy." [157]

Between 1948 and 1952 disarmament had been handled by four professional officers in the State Department and coordinated through the Executive Committe for the Reduction of Armaments (RAC), which included representatives of State, Defense, and the Atomic Energy Commission. In 1958 this pattern was resumed. Responsibility for overall policy rested with the Committee of Principals, consisting of the President's Special Assistant for Science and Technology and the heads of the State and Defense Departments, the Atomic Energy Commission, and the Central Intelligence Agency. In 1958 the State Department's disarmament staff still numbered only six or seven people. American preparation for four key international conferences on arms control measures in 1958, 1959, and 1960 reportedly left much to be desired. In the fall of 1960 the Administration created a new Disarmament Administration designed to have a staff of about fifty and to work under the Secretary of State. In its last six months in office, however, the Eisenhower Administration was unable to find a head for its Disarmament Administration.[158] Thus, after the disappearance of the Special Assistant, arms control policy, like civil defense, was administratively subordinated to an agency with other primary interests.[159]

The organizational dilemma of the alternative programs was reflected in the recommendations of their supporters. On one hand, it was frequently argued that the FCDA should be elevated into a cabinet department or that a new "peace" agency should be created, possibly also at the cabinet level, to handle arms limitation. Such arrangements, however, would institutionalize a clash of policy and organizations at the highest level of government. On the other

27. ASSIMILATION OF ALTERNATIVE PROGRAMS

hand, supporters of civil defense also urged that it be assigned to a fourth major department within the Department of Defense, and some disarmament advocates argued that disarmament properly belonged in the State Department. The military, however, repeatedly opposed placing civil defense in the Pentagon, and the State Department provided little support for its disarmament office. Neither organizational approach offered an escape from the policy dichotomy.[160]

Lacking strong and continuing organized support within the executive branch, the advocates of civil defense and arms limitation attempted to develop support elsewhere. Initially, however, neither activity had much support within Congress. The two principal centers of interest in civil defense were the Kefauver subcommittee of the Senate Armed Services Committee and the Holifield Military Operations subcommittee of the House Government Operations Committee. Neither carried great weight with Congress. In addition, until FY 1955, appropriations for civil defense were included in deficiency or supplemental appropriations bills. Thereafter they were made in the Independent Offices Bill, which again, however, meant that no Appropriations subcommittee was primarily concerned with civil defense. Similarly, congressional interest in disarmament was unorganized until the Humphrey subcommittee was created in 1955. This group played a significant role in prodding the executive branch to develop realistic proposals and more effective procedures on disarmament matters. Even so, until 1958 its activities were, as one Washington correspondent put it, treated with "massive indifference" by other members of Congress.[161] Restricted in their staff and support within the executive and legislative branches, the agencies concerned with disarmament and civil defense attempted to develop policies and to broaden support by utilizing ad hoc groups from outside the government. The Project East River panel made the most comprehensive study of civil defense in the early days of the FCDA. The Office of the Special Assistant for Disarmament employed eight task forces to aid in formulating policy. Similarly, the American positions for the surprise attack conference in November, 1958, the nuclear test conference in November, 1959, and the ten-nation disarmament conference in March, 1960, were all largely the work of hastily recruited ad hoc groups. Concern with the horror of nuclear war and scepticism about the efficacy of deterrence often led the same groups, such as the *Bulletin of the Atomic Scientists* and the National Planning Association, to take an active interest in both civil defense and disarmament. Similarly, in Congress, Senator Humphrey pushed the creation of a Joint Committee on Civil Defense at the same time that he was setting up the Subcommittee on Disarmament.

CHANGES IN THE ALTERNATIVE PROGRAMS

Civil defense and arms limitation had a continuing existence as potential alternatives to deterrence. In the mid-1950s, however, changes in military technology increased their compatibility with deterrence. This greater compatibility was not necessarily permanent; later technological changes might produce still different relationships. Nonetheless, for a while civil defense and arms control became not only alternative programs competing with deterrence but also supplementary programs contributing to it or at least not detracting from it.[162] The proponents of both civil defense and disarmament tended to abandon the "grand designs" of the late 1940s and early 1950s and instead advocated more limited measures, adoption of which would not necessarily imply a change in the fundamentals of defense policy. Strategists such as Kahn explored the relation between civil defense and deterrence, others such as Schelling that between arms control and deterrence.

The shift in arms control proposals towards a greater compatibility with deterrence was a product of the proliferation of nuclear weapons. The gap between the original American disarmament policy and the continuing American deterrent strategy increased steadily as the United States became more dependent upon the nuclear weapons which the Baruch plan proposed to abolish.[163] As the possibility of complete atomic disarmament became more and more unreal, arms control proposals became more and more specific. "Disarmament negotiations before 1955," one student has written, "revolved largely around comprehensive, step-by-step arms reduction plans. These plans either began or ended with the total prohibition and elimination of nuclear weapons and had to be agreed substantially in full before any real beginning could be made. The emphasis in 1955–56 upon lesser and more immediate steps as starting

27. ASSIMILATION OF ALTERNATIVE PROGRAMS

points offered greater promise." [164] The London conference in 1957 decided to adopt a separable, item-by-item agenda, considering proposals "point by point rather than plan against plan." That conference ended, nonetheless, with each side advancing a comprehensive "package proposal." The next year, however, the United States adopted a "functional approach." [165] Negotiations shifted from "disarmament plans" to "arms control measures," where agreement seemed more likely to be achieved and least likely to conflict with the needs of deterrence.

The two most important specific issues of arms control policy after 1957 were the prevention of surprise attack and the ending of nuclear tests. The former became an increasingly important goal of American policy after 1956 with the steady growth in the vulnerability of SAC. A situation in which either side could be reasonably certain that it could destroy the retaliatory power of the other by surprise seemed to be inherently unstable. Hardened, concealed, or mobile long-range missiles were one way to reduce this vulnerability and reintroduce stability. Agreement on measures to prevent surprise attack were another. They would thus reinforce the deterrent power of nuclear weapons. As Thomas C. Schelling put it, ". . . surprise-attack schemes—in contrast to other types of disarmament proposals—are based on *deterrence* as the fundamental protection against attack. They seek to perfect and to stabilize a situation of mutual deterrence. This means that they seek to enhance the integrity of particular weapons systems, not to dismantle or degrade those weapons systems." [166] The advocates of disarmament believe that the existence of the weapons themselves heightens tension and may provoke war. The advocates of inspection necessarily deny this premise.[167] The first major proposal for surprise attack prevention was the President's "open skies" suggestion at the 1955 Geneva conference. Although negotiations in 1956 and 1957 narrowed the gap between Soviet and American demands, Dulles, Strauss, and other top leaders were still suspicious of the effects of any significant arms control measure on existing policy. In 1957 and 1958, however, Killian and other scientists brought a new view to the higher reaches of policy-making. They "persuasively introduced the concept of inspection as a deterrent," and in November and December, 1958, a conference of experts explored with the Russians possible ways of preventing surprise attack.[168] The political obstacles to reaching agreement on anti-surprise attack measures, however, were greater than the technical obstacles to developing relatively invulnerable missile systems. With the shift from aircraft to missiles, effective inspection against surprise attack became more difficult. The rise and then decline in importance of anti-surprise attack measures in arms control policy thus directly reflected their changing value in achieving strategic deterrence.

In slightly different fashion the intense debate within the American government over ending nuclear tests was directed primarily to the effects which a ban would have upon weapons development and our deterrent posture. The initial impetus to end testing stemmed largely from concern over the increasing radiation in the earth's atmosphere. After underground and outer space testing emerged as possibilities, however, the proponents of the ban continued to argue that it would halt or slow down the development of nuclear weapons while the United States was still in the lead and would minimize future difficulties in deterrence by reducing the probability that other countries would develop nuclear weapons. The opponents held that no test inspection system could be completely proof against violation, that the temptations to violate and the probability of violation could leave other powers in a weakened position, incapable of preventing aggression. Moreover, they argued, even if the ban were completely enforceable it would prevent the United States from developing "clean" thermonuclear weapons, defensive nuclear weapons, and low-yield nuclear weapons, all of which would be desirable for future deterrence.[169] Here again an arms control issue was considered within the framework of existing policy.

In the late 1940s and early 1950s its supporters justified civil defense primarily on the grounds of the lives it would save if war should occur. In the mid-1950s, however, increasing attention was given to the potential contribution which civil defense might make to deterrence. Emphasizing its value in war, the supporters of civil defense also argued that it could become the third major deterrent after retaliatory power and military defense.[170] In its first phase the arms race focused primarily upon the means of destruction, nuclear and thermonuclear weapons. In its second phase the focus shifted to means of delivery, jet bombers and ballistic missiles. As both states began to acquire relatively invulnerable delivery techniques, the means of defense began to become more important. In the absence of an effective military defense against ballistic missiles, civil defense measures might be an essential element in a deterrent strategy. The more effective a nation's civil defense measures, the greater the range of enemy actions which it could deter by the threat of massive retaliation. Even "modest civil defense programs relying mainly on evacuation and improvisation" would help deter "extremely provocative behavior" by the Soviets short of an all-out attack on the United States.[171] Civil defense preparations would make other nations hesitate to stimulate a crisis with the United States. "There is an enormous difference in bargaining ability of a country," Herman Kahn also pointed out, "which can, for example, put its people in a place of safety in 24 hours' notice and one which cannot. If it is hard for the reader to visualize this, let him imagine a situation where the Russians had done exactly this and we had not. Then let him ask himself how he thinks he would come out at a subsequent bargaining table." [172] Increasingly, civil defense proponents stressed the necessity of balancing civil defense needs against needs of the strategic deterrent and continental defense and of developing in this light a realistic program reflecting "the willingness of U.S. voters to support appropriations for all national-defense purposes combined." [173] The 1957 fall-out shelter proposals were the last "grand design" of the civil defense advocates. Contrasting with it were the relatively mild measures suggested in a RAND Corporation study in July, 1958. The Gaither Committee had recommended a $22 billion shelter program; the RAND report pointed out the desirable features of such a program but suggested investing $500 million in research, development, planning, and inexpensive preparatory actions.[174] The importance of civil defense in the event of hostilities was still stressed; added to it, however, was a new appreciation of the role which civil defense might play in preventing hostilities. The research and preparatory activities advocated by the RAND experts were not massive alternatives to deterrence but inexpensive, reasonably feasible programs complementing and contributing to deterrence.

The assimilation of arms control and civil defense proposals reflected the changing requirements of deterrence. Future changes in those requirements might increase or decrease the relevance of specific arms control and civil defense measures. The merits of any measure would usually be debated in the same terms as the innovation of a major arms program: relevance to deterrence, balance, feasibility, timing.[175] The process of assimilation was a process of innovation, but it was a process which differed significantly from that which brought into existence the major deterrent arms programs. In general, the latter involved the accretion of new resources, forces, and weapons—a steady building out from existing strength. Assimilation, however, involved a tempering of earlier fears, hopes, and goals. It was, perhaps, an illustration of the policy-making pattern identified by Albert Hirschman in which the grand schemes and plans are first proposed and perform a useful, if negative function, by revealing their impracticality. They clear the way and generate support for more modest steps to deal with more immediate problems. The innovation of the deterrent arms programs involved the formulation and acceptance of new or broader goals. The assimilation of alternative programs involved a lowering of sights, an acceptance of limited goals requiring limited actions.

CHAPTER VI

The Competition of Strategic Programs

28. SERVICE INTERESTS AND INTERSERVICE COMPETITION

THE RISE OF INTERSERVICE COMPETITION

"General LeMay's statement that B-29s have rendered carriers obsolescent is the first overt act in the coming battle for funds," a leading admiral warned in April, 1945. "It is beginning to look to me that the war after the war will be more bitter than the actual war. Which, of course," the admiral concluded, "is a shame." A year later the commanding general of the Army Air Force asked, "Why should we have a Navy at all?" and answered himself by declaring, "There are no enemies for it to fight except apparently the Army Air Force."[1]

The premonitions of interservice war were well taken. The years from the beginning of the struggle over unification in 1944 until the beginning of the Korean war in 1950 stand out in American military history as a high-water mark of interservice competition. The issues at stake were vital to the services; the means employed were varied; the intensity and passion of the debate were unprecedented. An Air Force general could publicly refer to the Marines as "a small bitched-up army talking Navy lingo." "Power-hungry men in uniform," could reply a Marine general.[2] For two years, the Marine Commandant declared, the leaders of the Corps spent most of their time defending it against attacks. Navy officials charged the Air Force with irregularities in plane buying; Air Force officials gloated over the prospective decline in naval power. The Secretaries of the Navy and the Air Force resigned; the Chief of Naval Operations was fired; a major shake-up occurred in the naval high command. Charges and countercharges were traded. "The country is being flooded with speeches, articles, and talks by admirals on the potency of the submarine, and the omnipotence of large carriers," General H. H. Arnold wrote in October, 1949; "by ground generals proclaiming how the next war must be won by the doughboy plodding through the mud; by air generals telling the power of the large bombers. Partisans of the Marine Corps say the Marines must be the keystone in our war organization." [3]

Before World War II, service political controversy had two distinguishing characteristics. First, in most issues, a military service and a few satellite groups struggled against civilian isolationists, pacifists, and economizers. The Navy and the shipbuilding industry fought a lonely battle with the dominant groups in both political parties over naval disarmament. The Army lost its fight for universal service after World War I, but throughout the 1920s clashed with educational, labor, and religious groups over ROTC and with other groups over industrial mobilization preparations. In the annual budget encounters the issue was drawn between service supporters who stressed preparedness and associated values and their opponents who decried the necessity and the legitimacy of substantial military expenditures. To the extent that the services were in politics, they were involved in conflicts with civilian groups. Behind each specific opponent of the moment was the broad and deeply ingrained anti-military sentiment which had characterized American society since the eighteenth century.

A second crucial aspect of prewar service political battles was that each service waged its own independent of the other. Throughout the 1920s and 1930s the services cooperated in strategic planning through the Joint Board and in a few other enterprises. Strategic planning, however, involved no immediate claims upon scarce resources. It produced some disagreement but no real political conflict. The most significant intramilitary controversies involved the efforts of the two semi-services, the Air Corps and, to a lesser extent, the Marine Corps, to achieve greater autonomy and *de jure* recognition as services. The two major services, though, seldom fought each other politically and virtually never helped each other. They were distinct departments. Separate legislation, handled by separate Military and Naval Affairs committees, established and organized

28. INTERSERVICE COMPETITION

them, authorized their strengths, prescribed their systems of promotion and recruitment. Separate appropriations subcommittees provided their funds in separate supply bills. The political successes and failures of one service had little implication for the other: the National Defense Act of 1920 boded neither good nor ill for the Navy; the Vinson Acts of the 1920s neither assumed nor precluded an increase in the Army. Each service struggled along in its own world with its peculiarities and preoccupations, its own friends and enemies.

After World War II the traditional service-civilian conflict reappeared in the struggles between the Navy and the State Department over the Japanese mandates, the military and the scientists over the control of atomic energy, and the Army and civilian groups over universal military training. These conflicts were holdovers from a previous era. The primary locus of service political activity shifted drastically. World War II destroyed the separate political universes of the services. Service futures were now interdependent. The new role of the Army reflected not only its new weapons and responsibilities, but also what happened to the Navy and Air Force. Each service and would-be service was anxious to define a suitable role for itself before postwar relationships had jelled into enduring form. Service concerns over the future became fears of how the other services might affect that future. A unified defense organization meant competition over organizational position and strategic doctrine. A unified appropriations process meant competition for funds. The interservice struggle over unification between 1944 and 1947 was not only a model for future conflicts, but it also shaped the nature of those conflicts. Interservice rivalry was the child of unification. Both reflected the unity and complexity of modern war, and without the second, the first would never have come into existence.

The transition from civilian-service controversy to interservice controversy as the main focus of service political activity was graphically illustrated in the battle over UMT between 1945 and 1948. The lines of battle were initially drawn between the Army and some patriotic and veterans' groups, on the one hand, and various civilian educational, religious, pacifist, and farm groups on the other. The Army took its case for UMT to the country, employing press, radio, pamphlets, civilian advisory committees, the Fort Knox demonstration unit, organizational contacts, and all the vast panoply of modern public relations techniques. The opposition, one War Department consultant declared, included "subversive groups and a large section of the public which does not think."[4] UMT's opponents replied with dire warnings of the dangers of militarization. Here was a conflict in the classic pattern of the 1920s and 1930s, with all the familiar arguments, cliches, and symbolism. The resolution of the issue in 1948, however, reflected not so much the relative strength or persuasiveness of the two coalitions as it did the relative appeals of the Army and Air Force strategic doctrines. The issue was redefined from "UMT vs. no UMT" to "UMT vs. a seventy-group Air Force." "The effect of the Finletter report and of the Brewster-Hinshaw Board," Forrestal noted in his diary for March 8, 1948, "has been to convince the country that by a substantial increase in appropriations for Air, there would be no necessity for UMT . . ."[5] Congress added $822 million to Air Force appropriations, and the UMT legislation died in committee. The conflict of the military and a few affiliated groups against an extensive coalition of civilian groups had become a conflict of one service against another. The relative appeals of the services now determined the fate of military programs.

Organization and strategy were the two focal points of the interservice rivalry spawned by unification. The Air Force wanted independence of and equality with the other services. The Army backed the Air Force and in addition wanted an effective system of centralized control over all three services. The Navy and Marine Corps feared that independence for the Air Force and unification for the Army would mean subordination or elimination for themselves. Airpower advocates did not hesitate to challenge the need for substantial naval forces, and Dwight D. Eisenhower and other Army leaders made it clear that the Marine Corps ought to be maintained as only a minor landing force.[6] The battle over organization began in the spring of 1944. Eventually, the National Security Act, its 1949 amendments, and the allocation of roles and missions at the Key West and Newport conferences reassured the sea-going services of their future existence and importance. After the Marine Corps Act of 1952, the United States had four recognized services instead

28. INTERSERVICE COMPETITION

of the two it had had in 1940. After 1952, whatever the vicissitudes of budgets and strategy, the organizational existence of no service was seriously threatened by another. An equilibrium had been reached.

The tensions stimulated by the unification controversy were reinforced by those arising from the strategic controversy. During the continental phase of military policy, the purposes of the Indian-fighting Army on the frontier had little or no connection with those of the frigate-equipped Navy policing the slave trade in the South Atlantic. Each service had its own function or mission, and the only area of conflict or overlap was coastal defense, which was a secondary concern of both. Similarly, during the interwar period the strategic planning of the Navy was directed primarily toward the future war with Japan while that of the Army was implicitly oriented toward another Warld War I-type war in Europe. Where their strategic concerns did overlap, as in the defense of the Philippines, they were unable to reach agreement.[7] Otherwise, service planning was directed to different contingencies.

After World War II there appeared to be only one significant contingency for all the services. Each felt that it had to justify its existence in terms of its future importance in a general war with Russia. Agreed on the nature of the threat, the services sharply disagreed on the methods by which it should be met. The Air Force believed that a future war would consist of an initial decisive airpower stage in which victory would be irretrievably won or lost and then a second mopping-up stage in which possibly the other services might be of some use. In a war with Russia, airpower advocates held, a navy would have little role except to protect communications, and it would be impossible for the West to equal the Soviet advantages on land. Only strategic airpower represented the sure road to quick, decisive, and economic victory.

The surface services were less sure of what the war would be like, but both felt that it would be total and also more complex than the Air Force admitted. They tended to argue that no single type of power would in itself be decisive. The Army held that the initial air exchange between the two opposing states would be inconclusive until the surface forces had been built up to the point where they could move forward and seize bases and territories close to the enemy. After they had done their work, the air attack might play a more important role. But the final *coup de grâce* would still be administered by the ground forces moving in, defeating the enemy's land armies, and occupying his territory.[8] In the B-36 hearings, the Navy argued that the initial air offensive could never be decisive (if only because of the vulnerabilities and limitations of the B-36), and even if it were decisive, it would be poor policy and poor morals to utilize it. Thus the surface services arrived at the doctrine of balanced forces: air, sea, and land forces would all have important roles to play in the future total war and hence all three should be properly maintained in peace. Between their doctrines and that of the Air Force no compromise was possible. They were two different answers to the same problem of total war.

THE COMPETITION OF SERVICE PROGRAMS

In August, 1945, the President requested the Joint Chiefs to draw up a comprehensive statement of postwar military requirements, taking into consideration "our international commitments for the post-war world, the development of new weapons, and the relative position of the services as a result of these factors."[9] For nine months the Joint Chiefs struggled with the assignment. They could not agree on a postwar military program. In June, 1946, they gave up the effort. A unified strategy, they indicated, would have to wait upon a unified organization. By the time the organization was established in 1947, however, service program goals had hardened. After "unification" the Joint Chiefs were not significantly more successful in producing agreement than they had been before. The competition among military programs became preeminently the competition among service program goals.

The political environment impelled the services to articulate goals and also conditioned the nature of those goals. On the one hand, service leaders were aware that their goals should border upon the politically feasible. They often reduced the strength requirements submitted by subordinate echelons so they would not be abruptly rejected by Administration leaders and congressmen. On the other hand, some reduction or modification by the civilian agencies was inevitable, and the initial goals of the services had to be sufficient to permit this to take place without damaging effects.

28. INTERSERVICE COMPETITION

Also, it was in the interest of the service to have as a program goal a "salable" figure or force concept which would capture imagination and elicit enthusiasm. Ideally, it should be something which could be presented realistically but dramatically as the "absolute minimum" necessary for national security. Once a goal had been determined, moreover, a service was usually reluctant to abandon it, despite changes in its international applicability or domestic feasibility; to do so would cast doubt upon the soundness and objectivity of the process by which the goal was formulated. Service program goals became both the ends and the weapons of interservice controversy.

The initial program goals of the services were formulated before the end of World War II and were predicated on the assumption that the next war would be a general war similar to World War II. In the years that followed, the service programs were slowly adjusted to demands of the Cold War, and, conversely, the needs of the Cold War were employed to justify previously established service goals. Each goal was determined with little or no reference to the goals of the other services. Each goal was thus, in a sense, politically feasible in itself, when viewed from the perspective of a particular service, but all three service goals together were not feasible. Interservice competition stimulated the definition and articulation of service goals and at the same time frustrated their realization.

The Air Force objective of 70 groups emerged early in 1945. "In our new Air Force, as we see it," General Arnold declared on September 26, 1945, "we will have about 70 groups." During the next five years the 70-group goal became sanctified as "a carefully computed irreducible minimum" necessary for national security.[10] In the summer of 1947 the persistent Air Force emphasis on its need led to the creation of the Congressional Aviation Policy Board and the President's Air Policy Commission. The following winter both groups recommended an Air Force of 70 groups. The FY 1949 budget provided 48 groups. After the Czech coup, the Administration yielded and backed an Air Force of 55 groups in its spring rearmament program. Congress added additional funds to aid Air Force expansion to 70 groups. The Administration refused to utilize them, however, and in the gathering economy wave of the summer and fall of 1948, the Air Force goal was cut back again to 48 groups.

In 1949 the House of Representatives picked up the challenge and appropriated funds for 58 groups. The President impounded the money. In June, 1950, the Air Force had 48 groups.

The goals formulated by the Army during the war reflected the natural assumption that the mobilization strategy of the interwar period would be continued in the postwar years. General Marshall's Circular 347 of August 25, 1944, rejected the possibility and desirability of a large standing army in peacetime and stressed the need for citizen-soldiers and universal military training. In 1944 and 1945 several plans were drawn up proposing various levels of Regular Army strength, UMT trainees, and active reservists. Their implementation in the immediate postwar period was complicated, however, by the fact that through 1947 occupation was the Army's "primary mission" and the strength of the Army was "devoted largely to the consequences of victory." [11] Throughout the late 1940s the Army was caught between its long-term goal of UMT as a preparation for a future war and its immediate needs for manpower to discharge its current responsibilities. In 1946 Secretary Patterson agreed that extension of selective service was more important than UMT, and to avoid its becoming an issue in the 1946 elections no effort was made to push UMT in Congress. In 1947 UMT was endorsed by a presidential advisory committee (the Compton Commission) and a bill approved by the House Armed Services Committee. In March, 1948, the President included UMT in his "rearmament" program, but again the Army was forced to give a higher priority to the immediate need for selective service. Caught between this executive priority and Congressional enthusiasm for airpower, the UMT bills died with the 80th Congress. As a result, the Army turned to the build-up of its reserves. "Our mobilization planning concepts, prior to Korea," the Secretary of the Army accurately said, "reflected the expansion necessary in an 'all-out' war, based on our World War II experience. But since there has been no full mobilization or declaration of war, we have met certain unique problems." [12]

The Navy started its postwar planning before March, 1945, and its postwar Plan 1 was completed in the summer of 1945. The Navy, however, lacked a neatly packaged program goal such as seventy wings or UMT. In the past the Navy had defined meaningful and dramatic goals in terms of the relation between American naval strength and that of possible enemies: "a Navy second to none," "a two-ocean Navy." At the end of the war, however, the United States Navy was considerably larger than all the other navies of the world put together. Hence, not the Navy but its opponents cited the figures on relative naval strengths. "To maintain a five-ocean navy to fight a no-ocean opponent," as one Air Force general put it, "... is a foolish waste of time, men and resources."[13] In this position, airpower became the Navy's principal threat and its principal hope. On the one hand, the Air Force could maintain that airpower had made the traditional instruments of seapower vulnerable and obsolete. On the other, however, the development of naval airpower could open to the Navy a course in which its effectiveness would be judged not in terms of what was required to damage other navies, but rather what it could contribute to the attack on land targets. In the absence of competing navies, carrier airpower was the key to the Navy's future.

The expansion of carrier airpower required bigger planes, which required larger carriers. In 1945 Admiral Marc A. Mitscher recommended the construction of a large, flush-deck carrier, and in October the Navy began designing this ship. The Secretary of the Navy approved the ship for planning purposes in 1946. In May, 1948, the Secretary of Defense and three of the four members of the JCS approved its construction. The Senate and the House Armed Services committees approved the construction, and Congress appropriated funds for the carrier for FY 1949. In the spring of 1949, however, acting with the approval of the President, the new Secretary of Defense, Louis Johnson, canceled its construction. Thus, while the Administration had continually opposed the Air Force's principal program goal, and Congress had repeatedly refused to approve the Army's principal goal, the Administration first approved and then disapproved the Navy's goal, which left the Navy no worse off but considerably more disgruntled than the other two services. The combination of budgetary ceilings and interservice rivalry effectively prevented any one service from realizing its principal long-range program goals before the Korean War.

Between 1945 and 1950 the competition over UMT, the 70-group Air Force, and naval aviation was the heart of military policy. The Korean War expansion was also carried out primarily in terms of service goals, although the conflict among them was much less intense than it had been in the lean peacetime years. After the Korean War, Army leaders continued to speak of program goals such as 28 divisions, but since the Administration fairly continuously reduced the strength of the Army, these goals were hardly more than pious aspirations. The New Look, on the other hand, established a new expansion goal for the Air Force of 137 wings. The Air Force barely achieved this goal momentarily in 1957, however, when it was cut back because of changes in the estimates of the level of military strength required and the shifting emphasis from planes to missiles. After 1953 service goals declined in significance as they became less relevant to Cold War needs. Functional programs cut across service lines. STRAC divisions and anti-aircraft missile battalions could not be added together to make up a meaningful Army strategic program. The services became holding companies serving a variety of purposes rather than integrated companies devoted to a unifying goal.

INTERSERVICE RIVALRY AND CIVIL-MILITARY RELATIONS

The interservice struggles over organization, strategy, and program in the immediate postwar period had a lasting impact upon service political activity. Interservice rivalry became a permanent fixture of the military scene. It was built into the structure of the Department of Defense. Conflicts between one bureau and another occur in other departments of government, but nowhere else did intradepartmental conflict become institutionalized in quite the way it was in the military structure.

Interservice controversy also had a direct impact on civil-military relations. Potential conflict between civil and military institutions was sublimated and deflected into conflict among military groups. Interservice controversy substituted for civil-military controversy, and interservice controversy became a key aspect in the maintenance of civilian control. Two crucial foci of civil-military relations in modern states have been between the foreign office and the military and between the military and the budgetary agencies. Foreign offices make demands upon defense establishments for military support. The military make demands upon the budget agencies for the resources they want to maintain the forces required by foreign policy. American civil-military relations in the postwar decade, however, were characterized by the relative lack of sharp conflict between a united military establishment, on the one hand, and the State Department or Budget Bureau, on the other. Service rivalry permitted the civilian agencies to pick and choose. When the State Department wanted to reinforce Europe in 1950, the Air Force took a rather skeptical attitude, but the Army moved in to help develop and merchandise the policy. Conversely, when the Secretary of State spoke of massive retaliation, the Army dissented, but the now-favored Air Force congratulated the diplomats on their military common sense. When the budget was reduced in FY 1954, Vandenberg made his futile protests while the Army and Navy sat on the sidelines. When it was reduced in FY 1955, the Air Force was pleased with the new emphasis, and the Army fought alone against the cuts.

The extent to which interservice controversy moderated civil-military clashes was clearly reflected in the inverse relation between the intensity of the interservice conflict and size of the military budget. Civil-military relations before and after the Korean War would have been far different if the frustrations and anger generated by the Johnson and Wilson budgets had not in part been dissipated at other services and other strategic doctrines. At no point in the history of military policy after World War II were the President and his Budget Bureau confronted with a truly joint, integrated military program, publicly announced and supported by all military men as the indispensable minimum for national security. The civilians knew well enough that the imprimatur which the Joint Chiefs bestowed upon force level recommendations was seldom more than *pro forma*. The "minimum" programs were service minimum programs for 70, 143, or 137 wings; for one *United States*, 10 *Forrestals*, or a series of nuclear carriers; or for 12, 24, or 27 divisions. The conflict among the services not only permitted the civilians to pick and choose; it also facilitated the rejection of all service goals, as in the late 1940s, or as in 1958 when the Administration agreed with the Army and Navy on the lack of need to increase massive retaliatory strength and agreed with the Air Force on the undesirability of substantially increasing limited war capabilities. Each service chief tended to attack, not the overall ceiling on the military budget, but the allocation of the budget among the services.[14] The oft-commented-upon failure of the American military to have a distinctive "military viewpoint" on national policy after the war was not unrelated to the presence of distinctive service viewpoints.

Interservice controversy made unlikely any military rejection of the civilian world and civilian values such as occurred in the latter part of the nineteenth century and between the two World Wars. Civilian agencies were now more frequently arbiters than opponents, and each service was impelled to adjust its outlook to the prevailing political and social ideas or risk falling behind its rivals. Interservice conflicts thus tended to draw the military out of their service shells as far as civil-military relations were concerned, and then to drive them right back into those shells in intramilitary relations. Politicization of the military meant both a less military attitude in dealing with civilians and more sophisticated political techniques in dealing with other military groups.

In almost every modern state, the division of the military forces into two or more separate groups has been used to bolster civilian control. Totalitarian states create SS or MVD troops to check their regular forces. The Founding Fathers provided for both a militia and a regular army. After World War II, interservice rivalry played a similar role. "I want competition," Representative Vinson is quoted as declaring,[15] and congressional and civilian executive groups, at times without recognizing it, profited from its presence. Interservice rivalry not only strengthened the civilian agencies but also gave them a whipping boy upon whom to blame deficiencies in the military establishment for which just possibly they might be held responsible. The civilian deprecations of interservice rivalry were sincere and well meant, but, couched in generalities, they seldom resulted in concrete remedial action. In a sense, service political activities enhanced rather than challenged civilian control. In 1946 and 1947, when the War Department directly clashed with a number of powerful civilian groups, it was investigated and soundly denounced by a congressional committee for using public funds for its "military propaganda" promoting UMT legislation. The National Education Association and other anti-UMT organi-

28. INTERSERVICE COMPETITION

zations had every reason to focus attention on the alleged military malpractices. In interservice controversy, however, neither private groups nor congressional ones stood to gain by drastically reducing the service activities. After the B-36 investigation only an extremely virtuous or extremely foolhardy service would charge another with illegitimate political techniques. Service activity directed at other services was more acceptable than service activity directed at civilians. The services themselves undoubtedly found it easier and more virtuous to tangle with each other than to challenge civilian groups and arouse the hallowed shibboleths of civilian control.

THE INTERSERVICE RATIONALE OF POLITICAL ACTIVITY

After World War II competitive emulation among the services provoked the multiplication of service political activities. "The Jupiter," as Wernher von Braun explained, "involves several hundred million dollars of the taxpayers' money. One hundred percent security would mean no information for the public, no money for the Army, no Jupiter. . . . The Army has got to play the same game as the Air Force and the Navy." A new step by any one service was matched by comparable steps from the others. In the winter of 1955–1956, for instance, the Air Force prepared an elaborate press campaign to celebrate the tenth anniversary of SAC. In addition to an "extended worldwide campaign lasting through mid-1958" an intensive effort was scheduled to begin March 21, 1956, and to last several months. The program was designed to be "full of vitality" and to "implant logical conclusions" in the public mind rather than simply "flooding the public with facts." The intensive campaign was supposed to be a "true and inspired publicity effort" devoted to a "decade of security through global airpower" and designed to show the Air Force as "the dominant, decisive force" in "all forms of conflict." Almost simultaneously the Navy announced that it was adding to its "long range" public relations program a special six-month campaign beginning April 1, 1956, and designed to stress three themes: "(1) The U.S. depends on the Navy more today than ever before; (2) In global war the oceans become a giant, interconnected battlefield surrounding all continents; (3) The U.S. Navy is more important than ever." Army replies included the leaking to newspaper correspondents of staff studies with such titles as

"A Decade of Insecurity through Global Air Power," "The Facts Versus Billy Mitchell," and "A New Great Debate—Problems of National Security." The latter declared that: "The air power concept, unless modified, can only lead the United States to disaster; it is an unflexible, unrealistic philosophy of war . . ." [16]

Interservice competition came to justify service political activities. Traditionally, and again immediately after World War II, service appeals to their officers to be public relations-conscious stressed the close interrelation of political and military affairs and the general responsibility of military officers to enlighten the public on the needs of national security. Gradually, however, the stress on the public relations responsibility of the officer assumed a more service-oriented approach. Exhortations to political action were couched in terms of putting the service view across—informing the public of the indispensability of sea, air, or land power to national security.[17] From this concern it was only one step to justifying service political action in terms of the relative political position and status of the services. Each service, with the notable exception of the Marine Corps, developed an image of itself as the "silent service," politically underprivileged, misunderstood by the public, incapable of competing in the public arena with its more articulate and dramatic rivals. The ritualistic deploring of its inferiority furnished a perfect rationale for, and incentive to, service political action. Each service's feeling of inadequacy was undoubtedly real, and in this respect it was but another manifestation of the uncertainty and lack of self-confidence which lay at the root of interservice competition.

One might expect that the weaker a service was, the more frequently it would lament its poor public standing. In actuality, however, the reverse relationship appears to be closer to the truth. Perhaps the greater its power and the more extensive its activities, the more the service feels the need to justify them by stressing how weak it is. Conceivably, too, feelings of inadequacy derive more from the gap between a service's power and its aspirations than from its power compared to its rivals. Or, it may be that bemoaning the state of one's public relations is itself an inherent part of public relations activity and increases as the latter increases. By almost any standard, the Air Force was the strongest service politically during the postwar decade. It consistently outscored its rivals in public opinion polls, and after 1951 it regularly received the lion's share of the Defense Department budget. Yet the Air Force undoubtedly complained the most about its political weakness. The Air Force, one of its generals declared, had "a special problem in public relations," because most Americans did not understand the basic concepts of strategic air power and believed airpower to be too expensive. A distinguished lawyer and a brigadier general in the Air Force Reserve compiled an imposing list of obstacles to the development of American airpower:

Air power is the victim of cultural lag. . . . The military commentators were brought up in the older services. . . . The Air Force lacks representation in the Office of the Secretary of Defense. . . . The Congressional relations of the Air Force are inferior to those of the other services. . . . The Air Force is really the silent service. Its senior commanders do not write books and articles. . . . Those responsible for the development of national air power have not made use of the basic instrumentalities of information and enlightenment to get the public behind them.[18]

The *Air University Quarterly Review* endorsed these conclusions and went on to point out other deficiencies. Both the Army and the Navy had regular TV programs; the Air Force had none. Fewer motion pictures were made about the Air Force than about the other services. The *Review* found just one area of Air Force superiority. "Only in the mass medium of the comics does the Air Force come out ahead, with 'Steve Canyon' and 'Terry and the Pirates' far outstripping any competition in that field of communication and public relations." [19]

The complaints of the other services differed only in quantity, not quality, from those of the Air Force. The Army naturally felt that it was more likely to suffer from public misunderstanding because it was not romantic, clean, and technical like the Navy and Air Force. General Taylor urged the Army's generals to make sure that the Army maintained its standards and that it "gets due credit therefore from the Nation, which it deserves." The public, the Army's Chief of Information also declared, "is better acquainted with the roles of those two services (Navy and Air Force) than with the Army and has a better understanding of these roles." Army equipment could not catch the popular imagination "in the same degree as the range of the atomic submarine, the speed of a jet or the size of a super carrier." Because the Navy and Air Force "absorb the entire output of many individual corporations," it was argued, they "both benefit from a great deal of commercial advertising..."[20] In a similar vein, the Navy consistently maintained that it was on the short end of service public relations. "Whether or not the Navy is at fault for this lack of understanding," Admiral Radford declared in the B-36 hearings, "the fact is that we failed in our efforts to bring to our sister service—and to the American public at large—an effective, clear picture showing how further development of the aircraft carrier as a type, as well as the improved aircraft associated with it, would add to the future offensive power, not only of the Navy, but of all the armed services as a fighting team." Almost nine years later, Admiral Burke warned that the country must not "lose the benefit of sound naval thought by the default of an advocate's inability to put a point across."[21] At times, two or more services made similar or identical claims to inferiority. In 1949, for instance, Admiral Denfeld declared that the Navy lacked "adequate and appropriate representation in key positions within the Department of Defense." A few years later an Air Force writer held that since 1947 virtually no men with Air Force or Army backgrounds had occupied top civilian posts in the Defense Department and that "[m]en with an orientation toward the Navy have consistently held the most posts..."[22] Behind the conflicting claims lay a common psychology.

29. THE POLITICAL CASTELLATION OF THE SERVICES

Interservice competition tended to weaken the military as a whole but to strengthen the military services individually. Challenging the services, the rivalry also toughened them and forced them to develop the mechanisms and support necessary for survival in the pluralistic world of American politics. Neither Congress nor the general public decisively affected military programs, yet the spur of competition drove the services to great efforts to build up congressional and public support. The expansion of their political activities tended to resemble a process of castellation. Building out from the inner keep of the service itself, each service slowly constructed political, institutional, and legal defenses, coming to resemble an elaborate medieval castle with inner and outer walls, battlements and barbicans, watchtowers and moats. The services became well entrenched on the American political scene, as countless other interest groups, private and public, had done before them.

EXPANSION OF PUBLIC RELATIONS

After World War II, service public relations activities expanded tremendously.[23] They were directed to the general public, to selected elite groups, and to members of the service itself. All three major services attempted to elevate the prestige of public relations and to encourage recognition of it as an inherent aspect of military administration. Public relations, it was emphasized, is a function of command. Its changed status was reflected in the continuing admonitions that no person should be penalized for specializing in public information activities. The parallel between the military services and the large industrial corporations was pointed out, and the military were urged to adopt the public relations philosophy of industry. General Ridgway's call in 1954 for the "creation of a public relations-conscious Army" symbolized the trend of the times.[24]

Increased service emphasis upon reaching the public was reflected in the rise and expansion of the public information offices. During the 1920s and the 1930s, the Army and Navy public information sections occupied subordinate positions in the Intelligence branches of the services.* Inevitably the outlook and values associated with the collection and interpretation of intelligence were not those which encouraged the collection and dissemination of news to the mass media of communication. In February, 1941, Secretary Stimson created a War Department Bureau of Public Relations; two months later Secretary Knox followed suit with a separate Office of Public Relations for the Navy. After the war, all the

---

* Significantly perhaps, unlike the Army and Navy, the Marine Corps never subordinated public information to Intelligence. A Publicity Office was established by the Corps in 1925 and a full-blown Public Relations Section in 1933. Robert Lindsay, *This High Name: Public Relations and the U. S. Marine Corps* (Madison, Wis., 1956), p. 46.

services eventually established public information offices directly under the Secretary at the top of the administrative hierarchy. The Navy continued its wartime Office of Public Relations attached to the Office of the Secretary. Shortly after the end of hostilities, the Army Bureau of Public Relations declined to a Special Staff section, and the Director of Information was placed under a Deputy Chief of Staff. PR quickly began to creep up the military hierarchy, however, and in 1955 "full responsibility for public information policy" was transferred from the Office of the Chief of Staff to the Office of the Secretary of the Army.[25] After achieving its independence in 1947, the Air Force established an Office of Public Relations directly attached to the Secretary, where it remained except for a brief two years (1950–1952) when it was in Headquarters, U. S. Air Force. By 1959 each service reportedly had several hundred individuals engaged in information activities.

TABLE 15. PERSONNEL ENGAGED IN INFORMATION ACTIVITIES, 1959

	Officers	Enlisted Men	Civilians
Department of Defense	100	not available	not available
Army	600	2,150	200–300
Navy	212	500	not available
Air Force	650	1,400	230

Source: Morris Janowitz, *The Professional Soldier* (Glencoe, Ill., 1960), pp. 399, 413. "The low figure for the Navy is due, in part, to a narrowed definition."

The elevation of the public information offices was accompanied by an expansion and diversification of their activities. The Army Chief of Information, for instance, opened a branch office in Los Angeles in 1952 to improve relations between the Army and the movie industry, and another in 1956 in New York designed, in the words of the Chief of Staff, "to facilitate coverage in news media." A documentary film, "This Is Your Army," was released for distribution to commercial theaters across the country; the American Public Relations Association awarded three citations to Army organizations for outstanding public relations. Public relations was included in the Army Program System, and objectives were established quarterly, covering "those critical areas for which the Department of the Army particularly desires emphasis during the period." Guidance was sent to Major Commands in the form of information plans and speakers' fact sheets.[26] The other services paralleled the Army in employing a variety of public relations devices. Service war colleges invited civilian opinion leaders to participate in their annual strategy seminars. Weapons were displayed for inspection by selected civilian leaders. Spectacular demonstrations of or achievements by service weapons were timed to occur at the most propitious moment. Other efforts were made to suppress unfavorable news. A continuing struggle thus went on between the services and the Department of Defense and the Administration over the release of information concerning new weapons and weapons capabilities.

SERVICE COMPETITION AND CONGRESS

Increased service emphasis on congressional relations during the post-World War II period was also reflected in the loftier position in the service hierarchy given to offices responsible for this function. Army congressional relations had been handled by a variety of officials and staff offices before 1942, when a Legislative and Liaison Division was established in the Special Staff. In 1945, this division was placed for policy guidance under the Director of Information, who also handled public information and troop information and education. After a number of organizational shifts, the Office of the Chief of Legislative Liaison was set up in 1955 in the Office of the Secretary of the Army.[27] The Air Force also initially combined the functions of public information and legislative liaison. In 1949, however, a separate office for the latter was established directly under the Secretary of the Air Force. In the Navy, congressional relations were traditionally dispersed, with each bureau maintaining its own congressional contacts. In 1955, however, an Office of Legislative Affairs was established directly under the Secretary. Thus, by the middle 1950s all three major services had similar organizational arrangements for public information and legislative liaison: two distinct offices at the highest level directly responsible to the service secretary.

The congressional relations activities of the services fall into two subcategories. "Legislative" activities concern the preparation and presentation to Congress of bills which the service wants enacted, coordination of the service legislative program within the service and with other executive agencies, keeping track of bills in Congress affecting the service, and preparing service representatives who appear before congressional committees. "Liaison" work, on the other hand, involves helping individual congressmen who request information, explanations, or special assistance which the service might be able to offer. The liaison divisions "take the monkey off the congressman's back" when he receives demanding letters from constituents complaining about mistreatment by the service and demanding action by their congressman to remedy it. Reportedly, the total military L & L budget doubled between 1953 and 1958—a period in which military expenditures generally tended to decline or to remain stable.[28]

Three types of congressmen have special interests in the services and are specially cultivated by them. Often congressmen with *personal affiliations* with a service are dependable supporters of it in Congress. Army reservists included Major Generals (Representative) Leroy Anderson and (Senator) Strom Thurmond and Brigadier Generals (Senator) Kenneth Keating and (Representative) Robert Sikes. Senators Barry Goldwater and Howard Cannon were Brigadier Generals in the Air Force Reserve. In the Naval Reserve were Captain (Representative) James Van Zandt, Lt. (Representative) James G. Fulton, and the Marine Corps Reserve included Brigadier General (Representative) James Roosevelt and Colonel (Senator) Paul H. Douglas. If the affiliated congressmen are not on the Armed Services or Appropriations committees, their activity on behalf of a service is necessarily limited. Nonetheless, the services have definite interests in capitalizing upon congressional personal affiliations wherever they exist. In January, 1957, for instance, the Navy established a special Capitol Hill reserve unit for members of Congress and congressional employees. The unit operated under the sponsorship of the Navy Office of Legislative Liaison. The same year the Army announced the establishment of the U. S. Congressional Command and Operations Group (CCOG) for congressional reservists, assigned directly to the Office of the Chief of Staff and administered through its Office of Legislative Liaison. At the beginning of 1961, in a move which the Air Force Chief of Staff called "long overdue," the Air Force followed suit and established its congressional Air Reserve Squadron.[29] Weekly "drill" meetings of the congressional

29. POLITICAL CASTELLATION

units give the civilian and military leaders of the services excellent opportunities to present their views to sympathetic audiences.

A second form of congressional-service connection is through *constituency interest*. Congressmen naturally tend to support a service which long maintains important installations in their districts or which is supplied by industries important to the economy of the district. Often constituency interest is sufficient motivation for the congressman to get on the Armed Services Committee or the Military Appropriations subcommittee, where he can be of great help to the service. Presumably the interests of the Navy were not hurt by the membership of the congressmen from San Diego, Norfolk, Annapolis, and Charleston in the House Armed Services Committee. The last-named representative, indeed, was identified by one Navy officer simply as "Mendel Rivers of the Charleston Navy Yard." [30] Representative Paul Kilday, also on the Armed Services Committee, took an active interest in both the Army and the Air Force, as well as military personnel problems. His constituency included the Army's Fort Sam Houston in San Antonio, four Air Force bases, and reportedly more retired officers (including ninety generals) than any other district in the country. Although not on a military committee, Representative Yorty from Los Angeles was, as one might suspect, another vigorous supporter of the Air Force. In these instances, however, the interests of the congressman and the service coincide only at the constituency industry or installation. The congressman from Charleston is an ardent defender of the Navy—until the Navy wants to cut its operations at the Charleston Navy Yard.

The third and most important tie between congressmen and individual services is the *congressional responsibility* of the congressmen. Prior to 1946 the House and Senate Military Affairs and Naval Affairs committees were the principal centers of congressional interest in the service departments. As one congressman observed:

A gentleman is elected on the Committee on Naval Affairs because he has a predilection for the Navy. What is the result? The result soon is that they become "bugs" on the particular matter with which the committee deals. The naval committeeman soon grows into the belief that the Navy is the most important arm of the Government and that we ought to have the greatest Navy in the world. The Member who gets on the Committee on Military Affairs, where he associates with Chiefs of Staff and Secretaries of War, soon gets of the opinion that the Army is the outstanding branch of this Government.[31]

At the end of its existence, the House Naval Affairs Committee accurately described itself as "the body of the Legislature most avidly conscious of our need for sea power." [32] During the previous decades, its chairman, Representative Carl Vinson, established himself not only as the leading Navy spokesman in Congress but also as an authoritative figure within the Navy Department.

The replacement of the service committees by the Armed Services committees tended to weaken the ties between the committee members and any particular service. Neither Armed Services Committee was divided into subcommittees on service lines. The responsibility of the committee members was no longer for one service but for three, and the members liked to think of themselves not as service partisans but as the arbiters of interservice differences. "Carl Vinson has been unified too," was a journalistic heading accurately reflecting this change.[33] Other congressmen, such as Senators Symington and Jackson, similarly tended to broaden their original interests in the Air Force and nuclear weapons. Republican members of the Armed Services committees tended to vote considerably more "pro-defense" than nonmembers, but no significant differences existed between members and nonmembers in their patterns of service affiliation.* Membership on the committee gave those congressmen with prior service inclinations from constituency interest or personal affiliation greater opportunity to forward their inclinations. In itself, however, it did not seem to stimulate partiality toward any one service. If anything, it reduced that partiality.

The situation in the House Military Appropriations subcommittee was more complex. From 1952 to 1958 this subcommittee was regularly broken down into panels to handle the Army, Navy, and Air Force budgets. It is reasonable to suppose that appropriations

---

* Between 1947 and 1956 Republican representatives voted "pro-defense" 53.7 percent, while Republican members of the Armed Services Committee voted 71.2 percent pro-defense. Republican senators voted 37.2 percent pro-defense; Republican senators on the Armed Services committees voted 60.4 percent pro-defense. Democratic representatives and senators on the Armed Services committees also tended to vote more pro-defense than nonmembers, but the pro-defense averages in both cases were so high that the differences were not large enough to be significant. See Chapter V, Section 19.

units would be less sympathetic to agency interests than legislative committees. In this case, however, the appropriations panels became the only continuing congressional groups directly identified with particular services. Consequently, the panel members frequently emerged as strong advocates of their service viewpoint. Three of the five representatives who served longest on the Army panel—Representatives Sikes, Miller, and Ford—were on the Advisory Board of Directors of the Army Association, and two—Sikes and Miller—had served as officers in the Army. Representatives Sheppard and Wigglesworth, for seven years ranking Democrat and ranking Republican respectively on the Navy panel, were known as defenders of that service. Representative Mahon, ranking Democrat on the Air Force panel, early described his position: "I have always leaned over backwards, so to speak, to try to favor the Air Force with funds, and in a legislative way or in any way possible because I am a great believer in the Air Force for today and tomorrow." [34] The service panels were dropped in the 86th Congress. Their continued absence undoubtedly would weaken the identification between congressmen and particular services.

CULTIVATION OF THE "GRASS ROOTS"

The postwar period was marked by increased service activities designed specifically to reach public opinion at the "grass roots." Unlike many private associations and a fair number of governmental agencies, the services cannot easily mobilize sentiment across the country in support of a national program. The problem they face is similar to that confronted by the large industrial corporations. Both the corporation and the service are essentially national institutions. Political power in America, however, is to a large extent channeled through local organs. Individual political influence depends upon prolonged local residence: the employees of the corporation and the service are continually on the move. On the one hand, the economic health of the local community may depend upon decisions by a General Staff in Washington or a board of directors in New York. On the other hand, the small community normally possesses direct access to state and local governing bodies and frequently to Congress in a way which is denied to the national organization.

Corporations have attempted to adjust to the decentralization of political power by supplementing their general public relations activities with other efforts specifically designed to reach local publics. The armed services have done the same. Among them, the Army probably has been most active; more than the other services, it is concerned with issues where grass roots support is important. Shortly after World War II, for instance, when confronted with the need to stimulate recruiting and to arouse support for UMT, the Army sponsored the creation of Army advisory committees in many communities, each committee made up of leading local figures in business, religion, education, the press and radio, and civic organizations. "We are asking these groups," the Army's Chief of Information declared in 1947, "to present for us our plan for Universal Military Training. We furnish them information sheets from the War Department. . . . In that way, information on our actual policies and actual plans can be disseminated down through these advisory committees to all the various agencies that affect public opinion right out in the 'grass roots.' That is very important."[35] The civilian aides to the Secretary of the Army worked closely with the advisory committees in the postwar years. The aides developed originally from the Military Training Camps Association formed in 1916. In 1950 Secretary Pace greatly expanded their number and activities. Their duties included advising the Secretary on matters relating to the public standing of the Army, investigating specific problems at his request, and cooperating with the local Army commanders in furthering their programs. The Navy's counterpart to the Army advisory committees was the Advisory Council on Naval Affairs, founded in 1954. Sponsored by the Navy League, the members of the Advisory Council were appointed by the commandants of the various naval districts and furnished the Navy with a means of reaching local opinion groups.[36] In addition to these more broadly purposed programs, all the services emphasized the importance of "community relations" to the commanders of their posts and installations and urged them to carry on an active program of visits, support of local charities and projects, and sympathetic consideration of local interests.

The services also stressed the desirability of maintaining contact with national organizations through which the service viewpoint might be disseminated to local groups. The Navy, for instance, created an Office of Civil Relations in 1946. Its Director, in the words of the Secretary of the Navy,

> directs liaison with civil organizations in stimulating public good will and interest in the Navy. A program of establishing contacts with the national headquarters of organizations which are located in Washington was adopted and assistance was rendered these organizations in preparing naval matters for the agenda of their programs. Liaison contacts were made throughout the country with numerous veterans', women's, patriotic, youth, and other organizations both at the national level and at the local and state levels. Innumerable requests for naval speakers, representatives, sponsors and statements were evaluated and processed. The greatest problem was that of limited personnel in a field of constantly expanding activity.

A year later, the Secretary reported that naval contacts were maintained with 140 veterans' groups, compared with 5 previously, and that liaison existed with 291 civilian organizations of all types.[37] Similarly, in 1947, the Army embarked upon an extensive campaign to present its program for a 1,750,000-man M-day force to industrial, labor, press, farm, and educational groups. The effort, according to the Chief of Information, was designed to reach every representative group in the country.[38]

The services also use the reserve structure to reach local public opinion. The reserve organizations, and, to an even greater extent, the National Guard, are influential with Congress simply because they are organized for local political action. As more than one congressman noted, in contrast to the service "backstop" associations, the reserve organizations "have the votes." "Because the National Guard Association represents the fifty-one states and territories," one National Guard leader put it, "and is able through its membership to bring considerable pressure to bear on Congress, it has consistently enjoyed a high respect from Congress." The strength of the Guard, he continued, lies both "in the state representation" and in "the potential vote represented by the 500,000 and their families."[39] Army spokesmen and supporters frequently urged that efforts be made to utilize the reserves to put across the Army viewpoint. The very power of the reserve organizations, however, makes them less susceptible to use by the service leadership and more likely to have interests different from those of the service. The

Guard, for instance, is politically stronger than the reserve, but also more independent of the Regular Army.[40]

"BACKSTOP" ASSOCIATIONS AND THE ARTICULATION OF SERVICE INTERESTS

In the postwar decade the number, membership, and activities of service "backstop" organizations increased markedly.[41] The Navy League, oldest of the major associations, was formed by a group of civilians in 1902 to counterbalance the reaction against the Navy after the Spanish-American War. Before World War II, it was an active and devoted advocate of the Navy, but never a terribly large, affluent, or influential one.[42] In 1945 there appeared to be little reason to think that the League was on the verge of a new lease on life. Its great battles had been decades earlier supporting the programs of Theodore Roosevelt and opposing those of Calvin Coolidge. The unification controversy of 1945–1947, however, gave the League a new role to play, not in fighting anti-Navy midwesterners, but in fighting anti-Navy soldiers and airmen. Subsequently, as the B-36 controversy came to a head, the League embarked upon a large-scale program to "establish the Navy and Naval Aviation as an essential element of National Defense."[43] In 1958 the League once more took the lead in opposing the reorganization of the Defense Department. By 1959 it had 26,000 members. Meanwhile, comparable groups had developed for the other services. The Air Force Association was organized in January, 1946, by Army Air Force veterans to promote the cause of airpower. The following year, it took over the publication of the monthly *Air Force* magazine, previously published by the Army Air Force. In 1959, it had 50,000 members, of whom 30,000 were on active service. The Association of the U. S. Army grew out of the merger in 1950 of the Infantry and Field Artillery Associations, and in 1955 it assimilated the Anti-Aircraft Association. By 1958 it also had a membership of 50,000 and almost a hundred chapters.

Perhaps even more than among the services themselves, competitive emulation stimulated the development of the "backstop" organizations. "We can't flatter ourselves," the Secretary of the Navy told the Navy League in 1952, comparing its membership to that of the Air Force Association, "that one Navy League member is worth five Air Force Association members." The case for organizing an Army Association was put on a similar basis, the Army Chief of Information declaring that the Army had "a great need" for an organization like the Air Force Association and Navy League to help present its case to the public.[44]

The formation of the Army Association also reflected a tendency toward unification within the Army itself. More than the other services, the Army had been traditionally divided between regulars and reserves, combat forces and technical services, and between the various arms and services. The Army, as one officer said, was "its own worst enemy in dealings with the other two Services. In any attempt to harmonize the requirements of the several Services it is not at all unusual to encounter an Air Force position and a Navy position, with three, four, or half a dozen Army positions." [45] The constant theme of those arguing for an Army Association was the need for the "inner unification" of the Army. Originally the Association was designed primarily for officers in the combat arms; the technical services had their own associations which linked them with the appropriate industrial and civilian groups. In 1951, however, the Army Association added representatives to its executive council from the technical services, and four years later, it achieved full recognition as the official unofficial Army-wide group. The "unification" of the Army and the emergence of the Army Association as the "one strong voice" of the Army represented almost a classic Simmelian case of conflict furthering integration of a group.

The development and vitality of the "backstop" associations were particularly relevant to one major problem of service behavior in the postwar period: the definition and articulation of service interests. It was not an entirely new problem, but the increased political importance of the services after the war gave it new dimensions. Normally the leaders of a group are its natural advocates and defenders. For the services, however, this is not necessarily true. To be sure, the service secretary is free to articulate and to advance service interests except when they conflict with those of the Administration as defined by the President or the Secretary of Defense. In most civilian agencies, the definition, articulation, and promotion of the agency's interests are also a function of the top career leaders of the agency, those whose work-lives are continuously identified with it. The freedom of the military leaders to perform this function, however, is restricted by their presumedly instrumental character. The Department of Agriculture, for example, has a responsibility for and to the farmers of the country as well as a responsibility to the President and Congress. The military, on the other hand, are assumed to be responsible only to the higher political authorities of government; their representative role is minimal if not nonexistent; this is the essence of "civilian control." Thus, the top military leaders of a service—those who might be presumed to be most active and influential in the defense of its interests—must act with great circumspection. Hence, the problem arises: How are the interests of the service to be articulated and promoted?

One method is by subordinate groups within the service, which are less authoritative and responsible than its leaders. The internal structure of the service, however, frustrates and complicates this type of action. Often the leaders of an organization are more moderate in articulating and promoting the organization's interests than the nonleaders think desirable. In formally democratic organizations, such as labor unions, this may result in continuous pressure upon the leaders to adopt an "extreme" position. It may lead to subterfuges by which the leaders appear to press for union demands while really acting in ways they think desirable and realistic, if unjustifiable to the membership. The authoritarian structure of a military service, however, leaves the leadership relatively free of such membership pressure, except for considerations of service "morale." The commanders cannot be held responsible for the conclusions of Indian-level staff studies or the opinions of their subordinates, but they can be held responsible for allowing the staff studies to be made and for not disciplining the subordinates if they express their opinions in public. On the other hand, the leadership is also deprived of a possible source of strength in negotiations with other groups. In bargaining situations, discipline is disadvantageous. The very characteristics which enhance the combat effectiveness of a service reduce its political effectiveness. The egalitarian structure of the Senate has its benefits in conference committees; and in foreign negotiations, if the State Department did not have the Senate, it might well want to invent one. A Chief of Staff, however, has no organized opposition and cannot invent one. Nonetheless, his subordinates may well have a more positive view of the service interests than he does. The military leaders are thus placed in an extremely difficult position. The problem is not one of an apathetic membership or treacherous followers: it is one of compromised leaders. In a labor union, the rank-and-file may expel leaders who do not represent the group's interests aggressively enough. In a military service, the leaders may have to discipline subordinates who advance the group's interests too aggressively.

An alternative to subordinate action is action by an ally. The allies and supporters of a service are at times more royalist than the king. They do not necessarily identify more intensely with service interests than do the members of the service, but they do have a greater freedom to articulate those interests and to promote them through a wider variety of political means. Journalists, businessmen, retired officers, speak and act with a freedom denied to those on active duty. The most ardent proponents of airpower usually (with the exception of Billy Mitchell) have not been members of the Air Force. A private group can openly criticize the Administration while service leaders limit themselves to oblique suggestions under the prodding of sympathetic congressmen. Among the allies of a service, the "backstop" association is unique in its ability to act on the service's behalf. The Chief of Staff speaks for his service but also for the Administration and the Department of Defense. The service association speaks only for the service.

The association also can engage in political tactics and methods which are denied to the service. The Regular Army, for example, in its struggles with the National Guard Association and the Reserve Officers Association is, as one scholar has pointed out, handicapped "by its inability to throw charges—either reckless or responsible charges—into the headlines as its opponents frequently do." [46] Service associations are under no such restraints, and the less directly associated they are with the service, the greater freedom they will have. On the other hand, they cannot become completely detached. If they are too close to the service, they lose their freedom of action; if they are too distant from the service, they decrease their authority and responsibility and may misjudge the service's interests. A precarious balance must be maintained.

Preserving the balance poses problems with membership. From the start the Navy League protected its freedom of action by barring from membership military men on active duty. The Air Force Association permitted active personnel to be members only in a nonvoting, nonoffice-holding capacity. In contrast, the Army Association was originally organized by active officers. In 1956, however, it was reorganized, and the leadership was transferred to individuals not on active duty "so that the Association may exercise its right to express its own independent opinions." [47] By 1959 twenty percent of the membership was civilian. While they thus may have the freedom to do so, rarely, if ever, do the service associations take stands opposed by the leaders of their service. Through its long history, the Navy League disagreed only occasionally with the views of high-ranking officers and of agencies of the Navy Department.[48] The differences that do exist between a service association and its service usually result because the latter is not as free as the former to define its own interests. In 1959, for instance, the Administration advocated an Army of 870,000 men, the Chief of Staff one of 925,000 men, and the Army Association one of a million men.

Usually the service recognizes the unique position of the service association and the special relations which exist between them. At the same time, it also stresses the independence of the association. The Navy League, the Secretary of the Navy declared in 1958, is "the civilian arm of the service." Admiral Burke, however, also emphasized to a Navy League audience that the Navy "has absolutely no control over your fine organization." Air Force sources have informally referred to the AFA as "our lobby," and in 1949, General H. H. Arnold described the Association as "Air Force-controlled." Yet its private character is also emphasized. "We proudly bear the Air Force name," said the President of the AFA. "We are not, however, the 'civilian arm of the Air Force.' Nor are we the association of the U. S. Air Force." The Secretary of the Army has declared that the relationship between the Department and the Association "although unofficial, must be close and cooperative." The "success of the Association," he said, "is a matter of vital interest to the Department of the Army." [49]

INDUSTRIAL BARBICANS

The high level of military spending required by the Cold War and the heavy concentration of that spending on complex weapons brought into existence a significant peacetime munitions industry for the first time in American history. In their search for support in civil society the services could hardly overlook their contractors. In mobilizing industry the Navy and the Air Force started with two advantages over the Army. Both the Navy and the Air Force furnished a substantial portion of the demand for the products of two distinct industries. The shipbuilding industry would always encourage a larger Navy, and the aircraft industry a substantial Air Force. The Army, in contrast, had no such concentrated source of industrial support. Secondly, the research, development, and, in some cases, the production of Army weapons were traditionally done in government arsenals. The Navy made greater use of private industry, and the Air Force came into existence with little organized experience in research and development and hence depended very heavily upon the private aircraft companies. Army arsenals could generate support from the congressmen of their districts, but the aircraft companies could do this and also engage in all the public relations and propagandizing activities which their private status and funds permitted.

Interservice rivalry stimulated industrial competition, and industrial competition, in turn, fanned the flames of interservice rivalry. In 1959, as the conflict between the Army Nike and the Air Force Bomarc came to a head, Boeing took ads to counter the "misinformation" spread about Bomarc, and Army officials urged Western Electric to increase its advertising on behalf of Nike.[50] On the other hand, as General Gavin said, "what appears to be intense interservice rivalry . . . in most cases . . . is fundamentally industrial rivalry." Trade journals, Wernher von Braun declared, engage in "active instigation of interservice rivalry." They "often seem to feel that they owe it to their advertisers to go to bat for them" and to "publish quite frequently some rather vitriolic articles, taking a very one-sided stand in favor of one of the services." [51] In nationwide advertisements, Chrysler proudly heralded the Army's successful Jupiter C space shot. Two weeks later Douglas retaliated with ads declaring that the Air Force Thor was "already in mass production." The Army Director of Special Weapons replied by referring caustically to a missile with "an apogee of four feet." The Air Force struck back by leaking information concerning its new solid-fuel Minuteman missile and at the same time deprecating the expense of the Navy's solid-fuel Polaris missile. The Navy replied that Polaris was less vulnerable and much closer to operation than Minute Man. "Thus a publicity contest between two corporations," as William S. Fairfield observed, ". . . now involved the uniformed personnel of all three services." [52]

The Thor-Jupiter controversy was perhaps a classic example of how interservice rivalry initially can open a choice to the top civilian leaders of the defense establishment and then, in effect, shut off that choice through the competitive castellation of services. Thor and Jupiter were, as one general said, "about as alike as the Ford and the Chevrolet." [53] The Secretary of Defense repeatedly asserted that only one or the other would be put into production. He delayed his decision, however, and in the end choice was impossible. "If the Defense Department suggested canceling the Air Force's Thor program," a former Pentagon official declared, "a Congressional delegation from California would be down our necks. And elimination of the Army Jupiter program would have half the Alabama delegation plus a couple of representatives from the Detroit area fighting us." [54]

The most notable connection between a service and an industry was that between the aircraft industry and the Air Force. The industry expanded tremendously during World War II, and after the war it was repeatedly argued that military orders should maintain aircraft production as a base for expansion in the event of war. The desirability of supporting the aircraft industry was a major concern of the congressional and presidential groups investigating airpower policy in 1947. The aviation companies naturally contributed to the campaign for airpower and a larger Air Force. "The aircraft industry," Senator Barry Goldwater observed, "has probably done more to promote the Air Force than the Air Force has done itself." [55]

The shift from aircraft to missiles tended to broaden the ties of the aircraft industry with the services. Where the Air Force was the contractor, the old relationship continued with the new product. "Thor was a major bid by an airframe manufacturer to help capture the missile business for that industry," wrote the Army's missile commander. "The signboard was already up, pointing to a steady, but certain, reduction in the requirement for military aircraft. . . . We had saddled ourselves with a captive industry, and it could not be waved away or suddenly dissolved without painful results." [56] The captive industry, however, could also supply missiles to the other services. The Navy, of course, had always been a significant purchaser of aircraft, and increasingly in the 1950s the Army also turned to the aircraft companies for its missiles. The Army departed from its arsenal policy early in 1958 when it awarded a missile development contract to the Martin Company. "The aircraft industry," one Air Force legislative liaison officer reportedly admitted in 1958, "just isn't likely to be as good a source for lobbying as it was two years ago." [57] At that time, the Douglas Aircraft Company had contracts for one Air Force, two Navy, and three Army missiles. In the conflict between the Army Jupiter (Chrysler) and the Air Force Thor (Douglas), Douglas presumably was on the side of the Air Force. In the conflict between the Air Force Bomarc (Boeing) and the Army Nike (Douglas), Douglas presumably was on the side of the Army. As the major contractors increasingly worked for two or more services, the lines of industrial competition did not always coincide with, and sometimes actually blurred, the lines of interservice competition.

Associations also linked the corporations and the military. Corporation memberships in the backstop associations permitted the businesses to contribute financially to the association and corporation executives to participate in its activities. In 1959 the Air Force Association had 379 industrial associates, each of which had contributed at least $250. Navy League corporate membership also cost this amount. Sixty-four businesses, all defense contractors, subscribed $1,000 apiece for sustaining memberships in the Army Association. The military and the contractors were also linked through the American Ordnance Association and the National Security Industrial Association. The former had been founded as the Army Ordnance Association in 1919, but changed its name and attempted to broaden its affiliations in 1948. Nonetheless, its closest ties remained with the Army, and in the mid-1950s it was largely staffed by retired Army officers. In 1954 it had 35,000 individual members. The NSIA, on the other hand, was founded in 1944 as the Navy Industrial Association on the initiative of Secretary Forrestal, who wanted the Navy to have a counterpart to the AOA. It broadened its affiliations and changed its name in 1949, and in 1954 its membership included 600 industrial corporations, virtually all defense contractors. The Aircraft Industries Association, in turn, had its principal contracts with the Air Force but was also careful not to antagonize the Navy.[58]

THE PROLIFERATION OF DOCTRINE

After World War II, interservice competition contributed to increased service concern with doctrine and increased service output of doctrine. Every bureaucratic agency, military and civilian, tends to develop a "bureau philosophy" or "ideology." [59] The armed services differ from civilian groups, however, in the extent to which the bureau philosophy becomes formal, self-conscious, and explicit. The philosophies of civilian agencies may be just as real as those of the military, but they are seldom codified into written statements of "doctrine." The prominent role of doctrine in military thinking and the important place which its formulation occupies in military administration derives in large part from the extent to which the military groups are perceived to be and perceive themselves to be simply the instruments of a higher national policy. The justification for a Weather Bureau or even a Public Health Service, for instance, need hardly go beyond a statement of its functions. Such is not the case with the armed services. Except in a highly militarized or aristocratic society (such as, perhaps, Imperial Germany), they are not thought to possess inherent value. In the Anglo-American tradition they have been viewed as inherently dangerous, expensive, and undesirable. Consequently, their existence has to be explicitly rationalized in terms of a higher national end, and each activity and unit is justified only by its contribution to the realization of the prescribed hierarchy of values and purposes. Instrumentalism permeates military thinking. It is reflected in the emphasis, peculiar to the military, on the concept of "mission." "Military officers," as one Army publication puts it, "perhaps more than members of other professions, are accustomed to thinking of their duties in terms of specific missions. . . . Military forces that have no essential function [mission] are useless." [60] Thus the military are led to demand that national purposes and foreign policy objectives be expressed in concrete and meaningful form. If the nonmilitary agencies of government do not perform this task, the military fre-

29. POLITICAL CASTELLATION

quently feel compelled to do it implicitly or explicitly themselves. Given the ultimate goals, the roles and functions of a service can then be spelled out in service doctrine.

Prior to the 1930s, doctrine was reasonably well developed in the Navy, somewhat less so in the Army. The rise of airpower, however, was a powerful stimulant to the military quest for ideology. Lacking secure organizational existence or general acceptance during the 1920s and 1930s, the supporters of airpower—like any new, crusading group—needed to develop an intellectual rationale. The existence of the surface forces might be taken for granted; the need for an air force had to be demonstrated. Moreover, no longer was it possible for a service to elaborate a doctrine defining its importance to the nation and its relation to national policy without explicitly, and not just inferentially, defining the position of the other services also. Mahan had constructed a doctrine of seapower without specifically denigrating landpower. For the supporters of airpower, however, the attack on the surface forces was unavoidable. Once the Air Force was established, the intensity of their doctrinal concern perhaps moderated somewhat, but by this time the other services had felt compelled to reply in kind. Just as unification led to interservice political conflict, it also led to interservice doctrinal conflict.

Historically, the output of political theory correlates rather well with the presence of political crisis, turmoil, and conflict. So also, when vital controversies arise, military doctrine flourishes. After 1945 it proliferated in a variety of forms in manuals, speeches, journals, regulations, War College theses, and staff studies. The competitive spur was reflected in the creation of special staff units specifically designed to develop doctrine and arguments for use in the interservice debates. The prototype was the Navy's "Op-23," headed by Captain Arleigh Burke, during the B-36 hearings. A somewhat comparable unit was the Army's Policy Coordinating Group, the head of which retired shortly after the interservice blow-up in the spring of 1956. The services even found codification necessary. In 1953 the Air Force brought out a trim, concise statement of its position in AFM 1-2, "United States Air Force Basic Doctrine." Two years later, the Army responded with a new edition of FM 100-5, the first five pages of which forcefully explained why Army forces were "the decisive component of the military structure." In 1958, apparently feeling that a more elaborate statement was necessary, the Army came forth with a sixty-five page pamphlet entitled, perhaps significantly, "A Guide to Army *Philosophy*"![61]

30. CONFLICT AND CONSENSUS IN THE STRATEGIC MATRIX
SERVICES AND FUNCTIONS

The continuation of interservice rivalry and the innovation of functional programs produced a strategic matrix in which each service (except the Marines) contributed something to each major function. The Army devoted the five-division Seventh Army plus thousands of supporting troops to the defense of Europe. It maintained two divisions in Korea to deter renewed aggression there. It had the Strategic Army Corps of three divisions to deal with local aggressions elsewhere; it had the major responsibility for military assistance to allied nations. It contributed missile battalions to continental defense, a function which, it was estimated in 1957, absorbed 10 to 15 percent of the Army budget,[62] and it had primary responsibility for development of an antimissile missile. During the mid-1950s the Army developed the Jupiter missile for strategic deterrence. Until it lost its Redstone Arsenal to the National Aeronautics and Space Agency in 1959, the Army played a leading role in American space probes.

The Navy made similar diversified contributions. First its carrier aviation and then its Polaris submarines helped strategic deterrence. The Sixth Fleet and the Atlantic naval forces helped defend Europe. Naval aircraft and radar ships extended seaward the warning lines of continental defense. The carrier task forces and the Marine Corps were indispensable elements of the nation's limited war capabilities. The antisubmarine activities of the Navy were potentially important to European defense, continental defense, and limited war.

The Air Force's major commands reflected its contributions to the functions of deterrence. The Strategic Air Command with its planes, missiles, and 225,000 men was the core of the American strategic deterrent. The Air Defense Command, responsible for fighter interception and area defense with missiles, contained 115,000 men. The United States Air Forces in Europe supplied tactical support to the NATO ground forces and included 80,000 men. The 65,000 men in the Pacific Air Forces were the Air Force contribution to the deterrence or suppression of local aggression in East Asia. The Tactical Air Command, with 52,000 men, was concerned with limited war and included the 19th Air Force Composite Air Strike Force, designed, like the Army's Strategic Army Corps, to deal quickly with local aggressions wherever they might occur.[63]

While all the service departments thus made contributions to all major missions, the relative importance of the contribution to the mission and to the service varied considerably. For the Army, the defense of Europe was of primary importance, closely followed by its limited war functions. Continental defense ranked third, and strategic deterrence a poor fourth. To the Air Force, strategic deterrence was first, followed at some distance by continental defense, and with European defense and limited war of less importance. The Navy's functional contributions were more evenly distributed than those of the other services. Including the Marine Corps, it probably made its greatest contribution to limited war, with European defense and strategic deterrence contributions relatively evenly matched, and continental defense last. The relative importance of the missions to the services, of course, changed with technological developments and administrative decisions on weapons. The Polaris submarine increased the importance of strategic deterrence to the Navy. The assignment of operational responsibility for the Jupiter to the Air Force, the transfer of the Redstone Arsenal, and the limitations placed upon Army development of long-range missiles, all made the Army's role in strategic deterrence less important in 1960 than it had been a few years before. On the other hand, the increasing emphasis in the Army on limited war capabilities threatened to supplant the defense of western Europe as the primary Army concern.

The diversification of service activities had several important effects upon the political roles of the services. Although interservice rivalry remained the principal form of competition, intraservice rivalry among the competing claims of the functions began to rise in importance. In the late 1950s a continuing debate went on within the Army over the extent to which it should attempt to carve out a role for itself in strategic deterrence. The development of long-range missiles ate up funds which might be used for improving the Army's conventional weapons for ground combat. "For $5 billion worth of troop equipment," one division commander was quoted as saying in April, 1959, "I'd trade Huntsville away in a minute." [64] The Army commitment of five divisions to the defense of Europe also limited the effort to develop the Strategic Army Corps. Within the Air Force a natural rivalry developed among the major commands. As early as 1949 Air Force fighter pilots reportedly stimulated press leaks unfavorable to the B-36.[65] Junior officers identified with the Air Defense and Tactical Air Commands repeatedly warned of the dangers of giving overriding priority to the needs of strategic retaliation. Air Force leaders, such as Generals Vandenberg, Norstad, and Weyland, also stressed the importance of Air Force capabilities designed for purposes other than massive retaliation. On retiring in 1959, General Weyland, commander of the Tactical Air Command, "warned that the Pentagon's preoccupation with strategic bombing and long-range missiles may soon leave us unprepared to fight a limited war." [66] Officers of the Strategic Air Command, on the other hand, openly attacked the recommendations of the Air Force-sponsored Project Vista on tactical nuclear weapons and Project Lincoln on air defense. (Chapter V, Sections 23, 25.) Within the Navy, intraservice struggle was somewhat muted because of the diversified functions which individual naval weapons might serve. To some extent, intra-Navy lines of division tended to correspond more with the traditional differences between the submariners, aviators, and surface fighters than with the differences among functional groupings. Nonetheless, like the Army in the mid-1950s, the Navy in the early 1960s undoubtedly would be split betweeen those favoring increased emphasis upon strategic deterrence and those favoring more attention to the naval weapons and forces useful in limited and conventional war.

Appointments to the top positions within a service tended to reflect the relative importance of functions within the service. After General Vandenberg retired, the appointment of General Twining and then General LeMay to the two top positions in the Air Force reflected a shift toward massive retaliation. The successive

"Europeans" who served as Army Chiefs of Staff indicated the continued importance of European defense and NATO to the Army. While falling within this general pattern, the appointment of General Lemnitzer in 1959 was also said to mean that ground combat readiness would get top priority and that efforts would be made "to scale down the Army's space push to manageable proportions." [67]

For no service was intraservice competition ever equal in importance to competition among the services. Even though they performed different functions, officers generally put loyalty to the service ahead of loyalty to either a subordinate unit of the service or to a supraservice function. In a sense, the services are like nation states—intermediate groups, loyalty to which tends to override sectional or class affiliations and at the same time to be stronger than loyalties to higher or broader groups. Normally it is easier to change sectional or class affiliations within a nation state than it is to change citizenship from one state to another. Changes in the former, moreover, can be partial and gradual, while changes in the latter must be abrupt and clearcut. Intraservice controversy is mitigated by the relative ease of transfer among the various functional organizations within a service. The lines between the functional groupings within a service are never as clearcut as the lines between the services. If the Navy declines in size and functions, naval officers cannot easily transfer to the Air Force. On the other hand, if one naval function declines, no insuperable barriers prevent the transfer of its officers to other functions. All elements of a military service are united in a common hierarchy, obedience to a common headquarters, wearing of a common uniform, advancement through a common promotion list, identification with common symbols, and, to an increasing extent, attendance at a common undergraduate academy. The organizational and administrative ties which bind a service together preclude intraservice controversy from becoming as intense as interservice controversy.

CHANGES IN SERVICE DOCTRINE

The diversification of service activities affected the content of the proliferating doctrine stimulated by interservice competition. No longer could the services be justified in terms of exclusive missions or functions required by national policy. Before the innovation of the functional programs, military doctrine was service doctrine. So long as the significant missions were related to the command of the sea, the conquest of territory, and the control of the air, such doctrines were meaningful in policy terms. The functional requirements of deterrence, however, ended the strategic importance of elemental doctrines. The purpose of doctrine is to relate force to purpose, and airpower or seapower in and of themselves served no distinctive ends of policy. Mahan and Douhet were strategists of seapower and airpower; the Cold War produced strategists of massive retaliation and limited war.

The services thus were confronted with the increasing need to justify their existence in terms of national policy at a time when the possibility of a service's having a distinctive mission or even a clearly defined hierarchy of strategic missions was slowly disappearing. On the one hand, interservice competition stimulated the services to articulate doctrines. On the other hand, the requirements of deterrence undermined the traditional basis of their doctrines. They reacted to this problem in three ways. First, instead of stressing the function of the service as it related to the achievement of the higher goals of national policy, they tended to develop "essentialist" doctrine, to focus upon the inherent value or importance of the service and its element per se without reference to the functions it might perform. The Navy reiterated that three-quarters of the earth's surface is water, and the Army emphasized that man is a land animal. No longer able to link themselves directly to the ends of national policy, the services were compelled to hang on to the elemental categories. "Just as our Army and its soldiers are synonymous with land warfare and the Navy and its sailors with sea battles," the Chief of Staff of the Air Force declared in November 1957, "so are the United States Air Force and its airmen synonymous with air warfare . . . "[68] As a result, a curious disjunction developed between the doctrine directly relevant to interservice controversy and that directly relevant to major issues of national policy. Not infrequently, essentialist doctrine assumed a certain abstract or metaphysical quality. What did it mean in policy terms for its Secretary to say that the Army would be "a dominant force" in future war or for the Air Force to argue that "air forces are most likely to be the dominant force in war"?[69] Similarly, service debates over whether guided missiles were inherently aviation or artillery had little or no consequence for national strategy except, and it is a vital exception, as far as the future of the services was concerned.

Second, service spokesmen often attempted to identify the entire service with the functional doctrine most important to the service at the moment. Air Force spokesmen justified the preeminent role of the Air Force in terms of strategic deterrence, while Army and Navy advocates in the late 1950s employed doctrines of limited war. Yet functional doctrines could only be used with care. Exclusive emphasis on strategic deterrence by the Air Force would logically imply that the Army should take over tactical airpower. Exclusive Army or Navy emphasis on limited war could lead to Air Force claims to anti-aircraft forces and to sea-based strategic missiles. While each service could utilize functional doctrines for some purposes, no service could completely identify itself with any one doctrine. "The Army," as its Secretary declared in 1957, "cannot—and indeed assiduously seeks not to—commit itself to any particular doctrine, strategy or tactic." [70] Consequently, the services resorted to yet a third doctrinal emphasis, stressing the "flexibility" and "versatility" of their forces to serve a wide variety of functional ends. "The Army," the Army claimed, "is the most flexible form of military power." The "nature of the medium of space," the Air Force claimed, "gives to air forces a versatility not common to surface forces." [71] The more diverse its functions, the more extensive the claims which could be made on behalf of the service.

STRATEGIC CONSENSUS AND ITS LIMITS

The Korean War and the subsequent development of thermonuclear weapons changed the framework of strategic thought as it existed in the late 1940s. It became less and less likely that another war would be World War II plus nuclear weapons. The Air Force no longer stressed the decisive aspect of airpower, but its deterrent quality. The experience of the other services in Korea was codified into a doctrine of limited war. The basis was thus laid for a truce on the grand outlines of strategy. Previously, the Air Force concept and the surface forces concept of how to fight a general war had been completely incompatible. Strategic deterrence and limited war, on the other hand, were complementary and competitive but not incompatible. Previously, any increase in the effectiveness of strategic airpower meant a decrease in the probable roles of the other services. Now, the more effective the massive deterrent became, the greater the probability of the small-scale disturbances with which the other services were primarily concerned. To be sure, the debates still continued over how much of the effort should be devoted to one purpose and how much to the other. All the services, however, accepted the necessity of devoting some resources to each. Conflicting images of a single contingency future were replaced by general agreement on a multiple contingency future, although the priorities and probabilities of the various contingencies remained in dispute. In the earlier conflict the issue of how to fight a general war had been fought clearly along service lines: airpower vs. surface power. In the late 1950s the principal strategic issues cut across service boundaries. In the 1940s the Air Force had vigorously attacked the efforts of the Navy to develop larger carriers and longer range carrier aircraft. Strategic bombing, it had argued, was an Air Force responsibility; naval aviation should attack only naval targets. In the 1950s, however, the Air Force did not actively campaign against development of the Polaris submarines, and, in turn, the Navy did not feel compelled to maintain that they were only designed to attack naval targets. Both the Air Force and the Navy recognized the need for retaliatory forces and also recognized that both land- and sea-based forces contributed to meeting this need.

The strategic consensus was most obvious in the extent to which the services and others concerned with military policy agreed upon the requirements of deterrence and accepted the functional programs necessary to meet those needs. "Among the military planners of the Services," as one Army statement put it in 1958, "it is relatively easy to get agreement on the types of forces required to meet the national objective of deterrence of war. It is readily recognized by the Service representatives that this deterrence calls for the existence of a strategic air-retaliatory command, a Continental Air Defense Command, ground forces deployed overseas, a strategic mobile reserve, adequate seagoing forces and continued assistance to our allies." Similarly, Bernard Brodie noted that, "There has

30. CONFLICT AND CONSENSUS

indeed been general agreement on certain fundamentals—for example that any and all plans for the security of the United States must make provision for a strong strategic air power—and with the passage of time the area of basic agreement has tended to increase and the diversity to diminish." [72] Formulations of functional needs by leaders of different services showed a striking similarity. "The elements of a sound National Military Program," General Taylor declared in 1956, "must include adequate provision for: deterrence of general war, deterrence of local aggression, defeat of local aggression, and victory in general war conducive to a viable peace." [73] In July, 1956, the Air Force Chief of Staff similarly declared that "for the foreseeable future we must maintain in constant protected readiness a retaliatory force of sufficient strength to deter an attack or to insure ultimate victory if general war comes. We must also provide a deterrent to small wars and be able to win them if they do occur." [74] In phrases remarkably similar to those of the Army Chief of Staff, the Secretary of the Navy argued that the United States needed sufficient power, "First, to make it unthinkable to any aggressor to risk all-out war. Second, to prevent—if necessary to win decisively—any limited war or aggression. Third, to support the national policy in the Cold War." [75]

A measure of consensus thus existed among the military services on the nature of the threat, the probable contingencies which the United States would have to face, and the types of action it should take to deter or to deal with those contingencies. No Army general could admit that the Air Force was the dominant service, but he could agree that strategic deterrence demanded the highest priority. Similarly, no Air Force officer would give ground forces a decisive role in modern war, but he would not dispute the need to maintain forces to deal with local aggressions. The broad range of this agreement did not, however, preclude interservice struggles over priorities and relevancies. The same Army pamphlet which hailed the interservice agreement on the requirements of deterrence also argued that it was "not sufficient just to enumerate and create the forces required; the allocation of national assets must be made to these type forces." [76] The issue left in dispute was: "How much is enough?" The strategic consensus was bounded by the controversy which still existed: 1) over the relative priority of the functional programs and the adequacy of the resources assigned to them; and 2) the relative value of the weapons and forces which each service could contribute to each of the functional programs.

The continued interservice and interfunctional controversies limited the scope but not the significance of the area of consensus which existed in 1960. In the late 1940s a broad agreement had developed on a foreign policy of containment, as the potential alternatives of preventive war, appeasement, and isolationism were rejected. A decade later several major military programs had been created to support this foreign policy. By 1960 it was easy to take their existence for granted. Each of these major innovations in military policy, however, had initially encountered vigorous opposition. The hydrogen bomb and SAC, NATO and American forces in Europe, continental defense and warning systems, and limited war forces, had all involved major political battles. That these programs had all won general acceptance by 1961 was no mean achievement of the American political system.

INTERSERVICE CONTROVERSY: FROM STRATEGIC ISSUES
TO PROPRIETARY ISSUES

Despite the extent of strategic consensus, in the middle 1950s interservice debate was just as prevalent and intense as it had been previously. The issues at stake in the controversy, however, had changed in character. Strategic questions no longer dominated the discussion. Instead, proprietary issues had become prevalent. Neither the fundamental existence of the services nor fundamental alternatives of national strategy were at issue, but rather marginal gains and losses of resources, forces, and weapons. The question of what should be done was less controversial than the questions of who should do it and how much resources should be allocated to it. The B-36 controversy in 1949 had involved basic questions of "unification and strategy": the role of nuclear airpower in a future war; the feasibility of deterrence by retaliation; the future of carrier aviation; the place of the Navy in the defense structure. The Navy had attacked the entire theory and practice of strategic air warfare: ". . . the threat of instant retaliation," Admiral Radford had declared, "will not prevent it [war], and may even invite it." [77] In contrast, in 1956 the Army and the Air Force tangled neither over the doctrine of retaliation nor over the need to develop strategic missiles to implement that doctrine, but rather over who should build the missiles, who should operate them, and how much should be spent on one missile or another. The service partisans were still as passionate as ever, but their disputes involved proprietorship, not principle. The cause of Colonel Nickerson's martyrdom was hardly in the same class with that of John Crommelin, much less that of Billy Mitchell.

Interservice controversies over programs in the late 1950s included three categories. First, there was the recurring struggle for funds in the budgetary process. Before the Korean War the military budget was divided almost equally among the three services. This represented the uneasy situation in which each service had its own strategy and programs for fighting a future general war, in which the existence of each service apparently depended upon the acceptance of its strategy, and in which, as a result, choice among service strategies was impossible. In the New New Look a different pattern of budget allocations became relatively fixed, with the Air Force getting approximately 47 percent of Defense Department funds, the Navy approximately 29 percent, and the Army approximately 22 percent. These percentages, as Hanson Baldwin said, tended to become "sacrosanct and frozen"; the easiest way of resolving the budget disputes in any one year was to allocate the available funds on the same basis as the previous year. After considerable debate, for instance, the FY 1960 budget was consciously divided in the same ratios as the FY 1959 budget.[78] The fixed budget allocations, of course, had implications for strategy and the functional programs. They limited the likelihood of any major shift from one program to another. They did not, however, have the strategic significance of the equal three-way split of funds before the Korean War. In the earlier years it would have been unthinkable for the budget of one service to have been twice the size of the budget of another. By the late 1950s, however, the Army might not like receiving the smallest share of the budget, but it did not view this as a threat to its existence. Given the general pattern of service allocations, the service chiefs could still struggle among themselves over marginal gains and losses.

A second type of interservice competition concerned substantially similar weapons and forces developed by different services for the same mission. In these instances, the services involved agreed both on the nature and importance of the threat and upon the type of force necessary to meet that threat. But they disagreed over which service should provide that force. In 1955, for instance, both the Air Force and the Army were directed to proceed with the development of intermediate-range ballistic missiles. The development of Thor and Jupiter went along almost simultaneously. Leaders of the Department of Defense regularly asserted that at the appropriate moment a decision would be made on which one would be put into production. In November, 1956, it was decided that the Air Force would have operational responsibility for whichever one was produced. The choice between them, however, was steadily delayed. In the summer of 1957 Secretary Wilson declared that he would make this decision before retiring from office. A three-man committee was appointed to make recommendations. The committee was unable to make a choice. Mr. Wilson did not decide before retiring from office. Meanwhile, the failure to decide introduced delays and uncertainties into the program. After sputnik, Secretary McElroy put both missiles into production, thus maximizing interservice harmony at a cost of approximately $200 million in extra expenses which would have been avoided if only one had been selected.[79] Similar problems of choice among duplicating or similar programs came up with respect to the Army's Nike vs. the Navy's Talos, the Nike vs. the Air Force's Bomarc, the Army's Missile Master air defense control system vs. the Air Force's SAGE system, and the Army's STRAC vs. the Marine Corps. In some cases a choice was made between the competing programs, but more often the arrangement of political forces made a decisive choice one way or another virtually impossible. In the struggle over anti-aircraft missiles, the Army was supported by the House Military Appropriations Subcommittee and the Air Force by the Senate Armed Services Committee. The Administration's Master Air Defense Plan assigned roles to both missiles.[80] The tendency of the political system to frustrate choice, however, at times tended to increase overall American military capabilities. Both Army and Air Force IRBMs contributed to strategic deterrence. The three divisions of STRAC and the three divisions of the Marine Corps undoubtedly were a larger, if divided, limited war force than would have resulted if limited war had been made the exclusive responsibility of one service or the other.

A third form of interservice rivalry involved not rival programs but the allocation of responsibility for a single program or capability. The Air Force, for instance, argued it should properly exercise control over the Navy's P6M jet seaplane bomber and the Polaris submarine, since these weapons were designed for substantially the same mission as SAC. Similarly, the Air Force and the Army struggled with each other over the growth of the Army's organic aviation. In 1956 the Air Force persuaded Secretary Wilson to transfer responsibility for training Army helicopter pilots from the Army to the Air Force. The Army protested vigorously that this made as little sense as assigning to the Army responsibility for training Air Force truck drivers, and after the intervention of members of Congress the order was canceled.[81] Similarly, in 1958 and 1959 the Army and the National Aeronautics and Space Administration struggled over control of the missile development team at the Redstone Arsenal. The Army won the decision in 1958, but lost the following year. In all these instances the struggle was over the control of a unique activity or weapon initially developed by one service and then claimed by another service or organization. The controversies were often resolved by defining an arbitrary boundary to separate the weapons and forces of one service from those of another. In November, 1956, for example, in the continuing struggle between the Army and the Air Force over Army organic aviation, Secretary Wilson authorized the Army to operate fixed-wing aircraft with an empty weight not to exceed 5,000 pounds and rotary-wing aircraft not to exceed 20,000 pounds.

The recurring issues of interservice rivalry directly concerned the size and strength of the services but usually did not have significant implications for other groups in society. Interservice competition continued and became more intense at the same time that it became more limited in its effects. The issue of how much for the Air Force and how much for the Army or who should control what missile were political issues in the sense that they involved vigorous conflicts among competing *interests,* but they were not basic policy conflicts because they did not involve the allocation of resources among competing *purposes*. As a result, the services, in defending and advancing their interests against other services, reached out to arouse the support of other groups; but at the same time these other groups tended to see less and less of their own interests involved in the interservice controversy. Congressmen tended to become less the partisans of a particular service and more the partisans of defense in general against other interests and, within this general concern, the arbiters among competing service interests. Similarly, the once-strong identification of the aircraft industry with the Air Force declined as the industry filled Army, Navy, and Air Force orders for missiles. Also, the tendency of the general public to identify strongly with one service or another weakened, with more and more individuals declaring that all three services had important roles to play or that "balanced forces" were necessary.[82] This tendency among other groups to disassociate themselves from strong identifications with any one service reflected the reduced significance of the consequences of interservice rivalry for these other groups.

At the same time that the significance of interservice rivalry for other groups tended to decline, advantages to be gained by these groups by a lessening of interservice rivalry also tended to decrease. Interservice rivalry, outside groups often argued, was the source of many evils in the Department of Defense. Interservice harmony, the elimination of duplication (rational organization), reduced costs, and greater unification were often seen as directly related, and the achievement of interservice harmony, it was argued, was a step toward the achievement of the others. If this were actually the case, however, it was indeed strange that political and military leaders so persistently refused to realize these values. Why muddle along with interservice bickering, duplication, needless expenditure, and administrative disunity, if they could all be eliminated or reduced by taking a few simple steps? The relations among these goals were considerably more complex than they superficially appeared to be.

Interservice competition was not so much a cause of decentralization, duplication, and increased expenditures as it was the result of the desire to eliminate these supposed evils. More harmony among the services could be bought at the price of disunity, duplication, higher costs. It is generally conceded, for instance, that the less money there is in the military budgets, the more intense and bitter is the competition of the services for it. Similarly, interservice competition in the postwar decade originated in unification, and efforts to increase unification usually produced greater interservice competition. The steady tendency after 1947 toward more and more centralized control did not seriously reduce interservice conflicts. "If you try to put on the heat too much right now," Admiral Radford observed of the authority of the Secretary of Defense over the services, "they all take refuge in the law and you actually drive them apart." [83] On the other hand, the less unification there was, the greater was the freedom of the services to go their own way, the less fear they had of control by a central organ dominated by a hostile service, and hence the less likelihood there was of serious interservice rivalry. In comparable fashion, duplicating ambitions were a cause of interservice rivalry; duplicating programs and functions were a means of reducing that rivalry. Conflict developed when two services wanted to do the same thing. In one sense, duplication was a result of interservice rivalry, but it was a result which tended to reduce its cause, and certainly efforts to decrease duplication tended to increase interservice tensions.

Interservice harmony could thus be achieved at the sacrifice of reduced expenditures, rationalized organization, and greater unification. In addition, interservice peace would probably have certain costs in decreased civil-military harmony. Conversely, the achievement of these other values was only possible by accepting a considerable degree of interservice competition. One suspects that the real cause of the sustained deprecation of interservice competition was not its direct association with other evils in Defense Department management, but rather because it was a discomfort which had to be endured if these other evils were to be reduced. What people identified as the consequences of interservice competition were really the alternatives to it. Interservice competition became an ubiquitous, inherent, and permanent feature of the defense establishment simply because it would cost too much to eliminate it.

THE BALANCE OF FUNCTIONAL PROGRAMS

The balance among the functional programs was the product of at least four sets of decisions on two different levels. The Administration and the Secretary of Defense determined the relative priority of key elements of the functional programs, and each of the three services had some freedom, within the resources granted to it, to allocate those resources among the various functional programs to which it made contributions. The decisions were shaped by Administration preferences, service preferences, and the preferences of other groups.

Administration preferences affected not only its decisions but also service decisions. The existence—explicit or implicit—of a hierarchy of Administration priorities inevitably stimulated interservice conflict. Each service had to balance the advantages of making the principal contribution to a second priority Administration function against those of making a possibly secondary contribution to the Administration's top priority function. It had to weigh carefully the Administration's preferences versus its natural inclinations. During the Eisenhower Administration, for instance, the services had strong incentives to stress their contributions to strategic deterrence. In a 1954 budget conference, General Medaris told his Army colleagues that:

You're fighting a losing game. If you put all your energy and effort into justifying these conventional weapons and ammunition, even though I know we need them, I think you are going to get very little money of any kind. It is far easier to justify a budget with modern items that are popular, and I would strongly recommend that you increase the amount you show in the budget for the production of missiles, limiting yourself on the other items to the modest quantities that you know you can get by with. If you increase your demands for guided missiles, I think there is a fair chance you can get a decent budget. Why don't you accentuate the positive and go with that which is popular, since you cannot get the other stuff anyway? [84]

Similarly, after sputnik, Secretary McElroy asked the services to recommend funds to be included in a supplemental appropriation bill. "What was so revealing about this exercise," Charles J. V. Murphy commented, "was the overriding priorities that all three service chiefs attached to the weapons for a general war." [85] The 1950s produced a bewildering array of weapons related to strategic deterrence: Snark, Thor, Jupiter, Polaris, Atlas, Titan, Minuteman, B-47, B-52, B-70, carrier aviation. The scramble among the services to participate in strategic deterrence was the direct result of Administration policy, and the "duplication" it produced had the desired effect in strengthening the strategic deterrent forces. Inevitably, also, the Administration's preferences produced a somewhat different type of interservice conflict at the lower end of the priority scale. Those services which could establish major interests in higher priority functions had little incentive to bolster their contribution to lower priority functions in which other services had a primary interest. The Army regularly criticized the Air Force for its alleged neglect of tactical aviation and airlift. Both these services criticized the Navy for its alleged neglect of antisubmarine warfare and continental defense.

The relative commitments of the services to the various functions also affected the interfunctional balance. Strategic deterrence benefited from the overriding priority given it by the Air Force and the extent to which it could be related to traditional Air Force doctrine. European defense benefited from the early support of the Army and the traditional Army concern with western Europe. The scope of limited war programs broadened as first the Army and then the Navy began to give them a higher priority. Continental defense, on the other hand, suffered because it was a primary concern of no single service. In the spring of 1960, for instance, the Navy secured the approval of the Joint Chiefs to withdraw all but four of its thirty-six destroyer-escort radar picket ships from the North American Defense Command, despite the objections of the Chief of that command, General Kuter of the Air Force. Seventeen of the ships were to be assigned to other duties, primarily antisubmarine warfare, and fifteen were to be decommissioned and the resulting savings in funds used to modernize other vessels in the fleet.[86] Presumably the willingness of the Air Force and Army Chiefs to agree to this withdrawal reflected their own estimate of the importance of continental defense and the possibility that at some time they too might wish to withdraw forces assigned to that command.

The preferences and intensity of support of other groups outside the executive branch necessarily affected decisions on the functional programs. Strategic deterrence was easily identified with airpower and much of the popularity of airpower and the strength of the Air Force in Congress contributed to bolstering the forces required for the strategic deterrent mission. Its needs were strongly supported by the aircraft industry, and the Joint Committee on Atomic Energy was an influential lobby pushing the development of nuclear weapons and long-range missiles. European defense, on the other hand, received substantial support from the NATO powers. The possible reduction of American forces in Europe was mentioned during the formulation of the New Look in October, 1953, the discussion of the Radford Plan in the summer of 1956, the economy drive of 1957, and the formulation of the budget in the fall of 1959 and of 1960. In each case, the rumors triggered a barrage of anxious inquiries and vigorous protests from European capitals, Bonn in particular. In each case, the President, the Secretary of State, or the Secretary of Defense quickly reassured the Europeans that, despite the staff plans or Budget Bureau recommendations, no significant reduction would be made in American forces in Europe.[87] Continental defense and limited war, on the other hand, had neither the domestic constituency of strategic deterrence nor the influential foreign constituency of European defense.

Strategic deterrence was the most favored program, and its supporters argued that it should receive an "absolute" priority. In the formulation of the New Look, for instance, "a basic philosophical conflict [developed] within the Administration, between 'absolute priority' and 'relative priority' thinking." The absolute priority group included the President, the Secretary of the Treasury, and the leaders of the Air Force. They argued that all the needs of the first-priority function—strategic deterrence—should be met before resources were allocated to lower priority functions. The relative priority group, including primarily the leaders of the Army and Navy, accepted the first priority of strategic deterrence and the lower priorities of the other functions. They argued, however, that no needs were absolute, and that at some point the further allocation of resources to strategic deterrence produced less marginal utility than their allocation to other functional programs. In this and subsequent debates Army and Navy leaders held that a determination of "sufficiency" should be made for each program, and that each program should receive the minimum resources required for sufficiency before any program received resources to go beyond sufficiency.[88]

Critics of the allocation process attacked the decentralization of decisions among functional programs to the services. "In the absence of means to consider, at the NSC level, the relative balance among programs," one Hoover Commission study declared, "the real decisions appear to be made in part within the Service staffs of the Defense Department. Programs are often continued as a result of past momentums and because there exist powerful convictions within the Services to support certain ongoing activities." Similarly, General Taylor pointed out that the principal budget decisions were made on a "vertical" basis among the Army, Navy, and Air Force, and that little overall consideration was given to the requirements and capabilities on a "horizontal" or functional basis.[89] The interfunctional balance was thus in large part the product of intraservice decisions. Conceivably, such decisions could produce a very different result than would have been achieved by the direct allocation of resources to functional programs by the Administration and the Secretary of Defense. In actuality, however, service decisions were substantially influenced by Administration preferences. What General Taylor was objecting to, one suspects, was not so much the process of decision-making in the defense establishment, as the Administration's priorities which guided that process. A different Administration, which gave top priority to the development of limited war capabilities, could significantly alter the interfunctional balance by changing the framework in which service decisions were made without altering the authority of the services to make those decisions.

CONFLICT, CASTELLATION, AND UNIFICATION

In the strategic matrix, the relation of the services to fundamental issues of strategy tended to resemble the relation of the political parties to fundamental issues of national policy. The two parties have different centers of gravity on policy, and yet each includes groups representing almost all viewpoints on the political spectrum. Similarly, while the outlook and doctrine of each service differs somewhat from that of the others, each service also has interests all across the strategic spectrum. At times, of course, there may be party votes on major issues of policy, and at times, also, differences over strategy may coincide with differences between the services. Moreover, just as the parties exist independently of the issues of the moment, so also the existence of the service is independent of the strategy of the moment. The resolution of any particular set of issues, whether political or military, does not end the competition among the groups, whether parties or services. The competition continues, rising to peaks fixed by the calendar of biennial elections or annual budgets. Partisan debate and interservice debate are often carried on in cliches, slogans, and appeals, with little operational significance for governmental action. A member of a service is loyal to the service irrespective of its strategic function, just as a good organization Democrat or Republican is loyal to the party whatever its stand on policy. The existence of the services, moreover, like the existence of the parties, tends to obscure the issues of debate. It is often argued that the United States is well off to have non-ideological parties and that it would be unfortunate if the division between left and right coincided exactly with the division between Democrat and Republican. The same may be true with respect to the services and strategy, as strategic issues are blurred by the overlay of service competition.

Fifteen years of Cold War thus produced a multiplication of lines of controversy over military policy. Before World War II the principal conflicts had been between the military services and civilian groups. In the 1940s interservice rivalry predominated. In the 1950s the innovation of the functional programs produced new lines of tension. Further conflicts resulted from the alternative programs and the efforts to assimilate them into a strategy of deterrence. The multiplication of controversy, however, also tended to moderate its intensity. In this, the evolution of military politics followed a classic American path. Overlapping memberships in interest groups moderate the conflicts among those groups. The clash of interest groups within and across party lines moderates party conflict. Party struggles across institutional boundaries moderate executive-legislative conflict. Similarly, with the military, just as interservice rivalry moderated the potential conflict between military services and civilian agencies after World War II, the emergence of the functional programs tended to moderate interservice rivalry. A society, as E. A. Ross said, "which is ridden by a dozen oppositions along lines running in every direction may actually be in less danger of . . . falling to pieces than one split just along one line. For each new cleavage

30. CONFLICT AND CONSENSUS

contributes to narrow the cross clefts, so that one might say that society is *sewn together* by its inner conflicts." [90] Experts in military organization often argued that "unification" required either the merger of the four services into a single uniform or the abolition of the services and the organization of the Pentagon on a purely functional basis. The former proposal, however, was blindly utopian in rejecting the inevitability of pluralism, and conceivably the latter could intensify conflict to the point where it would be unbearable. "Unification" was more likely to come not from the reduction or elimination of intramilitary conflict but from its multiplication.

Diversification of function gave the services organizational flexibility and balance in freeing them from identification with and dependence upon any single strategic concept or functional mission. Noncommitment was the means of self-preservation. Shifts in emphasis in national policy from massive retaliation to limited war to continental defense would affect the relative standing of the services, but they were unlikely to threaten the existence of any service. The new role of the services was formally recognized in the Reorganization Act of 1958: the interservice and functional commands became clearly responsible for combat, the services for personnel, training, and logistics. By reducing the combat functions of the services, the act insured their continued existence. If this tendency continued, eventually the services could end up as English regiments on a grand scale—administrative organizations rather than fighting organizations.

The advantages to a service in not becoming peculiarly identified with any single strategic mission were well illustrated by the smooth sailing of the Navy in the interservice conflicts after 1950. The Air Force was identified primarily with strategic deterrence, the Army with European defense and then limited war. Traditionally, the Navy argued that it was not limited to any single medium, that it must include all the air, sea, and ground forces necessary to accomplish its mission. The Navy also maintained broadly diversified forces which could be interpreted as supporting one or more functional missions. A carrier task force could be used for strategic retaliation, European defense, or limited war. Antisubmarine warfare, similarly, was relevant to continental defense, European defense, and limited war. The Navy avoided primary identification with any single functional mission but at the same time made significant contributions to all four. The Navy, as General Taylor said, preferred "to advance along three parallel lines, seeking to expand its role in strategic bombardment and limited ground warfare while retaining its responsibility for antisubmarine warfare." Because of its combination of ground, sea, and air elements relevant to a variety of functional purposes, "the Navy has been a satisfied service and a staunch defender of the *status quo* in interservice relationships." [91]

The broad range of Navy capabilities meant that any single change in policy or technology, however great, was unlikely to increase or to decrease drastically the size and strength of the Navy. Between FY 1950 and FY 1961, for instance, the Navy's share of the Department of Defense appropriations varied only 4.4 percent, as contrasted with a variation of 18.1 percent in that of the Army and 15.3 percent in that of the Air Force. In 1951 the Army got 39.1 percent of the appropriations and the Air Force 33.7 percent. In 1958 the Army got only 21.0 percent and the Air Force 48.3 percent. The Navy's share, however, only changed from 26.2 percent in 1951 to 28.6 percent in 1958. Whether the emphasis was upon fighting a limited war in Korea or on massive retaliation, the Navy's capabilities were always relevant.

Diversification of function benefits not only the individual services but also the entire military establishment. The value of the services stems precisely from their incomplete commitment to any strategic doctrine. An organization, such as SAC or the Continental Defense Command, which exists for only one strategic purpose, cannot be receptive to changes in its purpose or to the creation of new organizations embodying competing purposes. The functional commands of today are the vested interests of tomorrow. So long as the existence of no service depends upon any single strategic purpose, no service has reason to oppose intransigently changes in strategic purposes. Organizational permanence is the partner of strategic flexibility. Thus, the unified and specified commands may become the instruments of strategy, and yet the political castles of the services may also continue to stand, with their storied keeps of service loyalty and tradition, their inner and outer walls in the executive and Congress, their towers and barbicans in industry, their moats flowing with the currents of public opinion. Perhaps, at some point, a major political or military innovation may, like gunpowder, bring these political structures down in a heap of broken masonry. The experience of other established organizations in American politics, however, suggests a different fate: that the castles of the services, like many of their medieval counterparts, will remain in existence, battered but untaken, long after the decisive battles—both political and military—have shifted to other fields.

CHAPTER VII

The Politics of Deterrence

31. THE CHANGES IN MILITARY POLICY

The drastic changes in the external environment following World War II made national security the overriding goal of the nation's foreign policy. Before World War II, security had been largely the result of distance, resources, and the European balance of power. Security concerns played a secondary role in American foreign policy. The United States emerged from World War II preeminent in world politics, but much less secure than it had been at any time since 1815. Security was no longer the gift of nature—the starting point of policy. Instead, it now had to be the product of conscious and substantial effort—the end result of policy. It became the dominant goal of foreign policy, with foreign policy itself often defined as a branch of national security policy.

The principal threat to national security came from the Soviet Union. The response to this threat could have been policies of accommodation and appeasement, withdrawal and isolation, or aggressive action and preventive war. The choices, however, were to preserve national security by containing the Soviet Union and preventing Communist aggression. The achievement of these goals required the use of traditional diplomatic methods, the United Nations, economic aid, information activities, collective security arrangements. In military policy it required a strategy of deterrence, which became the means of realizing the new goal of foreign policy with the least sacrifice of other values and purposes. Deterrence, in turn, required changes in the strategy and structure comparable to those major adjustments in military policy which took place at the beginning of the eighteenth and nineteenth centuries. These earlier

31. THE CHANGES IN MILITARY POLICY

adjustments produced satisfactory policies which lasted until new fundamental changes took place in the external environment of policy. Fifteen years after World War II, however, the environment was still rapidly changing. The expansion of world population, the emergence of new states in Asia and Africa, the growth in Soviet power, the truculence of Communist China, and the diffusion of nuclear weapons made the achievement of a stable equilibrium in military policy seem remote. Whether the United States was moving toward such an equilibrium depended upon the adequacy of national security as a goal of foreign policy, the adequacy of deterrence as a means to that goal, and the adequacy of the changes in strategy and structure to provide for deterrence.

STRATEGIC PROGRAMS

This book has dealt with the processes by which the new international environment and domestic politics shaped decisions on strategic programs. In terms of programs, the new strategy of deterrence *required:* 1) a total military effort of much greater scope than had ever before been maintained in peacetime; 2) the continued innovation of new strategic programs and weapons to meet the diversifying threats to security; and 3) a balance among strategic programs reflecting the probability and undesirability of the actions to be deterred. In the fifteen years after World War II the interaction of the foreign and domestic environments *produced:* 1) a military effort the level of which stabilized in the late 1950s at about 10 percent of the gross national product; 2) at least four major new strategic programs—strategic deterrence, European defense, continental defense, and, in part, limited war—and the repeated introduction and replacement of weapons; and 3) a balance among strategic programs favoring strategic deterrence and tilted against limited war capabilities. Were these responses adequate for deterrence?

The success of deterrent programs cannot be proved. Only failure is clearly visible. On the record, the decisions and policies on strategic programs down to the New New Look of 1956–1957 and the programs themselves down to 1960 did not fail to accomplish their purposes. The overall scope of the military effort was the product of a continuing battle between the competing claims of security and other values. In this competition, however, no one could deny that the security of the nation was essential for the achievement of other, more desirable, goals, at home and abroad. In World War II the American tendency to distinguish sharply between war and peace encouraged the belief that peace would be secured by eliminating the sources of war in the Axis countries, and that total victory as an absolute goal was the necessary prerequisite to total peace. Security was the Cold War equivalent of total victory. A minimum degree of national security became the indispensable prerequisite to the promotion of the goals of human freedom and welfare. It was thus an instrumental goal, but within its limits it was viewed as an absolute one. Up to some point its claims were overriding. Beyond that point they were unjustifiable. The location of the point was determined by the Administration. In the Cold War politics of fiscal policy, no significant group dared argue that the scope of the military effort should be less than the Administration wanted, and no significant group could compel the Administration to maintain a military establishment much larger than it wanted.

Similarly, the innovation of new programs, often directly helped by fortuitous "trigger events" in the external environment, seemed just rapid enough to keep pace with the multiplication of threats. The history of military policy after 1946 is a series of prophecies of disaster which never materialized. In 1950 and 1951 the Administration identified 1954 and 1955 as the danger years. In 1952 and 1953 scientists warned that in 1955 and 1956 the Soviet Union would have sufficient air-atomic power to attack the United States. In 1955 the Killian Committee pointed to the prospective Soviet advantage in long-range missiles. In 1955 and 1956 Air Force officers declared that the Soviets would have a decisive edge in strategic airpower by 1959. In 1957 the Gaither Committee warned that the years 1958–1960 would be a period of marked inferiority for the United States. In 1958 and 1959 critics of the Administration's policies placed the "missile gap" in the early 1960s. In each case the warning helped to avert the catastrophe. In a pluralistic society certain groups within and without the government were more sensitive to particular types of security needs than were others. They raised the danger signals and made the demands for "greater effort," "crash programs," "new weapons." Seldom, if ever, were their demands completely realized, but almost always they produced some action on the part of the Administration. The lobbying of congressional groups, the attacks from the opposition party, the potential "revolts" within the military services, the continuing attention and criticism of journalistic, university, and other groups, and the general diversity of interests within the executive branch provided safety valves through which the needs of security were articulated. Inevitably, no exact criteria existed by which to judge whether more or fewer programs were needed for national security. The continuing debate and discussion over the adequacy of the programs, however, and the conflict over what did constitute desirable criteria tended to insure that at least the minimum programs would be innovated in time and maintained sufficiently. Prophecies of disaster when credited by the right people are self-nonfulfilling. The innovation of deterrent programs was adequate as long as it kept disaster three years in the future.

The key problem was the ability of the political system to continue to innovate the strategic programs required for deterrence. Between 1949 and 1960, the change from a mobilization strategy was difficult, but there were no insurmountable obstacles to the innovation of the new programs of deterrence. Nonetheless, each successive strategic program was harder to innovate than its predecessor. The replacement of one deterrent program by another, moreover, was likely to be even more difficult than the replacement of a mobilization program by a deterrent program. The deterrent program inaugurated in 1955 would seem more relevant to the needs of 1965 than the mobilization program of 1945 had seemed to the deterrent needs of 1955. Thus, the problem of replacement could intensify, particularly as the earlier deterrent programs gradually were bulwarked by established interests and new traditions. A large-scale civil defense program, for instance, could at some point be the most urgent need for deterrence. The initiation of such a program, however, inevitably would require the disestablishment of many lower priority military programs, which would be vigorously resisted by the affected services, their industrial allies, and the localities concerned.

The balance among strategic programs reflected the apparent

relevance of those programs to the deterrence. The strategic programs most strongly supported were those most directly related to deterring unambiguous challenges to American security. Highest priority went to programs, such as strategic retaliation, designed to prevent a direct attack on the United States. A second priority went to other military programs designed to deter or to defeat less direct and more ambiguous forms of military aggression. Finally, support of a lesser order was available for foreign aid or scientific programs whose relevance to deterrence was still more subtle and complex. The natural tendency undoubtedly was to unbalance the military effort in favor of those programs designed to deal with the most terrifying contingencies.

The tendency toward absolute solutions was counterbalanced by the persistent pluralistic forces at work in the governmental system. The competition among the services and functions encouraged the multiplication of programs while obstructing choice among them. Field Marshal Montgomery and others have criticized the American World II strategy in Europe of advancing on a "broad front" in favor of the alternative of concentrating resources on a single decisive push. A somewhat similar "broad front" strategy existed in the Cold War contest over strategic programs. Few programs were eliminated and even fewer were ever given overriding and decisive priority. The tendency was to be partially prepared for most contingencies and well prepared for none. At the same time, however, the duplication of programs by various organizational units also tended to enhance overall military strength.

THE USES OF FORCE

The changes in strategic programs were only part of a larger adjustment involving the uses of force and the structural elements of policy. The changes in these areas have not been analyzed in this volume. They were, however, critically important in the overall change in military policy, and their principal elements may be briefly summarized here.

A government can use military force against another government in at least three ways. First, it can *initiate* the use of force to achieve some purpose it deems desirable, e.g., the acquisition of a particular piece of territory. Second, it can use force *responsively* as a reaction to the use of force by another government, e.g., defending by force the territory which another government is attempting to seize by force. Third, it can use force *deterrently* to persuade another government not to take actions which it wishes to prevent. Obviously these categories are closely related and overlap. Any specific use of force may involve all three considerations. A government may, for instance, initiate the use of force in one area as a response to the use of force by another government in another area and as a deterrent to action in yet a third area. Before 1945, however, the uses of force by the American government had been primarily either initiatory (1812, 1898) or responsive (World War II). A strategy of deterrence thus required not only major changes in military programs and capabilities but also major changes in the manner in which those capabilities were used in international politics. Deterrence required the government to identify the actions or contingencies it wished to deter, to communicate to the enemy its intention to respond if these contingencies should arise, and to convince the enemy that potential gain from the action would not be worth its cost.

Along with the development of the strategic programs necessary for deterrence, the United States also slowly developed the techniques of using force or promising to use force for deterrence. Military alliances were one means of communicating American intentions to respond to the uses of force by other powers. American intentions to preserve the independence of western Europe were formalized in the North Atlantic Treaty of 1949. American intentions in East Asia were spelled out in the Japanese treaty and the related Philippine and Anzus treaties of 1951, the Korean Treaty of 1953, the Southeast Asia Treaty and the Republic of China Treaty of 1954. Another means of communicating intentions was through a joint resolution of Congress, such as the Formosan resolution of 1955 or the "Eisenhower doctrine" Middle East resolution of 1957. A third technique was simply the declaration of interest or intention by the President or other high officials of the executive branch: the Truman Doctrine, the warnings in the spring of 1954 that the loss of Indochina was unacceptable under the "falling dominoes" theory, the statements of Secretary Dulles during the Formosan Straits crisis of 1958. A fourth means was through the deployment and demonstration of forces. The dispatch of American naval vessels to the eastern Mediterranean in 1946 and 1947 underwrote American intention to preserve the independence of Greece and Turkey.[1] The dispatch of B-29s to Britain in 1948 warned the Russians of the possible consequences of further interference with Berlin. The prolonged deployment of American forces in Europe and in Korea testified to American interests in those areas.

The initial development of the military capabilities for deterrence largely took place under the leadership of Secretary of State Acheson in the Truman Administration. The full development of American policy on the uses of force for deterrence was primarily the work of Secretary of State Dulles. Dulles explicitly articulated the doctrine that wars are normally the result of miscalculation and that the United States must clearly identify those actions to which it will respond by the use of force. Just as the requirements of deterrence in terms of program were not clearly seen at first during the late 1940s, neither were the requirements of deterrence in terms of the uses of force. American actions in 1949 and 1950 with respect to Korea, for instance, were hardly consonant with a deterrent strategy. American troops were withdrawn from Korea; the request of the Republic of Korea for a mutual defense alliance was rejected; economic and military aid to Korea was delayed or restricted; three top American officials concerned with U.S. policy in the area—the Supreme Commander of the American forces in the Far East, the Secretary of State, and the Chairman of the Senate Foreign Relations Committee—declared that Korea lay outside the defense perimeter of the United States. The Communist governments could hardly be blamed for concluding that the United States would not respond with force to an attack on Korea. The United States learned its lesson. Subsequently, the actions which the United States wished to deter were more carefully defined by treaties, policy statements, and military deployments.

STRUCTURE

After World War II, strategy evolved at a much faster rate than structure. The pre-Cold War structural policies had deep political, ideological, and institutional roots, which made them highly resistant to change. During the decade after World War II these policies became increasingly removed from the new requirements of strategy. As the differences over strategic concepts and the gap between strategy and foreign policy tended to narrow, the gap between strategy and structure tended to broaden. In many respects they were much further apart in 1957 than they had been ten years previously. Only in the late 1950s were significant changes made to bring the structural elements of policy more into line with the requirements of a strategy of deterrence.

In each area of structural policy, the needs deriving from the foreign environment were less acutely felt and perceived than they were in the area of strategy. The implications of the new threats for force levels, weapons, and alliances were naturally much clearer than they were for procurement and manpower policies, administrative and budgetary procedures. In addition, strategic decisions were made largely within the executive branch of government, while decisions on structural issues usually required the participation and acquiescence of congressional and nonofficial groups. In each area of structural policy specialized groups tended to give higher priority to purposes other than the adjustment of military policy to the needs of strategy. From their viewpoint, they were preserving important values. From the viewpoint of the "pure" strategist, they were vested interests. Just as the slower adjustment of strategy reacted upon foreign policy, defining the limits and sometimes defining the substance of policy, so also the slower adjustment of structure reacted back on strategy, defining its limits and in some cases its content. The slow processes of adjustment were visible in all areas of structure.[2] They can perhaps best be seen, however, in organization and manpower.

In 1947 the organization of the military establishment was frozen into a pattern embodying the lessons of World War II. This organization, not unnaturally, reflected the needs of a strategy of mobilization. In 1947, everyone agreed that no future war would be fought in separate air, land, and sea compartments. Implicitly, however, unification for combat was viewed as a phenomenon of war rather than peace. Consequently, the three services were established in their separate existences, the Joint Chiefs of Staff were legitimatized as a permanent peacetime planning agency, and a Secretary of Defense was created to coordinate these other elements. If it had been possible to return to the pre-World War II pattern of clear distinctions between war and peace and a substantial time lag in which to move from one to the other, this organization probably would have been adequate. Postwar strategy, however, required that the military forces be ready for action at a moment's notice. They had to be organized for combat, and yet the air, land, and sea services were not combat organizations. As a result, the most important issues of organization focused about the role of the services in the defense establishment. Three relationships were involved: 1) the relation of one service to another, i.e., roles and missions; 2) the relation of the services to the central defense organization, i.e., unification; and 3) the relation of the services to the unified commands, i.e., "functionalization."

The delicate political balance established among the services in the National Security Act did not permit any reallocation of roles and missions, which remained frozen throughout the 1950s. On the other hand, until the end of this period, the unified commands were too weak to encroach seriously upon the functions of the services; they were service creatures. Consequently, the great emphasis was upon unification. The centralization of power in the Office of the Secretary of Defense and the strengthening of the Chairman of the Joint Chiefs were seen as ways of reducing the roles of the services. In actuality, however, strategy required not the centralization of power but the reallocation of functions, the adjustment of military organization to the emergence of the strategic programs of deterrence.[3] Yet the reorganizations of 1949 and 1953 were concerned more with "unification" rather than with "functionalization." In each case the organizational superstructure was strengthened, but the underlying relationships were not significantly altered. The 1953 reorganization, in fact, while enhancing the power of the OSD also attempted to bolster the service departments and especially their secretaries by establishing a single combined political-military chain of command in the Defense Department and by making the service departments executive agents for the unified commands.

The 1958 reorganization continued the tendency toward unification. It also, however, dealt more directly than earlier reorgani-

31. THE CHANGES IN MILITARY POLICY 435

zations with the problem of the allocation of functions among the subordinate units of the Department. Significantly, perhaps, it was the first reorganization which was not associated with an economy wave. Its most distinctive features were the power it gave to the Secretary of Defense, subject to congressional veto, to transfer major combat functions among the services (i.e., to deal with the problem of roles and missions), and the increased status and power it gave to the unified commands. The service departments lost their role as executive agents, and two distinct lines of authority were established, a military chain of command from the Secretary through the JCS and the Joint Staff to the unified commands and a civilian-administrative line from the Secretary to the service departments, which were charged primarily with personnel and logistical functions. Previously the services had been responsible for the "conduct" of military operations. Now they became responsible for the "organization, training, and equipment" of the forces to be employed by the unified commands in performing the functions of deterrence. Thus, organization slowly adjusted to strategy, and the defense establishment moved toward a "balanced" system of organization and command.[4]

In manpower and personnel, as in organization, inherited policies, ideas, and practices conflicted with the new demands of deterrence. The idea of a small standing army supplemented in emergencies by a large citizen reserve had been basic doctrine since the establishment of the Republic. During the Cold War decade, continuous efforts were made to extend this idea and to adapt it to the new conditions. UMT, for instance, was frequently advanced on grounds which had relatively little to do with strategy. It came close to adoption in 1948 and again in 1951–1952. In each case, however, it was presented as a "long-term" program and was eventually sacrificed in favor of shorter-range proposals designed to meet immediate needs. Throughout the battles over UMT, the Army, the Administration, most veterans groups, and public opinion (as revealed through the polls) were in favor of it. The opposition came from religious, educational, pacifist, farm, and some business groups. Ironically, the opposing civilian groups, generally unconcerned with strategy and hostile to military needs, helped prevent the country from adopting a popular policy, backed by the Army, which would have been ill-suited to the military needs of the nation.

The Eisenhower Administration initially shifted emphasis from UMT to the creation of a large reserve force. It soon realized, however, that large reserves contributed relatively little to the purposes of deterrence. In 1957 it changed its ground and attempted to reduce the size of the reserves and to redirect those which were to be maintained to purposes more in line with overall strategic needs. Substantial opposition in Congress, however, led the Administration not to press its demands for reductions.[5]

Personnel policies for the regular forces were also only slowly altered. Selective service had been inherited from World War II, but by the late 1950s military requirements for draftees had fallen to the point where the operation of the system had become so selective that it often seemed quite arbitrary. Increasing dissatisfaction manifested itself in Congress with each renewal of the draft law. Theoretically, a strategy of deterrence would best be served by reliance upon career soldiers rather than citizen soldiers. Yet the problem of increasing the attractiveness of the military services so that the needs of the forces, particularly for skilled specialists, could be met by volunteers alone seemed insurmountable. Despite pay adjustments in 1949, 1952, and 1955, a significant gap still existed, as Chairman Cordiner of the advisory committee on compensation suggested in 1957, between military strategy, which had changed frequently after World War II, and the structure of military pay, which had not. The basic problem was "modernization of compensation practices" which were "clearly out of step with the times" and "inadequate" for "national defense."[6] After a year's delay for budgetary reasons, many of the recommendations of the Cordiner Committee were enacted in 1958.

The implications for personnel policy of the shift from mobilization to deterrence were also concretely seen in the changing functions of the ROTC. During the interwar years, the principal function of the college ROTC program was to train reserve officers who presumably could step in and assume military leadership roles when the nation mobilized for war. After World War II, however, the services had a decreasing need for large numbers of partially trained reserve officers and increasing requirements for career officers for active duty. Slowly, during the fifteen years after World War II, the goal of the ROTC programs shifted from the production of reserve officers to the production of active-duty officers. Even in 1959, however, the ROTC was still "not contributing adequately to the strong professional officer base required for the forces-in-being." [7]

Thus, by 1960 the United States had developed a strategy of deterrence, but in many important ways it still lacked the appropriate military structure to support that strategy. In each specific area of structural policy, strategic needs and values came into direct conflict with other values and established patterns of behavior. Disequilibrium still existed among the significant elements of military policy. If deterrence remained the strategy, however, presumably the structural elements of policy would eventually be brought into line with its needs. The more significant question concerned the adequacy of deterrence as a military policy in a still rapidly changing international environment.

32. BEYOND DETERRENCE?
THE SUCCESS OF DETERRENCE

Before 1960 the only spectacular failure of deterrence was the Korean War. Otherwise, American policy apparently deterred large-scale Soviet aggression against western Europe or the United States. The policies of the Korean War years and the New Look apparently deterred both large-scale and small-scale Communist military aggressions during the 1950s. Apart from its intervention in Hungary in 1956, the Soviet Union did not engage in direct aggression; apart from its conquest of Tibet and its intermittent shelling of the offshore islands, neither did Communist China. Once the Indochinese War was brought to a close in 1954, no other major military actions were initiated by Communist forces until the fall of 1960.

As an overall military response to needs of national security, deterrence was apparently a success. The question, however, was whether it could continue to be so in the future. Even the most ardent advocates of deterrence seldom presented it as more than an interim strategy, a policy with which to buy time until a more permanent and reliable solution to the problems of security could be worked out. The tentative character of deterrence is clearly revealed, for instance, if one compares it with an earlier fundamental strategy: the Monroe Doctrine. Designed to deter European states from intruding into western hemisphere politics, the Doctrine became a revered and even sanctified policy, an end in and of itself. The Cold War strategy of deterrence failed to achieve such exalted status in its first decade of existence; and the development of thermonuclear weapons in the mid-1950s reinforced the view that sustained deterrence could well lead to disaster.

Apart from war, the only major alternative proposed to deterrence was an effectively controlled system of disarmament. Even the supporters of deterrence agreed with Churchill that "we arm to parley." For fifteen years, however, the arming did not make the parleying successful, and the parleying did not reduce the need for arming. Deterrence was costly and uncertain, but it worked. Disarmament was desirable, but disarmament negotiations always failed. The record of fifteen years suggested that there was little likelihood of any substantial disarmament agreement between the United States and the Soviet Union. The obstacles in international politics seemed overwhelming and decisive. Even if these could be overcome, additional obstacles existed within the American political system (and probably also within the Soviet system). In the United States, the innovation of deterrence required many bitter political battles over the better part of a decade. Vast and powerful agencies of government had grown up to perform deterrent functions. Ten percent of the gross national product was directly devoted to implementing that strategy and a much larger share was indirectly devoted to supporting it. By 1960 the interests committed to deterrence were much stronger and more important in national politics than those which had been committed to a mobilization strategy ten years earlier. The replacement of deterrence probably would be even more difficult than its innovation.

Given the international and domestic obstacles, disarmament as an alternative to deterrence gradually lost support, and "arms control" emerged as a means of supplementing deterrence. Deterrence itself, after all, was a unilateral means of arms control. Conceivably the interests of both sides in deterring the other could lead to bilateral agreements on arms control. Such agreements, however, would be like continental defense or limited war, programs to meet the changing requirements of deterrence and to insure its success. This continued success of deterrence rather than its possible failure seemed likely to pose the principal problems of military and foreign policy in the 1960s.

SECURITY AND PURPOSE

In a sense, during the decade after World War II, world politics resembled a two-person zero-sum game. The western European countries were weak from the war. The Asian and African states had not emerged as a significant force on the world scene. Bipolarity prevailed, with the United States and the Soviet Union each dominating a bloc of allies and satellites. Moreover, the struggle between the two great powers and their allies was largely over territory. The principal Communist challenge was the effort to detach territory from the western side and add it to the eastern bloc. Direct and fierce struggles took place over Iran, Greece, Turkey, Berlin, China, Korea, Vietnam. A gain in territory for one side (e.g., China) was a direct loss for the other. Any such loss, consequently, was viewed by the loser as a direct threat to its security. National security naturally became the be-all and the end-all of policy.

In the mid-1950s, however, the structure of world politics began to change. This change was in part the product of the military policies of the major powers and in part the result of other forces. The relevant model of world politics was no longer a two-person, zero-sum game. Bipolarity declined. China and India emerged as major powers in Asia. Arab and African nationalisms developed as autonomous forces in world politics. Japan and the countries of western Europe put themselves back on their feet, developed prosperous economies, reconstituted their military strength. The nuclear duopoly was broken. The tight bonds of the two central alliances themselves showed signs of weakening with the unrest in eastern Europe in 1956, the disputes between Russia and China, the strains which developed in NATO as the American deterrent declined in credibility, and the restlessness among the Latin American countries. The United States and the Soviet Union were, to be sure, still the two great superpowers, but they did not bestride a stricken world as they had done in 1946. The power vacuums which had existed between them in Europe and Asia were now being filled by the recovery of old powers and the emergence of new ones. Increasingly, each of the superpowers had to give more attention to the effects of its actions not only upon the other but also upon the third forces pushing their way upward about the globe.

Simultaneous with the decline of bipolarity there was the change in the nature of the competition itself. Territory tended to become inviolate. Thermonuclear weapons, the United Nations, and the strengthening of the other powers, all made territorial aggression a dangerous and dubious method of increasing national power, and territory itself became less important as an element of national power. As a result, the struggle tended to become open-ended, a nonzero-sum game, in which a gain for one country did not automatically mean an equivalent loss for the other. The competition, in a sense, was internalized. A finite limit existed on territory, but there were no limits upon the goals which a government might set for itself in expanding its production, developing its military capabilities, and exploring outer space.

Deterrence, in short, was a success, and hence it was no longer enough. The change in the nature of the competition opened up a gap between the goal of security and the goal of preeminence in world politics. In a two-person zero-sum game, security and preeminence were identical. In a multi-person, nonzero-sum game, this was not necessarily true. Conceivably a nation could be reasonably secure, safe from attack and able to protect its vital interests, and be neither politically preeminent nor the strongest military and economic power. This gap was enhanced by nuclear technology, which meant that a power with a small military force might still be capable of deterring aggression by a power with a much larger one. In the 1940s General Arnold had argued that "the second best Air Force is as good as the second best poker hand." In the late 1950s airpower adherents still repeated this maxim, but technological changes were rapidly depriving it of whatever validity it may once have had. A nation could be second and still be secure. The United States, Khrushchev said in 1958, was in "the last years of its greatness." [8] He did not say the last years of its existence, its wealth, or its security. Between 1945 and 1958 the United States had demonstrated its ability to provide for these. The issue, instead, had become whether the United States was willing and able to compete in the pursuit of preeminence. Security alone is a mean goal for a great nation. At stake in world politics were not just security, but the prestige of the nation, the respect of its allies, the futures of the developing countries, and, most importantly, the confidence of Americans in themselves and their system of government. The record of 1945 to 1960, however, suggests that its political system and ideology might well hamper the United States in playing a more positive and creative role in world politics.

Ten years of Cold War had developed a substantial consensus on security as the prime value of foreign policy and on deterrence as the principal means of protecting it. Confronted with the need to choose between maximizing security and maximizing "prestige" or achieving "political" goals, the Eisenhower Administration almost always chose the former. Shortly after the sputniks, for instance, the Deputy Secretary of Defense said, "We must not be talked into hitting the moon with a rocket. . . . just to be first, unless by doing so we stand to gain something of real scientific or military significance." [9] Similarly, in 1958 the President named two major objectives of the nuclear aircraft program: "the earliest possible achievement of an operational military aircraft," and, secondly, "making sure that America is the first nation to produce a nuclear-powered aircraft, regardless of its utility, because of the possible worldwide significance of such an accomplishment." While both goals were inherently desirable, "unfortunately," the President said, "in present circumstances, they meet head on." In this situation it was his "conviction" that the "need for the development of high-priority military aircraft overrides the first nuclear flight objective." [10]

In so acting, the Administration reflected the underlying consensus and balance of interests in society. Many differing views existed on what was necessary for security and what was required for deterrence, but no goal could receive any broader support than security. An attempt to define and to apply broader goals for foreign policy inevitably would have produced serious disagreements over what those goals should be. In war, it has frequently been alleged, the United States has tended to make military victory its sole goal and to pay little attention to the political conditions which it desired to see prevail after the war. It has refused to define war aims beyond victory. Policy tends toward the lowest common denominator, that goal which has the broadest support and which produces the least discord among groups at home and among allies abroad. Lincoln defined the aim of the Union as the preservation of the Union, not the abolition or limitation of slavery or any other goal which might stir up controversy. Wilson declared that World War I was to be fought to make the world safe for democracy by the destruction of Imperial Germany, and Franklin D. Roosevelt described World War II as the War for Survival. As the Cold War equivalent of total victory, national security was an end which could be easily visualized and one upon which virtually everyone could agree. The effort to define any other goals for foreign policy would only cause controversy and disorder. In the Cold War, military forces were to be used only for national security, not to promote other political objectives. The Soviet Union, of course, used military forces, military developments, and scientific achievements for "political" purposes. In the United States, however, military actions and programs were justified in terms of military security. During the Eisenhower Administration the claims of security often served to limit or eliminate weapon developments and military programs that were justifiable only in terms of other "political" goals.

The difficulties in reaching agreement upon any foreign policy goal beyond security were markedly revealed in the discussions over "national purpose" in the late 1950s.[11] Such a debate could only take place in a society which was reasonably sure of survival. Underlying the search was the desire to pursue more positive purposes. Yet the principal participants in the debate were hard put to define acceptable political goals beyond security and yet below the generalities of the Declaration of Independence and Bill of Rights. Purpose demands priorities; priorities require choice; choice means controversy. Politics, however, eschews controversy, and thus policy settles upon security as a goal which accommodates all but satisfies none.

In addition, the competition of other interests in the fiscal politics of the 1950s inevitably tended to limit and reduce foreign policy goals. A goal broader than security and requiring larger foreign policy programs inevitably would have intensified the conflict with the demands of the domestic programs, tax limitation, and economic stability. Thus the pressure from these other goals encouraged the definition of minimal foreign policy objectives. Given the values dominant in the American political system, it was doubtful that any foreign policy goal apart from security could compete effectively with these other domestic goals of fiscal politics. Given the balance of forces in the American political system, any foreign policy goal was relatively weak when compared with the domestic goals, and any other goal would be weaker than security.

The dominance of security as a goal of military policy implied that foreign policy goals were justified primarily in terms of their domestic consequences. Closely related to this attitude was a fundamental conception of the nature of government and the relation between government and society. Government, in this view, existed to serve the ends of the individuals within society. Governmental actions are legitimate only in so far as they contribute to these ends. Governments are instituted among men to secure the rights to life, liberty, and the pursuit of happiness for individuals. Hence, governments do not have goals which are legitimate in and of themselves. If governmental goals do exist apart from the interests of the individuals in society, they are at best dubious and at worst illegitimate. Lockean tradition, the social contract theory of government, the liberal ideas of limited government and that the government is best which governs least, democratic ideas of representative and responsible government, all combined in the American tradition to deny to government legitimate ends apart from those of society.

The assumption of the identity of interest between government and society made little allowance for the ends which governments might desire to pursue in the world of international politics. International relations is very largely intergovernmental relations: the competition among governments for prestige, influence, territory. The individual in society has little interest in these stakes so long as his government maintains the minimum prerequisites of security and order. Only in special cases do individuals or groups have direct interests in the role which their government plays in international politics. The steady decline of the British Empire has not adversely affected the steady rise in material well-being of the average Britisher. That their governments are not major powers in international politics does not prevent individual Swiss and Swedes from leading the good life and realizing their own individual purposes. Indeed, the pursuit of goals in international politics by a government more often than not runs directly counter to the interests of individuals and groups in its society at home and imposes burdens and sacrifices upon them. Supporters of American policy have often pointed out that this is the case in the Soviet Union. "The price the Russian people are forced to pay," the *Wall Street Journal* commented after the first sputnik, "so that the Soviet Union can play a big power role is a frightful one." [12] Similarly, Vice President Nixon contrasted the growth in the military and economic power of the Soviet system with the fact that the "average Russian has poorer housing and poorer food than he had forty years ago." Russia he argued, is "a gigantic poorhouse by free world standards." The "Communist system has been good for the State and bad for the people." [13] The corollary would seem to be that the American system is good for the people and bad for the state.

Since the ends of government are assumed not to be valid apart from their contribution to individual welfare and freedom, democratic governments may be unable to do many things which are quite within the range of despotic governments. They may be unable to establish and to maintain major foreign policy programs, military or otherwise, which involve substantial resources and are devoted to some goal other than the common defense. By definition, a constitutional government is limited in what it can do. The limits imposed upon a constitutional government at home may restrict the goals it can pursue abroad. As Secretary Dulles pointed out in a concrete instance:

. . . I think whenever the Soviets register a first in an area that is spectacular, they gain greatly from it and we go down in popular estimation.

Getting to the moon first would certainly be spectacular. Now, one has to take into account . . . the fact that despotisms generally can achieve spectacular results which democracies don't achieve. You can look around the world today and the things that attract attention, things that visitors go to see are the products of despotisms. They are not the products of a democratic way of life. You can go to the pyramids of Egypt, and the Colosseum in Rome, and so forth. We cannot be drawn into the business of trying to compete in every way with despotisms, trying to do spectacular things, because they use up human labors in useless ways, or at least in ways which are not of immediate practicality, to the degree that we don't.

If you are going to spend a few hundred million dollars getting to the moon, that means a certain number of manhours people are going to have to work to do that, and it is not going to put any bread in their mouths or clothes on their backs to get to the moon.

Now, the despots, they don't mind tying their people down and have them work to produce this result as long as it glorifies their particular despotism, and that is one of the problems that we face. How much are we justified in making our taxpayers sweat to produce a result which has . . . no practical value.[14]

The limits on American military programs and on other foreign policy programs were thus set by the limits of American goals in world politics. The Constitution defines six purposes of government. Five are the achievement of unity, tranquillity, welfare, justice, and liberty *within* American society. These the American political system has been reasonably successful in achieving. The Constitution's sixth purpose is to "provide for the common defense." This mandate, too, the political system has discharged satisfactorily. The Constitution does not mention other purposes in foreign policy.

Yet in the long run, successful provision for the common defense may require the pursuit of goals other than security through means other than the deterrence of Communist aggression. Security in the broader sense could well demand more active and positive efforts to shape the evolution of world politics in directions compatible with American interests. It could demand a strategy of participation, more political than military, a strategy designed not to replace deterrence but to supplement it and to deal with its consequences. The innovation of such a strategy would be difficult. It would require additional sacrifices of domestic values, further changes in accepted doctrines and ideas, and a new relationship between government and society. It would also require the development of a new consensus to supplement the existing consensus on the military programs and actions necessary to deter Communist aggression. The key question of the 1960s may well be whether the United States can develop this consensus to move beyond deterrence.

Although the record reveals many limitations of the American political system, it also demonstrates many strengths. In a brief fifteen years the United States did adopt a new military strategy. This was a revolutionary achievement. Conceivably, a comparable revolution could take place in the future with the innovation of a new strategy to supplement deterrence. In any event, if the United States can successively innovate strategic programs and bring its structure into line with its strategy, it should be able to maintain indefinitely its new policy of deterrence. Even the probability that it can do this confounds some of the more pessimistic critics of the capabilities of democracy in foreign affairs. "Democracy," De Tocqueville said in a classic statement, "appears to me better adapted for the conduct of society in times of peace, or for a sudden effort of remarkable vigor, than for the prolonged endurance of the great storms which beset the political existence of nations . . . Foreign politics demand scarcely any of those qualities which are peculiar to democracy; they require, on the contrary, the perfect use of almost all those in which it is deficient . . . [A] democracy can only with great difficulty regulate the details of an important undertaking, persevere in a fixed design, and work out its execution in spite of serious obstacles. It cannot combine its measures with secrecy or await their consequences with patience . . ." [15] More recently, Lippmann declared that: ". . . The genius of American military power does not lie in holding positions indefinitely . . . It is, therefore, not an efficient instrument for a diplomatic policy of containment. It can only be the instrument of a policy which has as its objective a decision and a settlement." [16] The first fifteen years of the Cold War, however, suggest that the United States may have unforeseen powers of endurance in foreign policy. In a constitutional democracy, the forces of pluralism correct and counterbalance the instabilities, enthusiasms, and irrationalities of the prevailing mood. Indeed, in many respects, a constitutional democracy appears peculiarly suited for the "prolonged endurance" of the storms of international politics and "for holding positions indefinitely." It lacks not staying power but acting power. Yet the government which does have the capacity for sudden spectacular success usually also has the capacity for sudden spectacular failure. The American government may well be incapable of both, posing major obstacles to those who desire the more positive pursuit of preeminence and yet offering little grounds for despair to those concerned with national survival.

The record of American military policy between 1945 and 1960 suggests that not DeTocqueville but Fisher Ames provided the more accurate picture of constitutional democracy in foreign affairs.[17] A monarchy or despotism, Ames suggested, is like a full-rigged sailing ship. It moves swiftly and efficiently. It is beautiful to behold. It responds sharply to the helm. But in troubled waters, when it strikes a rock, its shell is pierced, and it quickly sinks to the bottom. A republic, however, is like a raft: slow, ungainly, impossible to steer, no place from which to control events, and yet endurable and safe. It will not sink, but one's feet are always wet.

Notes

I. THE DIMENSIONS OF MILITARY POLICY

1. My distinction between strategy and structure parallels that drawn by Charles H. Donnelly in his annual surveys of *United States Defense Policies* (H. Doc. 436, 85C2; H. Doc. 227, 86C1; H. Doc. 432, 86C2), between "strategic policies," and organization, manpower, budgetary, fiscal, and procurement policies. See also Paul H. Nitze's distinction between action policy and declaratory policy, "Atoms, Strategy and Policy," 34 *Foreign Affairs* (Jan. 1956), 187–88, and Roger Hilsman's categories of crisis policy, program policy, and anticipatory policy, "The Foreign Policy Consensus: An Interim Research Report," 8 *Jour. of Conflict Resolution* (Dec. 1959), 376–77. The distinction between strategy and structure in military *policy*, of course, should not be confused with the traditional distinction between strategy and tactics in military *science*.

2. Richard D. Challener, *The French Theory of the Nation in Arms, 1866–1939* (New York, 1955), pp. 264–65.

3. This historical summary is condensed from my more extensive analysis in "Equilibrium and Disequilibrium in American Military Policy," 76 *Political Science Quarterly* (Dec. 1961).

4. Gabriel Almond, *The American People and Foreign Policy* (New York, 1950), p. 106.

5. See my "To Choose Peace or War," 83 *U. S. Naval Institute Proceedings* (Apr. 1957), 363–66, and Bernard Brodie, *Strategy in the Missile Age* (Princeton, 1959), pp. 227–41, 392.

6. John Foster Dulles, "A Policy of Boldness," 32 *Life* (May 19, 1952), 146–60.

7. *New York Times*, Aug. 26, 1952, p. 12.

8. Paul Y. Hammond, "NSC 68: Prologue to Rearmament," MS, p. 42, to be published in Warner R. Schilling, Paul Y. Hammond, Glenn H. Snyder, *Making National Security Policy: Three Case Studies* (New York, 1962).

9. Glenn H. Snyder, "The New Look," MS, pp. 31–35, to be published in Schilling, Hammond, Snyder, *Making National Security Policy: Three Case Studies.*

II. THE SEARCH FOR A STABLE DETERRENT

1. Joseph and Stewart Alsop, *New York Herald Tribune,* Nov. 16, 1955, Sec. II, p. 3.
2. See, e.g., Harry Truman, *Memoirs* (Garden City, N. Y., 1955), I, 510–11; John C. Campbell, et al., *The United States in World Affairs, 1945–1947* (New York, 1947), pp. 456–57.
3. See, e.g., Secretary Lovett's statement, *Dept. of Defense (and related independent agencies) Appropriations for 1953,* Hears./HR CA SC/82C2/1952, p. 90.
4. Address, American Ordnance Association, New York, N. Y., Dec. 7, 1955.
5. Walter Millis, ed., *The Forrestal Diaries* (New York, 1951), p. 350.
6. Millis, *Forrestal Diaries,* pp. 38–41; Herbert Feis, *Churchill, Roosevelt, Stalin* (Princeton, N. J., 1957), pp. 597 ff.; Truman, *Memoirs,* I, 70–71.
7. H. Bradford Westerfield, *Foreign Policy and Party Politics: Pearl Harbor to Korea* (New Haven, 1955), p. 204.
8. Millis, *Forrestal Diaries,* p. 134; *New York Times,* Feb. 10, 1946, p. 1.
9. Millis, *Forrestal Diaries,* pp. 136–40.
10. See John C. Sparrow, *History of Personnel Demobilization in the United States Army* (Washington, 1951), pp. 187–219. For a summary of public opinion polls on demobilization, see Nancy Boardman Eddy, *Public Opinion and United States Foreign Policy, 1937–1956* (Massachusetts Institute of Technology, Center for International Studies, American Project, Working Paper I; mimeo.), pp. 49–62.
11. Sparrow, *Personnel Demobilization,* p. 360.
12. *Ibid.,* p. 379; Millis, *Forrestal Diaries,* p. 129; James F. Byrnes, *All In One Lifetime* (New York, 1958), p. 349.
13. Millis, *Forrestal Diaries,* pp. 102, 128–29, 139.
14. Admiral Radford, *Second Supplemental Surplus Appropriation Rescission Bill, 1946,* Hears./HR CA SC/79C2/1946, p. 559; Admiral Nimitz, *Navy Dept. Appropriation Bill for 1947,* Hears./HR CA SC/79C2/1946, p. 45.
15. "The Sources of Soviet Conduct," 25 *Foreign Affairs* (July 1947), 575–76.
16. Paul Y. Hammond, "NSC 68: Prologue to Rearmament," MS, p. 26, to be published in Warner R. Schilling, Paul Y. Hammond, and Glenn H. Snyder, *Making National Security Policy: Three Case Studies* (New York, 1962).
17. Millis, *Forrestal Diaries,* p. 508. As Millis points out, in formu-

II. SEARCH FOR A STABLE DETERRENT 451

lating the budget for that year the Joint Chiefs only considered capabilities "in case war should develop."

18. Sparrow, *Personnel Demobilization*, p. 380.
19. Millis, *Forrestal Diaries*, pp. 373–77.
20. Hammond, "NSC 68," pp. 17–18; Walter Millis, Harvey C. Mansfield, and Harold Stein, *Arms and the State* (New York, 1958), pp. 242–43.
21. Millis, *Forrestal Diaries*, p. 536.
22. Letter to Edwin G. Nourse, July 1, 1949, quoted in Nourse, *Economics in the Public Service* (New York, 1953), p. 250.
23. *Biennial Report of the Chief of Staff, United States Army, 1943–1945* (1945), p. 123; *Final Report, Chief of Staff, United States Army, February 7, 1948*, pp. 11–12; Gen. J. L. Collins, "National Security, The Military Viewpoint," 13 *Vital Speeches* (June 1, 1947), 489.
24. *Unification and Strategy*, H. Doc. 600/81C2/1950, p. 4. See also Ray S. Cline, *Washington Command Post: The Operations Division* (Washington, 1951), p. 352.
25. Brig. Gen. G. A. Lincoln, *Military Establishment Appropriations, 1948*, Hears./HR CA SC/80C1/1947, p. 4; *Final Report, Chief of Staff, Feb. 7, 1948*, pp. 8, 17.
26. *National Security Act of 1947*, Hears./HR CEED/80C1/1947, p. 582.
27. *Biennial Report, 1943–1945*, pp. 117–18; *First Supplemental Surplus Appropriation Rescission Bill, 1946*, Hears./HR CA SC/79C1/1945, II, 527, 531–32.
28. *Final Report, Feb. 7, 1948*, p. 2.
29. *Military Establishment Appropriation Bill for 1947*, Hears./HR CA SC/79C2/1946, p. 402.
30. Bernard Brodie, ed., *The Absolute Weapon* (New York, 1946), p. 88. "Determent" was Arnold Wolfers' word. He had his suffix wrong but his concept right.
31. *Final Report, Feb. 7, 1948*, p. 11; *The National Defense Program —Unification and Strategy*, Hears./HR CAS/81C1/1949, p. 544.
32. *Dept. of Defense Appropriations, 1951*, Hears./HR CA SC/81C2/1950, pp. 205 ff.
33. Campbell et al., *United States in World Affairs*, p. 12; Millis, *Forrestal Diaries*, pp. 397–98.
34. Hammond, "NSC 68," pp. 17–28. Except where otherwise noted, my description of the formulation and contents of NSC 68 is based on Hammond's exhaustive account.
35. *Ibid.*, p. 23.
36. *National Defense Program: Unification and Strategy*, Hears./HR CAS/81C1/1949, p. 518.
37. *Dept. of Defense Appropriations, 1951*, Hears./HR CA SC/81C2/1950, pp. 80–82; *Dept. of Defense Appropriations, 1951*, Hears./USS CA SC/81C2/1950, pp. 73–74.
38. Hammond, "NSC 68," pp. 31–32.

39. Paul H. Nitze, "The Need for a National Strategy," Address, Army War College, Carlisle Barracks, Pa., Aug. 27, 1958.

40. *Ibid.;* Hammond, "NSC 68," pp. 58–59.

41. Nitze, *loc. cit.*

42. Sen. Henry M. Jackson, "How Shall We Forge a Strategy for Survival?" Address, National War College, Washington, D. C., Apr. 16, 1959.

43. Harry S. Truman, *New York Times,* June 8, 1952, p. 67.

44. See Randolph Paul, *Taxation in the United States* (Boston, 1954), pp. 553–622.

45. *Semiannual Report of the Secretary of Defense, Jan. 1–June 30, 1951* (1951), p. 10.

46. *New York Times,* July 25, 1950, p. 25; *The Supplemental Appropriation Bill for 1951,* Hears./HR CA SC/81C2/1950, pp. 7–8, 16, 21, 232.

47. *Supplemental Appropriation for 1951,* Hears./HR CA SC/81C2/1950, pp. 9–22.

48. *Semiannual Report of the Secretary of Defense, Jan. 1–June 30, 1951,* pp. 2, 31, 71.

49. Herbert H. Rosenberg, "ODM: A Study of Civil-Military Relations during the Korean Mobilization" (Mimeo., Dec. 1953), p. 19; *Second Supplemental Appropriation Bill for 1951,* Hears./USS CA/81C2/1950, pp. 12–31; *Second Supplemental Appropriation Bill for 1951,* Hears./HR CA/81C2/1950, pp. 58–63; 96 *Cong. Record* (Dec. 15, 1950), 16650–58.

50. *Second Supplemental Appropriations, 1951,* Hears./USS CA/81C2/1950, p. 12; *Second Supplemental Appropriations, 1951,* Hears./HR CA/81C2/1950, pp. 24–25. For the role of the "year of maximum danger" concept in NATO planning, see Roger Hilsman, "NATO: The Developing Strategic Context," in Klaus Knorr, ed., *NATO and American Security* (Princeton, 1959), p. 20.

51. General Bradley, *Universal Military Training and Service Act of 1951,* Hears./USS CAS SC on Preparedness/82C1/1951, pp. 656–57.

52. *Ibid.,* p. 4; *New York Times,* Nov. 30, 1950, p. 1.

53. Rosenberg, "ODM," p. 12.

54. *Semiannual Report of the Secretary of Defense, Jan. 1–June 30, 1951,* p. 16.

55. For an early and informed, if anonymous, statement of the rationale of rearmament, see "The Balance of Military Power," 187 *Atlantic Monthly* (June 1951), 21–27. Cf. T. R. Phillips, "The 'Mister X' of Defense," 124 *New Republic* (June 11, 1951), 15–16.

56. *The Supplemental Appropriation for 1951,* Hears./HR CA SC/81C2/1950, pp. 7–8, 16, 21.

57. *Semiannual Report of the Secretary of Defense, Jan. 1–June 30, 1951,* p. 10.

58. *New York Times:* June 25, 1952, p. 1; June 27, 1952, p. 6; Aug. 24, 1952, p. 1; Dec. 10, 1952, p. 1; Jan. 5, 1953, p. 49. Rosenberg, "ODM," chaps. 3, 4.

59. See, e.g., *Developments in Military Technology and their Impact on United States Strategy and Foreign Policy*, Study prepared by The Washington Center of Foreign Policy Research, The Johns Hopkins University, Cmte. Print/USS CFR/86C1/1959, pp. 46 ff.; James E. King, Jr., "Collective Defense: the Military Commitment," in Arnold Wolfers, ed., *Alliance Policy in the Cold War* (Baltimore, 1959), pp. 119-21. Cf. Herman Kahn, *On Thermonuclear War* (Princeton, 1960), chap. 9.

60. *New York Times*, May 20, 1953, p. 24; C. J. V. Murphy, "The Eisenhower Shift," 53 *Fortune* (Jan. 1956), 87.

61. Murphy, 53 *Fortune* (Jan. 1956), 86-87.

62. Secretary Dulles, *Evolution of Foreign Policy* (Address, Council on Foreign Relations, New York, N. Y., January 12, 1954; Dept. of State Press Release No. 8), p. 2.

63. *New York Times*, Dec. 23, 1953, p. 4; *Dept. of the Army Appropriations, 1955*, Hears./HR CA SC/83C2/1954, p. 52.

64. *The Budget of the United States Government for the Fiscal Year Ending June 30, 1955*, p. M39.

65. *New York Times*, Jan. 27, 1955, pp. 1, 10; *Sundry Legislation Affecting the Naval and Military Establishments*, Hears./HR CAS/84C1/1955, pp. 217, 227-28; *New York Times*, Aug. 10, 1955, p. 1, Nov. 18, 1955, p. 18.

66. Except where otherwise indicated, the information in this discussion of the formulation of the New Look comes from Glenn Snyder's comprehensive study, "The New Look," MS to be published in Schilling, Hammond, and Snyder, *Making National Security Policy*. Professor Snyder is not responsible, however, for my interpretation of his data.

67. *Study of Airpower*, Hears./USS CAS SC on the Air Force/84C2/1956, pp. 1624-25. See also Robert J. Donovan, *Eisenhower: The Inside Story* (New York, 1956), p. 55.

68. Snyder, "New Look," pp. 12-13.

69. *Dept. of Defense (and related independent agencies) Appropriations, 1954*, Hears./HR CA SC/83C1/1953, p. 390; *Dept. of Defense Appropriation Bill, 1954*, Hears./USS CA SC/83C1/1954, p. 38.

70. Quoted in Snyder, "New Look," pp. 45-46.

71. *Ibid.*, pp. 31-35; Murphy, 53 *Fortune* (Mar. 1956), 232.

72. Snyder, "New Look," pp. 40-42; Murphy, 53 *Fortune* (Mar. 1956), 234.

73. Snyder, "New Look," p. 72.

74. For a more detailed summary, see Snyder, "New Look," pp. 95-99.

75. Snyder, "New Look," pp. 78-79.

76. "Assumptions Used in Developing Rough Budget Estimates for Fiscal Year 1955 (October)," *Study of Airpower*, Hears./USS CAS SC on the Air Force/84C2/1956, pp. 1643-44.

77. *The Budget of the United States Government for the Fiscal Year Ending June 30, 1956*, p. M13; Lewis H. Kimmel, *Federal Budget and Fiscal Policy, 1789-1958* (Washington, 1959), pp. 247-48.

78. Donovan, *Eisenhower*, p. 354.
79. Snyder, "New Look," pp. 41, 51.
80. *New York Times*, Dec. 15, 1953, p. 31; *Budget for Fiscal Year 1956*, p. M27; *Dept. of Defense Appropriations, 1956*, Hears./USS CA SC/84C1/1955, p. 6.
81. Secretary Dulles, *New York Times*, Mar. 20, 1954, p. 2.
82. Admiral Radford, *Dept. of Defense Appropriations, 1955*, Hears./USS CA SC/83C2/1954, pp. 88, 90.
83. Quoted in Murphy, 53 *Fortune* (Mar. 1956), 230.
84. Quoted, *ibid.*, p. 234. See also "Defense and Strategy," 48 *Fortune* (Dec. 1953), 78, 84; C. J. V. Murphy, "Is the H-Bomb Enough?" 49 *Fortune* (June 1954), 246–48.
85. *Dept. of Defense Appropriations, 1955*, Hears./USS CA SC/83C2/1954, p. 8.
86. *New York Times:* Mar. 17, 1955, p. 1; Apr. 24, 1955, Sec. IV, p. 10; 32 *Department of State Bulletin* (Mar. 21, 1955), 459–60.
87. 92 *Army-Navy-Air Force Journal* (Dec. 25, 1954), 498; *New York Times*, July 18, 1955, p. 1.
88. *Dept. of Defense Appropriations, 1955*, Hears./USS CA SC/83C2/1954, p. 60; "Defense and Strategy," 47 *Fortune* (June 1953), 90.
89. *Dept. of Defense Appropriations, 1954*, Hears./USS CA SC/83C1/1953, p. 23. Cf. *New York Times*, Dec. 9, 1954, p. 1.
90. *New York Times*, July 30, 1954, p. 4.
91. State of the Union Message, 100 *Cong. Record* (Jan. 7, 1954), 79; *Budget for Fiscal Year 1955*, p. M38.
92. See Snyder, "New Look," pp. 81, 97.
93. *New York Herald Tribune*, Mar. 18, 1954, p. 18; Murphy, 49 *Fortune* (June 1954), 246.
94. Quoted by Walter Millis, *New York Herald Tribune*, Mar. 18, 1954, p. 18.
95. Snyder, "New Look," p. 159.
96. 93 *Army-Navy-Air Force Journal* (Jan. 21, 1956), 630, 632; *New York Times*, Oct. 18, 1955, p. 1.
97. C. J. V. Murphy, "The New Air Situation," 52 *Fortune* (Sept. 1955), 221. See also Secretary Wilson's statements: *New York Times*, Oct. 7, 1953, p. 6, June 21, 1954, p. 1, May 25, 1955, pp. 1, 3; *Dept. of Defense Appropriations, 1954*, Hears./USS CA SC/83C1/1953, p. 9; *Dept. of Defense Appropriations, 1955*, Hears./HR CA SC/83C2/1954, p. 71.
98. See the Alsop reports, *New York Herald Tribune*, Sept. 19, 1955, p. 1, Oct. 11, 1957, p. 18, and also *New York Times*, Dec. 10, 1955, p. 5.
99. Quoted in Herbert S. Dinerstein, *War and the Soviet Union* (New York, 1959), pp. 80, 147; *New York Times*, July 19, 1956, p. 4.
100. On the Puerto Rico conference, see Secretary Wilson, *New York Times*, Jan. 13, 1956, p. 8, and President Eisenhower, *ibid.*, Oct. 31, 1957, p. 10; Secretary Wilson and Admiral Radford, *Dept. of Defense Appropri-*

ations, 1957; Amendments to the Budget, Hears./HR CA SC/84C2/1956, pp. 1–2, 13–14; *Dept. of Defense Appropriations, 1958,* Hears./USS CA SC/85C1/1957, p. 5; Gen. Maxwell D. Taylor, *The Uncertain Trumpet* (New York, 1960), pp. 36–38; C. J. V. Murphy, "Defense: The Revolution Gets Revolutionary," 53 *Fortune* (May 1956), 101–02.

101. *New York Times,* Oct. 13, 1956, p. 8; Murphy, "Eisenhower's Most Critical Defense Budget," 54 *Fortune* (Dec. 1956), 112–14, 246.

102. 94 *Army-Navy-Air Force Journal* (Feb. 9, 1957), 699.

103. *New York Times:* Aug. 18, 1957, p. 31; Sept. 29, 1957, p. 28. *New York Herald Tribune:* Sept. 20, 1957, p. 1; Oct. 6, 1957, Sec. 2, pp. 1, 10. 94 *Army-Navy-Air Force Journal* (Aug. 10, 1957), 1493. *Military Construction Approps. for 1958,* Hears./HR CA SC/85C1/1957, pp. 22–23.

104. *New York Times:* June 5, 1957, p. 17; June 14, 1957, p. 2; Sept. 29, 1957, p. 28. *New York Herald Tribune,* Sept. 20, 1957, p. 1. 94 *Army-Navy-Air Force Journal* (Aug. 10, 1957), 1520.

105. *New York Times,* July 5, 1958, p. 6.

106. *Ibid.:* Aug. 2, 1957, p. 2; Aug. 25, 1957, p. 44. C. J. V. Murphy, "America's Widening Military Margin," 56 *Fortune* (Aug. 1957), 218.

107. *New York Times,* Nov. 1, 1957, p. 8. See also *New York Times:* Oct. 10, 1957, p. 1; Oct. 11, 1957, p. 1; Oct. 14, 1957, p. 1, Oct. 21, 1957, pp. 1, 12.

108. *New York Herald Tribune,* Dec. 31, 1957, p. 7; Hanson W. Baldwin, *The Great Arms Race* (New York, 1958), p. 103.

109. "Air Force Industrial Production Readiness Policy," Department of Defense News Release No. 1226-55, Dec. 28, 1955, p. 1.

110. *Business Week:* Mar. 30, 1957, p. 43; Sept. 28, 1957, pp. 83–88.

111. *New York Times,* Jan. 20, 1957, p. E9.

112. 94 *Army-Navy-Air Force Journal* (Dec. 8, 1956), 440, (Dec. 15, 1956), 472; *New York Times,* Dec. 10, 1956, p. 17.

113. 94 *Army-Navy-Air Force Journal* (June 27, 1957), 1296, (Aug. 10, 1957), 1504, (Aug. 31, 1957), 1596; 95 *ibid.* (Sept. 14, 1957), p. 40; *Dept. of Defense Appropriations, 1958,* Hears./USS CA SC/85C1/1957, p. 83.

114. On the Radford plan, see page 1 of the *New York Times,* July 13, 14, 15, 17, 19, and Aug. 2, 1956, and Taylor, *Uncertain Trumpet,* pp. 39–43.

115. H. Rept. 2104/HR CA/84C2/1956, p. 40.

116. See the remarks of Senators Jackson and Russell, 102 *Cong. Record* (June 25, 1956), 10891, (June 26, 1956), 10973.

117. Secretary Wilson, *Dept. of Defense Appropriations, 1954,* Hears./ USS CA SC/83C1/1953, pp. 437–38; President Eisenhower, 92 *Army-Navy-Air Force Journal* (May 28, 1955), 1163.

118. For the salient portions of this address, see "How Much Is Enough?" 39 *Air Force* (Sept. 1956), 51–53. See also Quarles's statements: *Dept. of Defense Appropriations, 1957,* Hears./HR CA SC/84C2/1956, p. 830; *New York Times,* May 17, 1956, p. 15; *Study of Airpower,* Hears./

USS CAS, SC on the Air Force/84C2/1956, pp. 1545–46. See also Secretary Wilson, *New York Times*, Mar. 14, 1956, p. 18, *Dept. of Defense Appropriations, 1957*, Hears./USS CA SC/84C2/1956, p. 4, and President Eisenhower, *New York Times*, May 10, 1956, p. 16. Throughout the airpower debate, Administration supporters stressed the "absolute" character of nuclear airpower and Administration critics its "relative" character. See *Study of Airpower*, Hears./USS CAS, SC on the Air Force/84C2/1956, pp. 1, 28, 185, 219, 1683–85. On the significance of "absolute" and "relative" goals, see my "Arms Races: Prerequisites and Results," *Public Policy* (Yearbook of the Graduate School of Public Administration, Harvard University, 1958), VIII, 50–54.

119. For enlightening analyses of the issues involved in this controversy, see Henry A. Kissinger, *The Necessity for Choice: Prospects of American Foreign Policy* (New York, 1961), pp. 15–40, and Herman Kahn, *Thermonuclear War*, pp. 7–36.

120. See, e.g., *Dept. of Defense Appropriations, 1960*, Hears./HR CA SC/86C1/1959, Part 1, pp. 330, 506, 593–94.

121. Taylor, *Uncertain Trumpet*, pp. 26–27.

122. "Challenge and Response in U. S. Policy," 36 *Foreign Affairs* (Oct. 1957), 31. See also *New York Times*: Aug. 16, 1957, p. 7; Aug. 18, 1957, p. 1; Sept. 20, 1957, p. 12. S. Alsop, *New York Herald Tribune*, June 17, 1957, p. 14. Robert E. Osgood, *Limited War* (Chicago, 1957), p. 229.

123. The Gaither report was never made public. The description here is based on: Chalmers Roberts, *Washington Post and Times Herald*, Dec. 20, 1957, reprinted in 104 *Cong. Record* (Jan. 23, 1958), 358–59; S. Alsop, *New York Herald Tribune*, Nov. 25, 1957, p. 18 and Dec. 27, 1957, p. 10; A. T. Hadley, *New York Herald Tribune*, Dec. 22, 1957, p. 1; John W. Finney, *New York Times*, Dec. 21, 1957, p. 8; E. W. Kenworthy, *New York Times*, Dec. 29, 1957, p. 4E; and Morton H. Halperin's careful account, "The Gaither Committee and the Policy Process," 13 *World Politics* (Apr. 1961), 360–384. The Rockefeller study group recommendations apparently closely paralleled those of the Gaither Committee. See Rockefeller Brothers Fund, *International Security: The Military Aspect* (Garden City, N. Y., 1958). Four people who participated in the Gaither Committee work helped in the Rockefeller report. See also Klaus Knorr, "The Crisis in U. S. Defense," *The New Leader*, Section 2, Dec. 30, 1957.

124. Quoted by S. Alsop, *New York Herald Tribune*, Dec. 27, 1957, p. 10.

125. Halperin, 13 *World Politics*, 367.

126. William M. Holaday, *Inquiry Into Satellite and Missile Programs*, Hears./USS CAS SC on Preparedness/85C1/1957, p. 417.

127. Cf. Halperin, *ibid.*, n. 84.

128. *New York Times*, Dec. 21, 1957, p. 8; *New York Herald Tribune*, Dec. 31, 1957, p. 7.

III. STRATEGIC PROGRAMS AND POLITICAL PROCESS 457

129. Halperin, 13 *World Politics*, 373–74.
130. Chalmers Roberts, 104 *Cong. Record*, 858–59.
131. Raymond L. Garthoff, *Soviet Strategy in the Nuclear Age* (New York, 1958), pp. 12, 62.
132. *Ibid.*, pp. 63, 65.
133. Dinerstein, *War and the Soviet Union*, chap. 2.
134. Dinerstein, *War and the Soviet Union*, chap. 6, and Garthoff, *Soviet Strategy*, pp. 84–87.
135. Dinerstein, *War and the Soviet Union*, pp. 188 ff.; Garthoff, *Soviet Strategy*, pp. 72–75; Cyril E. Black and Frederick J. Yeager, "The USSR and NATO," in Knorr, ed., *NATO and American Security*, pp. 37 ff., 48–49.
136. *New York Times*, May 15, 1956, p. 8, May 16, 1956, p. 1.
137. Garthoff, *Soviet Strategy*, pp. 98–107.
138. Report to the Supreme Soviet, Embassy of the Union of Soviet Socialist Republics, Press Releases Nos. 16-22, Jan. 15–19, 1960. All subsequent quotations from Khrushchev's report are from this source. See also Maj. Gen. Nicolai A. Talensky, "On the Character of Modern War," 10 *International Affairs* (Oct. 1960), 23–27.
139. Garthoff, *Soviet Strategy*, p. 101 (italics omitted).
140. *New York Times*, Feb. 21, 1961, p. 7 (italics added).

III. STRATEGIC PROGRAMS AND THE POLITICAL PROCESS

1. *Organization of the Armed Services Committee*, Hears./HR CAS/83C1/1953, p. 2.
2. *The Federalist* (Modern Library ed.), No. 24, p. 148, No. 69, p. 448.
3. See, e.g., Howard White, *Executive Influence in Determining Military Policy in the United States* (Urbana, Ill., 1924), p. 44; Clarence A. Berdahl, *War Powers of the Executive in the United States* (Urbana, Ill., 1921), p. 101.
4. Gen. Maxwell D. Taylor, *The Uncertain Trumpet* (New York, 1960), pp. 81–82. I have adapted this discussion of the annual executive "legislation" from Taylor, *ibid.*, pp. 21–22, 80–87.
5. *Ibid.*, pp. 26–27, 29, 57–65; Paul H. Nitze, "The Need for a National Strategy," Address, Army War College, Carlisle Barracks, Pa., Aug. 27, 1958; Paul Y. Hammond, "NSC 68: Prologue to Rearmament," and Glenn H. Snyder, "The New Look," MSS to be published in Warner R. Schilling, Paul Y. Hammond, and Glenn H. Snyder, *Making National Security Policy: Three Case Studies* (New York, 1962).
6. Taylor, *Uncertain Trumpet*, p. 85.
7. *Ibid.*, pp. 22, 85–87; *Organizing for National Security*, Hears./USS GOC SC on National Policy Machinery/86C2/1960, p. 795.
8. See *Organizing for National Security: Selected Materials*, Cmte. Print/USS GOC SC on National Policy Machinery/86C2/1960, pp. 26–28.

Apparently, however, the annual "Basic National Security Policy" paper does not have a financial appendix. Taylor, *Uncertain Trumpet*, p. 82.

9. Roger Hilsman, "Congressional-Executive Relations and the Foreign Policy Consensus," 52 *American Political Science Review* (Sept. 1958), 725.

10. Lewis A. Dexter, "Congress and the Formation of Military Policy" (paper read at the American Association for the Advancement of Science, Dec. 31, 1958, Washington, D. C.), pp. 12–13; E. L. Katzenbach, Jr., "How Congress Strains at Gnats, Then Swallows Military Budgets," 11 *The Reporter* (July 20, 1954), 31–35.

11. Arthur F. Bentley, *The Process of Government* (Evanston, Ill., 1949), p. 359.

12. 103 *Cong. Record* (June 10, 1957), 8592. For the relevant statutes, see 60 Stat. 341 (1946), 62 Stat. 605 (1948), 64 Stat. 321, 408 (1950), 65 Stat. 88 (1951), 66 Stat. 282 (1952), 68 Stat. 27 (1954), 71 Stat. 208 (1957), 73 Stat. 13 (1959). See also Charles H. Donnelly, *United States Defense Policies in 1958*, H. Doc. 227/86C1/1959, pp. 72–73.

13. See, e.g., the actions of the House and Senate committees in the Bomarc-Nike dispute. *New York Times:* May 14, 1959, p. 15; May 24, 1959, p. 1. S. Rept. 434/86C1/1959, pp. 1–3.

14. The Army and Air Force Authorization Act of 1949, 64 Stat. 321, did authorize for the Air Force 24,000 aircraft or 225,000 airframe tons, whichever its Secretary deemed most in accordance with the purposes of the act. For perceptive analyses of the "Russell Amendment," Military Construction Authorization Act, 1959, 73 Stat. 302, I am much indebted to unpublished papers by Raymond H. Dawson, "Legislative Authorization of Weapons Programs: Congressional Intervention on Defense Policy," and Bernard K. Gordon, "The Military Budget: Congressional Phase."

15. Sen. Russell, *New York Times*, Mar. 15, 1953, p. 17; Sen. Chavez, "Influence of Congress on Military Strategy," 103 *Cong. Record* (Jan. 14, 1957), 598. See also *Unification and Strategy*, H. Doc. 600/81C2/1950, pp. 33–35, and Richard W. Hatch, *Notes on Congress and the National Interest: 1945–1951* (Massachusetts Institute of Technology, Center for International Studies, May, 1957), pp. 30–32.

16. 102 *Cong. Record* (Feb. 1, 1956), 1765.

17. *New York Times*, May 18, 1958, pp. 1, 26. On the lobbying activities of the Joint Committee in general, see Dorothy Fosdick, "Legislative Watchdog of the Atom," *New York Times Magazine*, June 26, 1955, pp. 25 ff.; Sen. H. M. Jackson, "Congress and the Atom," 290 *Annals of the American Academy of Political and Social Science* (Nov. 1953), 76–81; Sen. C. P. Anderson and J. T. Ramey, "Congress and Research: Experience in Atomic Research and Development," 327 *ibid.* (Jan. 1960), 85–94; Morgan Thomas, *Atomic Energy and Congress* (Ann Arbor, Mich., 1956), *passim;* Thomas E. Murray, *Nuclear Policy for War and Peace* (Cleveland, 1960), pp. 200–1; James T. Ramey, "The Joint Congressional

III. STRATEGIC PROGRAMS AND POLITICAL PROCESS 459

Committee on Atomic Energy and the Civilian Control of Atomic Energy," pp. 12–14, and Frank Smallwood, "The Joint Committee on Atomic Energy: Congressional 'Watchdog' of the Atom?", pp. 7–8, papers presented at the Annual Meeting, American Political Science Association, Sept. 8–10, 1960, New York, N. Y.

18. Secy. Wilson, 44 *U. S. News & World Report* (Jan. 10, 1958), 68; Pres. Eisenhower, letter to Rep. Price, Mar. 5, 1958, *New York Times*, Mar. 7, 1958, p. 9.

19. Anthony Leviero, *New York Times*, June 23, 1956, p. 8. See also: 102 *Cong. Record* (May 9, 1956), 7804–5, 7824–25; *Study of Airpower*, Hears./USS CAS SC on the Air Force /84C2/1956, pp. 1557–58, 1587–88.

20. 104 *Cong. Record* (Jan. 23, 1958), 860–63; *Inquiry Into Satellite and Missile Programs*, Hears./USS CAS Preparedness Investigating SC/85C1/1957, pp. 1003–4.

21. *New York Herald Tribune*, May 11, 1956, p. 1; *New York Times*: May 10, 1956, p. 1; June 29, 1956, p. 8; *Study of Airpower*, Hears./USS CAS SC on the Air Force/84C2/1956, p. 1715.

22. *Dept. of Defense Appropriations, 1957*, Hears./HR CA SC/84C2/1956, p. 126.

23. 105 *Cong. Record* (May 14, 1959), 8152–53.

24. Walter Millis, ed., *The Forrestal Diaries* (New York, 1951), p. 115.

25. *The Budget of the United States Government for the Fiscal Year Ending June 30, 1960*, p. M34.

26. *New York Times*, May 7, 1959, p. 6.

27. See *New York Times*, July 14, 1956, p. 34; 104 *Cong. Record* (June 4, 1958), 10180–90.

28. See 104 *Cong. Record* (July 21, 1958), 14487–94.

29. H. Rept. 2104/84C2/1956, p. 34.

30. See Sen. Chavez, 103 *Cong. Record* (Jan. 14, 1957), 599; Sen. Stennis, 104 *ibid.* (Feb. 5, 1958), 1735; Sen. Saltonstall, *Study of Airpower*, Hears./USS CAS SC on the Air Force/84C2/1956, p. 1803; Reps. Kilday and Mahon, *New York Times*, Feb. 6, 1955, p. 30; *New York Herald Tribune*, Aug. 16, 1960, p. 7; Rep. McCormack, 105 *Cong. Record* (Sept. 14, 1959), 19971. See also Martha Derthick, "Militia Lobby in the Missile Age: The Political Evolution of the National Guard," in Samuel P. Huntington, ed., *Changing Patterns of Military Politics* (New York, 1962).

31. See Samuel P. Huntington, *The Soldier and the State* (Cambridge, Mass., 1957), pp. 423 ff.

32. For valuable analyses of consensus building in foreign policy, see Hilsman, 52 *Amer. Pol. Sci. Review* (Sept. 1958), 725–44, and "The Foreign Policy Consensus: An Interim Research Report," 3 *Journal of Conflict Resolution* (Dec. 1959), 361–82.

33. On vertical bargaining, see Herbert A. Simon, "Notes on the Observation and Measurement of Political Power," *Models of Man: Social and Rational* (New York, 1957), pp. 66–68; Robert A. Dahl and Charles

E. Lindblom, *Politics, Economics, and Welfare* (New York, 1953), pp. 341–44; N. E. Long, "Public Policy and Administration: The Goals of Rationality and Responsibility," 14 *Public Administration Review* (Winter, 1954), 22–31; Richard E. Neustadt, *Presidential Power: The Politics of Leadership* (New York, 1960), chap. 3; Richard F. Fenno, *The President's Cabinet* (Cambridge, 1959), chap. 6.

34. See Morris Janowitz, *The Professional Soldier* (Glencoe, Ill., 1960), esp. chap. 3, and General Maxwell D. Taylor, "Budgeting for Deterrence," Address, National Security Industrial Association, New York, N. Y., Sept. 25, 1957: "Not only are there controls above but controls below. An effective military organization is not run arbitrarily by fiat. There is internal public opinion to be considered just as there is in any civilian enterprise. The Chief of Staff is watched very closely by his subordinates to see what kind of leadership he is giving and what results he is achieving in administering his important trust."

35. D. Norton-Taylor, "The Wilson Pentagon," 50 *Fortune* (Dec. 1954), 94; Gen. M. B. Ridgway, "My Battles in War and Peace," 228 *Sat. Evening Post* (Jan. 21, 1956), 46.

36. This account of the carrier confusion is taken from Paul Y. Hammond, "Super-Carriers and B-36 Bombers: Appropriations, Strategy, and Politics" (Twentieth Century Fund Project on Civil-Military Relations; mimeo.), pp. 17–18, 29–31, 139–41.

37. *The National Defense Program: Unification and Strategy*, Hears./HR CAS/81C1/1949, p. 567.

38. This incident comes from Glenn H. Snyder, "The New Look," pp. 102–7.

39. Lt. Gen. James M. Gavin, *War and Peace in the Space Age* (New York, 1958), pp. 156–57.

40. 96 *Army-Navy-Air Force Journal* (Feb. 7, 1959), 669. See also Taylor, *Uncertain Trumpet*, pp. 72–74.

41. See, e.g., Admiral Denfeld, "The Only Carrier the Air Force Ever Sunk," 125 *Collier's* (Mar. 25, 1950), 47, and Gen. Taylor, 93 *Army-Navy-Air Force Journal* (Oct. 29, 1955), 268.

42. Charles L. Bartlett, quoted by Arthur Krock, *New York Times*, Feb. 21, 1961, p. 34.

43. See, e.g., on manpower and reserve policy: Charles D. Story, "The Formulation of Army Reserve Forces Policy: Its Setting Amidst Pressure Group Activity" (Ph.D. dissertation, Oklahoma, 1958), p. 35; *Universal Military Training*, Hears./USS CAS/81C2/1950, pp. 22, 35; *Universal Military Training and Service Act of 1951*, Hears./USS CAS Preparedness SC/82C1/1951, pp. 22, 31, 38–39, 42–44; *Universal Military Training and Service Act*, S. Rept. 117/USS CAS/82C1/1951, p. 59; Gen. O. N. Bradley, "Toward a Long-Range Manpower Policy," 6 *Army Information Digest* (Mar. 1951), 14; *Reserve Components*, Hears./HR CAS SC on Civilian

III. STRATEGIC PROGRAMS AND POLITICAL PROCESS 461

Components/82C1/1951, pp. 188–91, 212–13, 327, 372–74. The 1955 Reserve Forces Act was prepared largely by ad hoc groups working under the Assistant Secretary of Defense (Manpower, Personnel, and Reserves). The NSC did, however, discuss this legislation several times. Timothy Stanley, *American Defense and National Security* (Washington, 1956), p. 124; *National Reserve Plan*, Hears./HR CAS SC No. 1/84C1/1955, pp. 1408, 1797–98. On NSC and JCS roles in the defense budget process, see: William R. Kintner and associates, *Forging a New Sword* (New York, 1958), pp. 30–31, 65, 77, 128; F. A. Lindsay, S. Livermore, C. E. Mills, T. F. Walkowicz, "Defense Procurement: The Vital Roles of the National Security Council and the Joint Chiefs of Staff" (Paper for Task Force on Procurement, Commission on Organization, 1955), p. A-59; Howard H. Cork et al., "Translation of Logistic Programs Into Procurement Requirements" (Paper for Task Force on Procurement, Commission on Organization, 1955), pp. B-13 ff.; Taylor, *Uncertain Trumpet*, pp. 69–70, 72, 92; *Study of Airpower*, Hears./USS CAS SC on the Air Force/84C2/1956, pp. 1447–49, 1468, 1496 ff.; *Organizing for National Security*, Hears./USS GOC SC on National Policy Machinery/86C2/1960, p. 795; *Military Posture Briefing*, Hears./HR CAS/86C1/1959, p. 918.

44. Taylor, *Uncertain Trumpet*, pp. 91, 108.

45. Henry L. Stimson and McGeorge Bundy, *On Active Service in Peace and War* (New York, 1947), p. 515.

46. See Thomas C. Schelling, *The Strategy of Conflict* (Cambridge, Mass., 1960), chap. 4.

47. *Satellite and Missile Programs*, Hears./USS CAS Preparedness Investigating SC/85C2/1958, p. 1520.

48. Taylor, *Uncertain Trumpet*, p. 107.

49. Snyder, "New Look," p. 40; C. J. V. Murphy, "The New Air Situation," 52 *Fortune* (Sept. 1955), 86.

50. Stimson and Bundy, *Active Service*, pp. 515–16; Taylor, *Uncertain Trumpet*, p. 94; Lindsay et al., "Defense Procurement," p. A-72.

51. *New York Times:* Sept. 18, 1951, p. 14; Sept. 25, 1951, p. 16; Oct. 3, 1951, p. 1.

52. *Nominations: Gen. L. L. Lemnitzer, Chairman, JCS, and Gen. G. H. Decker, Army Chief of Staff*, Hears./USS CAS/86C2/1960, p. 8; 97 *Army-Navy-Air Force Journal* (Jan. 16, 1960), 538; *New York Times*, Jan. 7, 1960, pp. 1, 6; *Organizing for National Security*, Hears./USS GOC SC on National Policy Machinery/86C2/1960, pp. 33, 730, 733.

53. Robert Cutler, *Organizing for National Security*, Hears./USS GOC SC on National Policy Machinery/86C2/1960, p. 582.

54. Virtually no one else has agreed with Vannevar Bush's repeated contentions that the Chiefs have failed to agree on war plans. See *Satellite and Missile Programs*, Hears./USS CAS Preparedness Investigating SC/85C2/1958, pp. 61, 479–80, 1519–20, 1524, 1527–28; Hanson W. Bald-

win, *The Great Arms Race* (New York, 1958), p. 84; Lindsay et al., "Defense Procurement," pp. A-47, A-71; Cork et al., "Translation of Logistic Programs," pp. B-5 ff.; Kintner et al., *Forging a New Sword*, pp. 128–29.

55. Anthony Leviero, "The Paradox That Is Admiral Radford," *New York Times Magazine*, Aug. 5, 1956, p. 50.

56. Denfeld, 125 *Collier's* (Mar. 25, 1950), 46–47.

57. Taylor, *Uncertain Trumpet*, p. 91; Denfeld, 125 *Collier's* (Mar. 25, 1950), 33; *Dept. of Defense Appropriations, 1951*, Hears./HR CA SC/81C2/1950, pp. 80–81, 1743; 99 *Cong. Record* (June 25, 1953), 7237–45; Snyder, "New Look," p. 53.

58. Taylor, *Uncertain Trumpet*, p. 91.

59. *Ibid.*, p. 94; Admiral Radford, *Study of Airpower*, Hears./USS CAS SC on the Air Force/84C2/1956, p. 1451.

60. *Dept. of Armed Forces, Dept. of Military Security*, Hears. on S. 84/USS CMA/79C1/1945, p. 50; Lindsay et al., "Defense Procurement," p. A-47.

61. Taylor, *Uncertain Trumpet*, p. 94.

62. H. Rept. 408/86C1/1959, p. 11; H. Doc. 600/81C2/1950, pp. 47–49; *Dept. of Defense Appropriations, 1958*, Hears./USS CAS SC/85C1/1957, pp. 348–49; *Study of Airpower*, Hears./USS CAS SC on the Air Force/84C2/1956, pp. 1495 ff.

63. *Organizing for National Security: The National Security Council*, Cmte. Print/USS GOC SC on National Policy Machinery/86C2/1960, pp. 3–4.

64. *Ibid.*, p. 3; V. Bush, "Planning," Address, Mayo Clinic, Rochester, Minn., Sept. 26, 1952; *New York Times*, Jan. 10, 1953, p. 4; Secy. of Defense Robert A. Lovett, Letter to the President, Nov. 18, 1952; Lindsay et al., "Defense Procurement," p. A-54.

65. Hilsman, 3 *Journal of Conflict Resolution* (Dec. 1959), 363.

66. Hammond, "Super-Carriers and B-36 Bombers," pp. 34–35.

67. V. Bush, *New York Times*, May 14, 1957, p. 46; *New York Times*, May 27, 1956, Sec. 2, p. 1.

68. Rep. Daniel J. Flood, 103 *Cong. Record* (May 27, 1957), 7733.

69. Taylor, *Uncertain Trumpet*, pp. 82–83; *National Security Council*, Cmte. Print./USS GOC SC on National Policy Machinery/86C2/1960, pp. 4–6; Kintner, *Forging a New Sword*, p. 52; S. Alsop, *New York Herald Tribune*, Mar. 30, 1956, p. 10; Lindsay et al., "Defense Procurement," p. A-43; Hilsman, 3 *Jour. of Conflict Resolution* (Dec. 1959), 378.

70. Taylor, *Uncertain Trumpet*, p. 94.

71. *New York Times*, Aug. 13, 1951, p. 10.

72. E. R. May, "The Development of Political-Military Consultation in the United States," 70 *Political Science Quarterly* (June 1955), 176–77.

73. Taylor, *Uncertain Trumpet*, p. 87; Cork et al., "Translation of Logistic Programs," pp. B-9 ff.

74. Snyder, "New Look," pp. 80–81, 97.

III. STRATEGIC PROGRAMS AND POLITICAL PROCESS

75. Many papers on the policy process have been brought together in *Organizing for National Security: Selected Materials,* Cmte. Print/USS GOC SC on National Policy Machinery/86C2/1960. For criticisms see particularly the comments of Messrs. Rostow, Kintner, Kissinger, Morgenthau, and Senator Jackson.
76. Walter Bagehot, *The English Constitution* (London, 1949), p. 202.
77. Henry A. Kissinger, *Nuclear Weapons and Foreign Policy* (New York, 1957), p. 407.
78. Hans J. Morgenthau, "Can We Entrust Defense to a Committee?" *New York Times Magazine,* June 7, 1959, in *Selected Materials,* Cmte. Print/USS GOC SC on National Policy Machinery/86C2/1960, p. 162.
79. A. L. Moffat, "The Legislative Process," 24 *Cornell Law Quarterly* (1939), 224, quoted in George Galloway, *The Legislative Process in Congress* (New York, 1955), p. 4.
80. Vice Admiral H. E. Orem, "Shall We Junk the Joint Chiefs of Staff?" 84 *U. S. Naval Institute Proceedings* (Feb. 1958), 57.
81. Dahl and Lindblom, *Politics, Economics, and Welfare,* chap. 13.
82. Woodrow Wilson, *Congressional Government* (Boston, 1885), p. 318.
83. See G. A. Almond, "Public Opinion and National Security Policy," 20 *Public Opinion Quarterly* (Summer 1956), 372.
84. See G. M. Lyons, "The New Civil Military Relations," 55 *American Political Science Review* (Mar. 1961), 59–61; S. P. Huntington, "Recent Writing in Military Politics: Foci and Corpora," to be published in Huntington, ed., *Changing Patterns of Military Politics;* G. M. Lyons and Louis Morton, "School for Strategy," 17 *Bulletin of the Atomic Scientists* (Mar. 1961), 103–6; "Defense Spending Lobby," 19 *Congressional Quarterly* (Mar. 24, 1961), 463–478; Henry A. Kissinger, *The Necessity for Choice* (New York, 1961), chap. 8.
85. Hilsman, 52 *Amer. Pol. Science Review* (Sept. 1958), 736–37.
86. See Arthur N. Holcombe, *Our More Perfect Union* (Cambridge, Mass., 1950), pp. 152–55; David B. Truman, *The Congressional Party: A Case Study* (New York, 1959), chaps. 3, 5, 7.
87. See, in general, H. Bradford Westerfield, *Foreign Policy and Party Politics: Pearl Harbor to Korea* (New Haven, 1955), *passim;* Cecil V. Crabb, *Bipartisan Foreign Policy: Myth or Reality* (Evanston, Ill., 1957), chaps. 7, 8.
88. See Huntington, *Soldier and State,* pp. 423–27.
89. Robert Cutler, "The Seamless Web," 57 *Harvard Alumni Bulletin* (June 4, 1955), 665.
90. *New York Times,* Oct. 30, 1949, quoted in Stephen K. Bailey and Howard D. Samuel, *Congress at Work* (New York, 1952), p. 381.
91. Millis, *The Forrestal Diaries,* p. 444.
92. See, e.g., Rep. Plumley's remarks, 95 *Cong. Record* (Apr. 12, 1949), 4433.

93. *New York Herald Tribune*, Mar. 30, 1956, p. 10.
94. *New York Times*, Dec. 8, 1956, p. 1; Harry S. Truman, *Memoirs* (Garden City, N. Y., 1956), II, 291–92.
95. See Samuel Lubell, "Sputnik and American Public Opinion," 1 *Columbia University Forum* (Winter 1957), 15–21; *New York Times:* Apr. 10, 1958, p. 1; Apr. 18, 1958, pp. 1, 8; May 29, 1958, p. 1; May 31, 1958, p. 1; June 7, 1958, p. 9; June 12, 1958, p. 17.
96. See E. L. Katzenbach, Jr., "Should Our Military Leaders Speak Up?" *New York Times Magazine*, Apr. 15, 1956, pp. 17 ff.; Huntington, *Soldier and State*, pp. 412–18.
97. *Military Establishment Appropriation Bill, 1948*, Hears./HR CA SC/80C1/1947, p. 631; Gen. J. L. Collins, "The War Department Spreads the News," 27 *Military Review* (Sept. 1947), 17–18; Gavin, *War and Peace in the Space Age*, p. 171; *New York Times*, Jan. 15, 1959, p. 19.
98. See Herman Kahn, *On Thermonuclear War* (Princeton, 1960), pp. 581–82.
99. Taylor, *Uncertain Trumpet*, p. 110.
100. Stimson and Bundy, *On Active Service in Peace and War*, p. 516.
101. Cutler, 57 *Harvard Alumni Bulletin* (June 4, 1955), 684.

IV. THE GREAT EQUATION

1. Quoted in C. J. V. Murphy, "The Eisenhower Shift," 53 *Fortune* (Jan. 1956), 87. My definition of the components of the "Great Equation" parallels the three choices suggested by W. W. Rostow, *The Stages of Economic Growth* (Cambridge, 1960), pp. 73 ff. See also his analysis in *The United States in the World Arena* (New York, 1960), Books 5 and 6.
2. Reps. Colmer and Madden, 104 *Cong. Record* (Jan. 15, 1958), 479–80.
3. See, e.g., Gen. J. L. Collins, *Dept. of Defense Appropriations, 1951*, Hears./HR CA SC/81C2/1950, pp. 205 ff.; Rep. Mahon, 95 *Cong. Record* (Apr. 12, 1949), 4427, quoted in Warner R. Schilling, "The Fiscal Fifty Military Budget," MS, p. 17, to be published in Warner R. Schilling, Paul Y. Hammond, Glenn H. Snyder, *Making National Security Policy: Three Case Studies* (New York, 1962).
4. See Schilling, "Fiscal Fifty," p. 34 for Truman's concern that it be made clear the American military effort was not related to a desire for war; D. Norton-Taylor, "The Wilson Pentagon," 50 *Fortune* (Dec. 1954), 95; Gen. Omar Bradley, "This Way Lies Peace," 222 *Saturday Evening Post* (Oct. 15, 1949), 33, 168.
5. Murphy, "The Eisenhower Shift," 53 *Fortune* (Jan. 1956), 87.
6. See *Organizing for National Security*, Hears./USS GOC SC on National Policy Machinery/86C2/1960, pp. 60–61.
7. "Russia's Growing Strength Could Be a Weakness," 40 *U. S. News and World Report* (May 11, 1956), 124 ff.

8. Schilling, "Fiscal Fifty," p. 17.

9. "The Nature and Feasibility of War and Deterrence," 3 *Stanford Research Institute Journal* (Oct. 1959), 136.

10. See Herbert S. Dinerstein, *War and the Soviet Union* (New York, 1959), pp. 92–93.

11. Committee for Economic Development, Research and Policy Committee, *The Budget and Economic Growth* (1959), p. 32.

12. Edwin L. Dale, Jr., *Conservatives in Power* (Garden City, N. Y., 1960), pp. 72–74.

13. Rockefeller Brothers Fund, Special Studies Project, *The Challenge to America: Its Economic and Social Aspects* (Garden City, N. Y., 1958), pp. 66–69; John K. Galbraith, *The Affluent Society* (Boston, 1958), *passim*.

14. Robert J. Donovan, *Eisenhower: The Inside Story* (New York, 1956), pp. 57–59.

15. *New York Times:* Nov. 14, 1957, p. 14; Dec. 2, 1957, p. 1; Jan. 15, 1958, p. 1; Jan. 19, 1958, p. 9E. 104 *Cong. Record* (Jan. 15, 1958), 480–81.

16. "The Sham Battle over 'Spending,'" 20 *The Reporter* (Jan. 8, 1959), 17.

17. William L. Cary, "Pressure Groups and the Increasing Erosion of the Revenue Laws," in U. S. Congress, Joint Economic Committee, *Federal Tax Policy for Economic Growth and Stability: Papers Submitted by Panelists* (84C1/1955), pp. 272–74. See also: in the same volume, Walter J. Blum, "The Effects of Special Provisions in the Income Tax on Taxpayer Morale," and Randolph E. Paul, "Erosion of the Tax Base and Rate Structure"; S. S. Surrey, "The Congress and the Tax Lobbyist—How Special Tax Provisions Get Enacted," 70 *Harvard Law Review* (May 1957), 1145–82; W. L. Cary, "Pressure Groups and the Revenue Code: A Requiem in Honor of the Departing Uniformity of the Tax Laws," 68 *ibid.* (Mar. 1955), 745–80; W. L. Cary, "Erosion of the Tax Laws," 33 *Harvard Business Review* (Sept.–Oct. 1955), 103–11; W. W. Heller, "Practical Limitations on the Federal Net Income Tax," 7 *Journal of Finance* (May 1952), 185–202.

18. A 100 percent increase in prices reportedly produces a 150 percent increase in personal income tax revenues. Otto Eckstein, *Trends in Public Expenditures In the Next Decade* (Committee for Economic Development, 1959), p. 8.

19. Walter Millis, ed., *The Forrestal Diaries* (New York, 1951), p. 536; Harry S. Truman, *Memoirs* (Garden City, N. Y., 1956), II, 37–38.

20. Murphy, 53 *Fortune* (Jan. 1956), 86–87; Arthur Krock, *New York Times*, July 23, 1959, p. 26.

21. *New York Times,* June 29, 1959, p. 16; and for typical Presidential statements: *ibid.*, Apr. 24, 1959, p. 1; May 14, 1959, p. 22.

22. See David B. Truman, *The Governmental Process* (New York, 1950), *passim*, but esp. pp. 265–70, 437 ff.

23. See Millis, *Forrestal Diaries*, pp. 501–2, 508–11.

24. Senator Henry M. Jackson, "Organizing for Survival," 38 *Foreign Affairs* (Apr. 1960), 451.

25. C. E. Silberman and S. S. Parker, "The Economic Impact of Defense," 57 *Fortune* (June 1958), 103.

26. *Military Posture Briefing*, Hears./HR CAS/86C1/1959, p. 907.

27. Truman, *Memoirs*, II, 34, 36–37.

28. *Ibid.*, p. 34.

29. President Eisenhower used this term to describe the views of General Ridgway in 1955 and Gen. Power, SAC commander, in 1960. *New York Times:* Feb. 3, 1955, p. 1; Feb. 4, 1960, p. 12.

30. Cf. James R. Schlesinger, *The Political Economy of National Security* (New York, 1960), pp. 116–17.

31. This name was suggested by Glenn H. Snyder. See his "The New Look," MS, p. 79, to be published in Schilling, Hammond, and Snyder, *Making National Security Policy*. See also Robert C. Sprague, *Organizing for National Security,* Hears./USS GOC SC on National Policy Machinery/86C2/1960, p. 51.

32. Millis, *Forrestal Diaries*, p. 162.

33. Paul Y. Hammond, "NSC 68: Prologue to Rearmament," MS, pp. 68–69, to be published in Schilling, Hammond, and Snyder, *Making National Security Policy*.

34. *Dept. of Defense Appropriations, 1955,* Hears./USS CA SC/83C2/1954, p. 83; Snyder, "New Look," p. 79.

35. C. J. V. Murphy, "Eisenhower's Most Critical Defense Budget," 54 *Fortune* (Dec. 1956), 114.

36. See *Major Defense Matters,* Hears./USS CAS Preparedness Investigating SC/86C1/1959, pp. 209–352; E. L. Katzenbach, "Bubud's Defense Policy," 22 *The Reporter* (June 23, 1960), 25–30; Capt. D. G. Gumz, "The Bureau of the Budget and Defense Fiscal Policy," 85 *U. S. Naval Institute Proceedings* (Apr. 1959), 80–89.

37. These distinctions are drawn by Glenn Snyder, "New Look," pp. 64–66, 172–74.

38. *First Deficiency Appropriation Bill, 1947,* Hears./HR CA SC/80C1/1947, pp. 303–5; Millis, *Forrestal Diaries,* p. 437.

39. Snyder, "New Look," p. 98.

40. *Ibid.*, p. 48; "Assumptions and Policies for Preparation of 1956 Budget," July 23, 1954, *Study of Airpower,* Hears./USS CAS SC on the Air Force/84C2/1956, p. 1651; *New York Times,* Dec. 3, 1955, p. 1; Secretary McElroy, *Inquiry Into Satellite and Missile Programs,* Hears./USS CAS Preparedness Investigating SC/85C1/1957, p. 228.

41. See *Dept. of Defense (and related independent agencies) Appropriations, 1953,* Hears./HR CA SC/82C2/1952, p. 143; Snyder, "New Look," p. 43; *Dept. of Defense Appropriations, 1960,* Hears./HR CA SC/86C1/1959, pp. 74–75, 79–80, 128–29.

IV. THE GREAT EQUATION

42. C. J. V. Murphy, "Defense: The Converging Decisions," 58 *Fortune* (Oct. 1958), 120.

43. Howard H. Cork et al., "Translation of Logistic Programs Into Procurement Requirements" (Paper for Task Force on Procurement, Commission on Organization, 1955), pp. B-39–40.

44. Snyder, "New Look," pp. 99–100.

45. 91 *Army-Navy-Air Force Journal* (Jan. 23, 1954), 624.

46. *New York Times:* Dec. 21, 1954, p. 1; Jan. 6, 1955, pp. 1, 14.

47. *Ibid.*, Nov. 29, 1956, p. 1; *New York Herald Tribune*, Dec. 31, 1957, pp. 1, 7; 44 *U. S. News & World Report* (Jan. 10, 1958), 67; 94 *Army-Navy-Air Force Journal* (Jan. 5, 1957), 556; C. J. V. Murphy, "The Budget—and Eisenhower," 56 *Fortune* (July 1957), 228.

48. *Washington Post & Times Herald*, Dec. 19, 1958, p. A2; *New York Times*, Nov. 26, 1959, p. 14.

49. Millis, *Forrestal Diaries*, p. 499.

50. See Samuel P. Huntington, *The Soldier and the State* (Cambridge, Mass., 1957), pp. 80 ff.

51. For a comprehensive analysis, see Snyder, "New Look," pp. 172 ff.

52. *Major Defense Matters*, Hears./USS CAS Preparedness Investigating SC/86C1/1959, pp. 112–14; Jack Raymond, *New York Times*, Jan. 10, 1959, pp. 1, 3; Gen. Maxwell D. Taylor, *The Uncertain Trumpet* (New York, 1960), pp. 70–72.

53. *Military Establishment Appropriation Bill, 1948*, Hears./HR CA SC/80C1/1947, pp. 172, 191–93; *First Deficiency Appropriation, 1947*, Hears./HR CA SC/80C1/1947, pp. 302–3; *Annual Report of the Secretary of the Navy for Fiscal Year 1947*, p. 63.

54. Paul Y. Hammond, "Super-Carriers and B-36 Bombers: Appropriations, Strategy, and Politics" (Twentieth Century Fund Project on Civil-Military Relations; mimeo.), pp. 76–77, 84, 92, 102, 169–70.

55. See 92 *Army-Navy-Air Force Journal* (Sept. 18, 1954), 58, 59, 66, 68.

56. *National Defense Program: Unification and Strategy*, Hears./HR CAS/81C1/1949, pp. 307, 627.

57. *New York Times*, July 13, 1957, p. 18.

58. See Rep. Cannon's summary of this story, 103 *Cong. Record* (Aug. 30, 1957), 16890–97, and Stewart Alsop, *New York Herald Tribune*, July 22, 1957, p. 14.

59. *Briefing on National Defense*, Hears./HR CAS/84C1/1955, pp. 311–12. I have been greatly aided on this point by George H. Shapiro's unpublished study, "Carl Vinson and Defense Legislation in 1955" (Harvard, May 21, 1957).

60. Murphy, 56 *Fortune* (July 1957), 99.

61. See Richard E. Neustadt, *Presidential Power: The Politics of Leadership* (New York, 1960), chap. 2.

62. Walter Lippmann, *The Public Philosophy* (Boston, 1955), pp. 19–20.

63. Roper Commercial Survey 24, May 1946, Roper Public Opinion Research Center, Williams College, Williamstown, Mass. Unless otherwise indicated, the polling data I have used come from the Roper Center. I am grateful to the Center and to its director, Professor Philip K. Hastings, for making available to me their survey data and for doing the tabulations and analyses which I requested.

64. Gallup Survey 391K&T, Feb. 26, 1947.
65. Gallup Survey 451K, Jan. 6, 1950.
66. Gallup Survey 453K, Feb. 24, 1950.
67. Gallup Survey 454K, Mar. 24, 1950.
68. Gallup Survey 459, July 28, 1950.
69. Gallup Surveys 467, Nov. 10, 1950, and 468K, Dec. 1, 1950.
70. Gallup Survey 508K, Nov. 12, 1952.
71. Gallup Survey 477, July 6, 1951.
72. Gallup Survey 514K, April 1953; Snyder, "New Look," pp. 46–47.
73. Gallup Survey 519K, August 1953.
74. Gallup Survey 553K, September 1955.
75. Three quotes, respectively, are from: *New York Herald Tribune,* Dec. 31, 1957, pp. 1, 7; *Ibid.,* Sept. 20, 1957, p. 1; 94 *Army-Navy-Air Force Journal* (Aug. 10, 1957), 28.
76. Gallup Survey 579K, February 1957.
77. Gallup Survey 583K, May 1957.
78. See *New York Herald Tribune,* Jan. 25, 1956, p. 11.
79. Gallup Survey 517K, July 1953.
80. Samuel Lubell, "Sputnik and American Public Opinion," 1 *Columbia University Forum* (Winter 1957), 18–19.
81. *New York Herald Tribune,* Apr. 10, 1960, p. 23.
82. See Lewis A. Dexter, "Congress and the Formation of Military Policy" (paper read at American Association for the Advancement of Science, Dec. 31, 1958, Washington, D. C.), p. 5; Anthony Leviero, *New York Times,* July 8, 1956, p. E3.
83. Gallup Survey 583K, May 1957.
84. Gallup Survey 468K, Dec. 1, 1950.
85. Gabriel A. Almond, "Public Opinion and the Development of Space Technology," in *International Political Implications of Activities in Outer Space: A Report of a Conference,* October 22–23, 1959, Joseph M. Goldsen, Chairman (RAND Corporation, Report R-362-RC, May 5, 1960), p. 128.
86. *New York Herald Tribune,* Apr. 13, 1960, p. 11.
87. See Gallup Surveys: 82, May 21, 1937; 101, Oct. 30, 1937; 133, Oct. 6, 1938; 139, Nov. 22, 1938; 143, Jan. 1939; 145, Jan. 1939, and Nancy Boardman Eddy, *Public Opinion and United States Foreign Policy, 1937–1956* (Massachusetts Institute of Technology, Center for International Studies, American Project, Working Paper I; mimeo.), pp. 28–32.

88. Gabriel Almond, *The American People and Foreign Policy* (New York, 1950), pp. 202–3, 206–8. It should also be noted that several foreign policies in Almond's typology—pacifism, radical appeasement, and, to some extent, internationalism—implied opposition to strong military forces. *Ibid.*, chap. 9, *passim*.

89. Edward A. Shils, *The Torment of Secrecy* (Glencoe, Ill., 1956), chap. 4.

90. Robert A. Dahl, *Congress and Foreign Policy* (New York, 1950), p. 84, citing *Science News Letter*, Nov. 11, 1949, p. 317.

91. Cornell University, *Public Reaction to the Atomic Bomb and World Affairs: A Nation-wide Survey of Attitudes and Information* (Ithaca, March 1947; mimeo.), Part I, Table 3 in Appendix C.

92. *Ibid.*, p. 13.

93. Gallup Surveys: 453, Feb. 1950; 508, Nov. 1952; 579, Feb. 1957.

94. AIPO Release, March 30, 1958. The question was: "In general how do you feel about foreign aid—are you for it or against it?" About one-third of each information group was against it.

95. For analysis of the extent to which congressmen select and shape the environmental pressures surrounding them, see Lewis A. Dexter, *Congressmen and the People They Listen To* (Communications Program Center for International Studies, Massachusetts Institute of Technology, Cambridge, Mass., 1955; mimeo.), chaps. 4–6.

96. Rep. Arends, 103 *Cong. Record* (May 28, 1957), 7899; Reps. Mahon and Scott, *ibid.* (May 24, 1957), 7607–8; (May 28, 1957), 7907; *Military Posture Briefing*, Hears./HR CAS/86C1/1959, pp. 845–46, 864, 905–06.

97. 102 *Cong. Record* (June 25, 1946), 10880. See also the results of Rep. Corbett's poll of his constituents, 104 *Cong. Record* (Aug. 5, 1958), 16301, and Sen. Richard L. Neuberger, "Are the People Ahead of Their Leaders?" *New York Times Magazine*, Aug. 23, 1959, pp. 13 ff.

98. See Bernard C. Cohen, *The Political Process and Foreign Policy* (Princeton, 1957), p. 4; R. Hilsman, "Congressional-Executive Relations and the Foreign Policy Consensus," 52 *Amer. Political Science Review* (Sept. 1958), 740.

99. For an eloquent statement by a leading critic, see Hans J. Morgenthau, *Dilemmas of Politics* (Chicago, 1958), p. 333.

100. George L. Grassmuck, *Sectional Biases in Congress on Foreign Policy* (Baltimore, 1951), pp. 32–33, 134–39; Julius Turner, *Party and Constituency: Pressures on Congress* (Baltimore, 1951), pp. 56–58, 70.

101. See Samuel Lubell, *Revolt of the Moderates* (New York, 1956), pp. 99–100; M. E. Jewell, "Evaluating the Decline of Southern Internationalism through Senatorial Roll Call Votes," 21 *Journal of Politics* (Nov. 1959), 624–46; H. Field Haviland, Jr., "Foreign Aid and the Policy Process: 1957," 52 *American Political Science Review* (Sept. 1958), 719–20;

H. Douglas Price, "Are Southern Democrats Different? An Application of Scale Analysis to Senate Voting Patterns" (Unpublished manuscript; mimeo.), pp. 16–18.

102. The definitions of "sharp" and "moderate" cleavage are from Turner, *Party and Constituency*, pp. 38, 69–71.

103. Grassmuck, *Sectional Biases in Congress*, chap. 2, esp. pp. 36–39; Turner, *Party and Constituency*, pp. 140–42, 155.

104. J. and S. Alsop, *New York Herald Tribune*, Jan. 29, 1956, Sec. 2, p. 3. See also Marguerite Higgins, *ibid.*, Jan. 23, 1956, p. 3, and Hanson Baldwin, *New York Times*, May 13, 1956, p. E3.

105. See Gallup surveys reported in *New York Herald Tribune*: June 14, 1957, p. 5; July 10, 1959, p. 15; Apr. 27, 1960, p. 10; and Angus Campbell, Philip E. Converse, Warren E. Miller, Donald E. Stokes, *The American Voter* (New York, 1960), pp. 187, 198–200.

106. Adlai E. Stevenson, "Why I Raised the H-Bomb Question," 21 *Look Magazine* (Feb. 5, 1957), 24. President Eisenhower refused to confirm or to deny the accuracy of Stevenson's allegation. *New York Times*, Jan. 24, 1957, p. 12. See also Thomas E. Murray, *Nuclear Policy for War and Peace* (Cleveland, 1960), p. 216.

107. See S. P. Huntington, "Radicalism and Conservatism in National Defense Policy," 8 *Journal of International Affairs* (1954), 206 ff.; Lt. Gen. James M. Gavin, *War and Peace in the Space Age* (New York, 1958), pp. 252–53.

108. Arthur N. Holcombe, *The New Party Politics* (New York, 1933), pp. 11, 35.

109. Lubell, 1 *Columbia University Forum* (Winter 1957), 18–19.

110. George H. Hildebrand, *Federal Expenditure Policy for Economic Growth and Stability*, Hears./USC JEC SC on Fiscal Policy/85C1/1957, p. 346.

111. *Federal Expenditure Policies for Economic Growth and Stability*, Committee Print/USC JEC SC on Fiscal Policy/85C2/1958, p. 3; Klaus Knorr, "The Crisis in U. S. Defense," *The New Leader*, Sec. 2, Dec. 30, 1957, p. 22; Committee for Economic Development, Research and Policy Committee, *The Problem of National Security: Some Economic and Administrative Aspects* (New York, 1958), p. 20.

112. Oskar Morgenstern, *The Question of National Defense* (New York, 1959), p. 201; James F. Brownlee, *The Defense We Can Afford* (New York, 1958), p. 5; David Novick, *Federal Expenditure Policy*, Hears./USC JEC SC on Fiscal Policy/85C1/1957, p. 355.

113. Gerhard Colm, *Can We Afford Additional Programs for National Security?* (National Planning Association Planning Pamphlet No. 84, October 1953), *passim;* Gerhard Colm and Manuel Helzner, "General Economic Feasibility of National Security Programs," in *Federal Expenditure Policy*, Hears./USC JEC SC on Fiscal Policy/85C1/1957, pp. 359–

IV. THE GREAT EQUATION

364; Arthur Smithies, *ibid.*, p. 364; Committee for Economic Development, *Problem of National Security*, p. 27. See also Bernard Brodie, *Strategy in the Missile Age* (Princeton, 1959), pp. 365–77.

114. *Control and Reduction of Armaments*, Hears./USS CFR SC on Disarmament/85C1/1957, p. 1317.

115. Committee for Economic Development, *Problem of National Security*, p. 27. See also Colm, *Can We Afford Additional Programs?*, p. iv. For a more pessimistic view, see Emile Benoit, *Economic Adjustments to Disarmament* (Institute for International Order, Program of Research No. 2, New York), pp. 3 ff.

116. Colm and Helzner, *Federal Expenditure Policy*, Hears./USC JEC SC on Fiscal Policy/85C1/1957, p. 356 (italics added).

117. Gerard Piel, "The Economics of Disarmament," 16 *Bulletin of the Atomic Scientists* (Apr. 1960), 121–22. For an acute recognition of the political problems of too many alternatives, see Benoit, *Economic Adjustments*, p. 8.

118. Committee for Economic Development, *Problem of National Security*, p. 28.

119. I am much indebted to James R. Schlesinger's similar discussion of the Korean War experience in *The Political Economy of National Security*, pp. 98–103.

120. For a brief discussion of the farm bloc and World War II price control legislation in Congress, see James M. Burns, *Congress On Trial* (New York, 1949), pp. 82–90.

121. Sec. 101, Defense Production Act of 1950, as amended. For an excellent brief description of the legislative battle over the amendments, see James A. Durham, "Congressional Response to Administrative Regulation: The 1951 and 1952 Price Control Amendments," 62 *Yale Law Journal* (Dec. 1952), 1–53.

122. Quoted in Durham, 62 *Yale Law Journal*, 43.

123. Durham, *ibid.*, p. 17.   124. *Ibid.*, p. 35.

125. *Ibid.*, pp. 33–35.

126. See Dale, *Conservatives in Power*, p. 132; Hildebrand, *Federal Expenditure Policy*, Hears./USC JEC SC on Fiscal Policy/85C1/1957, p. 344; William McC. Martin, *Control and Reduction of Armaments*, Hears./USS CFR SC on Disarmament/85C1/1957, p. 1254; Seymour Harris, *ibid.*, pp. 1266–68.

127. Silberman and Parker, 57 *Fortune* (June 1958), 103.

128. See *New York Times*: Sept. 7, 1957, p. 24; Sept. 27, 1957, p. 3; Sept. 28, 1957, p. 38; Oct. 9, 1957, p. 37; Oct. 22, 1957, p. 50; Oct. 29, 1957, p. 33; and the survey in 43 *U. S. News and World Report* (Nov. 15, 1957), 72–74.

129. C. J. V. Murphy, "The White House and the Recession," 57 *Fortune* (May 1958), 242.

130. Compare Meany's statement with that of Secretary of Labor James P. Mitchell, *New York Times,* Mar. 12, 1958, p. 22.

131. Dale, *Conservatives in Power,* pp. 140–41.

V. INNOVATION OF STRATEGIC PROGRAMS

1. On weapons innovation, see, for example: Bernard Brodie, *Sea Power in the Machine Age* (Princeton, 1941); James P. Baxter, III, *The Introduction of the Ironclad Warship* (Cambridge, Mass., 1933); Irving B. Holley, *Ideas and Weapons: Exploitation of the Aerial Weapon by the United States during World War I* (New Haven, 1953); Constance McL. Green, H. C. Thompson, P. C. Roots, *The Ordnance Department* (Washington, 1955); Edward L. Katzenbach, Jr., "The Horse Cavalry in the Twentieth Century: A Study in Policy Response," 8 *Public Policy* (Yearbook of the Graduate School of Public Administration, Harvard, 1958), 120–50. Studies of innovations in military organization include: D. D. Irvine, "The Origins of Capital Staffs," 10 *Journal of Modern History* (June 1938), 161–79; Maj. Gen. Otto L. Nelson, Jr., *National Security and the General Staff* (Washington, 1946); Harry Howe Ransom, "The Politics of Airpower: A Comparative Analysis," 8 *Public Policy* (1958), 87–119; Col. Lawrence J. Legere, Jr., *Unification of the Armed Forces* (Washington, n.d.); and Paul Y. Hammond, *Organizing for Defense* (Princeton, 1961).

2. Eli Ginzberg and Ewing W. Reilley, *Effecting Change in Large Organizations* (New York, 1957), p. 131.

3. James G. March and Herbert A. Simon, *Organizations* (New York, 1958), p. 190. My discussion here owes much to the brilliant analysis in chap. 7 of this volume.

4. *Ibid.,* p. 198.

5. See Ransom, 8 *Public Policy,* 87–88; Katzenbach, *ibid.,* 148; L. Berkner, "Science and Military Power," 9 *Bulletin of the Atomic Scientists* (Dec. 1953), 359–65; Morris Janowitz, *The Professional Soldier: A Social and Political Portrait* (Glencoe, Ill., 1960), pp. 22–31.

6. See M. W. Hoag, "Is Dual Preparedness More Expensive?" 13 *Bulletin of the Atomic Scientists* (Feb. 1957), 48–51.

7. See Ransom, 8 *Public Policy,* 107n., for the boards and commissions which studied airpower between 1919 and 1927.

8. March and Simon, *Organizations,* p. 131.

9. Quoted, 128 *New Republic* (Feb. 23, 1953), 7.

10. See March and Simon, *Organizations,* p. 174.

11. *Ibid.,* p. 173.

12. See Ransom, 8 *Public Policy,* 119, and Katzenbach, *ibid.,* p. 141, for the effect of "independence" on the development of airpower and armor.

V. INNOVATION OF STRATEGIC PROGRAMS

13. Quoted in Joseph and Stewart Alsop, *We Accuse!* (New York, 1954), p. 29.
14. *Assignment of Ground Forces of the United States to Duty in the European Area*, Hears./USS CFR/82C1/1951, p. 79.
15. J. R. Oppenheimer, "Atomic Weapons and American Policy," 31 *Foreign Affairs* (July 1953), 528, 534.
16. U. S. Atomic Energy Commission, Personnel Security Board, *In the Matter of J. Robert Oppenheimer* (Washington, 1954), pp. 79–80, 249–50, 362–63.
17. Laurence W. Martin, "The American Decision to Rearm Germany" (Twentieth Century Project on Civil-Military Relations; mimeo.), p. 18.
18. *Assignment of Ground Forces*, Hears./USS CFR/82C1/1951, p. 326.
19. Secretary Finletter in *Semiannual Report of the Secretary of Defense, Jan. 1–June 30, 1951*, p. 203.
20. March and Simon, *Organizations*, p. 184.
21. *Assignment of Ground Forces*, Hears./USS CFR/82C1/1951, pp. 341, 399; *New York Times*, Feb. 28, 1951, p. 1.
22. *Semiannual Report of the Secretary of Defense, Jan. 1–June 30, 1950*, p. 144; J. R. Killian, Jr. and A. G. Hill, "For a Continental Defense," 192 *The Atlantic Monthly* (Nov. 1953), 41; Gertrude Samuels, "A Plea for 'Candor' About the Atom," *New York Times Magazine*, June 21, 1953, pp. 20–21.
23. *Matter of J. Robert Oppenheimer*, pp. 242–43, 403.
24. *Assignment of Ground Forces*, Hears./USS CFR/82C1/1951, pp. 227, 403.
25. David Griggs, *Matter of J. Robert Oppenheimer*, p. 749.
26. 40 *Air Force* (Aug. 1957), 257.
27. *Matter of J. Robert Oppenheimer*, pp. 387, 751.
28. *Assignment of Ground Forces*, Hears./USS CFR/82C1/1951, p. 85.
29. James Reston, *New York Times*, Apr. 8, 1954, p. 20; I. I. Rabi, *Matter of J. Robert Oppenheimer*, p. 453.
30. "United We Stand Secure," 15 *Vital Speeches* (Apr. 1, 1949), 384.
31. *Unification and Strategy*, H. Doc. 600/HR CAS/81C2/1950, p. 26.
32. See Walter Millis, Harvey C. Mansfield, and Harold Stein, *Arms and the State* (New York, 1958), pp. 250–55, and Warner R. Schilling, "The H-Bomb Decision: How to Decide Without Actually Choosing," 76 *Political Science Quarterly* (March 1961), 30–36.
33. H. Doc. 600/HR CAS/81C2/1951, pp. 15, 33.
34. My description of the decision-making process on the hydrogen bomb is drawn from: 1) testimony of the participants in *In the Matter of J. Robert Oppenheimer*; Harry Truman, *Memoirs* (Garden City, N. Y., 1956), II, 308–9; E. Teller, "The Work of Many People," 121 *Science* (Feb. 25, 1955), 267–75; D. E. Lilienthal, "The Case for Candor on National Security," *New York Times Magazine*, Oct. 4, 1953, pp. 13 ff.;

Gordon Dean, "The Hydrogen Bomb," 10 *Bulletin of the Atomic Scientists* (Nov. 1954), 357 ff.; Lt. Gen. James M. Gavin, *War and Peace in the Space Age* (New York, 1958), pp. 114–15; 2) the detached accounts based on interviews by James Reston, "The H-Bomb Decision," *New York Times*, Apr. 8, 1954, p. 20; Morgan Thomas, *Atomic Energy and Congress* (Ann Arbor, Mich., 1956), pp. 86–94; Warner R. Schilling, "The H-Bomb Decision," 76 *Political Science Quarterly* (March 1961), 24–46; 3) the less detached accounts of James R. Shepley and Clay Blair, Jr., *The Hydrogen Bomb* (New York, 1954); Joseph and Stewart Alsop, *We Accuse!*, esp. chap. 3; "The Hidden Struggle for the H-Bomb," 47 *Fortune* (May 1953), 109 ff. Most importantly, I have benefited from the advice and counsel of my colleague, Professor Warner R. Schilling, whose full-length study of "The Hydrogen Bomb Controversy," will be the definitive account until the classified archives are opened. He has, of course, no responsibility for my interpretations of the process.

35. Letter to James B. Conant, Oct. 21, 1949, *Matter of J. Robert Oppenheimer*, p. 242.

36. *Ibid.*, pp. 77, 242, 682–83; Schilling, 76 *Political Science Quarterly* (March 1961), 33; Shepley and Blair, *Hydrogen Bomb*, pp. 74, 137–38.

37. Oppenheimer, *Matter of J. Robert Oppenheimer*, p. 243.

38. Thomas, *Atomic Energy and Congress*, p. 90.

39. Schilling, 76 *Political Science Quarterly* (March 1961), 38–39.

40. *N. Y. Times Magazine*, Oct. 4, 1953, pp. 60, 62. For Oppenheimer's views, see 6 *Bulletin of the Atomic Scientists* (March 1950), 75.

41. Quoted by Reston, *N. Y. Times*, Apr. 8, 1954, p. 20.

42. Truman, *Memoirs*, II, 306; *Matter of J. Robert Oppenheimer*, p. 258; Shepley and Blair, *Hydrogen Bomb*, p. 13; E. Rabinowitch, "Nuclear Physics and Creative Interference," 131 *New Republic* (Dec. 27, 1954), 16–17.

43. Teller, 121 *Science* (Feb. 25, 1955), 271.

44. *Matter of J. Robert Oppenheimer*, p. 242.

45. For the argument that the President's decision on January 31, 1950 was itself triggered by the arrest in England on January 27 of Klaus Fuchs, see Thomas, *Atomic Energy and Congress*, p. 91. By January 31, however, the Committee of Three had completed its work, and the White House press secretary denied that President Truman knew of the Fuchs case when he approved the bomb. *Soviet Atomic Espionage*, Cmte. Print/ U.S. Cong. Jt. Comte. on Atomic Energy/82C1/1951, p. 14.

46. 96 *Cong. Record* (Feb. 2, 1950), 1338–40.

47. See 6 *Bulletin of the Atomic Scientists* (March 1950), 75, (May 1950), 132.

48. Schilling, 76 *Political Science Quarterly* (March 1961), 37–38.

49. Truman, *Memoirs*, II, 310; Schilling, 76 *Political Science Quarterly* (March 1961), 44.

50. Schilling, *ibid.*, 45.

V. INNOVATION OF STRATEGIC PROGRAMS

51. *Matter of J. Robert Oppenheimer*, pp. 82–83, 304, 520, 605, 701, 706, 719–21.
52. *Ibid.*, pp. 83–84, 86, 898.
53. Schilling, 76 *Political Science Quarterly* (March 1961), 43–44; *Matter of J. Robert Oppenheimer*, pp. 95, 247–48; Shepley and Blair, *Hydrogen Bomb*, p. 207.
54. See *ibid.*, pp. 85–86, 248–49, 311–15, 722–24; Thomas, *Atomic Energy and Congress*, pp. 108–12.
55. 40 *Air Force* (Aug. 1957), 244.
56. Shepley and Blair, *Hydrogen Bomb*, pp. 166–67.
57. 40 *Air Force* (Aug. 1957), 244.
58. J. McDonald, "General LeMay's Management Problem," 49 *Fortune* (May 1954), 200.
59. *North Atlantic Treaty*, Hears./USS CFR/81C1/1949, p. 8. For development of the treaty, see Arthur H. Vandenberg, Jr., ed., *The Private Papers of Senator Vandenberg* (Boston, 1952), chaps. 21, 25; Daniel S. Cheever and H. Field Haviland, Jr., *American Foreign Policy and the Separation of Powers* (Cambridge, Mass., 1952), chap. 11; R. H. Heindel, T. V. Kalijarvi, F. O. Wilcox, "The North Atlantic Treaty in the United States Senate," 43 *American Journal of International Law* (Oct. 1949), 633–65; Stephen K. Bailey and Howard D. Samuel, *Congress at Work* (New York, 1952), chap. 14.
60. Vandenberg, *Private Papers*, p. 407.
61. Cheever and Haviland, *American Foreign Policy*, pp. 123, 126.
62. Vandenberg, *Private Papers*, pp. 479–80.
63. *Ibid.*, pp. 495–96.
64. Millis, Mansfield, and Stein, *Arms and the State*, p. 238.
65. *To Amend the Mutual Defense Assistance Act of 1949*, Hears./HR CFA/81C2/1950, p. 36; Institute of War and Peace Studies, *The Military Assistance Program of the United States*, Cmte. Print/USS Special Committee to Study the Foreign Aid Program/85C1/1957, pp. 36–41, 47.
66. *New York Times*: Apr. 10, 1950, pp. 1, 7; May 17, 1950, p. 2.
67. Laurence W. Martin, "The American Decision to Rearm Germany" (Twentieth Century Fund Project on Civil-Military Relations; mimeo.), pp. 10–12.
68. *Mutual Defense Assistance Program, 1950*, Hears./USS CFR/81C2/1950, p. 30; *New York Times*, May 19, 1950, p. 3.
69. *Amend the Mutual Defense Assistance Act of 1949*, Hears./HR CFA/81C2/1950, p. 22.
70. *Ibid.*, p. 31.
71. *The Supplemental Appropriation Bill for 1951*, Hears./HR CA SC/81C2/1950, p. 20.
72. William Reitzel, Morton A. Kaplan, Constance G. Coblenz, *United States Foreign Policy 1945–1955* (Washington, 1956), pp. 287–89.
73. Millis, Mansfield, and Stein, *Arms and the State*, p. 337.

74. Truman, *Memoirs*, II, 252.
75. Martin, "American Decision to Rearm Germany," p. 18. I am heavily indebted to this account for the events of the summer of 1950.
76. *Ibid.,* pp. 30–33; Millis, Mansfield, Stein, *Arms and the State,* pp. 336–39; Truman, *Memoirs,* II, 253–54.
77. Martin, "American Decision to Rearm Germany," pp. 20–21.
78. *Ibid.,* pp. 27–28. 79. *Ibid.,* pp. 28–30. 80. *Ibid.,* pp. 31–32.
81. Message to the President, Sept. 15, 1950, Truman *Memoirs,* II, 254.
82. Martin, "American Decision to Rearm Germany," p. 34.
83. *Assignment of Ground Forces,* Hears./USS CFR/82C1/1951, p. 401.
84. See Walter Millis' summary, *Arms and the State,* pp. 339 ff.
85. *New York Times,* Nov. 14, 1950, p. 1.
86. See *ibid.,* Dec. 21, 1950, p. 22.
87. See Roger Hilsman, "NATO: The Developing Strategic Context," in Klaus Knorr, ed., *NATO and American Security* (Princeton, 1959), pp. 13 ff.
88. Killian and Hill, 192 *The Atlantic Monthly* (Nov. 1953), 40.
89. Quoted in Steven R. Rivkin, "The Decision-Making Process for National Defense Policy" (Honors thesis, Harvard, 1958), p. 126.
90. See J. and S. Alsop, *New York Herald Tribune,* Mar. 16, 1953, p. 19; *New York Times,* Mar. 16, 1953, p. 1; Rivkin, "Decision-Making Process," pp. 130–33.
91. *New York Herald Tribune,* Mar. 16, 1953, p. 19.
92. 40 *Air Force* (Aug. 1957), 257; J. and S. Alsop, *New York Herald Tribune,* Nov. 5, 1952, p. 29.
93. J. and S. Alsop, *New York Herald Tribune:* May 8, 1953, p. 19; May 11, 1953, p. 17. Glenn H. Snyder, "The New Look," MS, p. 31, to be published in Warner R. Schilling, Paul Y. Hammond, Glenn H. Snyder, *Making National Security Policy: Three Case Studies* (New York, 1962).
94. Dept. of Defense Press Release No. 513–53, June 3, 1953; *New York Times,* Jan. 1, 1953, p. 15.
95. *New York Herald Tribune:* Mar. 16, 1953, p. 19; Mar. 20, 1953, p. 9.
96. 48 *Fortune* (July 1953), 40; *New York Herald Tribune,* May 29, 1953, p. 13.
97. Dept. of Defense Press Release No. 513–53, June 3, 1953.
98. J. Alsop, *New York Herald Tribune,* July 22, 1953, p. 17.
99. *Ibid.,* Aug. 24, 1953, p. 13.
100. Rivkin, "Decision-Making Process," p. 148.
101. Snyder, "New Look," pp. 41, 51; J. Alsop, *New York Herald Tribune,* Aug. 24, 1953, p. 13; *ibid.,* Aug. 27, 1953, p. 3, Sept. 25, 1953, p. 1.
102. Snyder, "New Look," pp. 34–35; Rivkin, "Decision-Making Process," p. 150; S. Alsop, *New York Herald Tribune,* Nov. 22, 1953, Sec. 2, p. 5.

V. INNOVATION OF STRATEGIC PROGRAMS

103. S. Alsop, *ibid.*

104. Gen. Omar N. Bradley, "A Soldier's Farewell," 226 *Saturday Evening Post* (Aug. 29, 1953), 48.

105. *Matter of J. Robert Oppenheimer*, pp. 749 ff., 763, 926; 40 *Air Force* (Aug. 1957), 257; Shepley and Blair, *The Hydrogen Bomb*, pp. 182–86.

106. "Organization of Military Research and Development," Memorandum, June 29, 1954, *Organization and Administration of the Military Research and Development Programs*, Hears./HR GOC SC on Military Operations/83C2/1954, p. 634.

107. J. Alsop, *New York Herald Tribune*, Aug. 24, 1953, p. 13.

108. "Atomic Weapons and American Policy," 31 *Foreign Affairs* (July 1953), 530.

109. *New York Times:* May 2, 1953, p. 1; June 21, 1953, Sec. VI, p. 20. G. Samuels, "A Plea for 'Candor' About the Atom," *New York Times Magazine*, June 21, 1953, pp. 20–21.

110. Killian and Hill, 192 *Atlantic Monthly* (Nov. 1953), 37.

111. See J. Lear, "Ike and the Peaceful Atom," 14 *The Reporter* (Jan. 12, 1956), 11–21; R. Lapp, "Atomic Candor," 10 *Bulletin of the Atomic Scientists* (Oct. 1954), 12–14.

112. *New York Times:* Oct. 5, 1953, pp. 1, 14; Oct. 11, 1953, p. 1; *New York Herald Tribune*, Mar. 26, 1954, p. 3.

113. *New York Times:* Oct. 9, 1953, p. 12; Oct. 20, 1953, p. 19; Nov. 15, 1953, p. 36.

114. *New York Herald Tribune*, Nov. 22, 1953, Sec. 2, p. 5.

115. *Ibid.*, Oct. 16, 1953, p. 10; *New York Times*, Oct. 7, 1953, p. 6.

116. Minister of Defence Brooke Claxton, *New York Times*, Nov. 27, 1953, p. 12.

117. Snyder, "New Look," pp. 115–16.

118. Secretary Wilson, *New York Times*, Apr. 9, 1954, p. 1.

119. Gen. Maxwell D. Taylor, *The Uncertain Trumpet* (New York, 1960), p. 16.

120. See Chapter II, Section 4, and Chapter V, Section 23; *Matter of J. Robert Oppenheimer*, pp. 46–47.

121. Gen. O. N. Bradley, "U. S. Military Policy: 1950," 1 *Combat Forces Journal* (Oct. 1950), 7.

122. Gen. J. L. Collins, "New Approaches to World Peace," 6 *Army Information Digest* (Jan. 1951), 3–4.

123. Gen. M. B. Ridgway, "The Army's Role in National Defense," Address, Cleveland Post, American Ordnance Association, 9 *Army Information Digest* (May 1954), 21–30. See also 'Colonel Unitas' "Battle Future of Our Army," 4 *Combat Forces Journal* (Apr. 1954), 13.

124. For a more extensive discussion of Army strategic concepts, see Richard O. Neville, "The Political Position of the United States Army, 1945–1958" (Honors thesis, Harvard, 1958), *passim.*

125. *Department of the Army Appropriations for 1955*, Hears./HR CA SC/83C2/1954, pp. 43–44, 49.
126. *New York Times*, Aug. 19, 1954, p. 2.
127. *Ibid.*, Jan. 4, 1955, pp. 1, 14.
128. 92 *Army-Navy-Air Force Journal* (Feb. 12, 1955), 690.
129. Ltr. to Secretary of Defense Wilson, June 27, 1955, *New York Times*, July 16, 1955, p. 8.
130. Taylor, *Uncertain Trumpet*, pp. 30–34, 98; *New York Times*, July 17, 1955, pp. 1, 26.
131. Gen. Taylor, *Department of Defense Appropriations for 1958*, Hears./USS CA SC/85C1/1957, p. 144.
132. Taylor, *Uncertain Trumpet*, pp. 55–56; Janowitz, *The Professional Soldier*, pp. 319–20.
133. William W. Kaufmann, *The Requirements of Deterrence* (Princeton, Center of International Studies, Memorandum No. 7, Nov. 15, 1954); Bernard Brodie, "Unlimited Weapons and Limited War," 11 *The Reporter* (Nov. 18, 1954), 16–21. See also Bernard Brodie, *Strategy in the Missile Age* (Princeton, 1959), p. 309, and "More About Limited War," 10 *World Politics* (Oct. 1957), 116; M. W. Cagle, "Sea Power and Limited War," 84 *U. S. Naval Institute Proceedings* (July 1958), 24. For a perceptive analysis of the evolution of limited war theory, see Morton H. Halperin, *Limited War: An Essay on the Development of the Theory* (Harvard, Center for International Affairs, Feb. 1961; mimeo.).
134. Taylor, *Uncertain Trumpet*, p. 26.
135. *New York Times*, Apr. 27, 1954, p. 1, May 10, 1954, p. 4.
136. Taylor, *Uncertain Trumpet*, pp. 26–27.
137. *New York Times*, Mar. 21, 1955, p. 1, July 16, 1955, p. 8.
138. Taylor, *Uncertain Trumpet*, pp. 37, 30–36.
139. *New York Times*, May 29, 1958, p. 1, Oct. 27, 1958, p. 1; General Twining, *Inquiry into Satellite and Missile Programs*, Hears./USS CAS SC/85C2/1958, pp. 2437–38.
140. *New York Times*, May 25, 1958, p. 28. See also Jack Raymond, *ibid.*, June 2, 1958, p. 14.
141. Taylor, *Uncertain Trumpet*, pp. 58, 63, 65; C. J. V. Murphy, "Defense: The Converging Decisions," 58 *Fortune* (Oct. 1958), 227–28.
142. Taylor, *Uncertain Trumpet*, pp. 55, 65.
143. *Ibid.*, pp. 142–43.
144. *Control and Reduction of Armaments*, S. Rept. 2501/USS CFR SC on Disarmament/85C2/1958, pp. 52, 65.
145. J. W. Deer, "Whatever Happened to Civil Defense?" 15 *Bulletin of the Atomic Scientists* (June 1959), 266; Chester Bowles, Introduction to Richard J. Barnet, *Who Wants Disarmament?* (Boston, 1960), p. xvi.
146. Federal Civil Defense Administration, *1955 Review of the Report of Project East River* (Battle Creek, Mich., 1955), p. 2.
147. *New York Herald Tribune*, Aug. 11, 1958, p. 17.

V. INNOVATION OF STRATEGIC PROGRAMS

148. *New York Times,* Aug. 20, 1951, p. 3, June 28, 1959, p. 6.

149. See Joseph Nogee, "The Diplomacy of Disarmament," *International Conciliation* (Jan. 1960), pp. 282 ff.

150. Project East River, *Information & Training for Civil Defense* (Pt. IX, Sept. 1952), p. 1. See also R. Daniel Sloan, Jr., "The Politics of Civil Defense: Great Britain and the United States" (Ph.D. dissertation, Chicago, 1958), pp. 164–66; and *Civil Defense for National Survival,* H. Rept. 2946/HR GOC SC/84C2/1956, p. 66: "the military authorities have only a dim regard for civil defense as a strategic concept."

151. FCDA, *1955 East River Review,* pp. 8–9. See also Sloan, "Politics of Civil Defense," pp. 159, 177 f., 180.

152. See *New York Times,* Dec. 22, 1957, p. 1, Dec. 25, 1957, p. 1; *New York Herald Tribune,* Feb. 12, 1958, p. 5.

153. *Control and Reduction of Armaments,* Hears./USS CFR SC/84C2/1956, p. 54.

154. *New York Times,* May 19, 1957, p. 1, May 20, 1957, p. 1.

155. Reston, *New York Times,* May 28, 1957, p. 13; S. Alsop, *New York Herald Tribune,* June 28, 1957, p. 14. See also Saville Davis, "Recent Policy Making in the United States Government," 89 *Daedalus* (Fall 1960), 954–57.

156. *New York Herald Tribune,* Feb. 24, 1958, p. 3; R. E. Matteson, "The Disarmament Dilemma," 2 *Orbis* (Fall 1958), 291–93.

157. *New York Times,* Feb. 8, 1958, p. 1.

158. *Strengthening the Government for Arms Control, A Report by the National Planning Association's Special Project Committee on Security Through Arms Control,* S. Doc. 123/86C2/1960, pp. 4 ff.; *Control and Reduction of Armaments,* S. Rept. 2501/USS CFR SC on Disarmament/85C2/1958, p. 16; Sen. Hubert H. Humphrey, "Government Organization for Arms Control," 89 *Daedalus* (Fall 1960), 973; *New York Times,* Sept. 10, 1960, p. 6.

159. Inglis, "Arms Control Effort Buried in State," 13 *Bulletin of the Atomic Scientists* (May 1957), 174 ff., and J. W. Deer, 15 *ibid.,* 266 ff.

160. See Sen. Humphrey's analysis of the pros and cons of various locations for disarmament, 89 *Daedalus,* 971 ff., and Sloan's discussion of the problem of locating civil defense in both the U. S. and Great Britain, "Politics of Civil Defense," pp. 147–55, 160 ff.

161. Tris Coffin, 41 *The New Leader* (May 5, 1958), 3. See also J. H. Spingarn, "The Humphrey Subcommittee: Was It Worthwhile?" 13 *Bulletin of the Atomic Scientists* (June 1957), 224 ff.

162. For a careful discussion of the relation of civil defense and arms control to deterrence, see Brodie, *Strategy in the Missile Age,* pp. 295–304.

163. See Barnet, *Who Wants Disarmament?,* pp. 26–27.

164. William E. Jackson, Jr., "Disarmament and Security: 1955 . . ." (M.A. thesis, North Carolina, 1959), p. 119.

165. U. S. Dept. of State, *Disarmament: The Intensified Effort, 1955–1958* (Washington, 1958), p. 35; *New York Times*, Oct. 14, 1958, p. 56. See also Barnet, *Who Wants Disarmament?*, pp. 45 ff., 99 ff.

166. "Surprise Attack and Disarmament," in Knorr, ed., *NATO and American Security*, p. 179. See also Brodie, *Strategy in the Missile Age*, pp. 300–1.

167. Barnet, *Who Wants Disarmament?*, p. 116.

168. Davis, 89 *Daedalus*, 958–59.

169. On the development of policy on the test ban, see Thomas E. Murray, *Nuclear Policy for War and Peace* (Cleveland, 1960), chaps. 4, 5; C. J. V. Murphy, "Nuclear Inspection: A Near Miss," 59 *Fortune* (Mar. 1959), 122 ff., and "The Case for Resuming Nuclear Tests," 61 *ibid.* (Apr. 1960), 148 ff.; C. M. Roberts, "The Hopes and Fears of an Atomic Test Ban," 22 *The Reporter* (Apr. 28, 1960), 20–23.

170. See, e.g., Merle A. Tuve, James R. Killian, Lloyd V. Berkner, *Civil Defense for National Survival*, Hears./HR GOC SC/84C2/1956, pp. 193, 215, 671; H. Rept. 2946/84C2, pp. v, 16–17. For the absence of any reference to deterrence in the early discussions of civil defense, see Sloan, "Politics of Civil Defense," *passim*, but esp. chaps. 11, 12, 15.

171. Herman Kahn, "How Many Can Be Saved?" 15 *Bulletin of the Atomic Scientists* (Jan. 1959), 32. See, generally, his *On Thermonuclear War* (Princeton, 1960).

172. Quoted in *New York Herald Tribune*, May 1, 1959, p. 10. See also: B. K. Gordon, "NATO's Missing Shield," 15 *Bulletin of the Atomic Scientists* (June 1959), 230, and Chet Holifield, "Civil Defense Shelters," 14 *ibid.* (Apr. 1958), 133.

173. *Report on a Study of Non-Military Defense* (RAND Corporation, R-322-RC, July 1, 1958), p. 37.

174. *Ibid., passim;* Herman Kahn et al., *Some Specific Suggestions for Achieving Early Non-Military Defense Capabilities and Initiating Long-Range Programs* (RAND Corporation, RM-2206-RC, July 1, 1958); Hanson Baldwin, "A Civil Defense Impasse," *New York Times*, Nov. 17, 1958, p. 11. See also the OCDM proposals to the Kennedy Administration, *New York Times*, Nov. 21, 1960, p. 19.

175. See Sloan, "Politics of Civil Defense," pp. 17 ff.

VI. THE COMPETITION OF STRATEGIC PROGRAMS

1. Gen. Carl Spaatz, quoted by Rear Adm. Ellis M. Zacharias, USN (Ret.), *National Security Act of 1947*, Hears./HR CEED/80C1/1947, p. 506; Vice Adm. John S. McCain to James Forrestal, April 28, 1945, quoted in Robert G. Albion and Robert H. Connery, "Forrestal and the Navy, 1940–1947," MS, p. 548.

2. Maj. Gen. Merritt A. Edson, USMC (Ret.), "Power-Hungry Men in

VI. COMPETITION OF STRATEGIC PROGRAMS

Uniform," 124 *Collier's* (Aug. 27, 1949), 16–17; Gen. Armstrong, USAAF, quoted by Rear Adm. Zacharias, *National Security Act of 1947*, Hears./HR CEED/80C1/1947, p. 505.

3. Gen. H. H. Arnold, "Tradition Can't Win Wars," 124 *Collier's* (Oct. 15, 1949), 13. See also *National Defense Program: Unification and Strategy*, Hears./HR CAS/81C1/1949, pp. 366–67, and Robert Lindsay, *This High Name: Public Relations and the United States Marine Corps* (Madison, Wis., 1956), pp. 73–77.

4. *War Department Publicity and Propaganda Relating to Universal Military Training*, Hears./HR CEED/80C1/1947, pp. 31, 38.

5. Walter Millis, ed., *The Forrestal Diaries* (New York, 1951), p. 388.

6. See *National Security Act of 1947*, H. Rept. 961/80C1/1947, pp. 12–14.

7. See Louis Morton, "War Plan Orange: Evolution of a Strategy," 11 *World Politics* (Jan. 1959), 221–50.

8. See *Final Report of the Chief of Staff, United States Army, February 7, 1948*, pp. 9–13; *Military Establishment Appropriation Bill for 1948*, Hears./HR CA SC/80C1/1947, p. 1241.

9. Memorandum of the President to Admiral Leahy, Aug. 21, 1945, quoted in Lawrence J. Legere, Jr., *Unification of the Armed Forces* (Washington, Office of the Chief of Military History, mimeo.; n.d.), pp. 316–22.

10. *Military Establishment Appropriation Bill for 1947*, Hears./HR CA SC/79C2/1946, p. 488; *First Supplemental Surplus Appropriation Rescission Bill, 1946*, Hears./HR CA SC/79C1/1945, II, 573.

11. *Final Report, Chief of Staff, Feb. 7, 1948*, p. 5; *Military Appropriation, 1948*, Hears./HR CA SC/80C1/1947, p. 75; John C. Sparrow, *History of Personnel Demobilization in the United States Army* (Washington, 1951), pp. 56 ff., 82 ff.; Charles D. Story, "The Formulation of Army Reserve Forces Policy: Its Setting Amidst Pressure Group Activity" (Ph.D. dissertation, Oklahoma, 1958), pp. 6–7.

12. *Semiannual Report of the Secretary of Defense, Jan. 1–June 30, 1951*, p. 79.

13. Maj. Gen. H. J. Knerr, USAF, "If We Should Fight Again," 27 *Military Review* (Dec. 1947), 24.

14. See, e.g., Gen. Maxwell D. Taylor, *The Uncertain Trumpet* (New York, 1960), pp. 63–64, 74.

15. J. L. McConaughy, Jr., "Congressmen and the Pentagon," 57 *Fortune* (Apr. 1958), 162.

16. *Availability of Information from Federal Departments and Agencies*, H. Rept. 1884/HR GOC/85C2/1958, pp. 248–51; *New York Times*, June 27, 1957, p. 8, quoted in Douglass Cater, *The Fourth Branch of Government* (Boston, 1959), pp. 10–11; Thomas Winship, *Boston Globe*, May 19, 1956, p. 3; 93 *Army-Navy-Air Force Journal* (Apr. 14, 1956), 1008;

67 *Time* (June 4, 1956), 20–23; Morris Janowitz, *The Professional Soldier: A Social and Political Portrait* (Glencoe, Ill., 1960), pp. 408–9.

17. See, e.g., Gen. J. L. Collins, "The War Department Spreads the News," 27 *Military Review* (Sept. 1947), 15; Lt. Cmdr. J. L. Howard, "The Navy and National Security," 77 *U. S. Naval Institute Proceedings* (July 1951), 753; Col. T. M. Smith, "Air Force Information at the Grass Roots," 5 *Air Univ. Quarterly Review* (Spring 1952), 83.

18. W. Barton Leach, "Obstacles to the Development of American Air Power," 299 *Annals of the American Academy* (May 1955), 71–74; Lt. Gen. E. W. Rawlings, "Public Opinion and Air Force Dollars," 8 *Army Information Digest* (Apr. 1953), 58; "The Big Look," 6 *Air Univ. Quarterly Review* (Winter 1953–54), 133.

19. "Approaches to Air-Age Education in American Schools and Communities," 8 *Air Univ. Quarterly Review* (Summer 1956), 116.

20. Letter, Gen. Maxwell D. Taylor to senior Army commanders, Sept. 15, 1955, 93 *Army-Navy-Air Force Journal* (Sept. 24, 1955), 91; Maj. Gen. Gilman C. Mudgett, 92 *ibid.* (July 5, 1958), 1312.

21. *National Defense Program—Unification and Strategy*, Hears./HR CAS/81C1/1949, p. 49; 95 *Army-Navy-Air Force Journal* (July 5, 1958), 1312.

22. Leach, 299 *Annals*, 72; *National Defense Program—Unification and Strategy*, Hears,/HR CAS/81C1/1949, pp. 350 f., 361, 616–18.

23. For perceptive discussions of service public relations, see: Hanson W. Baldwin, "When the Big Guns Speak," in Lester Markel, ed., *Public Opinion and Foreign Policy* (New York, 1949), pp. 97–120; W. S. Fairfield, "PR for the Services—In Uniform and in Mufti," 18 *The Reporter* (May 15, 1958), pp. 20–23; Janowitz, *Professional Soldier*, chap. 19; G. M. Lyons, "PR and the Pentagon," 43 *The New Leader* (Oct. 17, 1960), 10–12.

24. Gen. M. B. Ridgway, "Army Troop and Public Relations," 9 *Army Information Digest* (Aug. 1954), 5. The Army's concern was reflected in the bibliographies on subjects of special interest to it which it issued in 1957 and 1958. These included titles on: *Mobility in Modern Warfare; Limited War; Guided Missiles, Rockets and Artificial Satellites;* and *Community Relations and Public Relations.*

25. 10 *Army Information Digest* (Mar. 1955), 28.

26. See Ridgway, 9 *Army Information Digest* (Aug. 1954), 5; Gen. M. D. Taylor, "Biennial Report of the Chief of Staff," 12 *ibid.* (Sept. 1957), 61.

27. "Congress and the Army," 5 *Officer's Call* (No. 2, 1953); 10 *Army Information Digest* (May 1955), 23; McConaughy, 57 *Fortune* (Apr. 1958), 166; Story, "Army Reserve Forces Policy," p. 80.

28. McConaughy, 57 *Fortune* (Apr. 1958), 166; Janowitz, *Professional Soldier*, p. 358.

29. See 107 *Congressional Record* (Feb. 24, 1961), A1228 (daily ed.).

VI. COMPETITION OF STRATEGIC PROGRAMS 483

30. Quoted in Fairfield, 18 *The Reporter* (May 15, 1958), 21.
31. Rep. Connally, 60 *Cong. Record* (Jan. 29, 1921), 2271, quoted in Howard White, *Executive Influence in Determining Military Policy in the United States* (Urbana, Ill., 1924), p. 276.
32. *A History of the Committee on Naval Affairs of the House of Representatives,* Paper No. 287/HR CNA/79C2/1946, p. 3874.
33. William S. White, "Carl Vinson Has Been Unified, Too," *New York Times Magazine,* Sept. 10, 1950, p. 12.
34. *Military Appropriation Bill for 1948,* Hears./HR CA SC/80C1/1947, p. 627.
35. Collins, 27 *Military Review* (Sept. 1947), 11–12.
36. Lt. Col. T. J. Cleary, "Civilian Aides to the Secretary of the Army," 7 *Army Information Digest* (Nov. 1952), 13–18; *Employment of Retired Military and Civilian Personnel by Defense Industries,* Hears./HR CAS SC/86C1/1959, p. 439; *New York Times,* Apr. 13, 1958, p. 12; *New York Herald Tribune,* Apr. 15, 1958, p. 9.
37. *Annual Report of the Secretary of the Navy, 1946,* pp. 64–66; *Ibid., 1947,* p. 82.
38. Collins, 27 *Military Review* (Sept. 1947), 13–14.
39. Maj. Gen. James F. Cantwell, Chief of Staff, New York National Guard, July 23, 1957, quoted in Story, "Army Reserve Forces Policy," pp. 210–11.
40. See Maj. Gen. E. S. Bres, "The ORC, Too, Can Tell the Army's Story," 1 *Army Information Digest* (Oct. 1946), 3–5; "Representatives of National Security," 59 *Infantry Journal* (July 1946), 54–55; Col. S. Legree, "We Must Get Together," 60 *ibid.* (May 1947), 25–29. See, in general, Martha Derthick, "Militia Lobby in the Missile Age: The Political Evolution of the National Guard," in Samuel P. Huntington, ed., *Changing Patterns of Military Politics* (New York, 1962).
41. On backstop associations, see Janowitz, *Professional Soldier,* pp. 383–87; *Employment of Personnel by Defense Industries,* Hears./HR CAS SC/86C1/1959, pp. 390–476.
42. See Armin Rappaport, "The Navy League of the United States," 53 *South Atlantic Quarterly* (Apr. 1954), 203–12.
43. Quoted in Paul Y. Hammond, "Super-Carriers and B-36 Bombers: Appropriations, Strategy and Politics" (Twentieth Century Fund Project on Civil-Military Relations; mimeo.), p. 79.
44. *New York Times,* Dec. 6, 1952, p. 35; 92 *Army-Navy-Air Force Journal* (May 28, 1955), 1156; 2 *Combat Forces Journal* (June 1952), fac. p. 1.
45. Maj. Gen. John B. Medaris, *Countdown for Decision* (New York, 1960), p. 103.
46. Story, "Army Reserve Forces Policy," p. 257.
47. Secretary of the Army Brucker, 7 *Army* (Dec. 1956), 79.
48. Rappaport, 53 *South Atlantic Quarterly,* 208. For the rather

strained efforts of the Air Force Association leaders to distinguish their view from that of the Air Force, see *Employment of Personnel by Defense Industries*, Hears./HR CAS SC/86C1/1959, p. 407.

49. Secretary of the Army, 7 *Army* (Dec. 1956), 79; 104 *Cong. Record* (May 1, 1958), A4026; 95 *Army-Navy-Air Force Journal* (July 5, 1958), 1312; *New York Times*, Dec. 29, 1956, p. 2; *National Defense Program—Unification and Strategy*, Hears./HR CAS/81C1/1949, p. 70; *Employment of Personnel by Defense Industries*, Hears./HR CAS SC/86C1/1959, pp. 392, 455–56.

50. *Employment of Personnel by Defense Industries*, Hears./HR CAS SC/86C1/1959, pp. 570 ff., 739–44, 752, 910–11.

51. *Inquiry into Satellite and Missile Programs*, Hears./USS CAS SC/85C1/1957, p. 615; Lt. Gen. James M. Gavin, *War and Peace in the Space Age* (New York, 1958), pp. 256–57.

52. Fairfield, 18 *The Reporter* (May 15, 1958), 23.

53. *Satellite and Missile Programs*, Hears./USS CAS SC/85C1/1957, p. 959.

54. Quoted in Fairfield, 18 *The Reporter* (May 15, 1958), 21.

55. *Ibid.*, p. 22.

56. Medaris, *Countdown for Decision*, p. 161.

57. Quoted in Fairfield, 18 *The Reporter* (May 15, 1958), 23.

58. See *Employment of Personnel by Defense Industries*, Hears./HR CAS SC/86C1/1959, pp. 355–90, 394, 432, 464, 476–84; Walter H. McLaughlin, Jr., "Business Attitudes Towards Defense Policy During the Cold War" (Honors thesis, Harvard, 1955), pp. 43–57.

59. See Herbert A. Simon, Donald W. Smithburg, Victor A. Thompson, *Public Administration* (New York, 1950), pp. 543–44.

60. Dept. of the Army, *The Role of the Army* (Pamphlet 21–70, June 29, 1955), pp. 3–4.

61. Dept. of the Army, *A Guide to Army Philosophy* (Pamphlet 20–1, Jan. 22, 1958).

62. *Defense Department Appropriations for 1958*, Hears./USS CA SC/85C1/1957, p. 878.

63. Personnel figures for Air Force commands are from Tom Compere and William P. Vogel, Jr., eds., *The Air Force Blue Book* (New York, 1959), I, 267 ff.

64. "Forces on the Ground," 73 *Time* (May 11, 1959), 23; Medaris, *Countdown for Decision*, pp. 115–16.

65. Hammond, "Super-Carriers and B-36 Bombers," p. 59.

66. Jim G. Lucas, *Washington Daily News*, July 29, 1959, quoted in *Employment of Personnel by Defense Industries*, Hears./HR CAS SC/86C1/1959, p. 473; Janowitz, *Professional Soldier*, pp. 317–18.

67. 73 *Time* (May 11, 1959), 23; Janowitz, *Professional Soldier*, pp. 313–17.

VI. COMPETITION OF STRATEGIC PROGRAMS 485

68. 95 *Army-Navy-Air Force Journal* (Dec. 8, 1957), 411.

69. *New York Times*, Oct. 22, 1955, p. 10; *United States Air Force Basic Doctrine* (Air Force Manual 1–2, Apr. 1, 1954), p. 7.

70. W. M. Brucker, "A Year of Progress," 12 *Army Information Digest* (Feb. 1957), 2.

71. Dept. of the Army, *A Guide to Army Philosophy* (Pamphlet 20–1, Jan. 22, 1958), p. 32; *Air Force, Basic Doctrine*, p. 7.

72. Bernard Brodie, *Strategy in the Missile Age* (Princeton, 1959), p. 227; Dept. of the Army, *Army Philosophy*, p. 15.

73. "A National Military Program," October 1, 1956, in Taylor, *Uncertain Trumpet*, p. 31.

74. Gen. Nathan Twining, *Study of Airpower*, Hears./USS CAS SC/84C2/1956, p. 1486. See also Gen. Thomas D. White, "USAF Doctrine and National Policy," 41 *Air Force* (Jan. 1958), 51.

75. *Satellite and Missile Programs*, Hears./USS CAS SC/85C1/1957, p. 640.

76. Dept. of the Army, *Army Philosophy*, p. 15.

77. *National Defense Program—Unification and Strategy*, Hears./HR CAS/81C1/1949, p. 52.

78. *New York Times*, Jan. 25, 1959, p. E5; Taylor, *Uncertain Trumpet*, pp. 65–66, 71–72; *Defense Department Appropriations for 1960*, Hears./HR CA SC/86C1/1959, pp. 506–7.

79. *Satellite and Missile Programs*, Hears./USS CAS SC/85C1/1957, pp. 456, 858, 933, 959–61, 992–93.

80. See *New York Times:* May 14, 1959, p. 15; May 24, 1959, p. 1; May 25, 1959, p. 1; June 3, 1959, p. 14; June 7, 1959, p. 1; June 13, 1959, p. 1; June 14, 1959, p. 1; June 21, 1959, p. E7.

81. See Douglass Cater and A. T. Hadley, "The Army's Beefs Against the Air Force," 20 *The Reporter* (June 14, 1959), 16; *New York Times*, May 22, 1956, p. 15.

82. See Gary B. Christiansen, "Navy Political Tactics in Crisis" (Honors thesis, Harvard, 1956), p. 112.

83. *Defense Department Reorganization Act of 1958*, Hears./USS CAS/85C2/1958, p. 418. Admiral Radford used this point to urge statutory strengthening of the Secretary. Both the 1949 and 1953 reorganizations, however, had purported to establish his full authority over the Department.

84. Medaris, *Countdown for Decision*, pp. 64–65.

85. C. J. V. Murphy, "Defense: The Converging Decisions," 58 *Fortune* (Oct. 1958), 227.

86. *New York Times*, Mar. 5, 1960, p. 7.

87. Glenn H. Snyder, "The New Look," MS, p. 71, to be published in Warner R. Schilling, Paul Y. Hammond, Glenn H. Snyder, *Making National Security Policy: Three Case Studies* (New York, 1962); Taylor, *Un-*

certain Trumpet, p. 42. *New York Times:* July 19, 1956, p. 4; Aug. 16, 1957, p. 7; Sept. 20, 1957, p. 12; Nov. 16, 1957, p. 2; Nov. 18, 1959, pp. 2–3; Dec. 14, 1960.

88. Snyder, "New Look," p. 74n.; Dept. of the Army, *Army Philosophy,* pp. 15 ff.

89. Franklin A. Lindsay, S. Livermore, C. E. Mills, T. F. Walkowicz, "Defense Procurement: The Vital Roles of the National Security Council and the Joint Chiefs of Staff" (paper prepared for Task Force on Procurement, Commission on Organization, 1955), p. A-16; *Major Defense Matters,* Hears./USS CAS SC/86C1/1959, p. 69; *Defense Department Appropriations for 1960,* Hears./HR CA SC/86C1/1959, pp. 336–37.

90. Edward A. Ross, *The Principles of Sociology* (New York, 1920), p. 165. See also Lewis A. Coser, *The Functions of Social Conflict* (Glencoe, Ill., 1956), pp. 76–81.

91. Taylor, *Uncertain Trumpet,* pp. 102, 168. On this general point I am indebted to Christiansen, "Navy Political Tactics," pp. 113–15.

VII. THE POLITICS OF DETERRENCE

1. See Stephen Xydis, "The American Naval Visits to Greece and the Eastern Mediterranean in 1946: Their Impact on American-Soviet Relations" (Ph.D. thesis, Columbia, 1956).

2. Among the other elements of structural policy, see, for procurement: John Perry Miller, *Pricing of Military Procurement* (New Haven, 1949), chaps. 14, 15, and "Military Procurement Policies: World War II and Today," 42 *American Economic Review* (May 1952), 453–75; B. K. Gordon, "Conflicts in Military Procurement," 38 *Current History* (Apr. 1960), 234–39; Commission on Organization, Task Force on Procurement, *Report on Military Procurement* (Washington, 1955); Charles J. Hitch and Roland N. McKean, *The Economics of Defense in the Nuclear Age* (Cambridge, Mass., 1960), chap. 12, and Stephen Enke, "Logistics," chap. 14; *Military Procurement,* Hears./USS CAS SC/86C1/1959. On the military budget, see: Arthur Smithies, *The Budgetary Process in the United States* (New York, 1955), chaps. 11, 12; David Novick, *A New Approach to the Military Budget* (RAND Corp., RM-1759, June 12, 1956); Hitch and McKean, *Economics of Defense,* chap. 4; Frederick C. Mosher, *Program Budgeting: Theory and Practice with Particular Reference to the U. S. Department of the Army* (n.p., 1954); Commission on Organization, Task Force on Budget and Accounting, *Budget and Accounting* (Washington, 1955); Commission on Organization, *Report on Budget and Accounting* (Washington, 1955).

3. See H. A. Kissinger, "Strategy and Organization," 35 *Foreign Affairs* (Apr. 1957), 379–94; Col. A. P. Sights, Jr., "Major Tasks and Military Reorganization," 9 *Air Univ. Quarterly Rev.* (Winter, 1956–1957), 3–26; Wil-

liam R. Kintner and associates, *Forging a New Sword* (New York, 1958); Paul Y. Hammond, *Organizing for Defense* (Princeton, N. J., 1961).

4. See Samuel P. Huntington, *The Soldier and the State* (Cambridge, Mass., 1957), pp. 184–89, 428–55.

5. For a casual but more extensive summary, see my "Men at Arms?" 2 *Columbia University Forum* (Spring 1959), 42–47.

6. *Report of the Defense Advisory Committee on Profesional and Technical Compensation*, May 1957. Volume I, *Military Personnel*, p. 12.

7. Gene M. Lyons and John W. Masland, *Education and Military Leadership* (Princeton, N. J., 1959), p. 212. This volume is an excellent case study of the postwar disequilibrium in ROTC policy.

8. Quoted in Walter Lippmann, *The Communist World and Ours* (Boston, 1959), p. 23. See also Hans J. Morgenthau, "The Last Years of Our Greatness?" *The Purpose of American Politics* (New York, 1960), pp. 324–41.

9. Donald A. Quarles, Address, Wings Club, New York, N. Y. Nov. 18, 1957.

10. *New York Times*, March 7, 1958, p. 9.

11. See John K. Jessup, et al. *The National Purpose* (New York, 1960); *Goals for Americans: Report of the President's Commision on National Goals* (New York, 1960); Max Ways, *Beyond Survival* (New York, 1959); Walt W. Rostow, *The United States in the World Arena* (New York, 1960); Emmett Hughes, *America the Vincible* (Garden City, N. Y., 1959).

12. *Wall Street Journal*, Oct. 7, 1957, p. 10.

13. Richard M. Nixon, Address, National Association of Manufacturers, New York, N. Y., Dec. 6, 1957.

14. John Foster Dulles, *Mutual Security Act of 1958*, Hears./HR CFA/85C2/1958, pp. 230–31.

15. Alexis de Tocqueville, *Democracy in America* (New York, Vintage ed., 1954), I, 237, 243–44.

16. Walter Lippmann, *The Cold War* (New York, 1947), p. 20.

17. Fisher Ames, address in House of Representatives, 1795, quoted in Ralph W. Emerson, "Politics," *Essays: Second Series* (Philadelphia, 1893), p. 228. I am indebted to Harvey A. DeWeerd for first calling Ames's remarks to my attention.

Index

Absolute Weapon, The (Brodie), 451
Acheson, Dean, 112, 191, 313, 432; quoted, 316, 320–21
Action commitments and interventions, 124
Administration, the, *see* President (U. S.), Eisenhower Administration, Truman Administration
Administrative hierarchy, 171
Advisory Council on Naval Affairs, 392
Aeronautical and Space Sciences committees (congressional), 123
Africa: emergence of new nations, 15, 439
Agricultural surpluses, 2
Aircraft: nuclear powered, 137, 441
Aircraft carriers, 308, 377
Aircraft Industries Association, 402
Aircraft industry, 399–401
Air defense: Air Force study of, 307
Air Defense Command, 308
Air Force (U. S.): view of total war, 44; as strategic deterrent, 47, 74, 83–84; reduction of appropriations for, 71; technological innovations advanced by, 289; Project Lincoln and Project Vista, 307; views on European defense, 322 ff.; responsibility for continental defense, 328; political standing, 382 ff.; contributions to functional programs, 404 ff.
Air Force (periodical), 394
Air Force Air Defense Command, 326
Air Force Association, 394, 401
Air Force Organization Act (1951), 125n
Air University Quarterly Review, 383
Alliances, military, 431
All in One Lifetime (Byrnes), 450
Almond, Gabriel, 463; quoted, 15

Alsop, Joseph, 450
Alsop, Stewart, 450, 456
Alvarez, Luis, 300
"American Decision to Rearm Germany" (Martin), 476
American Ordnance Association, 401
American People and Foreign Policy, The (Almond), 449
Ames, Fisher, 447
Anderson, Orvil A., 17
Anglo-French plans (1954, 1956) for disarmament, 358
Appropriation and authorization (congressional), 129, 133 ff., 139–43
Arends, Leslie, quoted, 249
Armed forces (U. S.): postwar disintegration, 35 ff.; as deterrent, 39; deployment in Europe, 315 ff.
Armed Forces Reserve Act (1952), 125
Armed Services committees (congressional), 123, 125, 134, 138, 390
Armed Services Procurement Act (1947), 125
Arms and the State (Millis; Mansfield; Stein), 451
Arms limitation: as alternative to deterrence, 353 ff., 438; aspiration and achievement, 355–59; political aspects, 359–64; changes in program, 364–68
"Arms Races: Prerequisites and Results" (Huntington), 456
Army (U.S.): as supporter of limited war concept, 344 ff.; public relations activities, 392; contributions to functional programs, 404 ff.; *see also* Military services
Army and Air Force Vitalization and Retirement Equalization Act (1948), 125n

Army Antiaircraft Command, 326
Army Organization Act (1950), 125n
Arnold, H. H., quoted, 370, 375, 440
Asia: emergence of new nations, 15, 439
Association of the U. S. Army, 394
Atomic bomb: Soviet explosion of, 17; in support of political position, 40–41; as deterrent, 45, 298; see also Hydrogen bomb; Nuclear weapons
Atomic Energy Commission, 296, 300 ff.
"Atomic Weapons and American Policy" (Oppenheimer), 477
"Atoms-for-peace" speech (1953), 221, 337
Austrian peace treaty (1955), 90
Authorization, see Appropriation and authorization

B-36 debate, 299, 374, 381, 384, 412
Bacher, Robert, 305
"Backstop" associations, 394–98
Bagehot, Walter, quoted, 168
Baghdad Pact (1955), 315
Balaklava, battle of, 22
"Balance of Military Power, The" (anon.), 452
Balance-of-power system, 14
Balance of terror, 88–90, 91, 92, 101 ff., 116, 120, 207, 294, 341
Baldwin, Hanson, 482; quoted, 83, 97
Bargaining relationships, 148, 193
Bartlett, Charles L., quoted, 152
Baruch, Bernard, 46, 358
"Basic National Security Policy" (NSC), 128, 349, 350, 458
Bentley, Arthur F., quoted, 132
Berdahl, Clarence A., 457
Berkner, Lloyd, quoted, 335
Berlin crisis: *1948*, 124; *1960*, 205
Bethe, Hans, 305
Bipartisanship in foreign policy, 179
Bradley, Omar N., 46, 114; quoted, 49–50, 149–50, 334
Bres, E. S., 483
Brewster-Hinshaw Board, 372
Brodie, Bernard, 348, 449; quoted, 45–46, 410
Brooks, Overton, 144
"Brushfire" wars, 28, 41
Brussels Treaty (1948), 313
Budget (U. S.): Eisenhower Administration, 67, 70, 77–78, 197 ff., 209 ff.; as instrument of civilian control, 151; postwar period (1945–1960), 212–14;

total and major national security expenditures, 283; in debates on continental defense, 334; allocations to the services, 413 ff.; see also Military budget
Budget Bureau, 7, 72, 222 ff.
"Budgeting for Deterrence" (Taylor), 460
Bull Committee (1953), 332, 333
Bundy, McGeorge, 461
Bureaucratic groups: in determination of military policy, 123 ff.
"Bureaucratic innovator," 310
Bureaucratic pluralism, 168
Bureau of Investigation, 310
"Bureau philosophy," 402
Burns, James M., 471
Bush, Vannevar, 461
Byrnes, James F., 16, 35, 37, 450

Cabinet Committee on Price Stability for Economic Growth (1959), 213
Campbell, John C., 450, 451
Canada: adopts early warning system, 339–40
"Can We Entrust Defense to a Committee?" (Morgenthau), 463
Capabilities of other nations: as external influence on military effort, 199–207
Career Compensation Act (1949), 125n
Career Incentive Act (1955), 125n
Carrier airpower, 308, 377
Carroll, Holbert N., quoted, 180
Cary, William L., 465
"Challenge and Response in U. S. Policy" (Dulles), 456
Chiang Kai-shek, 19
Chidlaw, Benjamin W., 340–41
China, 14, 49
Churchill, Sir Winston, 63, 64; quoted, 89, 298
Churchill, Roosevelt, Stalin (Feis), 450
Civil defense, 58, 106 ff., 134; programs, 353–68
"Civilian Aides to the Secretary of the Army" (Cleary), 483
Civil-military relations, 6, 7, 190, 371, 378–81, 385–402, 419 ff.
Civil War (U.S.), 11
Class politics, 265
Cline, Ray S., 451
Cohen, Bernard C., 469
Cold War: military policies, 14–24, 27, 33, 38 ff.; strategic programs, 134;

INDEX

public opinion, 235; functional programs, 286; interservice controversies, 422 ff.; security as goal in, 428
"Collective Defense: The Military Commitment" (King), 453
Collective security, 14, 27, 60 ff.
Collins, J. L., 451; quoted, 46, 344
Colm, Gerhard, quoted, 269
Colonial systems, 15
Commercial expansion, 12, 13
Committee for Economic Development, quoted, 208
Committee system, 167 ff., 188 ff.
CONAD, 292, 340, 341
Conant, James B., 306
Conciliar structure, 123, 147, 154
Concurrent majority, 156
Congress: appropriations, 63, 110; appointment of Chiefs of Staff, 71; evaluation of Soviet threat (1956), 100; determination of military policy, 123 ff., 127, 290, 337 ff.; lobbying, 135–46; attitudes toward executive, 143–45; consensus in, 178 ff; hearings, 187–88; image of public opinion, 249; Administration and opposition parties in, 251 ff.; service competition in relation to, 387–91, 393 ff.; patterns of voting by members and nonmembers of service committees, 390n; joint resolutions, 431
"Congress and the Formation of Military Policy" (Dexter), 458
Congressional Aviation Policy Board, 375
"Congressional-Executive Relations and the Foreign Policy Consensus" (Hilsman), 458
Congressmen, 388–90
Connally, Tom, quoted, 389–90
Consensus: development of, 147 ff., 168–69, 174–75, 178, 184, 187, 193, 404, 409–12, 441, 445; disruption of, 287–88, 293
Conservatives in Power (Dale), 465
Constitutional pluralism, 168
Consumer prices, 212 ff.
Containment policy, 15 ff., 33, 39 ff.
Continental defense, 78; innovation of program, 294, 295 ff., 326–41
Continental Defense Command, 292, 340, 341
Continental expansion, 12
Cordiner Committee (1957), 436

Cork, Howard H., 467
Cornell University survey (1946), 267n
Council of Foreign Ministers: *1945*, 34, 36; *1947*, 312
Countercity strategy, 103 ff.
Counterforce strategy, 103 ff., 119
"Crisis in U. S. Defense, The" (Knorr), 456
"Critical program," 287, 289
Cutler, Robert, quoted, 182, 194

Dale, Edwin L., Jr., 465
Dean, Gordon, 306
Decision-making: loci of, 5; executive processes, 146 ff.; committees vs. individual executive, 167; arenas for domestic and military programs, 220; developing new programs, 287, 290, 291; hydrogen bomb debates, 298 ff., 473; European defense program, 312–26; continental defense program, 326–41; limited war program, 348 ff.
Declaration of war, 124
Defense, Secretary of, 6, 192 ff.
Defense Department, 49, 378–81
Defense Department Reorganization Act (1958), 109, 125n
Defense Production Act (1950), 271
De Gaulle, Charles, 10
Demobilization: postwar, 33 ff.
Democratic party, 252 ff., 266 ff.
Denfeld, Louis E., quoted, 160
"Determent," 45, 451
Deterrence, strategy of, 23; conflict with strategy of mobilization, 25 ff.; stability, 29; State Department statement (1948), 39–40; budgetary and doctrinal constraints, 43; forces-in-being, 45; NSC 68, 56; U. S.-Soviet military balance, 59; strategic airpower and nuclear weapons, 74, 78; continental defense, 78, 326–41; doctrine of "sufficiency," 99–105; counterforce vs. countercity strategy, 103; limited war, 105–6, 341–53; Soviet policy, 120; policy determinations, 124; external influences on, 199–207; functional programs, 284; new programs, 284 ff., 293–95, 427–30, 446; hydrogen bomb, 298–312; SAC, 309 ff.; European defense, 312–26; uses of force, 430–32; structural policies, 432–37, 486; success of, 437–39; security and purpose, 439–47

De Tocqueville, Alexis, quoted, 446
Developments in Military Technology and Their Impact on United States Strategy and Foreign Policy (Washington Center of Foreign Policy Research), 453
Dexter, Lewis A., 131, 468, 469
Dinerstein, Herbert S., 454, 465
Diplomatic issues: in innovation of functional programs, 286
Disarmament, *see* Arms limitation
Disequilibrium: in military policy, 7–14, 285, 437
Distant early warning system, 328, 329, 334
Doctrine proliferation, 402–4, 407–9
Dodge, Joseph M., 334; quoted, 209
Dollar stability, 213
Domestic expenditures, 207 ff., 242–43
Domestic policy: New Look, 64 ff.; military programs, 115, 214–18; foreign policy vs., 197 ff.; domestic programs, 90, 207–10; taxation, 210–12; balanced budgets, 212–14
Donnelly, Charles H., 449
Donovan, Robert J., 453
Dulles, Allen, quoted, 204
Dulles, John Foster, 74, 77, 84, 112, 115, 124, 191, 216, 351, 432, 453, 454; quoted, 18, 80, 90, 106, 444–45

East Germany, 19
Eckstein, Otto, 465
Economic controls, 271 ff.
Economic policy: of Eisenhower Administration, 65 ff.
Economics in the Public Service (Nourse), 451
Economic Stabilization Agency (1950), 271
Economic strength: in relation to military strength, 203
Economy (U. S.): military policy in relation to, 115–22, 268 ff.
Economy drives, 232–34
Eddy, Nancy Boardman, 450
Education and information: as factors in public opinion polls, 247 ff.
Edwards Committee (1953), 333
Effective decisions, 127
Eisenhower, Dwight D., 44, 62, 325; quoted, 18, 45, 66, 77, 80, 209, 210, 339
Eisenhower Administration: military budgets, 42, 218 ff., 223 ff., 232–34, 255; "New Look," 64–106; congressional relations, 143; control methods, 152; public interest in strategic programs, 176; components of the Great Equation, 197 ff.; domestic spending programs, 209; image of public opinion, 249 ff.; continental defense, 328; limited war, 343 ff.; civil defense, 360 ff.; preference for strategic deterrence weapons, 418; *see also* Gaither Committee Report; New Look; President (U. S.); Truman Administration
Eisenhower Doctrine, 124, 431
"Eisenhower Shift, The" (Murphy), 453
Eisenhower: The Inside Story (Donovan), 453
Elections, national: defense issue in, 259–64
English Constitution, The (Bagehot), 463
Environment, external, 14–15, 47, 116, 199–207, 426 ff.
"Essential Principles of a Disarmament Program," 358
European defense system, 62, 75, 312–26
Evolution of Foreign Policy (Dulles), 453
Excise Tax Reduction Act (1954), 76
Executive department: in determination of military policy, 123 ff., 127 ff.; congressional relations, 143–45; divergent interests, 169; attitudes toward innovation of functional program, 290; *see also* Eisenhower Administration; President (U. S.); Truman Administration
Executive Influence in Determining Military Policy in the United States (White), 457
Executive legislation: processes of policy-making, 146 ff.; unanimity and strategic legislatures, 155–62; producing agreement, 162–66; leadership in strategy, 188–96

Federal Budget and Fiscal Policy, 1789–1958 (Kimmel), 453
Federal Civil Defense Act (1950), 355
Federal Civil Defense Administration, 106, 355, 359, 360
Federalist policies, 12

INDEX

Feis, Herbert, 450
Finite deterrent strategy, *see* Countercity strategy
Finletter Commission, 190, 372
Finney, John W., 456
"Fiscal Fifty Military Budget, The" (Schilling), 464
Fiscal policy, 2, 4; Eisenhower Administration, 64 ff., 76; dollar softness, 96; politics of, 197–99, 266; foreign policy goals limited by, 443; *see also* Budget (U. S.); Military budget
Five-Year Plan (1946), 34
Flood, Daniel J., quoted, 164
Florida, purchase of, 12
Force: uses of, 430–32
Force levels: determination of, 130, 133, 142, 144, 145
Forces-in-being, 26, 27, 45, 56, 62
Foreign Affairs committee (congressional), 123
Foreign aid: appropriations requests, 134; public opinion toward, 235, 243, 247; congressional attitudes, 252 ff.
Foreign policy: historical development of, 12–14; containment and alternative policies, 15–20, 39 ff.; in Cold War period, 20, 33 ff.; expenditures, 42 ff., 51–54; 94, 95, 210; budgetary limitations, 48; NSC 162, 74; Eisenhower Administration, 76, 85, 97; military strategy in relation to, 115; congressional procedures, 179; European defense, 312–26; national security as goal of, 426, 439, 441–42; defined by limits of U. S. goals in world politics, 445
Foreign Policy and Party Politics: Pearl Harbor to Korea (Westerfield), 450, 463
Foreign Relations committee (congressional), 123
Forest Service, 310
Formosan crisis: *1955*, 69, 124, 201; *1958*, 201
Forrestal, James V., quoted, 31, 37, 42
Forrestal Diaries, The, 450, 451
Fortune poll (1946), 244–45
Fosdick, Dorothy, 458
France, 9
Fuchs, Klaus, 474
Functional programs: innovation of, 284 ff.; *see also* Structural policies

"Gaither Committee and the Policy Process, The" (Halperin), 456
Gaither Committee Report, 96, 104, 106–13, 115, 190, 205, 216, 221, 277, 350, 360, 367, 456
Galbraith, J. K., 117
Gallup surveys, 236–40, 242, 244, 248, 267n; *see also* Public opinion
Gamelin, Maurice G., 10
Garthoff, Raymond L., 119; quoted, 120
Gavin, James M., quoted, 150
"Generalist-specialist" conflict, 219
Geneva Conference (1955), 69, 90
Geological Survey, 310
George, Harold, 322
Germany: participation in defense efforts, 62; rearmament, 75, 316 ff.
"Gibraltar" speech (Hoover), 16, 323
Ginzberg, Eli, quoted, 287
Government: concept of nature of, 443 ff.
Governmental Process, The (Truman), 465
Grassmuck, George L., 253n, 469
"Grass roots" cultivation by military services, 391–94
Great Britain: maritime supremacy, 12; defense concepts (1952), 63, 64; military policies, 118; public opinion toward defense expenditures, 243n
"Great Debate" (1951), 16
Gross national product, 211–12, 269, 275, 282
Ground forces: contraction of, 79
Gruenther, Alfred M., 44
"Guide to Army Philosophy, A," 404

Hadley, A. T., 456
Halperin, Morton H., 112, 456, 478
Hamilton, Alexander, quoted, 127
Hammond, Paul Y., 449, 450, 451; quoted, 50
Harriman, W. Averell, quoted, 33
Helena Conference (1952), 66, 197, 213
Hierarchical structure, 123, 147, 154, 171
Hill, A. G., 329
Hilsman, Roger, 449, 452, 459; quoted, 130
Hirschman, Albert, 368
History of Personnel Demobilization in the United States Army (Sparrow), 450
Hoag, M. W., 472

Holaday, William M., 456
Holcombe, Arthur N., 463; quoted, 265
Holifield Military Operations subcommittee, 363
Hoover, Herbert, 16
Hoover, J. Edgar, 310
Hoover Commission, quoted, 225, 421
House Military Appropriations subcommittee, 390
Humphrey, George, 72, 114–15, 334; quoted, 79
Humphrey, Hubert, 364, 479
Hungarian crisis (1956), 19, 201, 352
Hydrogen bomb, 48–49, 294, 298 ff.; *see also* Atomic bomb; Nuclear weapons

Ickes, Harold L., 37, 38
"Ideology" of bureaucracies, 402
"Ike and the Peaceful Atom" (Lear), 477
Indochina crisis (1954), 69, 124, 201, 349
Industrial potential, 45, 46, 275
Infinite deterrent strategy, *see* Counterforce strategy
Inflation, 66, 91, 212 ff.
Information: restrictive policies, 184–85
Innovation: dialogue of, 293–98; bureaucratic, 310; *see also* Strategic programs, innovation of
Interest groups: conflicting pressures of, 132; pressures on domestic spending, 208; resistance to economic controls, 271 ff.
Internationalism, 14
International politics: structure, 439 ff.
International Security: The Military Aspect (Rockefeller Brothers Fund), 456
Interservice rivalry, 160, 164, 217–18; in development of continental defense, 340; role in Army's support of limited war concept, 345; rise of, 369–74; competition of programs, 374–78; civil-military relations, 378–81; rationale of political activity, 381–84; relations with Congress, 387–91, 393 ff.; industrial competition stimulated by, 399; proliferation of doctrine, 402–4; changes in doctrine, 407–9; proprietary issues, 412–17; affected by Administration preferences, 417–21; conflict and unification, 421–25
Intraservice rivalry, 405 ff.
Investigation, congressional, 138–39
Isolationism, 12, 16, 30
"Is the H-Bomb Enough?" (Murphy), 80

Jackson, Henry M., 452; quoted, 51, 136, 216
Janowitz, Morris, 460, 483
Japan, 75
Jewell, M. E., 253, 469
Johnson, Louis, 17, 49
Johnson missile investigation (1957–1958), 139
Joint Chiefs of Staff: budgetary estimates, 49, 50, 70, 72; *Sequoia* paper (1953), 73, 74, 75; policy formulation, 74–76, 84, 114 ff., 129, 149, 153 ff., 192 ff.; Puerto Rico meeting (1956), 92–93, 454; conciliar structure, 123; agreement and disagreement, 159, 162–66; criticism of, 170 ff.; hydrogen bomb, 300 ff.; European defense plans, 319 ff.
Joint Committee on Atomic Energy, 123, 136 ff., 300
Joint Strategic Objectives Plan, 129

Kahn, Herman, 106, 206, 453; quoted, 367
Katzenbach, E. L., Jr., 464
Kaufmann, William W., 348
Kefauver subcommittee of the Senate Armed Services Committee, 363
Kelly Committee (1952), 331, 332, 336
Kennan, George F., 15, 302, 343, 348; quoted, 34–35, 37–38, 39
Kennedy, John F., 264, 349
Kenney, George, 308
Kenworthy, E. W., 456
Key West conference (1948), 149
Khrushchev, N., quoted, 90, 120, 121
Killian, James R., 365
Killian Committee, 89, 190
Kimmel, Lewis H., 453
King, James E., Jr., 453
Kissinger, Henry A., 348, 456, 486; quoted, 168
Knorr, Klaus, 452, 456
Korean War, 16, 17, 53, 124; military budget increased by, 201; economic controls, 271 ff.; effects on European

defense plans, 316 ff.; as limited war, 342 ff.; as failure of deterrence, 437
Landon, Truman H., 50, 114
Latin America, 12
Lawrence, Ernest O., 300
"Leakage" of information, 185
Lear, J., 477
Lebanon crisis (1958), 96, 124, 201, 352
Legislative activities of military services, 387 ff.
"Legislative Watchdog of the Atom" (Fosdick), 458
Le May, Curtis E., 309 ff., 324, 406
Lemnitzer, Lyman, 407
Liaison activities of military services, 388
Liberal reform, 172
"Liberation": as Cold War policy, 18
Lilienthal, David E., 48, 301, 343; quoted, 303, 304
Limited war: as strategic program, 341–53
Limited War (Osgood), 348
Lincoln, G. A., 451
Lincoln Laboratory, 329
Lincoln Summer Study Group, 190, 295, 329 ff., 335
Lippmann, Walter, quoted, 85, 234–35, 446
Lisbon Conference (1952), 62, 63, 64, 80
Livermore (California), 307
Lloyd, David D., quoted, 210
London Conference (1957), 361, 365
Long-range ballistic missile programs, 96
Los Alamos (New Mexico), 307
Louisiana Purchase, 12
Lovett, Robert, 113, 313, 450
Lubell, Samuel, 464, 469; quoted, 240–41
Lyons, G. M., 463

MacArthur, Douglas, 16, 18, 139
McCloy, John J., 113
McDonald, John, quoted, 312
McMahon, Brien, 136
McNarney Board (1948), 227
Maginot Line, 10
Making National Security Policy: Three Case Studies (Schilling; Hammond; Snyder), 449, 453
Manpower potential, 46, 58

Mansfield, Harvey C., 451
March, James G., quoted, 287, 289
Marine Corps: public relations section, 385n
Marine Corps Act (1952), 140, 372
Marshall, George C., 45; quoted, 40, 44, 54, 56, 57, 58, 59, 62
Martin, L. W., 476; quoted, 317–18, 320, 321
"Massive retaliation" speech (Dulles), 74, 84, 348
Mass opinion, *see* Public opinion
Matthews, Francis, 17
"Maximum danger," period of, 57, 67–68, 452
Meany, George L., 277
Medaris, John B., quoted, 418
Memoirs (Truman), 450
Middle East Doctrine, *see* Eisenhower Doctrine
Military alliances, 28
Military Appropriations subcommittees (congressional), 123
Military assistance program, 314 ff.
Military budget: "remainder method," 42, 75, 221, 466; industrial and manpower potential, 46; Korean War, 53; Eisenhower policies, 76 ff.; domestic and foreign pressures, 90 ff., 214–18; expansion of, 117; congressional appropriations, 129; external influences, 199–207; process phases, 222 ff.; pre-Congress controls, 223–29; post-Congress controls, 229–32; economy drives, 232–34; public opinion, 242–43; party differences, 254 ff.; political consequences of drastic changes in, 268–77; magnitude of security effort, 1945–1960, 277–83; *see also* Budget (U. S.); Foreign policy
Military budgets, Fiscal years: *1946,* 42; *1947,* 42, 230; *1948,* 42, 221, 223, 278; *1949,* 42, 223, 375; *1950,* 42, 43, 54, 90, 223–226, 230, 231; *1951,* 43, 50, 52, 161, 223, 227n, 230; *1952,* 54, 55, 60, 227; *1953,* 55; *1954,* 65, 70; *1955,* 72, 73, 74, 76, 78, 83, 84, 150, 209, 225, 228, 230; *1956,* 77, 79, 216, 230; *1957,* 87, 88, 91, 94, 279; *1958,* 93, 94, 231; *1959,* 96; *1960,* 96, 150, 224; *1961,* 96
Military leaders: role in policy-making and implementation of policy, 114 ff.
Military Pay Act (1958), 125n

Military policy: purpose, 2–3, 26; equilibrium and disequilibrium, 7–14, 285, 437; development of, 12–14, 65 ff., 284, 426–37; environmental factors, 14–15, 28, 32, 47, 116, 199–207, 426 ff.; stability, 29–32, 200 ff.; phases, 32; conflicts in, 39–47; rearmament, 53–54; mobilization vs. deterrence, 56; European defense, 62, 75, 312–26; Eisenhower Administration, 64, 69–70; continental defense, 78, 294, 295 ff., 326–41; Administration's role, 113 ff., 124, 218–23, 291, 417 ff.; Congress, 127, 253 ff.; public opinion, 234–42, 263, 428; strategic deterrence, 298–312; SAC, 309 ff.; consensus, 409–12; uses of force, 430–32; limits set by U. S. goals in world politics, 445; *see also* Decision-making; Eisenhower Administration; National Security Council Reports; Strategic decisions; Strategic programs, innovation of; Structural policies; Truman Administration

Military Policy and the National Security (Kaufmann), 348

Military Policy of the United States, The (Upton), 21

Military services: political aspects, 370 ff., 381–85, 405; public relations, 385–87; cultivation of "grass roots," 391; articulation of interests, 394–98; "backstop" associations, 394–98; proliferation of doctrine, 402–4, 407–9; balance of functional programs, 417–21; conflict and unification, 421–25; structural policies, 432–37, 486; *see also* Interservice rivalry

Military Training Camps Association, 392

Millis, Walter, 450–451; quoted, 221, 317

Mission capability, 101

Mobilization, 13, 25, 56–59, 67, 81–82, 97, 237, 240

Monetary policy, 213; *see also* Fiscal policy

Monroe Doctrine, 12, 438

Montgomery, B. L., Viscount, quoted, 161–62*n*

Mooney, Richard E., quoted, 231–32

Morgenthau, Hans J., 469; quoted, 168–69

Morton, Louis, 481

Munitions, 216, 398–402

Murphy, C. J. V., 453, 454; quoted, 222

Mutual Defense Assistance Program, 48, 314

National debt, 94

National Defense Act: *1916*, 21; *1920*, 21, 371

National Defense Education Act (1958), 110

National Guard, 393

National Planning Association, 269

National policy, 5, 8 ff., 51, 66–69, 73, 203, 408 ff.; *see also* Military policy

"National purpose" discussions, 442

National Reserve Plan, 81

National Security Act (1947), 125*n*, 372, 434

National Security Council, 20, 123, 128, 153 ff., 162–66, 170 ff., 190 ff., 224 ff., 302

National Security Council Papers: NSC 20, 39, 51; NSC 68, 19, 47–53, 59–60, 64, 65, 69, 111–13, 128, 221, 304, 326; NSC 141, 331; NSC 162, 20, 73 ff., 128, 333, 334, 338

National Security Industrial Association, 401

National Security Training Commission, 59, 81

NATO, 62, 63, 64, 80, 124, 294, 312, 314 ff.

NATO and American Security (Knorr), 452

NATO Conference (1958), 110

"NATO: The Developing Strategic Context" (Hilsman), 452

Navy (U. S.): strategic retaliation weapons developed, 308; attitudes toward limited war concept, 347 ff.; post-World War II plans, 376 ff.; contributions to functional programs, 404 ff.; interservice relationships of, 423–24

Navy League, 394 ff., 401

Navy Organization Act (1948), 125*n*

Necessity for Choice: Prospects of American Foreign Policy, The (Kissinger), 456

Negotiation and concession, 15

Neustadt, Richard E., 467

Neutrality, 12

Neville, Richard O., 477

"New Civil Military Relations, The" (Lyons), 463

INDEX

New Look (1953–1960), 64–106; *see also* Eisenhower Administration
"New Look, The" (Snyder), 453
Nike antiaircraft missiles, 340
Nimitz, Chester W., 450
Nitze, Paul, 49, 449, 452; quoted, 51
Nixon, Richard M., 263
North American Air Defense Command, 341
North Atlantic Council, 317 ff.
North Atlantic Treaty (1949), 43, 312 ff.
"Notes on the Observation and Measurement of Political Power" (Simon), 459
Nourse, Edwin G., 451
NSC, *see* National Security Council
Nuclear test ban, 366, 480
Nuclear weapons, 15, 45, 48, 65, 74, 79–81, 89, 105, 136 ff., 300 ff., 307; *see also* Atomic bomb; Hydrogen bomb
Nuclear Weapons and Foreign Policy (Kissinger), 348, 463

Office of Civil Relations, 393
Office of Defense Mobilization, 58
Office of Legislative Affairs, 387
Office of the Chief of Legislative Liaison, 387
Office of the Special Assistant for Disarmament, 361, 363
Officer Personnel Act (1947), 125*n*
"On the Character of Modern War" (Talensky), 457
On Thermonuclear War (Kahn), 453
"Op-23," 403
"Open Skies" proposal for disarmament, 358, 365
"Operation Candor," 220, 336
"Operation Paperclip," 164
"Operation Solarium," 73, 332, 333
Oppenheimer, J. Robert, 303, 343; quoted, 300, 301, 305, 306, 336–37
Opposition party, 251 ff.
Orem, H. E., quoted, 170
Organizational autonomy, 293
Organizing for National Security: Selected Materials, 463
Osgood, Robert E., 348
Our More Perfect Union (Holcombe), 463
Overseas bases, 60, 308

Paris conference (1960), 205

Paris Peace Conference (1946), 36
Parker, S. S., quoted, 276
Partisanship: on controversial military policy, 178–81
Phillips, T. R., 452
Pike, Sumner, 306
Pinchot, Gifford, 310
Poland, 19
Policy Coordinating Group (Army), 403
Policy Planning Staff (U. S. State Department), 48
Political Economy of National Security, The (Schlesinger), 466
Political parties, 251–59, 264, 266
"Political Position of the United States Army, 1945–1958, The" (Neville), 477
Politics, domestic, 2, 41, 51 ff., 63, 131 ff.
Powell, John Wesley, 310
"Pre-emptive war," doctrine of, 119
"Preparedness," 26
President (U. S.): decision-making, 124, 218–23, 234, 291, 417 ff.; executive legislation, 147 ff.; leadership, 181 ff., 193, 240, 241; pre-Congress and post-Congress budgetary process, 223–32; economy drives, 232–34; intervention in labor disputes, 274; declarations of interest or intention, 431
Presidential Power: The Politics of Leadership (Neustadt), 467
President's Air Policy Commission, 375
"Pressure Groups and the Increasing Erosion of the Revenue Laws" (Cary), 465
Preventive war, 7
Price, Melvin, 137
Price controls, *see* Economic controls
Prices, *see* Consumer prices; Wholesale price index
Process of Government, The (Bentley), 458
Productive capacity, 31, 40–41
Professional Soldier, The (Janowitz), 460
Project Charles, 329
Project East River, 357, 363
Project Lincoln (1951), 307
Project Vista (1952), 307
"Proposals for Partial Measures of Disarmament," 358
"Proposals for Progressive and Continuous Disclosure and Verification of Armed Forces and Armaments," 358

Public debate, 174 ff., 299, 303 ff., 323 ff., 337 ff., 348 ff.
Public opinion: defense effort, 234–48; images of, 248–51; "grass roots" activities of military services, 391–94; *see also* Gallup surveys
"Public Opinion and National Security Policy" (Almond), 463
Public Opinion and United States Foreign Policy, 1937–1956 (Eddy), 450
Public relations: military services, 385–87, 391–94
Puerto Rico meeting of JCS, 92–93, 115, 350, 454

Quarles, Donald, 455; quoted, 101, 102
Quemoy crisis (1958), 96, 124, 352

Radar stations, 326
Radford, Arthur W., 74, 114, 450, 485; quoted, 44–45, 221–22, 417
Radford Plan, 93, 99, 102, 262, 455
RAND Corporation study (1958), 367
Raw material stockpiling, 58
Rearmament, 53–56, 62, 75
Recession (1957–1958), 276
Redstone Arsenal, 404
Regulatory commissions, 153n
Reilley, Ewing W., quoted, 287
"Remainder method," 42, 75, 221, 466
Reorganization Act (1958), 115, 423
Reorganization Plan No. 6 (1955), 125n
Republican Party, 87, 113, 252 ff., 266 ff.
Requirements of Deterrence, The (Kaufmann), 478
Reserve forces, 81–82, 97–99, 436
Reserve Forces Act (1955), 81, 98, 125
Reserve military organizations, 393 ff.
Reserve Officer Personnel Act (1954), 125n
Reynaud, Paul, 10
Rhineland, remilitarization of, 10
Rickover, H., 311n
Ridenour, Louis, 329
Ridgway, Matthew B., 84; quoted, 82, 149, 345, 346
Rio Treaty (1948), 315
Rivkin, Steven, quoted, 333
Roberts, Chalmers, 456
Rockefeller, Nelson A., 263
Rockefeller Brothers Fund Report, 209, 277, 456
Root, Elihu, 311
Roper Commercial Survey (1946), 236
Ross, E. A., quoted, 422–23

Rostow, W. W., 464
Rotation of duty, 311
ROTC, 436–37, 487
Russell, Richard B., quoted, 135
Russia, *see* Soviet Union

SAC, *see* Strategic Air Command
SAGE system communications system, 340
Schilling, Warner R., 204, 305, 449, 464, 474; quoted, 306
Schlesinger, James R., 466, 471
Science and Astronautics committees (congressional), 123
Scientists, civilian, 300
Seapower, 41
SEATO, 124
Sectional patterns, 257 ff., 265
Security Act Amendments (1949), 125n
Security expenditures, *see* Military budget
Selective service, 436; *1946*, 133; *1948*, 125n
Sequoia meeting (1953), 73, 74, 333
Service interests, *see* Interservice rivalry
"Seven Wise Men," 331, 333, 335
"Sham Battle over 'Spending,' The" (Lloyd), 465
SHAPE, 62, 80–81, 292, 325–26
Shelling, Thomas C., quoted, 365
Shils, Edward, 247
Shipbuilding industry, 399
Silberman, Charles, quoted, 276
Simon, Herbert A., 459; quoted, 287, 289
Slessor, Sir John, 63
Snyder, Glenn H., 449, 450, 453, 466; quoted, 74, 87
Socio-economic pluralism, 168
Sokolovsky, V. D., quoted, 121
Souers, Sidney, 48
"Sources of Soviet Conduct, The" (Kennan), 15, 450
Southeast Asia Treaty (1954), 315
Soviet bloc, 14
Soviet Strategy in the Nuclear Age (Garthoff), 457
Soviet Union: U. S. relations, 14, 39, 185–86, 426 ff.; strategy, 31, 66, 118, 119 ff.; foreign policy, 33 ff., 90; atomic and nuclear weapons, 47, 59, 300, 304, 333, 358; capabilities, 88, 203 ff., 285; sputniks, 95, 96; limited war threat, 341 ff.
Spaatz, Carl A., quoted, 45, 369

Spanish-American War, 11
Sparrow, John C., 450
"Sputnik and American Public Opinion" (Lubell), 468
Stages of Economic Growth, The (Rostow), 464
Stalin, Joseph V., 68; quoted, 34
Stassen, Harold, 359, 361, 362
State Department, 7, 39–40, 49, 191, 214 ff., 302, 319 ff.
State of the Union Message (1954), 454
Statutory authorization, 129
Steel strike (1952), 63, 274
Stein, Harold, 451
Stevenson, Adlai E., 260; quoted, 262
Stimson, Henry L., quoted, 156
Stockpiling Act (1946), 58
Story, Charles D., 460
STRAC, *see* Strategic Army Corps
Strategic Air Command, 83, 107, 292, 308 ff.
Strategic Army Corps, 292, 352, 378
Strategic decisions, 3, 5; Cold War, 20–24; stability, 29–32; containment policy, 39 ff.; Eisenhower policies, 71 ff.; balance, 113–15; congressional lobbying, 135–46; legislation, 146–66; program development, 147–55, 427–30; strategy-making process, 166–96, 124 ff.; limited war concept, 342; *see also* Structural policy
"Strategic pluralism," 264
Strategic programs, innovation of: partisanship, 178–81; patterns, 284–98; process of, 286–93; issues, 293–98; thermonuclear weapons, 298–312; European defense, 312–26; continental defense, 326–41; limited war, 341–53; alternative programs, 353–68; competition of, 369–84, 404–25, 417–21; continuance of innovation, 429 ff.
"Strategy and Organization" (Kissinger), 486
Strategy-making, 174–96
Strauss, Lewis L., 300, 301
Structural policies, 3–7, 20–24, 123–35, 177, 186–87, 432–37, 486
Suez crisis (1956), 201, 352
Sufficiency, doctrine of, 101, 105, 106
Symington airpower hearings (1956), 139

Tactical Air Command, 83, 308, 352
Taft, Robert A., 71, 85, 323
Talensky, Nicolai A., 457

Taxation, 53, 54, 76, 77, 210–12, 243–45
Taylor, Maxwell D., 350, 455, 456, 457; quoted, 31, 161, 165, 346, 348, 351, 411, 460
Technological innovation, 118, 286
Teller, Edward, 300, 307; quoted, 304
Territorial aggression, 439, 440
Thayer, Sylvanus, 310
"This Is Your Army" (film), 386
Thor-Jupiter controversy, 400, 414
Torment of Secrecy, The (Shils), 247
Trends in Public Expenditures in the Next Decade (Eckstein), 465
Truman, David B., 465
Truman, Harry S., 37, 38, 41, 304, 450, 474; quoted, 43, 53, 55, 143, 183, 218, 219, 317
Truman Administration: budgets, 42–43, 218 ff., 223 ff., 232–34, 255; hydrogen bomb program, 48–49; NSC 68, 52–53, 68, 111–12; UMT, 59; military and foreign policies, 64; attitude toward Congress, 143; public interest in strategic programs, 176; image of public opinion, 249 ff.; NATO, 312 ff.; limited war, 343 ff.; *see also* Eisenhower Administration; President (U. S.)
Truman Doctrine, 15, 431
Turner, Julius, 257
Twining, Nathan, 406; quoted, 411

UMT, 59, 240, 371, 435
Uncertain Trumpet, The (Taylor), 455, 456
"Unification and Strategy" (hearings, 1949), 138–39
Unification of services, 371 ff., 421 ff., 434 ff.
Uniform Code of Military Justice (1950), 125
Uniformed Services Pay Increase Act (1952), 125n
United Nations, 90
"United States Air Force Basic Doctrine," 403
United States in World Affairs, 1945–1947, The (Campbell), 450
Universal Military Training, 59, 240, 371, 435
Universal Military Training and Service Act (1951), 125n
"Unlimited Weapons and Limited War" (Brodie), 478
USSR, *see* Soviet Union

U-2 crisis (1960), 201, 205

Valley, George E., Jr., 329
Vandenburg, Arthur H., quoted, 313, 314
Vandenburg, Hoyt S., 329; quoted, 300–1
Veto power of Congress, 132, 133, 134, 135, 140
Vinson, Carl. 144, 390; quoted, 231
Vinson Acts (1920s), 371
von Braun, Wernher, quoted, 381, 399

Wage boards, 274 ff.
Wage controls, *see* Economic controls
Wallace, Henry, 16
War and Peace in the Space Age (Gavin), 460
War and the Soviet Union (Dinerstein), 454, 465
War Powers of the Executive in the United States (Berdahl), 457
Washington Command Post: The Operations Division (Cline), 451
Weapons, innovation, 136, 137, 286, 298–312, 414 ff., 418, 472; *see also* Atomic bomb; Hydrogen bomb; Nuclear weapons
Westerfield, H. Bradford, 450, 463
"When the Big Guns Speak" (Baldwin), 482
White, Howard, 457
Wholesale price index, 212 ff., 271
Wilson, Charles E., 77, 93; quoted, 69, 72, 81, 82, 141
Wilson, Woodrow, quoted, 172
Wolfers, Arnold, 451

Xydis, Stephen, 486